INTRODUCTION TO SOCIOLOGY
Second Edition

James B. McKee
Michigan State University

INTRODUCTION
to
SOCIOLOGY

SECOND EDITION

HOLT, RINEHART AND WINSTON, INC.
New York   Chicago   San Francisco   Atlanta
Dallas   Montreal   Toronto   London   Sydney

Photographs for the part titles were supplied by Wide World Photos (Parts I and IV); Magnum (Parts II and VII); The City University of New York (Part III); the U.S. Capitol Historical Society, George F. Mobley (Part V): and UPI International (Part VI).

Library of Congress Cataloging in Publication Data

McKee, James B., 1919–
   Introduction to sociology.
   1. Sociology. I. Title
     HM51.M197   1974   301   73-5200
     ISBN: 0-03-091557-0

Preface

The teaching of the elementary course in sociology is not an elementary task; to convey to beginning students an appropriate sense of the range and scope of the discipline and its distinctive problematic setting within the social sciences, in the limitations of a term or semester, is a challenging and often frustrating undertaking. In that task the introductory textbook plays an important part, for its discussions of the nature and substance of sociology can be read and reread, studied and underlined by the student. Whether it reads well and interests him, and whether it conveys in any systematic way some organized sense of the discipline of sociology, has a great deal to do with what the teacher can accomplish in the course.

There seem to be two different and even conflicting strains today in sociology that bear significantly on the teaching of the discipline, particularly to undergraduates. One is to demonstrate the *scientific* worth and commitment of sociology, the other is to show its *relevance* to the vexing social issues that beset modern society. I have sought a judicious balance between these two on the simple assumption that neither one alone properly reflects the temper or concerns of working sociologists.

In revising this book I have tried to preserve what many readers and users felt was most valuable about it, while undertaking a thorough rewriting. In particular, I have tried to preserve a humanistic tone, a sense that sociology is a discipline relevant because it has something to say about the human condition in a world grown larger, more complex, and more interdependent, while at the same time maintaining an appreciation of the effort to make that voice a rational and scientific one.

Following the advice of many colleagues and users, the main intent of this revision has been to make the text more readable for a much larger body of undergraduate students. I have attempted to do this by rewriting the text, by using more concrete examples, by avoiding too many scholarly phrases and abstruse words, by changes in format, and by the more liberal use of boxed and graphic material. I have provided a summary for each chapter, as well as a list of suggested readings.

The basic organization of the text has been retained, with only slight alterations in the chapters. Chapter 2 of the first edition, on the historical origins of sociology, has been omitted, yet elsewhere I have made the point that sociology emerged under specific historical circumstance at the same time that modern society came into being. Two chapters on minorities and the poor have been incorporated into a single chapter, and the same has been done with the formerly separate chapters on science and religion. In addition, the last two chapters have been combined. However, a chapter on society (Chapter 6) has been added. This reduces the number of chapters from 23 to 20. Also, what was originally a chapter on population has become a chapter on ecology and population (Chapter 19).

The usual updating that one expects of a new edition has been carried out. All census material includes the 1970 census, and in some cases even more recent census data has been used. Perhaps the major updating, however, has been to bring the book abreast of contemporary issues and developments for which sociology has relevance: counterculture and the renewed interest in community, for example, or the significance of the Coleman Report, the Jencks work on inequality, and the Moynihan report, as well as sex roles, women's liberation, and ecology.

A number of anonymous critics read earlier drafts of this edition, and I appreciate their careful reading and critical comments. I owe a particular debt to Charles Warriner and Larry Reynolds, whose critical reading did so much to improve the text and to enable me to avoid egregious errors. As usual, my colleague John Useem made a number of very helpful suggestions and provided useful material. William Tregea helped with suggestions and material for Chapter 19.

Richard Owen has been supportive and encouraging, and Louise Waller's sensitive and intelligent editing has made me aware of how valuable a really good editor is to an author. And, as always, I am immeasurably indebted to my wife, Alice, for her patience and unstinting support, and for the enormous amount of work she did in helping me to meet deadlines.

East Lansing, Michigan   —J. B. McK.
December 1973

Contents

INTRODUCTION TO SOCIOLOGY
Second Edition

PART I

SOCIOLOGY
AND SOCIETY

No man is an island entire of itself.
— *John Donne*

Chapter 1

The Study
of Society

Suppose you could choose any life you wanted, limited only by your imagination. It is a good sociological bet that, whatever you came up with, it would fall somewhere among the following:

. . . you would change who you are but keep yourself in your society, though perhaps in another place.
. . . you would change your society, a lot or a little.
. . . you would change both yourself and your society.
. . . you would put yourself into another society, past or present.
. . . or you would construct, in science-fiction fashion, a wholly imagined society of the future.

In every one of these possibilities you would take for granted the existence of society, this one or another. Why? Because we all know that to be human is to live in society, not outside of it. Only in a fearful nightmare are we likely to imagine ourselves all alone, isolated from others, devoid of human contact.

It does not seem particularly profound to say this, for surely we know it so well we need hardly be told it. In growing up we discover for ourselves how much being human involves us in a life shared with others. We do so,

4

not all at once, but gradually, so gradually in fact that it may not crystallize in our minds as a conscious thought. We become aware we know it only when somebody else has reason to state it.

Yet the recognition that our lives are always bounded by society is profound in its implications. It means, for one thing, that we become a particular person, unique among all other persons, only within a society; outside of society this would not be possible. It means also that we achieve our personal development within the limits of human variety possible in our society. No one society encompasses the entire range of the humanly possible.

There are other meanings, too. What we do every day in living our own lives is to act within the constraints and routines of society. We never escape society, only (sometimes) a particular society. We are born into a society, which was there before us and will be there after us, though it may change during our lifetime a little or much.

To live within society means to be involved, first of all, in a small and personal world of immediate experience, of the familiar and manageable, of people we know and love (or even hate). We experience in face-to-face relations family, friends, neighbors, co-workers, fellow students, teachers, employers, local merchants, and the like. Our daily activities interlock with theirs.

It is rarely so that this small world of ours is the limits of our society, though such has been the case for some isolated small societies. For the vast majority society extends into a larger world to which we more impersonally and indirectly relate. Large and remote systems penetrate our small worlds. Our neighbor down the street, for example, sits on the local draft board, an *agent* of a vast impersonal system, the rules and regulations of which can provide a common fate for many young men who will never know one another.

Why Is There Society?

Perhaps it is foolish to ask this question. After all, nobody is advocating society be abolished; intuitively we all take its existence for granted. Yet it may still be useful to pursue the matter briefly, since understanding why society exists helps us to understand what it is.

There are two basic arguments for the necessity of society, one based on a conception of human nature, the other on the problem of human survival. Compressed into brief statements, they are as follows:

1. At birth the individual organism is not yet human and is helpless to meet its own needs. Others must protect and sustain it, else it will quickly perish. Also, it needs others from whom it can learn how to do things necessary to live. Human life can be sustained only if the prolonged dependency of each new human organism is provided for by some social process.

   This argument assumes that the human organism is not genetically programmed; that is, its behavior is not a pattern of inherited instincts. What is required of the human organism, instead, is a complex learning process. This requires prolonged association with others, which in turn requires at least an elementary form of society.

   From this, in turn, a derivative argument is developed. From prolonged association with others, the organism realizes its potentiality to acquire a *human* nature and so to become a person. Once that occurs, the individual is bound more firmly than ever to relations with others. He needs now to love and to be loved, to give and receive respect and consideration. It is painful to be rejected by others, and it hurts not to be respected. Isolation from others produces the painful experience of loneliness, and enforced isolation can be used as severe punishment. A human being will destroy himself (commit suicide) if his relations with others do not give sufficient meaning to his existence. Becoming human means sharing in an existence that is always more than physical survival.

The other argument shifts the focus to the issue of human survival.

2. Human survival in a sometimes capricious, often hostile, and always stubbornly resistant environment can only be accomplished if human beings act collectively. Cooperation can accomplish things no one could manage alone. From this perspective human society is defined as a product of collective *adaptation* to a natural environment, a process of finding how to live cooperatively in such a way as to make the natural order yield enough to sustain life. By cooperative activity among an aggregate of learning organisms, skills are acquired; knowledge is accumulated; techniques and tools are developed; and all are transmitted to the next generation.

From this argument, too, comes a derivative one. For any society to be a society, it must organize people; sustaining organization makes additional demands on people to accept the requirements of a collective existence. Social organization requires coordination and control processes; it requires procedures for assigning individuals to roles and tasks; and it requires means to process organisms in order to produce reasonably competent members of the society. A society is carried on by the actions of its members; each new member must learn what the necessary actions are. This is the source of the compulsions and constraints that any society imposes upon its members.

The recognition that human beings cannot even survive physically except through cooperation is the basis for viewing work as a central human activity and for insisting that the economy is the basic structure of society, from which all else is derivative. The activity necessary to provide the material basis for life is interpreted as fundamental in forming society and in giving it a particular organization.

This is a conception of society shared by Marxists and non-Marxists alike, including social scientists who emphasize the significance of technology in the *evolution* of society from primitive forms to an advanced industrial structure. Not only does this evolutionary perspective define society as an adaptation to the natural environment, but it also asserts that even with the most advanced technology, such adaptation does not allow society to acquire just any form. The structure of society, so goes the argument, is bound to requirements set by the nature of the environment.

To stress the issue of survival may seem quaint in this latter day when modern people possess powerful technologies that spare them mindless subservience to the forces of nature. They mine the earth for coal and minerals, extract oil and gas from deep within the ground, change the course of rivers and dam them to create great bodies of water, change arid land into fertile soil by irrigation, drain swamps, tunnel through mountains, domesticate wildlife, and in so many other ways turn the natural environment to their own use.

Until recently, they exploited and altered the environment without concern for the consequences, but extensive pollution and the destruction and depletion of natural resources rudely reminded them that they are still dependent on a viable physical environment. Modern populations are not released from the need to adapt to the environment, though technology has radically altered the terms of that adaptation.

But the more technology makes possible a society that places us beyond the edge

Figure 1.1 The campus is an example of a social community where people experience each other in face-to-face relationships. *(Wide World Photos)*

of survival, the more are we individually dependent on the complex social organization needed to sustain life at new levels of material living. As individuals we may worry less about collective survival, more about our individual fate; even so, we are forced to recognize that our personal destiny, for good or bad, is inextricably tied into the social organization of our society. We depend on teachers and schools in order to learn an occupation, for example. We may be aware, though vaguely, that what chance we have to learn a given occupation, particularly one that ranks high, may depend on other than our individual talents and energies; it may depend, for instance, on where our family is located in the hierarchy of society. And we may even come to recognize that the reason some occupations are highly rewarded and others are not is also a consequence of the organization of society.

Interaction: The Basis of Social Life

Examining these arguments for the necessity of society has told us that (1.) society is produced by the cooperative activity of human beings, and (2.) a human organism becomes human only in a society. Neither the fully human organism—the person—nor society comes from nature ready made; neither, that is, is genetically produced. Both are the product of extensive and constant *interaction*.

Nor is that all. Interaction cannot proceed except as the interacting individuals develop some common understandings and some collective meaning; a shared language is a common denominator for interaction. Like society and person, these *cultural* phenomena do not come ready made from nature either. Culture also is produced through interaction.

Interaction, then, is the basis of social

life; through it the person, society, and culture emerge. No one of them can come into existence in any other way. Interaction produces something psychological, social, and cultural that did not exist before and cannot be accounted for in terms of the prior characteristics of the interacting organism.

Is Society Real?

If society emerges from social interaction, the same as the person does, then is society as real as the person? Émile Durkheim argued persuasively that society is a reality *sui generis* (of its own kind), a thing apart from and external to individu-

als. While not all sociologists would take so forthright a philosophical position, they would all probably agree that a person *experiences* society as an objective reality that constrains and coerces him. Furthermore, it is agreed, society and person are interdependent phenomena. Society does not exist without individuals through whose action it is carried on.

To this point we have only stated that society is an emergent phenomenon, is experienced as an objective reality, and is carried on through the actions of persons; we have not explored and developed that idea. That will be the task of Chapter 3. But for now such a statement serves as the basis for defining sociology as the study of society.

EMILE DURKHEIM: THE REALITY OF SOCIETY

Figure 1.2 Émile Durkheim, one of the founders of the discipline. *(The Bettmann Archive, Inc.)*

One of the great names in the founding of sociology, Émile Durkheim (1858–1917) argued, forcefully and polemically, for the independent existence of society. Society was a reality sui generis, created from the association of individuals, but being more than the attributes of these individuals; the whole is greater than the sum of its parts. "We can see . . . that society does not depend upon the nature of the individual personality."

In *The Rules of Sociological Method* Durkheim pressed the idea that the social

SOCIOLOGY: THE STUDY OF SOCIETY

As one among several social-science disciplines, sociology shares in the larger task of studying social life in its manifest forms — personality, culture, and society. Studying society can hardly be claimed to be anything new; as far back as we have records, scholars and scribes have described and analyzed the collective social life shared by a people. Yet sociology as a discipline goes back in name and identity only to the early decades of the nineteenth century, barely a century and a half.

Sociology grew at a time of new and creative social thought that transformed and modernized all of the social sciences. New specialized disciplines broke away from the long-established fields of history and philosophy. The specialized study of economic phenomena, for example, only became *economics* when, under laissez-faire capitalism, the economic system was thought of as separate and apart from the political process, especially the state.

Later on, anthropology and sociology were defined, not as studying a limited institutional area of society (such as the political or economic) but as new ways to look at and understand social life. Anthropology originated in the interest that Europeans developed in non-Western peoples as a result of three centuries of exploration, colonization, and trade. After the explorers, colonizers, traders, and the missionaries seeking converts to Christianity came the anthropologist, the Western intellectual specialist on non-Western peoples.

---

realm was one of *social facts,* defined as *things* external to individuals and constraining them. The social fact is experienced by the individual as an independent reality which he did not create and which he cannot wish away, such as moral rules, laws, customs, rituals, and official (bureaucratic) practices, among others. "All are expressly obligatory, and this obligation is the proof that these ways of acting and thinking are not the work of the individual but come from a moral power above him, that which the mystics call God or which can be more scientifically conceived."

Social facts, said Durkheim, are to be explained by other social facts: "The determining cause of a social fact should be sought among the social facts preceding it and not among the states of the individual consciousness." The existence of society, Durkheim thought, could not be explained by resorting to the psychological characteristics of its members. Sociology must have its own object of study, and this could only be social facts, realities external to the individual. "If no reality exists outside of individual consciousness, it [sociology] wholly lacks any material of its own." Then there can only be psychology.

"It is not realized that there can be no sociology unless societies exist, and that societies cannot exist if there are only individuals."

Among Durkheim's writings were four influential monographs of great scope and intellectual power:

> *The Rules of Sociological Method*
> *Suicide*
> *On the Division of Labor*
> *The Elementary Forms of Religious Life*

The Origin of Sociology

The emergence of sociology, in contrast, stemmed from an intellectual crisis brought on by the Industrial Revolution, which radically changed the structure of human society. The Industrial Revolution moved rural people into urban centers, changed peasants into workers, and produced cities where villages had once stood. Two significant consequences followed from this: (1.) the individual's daily range of personal experiences became too limited in scope to provide him with sufficient familiarity with his own social world, for that world was growing to be vast and complex; (2.) his world changed before his eyes even as he learned about it. No one could assume that his world would be the same as the world of his parents, or that the world of his children would be like his own.

For many social thinkers the radical transformation of society produced both hope and anxiety. Democratization and rising standards of living were sources of hope. Yet there also emerged a deep anxiety over the future. Did all this change threaten the continuity of society itself? Did the breaking loose of fixed social position and the decline of once sacred and unquestioned values bode ill for the future of the family and community?

Scholars of divergent perspectives recognized that an old order—the Christian unity of medieval society—was breaking up, to be replaced by a new order of unfamiliar and uncertain features. Among a varied group of intellectuals in nineteenth-century Europe—some radical, some conservative—there developed a new consciousness about society, a recognition of how revolutionary the change in human society had been, how uncertain had the future become. Society, which people always took for granted, now became an object of conscious, intellectual examination. Society had become a problem—and from that sociology was born.

Human Society as Problematic

Any time social change so alters the familiar social world that it is no longer adequately understandable or explainable by the usual ways of thinking common to a society, people examine it with a new level of social awareness. The modern world has provoked such a sustained and intense level of social awareness for over a century, a social consciousness rooted in the vastly impressive reordering of social life under the impact of industrialization and urbanization. It has created social ideologies and social sciences that have one thing in common: They attempt to provide answers to questions generated from this consciousness.

There were questions such as these: How are people able to sustain social order and avoid chaos and disorder? What are the basic elements necessary to the existence of society? Is common religious belief necessary to sustain society? What are the sources of social change? How does society control individual conduct? What is the necessary relationship of the individual to the group? What is the importance of the small and traditional group in society—family and community, for example—both for the individual and his relationship to society, and for the organization of society? What are the relationships between social classes? Is social hierarchy necessary in human society? Does class conflict necessarily lead to social revolution?

Throughout the nineteenth century sociology took shape and substance from intellectual debates that grappled with these

Figure 1.3 Beginning in England about the middle of the eighteenth century, the Industrial Revolution heralded the development of large-scale manufacturing. *(Culver Pictures, Inc.)*

many questions. The founders of sociology tended to ask global, all-encompassing questions posed at the highest level of generality. And for good reason. They were trying to get a basic theoretical grasp of fundamental change from a feudal, authoritarian, pre-industrial society to an industrial, democratic, urban society, which had never before existed in human experience.

If many early sociologists were intellectuals inquiring into the larger meaning of societal transformation, there were still many others asking more specific questions, and answering them by going out and observing the empirical world. Among these were some exploring the vast unmapped dimensions of the social worlds of the working poor, who in nineteenth-century industrial England were probably a majority of the population. Perhaps the most influential of these was a detailed, factual study of the living conditions of the poor in London in the 1880s and 1890s,

undertaken by a wealthy British industrialist, Charles Booth, and published in several volumes from 1891 to 1903 as *Life and Labour of the People of London.*

Novelists, too—Charles Dickens in England; Stendhal, Honoré de Balzac, Gustave Flaubert, and Émile Zola in France, for example—undertook explorations of the social worlds brought into being by the emergence of industrial cities and the new social classes dwelling therein, especially the new propertied bourgeoisie and the impoverished and depressed working classes. In the United States, Jacob Riis' *How the Other Half Lives* probed the world of the immigrant poor in rapidly growing American cities.[1]

The origin of sociology, then, is rooted equally in two different though related

[1] For a selection from Riis' writings on the lives of the poor *see* Francesco Cordasco, ed., *Jacob Riis Revisited: Poverty and the Slum in Another Era* (Garden City, N.Y.: Doubleday & Company, Inc., 1968).

11

tasks: The theoretical reformulation of a conception of society and empirical observation and description of the lives of people in new, urbanized structures. If sociology emerged as a distinct social science from this process, many others besides sociologists engaged in the task, particularly the empirical exploration and description. Looking at the world sociologically is not the monopoly of sociologists. And so it is today; sociologists share with others, particularly journalists, the task of describing divergent, even contradictory patterns in personalities, cultures, and groups found within the boundaries of modern society. The best journalists and novelists have often been good descriptive sociologists. But the sociologist intends to be both describer and theorist, moving carefully back and forth from the empirical level of observable facts to the more abstract level of theory based on those descriptions.

THE SOCIOLOGICAL PERSPECTIVE

Hopefully, we have by now made the point that sociology is a way of looking at the world, a focus on reality that brings some things to the fore and leaves other things in the background. It is selective in its perception. All thinking is selective, of course; what is distinctive about sociology is its manner of selection, its particular perspective.

Some of that perspective we have already established. Sociologists look not at particular persons as persons but as *actors* in social relationships. When sociologists study social relationships they examine the small microworlds of actors in limited systems of interaction. Such microworlds, to be sure, do not exist in a vacuum; they exist in a larger context of groups and

structures. These larger structures reach into the ongoing relationship and constrain it, as when, for example, the authority structure of the university constrains the relations of students and professors. Whatever may be the attitudes and intentions of a particular student or teacher, *as actors in social roles* they are not social equals within the structure of the university (however they may be in other ways), and this stubborn fact is one decisive element in shaping their interaction.

But not all sociologists make the close-up study of social interaction their way of doing sociology. Established interaction sustains already existing social groups and societies, and these may be the places where a sociologist cuts into reality. Any group or society is organized in some way; it has a *social structure*. When a sociologist seeks to provide a fairly detailed description of the urban middle-class family in the United States, he may be trying to relate this family structure to the class structure of American society. A sociologist who asks a sample of industrial workers in Detroit or Chicago about their political beliefs is probably less interested in whether workers will continue to vote Democratic than in more basic theoretical issues about the relationship of class structure to political groups, such as parties and labor unions.

Another sociologist might examine the world of higher education as a social system changing in response to pressures to provide educational opportunity for social classes and minorities previously left out of the system, while yet continuing to train the professional classes, serve the nation-state, and stay in the forefront of scientific research and training. He might then look for the emergence of different patterns of specialization among universities and col-

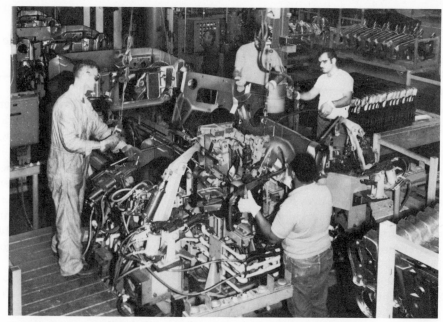

Figure 1.4 By working with existing social groups, such as these Detroit automotive industry workers, the sociologist cuts into real-life situations. *(Wide World Photos)*

leges: highly selective liberal arts colleges providing academically and socially "superior" students with assured admission to professional and graduate schools; large universities, while taking "better" undergraduates, providing the professional and graduate training and carrying on scientific research; and state and community colleges educating students who are the academic non-elite. He would expect to find a functional differentiation in higher education that reflects, among other things, unequal accessibility of social classes to the mobility opportunities provided by a college education.

Yet another could study higher education on a worldwide basis, comparing how it is organized within modern societies and still-modernizing ones, within societies committed to different degrees of educational opportunity, within socialist and capitalist societies. In these cases the uni-

versity is only understood in relation to the structure of the society of which it is a part. This is truly a *macro-sociological* analysis, a long way from the micro-sociology of social relations in the small context of social interaction.

These few examples provide some indication of variations in the ways sociologists look at social life. Yet, from the micro-perspective of two-person social relations to the macro-perspectives of large structures, even total societies, sociologists maintain a consistent perspective; they look at social relations, at groups and organizations, at social structures, or at total societies.

Defining sociology as the study of society, then, means studying all the social forms that emerge and take shape from persistent social interaction, from the smallest of groups to the largest of societies. As systems of interaction some are

13

remarkably persistent and continuous over time, others are not; some are stable and little modified over time; some change radically.

Sociological Consciousness

Sociology at its best induces in all of us an acute awareness of other social worlds lying beyond our immediate and familiar surroundings. It conveys to us an awareness of social worlds undergoing rapid and often difficult-to-predict social change. At such times sociology provides us with a clear "window" on worlds other than our own, when common sense or official ideologies provide only opaque or distorted glimpses, if indeed, we can see any other reality at all through them.

Peter Berger has argued convincingly that sociology as a form of *social consciousness* includes skepticism about the official claims or common-sense explanations of human behavior.[2] The sociological perspective becomes a process of "seeing through" the façades of social structure. Behind the visible political or bureaucratic organization of social life is a social reality that may be more enduring than the official structures. The sociologist tries to describe social actions and patternings of human relationships that may go unnoticed or even be denied by official explanations. Sociology, therefore, may undertake, even if unintentionally, a *debunking* function.

Sociologists have long been fascinated by the underside of society, the unrespectable phases of life where official explanations are disbelieved and quite different and sometimes contradictory versions of social reality prevail—neither of which are to be

[2] Peter Berger, *Invitation to Sociology: A Humanistic Perspective* (Garden City, N.Y.: Anchor Books, 1963).

uncritically accepted by the sociologist. In the ghetto and the slums, in the underworld and deviant communities, in the subworlds of those of marginal status in society, we find other languages, other values, other life styles. These other worlds, says Berger, have always exercised a powerful attraction for sociologists.

The attraction is not sociology's alone: the middle classes of modern society have been both fascinated and repelled by the alienated social realities lying just beyond the world of the respectable. Sociologists have been one of respectable society's emissaries—an intellectual ambassador, if you will—to these other realities somehow connected to society. (In the same fashion the anthropologist has been a Western ambassador to the lands of "heathens" and "primitives," for which similar fascination exists.)

Modern society is characterized by social mobility and geographic movement so that large segments of the population are exposed to other ways of life, other moral outlooks and social values. The mass media further contribute to this cultural exposure. It is difficult to be totally insulated within a single, conventional perspective in modern society. Although for many this broader exposure remains a rather superficial experience, there are few indeed who escape the awareness that the values of their culture are quite relative to time and place. Sociology manifests a modern consciousness of a world in which all values have been radically relativized. It does not permit us to ignore the fact that any modern society is an arrangement of multiple social realities, of varied social worlds sometimes complementary, sometimes incompatible and in conflict.

No less than Peter Berger, the late C. Wright Mills claimed for sociology a con-

Figure 1.5 Geographic movement and social mobility characterize the society of the United States. *(Wide World Photos)*

sciousness peculiar to the sociological outlook which he called the sociological imagination.[3] It involved a capacity to shift from the micro-perspective of intimate human relations to the macro-perspectives of large structures. "It is a capacity to range from the most impersonal and remote transformations to the most intimate features of the human self—and to see the relations between the two."[4] And its intention is clear: to enable us to grasp what is going on in our world and so to understand what is happening to us as persons unavoidably bound into massive structures undergoing historical transformation.

In large part, contemporary man's self-conscious view of himself of at least an outsider, if not a permanent stranger, rests upon an absorbed realization of social relativity and of the transformative power of history. The sociological imagination is the most fruitful form of this self consciousness.[5] . . .

[3] C. Wright Mills, *The Sociological Imagination* (New York: Oxford University Press, 1959; Grove Press, paperback edition, 1961).

[4] Mills, p. 7 (paperback edition).

[5] Mills, p. 7 (paperback edition).

SUMMARY

Society is a necessary phenomenon because (1.) the human organism can neither survive nor develop into a person without prolonged association with others; and (2.) human survival in the natural environment requires human cooperation; society is an adaptation to environment.

Interaction is the basis of social life. From persistent interaction comes society as an *emergent phenomenon,* as does the person and culture. Society is then a *reality sui generis,* different from, though interdependent with, persons and culture.

Sociology is the study of society, which means it studies all the social forms —from small to large—that emerge from interaction. Sociology developed from the intellectual crisis about the radical transformation of society brought about by the Industrial Revolution. Its *perspective* is a consciousness of society as multiple realities of relativized values; it seeks to be a window on these realities when common sense and official ideologies cannot be such a window.

Suggested Readings

Peter Berger, *Invitation to Sociology* (Garden City, N.Y.: Anchor Books, 1963). An influential and effective "invitation" to partake of sociology from a humanistic perspective on the human scene.

Randall Collins and Michael Makowsky, *The Discovery of Society* (New York: Random House, Inc., 1972). An introduction to sociology which examines in historical context the lives of the brilliant men who made it possible—not all are sociologists.

R. P. Cuzzort, *Humanity and Modern Sociological Thought* (New York: Holt, Rinehart and Winston, Inc., 1969). A fascinating examination of sociology through the ideas of some of its more imaginative and creative contributors.

Jack D. Douglas, ed., *The Relevance of Sociology* (New York: Appleton-Century-Crofts, 1970). A series of provocative essays on the relevance of sociology for understanding and solving social problems.

Roscoe and Gisela Hinkle, *The Development of Modern Sociology* (New York: Random House, Inc., 1954). A small, useful study that explores the origins of American sociology in the first half of this century.

Alex Inkeles, *What Is Sociology? An Introduction to the Discipline and Profession* (Englewood Cliffs, N.J.: Prentice-Hall, Inc., 1964). A short, concise analysis of the range and perspective of sociology as a discipline and as a profession.

C. Wright Mills, *The Sociological Imagination* (New York: Oxford University Press, 1959; paperback edition, Grove Press, 1961). One of the most influential books in sociology in the last two decades, it pleads for the critical and probing use of sociological imagination in order to understand ourselves and the times in which we struggle to create a sane and humane world.

Bernard Rosenberg, *The Province of Sociology: Freedom and Constraint* (New York: Thomas Y. Crowell Company, 1972). A look, both historical and contemporary, at the effort of sociology to understand society as the contradictory process that engenders both freedom and constraint.

Charles K. Warriner, *The Emergence of Society* (Homewood, Ill.: Dorsey Press, 1960). A small study that makes clear what it means when we say society is emergent and a reality sui generis.

Man is the measure of all things.
  — *Protagoras*

Chapter 2

The Sociological Enterprise

Sociologists study society; the task ahead is, therefore, to examine the form and substance of society, from the micro-perspective of small-scale social relations to the macro-perspective of large structures and total societies. But before we turn fully to *what* sociology studies, there may be value in knowing *how* sociology studies society, and, beyond that, how sociologists perceive the sociological enterprise: its value to society, its practical and political meaning.

Throughout its brief history sociology has exhibited tension between two competing, sometimes contradictory, sometimes compatible imperatives: to be *scientific* and to be morally and politically *relevant*. While among them some would insist there is no inherent difficulty in being both, sociologists have often differed considerably in their views of what they should be doing.

SCIENTIFIC SOCIOLOGY

If there can be scientific study of social life—and from its beginning sociology has been defined by its practitioners as a science—there must be order in social phenomena. Without order no one thing relates to any other;

there could be no generalizing about people and their actions, no predictions made.

Philosophers of science disagree on whether science *discovers* order in phenomena or whether it *imposes* order on phenomena. In either case, however, the existence of order is basically affirmed in the knowledge scientists create, for their knowledge is about interrelatedness, patterning, and structure in phenomena.

Whether he assumes order is imposed or discovered, the social scientist assumes with the natural scientist that orderliness makes possible the use of rigorously logical reasoning; science is a *rational* process. But it is not that alone; science is not primarily a speculative process, however ingenious and imaginative speculation might be, and however useful the capacity to speculate is in the working out of theory. Science is also an *empirical* process, for it reasons with and from *facts*.

The Sociological Problem

There is an old saying: Ask a stupid question and you'll get a stupid answer. An updated version of that speaks to the limitations of those wonderfully ingenious machines, the computers: Put garbage in and you'll get garbage out. Sociological research is never any better than the questions sociologists ask. Poor questions produce nothing, or garbage. Good questions formulate a problem worth pursuing.

Carefully formulating a statement of the problem is the beginning of sociological research, an effort to ask the right question and to determine what needs to be known to answer it. This has never been a simple or obvious matter in any science. One can ask *why* about anything, but scientists have to decide what questions are worth asking, as well as how they are best asked.

Asking the wrong question is a frequent error in science. A case in point is the nature-nurture controversy: Does heredity *or* environment determine behavior? The question as posed is unanswerable, for it is not an either/or matter; both heredity and environment affect behavior, and they seem not even to be clearly separable from one another. Only when social scientists stopped asking the question in either/or terms could any progress be made.[1]

While some questions are wrong, others are merely trivial; not every question matters for science. Those that do, according to Robert Merton:

. . . are questions so formulated that the answers to them will confirm, amplify, or variously revise some part of what is currently taken as knowledge in the field. In short, although every problem in science involves a question, or series of questions, not every question qualifies as a scientific problem.[2]

When sociologists formulate questions, therefore, they do so only after taking account of what the state of knowledge is. If much is already known, questions may challenge the adequacy of already formulated hypotheses, even theories, or find ways to choose among competing models. When Swedish sociologist Walter Korpi, for example, wanted to explore further the problem of whether voters choose rationally, he decided to study Communist voting, since available theories on that issue mostly assumed voting Communist not to be rational.

[1] *See* Nicholas Pastore, *The Nature-Nurture Controversy* (New York: King's Crown Press, 1949).
[2] Robert K. Merton, "Notes on Problem-finding in Sociology," in Robert K. Merton, Leonard Broom, and Leonard J. Cottrell, Jr., eds., *Sociology Today: Problems and Prospects* (New York: Basic Books, Inc., 1959), p. x.

Figure 2.1 Little sociological research has dealt with the educated, stable, employed black adult who has "made it." *(Hugh Rogers, Monkmeyer)*

The purpose of this paper is to discuss the question of rationality in the area of Communist voting among workers. Two different theories of Communist voting, that of Lipset . . . and of Allardt . . . assume that it is in whole or in part nonrational. These two theories will be analyzed and compared with a model which assumes rational choice . . .[3]

But often research is undertaken where there are gaps in knowledge. This was the reason, for example, why two sociologists undertook to study stable, employed black workers; as they noted, most sociological research has been about the poorest blacks, uneducated and unemployed, or underemployed:

Little attempt has been made to study those who have steady jobs, live with stable families in respectable neighborhoods, and stay out of trouble. What about working-class and middle-class blacks who have made it?[4]

In another case a sociologist undertook a study where little was actually known, though much had been assumed, namely, that bureaucracy encourages conformist, unthinking behavior.

But does working in a bureaucracy merely make automatons of men, or are there compensating features that encourage individualistic qualities? Surprisingly, there has been little empirical study of how bureaucracy affects those who spend their working hours in its employ. One objective of this study is to ascertain whether "bureaucrats" really are con-

[3] Walter Korpi, "Working Class Communism in Western Europe: Rational or Nonrational," *American Sociological Review,* 36 (December, 1971), p. 971.

[4] Joseph A. Kahl and John M. Goering, "Stable Workers, Black and White," *Social Problems,* 18 (Winter 1971), p. 307.

formist in their values and in their appraisal of social reality . . .⁵

Social change brings new events and an opportunity to study things never before studied. A new event may provide new data for reexamining old problems and asking again questions that were asked in other situations. Medicare, for example, might be studied to answer a practical question: Does it deliver medical care more adequately than was done before? Studying Medicare might serve to answer other questions, too. Noting that Medicare was bitterly opposed by the medical profession, for example, one sociologist decided to find out what happened after it was introduced:

This paper examines how individual physicians reacted, in their behavior and their thinking, to Medicare after it became law. The more general issue raised by this question is the role of law as an instrument of social change, an old sociological problem.⁶

Theory: The Effort to Explain

No matter how interesting the social phenomena being studied, and no matter how descriptively rich is the available data, more than description is intended by sociological research. Any effort to state a problem or to formulate a question is meant to relate description of facts to theory. While accurate description focuses attention on *particulars*, theory is constructed in an effort to provide explanation. And that requires generalizations.

Generalizing from facts and constructing explanations of what we observe is natural to human beings. Scientists did not invent explanation, but they do insist that scientific explanations be constructed *logically* and always be tested *empirically* (based on observations or experiments) against the facts. Untestable propositions cannot enter into scientific theory.

We generalize first when we sum up some data: For example, whites on the average get more education and earn more income than blacks do. Such an empirical statement requires some theory, however simple, to explain it. A sociologist might assert, for example, that education correlates closely with income—high education, high income; low education, low income— and that whites achieve more education than blacks do. Better-educated whites thus attain better jobs.

But this is hardly likely to satisfy as an explanation; it raises a more pressing question: *Why* do whites achieve more education than blacks do? One direction in which to theorize might be that whites possess the power to discriminate, so that discrimination in education gives them preferred access to jobs requiring education. Educational discrimination leaves blacks less qualified. Explaining these differences between blacks and whites in terms of a theory of discriminatory processes—stated here only in crude simplicity—has found favor with most sociologists, but there are other theories, from that of differential achievement aspirations among diverse ethnic and racial groups to an old, controversial one about inherent differences in natural ability.⁷

⁵ Melvin L. Kohn, "Bureaucratic Man: A Portrait and an Interpretation," *American Sociological Review*, 36 (June 1971), pp. 461–462.

⁶ John Colombotos, "Physicians and Medicare: A Before-after Study of the Effects of Legislation on Attitudes," *American Sociological Review*, 34 (June 1969), p. 318.

⁷ For a review of the argument about educational discrimination *see* Thomas F. Pettigrew, "The Negro and Education: Problems and Proposals," in Irwin Katz and Patricia Gurin, eds., *Race and the Social Sciences* (New York: Basic Books, Inc., 1969), pp. 49–112.

Competing theories often exist side by side for a long time, each providing plausible explanations for some set of facts; each is strongly adhered to, but sometimes for ideological reasons. Explaining why blacks have less education and income than whites do by a theory of discrimination fits a liberal ideology, and most sociologists find that palatable. For the same reason they find unpalatable a biological theory that asserts genetically-based differences account for differences in levels of individual achievement in education and income. But for the same ideological reason they also tend to reject more radical (and particularly Marxian) theories that explain race relations in terms of class structure in a capitalist society.

Eventually the weight of empirical evidence brought to bear on the problem, and the relatively greater success of one theory in accounting for a greater range of facts, should lead to progressive acceptance of that theory and to rejection of other, competing ones. But many times in sociology, competing theories are all too tentative and incomplete, and continuing sociological research modifies all of them and brings forth a new, more inclusive theory.

Theories are of all kinds—some being highly ambitious attempts to account for much, others quite modest and limited. They can also be culturally specific: a theory of community power applicable only

to American cities and towns, for example. Some sociologists insist on reserving the term "theory" only for a tightly worked out logico-deductive system of general postulates or assumptions from which testable hypotheses can be deduced. But other sociologists argue that such a narrow definition of theory may be more inhibiting than necessary, and so they argue for a "looser" version of sociological theory.[8]

On Concepts

Nowhere are theory and research more closely linked than through *concepts*. In contrast to the names of *particular* things, a concept is a *general* term that names a class of objects, persons, relationships, processes, or events. Miss Jones is the name of a particular woman, but "woman" is a concept. Probably most words in any language are concepts, for without them people could not communicate except in the most concrete and particular terms. Scientific concepts differ from the concepts of ordinary language only in the effort to be more precise and abstract.

Since most of the concepts of sociology come from ordinary language, they often retain some imprecision and ambiguity. They can be given a more precise definition, but this often proves easier to say than to do. Concepts such as *status* or *role* or *community* or *group* not only reflect varying and imprecise meanings but sociologists define these concepts in different ways.

So significant are concepts that much of

For a recent review on the issue of inherent differences in ability *see* several articles in John Brigham and Theodore Weissbach, eds., *Racial Attitudes in America: Analyses and Findings in Social Psychology* (New York: Harper & Row, 1972), pp. 275–319.

On different achievement aspirations *see* Bernard C. Rosen, Harry J. Crockett, and Clyde Z. Nunn, *Achievement in American Society* (Cambridge, Mass.: Schenkman, 1968); and Bernard C. Rosen, "Race, Ethnicity, and the Achievement Syndrome," *American Sociological Review*, 24 (February 1969), pp. 47–60.

[8] For such a position *see* Gideon Sjoberg and Roger Nett, *A Methodology for Social Research* (New York: Harper & Row, 1968), pp. 29–30. For explicit disagreement with them *see* Jack Gibbs, *Sociological Theory Construction* (Hinsdale, Ill.: The Dryden Press Inc., 1972), pp. 4–5.

the history of social science is a history of the creation, development, and modification of concepts. A new concept may give us radically new insights into human action. Great intellectual innovators like Sigmund Freud and Karl Marx, for example, created new sets of concepts that enabled us to see and think in radical new ways about the social world.[9] Human character has never seemed the same since Freud taught us about *id, ego,* and *super-ego, sublimation,* and *repression.* Nor can

[9] *See* Sigmund Freud, *An Outline of Psychoanalysis* (New York: W. W. Norton & Company, Inc., 1949); and T. B. Bottomore, ed. and trans., *Karl Marx: Selected Writings in Sociology and Social Philosophy* (New York: McGraw-Hill, Inc., 1964).

society in historical change ever again be discussed without some reference to Marx's concepts of *class conflict, class consciousness,* and *ideology.*

While sociological concepts usually originate in ordinary language, sometimes they come from special languages. *Role* and *actor,* for example, obviously come from the language of the theater; *charisma* came from theology (it meant a gift of grace). Other concepts emerge over time, transformed through historical change from once quite different meanings. *Culture* evolved from a pre-nineteenth-century meaning of "tendency of natural growth" and then human training. According to the British scholar, Raymond Williams, it

SOME PIONEERS OF EMPIRICAL RESEARCH

The several ways of doing social research did not spring up overnight, or develop solely in the twentieth century. There is a long, creative history of innovating, developing, and refining various techniques of social research, particularly *statistical* techniques making quantitative data possible and *observational* techniques for obtaining information, particularly about workers and poor people (the majority of the population at that time) never before available. While much of this research has come to mature development only in this century, some early innovative pioneers undertook work that in each case marks a large step forward. Here are some of the major ones:

Adolph Quetelet (1796–1874), a Belgian astronomer and mathematician, who as early as the 1820s was working on making a better census in the Netherlands (and later Belgium) by improving the forms of schedules, kinds of questions to be asked, methods to tabulate data, and the like. He also tried to abstract "laws" from such quantitative data. He coined the term *social physics,* which angered Comte, who had wanted to name the study of society that; so Comte thought up a new name, *sociology.* Later, Quetelet was an important influence in establishing the Statistical Society of London (later the Royal Statistical Society), an organization important in seeking to develop a body of facts about the social conditions of the working classes.

Charles Booth (1840–1916), an English industrialist, pioneered in studying the urban poor. In the 1880s and 1890s Booth undertook what was probably the first great empirical social scientific study, a detailed investigation on the conditions of life among the people of London reported in the several volumes of his *Life and Labour of the London Poor* from 1893 to 1901.

Frederick LePlay (1806–1882) undertook to understand the life of European

came to be used with its present meaning only with the onset of industrial society. Furthermore, he argued, *culture* was one of five key words—the others were *industry, democracy, class,* and *art*—that became significant in giving meaning to the social transformation accompanying the Industrial Revolution.[10]

Sociological and psychological concepts often quickly capture the interest and attention of the same human beings they are intended to help analyze. With remarkable swiftness they are incorporated into everyday speech. Psychological concepts like *neurosis, tension, ego, IQ, self,* and *identity* have readily become parts of the speech of literate Americans. The concept of *role* is now in such general use that few realize it entered the general vocabulary through sociology. Such basic terms as *culture* and *society* have been common in our speech for only about a hundred years, while *status* has become common to ordinary speech only in recent decades.

Data-gathering: Observing the World

Any social research must be carefully designed so that questions. can be answered; it is surprisingly easy to gather

[10] Raymond Williams, *Culture and Society 1780–1950* (New York: Anchor Books, 1959).

---

workers by examining their family lives in terms of income and expenditures. His work involved studying families in their natural surroundings and winning their confidence so as to get detailed data on family budgets. His *Les Ouvriers Européens* (1855) is an early but influential effort in social research to give a quantitative picture of social life.

Émile Durkheim (1858–1916), whose great work we have already introduced, undertook in *Suicide* a study that pioneered in the application of statistical methods to a sociological issue that was theoretically significant. He stands out among early sociologists as both a theorist and a pioneer in the development of empirical research.

For further discussion of the development of social research see the following sources:

1. Daniel Lerner, "Social Science: Whence and Whither?", Nathan Glazer, "The Rise of Social Research in Europe," and Harry Alpert, "The Growth of Social Research in the United States," in Daniel Lerner, ed., *The Human Meaning of the Social Sciences* (New York: Meridian Books, Inc., 1959).

2. John Madge, *The Origins of Scientific Sociology* (New York: The Free Press, 1962), which begins with a chapter on Durkheim's *Suicide* and then examines the pioneering studies that shaped American sociological research throughout the first half of the twentieth century.

3. Anthony Oberschall, ed., *The Establishment of Empirical Sociology: Studies in Continuity, Discontinuity, and Institutionalization* (New York: Harper & Row, 1972). Here is evidence of recent interest among sociologists in the origins of empirical research; in this book several of them carefully reexamine the nineteenth- and early twentieth-century pioneering work from which today's more sophisticated empirical research grew.

interesting data that never manage to answer the question first posed. A researcher must decide what kind of data he needs and how to obtain it.

Observing the social world always encounters a particular difficulty: Many phenomena are *invisible*. Did you ever "see" a group's *morale,* a person's *attitude,* an organization's *goal?* In fact, did you ever see a *role* or a *group?* Quite literally the answer is no. What you do see, when you try to observe, are people's actions, and from these you *infer* that a group's morale is low, or that some people hold certain attitudes, or that a particular role exists.

Making *valid* inferences from observations can be a tricky matter; too often the same observation yields quite different inferences. A careful researcher, therefore, usually constructs *indicators;* he specifies the particular observations from which his inferences are made. Then others can check him out. Low morale in an army, for example, might be inferred from such indicators as reenlistment rates, proportions of AWOLs, maintenance of military discipline, or the extent of griping. In a factory absenteeism, job turnover, quality of work, unauthorized work stoppages, and complaints filed with the grievance procedure might serve as indicators.

To Sample or Not

Guided by what he wants to know, a sociologist has to decide whether it is useful and also feasible to observe all of the population of people (or behaviors) under study. Practical considerations may lead him to use a *sample,* a small proportion of the total population drawn so that the variation in its characteristics will be present in the sample in the same proportion they appear in the universe of study. Or,

he may decide to do a *case* study, a fairly detailed analysis of but one instance: one person, one family, one divorce, one community, one riot.

What is best done depends on the research objective and on the existing state of knowledge. The larger the sample, the more representative it can be, but usually less data are gathered about each unit. With a large national sample, for example, interviewers will conduct only a brief interview. A case study cannot claim representativeness, but if there is little yet known anyway one detailed case may offer rich insights useful in developing better hypotheses for future research. (Social scientists never assume that one study is going to do it all; it is always conceived of as building on what went before and contributing to what will yet be done.)

Between the large, representative sample and the case study, a compromise may be struck. A small and less representative sample may offer an opportunity to explore in greater depth, to have longer, more probing interviews. In any case, interviewing people and having them fill out questionnaires is an indirect though more economical way to observe action. The problem is to insure the accuracy (and honesty) of responses.

Fieldwork

There is a long tradition in sociology of fieldwork: gathering data by direct observation in natural situations. Like anthropologists, some sociologists choose to be *participant-observers,* taking part in the social life of some group or community to make observations from the inside, often by this means finding out things that would not readily (perhaps never) be revealed by interviews or questionnaires.

(Figure 2.2) Sigmund Freud and (Figure 2.3) Karl Marx *(right)* Two intellectual innovators whose radical ideas have stimulated new ways of thinking about the social world. *(Courtesy of Mrs. E.L. Freud, and The Bettmann Archive)*

William F. Whyte's *Street Corner Society,* a participant study among young men in their twenties in an Italian community in Boston, is now a sociological classic of participant fieldwork.[11] Twenty years later Herbert Gans studied a Boston working-class Italian neighborhood by participant observation.[12] Later, he resided in a new suburban community where he combined participant observation with a sample survey to find out how a new community was settled and organized.[13] Howard Becker used his consummate skill as a jazz pianist in studying jazz musicians;[14] in similar unique fashion Ned Polsky combined his early experience as a pool-hall hustler with historical materials to study that declining and illegal occupation.[15]

Using Documents But some sociological problems do not lend themselves to fieldwork. Macro-sociological studies of whole societies, for example, may utilize *documentary* sources: official records and reports, the census, Congressional hearings, annual reports of government agencies and corporations, as well as historical documents, including biographies and auto-

[11] William F. Whyte, *Street Corner Society* (Chicago: University of Chicago Press, 1942).

[12] Herbert Gans, *The Urban Villagers* (New York: The Free Press, 1962).

[13] Herbert Gans, *The Levittowners: Ways of Life and Politics in a New Suburban Community* (New York: Pantheon Books, Inc., 1967).

[14] Howard Becker, *Outsiders: Studies in the Sociology of Deviance* (New York: The Free Press, 1963), Chs. 5 and 6.

[15] Ned Polsky, *Hustlers, Beats, and Others* (Chicago: Aldine Publishing Co., 1967).

biographies of people who were significant actors in events under study.

Among these, the United States Census is worth singling out; its rich source of data on the American population, continuously collected since 1790, is undoubtedly one of sociology's — indeed, social science's — most useful sources of data.

OBJECTIVITY AND PERSPECTIVE

Most sociologists believe their task is not to moralize about social life but to develop a science of society. To do that, sociological knowledge must be separated from moral and ideological discourse — something easier to say than to do — and the study of society must always be *objective*.

Objectivity is social thought sufficiently disciplined to reduce the possible distortions in observation and analysis produced by one's more personal attitudes, emotions, values, and dislikes. Anyone is capable of being more objective in one situation, less so in another. Experimental psychology has taught us, for example, that if we are emotionally involved in something, or intensely prejudiced about it, or if we have interests at stake, our social perceptions are likely to be strongly influenced. We will not see the situation as others do; our emotions and attitudes will stand between us and the more dispassionate definition of reality.

Though thinking objectively about social phenomena does not come easily, there are situations in which anyone must be guided, for his own self-interest if nothing else, by an objective assessment of what is likely to happen. A businessman, for example, must objectively assess market conditions, the state of his own industry and his firm, the abilities of his competitors, the likely demands of labor unions, and a host of other factors in order to work out policies of successful business operation.

Objectivity as a Norm

In social research objectivity is a *norm*, a standard governing research behavior. To make objectivity more likely, some useful techniques have been devised. Random sampling, for example, insures representativeness of data, thus avoiding a biased sample from which invalid inferences might otherwise be made. Also, long experience in devising questionnaires and conducting interviews has provided a substantial stock of knowledge about sources of bias. *Loaded* (emotionally-tinged) words bring distorted responses; complex and ambiguous language fails to communicate.

Good interviewing requires practiced skill. The interview is an interaction situation in which the relative status of the interviewer and the interviewed person can easily affect results. Differences in sex and race, for example, as when women interview men and whites interview blacks, may make a difference in some interview situations. What is at issue here is the willingness of those interviewed to speak frankly and fully. Men are not likely to be frank with women interviewers on matters about which men hold a perspective not shared with women. Blacks might not be open to whites on some matters of race. People of lower status sometimes tell a higher-status interviewer what they think the interviewer wants to hear. Thus, accumulated experience in interviewing provides some knowledge of how to minimize the bias inherent in the interview situation.

The Norm of Publicity

Techniques and procedures based on past experience are certainly useful, but social researchers always invoke a basic principle for insuring objectivity found in all sciences, namely, the requirement that any scientific work be open to public scrutiny by competent students. This "norm of publicity," as Scott Greer calls it, requires the social researcher to submit his work to a jury of his peers.[16] Whatever idiosyncratic bias is evident in his work will be challenged by others who hold no such bias. The very threat of that, presumably, will promote a self-conscious discipline in social scientists.[17] Objectivity is sustained, then, not primarily by individual objectivity, but by institutional practices, such as public scrutiny, and also by replication of studies to see if other researchers can get comparable results.

Bias as Perspective

Like all human beings, social scientists share the values and premises of their society, often of their social classes. Contemporary American sociologists are Western, urban, professional, educated, middle-class people, and not all of the assumptions inherent in the world-view of such people can be consciously guarded against when doing research. Bias in research now becomes the *collective bias* of the community of scholars. The norm of publicity will not suffice in this case.

There are some notable examples in the sociological record of such collective bias,

Figure 2.4 In order to understand the meaning and intent of social interaction among groups sociologists observe and often live with such groups. This was true of Elliott Liebow when he studied black street-corner men. *(Homer Page, The Ford Foundation)*

a matter of shared perspectives. Here are four:

The City The study of the city in American sociology developed by contrasting it to the rural community, unconsciously invoking rural and communal values in the process, thus leading to the study of the city from an anti-urban perspective (*see* Chapter 8).[18]

The Family Despite familiarity with ethnographic data on wide variations in the structure of the family, many American sociologists have treated the black mother-centered family as a "breakdown" in the normal American family pattern rather than

[16] Scott Greer, *The Logic of Social Inquiry* (Chicago: Aldine Publishing Co., 1969), pp. 6–7.

[17] Even that does not always suffice however; *see,* for example, Larry Reynolds, "A Note on the Perpetuation of a 'Scientific' Fiction," *Sociometry,* 29 (March 1966), pp. 85–88.

[18] *See* Morton and Lucia White, *The Intellectual versus the City* (Cambridge, Mass.: Harvard University Press and M.I.T. Press, 1962).

as an adaptation to historical and structural conditions (*see* Chapter 11).[19]

Social Change   Robert Nisbet has argued brilliantly that for 2,500 years the Western mind has spoken of "growth" and "development," a metaphorical borrowing from biology, where plants and animals do grow and develop according to their inherent nature.[20] There is an unfolding from seed to fully developed plant or organism. Applying that to the study of society, Western thinkers since and including the ancient Greeks have imposed on the fact of social change the idea that it is directional, is cumulative, is irreversible, moves through stages, and possesses purpose. In civilization, as in biological life, it is believed, there is growth and decay.

In a perceptive piece of scholarship Nisbet shows us that this is a persuasive but nonetheless Western ethnocentricity. Only because we hold such powerful preconceptions do we ever "see" a society grow and decay; in fact, he says, we do not; we see, or see evidence of, a bewildering record of historical change. Seeing it as evidence of the growth and decay of something called Civilization is an immensely powerful built-in preconception of Western thought.

Race Relations   American sociologists since the 1940s have viewed race relations in the United States from a liberal perspective that claims slow but steady progress toward desegregation and integration, and accepts movement toward this goal as an adequate sociological model of race relations in American society. Whether con-

sciously or not, sociologists have been providing scientific justification for liberal ideology (*see* Chapter 11).

Ideas Have Social Roots

The presence of collective bias compels us to recognize that all ideas, including social-scientific ones, emerge out of particular human situations and interests; all ideas have social roots. It was Karl Marx who made us most conscious of that fact, as when he said, "It is not the consciousness of men that determines their being, but, on the contrary, their social being that determines their consciousness."[21]

But could not consciousness sometimes emerge from significant social formations other than social class? Karl Mannheim (1893–1947), a brilliant student of the sociology of knowledge (the study of the relation of ideas to social structure), argued that it could, and extended Marx' original thesis to include status groups, sects, generational groups, integrated groups, and groups formed by socially-uprooted individuals.[22]

That all ideas, even scientific ones, do not spring virginal from the human brow but are the product of human effort and struggle with the conditions of life is an important insight, but one which has discouraging implications for the problem of objectivity; it invites despair over the possibility of objective truth. Yet Mannheim, for one, felt no despair and saw the possibility for an objective social science.

[19] *See* Lee Rainwater and William L. Yancey, *The Moynihan Report and the Politics of Controversy* (Cambridge, Mass.: M.I.T. Press, 1967).
[20] Robert Nisbet, *Social Change and History* (New York: Oxford University Press, 1969).
[21] Karl Marx, Preface, *A Contribution to the Critique of Political Economy* in Karl Marx and Frederick Engels, *Selected Works* (Moscow: Progress Publishers, 1968), p. 182.
[22] *See* Karl Mannheim, *Ideology and Utopia* (New York: Harcourt, 1936); also, Kurt H. Wolff, ed., *From Karl Mannheim* (New York: Oxford University Press, 1971).

His answer was found in a particular kind of human experience, that which occurs when the individual is *marginal* to several social groups, not fully integrated into any one, thus not "captured" by the perspective of any single class or group. Mannheim saw in the mobile and uprooted conditions of post-World War I Germany a body of "unattached intellectuals"—he was one of them—who possessed the capacity to transcend the dogmas and doctrines of particular social groups. These individuals could be the "seedground for objective knowledge," as Scott Greer so aptly phrased it.[23]

Mannheim's answer has not satisfied most social scientists, however. He tells us, Greer notes, of "the kind of individuals who have socially detached perspectives," and also, "what kinds of situations may produce hypotheses transcending the folk thought and interests of specific groups within the society."[24] But he does not tell us how to determine if these individuals are objective or even accurate. Nor can he assure us, we might add, that a collection of socially-detached intellectuals can constitute a continuing community of social-scientific scholars sharing some consensus about methods of study and about the knowledge obtained by these methods.

Approaching the issues in a different manner, Gideon Sjoberg and Roger Nett argue that the researcher needs to examine himself in crosscultural perspective:

If the researcher compares his own actions with those of scientists in other sociocultural settings or in an earlier era within his own society, he can attain an understanding of the universal problems that face anyone who seeks to analyze human action.[25]

What Sjoberg and Nett call for is full recognition that various social forces impinge on the mind of the social researcher, and that these should be brought to the level of consciousness to be identified and confronted. "This objectification of the social pressures upon the scientist is a necessary, if not a sufficient, condition for achieving some measure of control over them. Sheer knowledge of the hidden biases makes it possible to bypass them or eliminate them completely from the research design."[26]

As long as American sociologists were confined to a sociological community that was almost exclusively American, few of them knew how to examine themselves in crosscultural perspective, but now sociology is more and more an international community. The *American-ness* of American sociologists is subject to check by non-American sociologists. Furthermore, though most American sociologists still do their research in American society, more and more their work is deliberately comparative. Increasingly their generalizations are based on at least some data drawn from societies other than their own.

All of this increases the potential for an objective, crosscultural, crossnational sociology. None of it is a guarantee, however; the problem of collective bias remains difficult. But recognizing the difficulty is no warrant for sociologists to abandon the aim. Instead, it presses them to find ways to break through the closed minds that everyone suffers as a consequence of sharing membership in particular social groups. We cannot have an objective social science unless we find some way to break out of group-imposed cultural shells.

[23] Greer, *op. cit.*, p. 6.
[24] Greer, *op. cit.*, p. 6.
[25] Sjoberg and Nett, *op. cit.*, p. 11.

[26] Sjoberg and Nett, *op. cit.*, p. 11.

The Obtrusive Observer

For many social scientists, and for others, these complex issues have been the basis for arguing that social science cannot reach the level of objectivity that natural science can, because the social scientist is part of the phenomena he analyzes. But physical scientists now recognize that even they do not escape this problem: The method of observation always affects the phenomenon being observed; the observer is always an obtrusive factor. There can be no avoidance of that fact in any science; scientists can only confront it and find ways to take account of it. Kai Erikson summed it up well:

Recent critiques of sociology, then, focus attention on something we have really known for a long time—that the sociological enterprise, for all its internal consistencies and balances, nonetheless rests on a soft substratum of human biases and assumptions. This is inconvenient, perhaps, but inescapable; and we can only take what comfort we can from the fact that the older and more confident sciences have known it for years and have learned to regard it as a natural condition of their work.[27]

Traditions in Social Research

Sociology did not develop in any single way but grew from diverse strands of research and theorizing. It is still a multifaceted field and one aspect of that is two contrasting traditions of research. Though they have no well-defined names, let us call them *positivist* and *qualitative* sociology.

The Tradition of Positivism

Admiration for the rigor and exactness of natural science and conviction that all

sciences are alike in sharing the logical structure of the scientific method led positivists to utilize physical science as a model for developing sociology. Differences among the sciences are simply taken to be a consequence of the particular phenomena each science studies.

Positivists have led the way in emphasizing social *measurement* and the development of *quantitative* techniques in analyzing social data. Innovations in random sampling and in developing sample-survey research of various social populations are achievements of positivists; so is the refinement and innovation in statistical techniques useful to social scientists. This has been accompanied by refinement in the construction of questionnaires as instruments for gathering data, and in devising *scales* to measure such subjective phenomena as attitudes, degrees of commitment, and feelings of alienation. They are innovators in the use of the computer, permitting analysis of large bodies of data.

But size is not decisive for what positivists do. They have also, in fact, undertaken rigorously-controlled experiments with small groups under laboratory conditions. In a somewhat newer direction they have also pioneered in constructing *mathematical models* that in logic and technique go beyond the conventional statistical tools that most sociologists know well. Whether in a sample survey or in a small-groups laboratory, positivists hold as ideal, and seek to maximize, the carefully designed and rigorously-controlled scientific experiment.

The Qualitative Tradition

Qualitative sociology is built on the rich and varied experiences of fieldworkers who involve themselves closely in the lives of those they study. Its rationale comes from

---

[27] Kai T. Erikson, "Sociology: That Awkward Age," *Social Problems,* 19 (Spring 1972), p. 433.

a philosophical tradition that, in contrast to positivism, claims a radical difference exists between society and nature. Nature, it is asserted, can only be observed from the outside, and observed relations among natural phenomena are mechanical relations of causality. But society can (and must) be understood and studied from the inside, and that we can do because we are already in society. We can comprehend its relations, not as mechanical relations of causation but as relations of meaning and intent.

For the qualitative sociologist as field-worker, it is not only essential to observe what people do, it is important to know what they *mean* by what they do. The interest here is not to know what is inside somebody's head but to find out what is inside the social world of shared meanings that actors build up with one another through interaction.

From this perspective, explaining human action requires that the subjective meaning held by the actors be incorporated into the explanation. Max Weber, a great sociological scholar, insisted that sociological explanation be adequate at the level of *causation*—that is, explained logically according to scientific procedures—and also be adequate at the level of *meaning*—that is, understandable from the perspective of those involved. For Weber, sociology was *verstehende* (understanding) *sociologie*.

Sustained observation over time, as well as participant observation, remains the creative skill of those sociologists who believe in close and detailed observation *in vivo* of their human subjects. Such classics as William F. Whyte's *Street Corner Society* have served as models for generations of sociologists to emulate. Herbert Gans' *The Urban Villagers* is a contemporary model. Recent studies like *Tally's Corner*, an inti-

mate portrait of black street-corner men (done, incidentally, by a white social scientist), and *Justice without Trial*, an analysis of how policemen actually enforce law in their daily routines, are recent examples of the kinds of qualitative studies that seek to explore the "inner" world of its subjects through close observation and participation.[28]

The Problem Chooses the Method

The sharp contrast we have drawn here does not warrant any notion that these two traditions are warring camps. Most sociologists probably make no clearcut identification with either one. Indeed, over time many of the differences between them have been blurred; positivists, for example, do not deny the importance of knowing the values and intentions of actors in a situation. Imaginative sociologists borrow shamelessly from both traditions in constructing their own research projects.

And why not? It is a principle of scientific research that the method employed is determined by the needs of the study. Some sociologists may be primarily field-workers, and gifted ones at that; others may be experts in doing sample surveys. But their skill in and preference for one technique over another does not justify using that technique in every study. Rather, what technique to employ in gathering data should be decided solely by what needs to be known and how appropriate data might best be gathered. The problem determines the method, not the other way around.

Whatever the method chosen, the find-

[28] Elliott Liebow, *Tally's Corner* (Boston: Little, Brown & Company, 1967); Jerome H. Skolnick, *Justice without Trial: Law Enforcement in Democratic Society* (New York: John Wiley & Sons, Inc., 1966).

ings of any study are always tentative. As in all of science no problem is ever closed forever, no matter how certain its theoretical status at one time seems. As Scott Greer notes:

This is another way of saying that scientific knowledge is perpetually hypothetical in nature: at any one point in history it amounts to humanity's best guess about the nature of things.[29]

SOCIOLOGY AND SOCIETY

The intention to be scientific has been a powerful pull on sociologists, but the desire to be relevant has also been strong. Sociology grew in part out of empirical work that explored the lives of the "other half," and a concern for understanding and solving social problems has long been a vigorous impulse within American sociology.

But that is only one conception of what it means to be relevant. For other sociologists the relevance of sociology is in the contribution it can make by its growth as a science of society. If there could be a science of society, then society would be more rational than at any time in history.

Sociology and Values

The question of values has always been troublesome for sociology. The aim to create an objective social science has forced sociologists to confront values in at least three ways.

The Values of Science

First, like all scientists, sociologists accept some values as basic to the scientific

[29] Greer, *op. cit.*, p. 7.

enterprise. There is consensus in sociology about the value of objectivity; it is the major norm governing research action. Behind that, and making sense of it, is the value placed on knowledge; science seeks to create knowledge and values it over ignorance. Concomitantly, science chooses truth over error and reason over blind faith or superstition.

There has also been much concern over, but much less consensus on, the idea that certain other values are necessary in order for sociologists to do their work well. Sociologists, it would seem, work better in a free environment, one that is tolerant of their inquiries into practices and actions found in society. A democratic society would, therefore, seem more likely to support sociology than would authoritarian or totalitarian ones. But the rapid growth of sociology in Communist countries, including the Soviet Union, clouds the issue. It suggests that sociology can be conceived in different ways, specifically, as an autonomous scientific discipline on the one hand, or as a skilled, technical source of useful data on the other. When it is the latter, it is eminently useful in the most unfree of milieus.

Values as Facts

A second way in which sociology confronts values is to define them, for purposes of analysis, as social facts; it is a fact that particular values are held by particular people, or are related to certain social actions; it is equally a fact that others do not hold such values, and do not seem to act upon them. Values, then, are relative; not everyone holds the same values. But they are real in the lives of people and must be taken into account in explaining social action.

Value-neutrality

A third way is to claim that, except for the basic values of science, sociology is neutral toward all values. To demand of the sociologist that he be value-free is to claim that his commitment to the search for knowledge does not allow him, *as a scientist,* to make value-judgments or to advocate any moral or political position. He is then ethnically neutral.

A rationale for value-neutrality often offers an instrumental view of science as a means to an end. Science can presumably tell us *how* to achieve our goals, but not *what* goals we should seek. This is based on a philosophical premise: *What is* does not tell us *what should be.* No one can ever decide what he ought to do simply by knowing what is. The empirical situation can never dictate the moral one.

There is an additional argument that points to scientific knowledge as a two-edged sword; it can be used for both moral and immoral purposes. A biological knowledge of germs, for example, can be used to reduce disease among humans and animals; it can also be used to conduct germ warfare. For which of these purposes it is used is a political decision, and scientists alone (or even at all), so goes the argument, do not and should not decide on the uses to which scientific knowledge is put.

On this point the advocates of value-neutrality are on firm ground. It is true that knowledge once discovered can be used in many ways, for many human purposes. Furthermore, science views its knowledge not as property—there are no patents or private rights for scientific discoveries—but declares that it is there for all who take the trouble to learn.

Yet there is something unsatisfactory about this argument. If science can serve moral and immoral purposes equally well, then increasing scientific knowledge does not necessarily better the lot of mankind; it merely increases the capability with which people can pursue both moral and immoral goals. What the right hand can more effectively cure, the left hand can more effectively kill.

Surely scientists intend more than this as their contribution to society. They have always believed that increased scientific knowledge would not simply put much greater know-how in the hands of moral barbarians but would make it possible for mankind to create a more humane existence. But that is less likely if science is viewed merely as a tool by which someone else (usually the powerful) can more effectively achieve group or organizational goals.

Is Value-neutrality Possible?

Some sociologists construct a different argument: that it is not possible to be value-neutral. The sociologist, they assert, is not a sociologist twenty-four hours a day. He is also a parent, teacher, citizen, and neighbor; he belongs to a family, a university, a community, a professional organization, or a political party. In these groups he shares with others values that cannot help but be carried over into his work. Values cannot be shed easily like a coat on a warm day; they are woven into any person's perspective on life.

Furthermore, sociologists—and other scientists, as well—have never in practice been as neutral as they claimed to be. Throughout this century scientists did not remain indifferent to organized expressions of racial or religious bigotry. They have strongly asserted a scientific basis for treating racial groupings as equal, and they resolutely opposed the brutal treatment of the Jewish people by the Nazis. In the United States the scientific community as a whole—with a few individual exceptions—has challenged racist myths that assert the superiority of whites over nonwhites.

In doing this, to be sure, they were standing firmly on scientific findings and were challenging whatever cultural myths and beliefs made claims of fact contrary to scientific evidence. Critics of value-neutrality, however, have often meant something different: the intrusion into scientific work of values that were not based on scientific findings; the instances of collective bias just given are examples of what is meant.

Is Value-neutrality Desirable?

While some sociologists claim value-neutrality is not even possible, others argue it is not desirable. It is not that these latter sociologists think it possible, so much as they believe that acting as if it *were* possible leads to undesirable consequences. Alvin Gouldner challenged the commitment to value-neutrality, while arguing that, first, it had served sociologists well in the past:

Without doubt the value-free principle did enhance the autonomy of sociology; it was one way in which our discipline pried itself loose—in some modest measure—from the clutch of its society, in Europe freer from political party influence, in the United States freer of ministerial influence. In both places, the value-free doctrine gave sociology a larger area of autonomy in which it could steadily pursue basic problems . . .[30]

But now there are other, less admirable consequences. For one thing, it became for some an excuse for being morally indifferent or morally irresponsible, while pursuing personal interests in the name of science. In other cases it became a reason for not doing what often took courage anyway—to criticize society. "*One* latent meaning then of a value-free sociology is this: 'Thou shalt not commit a critical or negative value-judgment—especially of one's own society.' "[31]

During the 1960s, radical sociologists emphasized this point.[32] They often charged that value-neutrality served as a cloak behind which sociologists accepted the prevailing social structure uncritically in return for improved status, professional recognition, and more material support. Put mildly, sociologists had been coopted; put harshly, they had sold out. Gouldner was not so harsh:

What seems more likely is that it entails something in the nature of a tacit bargain; in return for a measure of autonomy and social support, many social scientists have surrendered their critical impulses. This was not usually a callous "sell-out" but a slow process of mutual accommodation; both parties suddenly found themselves betrothed without a formal ceremony.[33]

Obviously, value-neutrality does not actually mean sociologists can be devoid of values—a psychological and cultural impossibility—but it refers to a relationship between society and the community of soci-

---

[30] Alvin Gouldner, "Anti-Minotaur: The Myth of a Value-free Sociology," *Social Problems*, 9 (1962), p. 203.

[31] Gouldner, *op. cit.*, p. 205.

[32] *See*, for example, essays by Richard Lichtman, John Horton and Howard Ehrlich in J. David Colfax and Jack L. Roach, eds., *Radical Sociology* (New York: Basic Books, Inc., 1971); and essays by Sidney Wilhelm, Martin Nicolaus, and Alvin Gouldner, in Larry T. Reynolds and Janice M. Reynolds, eds., *The Sociology of Sociology* (New York: David McKay Company, Inc., 1970).

[33] Gouldner, *op. cit.*, p. 206.

ologists. If not *that* relationship, some other must exist. There must be understanding in society as to what sociologists are doing, and they must gain some support in order to teach and do research. The issue resolves into varying conceptions of the uses of sociology in society.

The Uses of Sociology

From its very beginning sociology has been regarded by its practitioners as useful to society in some way. August Comte (1798–1857) saw in sociology a means to provide reorganization of society and to create social order where little seemed to exist.[34] Being useful, then, has never been the issue, for all sciences are useful. But how and in what way—that has been argued about.

Practical Uses

Some of the rapid growth of sociology can be accounted for by its practical use to government agencies making policy and evaluating programs, to politicians seeking office, to administrators trying to control and direct people's actions, to corporations wanting to "handle" employees or market their products better. Most large organizations in modern society use sociological research to advance specific goals.

Such practical usefulness brings customers to sociology, provides a source of research funds, and makes sociologists seem like useful, practical people. But other sociologists deplore and criticize this practicalness. To them, such use seems always to help the powerful and those with special interests to have their way with ordi-

[34] For selections from Comte's writings, *see* George Simpson, *August Comte: Sire of Sociology* (New York: Thomas Y. Crowell Company, 1969).

Figure 2.5 Sociological research often meets the needs of the powerful and on-going organizations in society. *(Wide World Photos)*

nary people who, as publics, or clients, or customers are manipulated, controlled, or administered. Practical for whom, then, becomes a critical question.

Ideological Uses

In a society in which change is constant, in which old institutions and organizations find their authority challenged, and in which new and powerful groups emerge without clearly defined legitimacy, the very study of society has meaning, intended or not, which supports or denies claims to authority and legitimacy. As C. Wright Mills noted:

Every society holds images of its own nature —in particular images and slogans that justify its system of power and the ways of the powerful. The images and ideas produced by social scientists may or may not be consistent with

35

these prevailing images, but they always carry implications for them.[35]

Implications like these can be both helpful and hurtful to those whose interests are served by sustaining such images. But they do not leave it to chance; they seek out social researchers to provide what Mills called "ideological ammunition."[36] There seem always to be some social researchers to provide it.

Both practical and ideological uses of sociology are most likely to meet the needs and help to resolve the problems of the on-going organizations of society. In this particular sense, sociology can be a "managerial sociology," as sociologist Harold Sheppard once termed it.[37] In the sense, too, that such sociological work is basically supportive of society's institutions and organizations, its power structure and its class structure, it is conservative in its political meaning, even if not in conscious intent.

Critical Uses

There are many sociologists who do not wish deliberately to engage in ideological attack for or against the established structures of society, but who do want sociology to address itself to issues that are relevant for the lives of its members. They want a sociology not committed to existing social institutions, though not automatically opposed to whatever is just because it is. They want a sociology free from partisan commitment, whether that be to General Motors Corporation, the Department of Defense, the Democratic Party, or the Black Panthers. They want a sociology whose claims to independent status free it from being a servant of power—any power. They want a sociology which examines with interest and sympathy the emergence of social movements among the oppressed, without being propagandist for such movements. They want, in short, a critical, inquiring sociology which asks questions of social and political significance while also asking questions of theoretical import.

Over thirty years ago Robert Lynd called for such a sociology in his renowned book, *Knowledge for What?*:

No protestations of scientific objectivity and ethical neutrality can excuse the social scientist from coming down into the arena and accepting as his guiding values, *in selecting and defining his problems,* these deep, more widely based, cravings which living personalities seek to realize.[38]

At the outset of the book he had said: "Social science is not a scholarly arcanum, but an organized part of the culture which exists to help man in continually understanding and rebuilding his culture."[39]

For a more recent generation C. Wright Mills provided brilliant instruction on how to make critical use of sociology; his *The Sociological Imagination* was a sustained argument in behalf of such study. In the work of Lynd and Mills, and in a long line of sociological thinkers back to Karl Marx, a new generation found the conviction that

[35] C. Wright Mills, *The Sociological Imagination* (New York: Oxford University Press, 1959, *see* all of Chapter 4, pp. 76–99; paperback edition, Grove Press, 1961, p. 80).
[36] Mills, *op. cit.,* p. 81.
[37] *See* Harold Sheppard, "The Treatment of Unionism in 'Managerial Sociology,'" *American Sociological Review,* 14 (April 1949), pp. 310–313.
[38] Robert S. Lynd, *Knowledge for What?* (Princeton, N.J.: Princeton University Press, 1939; paperback edition, 1966), p. 191
[39] Lynd, *op. cit.,* p. ix.

knowledge was intended to solve our problems and to change the world.

The Sociologist in Society

What, then, does this all add up to? The problem of values in sociological work, and their implication in the varied uses of sociology, offer no easy solution, possibly no solution at all. For sociologists, to make a critical use of sociology requires that sociology be reasonably independent, reasonably autonomous. That cannot be accomplished from the principle that science is an *instrumental* means to any and all human purposes. To be sure, sociology—and any science—can be used as an instrument; that is why sociology is growing in use in the Soviet Union and other Communist nations.

But for a critical use of sociology to be a dominant commitment of sociologists, sociology, and all of science—for sociology is but one modest room in the house of science—must claim to be an institution in its own right, with its own goals and values, its own sense of purpose. Yet, if that sense of purpose is to warrant a reasonable degree of autonomy in society, it must not be a purpose that serves only the interests of elites or is indifferent to "the lives of quiet desperation" of ordinary men. Alvin Gouldner put it well when he said:

Social science can never be fully accepted in a society, or by a part of it, without paying its way; this means it must manifest both its relevance and its concern for the contemporary human predicament. Unless the value-relevances of sociological inquiry are made plainly evident, unless there are at least some bridges between it and larger human hopes and purposes, it must inevitably be scorned by laymen as pretentious word-mongering.[40]

We hope to make it plain that sociology at its best is much more than "pretentious word-mongering."

[40] Gouldner, *op. cit.*, p. 205.

SUMMARY

A scientific sociology requires:

1. A carefully formulated *statement of the problem* and useful questions, the answers to which confirm, amplify, or revise knowledge.
2. *Theory,* an effort at explanation that is constructed logically and tested empirically.
3. *Concepts,* terms denoting a *general* class of objects, rendered as precise as possible. The origin of sociological concepts in ordinary language, or in special non-sociological languages, makes this difficult.
4. *Data-gathering,* a process of observing the world by techniques and tools devised for that purpose: sampling, questionnaires, interviews, fieldwork, including participant observation, and documents.

A major norm governing social research is *objectivity*. Individual bias is checked by requiring that all work be subject to scrutiny by a jury of peers (the norm of publicity), but *collective bias* is not checked in this way unless the community of sociologists is cross-cultural and cross-national.

There have been two major traditions in sociological research. One is *positivism,* based on admiration for the rigor of natural science and emphasizing quantification and measurement. The other is the *qualitative*, based on close-up, often participant observation of social action, which includes finding out what *meanings* people share in their interaction.

Sociology confronts values in three ways: first, there are values held by science—objectivity, knowledge, truth, reason—second, it is a fact that particular people hold particular values, and these must be accounted for in explaining their actions; and third, sociology claims neutrality toward all values other than scientific ones.

Value-neutrality is an effort to attain some autonomy for sociology, but its use of an *instrumental* conception of science makes an unsatisfactory argument and justifies an uncritical, therefore conservative acceptance of the sociologists' own society.

Sociology can become of *practical* use to organizations and powerful groups, and it has *ideological* use in justifying and legitimizing powerful groups. But most sociologists desire a *critical* use, in which sociologists are neither automatically for or against anything but are free to examine critically any social institution or group. This requires, not an instrumental view of science but a conception of sociology as having a purpose of its own worthy of some autonomy and as paying its own way by addressing itself to concerns significant to members of the society.

Suggested Readings

Severyn T. Bruyn, *The Human Perspective in Sociology: The Methodology of Participant Observation* (Englewood Cliffs, N.J.: Prentice-Hall, Inc., 1966). A careful, detailed examination of how and why participant observation provides a means of getting at the "inner" perspective.

William J. Filstead, *Qualitative Sociology* (Chicago: Markham, 1970). A book of essays on the problems and promise of qualitative sociology by skilled practitioners.

Scott Greer, *The Logic of Social Inquiry* (Chicago: Aldine Publishing Co., 1969). A sophisticated treatise on the problems of social research by a distinguished practitioner.

Phillip Hammond, ed., *Sociologists at Work: Essays on the Craft of Social Research* (New York: Basic Books, Inc., 1964). An interesting set of essays by the authors of some noted research about what it is really like to do good research.

Abraham Kaplan, *The Conduct of Social Inquiry* (San Francisco: Chandler Publishing Company, 1964). A noted philosopher probes the problems of scientific analysis in social science.

Sanford Labovitz and Robert Hagedorn, *Introduction to Social Research* (New York: McGraw-Hill, Inc., 1971). A brief paperback introduction to the basics of social research.

Robert S. Lynd, *Knowledge for What?* (Princeton, N.J.: Princeton University Press, 1939; paperback edition, 1966). A sociological classic that challenged value-neutrality over thirty years ago.

John Madge, *The Origins of Scientific Sociology* (New York: The Free Press, 1962). An examination of great classics of social investigation provides an historical view of the development of sociological research.

Karl Mannheim, *Ideology and Utopia* (New York: Harcourt, 1936; paperback edition, 1949). The classic work that introduced American sociologists to Mannheim and the sociology of knowledge.

Larry T. Reynolds and Janice M. Reynolds, *The Sociology of Sociology* (New York: David McKay Company, Inc., 1970). A fine collection of essays in which sociologists critically examine sociology from a sociological perspective.

Gideon Sjoberg and Roger Nett, *A Methodology for Research* (New York: Harper & Row, 1968). An exploration of the problems of social research, using the perspective of the sociology of knowledge.

Gideon Sjoberg, *Ethics, Politics, and Social Research* (Cambridge, Mass.: Schenkman, 1967). A series of essays exploring the ethical issues that emerge in doing research and the political constraints and pressures that often plague research on social issues.

PART **II**

THE STUDY OF
SOCIAL LIFE

No longer in a merely physical universe, man lives
in a symbolic universe.
—*Ernst Cassirer*

Chapter 3

Interaction:
Structure and Process

It frequently happens that to learn new ideas people have to unlearn old
ones. So it has been in the study of society. To learn that society emerges
from interaction, it was necessary to free the conception of man from older
ideas that located the determination of human behavior solely in instincts
or in such external factors as geography, climate, or race. Modern sociology
—indeed, all of modern social science—draws its inspiration from the
simple but fundamental idea that neither individual conduct nor the organization of society is to be explained by nonsocial factors. Person and
society in all their human variety emerge from social interaction. (Yet that
basic point does not permit us to dismiss nonsocial factors as insignificant.
Interaction occurs in a physical environment which always conditions or
limits the possibilities of interaction.)

INTERACTION: SOCIAL AND SYMBOLIC

Whatever else man may usefully be imagined to be, sociology concerns
itself with man as an *actor*; when he *acts* he initiates and directs action
toward objects (including persons) in the world around him. In observing

social life we see people acting: conversing, praying, working, arguing. All around us is a stream of on-going activity, and this action is the "stuff" of which society is made.

The Social Act

When a person acts, he does something that he and others understand and give a name to: "eating dinner," "taking a test," "writing a paper," "reading a book," "watching TV," "playing baseball," "making love," "borrowing money," "going to work." To name it is to identify it, separate it out from the stream of on-going activity, and mark it off by conventional understandings shared by members of the society. By knowing the language, each of us knows what it is and what it does.

By not knowing the language we do not know what the act is or means, even though we observe it directly. If we came upon a group of crouching young men and asked, "What are they doing?" And someone said, "Shooting craps"; we would then understand their actions *if* we knew what dice were and how they were used in a game of chance. Otherwise, watching a group of young men crouching down in a circle, each in turn rolling two small objects around in their hands and then throwing them down on the ground while making strange sounds would seem to be odd behavior indeed. Any action seems odd when you do not understand what it means to the actors involved; only when we understand the meanings the actors give to their actions do we understand what they are doing.

Interaction

Social acts connect with other social acts in an on-going stream of human activity, in *interaction,* which is the process by which two or more persons are acting toward and responding to one another at the same time. A conversation between two or more persons is a simple example. Each person speaks to others and simultaneously responds to what others are saying. Furthermore, each person takes account of the others. To "take account" means to be aware of the others, to define each of them as a social object of particular meaning (he is a friend, teacher, salesman; he is friendly, cold, impersonal; he is important, prestigious, lowly), and to include that definition of the other in deciding how to act toward him. Thus, the action of persons in social interaction is *meaningful* action.

To converse, then, is not just to emit sounds but to express some cultural meaning through gestures and words. Cultural meaning is meaning held in common by the actors in the interaction. Each actor must respond to the others' gestures and words in a like manner; they must assign common meaning to the interaction. When this occurs, there is communication. Communication, in turn, requires *language,* a complex system of verbal, written, and gestural *symbols* that are "conventional," socially-created, and adopted by men to convey meaning.

Signs and Symbols

It is not a new idea that man lives with and through symbols, and that language is his most basic symbolic process. René Descartes and John Locke said this centuries ago. But only within this century has the importance of man's symbolic capacities become a firm pillar of our assumptions about man. The anthropologist, Leslie White, offers a vigorous argument for the idea that the symbol is basic to making man human and to building civilization.[1]

Signs

Acknowledging that there are impressive similarities between animal and human behavior (and that in some important ways man *is* an animal), White insists there is nonetheless a basic difference: Animals do not enter into the world of man—the symbolic world. Animals, agrees White, can be taught to respond to a vocal command, and any kind of vocal sound can be used for such a purpose. Here we are dealing with *signs*. A sign is "a physical thing or event whose function is to indicate some other thing or event."[2] Some signs occur in nature, such as dark clouds and wind signifying a coming storm; others are conventional; that is, human-made, such as a traffic signal.

Animals can learn very complex sign systems, and animals (including human ones) can be conditioned to respond in set ways to contrived signs. White, however, makes the significant point that although a dog can learn appropriate signs, it is only man that "*can and does play an active role in determining what value the vocal stimulus is to have . . .*"[3] In short, a dog only passively *learns* signs, but man can *create* signs.

Symbols

When signs are conventional; that is, human-made, they are *symbols*. Symbols are all those objects (including words) for which human beings have a set of shared

meanings and values. Symbols always signify something; but not always a particular, specific event, like dark clouds signifying coming rain, or like a traffic signal telling us to stop or go. Thus, the "sign" of the cross is not a form to signify any particular event or action (though its origin is in the crucifixion of Jesus Christ), but to represent the *meanings* and *values* of the Christian faith.

One of the major philosophers of this century, Ernst Cassirer (1874–1945) saw in symbol-creating the distinctiveness of what is human, and credited man alone with having the "symbolic system."[4] "This new acquisition," he said, "transforms the whole of human life. As compared with other animals, man lives not merely in a broader reality; he lives, so to speak, in a new dimension of reality."[5] On this basis, Cassirer asserts that man should be defined as an *animal symbolicum*.[6]

The Social Nature of Language

Though the capacity to speak is universal, men do not inherit language as a dimension of their biological organism but must create it. They do so through the social interaction that goes on among those who share common experiences within a human community. This is a universal process; it is also a relative process— a particular language emerges among a particular people.

By possessing language a people can be conscious of the attributes and qualities of

---

[1] Leslie A. White, *The Science of Culture* (New York: Farrar, Straus, 1949; paperback edition, Grove Press, 1958). *See particularly* Chapter 2, "The Symbol: The Origin and Basis of Human Behavior."

[2] White, *op. cit.*, p. 27.

[3] White, *op. cit.*, p. 29.

[4] Ernst Cassirer, *An Essay on Man: Introduction of a Philosophy of Human Culture* (New Haven, Conn.: Yale University Press, 1944; paperback edition, Doubleday, 1953, p. 43).

[5] Cassirer, *op. cit.*, p. 43.

[6] Cassirer, *op. cit.*, p. 44.

THE SYMBOLIC WORLD

The world we live in is rich with symbols, some ancient and honored, some new, but always in use. When used, symbols sometimes fade out; they change in meaning; new ones replace old ones. Here are some familiar symbols of Western culture.

I. *Political* symbols: the *flag* of any nation; the *hammer* and *sickle* of world communism; the Nazi *swastika;* the *donkey* and *elephant* of the two American parties.

II. *American national* symbols: the American flag; the 4th of July; Memorial Day; George Washington, Abraham Lincoln; Bunker Hill; Boston tea party; Gettysburg Address; Declaration of Independence; the Constitution; the Bill of Rights.

III. *Colors* are symbols: *red* (blood) for courage (but red is also communism's symbolic color); *yellow* for cowardice; *black* for darkness, fear, and evil, for mourning; *white* for innocence and purity (the white bridal gown).

IV. The *animal kingdom:* doves for peace; hawks for war and aggressiveness; sparrows are insignificant but belong in God's kingdom; eagles for strength and majestic courage; foxes for cunning; lions for strength (king of the jungle); jackals for low, dishonest action; snakes for treachery and deceit.

V. Physical *gestures* are symbols: the military salute; the handshake; waving goodbye or hello; thumbs up; thumbs down; thumbing your nose; shrugging your shoulders; smiling or frowning; the two-fingered "V" sign; winking; raising an eyebrow.

the phenomena they encounter—whether physical, biological, or social—and of what happens in such encounters; they can assess and compare and so derive some meaning from them. In that way an encounter or event remembered and assessed becomes an *experience.* The meaning assigned to all experienced objects is not the product of the single individual but is based, as the educator John Dewey noted, on *consensus.*[7] It is the outcome of a social act of communication and agreement; for experience to have meaning, it must be shared and communicated.

[7] John Dewey, *Experience and Nature* (New York: Open Court, 1925), p. 179.

But to confer meaning on objects and events and to communicate those meanings requires that they be given cognitive form; that is, named and categorized. The blurring, buzzing confusion of sensations that an encounter with the world first gives to us requires an act of conceptualization. The array of separate perceptions must be integrated into concepts that specify qualities or relations; thus, concepts are necessary for there to be "facts." The simple perception that rain follows hard wind and dark clouds would not be mentally possible except through the cognitive process of naming and categorizing "wind," "clouds," and "rain," and specifying the sequence in which they are perceived.

Language and Reality

This cognitive process of naming, identifying, and categorizing enables us to represent experience by symbols. Through this symbolic representation we define and understand reality. This "reality" is not the array of raw impressions and perceptions that bombard our senses; and it is not something outside of us, an objective environment independent of our existence. Instead, raw sense impressions and perceptions are sifted through a symbolic screen and are given recognizable form by man-made symbols. They are organized into a system of meanings that define what is and what can be.

The sounds of a summer night, for example, are for most persons today the sounds of a *natural* reality, that of wind and animals. But in an earlier time every sound was acutely recorded as evidence of evil spirits, of ghosts, for the darkness of night was the habitat of evil. In such cases people were inhabiting different "realities." As another example note that in our time someone's bizarre and "unreal" behavior may be perceived as evidence of mental illness, that the person is "really sick." But in an earlier time it would be construed differently—that the person was possessed of the devil, bewitched. In these cases different symbolic systems give us different "realities" from the same raw sense data.

Thus, reality is humanly constructed; it is a symbolic environment, and it is this which man inhabits.[8] Reality is defined for us by our symbols.

[8] For a discussion of society as socially-constructed reality, *see* Peter Berger and Thomas Luckmann, *The Social Construction of Reality* (New York: Doubleday & Company, Inc., 1966; Anchor paperback edition, 1967).

Furthermore, language does not simply name and categorize objects or events that are concretely given and are already present in the environment, like wind, rain, and trees. It also names and identifies "invisible" objects, like "friendship" and "marriage." These could not be mentally grasped except through symbols, and so could only come into being through conceptualization. In his classic, *Mind, Self, and Society,* theorist George Herbert Mead (1863–1931) put it this way:

Symbolization constitutes objects not constituted before, objects which would not exist except for the context of social relationships wherein symbolization occurs. Language does not simply symbolize a situation or object which is already there in advance; it makes possible the existence or the appearance of that situation or object, for it is part of the mechanism whereby that situation or object is created.[9]

What Language Does

Once language is established, even what we perceive depends on the naming and identifying words available to us in our language. They become the spectacles by which we "see" the world. Journalist Walter Lippmann's famous aphorism is apropos: "First we look, then we name, and only then do we see." In short, language *organizes* our perceiving process; it identifies, selects, and also omits. What we do not have a word for may go unperceived. Without the concept of *neurosis*, for example, we would not perceive neurotic behavior but only some erratic actions, if we even noticed those. Perception is always highly selective, and words are the instruments of selection.

However, we do more than perceive

[9] George Herbert Mead, *Mind, Self, and Society* (Chicago: The University of Chicago Press, 1934), p. 78.

with the aid of language, we *think* with language. To think is to speak, and there is neither thinking without speaking nor speaking without thinking. Without the grammatical ordering of words, thought is vague and rudimentary. Plato had Socrates say: "When the mind is thinking, it is talking to itself." Yet, this ancient recognition of the dependence of thought on language was by no means commonplace. When Max Muller, a pioneering student of language, delivered his famous dictum: "No thought without words" in his *Three Lectures* in 1887, it became a source of controversy just because the idea was not obvious. Today, from the perspective of symbolic interaction (which we will next turn to), it is accepted without serious dispute.

Figure 3.1 Businessmen may meet in a restaurant to discuss a transaction away from the hectic atmosphere of an office. (*The New York Hilton at Rockefeller Center.*)

Symbolic Interaction

When interaction proceeds through the communication of meanings by language or other symbol-using processes, it is *symbolic interaction.* Persons in social interaction communicate meanings by their verbal behavior, as well as by conventionally defined (thus symbolic) gestures, such as winking or thumbing their noses. These gestures, according to George Herbert Mead, become *significant symbols* when they are *conscious* gestures by one actor which are then responded to by a second actor. Mead said: "The meaning of a gesture on the part of one organism is the adjustive response of another organism to it . . ."[10]

Defining the Situation

By the use of symbols, actors define the situation in which interaction occurs, for

[10] George H. Mead, *op. cit.,* p. 80.

it never occurs in a vacuum; there is always a larger context in which interaction takes place. For example, people conversing over dinner may be guests in the home of a host; or they may be businessmen carrying out a business transaction in an expensive restaurant, with one of them paying the bill and putting it on his expense account; or, yet again, the host may be entertaining his employer at dinner in his home.

"Conversation over dinner," then, takes place in different social situations, and this has consequences for the actors' conduct. Friends at dinner may engage in serious discussions, feel able to express themselves freely, and even dare to disagree while yet remaining friends. Businessmen intent on a transaction are likely to avoid serious subjects (other than the business deal) and stick to sports or shop-talk. The host entertaining his employer, and his wife-hostess, are likely to act in such a way as to maximize what they see as a good impression, which is likely to limit the kind of conversation carried on.

In each of these instances social interaction goes on in particular kinds of social situations. And it is the kind of social situation it is because it is *defined* that way by the actors in the situation. They acted, in short, in terms of how they defined the situation.

All of this leads to the idea that "if men define a situation as real, it *is* real in its consequences," which is what sociologist W. I. Thomas (1863–1947) meant by *the definition of the situation*. Thus, if actors define a situation as hostile and threatening, they will act to defend themselves, perhaps to respond hostilely themselves. To assert that, objectively, they were not correct may be true, but it is irrelevant for the purpose of understanding their actions.

Action Is Situational

Using symbols to define interaction also leads to the idea that action is *situational;* that is, the conduct of interacting persons occurs in a situation that has been symbolically defined. One type of situation, such as a party, permits one kind of action; whereas a work setting requires another. Interaction on the job is not the same as interaction after the job relaxing over a beer, even though the people are the same.

Though action is situational, every circumstance also contains elements which necessarily constrain and limit the act of defining the situation. Actors are not free to construct just any symbolic definition of a situation. They cannot avoid taking account of physical reality which is not man-made:

Man cannot act without some reference to the phenomenal character of his environment for long without being reminded by his senses that stone walls are impenetrable, that thorns do prick, that fires do burn, and the fists of another can contuse one's chin. The "pictures in our heads" do and must have some relation to the existential world.[11]

PATTERNS OF INTERACTION: ROLES AND RELATIONS

The concept of interaction is basic to all the social sciences; even the individual person can be understood only with reference to the social interactions significant in his life-experience. Sociological concepts are extensions of the concept of interaction, focusing upon those interactions that occur with some regularity, rather than transitory and ephemeral ones.

Roles and Relations

Interaction that is not fleeting and ephemeral involves an actor in a somewhat stable and persistent pattern: a *social relation*. Marriage is a social relation, so is friendship. There is an almost endless list: the relationship of foreman to worker, of parent to child, of doctor to patient, of student to teacher. These social relations can, in turn, be analyzed into constituent parts: *positions* and *roles*.

A social position is a socially identified place in a system of interaction: professor in a university, parent in a family, mayor of a city, secretary in an office, chairman of a committee. A role points out that the occupants of these positions interact with the occupants of other positions—husband with his wife, a doctor with his patients—

[11] Charles K. Warriner, *The Emergence of Society* (Homewood, Ill.: The Dorsey Press, 1970), pp. 58–59.

in patterned ways, and that both occupants always share some mutual *expectations* about how each will act toward the other. A social role, then, defines the action "expected" by the actors in social relations.

Role Expectations

Expectations are seldom spelled out precisely, as if they were lines in a play, carefully learned by an actor who then acts out his part as an author wrote it on cue; they do not specify particular conduct for all foreseeable situations. Instead, they denote an *orientation* to other actors. A role is better seen as *consistency* in orientation to others rather than as *conformity* to prescribed actions.[12] Consistency prescribes no specific conduct, though it suggests the range within which acceptable action will occur and also the range beyond which it cannot go without violating expectations.

Two people who are friends expect of each other actions they would never expect of strangers, but there is no blueprint to prescribe exactly what each is supposed to do for the other. In interaction among friends the specifics are worked out. "That's what a friend is for"—this suggests one can expect more from friends than from others; "a friend in need is a friend indeed"—friends are there when help is needed. But how far can this be carried—to helping a friend escape the clutches of the law, for example? In some situations and groups that would be a legitimate expectation; in others it would be much more problematic.

Let us take a more detailed example. A woman learns to act toward others in a

Figure 3.2 The mother role encompasses caring for the child, meeting both his physical and psychological needs. *(Wide World Photos)*

way consistent with shared expectations—shared by both men and women—of what acting like a woman means. When she marries, she must act like a wife, an expectation that may not prescribe conduct in all details though it may specify some, such as cooking meals and caring for a house. She will need to act in such a way as to validate her claim to being a woman and a wife. When she becomes a mother other expectations orient her to act so as to validate her claims to being a mother. She must act as a mother is supposed to act.

And how is that? The blueprint does not exist, so each woman constructs the role of mother for herself. What she constructs is oriented to the most general expectations in society that she *ought* to care for her child—nurture and comfort it, tend to its material and physical needs, train it, and, when necessary, discipline it. A mother is

[12] *See* Ralph Turner, "Role Taking: Process versus Conformity," in Arnold M. Rose, ed., *Human Behavior and Social Processes* (Boston: Houghton-Mifflin Company, 1962), pp. 20–40.

expected to have the sentiments of "motherhood," combining caring, patience, devotion, and gentleness. (Today the women's liberation movement wants to redefine radically the traditional expectations held by both women and men of what is womanly, wifely, and motherly conduct. *See* Chapter 18.)

Levels of Role Expectation

In the case just described, as in most others, it would be an error to think that role expectations are pervasive throughout society and that they coerce us into specific actions, however unwelcome. Role expectation occurs at different levels of generality. At the society-wide level, they are the most general expectations of the kind we have been discussing. But within social classes and ethnic groups, variations occur. The female role expectations that the wife of a corporation executive encounters are not the same for the wife of a blue-collar worker, and are still different for a black woman in the inner-city ghetto. Generations, too, can make a difference. Younger women support one another in feeling freer to ignore some traditional expectations that were more compelling for their mothers, such as those about education, having children, training for a profession, and living with a man before marriage. In interacting among themselves and with young men, they are creating new expectations for their roles, and, incidentally, for male roles too.

There is no escaping the fact that when two young persons develop a relationship, the more general expectations learned from society, from their class, from their families, from their generation will be modified as they work out very particular role expectations applied only to one another. Expectations are not merely learned, they

are always redefined and altered in interaction. Furthermore, since roles are always ambiguous in at least some aspects of the relationship, role-taking is continuously subject to redefinition and remaking.

Role Set

Up to this point we have spoken as if there were but one role associated with a social position, but that is not so. A student, for example, finds himself in a relationship with fellow students, which invokes one set of expectations, and in a relationship with professors, which brings forth somewhat different expectations. He finds that interacting with administrators and other rule-enforcers manifests still other expectations; and even quite different expectations may emerge from interacting outside the university, as, for example, with the local police. For the position of student, then, there is not one role but a *role set*, a differentiated set of role expectations that orient him toward other actors in the several different relationships in which he as student becomes involved.[13]

Role Strain

These different role expectations often create strain and tension for the actor when they are not merely different but incompatible.[14] He cannot seem to meet one role expectation fully without violating another. During the late 1960s many university presidents were expected by alumni to "handle" student demonstrators forcefully and were severely criticized when they

---

[13] *See* Robert K. Merton, "The Role-Set: Problems in Sociological Theory," The British Journal of Sociology, vol. 8 (June 1957), pp. 110–111.

[14] *See* William J. Goode, "A Theory of Role Strain," in his *Explorations in Social Theory* (New York: Oxford University Press, 1973), pp. 97–120.

Figure 3.3 A teacher, her assistants, and the children in school all expect certain kinds of behavior of each other, based on their relative positions in a well-established group. *(Elizabeth Wilcox, The Ford Foundation)*

seemed not to do so. But they were often subject to different expectations by various faculty groups, and still others by students. For presidents of public universities, legislators were yet another source of conflicting role expectations. A high turnover in university presidents signifies how punishing many found these incompatible expectations to be.

Here is another example. A foreman becomes a "man in the middle" when management expects him to carry out managerial authority in organizing and controlling the work situation, while the workers expect him to consider sympathetically their problems and needs, speak for their interests, and so sustain good morale without which production will suffer. Being a good leader of workers and being a representative of management may be incompatible roles.

Often such role strain is never resolved,

only lived with. It may be alleviated when a "human relations" perspective on the part of management leads them to allow foremen to emphasize their closeness to the men they supervise. From the other side, unionization may lead workers to redefine the foreman as solely a representative of management, and then to create a new role, that of shop steward, to speak for the workers.

Roles, Positions, and Persons

Some roles are not obviously linked to a well-identified social position, and may instead be identified—in people's minds—primarily with personality types, such as "peacemaker" or "clown." Wife and mother, as roles, and teacher and policeman, easily link a role expectation to a position in a well-established group. Other roles, however, do not; but they are roles, nonetheless. Where tension and conflict disrupt social relations in a group, for example, one member may act as peacemaker, mediating between contending factions. In a family situation a mother may mediate between a stern father and his rebellious children for the sake of family peace.

These are roles that arise in situations for which no specific position has been defined, nor, in small contexts, need it be. In larger organizational situations, however, the emerging role of mediator may be converted into a specified position, provided with resources and authority in order to act permanently to maintain the "antagonistic cooperation" that best describes social relations in large groups with unequal rewards and status.

There are further examples. The "life of the party" type may be an outgoing extrovert who enjoys being the center of attraction and can perform well to amuse his friends; in school the class "clown" may do the same. In smaller settings there are no positions to accommodate these roles; there are only situations in which these expectations become appropriate. But where talent is sufficient such persons can move on in larger, societal contexts in which the occupational positions of performer or comic do exist.

Whether it is as a mediator in tense relationships or as the clown in an informal group, roles emerge from on-going interaction to meet situational needs or to fulfill desired group functions; and these roles may better "fit" some persons than others. An aggressive, combative person will not easily be a mediator for his group. When mediator becomes an official position, qualifying for it requires individuals with certain skills, and also with a certain temperament and self-discipline. Mediators who "blow their stacks" easily will often fail at their tasks.

SOCIAL PROCESS AND SOCIAL STRUCTURE

Understanding roles and relations enables us to grasp the idea that human society is created by man through symbolic interaction. Social life becomes organized when ways of interacting indicated by such concepts as roles, relations, and structure emerge.

When there is persistent interaction among the same people, social collectivities, both large and small, such as a *group* or a *society*, evolve. Groups and societies exist by the coming together of an identifiable people who build and develop social relations over time into a stable pattern— a social structure—and who identify to some extent with others with whom they share this social structure. Thus, group and society differ analytically from a social structure; a group *has* a structure.

Social Structure

In a dictionary sense *structure* means the arrangement or interrelation of the parts of a whole. Bricks and boards do not constitute a building until they are put together in some manner; the notes of the musical scale must be arranged in some creative order by a composer to make music.

In these examples the concept of structure is not difficult to grasp, for it materializes before our eyes. But *social* structure is not a material thing; rather, as a concept it conveys to us the idea that people interact in roles which are related to one another in some systematic way, that there is a *pattern* by which roles are linked to one another. The family, for example, includes (at a minimum) the roles of mother, father, daughter, son. But to make these several roles into a family, there must be some coherence in the patterning of interaction. Any one relationship, like that of father to son, must fit into the network of other relationships so that all of them together make sense. Social structure, then, is the integration of social roles into a relatively coherent pattern of interaction.

Structures, however, are only *relatively* coherent, some more so, some less so; there is never a perfect integration of roles. Some strain exists even in the most coherent and stable of social structures; many structures reveal a good deal of internal inconsistency.' As a consequence these strains and tensions in social structure are the basis for internal conflict and exert pressure for social change.

The "Unstructured" Situation

It happens sometimes that social change brings about "unstructured" situations, where there are no role expectations, no established relations to orient people to one another. They do not know how to act or what to expect of others. They do not have a role to take, so they do not know what kind of an actor to be.

When people come together without prior definition of the situation and without any structure to their social relations, the circumstance is one of *collective behavior*. Conditions of conflict and change are likely to bring about collective behavior, where milling around in an unorganized crowd situation, for example, can lead to a new definition of the situation that serves to justify a potentially violent confrontation (*see* Chapter 17).

Collective behavior, then, contrasts with conventional interaction in that established role expectations do not control the interaction; new circumstances and unresolved problems lead to breaks in established relations. From unstructured interaction, new definitions of the situation emerge, new role expectations are created, a new group or society may be in the making.

Social Structure, Social Organization, and Social System

What some sociologists call social structure, others call social organization or social system. In each case the concept conveys the same idea: that social interaction builds up into complex systems of interaction which are relatively stable and persistent.

Once systems of interaction come into being, however, they provide a structural context which then affects how interaction goes on. A large social structure, for example, ranks its positions, and this ranking may exclude some from interacting with others at all, and may limit interaction to concerns about the job for others, as when the employer assigns tasks to employees, the professor instructs the students and the major gives orders to his men. Off-duty, high rank may not want to, or even be allowed to interact with low rank. Thus, the most inclusive interaction is likely to occur among social equals in large social structures, while up and down the hierarchy it is inhibited and restricted to specified functions.

What such an example tells us is that social structure provides a context that limits, inhibits, and constrains social interaction, as well as focuses it on tasks specific to the interactional system. Interaction cannot develop equally and in the same way among all actors in the system.

Social Process

Social process refers to *modes* or *forms* of social interaction, such as cooperation, competition, accommodation, assimilation, and conflict. Process designates human beings acting or doing things, and so the concept seems to be "dynamic" in contrast to the "static" idea of structure. This is an oversimplified distinction, but process does emphasize the forms of on-going activity, while structure denotes the more stable, "fixed," and even routinized interaction that gives coherence to the social relations of any group.

An earlier generation of American sociologists interpreted the study of social process to be the study of sequences of social development; that is, the bringing about of change in human affairs.[15] From the perspective of process, social life is not only organized, it is continually *reorganized*; it is assumed to be ever in flux, to be in process rather than set into static patterns.

Social Change

Social change is always going on in society, so we cannot assume social structure to be unchanging. Nor is it adequate to identify change solely with disturbance, instability, and disruption.

It has been usual to view social change as lessening the integration of society; that is, weakening the social structure, possibly to the point of disorganization. Émile Durkheim used the concept, *anomie*, to identify a possible endpoint of change, where social relations had so disintegrated

that moral rules no longer effectively regulated social action. From this perspective social change is interpreted as a threat to social structure.

Yet a social structure does not necessarily disintegrate completely; a disorganizing process is often the prelude to the emergence of new social relations. Reorganization follows disorganization. If change sometimes means social disruption, it also means the rebuilding of disrupted relations, the creation of new relations, the further integration of a poorly organized group, and the acceptance of new beliefs and attitudes and the actions made legitimate by them. If change is sometimes sudden and painful to many, it is often at times also slow and cumulative, so that people can adjust to it without sensing disruption and a threat to their interests and established ways of life. Nor is change always resisted; sometimes it signifies a welcome improvement in material conditions or a lessening in coercive social relations and may be called *progress*.

The study of social change has been important in sociology from still another perspective: that modern history is a major trend from smaller, simpler, and more integrated societies to larger, more complex ones. The *division of labor* refers to a process whereby specialization in occupational and other social roles—*role differentiation*—leads to a more complex social structure. Complexity in social organization leads to *segmentalization*, the emergence of differentiated subgroups where before there was but a single structure.

In a classic study, *The Division of Labor in Society*, Durkheim pursued the full implication of this historic transformation of social structure. To do so, he constructed two types of social *solidarity*, by which he meant the cohesion of social groups into

---

[15] *See* Robert Park and Ernest Burgess, *An Introduction to the Science of Sociology* (Chicago: University of Chicago Press, 1921).

Figure 3.4 Conflict focuses on disorganization and differentiation which often lead to social change. *(A. Devaney, Inc., N.Y.)*

a unified structure. *Mechanical* solidarity occurs in "simple" societies where there is little division of labor. The individual is so little differentiated from others in skills and knowledge, and in tasks to perform, that he is also little differentiated in personality.

The solidarity which is based on likeness is at its maximum when the collective conscience completely envelopes our whole conscience and coincides in all points with it. But then individuality is nil.[16]

In such a social structure interaction occurs among persons who are much alike and share more common meanings and actions than not; their styles of life are identical. Furthermore, there is much stability to their interaction, much more learn-

ing of established role expectations and following them, less innovating and creating new relations through social interaction.

In *organic* solidarity, by contrast, the division of labor so differentiates the parts of society that autonomous and distinct social groups emerge, and with them a more differentiated human individual. The division of labor now creates interdependence. While people and small groups perform different functions, these specialized functions are incomplete in themselves, except as they are coordinated with those of others.

The greater the division of labor, the greater the dependence of the individual on society, on the one hand; on the other hand, the more specialized the individual, the more personal his activity.[17]

[16] Émile Durkheim, *The Division of Labor in Society,* George Simpson, trans. (New York: The Free Press, 1947), p. 130.

[17] Durkheim, *op. cit.,* p. 131.

There is more play for initiative here, more opportunity to enter into a greater variety of social relations. But there is also a loss of common meanings; more relations are impersonal and instrumental only, entered into just for utilitarian purposes. When there is independence of social action, people are less bound to common moral rules; a sense of shared morality may decline and anomie grow.

Social Conflict

Since no social structure is ever perfectly integrated, social conflict is always present, though sometimes latent and unrecognized. Conflict is struggle over values or over scarce resources, in which two contesting groups each seek to impose their definition of the situation. To do so, they seek to maintain or to change the social structure in terms of their values or on behalf of their interests.

The Functions of Social Conflict

Conflict is easily perceived as *dysfunctional;* that is, destructive of established social relations and producing social disorganization. Conflict is then viewed as negatively as change sometimes is. But Georg Simmel, a gifted and seminal European sociologist, argued that conflict can be positive in its functions for social groups.[18] Positive outcomes of conflict, he pointed out, can offset negative ones. Some of these are:

---

[18] *See* Georg Simmel, *Conflict and the Web of Group Affiliations,* Kurt H. Wolff, trans. (New York: The Free Press, 1955); a brilliant rendering of Simmel's theory of conflict is in Lewis A. Coser, *The Functions of Social Conflict* (New York: The Free Press, 1956).

Clarifies Issues Conflict may "clear the air" by making it evident what actors and subgroups want and what price others have to pay to achieve a resolution of long-standing resentments and tensions. It may also make clear that two groups have an unresolvable conflict of interest that can only lead to further problems.

Conflict may clarify and sharpen other matters, too: the extent and limits of authority; the boundaries of groups, including their physical boundaries; the distribution of rights and privileges for various categories of members.

Identifies Sources Conflict may pinpoint the source of tensions in specific relations and structures, when earlier it may have been rationalized or scapegoated in different ways.

Unifies Group Conflict against an *external* threat to a group is integrating in its *internal* effect. Members can put aside other differences and reaffirm their common values and interests. Solidarity and morale increases. On the other hand, such a situation decreases the tolerance for deviation; loyalty to the group is more closely measured.

Induces Change Since conflict needs to be resolved, the outbreak of overt conflict induces those changes in relations and in values and attitudes that enable a group to move to conflict resolution.

Structure and Process

Through the *processes* of change and conflict our attention is focused on disorganization and differentiation which marks a transformation from one pattern of social relations to another. In turn, through the concept of *structure,* we focus on the stable patterning of social interactions. The study of society requires that we use both process and structure, looking at societal phenom-ena first from one angle, then from the other. Both angles of vision are necessary, for there is continuing process and there is stable patterning; neither alone provides us with a full sociological perspective; each is complementary to the other.

SUMMARY

Social interaction occurs when two or more persons are acting toward one another at the same time. In interaction, individuals take account of one another by defining each other as social objects (that is, friends) and act accordingly.

Interaction requires communication through language. Once established, language organizes our experience and gives it cognitive form, and by consensus gives it a common meaning. "First we look, then we name, and only then do we see." We think through language: "No thought without words."

Because interaction proceeds through language and other symbols, it is symbolic interaction. Through symbols we define situations so as to define appropriate conduct; this *definition of the situation* says: "If men define a situation as real, it is real in its consequences."

A *role* is an expectation of behavior shared among actors in a social rela-tionship. It does not mean conformity to a specifically prescribed behavior; rather, actors share some understanding of what to expect from one another, as friends do. A *role set* is the several roles attached to a single position, because the actor's interaction differs in different relations (professor to student, professor to colleague, and so on). Incompatible role expectations produce *role strain.*

Social structure is the systematic organization of social roles into a rela-tively coherent whole. Social *process* is on-going activity in contrast to the more "fixed" structure.

Social change is constant, for social relations never remain unchanged. Change may lessen the integration of society, but the resulting *anomie,* or disorganization, precedes a reorganization. Change in the modern world also means a transition from a smaller, simpler society to a larger, more complex one, where the division of labor points to increasing *role differ-entiation.*

When change alters the patterns of integration and consensus, the result-ing strains and tensions produce *social conflict.* Conflict is the struggle, or contest, over values and over scarce resources, in which two contesting groups seek to impose their definitions on the situation and so to change or maintain the social order in terms of their values. Conflict can be *dysfunctional,* but it can also have positive functions.

The study of society requires that it be examined from the perspective of *processes* of change and conflict, and also from the perspective of relatively stable *structure.*

Suggested Readings

Peter Berger and Thomas Luckmann, *The Social Construction of Reality* (New York: Doubleday & Company, Inc., 1966; Anchor edition, 1967). An examination of our humanly-created reality as being both subjective and objective.

Ernst Cassirer, *An Essay on Man: An Introduction to a Philosophy of Human Culture* (New Haven, Conn.: Yale University Press, 1944; Doubleday paperback edition, 1953). A famous philosopher develops a cogent philosophical argument that man alone creates a symbolic reality; he is the *animal symbolicum.*

Lewis Coser, *The Functions of Social Conflict* (New York: The Free Press, 1956). An influential book, based on Georg Simmel's work, that made an impressive case for the positive functions of conflict.

George Herbert Mead, *Mind, Self, and Society* (Chicago: The University of Chicago Press, 1934). The classic work of America's foremost symbolic interactionist.

George Herbert Mead, *On Social Psychology,* Anselm Strauss, ed. (Chicago: University of Chicago Press, 1956). A selection of Mead's more important writings on symbolic interaction.

Arnold Rose, *Human Behavior and Social Process* (Boston: Houghton-Mifflin Company, 1962). An interesting set of papers by sociology's leading symbolic interactionists. Of particular interest here are essays by Arnold Rose, Ralph Turner, and Herbert Blumer.

W. Lloyd Warner, *The Living and the Dead: A Study of the Symbolic Life of Americans* (New Haven, Conn.: Yale University Press, 1959). The foremost study of the symbols central to the organization of American life.

Charles K. Warriner, *The Emergence of Society* (Homewood, Ill.: The Dorsey Press, 1970). An impressively detailed analysis of how human society emerges from symbolic interaction.

Leslie A. White, *The Science of Culture* (New York: Farrar, Straus & Giroux, Inc., 1949). A provocative and influential assertion of the uniquely human capacity to create a symbolic environment.

Benjamin Lee Whorf, *Language, Thought, and Reality* (New York: John Wiley & Sons, Inc., 1956). A now-classic set of papers about the place of language in the human construction of society.

Culture implies all that which gives the mind possession of its own powers; as languages to the critic, telescope to the astronomer.
— *Ralph Waldo Emerson*

Chapter 4

Culture

The study of society cannot go forward without consideration of *culture*. As he creates society, man—and no other creature—creates culture through interaction, for as we have noted, culture does not come from nature readymade.

The concept of culture becomes understandable when we remember that man is a flexible and learning creature who invents ways to adjust to his environment and to develop some limited mastery and control over it. He must do this, for he is not genetically programmed to survive. It is man's nature, then, that requires culture.

THE MEANING OF CULTURE

For mid-nineteenth century anthropologists *culture* and *civilization* were used to characterize one kind of society, and *savage* and *barbaric* to characterize another. The concept of culture once drew invidious distinctions about the quality of social life among the earth's peoples. However, when Edward B. Tylor published his classic work, *Primitive Culture*, in 1871, the anthropological meaning of culture applied to all people without exception. In that work Tylor defined culture as "... that complex whole which includes knowledge, belief, art, morals, law, custom, and any other capabilities and habits acquired by man as a member of society."[1]

Tylor's definition of culture—long used by social scientists—emphasized two things: that each of us acquired culture as a member of society, and that culture includes *ideational* phenomena: language, myth, philosophy, custom, and the like. Culture does not consist of things and events that we can observe, count, and measure. It consists of "invisible" things about which we make inferences from what we see going on around us. A woman shopping for a new dress is not a part of her culture, but the pattern of meanings that makes her act intelligible is.

Culture is the term that refers to the symbolic world of meanings and understandings built up through social interaction. Culture is *an ordered system of symbolic meanings and understandings.*

Culture and Social Structure

Though culture emerges from social interaction, it is not to be confused with society; it is a different order of phenomena. As anthropologist Clifford Geertz notes:

Culture is the fabric of meaning in terms of which human beings interpret their experience and guide their actions; social structure is the form that action takes, the actually existing network of social relations. Culture and social structure are then but different abstractions from the same phenomena.[2]

[1] Edward Tylor, *Primitive Culture: Researches into the Development of Mythology, Philosophy, Religion, Language, Art and Custom* (London: John Murray, 1871), p. 1.
[2] Clifford Geertz, "Ritual and Social Change: A Javanese Example," *American Anthropologist*, vol. 59 (1957), p. 34.

Culture as Social Heritage

Older definitions often did not clearly distinguish between culture and society. What was given emphasis was that culture included all that had been humanly created and then transmitted from one generation to the next. Culture was the social heritage —an emphasis that has been retained in much sociological discussion.[3]

This stress on culture as social heritage originated in the nineteenth-century effort to distinguish the *cultural* world from the *biological*, and to identify those aspects of human behavior not biologically determined. During the latter decades of that century, spurred by Charles Darwin's discoveries, a new and exciting biology seemed able to tell people more about themselves that was scientifically sound than could any other science. There was a powerful impulse, therefore, to extend biological explanations into social life. This led to theories of biological differences between races and classes, between the "fit" and the "unfit," which gave scientific support for antidemocratic, reactionary ideologies.[4] Notions of inherited traits and social instincts persisted in the social sciences for several decades into the twentieth century.

To view as culture all that was not genetically inherited was a definition of reality that was part of a larger struggle—partly scientific, partly ideological—to redefine human nature to fit a democratic perspec-

[3] Typical of the kind of definition long used by sociologists—and still used by some—is the following: Culture "embraces all modes of thought and behavior that are handed down by communicative interaction—i.e. by symbolic transmission—rather than by genetic inheritance. It is what we learn from others through speech, gesture, and example..." Kingsley Davis, *Human Society* (New York: The Macmillan Company, 1949), pp. 3–4.
[4] *See* Richard Hofstadter, *Social Darwinism in American Thought* (Boston: The Beacon Press, 1955).

Figure 4.1 A religious ceremony in a Nigerian village of under 1,000 people. *(Philip E. Leis)*

tive. From this perspective a great deal was cultural, and therefore socially inherited, not genetically inherited. Describing the dimension of man that was cultural served to set the limits of biology and to establish the legitimate boundaries of the social sciences. Valuable as this was, however, it did one-sidedly emphasize culture as social heritage while playing down the equally important fact that culture is created in interaction, and is continually recreated in the same way.

The Integration of Culture

If culture is an "ordered system," then it is not merely an aggregate or unorganized grabbag of cultural items. In studying preliterate and peasant peoples in small societies, anthropologists usually looked for some internal consistency among the cultural elements, a relationship of one to another that revealed an internal logic. A culture was perceived to be an organized entity, with coherence and pattern.

From that perspective, *a* culture is characteristic of *a* people. There is Navaho culture, Hopi culture, Japanese culture, Trobriand culture, and so on. By the same token, there is German culture, French culture, Canadian culture, and American culture. Mapping the culture of a large and extensive national structure such as that of the United States, though, is a forbidding task, and most sociologists have avoided the challenge.

Even though cultures are integrated wholes, there are often great differences in the degrees of integration. Traditional cultures that have persisted over many generations in the same environment, with little change in technology or social structure, are likely to be reasonably well-integrated; religious beliefs, kinship values, and technical knowledge link together coherently. But any modern culture is much

61

less integrated. The relatively rapid rate of social change and the complexity and size of the social structure produces many inconsistencies and strains, even contradictions; there emerge many subgroups which carry particular values or beliefs that vary from, even contradict the major cultural patterns. (Further on in this chapter we take up the issues of subcultures and countercultures.)

It is easy, particularly in the study of more traditional societies, to overemphasize the integration of a culture, to view it as a "seamless web" tightly knit and fitted together into a systematic design. Anthropologist Clifford Geertz doubts this design idea: "The problem of cultural analysis is as much a matter of determining independencies as interconnections, gulfs as well as bridges."[5] He goes on to make the point that an appropriate image of cultural organization is neither the spider web nor the pile of sand:

> It is more the octopus, whose tentacles are in large part separately integrated, neurally quite poorly connected with one another and with what in the octopus passes for a brain, and yet who nonetheless manages to get around and to preserve himself, for a while anyway, as a viable, if somewhat ungainly entity.[6]

The Carriers of Culture

Just as there cannot be social interaction and social relations without actors, so there cannot be culture without *carriers*, persons who know and share in the culture and exemplify it in their social action. It is in the observation of their actions that we infer the existence of culture.

The boundaries of the population of

people who are the carriers of a culture are always something to be determined empirically. In many cases it is reasonably obvious—a tribe, a village, any small and relatively separate population of people. Even in larger cases it may still be reasonable to attribute a culture to the French, for instance, in contrast to Germans, Irish, or Americans. In such cases language, history, and national boundaries are significant in giving to a carrier population an identity as a distinct people.

But there are complications. While the French people may have a distinct culture, they nonetheless share many cultural elements with other people: the Roman Catholic religion, for one; the culture of capitalism, for another; political beliefs in democracy, personal liberty, and the like. They also share in scientific knowledge and in technical know-how. Many of these cultural elements are common to a wider body of carriers, all the Western peoples, so they are elements of Western culture. And all of them have now diffused to non-Western parts of the world. Thus, while Catholicism and a belief in personal liberty are elements of the whole that is French culture, they did not necessarily originate among the French, or at least not alone among them, and are not peculiar to them alone.

There is another problem. Many French are devoted Catholics; many others are only nominally so; many are not even that. Though France is culturally Catholic, not all Frenchmen are Catholics. Though French culture is historically bourgeois, millions of French people are Socialists and Communists; in March 1973, 46 percent of the French electorate voted for a Socialist-Communist coalition.

What is the significance of this fact? It means that any culture, as a whole, is not perfectly reflected in its presumed car-

[5] Clifford Geertz, *Person, Time, and Conduct in Bali: An Essay in Cultural Analysis* (New Haven, Conn.: Southeast Asia Studies, Cultural Report Studies 14), p. 67.
[6] Geertz, *op. cit.*, p. 67.

Figure 4.2 Parisians relax and enjoy life at a sidewalk café. *(Wide World Photos)*

riers. For one thing not every cultural element is equally significant to everyone, or equally valued. Some people may ignore some cultural elements. In other cases people are simply ignorant, as when they lack training or sufficient level of education. Furthermore, a culture changes, and some members of the society may be *creators* of new cultures, while others are still carriers of more traditional cultural elements. We must also realize that each person interprets his culture in his own way; an observer's statement of what a culture is, then, is always a generalization from observation of actions, each of which varies a little from another.

Some individuals in a culture reject specific elements of their culture: the agnostic Frenchman, for example. But sometimes this rejection may be true of whole segments of the society, such as social classes. In France the large vote for Socialists and Communists is an anti-Capitalist vote, which has deep roots in the working class as well as in some sectors of the intellectual population and university students.

These examples and others are evidence of the problem of identifying a culture; not all members of the society are carriers of all elements of the culture, as has been illustrated, and some members of the society carry contradictory cultural elements. No one person can know all of his culture, nor are most people conscious of their fundamental beliefs and assumptions; consequently, each person's action is an interpretation which stresses some elements over others and reveals different degrees of commitment to custom and value.

THE ELEMENTS OF CULTURE

Culture can be categorized in many ways, but sociological purposes can be served by emphasizing three categories of cultural elements: cognitions, norms and values, and world views and ideologies.

Cognition: The Known World

A major set of elements in any culture is the cognitive, the world of known facts available as a store of empirical knowledge. Even the most technologically simple people know a great deal of matter-of-fact things about nature and about how to manipulate it. Whether they hunt or fish or gather, or some combination of these, they know a lot about plants and animals; and they possess considerable skill in turning this knowledge to their own use.

There are always limits to factual knowledge, and in simple societies there may be frequent resort to magic and religion to placate nature or to curry favor with the gods; but none of this should hide the fact that day-to-day survival behavior is organized around a great deal of factual knowledge.[7]

The evolution of human societies was made possible by the growth of cognitive elements: knowledge of how to domesticate animals, and how to grow crops, fell trees and turn them into lumber for building, refine and develop tools—all leading over the long centuries to the Industrial Revolution and then to the advanced technology of today. There has also grown a more theoretical knowledge, *science*, which can abstract from practical techniques and tools in order to build conceptions, not just of what works and how but why it works—a conception of abstract principles that lie behind observations of successful practice and knowledge of natural process and mechanical technique.

The growth of these cognitive elements of culture has had enormous impact on social structure; new technology often changes social structure in ways never anticipated, as when the development of large machines relocates work in factories, removing it from homes and thus affecting the internal structure of the family (*see* Chapter 11). In addition, the rational mode of scientific reasoning comes to permeate so many aspects of modern social life that the scientific element becomes increasingly dominant; scientific knowledge effectively challenges the credibility of other modes of knowing (*see* Chapter 16).

Norms and Values

Among other elements a culture always provides, out of past experience within the group or society, a set of general themes and specific rules to guide social interaction. There is always an active moral perspective involved in interaction; *norms* and *values* are these elements.

Norms

All social action is normatively oriented; that is, given direction and definition by norms, which are rules of conduct that specify what "should" be done in social situations. Norms vary in their importance to the group and in the intensity with which they are believed.

William Graham Sumner once made a distinction between *folkways* and *mores* that has since become a standard part of the sociological vocabulary.[8] Folkways are those customary ways of doing things that are usually accepted as the right way, such as manners, ways of greeting people, cor-

[7] *See* Bronislaw Malinowski, *Magic, Science and Religion* (Boston: The Beacon Press, 1954).

[8] William Graham Sumner, *Folkways* (Boston: Ginn & Company, 1907; paperback edition, New York: New American Library, 1960).

rectness of attire. Violation of folkways does not bring punishment, though it may result in ridicule or gossip; such violation suggests that the person is somewhat incompetent in knowing the customs of the group. The desire for good standing exacts conformity to the folkways—you try to show you "learned your manners" in childhood—but those who deliberately persit in violating some folkways are not likely to suffer too severely. Sometimes they may even gain by building a reputation for being different, interesting, independent, or nonconformist.

Mores are those standards which people regard as crucial for the welfare of the group. Here violation is a serious matter and some kind of group-enforced punishment will be invoked. It is one thing not to wear a necktie in a situation which usually prescribes one, but it is quite another thing to violate group standards about the rights of persons to their lives, property, and social opportunities. Also, it is a serious matter to abrogate one's obligations to wife and children, to a business partner, or to anyone with whom one has a contractual relationship.

When mores are put into a written code, with specified punishments for violations, and when social agencies are created with authority to enforce them and punish violators, then mores are *laws.*

Like the actions they serve to regulate, social norms change as new situations and problems develop for a group. Folkways are more easily subject to change than mores. Moral standards intensely held and defining social action thought to be crucial for the meaning and identity of a group, particularly if given sacred even supernatural support, are especially resistant to change. Efforts to make a change can produce intense conflict within a group.

Legal norms are particularly susceptible to conflict, for they are backed by agencies that have the obligation to enforce them, even when cultural change has left them without strong support. Although laws are frequently repealed, they can often be more resistant to change than nonlegal norms. Protestant groups, for example, have often put laws on the books, such as the Prohibition amendment, or kept anti-gambling laws alive even when the majority of the public felt otherwise. Similarly, Catholic groups have been effective supporters of laws against birth control and abortion, even though Catholics are a numerical minority.

Values

In every culture there are conceptions of what is good and desirable, of end states that people would like to achieve. These are the values of a society. They constitute standards by which choices can be made among alternatives and by which specific courses of action can be judged. Thus, for Americans, being *democratic* is a value, but so is being *efficient.* These two values can be in opposition when judging alternative actions in a given situation.

Many of the values of a society are not easy for its members to verbalize, for they may be so taken for granted that people are not conscious of them. Nor are they therefore immediately apparent to the observer. Determining what values are basic to the organization of a society may be a difficult task in sociological observation and analysis.

Relation of Norms to Values

In any society norms are more readily apparent to observation, for their constant application in daily interaction bring them more readily to mind for actors, who are more conscious of the do's and don't's, the statements of "you should," "you must," "you can't," the statements that say "thou shalt, thou shalt not." Values, in contrast, are less obvious, for they are more general principles.

Sociologists Blake and Davis argue that through norms we infer the existence of values:

In practice, we tend to find the best evidence of values in the norms themselves. If people manifest a dislike of cheating in examinations, of dishonest advertising in business, and of unnecessary roughness in sports, we infer something like a "value of fair competition."[9]

This gives them reason to place more importance on norms than on values in sociological investigation:

It is the norms, not the values, that have the pressure of reality upon them. It is the norms that are enforced by sanctions, that are subject to the necessity of action and the agony of decision. It is therefore the norms that represent the cutting edge of social control. In this regard Sumner seems to have been more correct than some of his successors, for he emphasized the importance of the folkways and mores in understanding society rather than the vague, slippery ideologies, rationalizations and generalizations people use in justifying their observance and nonobservance of norms.[10]

That values may be invoked to justify an action decided upon for quite other reasons, however, is no reason to think of values as only "vague and slippery." They can be and often are that, but so are norms; even action in some situations is indecisive, vacillating, uncertain. Let actors be unsure of the *meaning* of a situation and they will be uncertain as to what norms apply, what action is appropriate.

Nonetheless, it is useful to heed the warning that Blake and Davis give us and not try to use value or norms as *the* principle for explaining action. In saying this they are arguing against a "blueprint theory" of society which asserts "a set of 'culture-patterns' which are, so to speak, laid down in advance and followed by the members of the society."[11] This, they argue, is inadequate for understanding society:

The blueprint theory of society does not fit the facts of social existence. Societies as we know them are highly active and dynamic, filled with conflict, striving, deceit, cunning. Behavior in a given situation tends to be closely related to that situation, to be strongly affected by individual interests, to be unpredictable from a knowledge of the norms alone. Far from being fully determinative, the norms themselves tend to be a product of the constant interaction involving the interplay of interests, changing conditions, power, dominance, force, fraud, ignorance, and knowledge.[12]

Culture as World View

If Blake and Davis properly warn us not to overestimate the significance of norms and values in social action, neither should we make the opposite mistake and underestimate their significance. Values and norms are elements of culture; in particular, they are components of the belief system of a people, of their *world view*. The actions of people become meaningful to themselves, and the actions of others are also meaningful, only within a framework of meaning derived from long group experience. Life makes sense, in short, only because the

---

[9] Judith Blake and Kingsley Davis, "Norms, Values, and Sanctions," in Robert E. L. Faris, ed., *Handbook of Modern Sociology* (Skokie, Ill.: Rand-McNally & Company, 1964), pp. 460–461.

[10] Blake and Davis, *op. cit.*, p. 461.

[11] Blake and Davis, *op. cit.*, p. 462.

[12] Blake and Davis, *op. cit.*, p. 464.

actions of people and the events of nature can be made sense of by reference to some basic, even ultimate ideas.

A world view makes sense of the world in empirical, factual, and scientific terms, but also in sacred, mythical, even magical and supernatural terms. It incorporates values as well as knowledge; it is an assertion of what *really is* as a people see it, of what is important and fateful, of what is honorable and good, dishonorable and evil. It implies a conception of human origins and causality in nature and in human affairs. It constitutes the mentality that enables a people to assume that some things are "unreal" or "impossible," while another people take them to be both real and possible. God is real and intervenes in human affairs from one perspective; from another, he is the Creator and source of life but does not possess human characteristics and does not intervene in human affairs.

At most times in the past there has been only a single dominant perspective within a society, although there may be variations, as between an educated upper class and the common people. A single world view is an integrating perspective, but in the modern world rapid social change and vastly complex and varied social structures lead to different world views, often in conflict with one another.[13]

Ideologies

When world views come into conflict, *ideologies* emerge to give expression to the

[13] For a study in the United States, *see* Philip E. Converse, "The Nature of Belief Systems in Mass Publics," in David E. Apter, ed., *Ideologies and Discontent* (New York: The Free Press, 1964), pp. 206–261. For an historical perspective on Europe, *see* Karl Mannheim, *Ideology and Utopia* (New York: Harcourt, Brace and Company, Inc., 1936), particularly pp. 211–263.

effort to change or defend the social structure. Ideologies are active formulations of specific aspects of world views, particularly in relation to social structure. They are likely to be primarily focused around economic or political dimensions; they may differ on the basis of stratification, as in working-class and middle-class ideologies. In short, ideologies give active expression to ideas about how to organize social life; there are *conservative* ideologies in support of an existing structure; *reformist* ideologies that seek change without altering the basic structural pattern, as when welfare measures are introduced into capitalism without eliminating private property and unequal wealth; and *radical* ideologies, which seek a reorganization of the basic patterning of the social structure, as when power is shifted from an inherited aristocracy to a democratic citizenry.

CULTURAL CHANGE AND ADAPTATION

Culture, like society, emerges from the human effort to survive. Survival requires human cooperation; it also requires skills and tools and knowledge about nature. From this perspective culture is an adaptation to environment, a cognitive body of knowledge and techniques developed by man as *homo faber* (man the maker).

Culture and the Ecosystem

The need to survive forces men to adapt to their physical environment; that obvious fact has long raised for social scientists, particularly anthropologists, the problem of the relation between culture and environment. No matter how imaginative and creative the symbolic system which a people creates is, the shape of their lives must always begin with the physical environment in which they are anchored.

The action necessary to wrest a living from the environment with whatever tools and techniques he possesses emphasizes man as worker, as pragmatist, doing what he can in circumstances never entirely of his own choosing and making. He is a struggling organism living in relations of interdependence with other organisms in an environment that is both physical and related to life. The study of the relations of organisms to environment is *ecology;* the interconnected, interdependent system of relations between organisms and environment is an *ecosystem.*[14]

Unlike other living organisms man is not genetically equipped to survive in specific environments. Instead, he adapts to a wide range of environments, for he relies on his capacity to learn and create tools and techniques to insure his survival. Unlike other animals, he does not stand in direct relation to his environment; instead he creates a culture, however technically primitive at the outset, which mediates his relations with his environment. The way he adapts to his ecosystem shapes his culture, but his culture shapes his ecosystem.

The lower the technological level of a people, the more directly dependent they are on the nature of the environment, and the more their life is directly tied to seasonal and cyclical changes in nature. But as technology develops, they are less threatened by natural occurrences—floods, storms, drought—and they are more able to reshape the environment to make it yield greater material comfort for an ever-larger human population.

At one time primitive techniques enabled man to sustain himself only in small bands; human population was necessarily limited and human groups were sparsely scattered over the earth. Now, huge populations cluster in vast urban settlements, and the growth of human population has kept pace over the centuries with rapid technological advance. Since at least the time that Thomas Malthus wrote on population a new worry has crept into the human mind: that the enormous growth of human population, which culture in the form of science and technology makes possible, may eventually, and perhaps soon, exceed the sustenance capacity of the whole earth. The growth of the world's population now looms as a major social problem (*see* Chapter 19).

Technology and Ecology

A knowledge that we survive by adjustment to an interdependent ecosystem has probably never been more than a fragmentary conception for most of mankind in the past. It was possible for early man to act out of ignorance to disrupt and damage that interdependent process. In the long time span of primitive technologies and sparse populations probably only short-run disruptions were produced, as in hunting out particular animals or changing migration patterns; these were only temporary. Such people, bound tightly to the web of nature, were then forced to seek a new environment as the old one changed. Nature usually restored the abandoned territory in time.

But when technology transformed man

[14] *See* Otis Dudley Duncan, "Social Organization and the Ecosystem," in Robert E. L. Faris, ed., *Handbook of Modern Sociology* (Skokie, Ill.: Rand-McNally & Company, 1964), pp. 36–82.

into a new and different kind of creature, making it possible for him "to be fruitful and multiply," as the Old Testament urged, the human capacity to influence ecosystems grew enormously. The ability to be disruptive and destructive grew apace with scientific knowledge and technology.

Only in this century have we really become aware of how complex and intricate any ecosystem is, and how disrupted it can be if but one component is altered. Polluting air and water because of extensive use of modern technology, using rivers and lakes as dumping grounds for industrial and human waste, unintentionally endangering animal and human life through pesticides—these and other issues are but a new chapter, more complicated, more subtle, in the relation of technology and the ecosystem. As long as we are bound to this planet, adaptation to it remains essential for human survival.

Culture and Evolution

The effort to understand the relation of culture and ecosystem has often focused on the great sweep of change from human wandering bands of food-gatherers to vast urban societies; this process of change made possible by technological mastery is the theme of *evolutionary* theory. In the nineteenth century the idea of social evolution dominated both sociological and anthropological theory. But the models of evolutionary progress postulated that all cultures passed through similar stages of development, and scathing criticism of this theory by anthropologists and other scholars arguing from sound evidence soon put evolutionary theory into disrepute.

But now, building on the work of anthropologists such as Leslie White, a renewed conception of evolution has been restored to social theory.[15] Technological advance is seen as the source of cultural development, permitting new levels of integration of human populations from the small social structures of primitive hunters to modern nation-states, each level in turn encompassing a greater span of integration and control of population accompanied by greater internal differentiation, and so greater social complexity. The higher social forms of evolution have greater adaptability, and replace lower social forms whenever these come into contact.

However useful it is to see the great sweep of evolutionary progress from the beginnings of human life to now, many anthropologists still find problems with this idea; the theory of *general evolution* does not meet their scholarly concern to specify the way in which adaptation in specific environments leads to diversification and variability of cultural forms. Thus, according to anthropologist M. Sahlins, they deal in *specific evolution*,[16] which suggests that:

Adaptation, not evolution, is the key concept; and it is here that a view of man as part of an ecosystem is most useful. Many scholars who are dubious about vast evolutionary models share a common ground with followers of White in their concern with cultural adaptation to ecosystems.[17]

[15] See Leslie White, *The Science of Culture: A Study of Man and Civilization* (New York: Farrar, Straus, & Cudahy, Inc., 1949).

[16] M. Sahlins, "Evolution: Specific and General," in M. Sahlins and E. Service, eds., *Evolution and Culture* (Ann Arbor: University of Michigan Press, 1960).

[17] Roger M. Keesing and Felix M. Keesing, *New Perspectives in Cultural Anthropology* (New York: Holt, Rinehart, and Winston, Inc., 1971), p. 145.

Does Environment Determine Culture?

It is possible to conceive of the need to survive and adapt to an environment as being so compelling that it leads to the proposition that environment determines culture. Many scholars once argued just that; but now alternative views prevail.[18] A conventional position in anthropology has been that environment "poses problems and restricts alternatives, but the cultural forms are not *determined* by ecological adaptation."[19]

Perhaps a more fruitful way to look at it is to recognize that it is fairly evident that environment sets limits to what is culturally possible if we restrict culture to those cognitive forms which aid survival. Human beings will eat the food that is available in the environment and develop a strong liking for it, but that is only one dimension of the relation of culture to environment. Humans can also take other material from the physical environment and endow it with rich symbolic significance that has little to do with adaptation as a survival process. In this case environment restricts available material, and important human experiences occur in interaction with that environment—hunting, fishing, tilling the soil—but what human beings imaginatively make of these things symbolically, what larger meanings of life they give their adaptive existence cannot be explained only by knowing about their environment.

Man is a pragmatic, adaptive creature, and what he does to adapt is closely shaped by the demands of the environment; but he is also a creative symbol-manipulator, and this rich potential for elaborating complex cultural systems is not narrowly restricted by the shape of the physical world around him. Man's necessary adaptive capacity reveals only one aspect of his many-sided nature.

Furthermore, as technology grows, human beings are less tied to the immediate demands of nature, and then culture shapes environment. Culture and environment are always in an interactive process, and the terms of that interaction are always altered when technology grows.

Cultural Progress and Relativism

Early evolutionary theory made use of the concept of *progress*. Highly evolved cultures were viewed as evidence of human progress and were therefore considered superior to the less evolved. But this interpretation came under severe attack.[20] For one thing, such statements were taken to be *ethnocentric*, defined as judgments of the superiority of one culture over others; and ethnocentrism lent itself to nationalistic and racial chauvinism, providing reasons for exploiting, even destroying powerless people by the technologically powerful.

One major anthropological observation is important here. A people who are technologically primitive are not necessarily simple in their social organization, in their religion and mythology, or in the complexity of their language. The limits of technological development are not matched by limits in a range of symbolic development.

As a consequence evolutionary progress has now come to mean the technological development of mankind in adaptation to

---

[18] For a review of such works, *see* Pitirim Sorokin, *Contemporary Sociological Theories* (New York: Harper & Row, 1928), Chapter III, pp. 99–193.
[19] Keesing and Keesing, *op. cit.*, p. 145.

[20] *See* Keesing and Keesing, *op. cit.*, pp. 377–381; *see also*, George W. Stocking, Jr., *Race, Culture, and Evolution: Essays in the History of Anthropology* (New York: The Free Press, 1969).

Figure 4.3 With the growth of cities have come additional social problems—and the diversification and variability of life in a large industrial complex. *(UPI Photo)*

environment, with no intended ethnocentric judgments about the superiority of the technically advanced. It is doubtful, however, whether such judgments can be kept from creeping into the concept of progress, particularly in cultures which place high value on technology and its use.

To counterbalance ethnocentric judgments, cultural *relativism* serves as an argument asserting the equal legitimacy and essential integrity of all human cultures; each in turn was developed by the human struggle to create a symbolic life in circumstances limited by environment. Varied as they may be, none was to be preferred over another. Indeed, anyone's preference was merely evidence that his values had been shaped by his own culture. What was then taken empirically to be cultural relativism—man had developed differently under different circumstances—came with small modification to be *ethical* relativism,

the idea that each culture can only be evaluated by its own cultural standards.

But this idea also has its problems. Most simply, it is a position extremely hard to live with; carried out rigorously, it prevents anyone from passing judgment on slavery, racial bigotry, race genocide, and other cases of cultural justification for human mistreatment. Presumably slave-labor camps and gas chambers could not be judged inferior to fair trials and the right of political dissent under this position. Few if any people can be so ethically relative.

One response has been to look for cultural *universals,* some presumably enduring moral patterns which can be found beneath the surface manifestation of diversity in cultural customs and standards. Murder is wrong in all cultures, it is asserted; but such an argument is a tautology if *murder* is defined as *illegitimate* killing of another.

All cultures permit the taking of life under some circumstances, and the permissible circumstances vary considerably.

Cultural relativism, then, is not an ethical guide for conduct, for each society must proceed according to cultural standards. But cultural relativism is still useful in teaching us much about how man has learned to live as a human being on this one planet; of the varied ways, cruel and ennobling, in which to be human; and something of the human possibilities that can be conceived of by human beings and then acted upon, sometimes bravely but foolishly, sometimes meanly. It is worth knowing from the human record what it means to be part of the company of man as it has existed in culturally varied forms since the beginning of human life.

SUBCULTURE AND COUNTERCULTURE

In peasant communities, in African tribes, and in all small traditional societies, there usually seems to be but a single, homogeneous culture. But in large, complex societies there is much more variation in how the culture is perceived and given expression among various segments and groups of the society. In addition, there are always segments and groups which display cultural elements that are simply contrary to or even in violation of the values of the culture. Social complexity is accompanied by cultural complexity. This is when sociologists find it useful to speak of *subcultures and countercultures.*

The Subculture

Sociologists studying prisons, military organizations, or high schools, or observing street-corner gangs, dope addicts, hippies, or professional thieves have looked for some integrating pattern of values and beliefs that constitute a distinctive interpretation of human experience—distinctive because the experience itself is distinctive. Being in prison or in the army or in the ghetto is in each case a particular setting for experiencing life. Yet in each case it is not a life entirely cut off from the larger society and the dominant culture. These distinctive versions of the culture carried by particular segments and groups of the society are subcultures.[21]

Other sociologists have done the same in speaking of a "suburban life-style," invoking a conception of a somewhat consistent way of living among middle-class Americans who reside in homogeneous suburbs and who share a pattern of beliefs and values evident in their social actions.[22] *Life style,* then, is sometimes a synonym for subculture.

Subcultures are most evident in regions of a society—such as the Southern, Midwestern, Eastern and Western in the United States—in social classes and ethnic and religious groups, and in particular occupations. In the first instance there is persistent regional variation in the culture, based in part on unique historical origins and settlement patterns, as well as on economic and social differences in the region. Ethnic subcultures originate in the persistence of immigrant groups maintained over generations. When intermarriage within the group is maintained, and also a strong community structure, while yet much adap-

---

[21] *See* David O. Arnold, *The Sociology of Subcultures* (Berkeley, Calif.: Glendessary Press, 1970).

[22] *See* Dennis H. Wrong, "Suburbs and Myths of Suburbia," in Dennis H. Wrong and Harry L. Gracey, eds., *Readings in Introductory Sociology,* 2nd ed. (New York: The Macmillan Company, 1972), pp. 305–311.

Figure 4.4 Wall Street organizes people into a financial world preoccupied with banking and the stock market. *(Wide World Photos)*

tation to and acceptance of the dominant culture occurs, an ethnic subculture emerges.

It is doubtful that all occupations can be thought of as subcultures; too many of them are little more than a particular set of skills or occupational actions. But some occupations occur in larger settings, for which we have labels like *Wall Street, Madison Avenue,* or *Broadway,* identifying *social worlds* linking and integrating related sets of occupations around common activities. Thus, Wall Street signifies banking, stockbrokers, and the stock market, the *financial world,* where an intense preoccupation with the exchange of money and stocks induces a distinctive set of experiences and a distinctive subculture.

Other occupations become subcultures when they create life patterns which segregate people from the more routine, family-oriented lives of other people. Professional athletes, who train and work away from their families for long periods, are an example; but they also belong to a subculture because there is glamour and riches for those who make it, however briefly, in such youth-oriented occupations. The lives of boxers, musicians, soldiers, jockeys, and horse-trainers, carnival and circus performers are other examples.

Deviant Subcultures

Some subcultures are not merely distinctive in values and life styles but produce cultural elements in opposition to the dominant culture, or at least to some of its values. Delinquent boys reject some major values of the culture, such as academic achievement and occupational success, and act instead to assert some quite opposed values—such as "toughness," violence, or illegal action—from which they can gain a status and self-respect not available from the larger society.[23] Professional thieves develop a subculture around illegal activities: their need for secrecy; for reliance on networks of others who provide assistance; the need for "fences," illegal dealers to market stolen goods. There are other examples of *illegal* occupations as subcultures: prostitutes, pimps, gamblers, pickpockets, dope-peddlers, bootleggers, and rum-runners.

Illegal activities constitute one kind of *deviant* status in society, but so does activity that is morally disapproved of and even legally punished, such as homosexuality. Here, concealment of activity and relations with others produce a "gay" subworld that conceals from the "straight" world what is going on. (Only very recently homosexuals have come into the open and claimed their right to be homosexual without fear of punishment from society.)

When the concept of subculture came to be used more frequently to characterize the cultural values and outlooks of delinquents, criminals, and those in illegal occupations, sociologist J. Milton Yinger suggested that *contra culture* be used for these cases, retaining subculture for the values and life styles of other, legitimate subgroups in the society.[24] The term never caught on, but it did serve to emphasize that such groups oppose some major values of the culture and in practice give evidence of contrary ones.

This is still a selective process. In many other ways the carriers of deviant subcul-

tures adhere to many dominant values: to consumption styles, to the importance of making money, to gaining status, even though they may use illegitimate ways to achieve such values. Furthermore, deviant subcultures often contain conservative political values: inmates of prisons can be patriotic and nationalistic. (The emergence of a radical political consciousness among black prisoners, evident at the Attica prison uprising, is a recent development.)

However sharply, then, subcultures differ from the dominant culture on specific values, they are not a conscious effort to judge and find the dominant culture wanting across a wide span of major values. But when a radical cultural opposition to most of its dominant cultural themes and values, accompanied by a conscious effort to construct alternative values and life styles, emerges in a society then there is a *counterculture*.

The Counterculture

When the actions of rebellious youth in the 1960s directly confronted and contradicted dominant American values, the concept of counterculture was born. This has come to be a specific concept, descriptive of a particular counterculture found among some American youth at the present time. But *this* counterculture should be seen as but one example of a phenomenon that has occurred before and undoubtedly will occur again.

The American counterculture of the 1960s cannot be understood except with reference to the dominant culture which in some important ways it *counters;* that is, opposes, goes against. American culture is a vast, complex, and intricately inconsistent pattern of values and themes; but the counterculture confronts only some of these, albeit

---

[23] *See* Albert K. Cohen, *Delinquent Boys* (New York: The Free Press, 1945).

[24] J. Milton Yinger, "Contraculture and Subculture," *American Sociological Review,* vol. 25 (October 1960), pp. 625–635; reprinted in Arnold, *The Sociology of Subcultures,* pp. 121–134.

Figure 4.5 Counterculture youth espouse values and a life style in opposition to the culture and morality of the dominant culture. *(Magnum Photos)*

some major ones. For the following discussion the analysis of American culture by Robin Williams provides a useful summary against which to contrast the counterculture (*see* boxed material).

The Origins of Counterculture

The origins of the contemporary American counterculture can be traced back to the *bohemian* life style which first appeared in the middle of the nineteenth century in France and was intended as a counter-personality to capitalism's ideal man, the *bourgeois*, who exhibited a life style of sobriety, discipline, respectability, conformity, logical reasoning, and practical and acquisitive behavior.[25]

In the United States in the early twen-

tieth century Greenwich Village served as both place and symbol of bohemian life, where artists and writers could live on the margins of respectable society, creating a life style that was "liberated" from the conventional moral constraints of middle-class life. It reappeared again among the *beats* of the 1950s. But the counterculture today is no longer restricted to a small circle of largely artistic individuals; rather, it is masses of people, most of them young. These two facts—numbers and youthfulness —make the counterculture something historically new.

The Carriers of the Counterculture

Not all contemporary youth are carriers of the counterculture; only some are. Excluded are those more conservative and conventional young and also liberal youth still anxious to be active in the mainstream

[25] For a fine sociological analysis of the creation of the bohemian, *see* Cesar Grana, *Bohemian vs. Bourgeois* (New York: Basic Books, Inc., 1964).

of American politics; also not in the counterculture are black youth whose cause leads them in a different direction. But perhaps most fundamental is a class difference. Counterculture youth are more likely to be middle class than working class, more likely to be college youth than working youth.[26]

Theodore Roszak, among others, explains this by centering on the permissive child-rearing of upper-middle-class children for whom there are no economic pressures.[27] The postwar affluent society simply does not need masses of highly trained young people funneled rapidly and early into the labor force, so college-bound

[26] *See* Richard Flacks, *Youth and Social Change* (Chicago: Markham Publishing, 1971), pp. 47–56.

[27] *See* Theodore Roszak, *The Making of a Counter Culture* (Garden City: Doubleday & Co., Inc., 1969).

MAJOR VALUE-ORIENTATIONS IN AMERICA*

Perhaps the most impressive effort to identify the major values and cultural themes of American life has been carried out by Robin Williams. He worked out fifteen such "value-orientations." An inspection makes evident that they are not all consistent, nor can they all be said to characterize all Americans, perhaps not any American some of the time.

1. *Achievement and Success* Personal achievement, especially occupational achievement, in a competitive process brings the rewards of success: wealth and prestige. Working hard and striving to climb the organizational or professional ladder to respected heights is inculcated by family and school in most youth.
2. *Activity and Work* Americans are an active, doing people, always busy, and work—"directed and disciplined activity in a regular occupation"—is the most highly valued form of activity. It is incorporated into personality so thoroughly that work often becomes an end in itself, a major source of respect from others.
3. *Moral Orientation* Americans tend to see the world always and in every way in moral terms, feeling it necessary to make moral judgments on all situations and all personal conduct as right or wrong, good or bad.
4. *Humanitarian Mores* Americans have long demonstrated a capacity to respond sympathetically to the plight of unfortunate people, spontaneously to provide aid when disaster strikes, to engage in numerous community projects to help others, and to side with the underdog.
5. *Efficiency and Practicality* The activism of Americans leads them to value highly efficient and practical action; to emphasize invention, expansion, "getting things done." Engineers are admired; poets are ignored.
6. *Progress* A faith in progress means an optimism about the future, a looking ahead not back ("history is bunk," said Henry Ford), a willingness to change, a belief in the perfectibility of the common man.
7. *Material Comfort* A high level of material comfort proclaims the superiority

*Robin M. Williams, Jr., *American Society: A Sociological Interpretation*, 3rd ed. (New York: Alfred A. Knopf, 1970), pp. 438–504.

middle-class youth experience a less demanding childhood. If the young are "spoiled," Roszak notes, it means "they are influenced to believe that being human has something to do with pleasure and freedom."[28] Taking economic security for granted, he says, they build upon it "a new, uncompromised personality,

flawed perhaps by irresponsible ease, but also touched with some outspoken spirit."[29] Though probably most of the young eventually assume a "responsible" place in the adult world; some do not. "They continue to assert pleasure and freedom as human rights and begin to ask aggressive questions of those forces that insist, amid

[28] Roszak, *op. cit.*, p. 31.

[29] Roszak, *op. cit.*, p. 31.

of the "American standard of living." A passive gratification, and consumption values now increase in importance.

8. *Equality* The persistent theme of equality means equality of opportunity and equality of formal rights and obligations; it also is exhibited in the ways individuals relate to one another. This sense of equality nonetheless fits into a social structure that is hierarchical and given to distributing its material comforts unequally.

9. *Freedom* To be free is to be unrestrained by powerful groups or authority; to be free is to possess freedom of speech and the press. It also means freedom to choose one's church, one's residence, one's occupation.

10. *External Conformity* Despite personal independence and "rugged individualism," Americans display considerable uniformity in speech, manners, dress, grooming, recreation, and political ideas. There is a standardization of individuality. In a nation of joiners, Americans conform easily to their social groups.

11. *Science and Secular Rationality* Science is rational, functional, disciplined, active; it requires systematic diligence and honesty. It fits an engineering civilization, for it has practical utility and encourages efficiency.

12. *Nationalism-Patriotism* Americans are nationalistic, elevate loyalty to country and its life-ways—"Americanism"—to a supreme virtue; "un-American" is an epithet for disallowed deviance, thus encouraging conformity.

13. *Democracy* The belief in democracy is a commitment to majority rule and representative government, but also reserves certain "inalienable rights" for the individual.

14. *Individual Personality* There is a value placed on the development of individual personality and an aversion to invasion of individual integrity. To be a responsible, self-respecting individual is important.

15. *Racism and Related Group-superiority Themes* A pervasive and powerful countercurrent to many of the above is the assignment of value and privilege to individuals by virtue of race or a particular group membership.

Note: These highly abbreviated statements do not do justice to Williams' subtle discussion of these cultural themes, each of which is inconsistently reflected in the actions of Americans, many of which are regularly violated, and some of which are inconsistent with one another.

obvious affluence, on the continued necessity of discipline, no matter how subliminal."[30]

There are other factors, too. One of these is the sheer numbers of young people. With so many of them attending college now, large campuses are major gathering centers where the young interact preponderately with their own. Aware of their numbers and possessing an affluence that makes them a market to which the mass media pay serious attention, young people develop a group identity around the basic fact of age. Here is fertile soil for the growth of the counterculture.

Culture versus Counterculture

What specifically does the counterculture oppose in the dominant American culture? Using Robin Williams' assessment of American value orientations, we can locate basic countercultural opposition to and rejection of a number of these values:

1. A fundamental premise of the counterculture is a far-reaching opposition to the kind of society that technology and industrialism, supported by science, brings into being. Thus, it stands opposed to *efficiency* and *practicality*, writ large as engineering and technology. It did not first create but has enlarged an indictment of such a society as cold and mechanical, drying up the wellsprings of human feeling; of shaping a typical modern technocrat who distrusts emotion and relies only on objective reasoning and cold logic.
2. The counterculture is a challenge to the hitherto unchallenged status of science as the only legitimate source of knowledge, thus rejecting the value orientation of *science and rationality*. Its carriers have sought to restore a respect for intuitive ways of understanding reality and for ways to know

[30] Roszak, *op. cit.*, p. 33.

things other than through objective science. They seek out other sources of knowledge for guidance, such as the ancient wisdom of the East, whose wise men (gurus) offer ways of learning that are strange to the scientifically educated mind. Many pursue an interest in the occult: I Ching, the Tarot, astrology, and the like. Others find answers in wholly Western perspectives, like romanticism and existentialism.

3. The counterculture has sought to restore the human emotions to a central and celebrated place in life, to release human feeling and human activity from the discipline imposed by science, technology, and routinized work. To do this it rejects the commitment to success and material consumption that its adherents claim dominate American life. It rejects the value orientations of *achievement and success, material comfort and consumption,* and *activity and work.* It refuses to accept the disciplined constraints imposed by the logic of industrial capitalism, the value on money-making, and the primary emphasis on work-derived status.

Affirming Dominant Values

However radical is the counterculture's opposition to these deeply ingrained American values, the youthful carriers of the counterculture are nonetheless human "products" of American society. In some important ways they reaffirm basic American values, rather than countering them, though the actions by which they do so are often strikingly different than the standard ways.

Like their parental generation, for example, they are as inclined to a *moral orientation,* expressing strong moral judgments on the actions of others, passionate in their demand for honesty and their condemnation of hypocrisy; only now, they often condemn what conventional Americans praise and praise what others condemn. Like their parents, too, they display *humanistic mores,* a concern for others, a sharing of goods, a providing of shelter. And, no less than more conventional Americans, they claim *freedom* as theirs, particularly freedom from the "oppressive" demands of *external conformity* to the standards of conventional life. Yet, they often exhibit a remarkable conformity—in dress and grooming, in speech, in ideas and musical interests—to the standards of their own counterculture group.

Nonetheless, counterculture youth strongly reaffirm the value of *individual personality.* They stress being *authentic* as a person and "doing your own thing." In many ways their reaffirmation of this value is an intended rebuke to a society which they see as having departed too much from its own claimed commitment to the integrity of the individual person.

Assessing the Counterculture

Now that its groups and communes seem to be in decline, one might ask: Has counterculture's influence declined? No adequate assessment has been or can yet be made, but one can note that its influence permeates well beyond the more limited circle of the committed; there are millions of youth who exemplify in some way or another a countercultural life style.

Still the counterculture also has stern critics. It affronts those who place unquestioned confidence in the scientific method as the only valid way of knowing. It frightens those who see in the affirmation of the nonrational the potential for an irrationality that can be captured and used for totalitarian purposes—as the Nazis captured and absorbed German youth, who were like the present countercultural youth in a number of ways. And it dismays those who see in the pursuit of psychedelic pleasures a copout on the hard political action necessary to create a social structure in which humanistic, nontechnocratic values could be made real.

Beneath the psychedelic trappings of the counterculture are a set of concerns and values by no means alien to American thought: the assertion of individuality and the fear of human subordination to some technological monstrosity. It is a fear long expressed in Western literature and the arts; the counterculture has honorable ancestors. But to many otherwise sympathetic people abandoning science and rationality may be an extraordinarily heavy price to pay for escaping subordination to the technological order spawned by science. The task now may be to find what conscious choices can be made, what alternatives can be constructed.

SUMMARY

Culture is an ordered system of symbolic meanings and understandings. It is humanly created through social interaction and is transmitted over generations as a social heritage. A culture is always integrated to some degree, never perfectly. Its carriers are a people defined by language, boundaries, and social heritage, such as a tribe or a nation.

The elements of culture are: *cognition,* the world of facts, up to and including science and technology; *norms* and *values;* and *world views* and *ideologies.*

Culture mediates man's *adaptation* to the environment; technology aids survival, and in time alters the ecosystem. Through adaptation there is an *evolution* of cultures in technological terms, and only this is progress.

Subcultures are the cultural variations found in large, complex societies among regions, in ethnic groups, and in particular occupations. *Deviant* subcultures occur among subgroups that reject some dominant cultural values, as among delinquent boys. A *counterculture* emerges when a group or segment of society comes into opposition to at least some dominant values.

Suggested Readings

David O. Arnold, *The Sociology of Subculture* (Berkeley, Calif.: Glendessary Press, 1970). A series of essays that explore the development and meaning of subculture.

Ruth Benedict, *Patterns of Culture* (Baltimore, Md.: Penguin Books, Inc., 1946). A world-famous study of variations in human culture.

Serge Denisoff and Richard A. Peterson, *The Sounds of Social Change* (Skokie, Ill.: Rand-McNally & Company, 1972). A series of provocative essays exploring music (especially jazz, blues, folk, and rock) as popular culture and counterculture.

Cesar Grana, *Bohemian versus Bourgeois* (New York: Basic Books, Inc., 1964). A superb sociological analysis of the origins of the counterculture.

Jules Henry, *Culture against Man* (New York: Random House, Inc., 1963). An anthropologist's impressively severe critique of the negative side of American culture.

Robert Redfield, *The Folk Culture of Yucatan* (Chicago: The University of Chicago Press, 1941). A classic field study of village culture in pre-industrial contexts.

Theodore Roszak, *The Making of a Counter Culture* (Garden City: Doubleday & Company, Inc., 1969). Still the best of the analyses of the counterculture, basically but critically sympathetic.

Philip Slater, *The Pursuit of Loneliness* (Boston, Mass.: The Beacon Press, 1970). A penetrating critique of American culture that, along with Roszak, makes the best case for the counterculture.

William Graham Sumner, *Folkways* (Boston, Mass.: Ginn & Company, 1907; paperback edition, New York: New American Library, 1960). The first presentation of folkways and mores in an original and influential analysis of culture.

Raymond Williams, *Culture and Society 1780–1950* (New York: Anchor Books, 1959). A British scholar traces the emergence of the concept of culture as one key term in understanding the onset of industrial society.

Robin M. Williams, *American Society: A Sociological Interpretation* 3rd ed. (New York: Alfred A. Knopf, 1970). Chapter XI on values and beliefs is a classic analysis of American culture.

Tell me what company you keep, and I'll tell you
what you are.
                                    —*Cervantes*

Chapter 5

The Person
in Society

Though the study of human personality belongs to the discipline of
psychology, some conception of human nature and of the relation of the
individual to society is necessarily built into sociological work. For sociologists there is no separation between the individual and society. Human
nature is shaped and developed within and through society, not prior to
or outside of it. *Socialization* is the basic process by which the human organism becomes a person and a functioning member of society and by
which such persons are continually integrated into groups by acquiring as
their own the norms, values, and perspectives of such groups. It is, therefore, a process essential for individuals, else they would not become human,
and also a process essential for groups, for they could not persist without
continually socializing new members.

SOCIALIZATION

The existence of any society depends on the existence of people who
share in the culture, and who take roles and otherwise manifest the actions
that make the society an on-going process. But such people do not come

ready-made. At birth the human organism knows nothing and can do nothing; totally helpless and dependent on others, he has, relative to other organisms, a longer period of learning and developing in which he remains dependent. His social and human characteristics develop over time only when and if the individual is involved with others in the experiences of living in society.

Since a child is always cared for by others and would die if this were not so, there is little contrary evidence against which to test the proposition that one becomes human only by being in society. How do we know how much a person gets from interaction with others and how much is inborn and native, if all persons exist from birth in a society?

Feral Children

What evidence there is comes from a very few cases of children who survived physically even though in virtual isolation from human contact—*feral* children—who were thus denied the humanizing influence of the socialization process. Two actual cases observed by sociologist Kingsley Davis[1] were girls who had missed the first six years of normal socialization because, being illegitimate, they had been hidden in dark rooms and attics and thus denied normal human company. Both were unable to speak, and one could not walk or in fact make any move for herself. They had no "mind," as we know the term; one was completely apathetic and apparently without emotion, whereas the other manifested fear and hostility toward others. Both were believed to be feebleminded at first, but in fact they later made considerable prog-

ress toward recovering the pattern of learning and cultural meaning they had failed to acquire earlier.

But the condition Davis observed in both is an impressive argument that human development requires interaction and communication with others. As further evidence, studies by René Spitz and William Goldfarb[2] have compared impersonal if physically adequate infant care to the normal mothering a child receives. Infants—orphans, for instance—without mothering displayed apathy and little emotional response, and their death rates, despite good physical conditions, was much higher than for those cared for by their mothers.

Such evidence as this does seem to give reason for saying that the individual *acquires* his social nature. Individual and society, then, exist within the same social process. Sociologist Charles Horton Cooley (1864–1929) put it this way: "A separate individual is an abstraction unknown to experience, and so likewise is society when regarded as something apart from individuals."[3] Human society is the system of interactions which occur among individuals, but the person is also a product of those same interactions. Thus, the individual is no more (and no less) "real" than is society. Indeed, *person* and *character* are abstract concepts just as *society* and *group* are. None of these words denotes physical entities; the physical substance of the body is essential to being a person, but is not to be confused with the person.

---

[1] Kingsley Davis, *Human Society* (New York: The Macmillan Company, 1949), pp. 204–208.

[2] For a review of evidence and sources, *see* Judith Blake and Kingsley Davis, "Norms, Values, and Sanctions," in Robert E. L. Faris, ed., *Handbook of Modern Sociology* (Skokie, Ill.: Rand-McNally & Company, 1964), p. 471.

[3] Charles Horton Cooley, *Human Nature and the Social Order* (New York: Charles Scribner's, Sons, 1902), p. 236.

Becoming a Person

No matter how devoid of personality the newborn infant may be, he is loved and nurtured as a person by loving parents — at least, most infants are, and those who are not fail to develop and mature in the same manner as others. From the outset other persons treat him as a valued individual, care for him, respond to his cries, and engage him in interaction from the earliest moment when he responds to others.

Through this interaction the new human begins to enter the complex symbolic world and to learn and share in its culture. The early acquisition of language enables him to participate in more complex social interaction and to acquire distinctly social characteristics.

George Herbert Mead, a philosopher important in the development of the symbolic interaction perspective, stressed this crucial role of language in this process.[4] He started from the fact that interaction and communication could and indeed do exist for animals without language. Each newborn human also engages in interaction before he learns any language; through this interaction he learns the meaning of facial expressions and voice tones, for example, so that he soon knows when another is pleased or angry. The learning of *gestures* forms the basis for learning language; the child already knows the meaning of many objects and events — food, milk, spoon, highchair, getting washed, taking a nap — before he learns the words for them. Once language is a part of the socialization process, however, it makes possible ideas about behavior; now he can engage in the mental process we call thinking. To learn language is to acquire a mind. The child can now reflect upon others' actions toward him and also about the meaning of his own actions.

The interaction between child and significant other — such as mother — now involves learning attitudes that are expressed in words, which convey emotional responses of liking and disliking, approving and disapproving. He not only learns to speak like others, he also learns to use language to convey the same ideas and feelings as others do toward the familiar objects in the environment; he learns to respond in similar fashion.

Internalization

Like Cooley, Mead noticed how children imitate adults in their actions and how significant this is in their learning. For Mead this meant that *by taking the roles of others* the child learns how they respond to objects around them; thus, he is able to *internalize* these responses as his own. By taking their roles he learns to feel and think as they do. For example, watch a small child scold a doll, using the words and voice tone of its mother.

At first this process is one of taking the role of a *particular* other, such as mother or father, but later it becomes taking the role of the *generalized other*. When children play games, for example, there are rules and general expectations about the actions of each participant. This generalized attitude of the group becomes evident to the individual child through his own participation and through his sharing in the rules of the game. He learns what is "fair" and "no fair."

When he has taken on general expectations of performance for every participant,

[4] George Herbert Mead, *Mind, Self, and Society* (Chicago, Ill.: University of Chicago Press, 1934), especially Chs. II and III.

including himself, he has invoked the generalized other within himself. He has now internalized social attitudes. What was once external is now within himself; what others expected of him, he now expects of himself.

He has, in ordinary terms, a *conscience.* Mead called this the "me," whereas Freud called it the *superego.* It is the *internalization* of the norms of society. It enables the individual to respond morally to his own actions and thoughts, and to judge himself as he perceives he would be judged by the community. Such a capacity for self-judgment means the individual now has a *self* that has developed through the individual's social interaction with others.

The Emergence of Self

Prior to internalization society is experienced by the child as an *external* process, something "out there" which controls and constrains him, which compels him to do some things and does not let him do others. The notable Swiss psychologist, Jean Piaget, has made the point that morality is external to the very young child and exists only by virtue of the authority of the parent.[5]

Perhaps the first step toward the development of a self occurs very early, when the child is first able to discriminate among objects in his experience. At some quite early point the new human knows that the world around him is made up of separate and distinct objects; and he learns to tell one from another. He can tell mother from father long before he knows the words or understands the relationships. This permits him to engage in differential interaction with others. But while other persons are objects to him, he is not as yet an

object to himself. He is conscious of others, but he is not yet self-conscious.

The concept of *self* finds its meaning in becoming aware of and responding to oneself, even as one responds to others. To be able to respond to oneself, to evaluate oneself, to approve or disapprove of oneself requires being able to look at oneself from the outside—to be an object to oneself. Cooley suggested that we all undergo a process of imagining how we appear to the eyes of others, depending on what judgments or responses those others make, and of then feeling mortified or pleased or whatever else about this. He called this the "looking glass self."[6]

Self and Society

Mead's perspective lets us see how society "gets into" the person, so that self and society are inseparable phenomena. But Mead insisted that the self, while clearly *social,* is not determined in every aspect by society. He distinguished between the "I" and the "me" as two aspects of self: the "me" is the socialized side, made up of internalized attitudes; whereas the "I" is a spontaneous, creative, even impulsive side, a *self-interested* side that takes into account the "me" but is not entirely controlled by it.

Mead did not grant to society any complete victory over the person. He recognized an element of the individual that is not fully socialized, so that the conduct of the person can never be totally explained as conformity to the norms of society.

The Problem of Socialized Man

Mead's distinction between the "I" and the "me" warns us not to exaggerate the

---

[5] *See* Jean Piaget, *The Moral Judgment of the Child* (New York: The Free Press, 1948).

[6] Cooley, *op. cit.,* pp. 183–184.

power of socialization to produce persons who fit with unconscious ease into society. There is a quality in all persons resistant to the expectations built into the social structure. But how to account for that remains an issue.

Some social scientists seem to stress the cultural fit between person and society, as when Ruth Benedict said:

Most people are shaped to the form of their culture because of the enormous malleability of their original endowment. They are plastic to the moulding force of the society into which they are born.[7]

Such a view of man Charles K. Warriner calls the "culture-man approach which sees man as an empty vessel capable of learning, whose character and nature and behavior are to be understood in terms of that which he learns."[8]

But there have always been, in sharp contrast, strong proponents of the idea that some human attributes are not derived from society, though they may be influenced by social experience. Sigmund Freud is the most notable name to argue for an image of the human being that imputes to him "instinctual endowments," among which is a "powerful share of aggressiveness."[9] Freud spoke glumly of the rapacity and exploitation of man by other men: *"Homo homini lupus"* (man is a wolf to man), he said.[10] More recently there has been a resurgent literature purporting to prove that man is "a naked ape" impelled by his aggressive nature to dominate or be dominated, and pushed by a "territorial

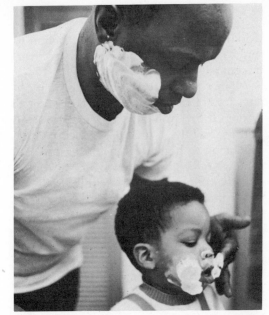

Figure 5.1 By imitating his parent, a child learns how the adult responds and then begins to internalize these responses as his own. *(Magnum Photos)*

imperative" to fight for "turf," presumably like the great apes to which he is linked by biological evolution.[11]

The Oversocialized Image of Man

Reacting against the "culture-man" approach, while not embracing biological explanations, Dennis Wrong claimed that contemporary sociology too easily slips into an *oversocialized* view of man and an *overintegrated* view of society. What Wrong objects to is the view of the person as nothing but the *role-player*, so thoroughly socialized by society that there is a complete internalization of its norms producing a high consistency between person and society. Such a mythical society, where role expectations mesh into a smoothly

---

[7] Ruth Benedict, *Patterns of Culture* (Baltimore, Md.: Penguin Books, Inc., 1946), p. 232.

[8] Charles K. Warriner, *The Emergence of Society* (Homewood, Ill.: The Dorsey Press, 1970), p. 4.

[9] Sigmund Freud, *Civilization and Its Discontents* (New York: W. W. Norton & Company, Inc., 1961), p. 58.

[10] Freud, *op. cit.*, p. 58.

[11] *See* Desmond Morris, *The Naked Ape* (New York: McGraw-Hill, Inc., 1968); and Robert Ardrey, *The Territorial Imperative* (New York: Atheneum Publishers, 1968).

working social system without friction or conflicts, is what Wrong means by over-integrated.

When sociologists stress a thorough *internalization* of social norms, according to Wrong, they are likely to view social control as largely a matter of self-control, producing a high degree of self-induced conformity while minimizing how frequently conformity is a result of coercion rather than conviction. Indeed, if the over-socialized view is correct, he asks, how is it that violence and conflict and the individual's sense of being coerced by society exist?[12] Man, he tells us, is as Freud saw him: ". . . a social animal without being entirely a *socialized* animal."[13]

Man: A Contra-normative Actor

But some sociologists who agree with Wrong's assertion about an oversocialized view of man nonetheless disagree with his resolution of the issue. To them, Wrong falls back on drives and instincts and assumes some universal biological nature that resists socialization. They, in turn, locate the issue not in human nature but in the nature of society. There must always be norm-violating (*contra-normative*) action just because the norms of any society are always inconsistent and contradictory, and this is particularly true in a large, complex society.[14] The process of socialization, then, cannot help but yield inconsistencies and

conflicts rather than any easy fit in the relation of the individual to society.

Robert Merton has addressed himself to the issue in another way, pointing out that normative violations can occur when people cannot achieve such a culturally prescribed *goal* as "success" simply by conforming to normatively prescribed *means*.[15] A society can value success so highly that it unintentionally encourages cheating and sharp-dealing in business, for example; much white collar and especially corporate crime stems from this. For those at the bottom of society, such normative means as individual competition may be unavailable because of ethnic and class discrimination. Then, success may be sought in illegitimate ways, as in crime and the rackets.

Even sociology's classic literature gives us no reason to assume that man is other than a *contra-normative* actor. Émile Durkheim, for example, saw a double significance in criminal action. First of all, a criminal act evokes punishment of some kind by arousing collective sentiments against the act, and thus against the perpetrator of the act. This reaction against criminal acts strengthens the sense of agreement about what is normative and what is not. "Crime brings together upright consciences and concentrates them."[16]

In the second instance, crime, according to Durkheim, is "normal" not "pathological," in that no society can enforce total conformity to its norms; to try to do so a society would become so repressive as to

[12] Dennis Wrong, "The Oversocialized Conception of Man in Modern Sociology," *American Sociological Review*, 26 (April 1961), pp. 183–193.

[13] Wrong, *op. cit.*, p. 192.

[14] For a review of literature that demonstrates how the sources of contra-normative action lie not in biological drives but in the complex relation of the individual to society, *see* Blake and Davis, pp. 456–484.

[15] Robert K. Merton, "Social Structure and Anomie," in his *Social Theory and Social Structure*, rev. and enlgd. ed. (New York: The Free Press, 1957), pp. 131–160.

[16] Émile Durkheim, *The Division of Labor in Society* (New York: The Free Press, 1956), p. 103.

lose the necessary capacity for change and adaptation.

Where crime exists, collective sentiments are sufficiently flexible to take on a new form, and crime sometimes helps to determine the form they will take. How many times, indeed, it is only an anticipation of future morality—a step toward what will be.[17]

Bootlegging liquor and running "speak-easies" were once criminal acts; in time they were replaced by quite legal liquor stores and bars. Similarly, in some states, the numbers racket has been partially replaced by legal track-betting and now by state lotteries. In some states, criminal abortion has become legalized abortion.

Social life, then, is always normatively regulated, and norms are both internalized and enforced—but never fully. The over-socialized man in an overintegrated society does not exist in the real world. But the opposite of that—an aggregate of free and unregulated individuals each pursuing his own self-interest exclusively—is equally unreal.

Agencies of Socialization

Social groups within which the newborn organism can be socialized are a basic part of the structure of society. They are agencies of socialization, and the family unit is the most obvious one.

The Family as Socializing Agency

Though the structure of the family varies from one society to another, some arrangement of familial relationships occurs to provide responsibility for the care and nurturing of the very young. Such a group does more than meet the needs of the dependent child; it provides—partly unconsciously and informally, partly consciously and deliberately—instruction in moral conduct and in socially valued skills. Accordingly, it becomes for such purposes the representative of more general cultural standards and expectations.

In small, traditional societies the family can be regarded as a means for socializing the child into society's norms and values; parents reflect more directly a general social standard of moral conduct evident, though imperfectly, in individual adult conduct. But in large, complex societies the family does not encompass the range of social experience in the society; more to the point, each family is located somewhere within a complex social structure, particularly somewhere within a class structure. Socialization, then, transmits the attitudes and values, modes of conduct, and life styles that are typical of the parents' social class.

Family and Class in Socialization

During the 1940s Allison Davis and Robert Havighurst demonstrated that middle-class mothers followed a rather rigid, inflexible schedule of feeding, attempted toilet-training early, and sought early attainment of habits of cleanliness.[18] Lower-class mothers, in contrast, seemed to proceed flexibly without a rigid schedule, and to allow greater freedom for impulsive and even aggressive behavior. One important consequence was a presumed greater neuroticism among middle-class children.

By the 1950s new research seemed to sug-

[17] Émile Durkheim, *The Rules of Sociological Method* (New York: The Free Press, 1950), p. 71.

[18] Allison Davis and Robert J. Havighurst, "Social Class and Color Differences in Child-rearing," *American Sociological Review*, 11 (February 1946), pp. 31–41.

gest just the opposite; now the middle class appeared permissive and less demanding in its child-rearing practices, whereas the lower class seemed rigid and demanding, exerting strong parental controls and insisting on close conformity to parental demands and rules. Urie Bronfenbrenner analyzed these seemingly contradictory findings and pointed out that middle-class child-rearing practices had, indeed, changed.[19] Since World War I middle-class parents had been following professional advice, particularly that of the highly influential manuals of the United States Government Children's Bureau and such authorities as Arnold Gesell and Benjamin Spock. Changing advice had brought about changing practices.

In addition, many of the studies had lumped together all families below the middle class; but lower class and working class are not the same in family patterns or in child-rearing. The stable working-class family usually makes strong demands on its children, but they are also gradually learning the child-rearing styles of the middle class.

Intraclass Differences

These studies were trying to establish *inter*class differences in family child-rearing practices, thus slighting *intra*class differences. But classes are wide and varied strata. A study in the Detroit area compared "entrepreneurial" and "bureaucratic" families in terms of child training.[20]

In effect, this was a comparison of families of the "old" middle class of independent businessmen and free professionals and of the "new" middle class of salaried executives and professionals employed in large organizations.

What was discovered was that the new middle-class ("bureaucratic") parents teach their children the importance of adjustment, security, and getting along with peers, an orientation consistent with the newer child-training literature and fitting in with an "organization-man" perspective of the world. The old middle-class ("entrepreneurial") parents instill in their children a more active and manipulative approach to life; the child learns the necessity of strong aspirations and hard striving toward his goals. These familiar historic values are also the child-training values found in the professional literature thirty years ago.

In a thorough review of the literature on social class and child-rearing practices, William Sewell has come to the conclusion that there is *some* relationship of social class to personality development in children, as mediated through socialization by the family, but that the frequent assertion of greater neuroticism of middle-class children is invalid.[21] A greater permissiveness in child-training by middle-class parents is clear enough at present. What is less clear is what effect this has on personality development for members of different social classes, and what significance this has, in turn, for their life chances.

The Family as Primary Group

The family is the most significant *primary group* within which the new human is

[19] Urie Bronfenbrenner, "Socialization and Social Class through Time and Space," in E. E. Maccoby, T. M. Newcomb, and E. L. Hartley, eds., *Readings in Social Psychology* (New York: Holt, Rinehart and Winston, Inc., 1958), p. 400.

[20] Daniel R. Miller and Guy E. Swanson, *The Changing American Parent* (New York: John Wiley & Sons, Inc., 1958).

[21] William Sewell, "Social Class and Childhood Personality," *Sociometry*, 24 (December 1961), pp. 340–356.

Figure 5.2 The school provides a training ground for the growing child and also exposes him to his peer group. *(The Ford Foundation, Roy Stevens)*

given a place. Charles Horton Cooley developed the concept of the primary group from observations of his own children in the family situation. Cooley defined primary groups as "characterized by intimate, face-to-face cooperation and association."[22] Within the primary group it was possible for the new human to be significant to others, to be loved and wanted, and to be treated compassionately. The growth of love and affection and the creation of the moral sentiments of a mature human being could occur here.

As Cooley saw it, within the primary group the organism acquires a human nature. By this he meant not biological instincts and innate aggressive drives but those "sentiments and impulses" that separate the human from the animal and are universally characteristic of mankind. The

primary group is the cradle of human morality and ideals, for it fosters a sense of decency and worth that becomes part of the human being for the whole of his existence.

The Peer Group

While family is the first and therefore the most primary of the primary groups, in time the socializing organism moves into more frequent interaction with others. This occurs in the *peer group*, the play group for the small child and the teenage gang or clique for the adolescent. Within its interaction the highly personal authority of the parent is replaced by the impersonal authority of the groups. (In Mead's language, the generalized other replaces the particular other.) The peer group provides significant experiences in learning how to interact with others, how to be accepted

[22] *See* Cooley, *Social Organization* (New York: Charles Scribner's Sons, 1909), p. 23.

by others, and how to achieve status in a circle of friends.

Other Agencies

Other, more formal, agencies share in socializing the child, but their influence is much less than that of family and peer group. Of these others—church, Boy and Girl Scouts, and similar "character-building" organizations—few besides the school have any measurable impact. The school provides training and experiences which are often beyond the capacity of the family to provide, yet seems to have much less impact on the teaching of morals and values than do primary groups.

THE FUND OF SOCIABILITY

The person who is produced by socialization has a continuing need to interact with others, a need to be *sociable*. Separated from friends and family we are lonely. This observation led sociologist Robert S. Weiss to hypothesize a *fund of sociability:* "...individuals require a certain amount of interaction with others, which they may find in various ways."* They may have fewer, more intense relationships, or more but less intense ones. The loss of one relationship, as by divorce, suggested Weiss, could be compensated for by increased sociability with others.

But Weiss and a colleague studied men and women who met as "Parents without Partners," and their findings did not support this hypothesis. Though belonging to "Parents without Partners" proved useful to these divorced parents, it did not diminish their sense of loneliness. This was even true when good friends were made.

This led Weiss to study next married couples who had recently moved to Boston from some distance away, where they were out of contact with old friends and family. The wives, it appeared, suffered for lack of friends with whom they could share the concerns of their daily lives. Their husbands, even when they tried, simply could not function as friends.

It seemed apparent, then, that friendships do not provide the functions ordinarily provided by marriage, but neither does marriage give the functions provided by friendship. There seem to be different kinds of relationships providing different functions.

Weiss and his associates then worked out a theory of functional specificity of relationships: "...individuals have needs which can only be met within relationships, that relationships tend to become relatively specialized in the needs for which they provide, and as a result individuals require a number of different

---

* Robert Weiss, "The Fund of Sociability"; published by permission of Transaction, Inc. from *Trans-Action*, Vol. 6 #9 July/Aug 1969, Copyright © 1969, by Transaction. Also reprinted in Morris L. Medley and James E. Conyers, eds., *Sociology for the Seventies: A Contemporary Perspective* (New York: John Wiley & Sons, Inc., 1972), pp. 68–77, and *also* in John W. Kinch, *Sociology in the World Today* (Reading, Mass.: Addison-Wesley Publishing Company, Inc., 1971), pp. 29–38.

Adult Socialization

Many social scientists once assumed — as many other people still do — that socialization formed the character structure of a person into a firm and definite mold that was not to change much throughout life. But socialization is a continuing process. Indeed, in modern, mobile societies continuing socialization during the adult years is essential, since a person's life situation may change rapidly and, as a result, the early agents of socialization can provide little specific preparation for many later roles.

Going from home town and high school to a distant college, or to a job in a factory or office, or to the army requires further

relationships for well-being."** Weiss suggests five categories of these relationships:

1. *Intimacy,* a relationship in which individuals can express their feelings freely and without self-consciousness. It requires trust, understanding, and ready access. Marriage provides such a relationship, and so can friendship.
2. *Social integration,* a relationship in which participants share similar concerns or are striving for similar objectives. People help one another, exchange information and ideas, do favors for one another. Among women (wives), Weiss says, this function is provided by friends; among men, by relations with colleagues, as well as by friends. A sense of isolation and boredom occurs when such a relationship is absent.
3. *Opportunity for nurturant behavior,* a relationship in which adults take responsibility for the well-being of a child. Weiss says that, based on his experience, men seem more able to act as foster fathers than women do as foster mothers. The absence of this function produces a sense of life as unfulfilled, meaningless, and empty of purpose.
4. *Reassurance of worth,* a relationship that proves an individual's competence in some role. Men and women who work find this reassurance in work relations, and some men find this in family life, too. Women who do not work outside the home look to their relations with husband, children, and acquaintances for recognizing their competence in managing a home and family. A loss here results in decreased self-esteem.
5. *Assistance,* a relationship of providing services or making resources available, is basic to kin relationships, but also neighbors and friendships. Its absence produces a sense of anxiety and vulnerability.

These are tentative generalizations, derived from one piece of research and in no sense definitive. But they point up a significant relationship between the person and society. Once the human organism has been socialized, Weiss tells us, and a self has emerged, there is a continuing need to interact with others. This much has often been stated before, but what Weiss' work adds is the recognition that just any relationship cannot be substituted for another. Different relationships meet different kinds of needs, and Weiss' categories are one effort to specify what these might be.

** Weiss, *op. cit.,* p. 38.

socialization. Learning an occupation is always more than acquiring skills and knowledge; it means the growth of an *occupational personality*. The apprentice absorbs new attitudes and values toward the work and toward the situation in which work occurs; and he also learns a new set of status definitions which relate people to one another—where authority is located, who are his peers, who are not. From this he gains a new image of himself, an occupational identity.[23] But this process is important for the group, too, for its continuity depends on recruiting and socializing new members.

Anticipatory Socialization

In a society in which age-grading creates significant subcultural differences and varying life styles, growing older requires continuing socialization to successive new statuses, such as becoming a grandparent and a retired person. Talking to others who have done the same provides some readiness, some knowledge of what to expect, in short, an *anticipatory socialization*.

The adult couple whose children have married and moved away, leaving an "empty nest," for example, must adjust to a new life situation. In a sample of urban middle-class postparental couples, Irwin Deutscher discovered that this change in life "does not appear to have been insurmountable and the adaptations are seldom pathological."[24] There was sufficient anticipatory socialization made possible by such

things as an acceptance of the inevitability of change, including that of family cycle, the temporary departure of children for college or military service, and the intent of the mother not to be "the mother-in-law you read about."

The Socialization of Generations

To come of age in a depression or in war or revolution is to undergo socialization at a time when major values and social perspectives are being radically altered, and when people develop new outlooks and expectations which they may then carry throughout life. Sociologists speak of *political generations* as shaped in this way.[25]

What a generation is, has no precise meaning. Most commonly it means those who have experienced at about the same age some major socializing influence: war, depression, social movements, or the innovation of new life styles. When that is the case, then it tends to be restricted to those in their late teens and early twenties who have shared crucial experiences in first testing and trying out adult roles.

Defined this way, a socialized generation is not simply a chronological generation. Karl Mannheim made just this point in suggesting a generation be conceived of as time internalized, based on a common sharing of qualitative experience and lasting just as long as its modes of expression prevail.[26] Nelson Foote said something similar in asserting that what separates one generation from another is "marked

---

[23] *See* Howard Becker and J. W. Carper, "The Development of Identification with an Occupation," *American Sociological Review,* 61 (June 1956), pp. 289–298.

[24] Irwin Deutscher, "Socialization for Postparental Life," in Arnold Rose, ed., *Human Behavior and Social Processes* (Boston, Mass.: Houghton Mifflin Company, 1962), pp. 506–525.

[25] *See* Rudolf Heberle, *Social Movements* (New York: Appleton, Century, Crofts, 1951).

[26] Karl Mannheim, "The Problem of Generations," in his *Essays on the Sociology of Knowledge,* Paul Kecskemeti, tr. and ed. (New York: Oxford University Press, 1952), pp. 276–322.

qualitative divergences, occurring rather suddenly."[27]

Many adults viewed the college generation of the middle 1950s as apathetic and subdued, a "silent generation" decisively shaped by the Cold War and the impact of anti-Communist investigations and accusations associated most with the name of the late Senator Joseph McCarthy. That generation contrasted sharply with the renewed political activism and outspoken dissent that surfaced rapidly among college students in the 1960s. Political radicalism born out of involvement in civil rights actions and anti-Vietnam protest, as well as the countercultural life style that spread so widely, made "generation gap" a household word in the United States, particularly among middle-class people.

This meaning of generation can define a shorter or longer period of time; but it also includes only some of those who are the generation of chronological age. While political activists and countercultural youth in the 1960s constituted a significant generation, many other college students knew little of either one. In small, conservative colleges, particularly church-related ones, and in military colleges, there was social insulation from these broader, pervasive generational influences.

But college youth are still a largely middle-class youth, and it is they who were radicalized. The sons and daughters of the working class, who went, not to college but to work, and often (for the males) to military service, were another generation altogether, very little involved in the political activities of that time. They were so far removed from the college generations in socializing experiences that perhaps the only thing they shared in common was their age. Black youth, too, were not the same as whites in generational terms, but they were a significant generation within the black community.

Resocialization

There are some circumstances in which socialization later in life makes a sharp break with an individual's past; early socialization is undone and an older way of life is abandoned for a radically new and different one. This transformation of the person in a short period is *resocialization*. Religious conversion is a notable example of resocialization, as is "brainwashing."[28]

Resocialization occurs regularly as a basis for induction into social groups which define themselves as culturally and socially different from most others in society, but which recruit their members from those other groups. Recruitment from citizen ranks into a military elite is a prime example, as is recruitment into such religious roles as priest and nun.

The resocialization techniques of such groups as these begin with the maximum isolation of the individual from society, a situation that gives the new group sole access to the individual. Its socializing influences then cannot be offset by countervailing exposure to the larger society. In addition, the individual is often stripped of all overt symbols of prior status. His clothes are taken away and a uniform is supplied; shaving the head removes whatever symbolic significance hair style may have had.

---

[27] Nelson Foote, "The Old Generation and the New," in Eli Ginsberg, ed., *The Nation's Children,* vol. 3, *Problems and Prospects* (New York: Columbia University Press, 1960), pp. 1–24.

[28] For a study of brainwashing as resocialization, *see* Robert Jay Lifton, *Thought Control and the Psychology of Totalism* (New York: W. W. Norton & Company, Inc., 1961).

The early stages of resocialization often include deliberate humiliation and degrading, reducing all sense of self-esteem and self-respect acquired from past interaction in society. Past status is suppressed as a prelude to a new status. Basic training in the Marine Corps utilizes this extensively; the low status of first-year students in military academies often includes much harassment by older cadets, petty sanctions, and few if any privileges.

Stripping away old identities precedes the effort to build new ones, which also requires close involvement with a peer group and removal from society. Peers support and reward one another and provide a sustaining milieu through a solidarity built up from sharing together the identity debasement and personality reconstruction that is the core of their resocialization.

Since commitment to a new identity is deliberately induced, it is often tested. Passing a series of tests is necessary if one is to be a priest or a military officer, for the basic issue is not skill or knowledge but thorough socialization into and commitment to a role and its life style.

In this process strong sanctions may be invoked. They can be the harsh punishment of military discipline, the torture of "brainwashing" programs, or enforced isolation. Positively, they can be the promise of membership in an elite group, high social status, or the promise of eternal salvation.

Making a Black Muslim

John R. Howard interviewed in depth a group of recruits to the Black Muslims in order to understand their socialization into the black nationalist organization.[29] What

[29] *See* John R. Howard, "The Making of a Black Muslim," *Transaction* (December 1966).

he discovered was a process much like resocialization. The recruits he interviewed were all drawn to the Black Muslims out of life situations marked by instability and a breaking of ties with regular institutions, including unstable marital histories. Each felt that being black was the most important factor in accounting for what happened to him. Thus, some anticipatory socialization had already occurred when these men sought out their new organization, a readiness to accept its message on the ultimate superiority and assured victory of blacks over whites.

To be a Black Muslim required undergoing a religious conversion to a Protestant ethic that demands ascetic denial of the pleasures of sex and alcohol, and a sober, industrious life in support of family and children.

"Getting into the thing deep" — getting increasingly more involved and committed — usually involves three stages:

1. Participation in the group's activities, such as attending and assisting in running meetings, eating at Muslim restaurants, and selling its newspapers on the street.
2. Isolation from other social contacts by gradually drifting away from old friends and associates and former activities.
3. Making a full commitment by absorbing the ideology. When that occurs, the individual uses the Muslim doctrines to guide and interpret his own actions in the world. His world view has undergone a radical transformation.

Such a commitment has had a dramatic effect on some persons, transforming alcoholics and drug addicts into puritanical people. Men have been converted in prisons (as was Malcolm X, the Black Muslims' most famous recruit and most dynamic leader), turning away from the criminal activities that had once dominated their lives.

SOCIAL CONTROL

Through socialization individuals internalize the values and norms of society and are able to exercise self-control. Yet no society can rely entirely on socialization and self-control. There are laws and customs; and there are ways of enforcing them, including *sanctions* meted out to violators. In addition, there are agents and agencies of society to assume responsibility for seeing that the group's norms are upheld. In informal but no less compelling ways any social group can invoke pressures and demands on its members as the price for acceptance by the group. All of this is *social control.*

But modes of compulsion, with threats of punishment (*negative sanctions*), are not the only complements to self-control. Individuals may also be induced through social rewards (*positive sanctions*) to undertake an activity of value to the society. In this way they may be willing to submit to rigorous training and hard work for some future reward, such as getting into and through graduate school or a professional program, like medicine.

Using Negative Sanctions

In any social group, from a family or group of friends to a large organization, formal and informal mechanisms of control are used to contain action within established limits. These can range from the mildest rebuke to the ultimate penalty —death. While only a political authority can invoke the legitimate sanction to deprive a person of his life, social groups have always resorted to ostracism or isolation, cutting an offending person off from social interaction with others. In formal organizations this may take the form of removing the person from membership; a

Figure 5.3 The anonymity of the individual is stressed in such organizations as the military, where prior symbols of status and even of identity are stripped away. *(Magnum Photos)*

company fires an employee; a school expels a student. Lesser sanctions can be suspension, a fine, and demotion. Political authority can use jail sentences and fines.

Informal Sanctions

It does not require official authority to invoke sanctions for social control. Even the smallest group, or the most loosely organized, manages to do so. *Ridicule,* for example, effectively threatens the group's esteem of the individual and so also his self-esteem. His good standing and personal reputation may be at stake.

It is because of this that *gossip* is a control mechanism. To avoid gossip the individual must avoid the conduct that, if gossiped about, would damage his reputation in the community. "What will the neighbors think" controls conduct among all those who in fact do care what the neighbors think.

An earlier generation of sociologists emphasized this informal process of social control, asserting that in the small rural community and cohesive neighborhood of the past, controls such as gossip worked well just because a person lived entirely among people before whom his conduct was always visible. The anonymity and impersonality of the city, however, made this kind of control less effective. Such formal mechanisms as law then take over from informal controls. Yet, for many urban people the neighbors do still count; but it may now be fellow church members, fellow employees, or even bosses. What somebody thinks of you counts; and much social control depends on that.

Peer Control

Informal sanctions rest on the principle that the more the individual values acceptance by his peers, the more he is susceptible to the pressures of the group. Most people can anticipate what the response of their group will be for any conduct, and this is a built-in control. Thus, small and intimate groups, such as family and close friends, are in a strategic position to exact a far-reaching conformity from their members.

Thus we have a paradox of human existence: that the individual may be controlled most effectively in that group in which he feels most free. His most valued group may be his most coercive, for he can least avoid living up to the expectations of those most significant to him.

Using Positive Sanctions

Rewards and other inducements are a familiar aspect of social life. Trophies and championships reward outstanding individual and team performance. High grades and scholarships reward academic excellence. Gold stars send small school children proudly home to show their mothers their good papers. Remove these, and the activity itself, even if valued, may not induce as concerted and sustained an effort.

In modern societies such rewards won in competitive action induce people to mobilize their energies and organize their actions to pursue difficult goals. Those who are led to seek high status as a social reward can be motivated to set long-term goals for themselves, to work hard and long for small immediate rewards, to endure discomfort and even hardship—all in order to realize a dream in the future.

The belief in "rags to riches" in American life has been a powerful myth leading generations of Americans to believe that a sustained effort on their part could lead to great personal success, if they also had the necessary personal attributes of ability and moral character. This is the *Horatio Alger myth*, the story of the poor but hardworking boy who eventually achieves the pinnacle of success in American society.[30]

After a century the Horatio Alger myth has not survived intact. A society in which success is found increasingly within the framework of organizational careers places a premium on the capacity of individuals to work well with others, to get along cooperatively. Relations with others become as important as hard work and ability; "personality" is the term that symbolizes this new aspect. Without an acceptable "personality" an individual has less chance to succeed.

Aspiring to achieve success today re-

---

[30] Horatio Alger (1834–1899) was a writer of popular inspirational novels, whose name came, in time, to symbolize the myth.

Figure 5.4 Ridicule, gossip, and isolation from the group are informal negative sanctions for social control. *(Magnum Photos)*

quires much more than a willingness to work hard; it usually takes education and training. Yet there are always those who lack the formal education necessary for business or professional careers, but who still aspire to succeed. For them there has long been an alternate route to success, the vast world of popular entertainment, including professional sports, where hard work, extensive practice, and amateur and professional apprenticeship may eventually bring success.

Professional baseball and boxing once provided channels for the aspirations of lower-status youths whose athletic skills were their only possible routes to fame and fortune. The minor leagues of baseball and the small tank-town boxing circuits paid poorly, yet thousands of young men endured them while sustaining the hope of making "the big time." The old-time baseball managers had a word for them:

They were "hungry." They could endure uncomfortable travel, poor accommodations, indifferent food, and poor pay, partly because they had little option for anything better but primarily because they clung to the hope of achieving the success that went with making it into the big leagues.

The dream factory that is Hollywood has also nurtured and channeled such aspirations.[31] The myth of the young starbound actress discovered at a drugstore counter was sufficient to send thousands of young women to Hollywood to endure years of sacrifice in the hope of eventual discovery and stardom. That few made it was no deterrent.

It is different now. The minor leagues are few, and small-town boxing clubs are

[31] Hortense Powdermaker, *Hollywood: The Dream Factory* (Boston, Mass.: Little, Brown & Company, 1950).

gone; the mode of recruitment has changed. Athletes are found at college and high-school campuses and are paid bonuses; they expect to make it big in a short time or else to quit for whatever other middle-class career is available. The young actresses who appear in Hollywood movies and television are recruited less from behind a drugstore counter and more from college campuses, local television stations, and actors' training studios.

During the 1950s and 1960s the world of rock music encouraged many young people to give concerts and make records for a market oriented largely to mass tastes among adolescents. Again, the success of the few encouraged the many to try. It was a way to reach fame and fortune without much in the way of education, professional training, or even long experience.

Controlling Reward by Policy

These examples of efforts to succeed in competitive markets where performers either please audiences or do not are familiar ones. Yet political authority can also deliberately harness human talent and shape social aspirations. The political and ideological concerns arising from the Cold War climate of the 1950s, for example, led the federal government to adopt a policy of encouraging the development of scientific and technological talent. Federal grants subsidized programs to steer large numbers of talented youngsters into careers in science. What may then seem at one level to be the personal decisions of millions of young people to seek a college education and pursue science as a career may also be the consequence of deliberate efforts to induce such intentions in choosing one career over another.

Limiting Aspiration

A mobile society encourages aspirations to be widely distributed among its young. But aspiration makes no sense to the young if available channels are not accessible, if there is too great an observable discrepancy between aspiration and achievement possibilities. Often in the past it has proven difficult to encourage minority youth to take an interest in education when they quite realistically assessed the actual opportunity for achievement to be low because of discrimination. Where a desire for achievement did become internalized in disadvantaged youngsters, it often harnessed energy and talent into alternate channels, such as athletics and entertainment, where discrimination, though still prevalent, was less of an obstacle to success.

Control and Freedom

To dwell on the mechanisms of social control, whether positive or negative, seems to emphasize how the group demands conformity by the individual, denying the freedom and individuality that are such important values in American culture. But there is no freedom and individuality outside of human society; to polarize society against the individual distorts what is a real and difficult issue.

Achieving social control in a large, complex society is much less assured than in the small group, a fact some people see as a problem and others see as a guarantee of individual freedom. The new electronic techniques for eavesdropping on private conversations can be a means of controlling the behavior of less-conforming persons. The accumulation of information stored in computers—data banks—can be a means to control large numbers of persons.

Imaginative minds have created versions of society in which the fit between person and society is frictionless. In *Brave New World* Aldous Huxley designed an anti-utopian society in which individual human beings are biologically manufactured to specification and socialization in a way so effectively carried out that there is never any problem of social control.[32] People are designed to fit society, to have only those abilities, emotions, and aspirations required to perform specified social functions. Based as it was on biological engineering, Huxley's conception of a controlled, freedomless future, however chilling, seemed unlikely in 1932. But in the 1970s the science of biology has moved nearer to effective genetic control, and Huxley's science-fiction nightmare of forty years ago no longer seems beyond scientific achievement and aspiration, presenting almost undreamed of problems of the ethics of social control for free societies.

What Huxley imagined in biological terms B. F. Skinner has put forth in psychological terms. His *Walden Two* is a science-fiction novel about a utopian society in which socialization is perfected to eliminate the emotions of fear, hate, and envy in completely controlled environments.[33] Skinner has become world-renowned for advocating a technique of psychological reinforcement that will make people fit culturally-desired standards. His most recent work, *Beyond Freedom and Dignity*, has aroused enormous controversy for its outright advocacy of instituting behavioral controls over individual citizens.[34]

Both Huxley and Skinner point to the possibilities of controlling human beings by a powerful science, biological in the one case, social in the other. Social science is not able as yet to prescribe for society's leaders and ruling institutions the behavioral mechanisms for fully effective control of people; and even though many social scientists aspire to such an achievement, others thoroughly oppose it. But biology has made vast strides toward a genetic control undreamed of but a few years ago and still not understood by most people. Its potentialities raise issues about freedom and control for which conventional values and morality have no answer.

INDIVIDUALISM, IDENTITY, AND ALIENATION

Social scientists concerned with the relationship of the individual to society have stressed that socialization produces a good fit between the two. But in recent years a new interest has emphasized instead tensions between the individual and society. For the past quarter-century a pressing concern has been the impact of vast and powerful social organizations on individual human beings, on the potential loss of integrity and individuality to the fact of a conformity-demanding social structure, and on the hypnotizing sameness and routinization of life in modern society. The common argument is that modern society forces a loss of identity for the individual, that he becomes a nonself, a face in a crowd, a number on an IBM card.

[32] Aldous Huxley, *Brave New World* (New York: Harper & Row, 1932).

[33] B. F. Skinner, *Walden Two* (New York: The Macmillan Company, 1948).

[34] B. F. Skinner, *Beyond Freedom and Dignity* (New York: Alfred A. Knopf, 1971).

Individuality and Conformity

There is in any society variation among individuals, but in modern societies there is much greater development of individuality, the uniquely individual character of each person. Earlier (Chapter 3) we quoted Émile Durkheim's observation that a society with little division of labor was one in which "individuality is nil," but that where the division of labor was greater, "the more specialized the individual, the more personal his activity." Durkheim's telling point was: "Individuality arises only if the community recedes."[35]

Individuality, then, is a *fact* of modern social structure, but it is also a *value*. Being a unique individual with a mind of one's own is respected. However, in American society it is a value about which there is ambivalence. Sociologist Robin Williams has indicated (Chapter 4) that in American society there is both the value of *individual personality* and the value of *external conformity*. As Alfred McClung Lee notes:

> To the nervous amusement and even grave concern of many friendly European students of the United States situation, we vaunt our personal independence, our respect for "individualism," and our opposition to "authoritarianism" and then, without appearing to realize our inconsistency, rationalize our conformism. In terms of our behavior, we hold conforming to be one of our highest virtues.[36]

The Peer-oriented Conformist

More recently the tension between individual and society has taken a new form.

The growth of large and encompassing social structures, often bureaucratic in nature, led to the idea that bureaucratic structures both produced and wanted a type of person who accommodated flexibly to diverse situations for interaction and who excelled in relating well to others. Not individual, self-motivated performers but cooperative team-workers was the presumed new requirement for human personality. Some degree of individuality gave way before the demand for conformity to effective work relations.

Sociologist David Riesman's seminal work, *The Lonely Crowd,* first set forth this idea almost a quarter-century ago.[37] Riesman argued that a highly urbanized society organized through large, bureaucratized structures demands a highly flexible, continually socializing type of person, now beginning to emerge among the urban, college-educated, bureaucratically-employed middle classes. He called this *other-directed,* a personality type particularly sensitive to the demands and expectations of the immediate situation and readily responding to the cues expertly detected in the actions of others.

The other-directed person is socialized early to be particularly dependent on the peer group, to be well-liked and accepted, and to make those adjustments in his own conduct that will insure acceptance by his peers. His direction, then, comes less from parental values internalized in early childhood and more from a ready response to peers and to the larger contemporary world to which he is oriented through his peers. The "bureaucratic" family studied by Miller and Swanson in Detroit (*see* footnote

[35] Émile Durkheim, *Division of Labor in Society* (New York: The Free Press, 1947), p. 130.

[36] Alfred McClung Lee, *Multivalent Man* (New York: George Braziller, Inc., 1966), p. x.

[37] David Riesman, with Nathan Glazer and Reul Denny, *The Lonely Crowd* (New Haven, Conn.: Yale University Press, 1950).

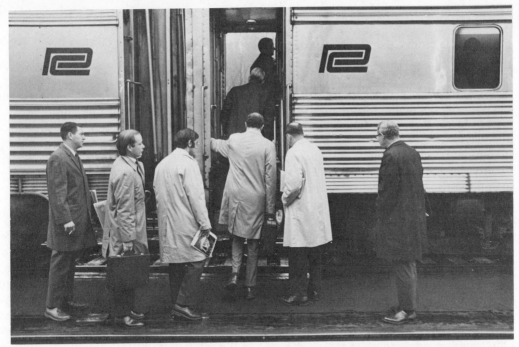

Figure 5.5 Do other-directed persons, largely dependent on their peer groups, signal the decline of individualism in American society? *(Mimi Forsyth, Monkmeyer)*

20 of this chapter), socializing its children to get along well with peers, provides support for this conception of a new pattern of personality development.

Riesman's work was interpreted by many to be describing a decline in individualism in American society. But Riesman intended no such idea; instead, he was describing what seemed to him to be a new way in which society constructed a "mode of conformity." Nonetheless, his work was the basis for an extended discussion about the threat of large-scale organization to individualism. A popularization of his ideas by William Whyte used middle-level corporate executives, their wives, and their suburban lives as evidence of a vastly conforming trend in modern life.[38] Indeed, "organization man" entered the American vocabulary

as a denigrating term for upwardly mobile men in large organizations whose career aspirations led them to overconform to the social world.

Yet much of this literature was a cry of alarm based, first, on a romanticized misreading of history, mistakenly attributing a rugged individualism as a normal aspect of life in American society prior to the present period; secondly, on a romantic mythology about the freedom and individualism inherent in small-scale social worlds and the loss of these qualities through the growth of social structure.

Furthermore, its claims were based on very little, if any, empirical analysis. A careful examination of the thesis that upwardly mobile American men overconform to the political norms of the middle class, for example, was found to be invalid by sociologist Andrew Hopkins: "... upwardly mobile American men are politically indis-

[38] William H. Whyte, *The Organization Man* (New York: Simon and Schuster, Inc., 1956).

tinguishable from their stable middle class compatriots.[39]

A comparable myth generated the image of the typical bureaucrat as rigidly adhering to rules; a petty, unimaginative conformer to routine procedures. But sociologist Melvin Kohn not only found this was not so, but found some modestly greater quality of intellectual flexibility, more openness to experience, and more self-direction in bureaucratically-employed men than in men who work in nonbureaucratic organizations.[40]

A great deal more needs to be known about how individuals adapt to large, complex social structures before we can adequately balance out what combination of gains and losses for individuality are inherent in the growth of social structure. One experienced sociologist asserts that we do not have the alternatives of living with or destroying giant social structures which currently so diminish the individual. Instead, the alternatives, he suggests, are whether "our relations with leviathan shall become more manipulative, oppressive, and impersonal or can become more humanistic and individually more stimulating and satisfying."[41]

Identity and Alienation

While conformity as a threat to individuality is one way to examine tensions between the individual and society, another is in terms of *identity* and *alienation*. Each person carries around a self-identity, an image obtained from membership and roles in groups that are particularly valued or in some cases are most inclusive of the individual's roles and available interactions with others. Identities are built up in life through attachments that grow and are valued, through membership in groups into which one is born, and by choices from among whatever options a person has.

Ascribed and Achieved

No one has a completely free choice in establishing his identity. To be male or female is basic to identity, as it is to be black or white; such identities are imposed —that is, *ascribed* to a person by others. Membership in an ethnic or religious group assigned at birth is also an ascribed identity, but here an individual can by choice escape such an identity in a way he cannot for sex and race. He can reduce his interaction with ethnic peers and consciously discard the clues that others use to establish his identity in their minds— speech, mannerisms, cultural interests. The immigrant of the second generation who looks for *role models* in people outside his ethnic group and tries hard to be like them, is an example. (Note, also, that anticipatory socialization is going on in this example.)

Yet in the modern world ascribed identity is never the whole of any person's identity, as it would be for the peasant or aristocrat in a medieval society. To a large extent modern people choose their identities among some range of options, though not all options are equally available to everyone. Their identities are *achieved*.

Occupation as Identity

Occupation is the most significant achieved identity in modern societies. For those with highly regarded occupations,

[39] Andrew Hopkins, "Political Overconformity by Upwardly Mobile American Men," *American Sociological Review*, 38 (February 1973), p. 147.

[40] Melvin L. Kohn, "Bureaucratic Man: A Portrait and an Interpretation," *American Sociological Review*, 36 (June 1971), pp. 461–474.

[41] Lee, *op. cit.*, p. x.

their involvement in work is often their central life interest; they pursue a career. For those with less-regarded occupations, work will not be their central life interest, even though work itself will remain a valued activity. This has been true for a long time of blue-collar workers, for example.[42] They build their self-identity largely from involvement in groups outside the world of work.

Sometimes such involvements may occur entirely within an ethnic group. When this is the case identity is largely formed, if not exclusively, from within a narrow circle of interaction. Herbert Gans describes life in a community of working-class second-generation Italians in the West End of Boston where life is largely circumscribed within the family and ethnic peers.[43] For these people work takes the individual into a hostile outside world where "they" control affairs.

The ideal job for them pays the most money for the least physical discomfort, one that does not demand any emotional involvement, such as "taking the job home with you." It is not that West Enders dislike work; on the contrary, they value hard work and doing a good job. But they will try to minimize involvement in it to only that required to do the job. Their work is a means to an end, not an end in itself.[44]

Work and occupation for such people, then, is a small factor in establishing their identity. As Gans notes, the West Ender and the middle-class person differ greatly in their attitudes toward a career. Work can be a central purpose in life, and it should be organized into a series of related jobs that make a career, these are not ideas to be found among the second generation of West Enders.[45]

Negative Identities

That working-class ethnics might stress their ethnicity rather than their semiskilled occupations in establishing identity is evidence that options are exercised among available choices and that not all social identities are positive and rewarding. Low-status occupations, as well as little education, put people into disesteemed identities. Being poor, for example, is a negative identity in the United States; being on welfare is more so. A minority person who experiences prejudice and discrimination knows in a painful way what it means to be negatively identified by others. From this perspective, women's liberation is a struggle to create a more positive identity for females, first in women's own minds, subsequently in men's.[46]

Nonetheless, people try to build self-respected identities out of the roles and memberships available to them. A working-class girl who marries soon after she leaves high school and equally soon gives birth to a child has few options on which to build an identity. She will probably emphasize a good marriage, being a "good wife," and the conscientious way she undertakes the responsibilities of being a mother. A small circle of girlhood friends and some friendships in her neighborhood,

---

[42] *See* Robert Dubin, "Industrial Workers' Worlds: A Study of the 'Central Life Interests' of Industrial Workers," *Social Problems*, 3 (1956), pp. 131–142.

[43] Herbert J. Gans, *The Urban Villagers: Group and Class in the Life of Italian-Americans* (New York: The Free Press, 1962).

[44] Gans, *op. cit.*, pp. 123–124.

[45] Gans, *op. cit.*, p. 124.

[46] For some useful papers on this point *see* Vivian Gornick and Barbara K. Moran, eds., *Woman in Sexist Society: Studies in Power and Powerlessness* (New York: Basic Books, Inc., 1971).

as well as the close attachments of family, will mark the range of her social world. It is within these relationships that she can establish an identity respected by others significant to her.[47]

Identity Crisis

The recent sociological literature on identity has rarely touched on these problems of disesteemed identities or on the problems experienced by so many ordinary citizens in establishing self-respected identities. Instead, as a consequence of the social disruptions of the 1960s, it has focused on the search for viable identities by middle-class college youth. Here the problem is different; these individuals find it difficult to accept the career-oriented identities for which a college education is essential. They remain uncommitted to the social roles and structures through which they are expected to pursue a rewarding adult career.[48] They experience an *identity crisis,* a difficulty in knowing what socially-recognized identities offer a mode of participation in society that will allow them to become the persons they want to be and to live in accordance with the values they hold dear.[49]

To some extent probably all youth in modern society face an identity crisis as part of coming of age, for identities and roles must be chosen for adult life; they are not simply transmitted by a process of inheritance. Each generation faces new circumstances, and only a few people inherit the specific statuses of their parental generation. Most youth must choose an occupation, at least seek a job; only some get to choose a career.

Alienation

To call "uncommitted" youth *alienated,* as Kenneth Kenniston did, is to invoke a concept with a long history and varied use;[50] but one recent idea is to define it as a *subjective* feeling of actors in social situations. Sociologist Melvin Seeman has developed five dimensions of alienation as psychologically experienced by the individual:[51]

1. *Powerlessness* is experienced when an individual realizes he cannot influence his own destiny in the social structure to which he belongs.
2. *Meaninglessness* is experienced when the individual no longer understands the functioning of the social structure, and so cannot understand the meaning of his own actions.
3. *Normlessness* is experiencing the inability to reach socially-acceptable and desirable goals through channels acceptable to society or through the individual's social groups; it is also experienced in the feeling that work is no longer a goal in itself.
4. *Isolation* is experiencing a sense of with-

[47] For some studies bearing on this issue *see* Lee Rainwater, Richard P. Coleman, and Gerald Handel, *Workingman's Wife: Her Personality, World and Life Style* (New York: MacFadden-Bartell, 1962); and Mirra Komarovsky, *Blue-Collar Marriage* (New York: Random House, Inc., 1964).

[48] *See* Kenneth Kenniston, *The Uncommitted: Alienated Youth in American Society* (New York: Harcourt, Brace, Jovanovich, 1965).

[49] Erik Erikson first developed the concepts of identity and identity crisis. *See* his *Childhood and Society* (New York: W. W. Norton & Company, Inc., 1950), pp. 227 ff., and "The Problem of Ego Identity," in Maurice Stein, Arthur J. Vidich, and David White, eds., *Identity and Anxiety* (New York: The Free Press, 1960).

[50] For an analysis of the development of this concept since Marx *see* Joachim Israel, *Alienation: From Marx to Modern Society* (Boston: Allyn and Bacon, Inc., 1971).

[51] Melvin Seeman, "On the Meaning of Alienation," *American Sociological Review,* 24 (December 1959), pp. 753–759.

drawal from goals not obtainable in socially-acceptable ways, a sense of negation so strong it may lead to retreating from social roles and thus a self-imposed isolation.

5. *Self-estrangement* is experiencing a loss of interest or involvement in necessary activities, such as work; these activities are no longer goals but are simply endured as means to other needed things, such as income.

A sense of alienation as the experience of one or more of these feelings is not uncommon in the relation of individuals to modern society. To feel powerless and also to experience meaninglessness is a common occurrence for large masses of people in a large, complex society, for that society seems neither understandable nor controllable by the political and economic means available to them. And it is then they realize how few are any such means controlled by other than powerful elites. Then alienation is no longer an issue about the *feelings* of individuals concerning society but a statement about structurally induced *conditions* in society (*see* Chapter 14).

SUMMARY

Socialization is the process of interaction whereby the organism becomes human and acquires a nature by internalizing the culture. The *self* emerges in socialization when the individual learns to be conscious of himself as a social object and to respond to himself with approval and disapproval. Socialization requires gesture and language (communication), and *taking the role of the other*.

The family and, later, peer groups are the primary *agents* of socialization. Adults undergo *continuing socialization* when they are socialized to new roles in new situations. *Anticipatory* socialization occurs when people socialize to new roles prior to actual occupancy of the role.

The socialization of *generations* means the common sharing of socializing experiences—depressions, wars, and social movements—for as long as the significant experiences last and including only those exposed to it.

Resocialization is the radical transformation of the person in a short period, whereby early socialization is abandoned and a new self emerges.

Social *control* relies on more than socialization and self-control. Social groups enforce norms by a variety of means, from rebuke to death. Peer groups can exercise effective control just because the individual values acceptance by his peers. There are negative sanctions (punishment) and positive sanctions (rewards).

Individuality is a fact in modern society, but it is also a value; however, it is countered by pressures to conform. Peer-oriented conformity (the other-directed person) is presumably a powerful control in bureaucratized society, though the case may be overstated.

Group memberships significant to us are the source of our *identities*. Some identities are ascribed, some achieved. Negative identities are assigned to people who cannot escape disadvantaged or minority status.

Youth often face an *identity crisis,* a difficulty in knowing what combination of roles so fit their character that they can participate in society in ways that allow them to become the persons they want to and live in accordance with their values.

For the individual, *alienation* is a feeling of powerlessness, meaninglessness, normlessness, isolation, and self-estrangement.

Suggested Readings

Charles Horton Cooley, *Human Nature and the Social Order* (New York: Charles Scribner's Sons, 1902). A still-readable classic on how we become human.

Émile Durkheim, *Suicide,* trans., John A. Spaulding and George Simpson (New York: The Free Press, 1951). A profound analysis of the problem of the integration of the person into society, with suicide rates as one index for measuring integration.

Erik Erikson, *Childhood and Society* (New York: W. W. Norton & Company, Inc., 1950). Erikson's notable study of becoming a person in society, including his concept of identity-crisis.

Erik Erikson, *Identity: Youth and Crisis* (New York: W. W. Norton & Company, Inc., 1968). In this more recent work, Erikson re-evaluates his own theories about identity.

Sigmund Freud, *Civilization and Its Discontents* (New York: W. W. Norton & Company, Inc., 1961). Freud's never-optimistic views of human nature and its relations to civilized life.

Joachim Israel, *Alienation: From Marx to Modern Society* (Boston, Mass.: Allyn and Bacon, Inc., 1971). A thorough review and analysis by a European sociologist of alienation as a concept, from Marx' first provocative use to contemporary sociological usage.

Kenneth Kenniston, *The Uncommitted: Alienated Youth in American Society* (New York: Harcourt, Brace, Jovanovich, 1965). Kenniston's influential examination of the alienation of middle-class youth in the 1960s.

Alfred McClung Lee, *Multivalent Man* (New York: George Braziller, Inc., 1966). The problem of individuality and conformity explored with insight and wisdom in terms of the many-valued and often value-conflicting society in which the individual functions.

George Herbert Mead, *Mind, Self, and Society* (Chicago, Ill.: University of Chicago Press, 1934). The classic presentation of the Meadian perspective.

Jean Piaget, *The Moral Judgment of the Child* (Glencoe, Ill.: The Free Press, 1948). An impressive analysis of how children acquire morality.

David Riesman, with Nathan Glazer and Reul Denny, *The Lonely Crowd* (New Haven, Conn.: Yale University Press, 1950). The best-known work of our time on the relationship of character to society.

Allen Wheelis, *The Quest for Identity* (New York: W. W. Norton & Company, Inc., 1958). A gifted psychoanalyst probes brilliantly into the changing character of modern Americans, their loss of old identities and their search for new ones.

PART **III**

SOCIETY
AND GROUPS

What is society, whatever its form may be? The product of men's reciprocal action. Are men free to choose this or that form of society? By no means.

—*Karl Marx*

Chapter 6

Society

In the preceding chapters we have examined those concepts we need in order to proceed with the study of society, but these are not that study itself. We must understand interaction as the basic social process underlying all social life, and we need to understand culture and person as social phenomena that emerge from interaction and are complexly interwoven with society. But person and culture are not the phenomena we want to focus on most specifically; that we will leave to social psychologists and anthropologists, respectively. We want to examine society, and we begin that process in this chapter by taking a close look at what a society is.

THE CONCEPT OF SOCIETY

So far we have said only that sociology is the study of society and that society emerges from human interaction, but nothing yet about what the concept of society means. We have proceeded on the assumption that a common-sense conception would suffice—up to now it has. However, it is time to make clear what it is we are talking about when we say "society."

Most people, sociologists included, seem to have little need to define society. Often society means something like the fabric of social life, the larger context in which particular actions occur, reminding us that events and actions do not happen in a vacuum, and that somehow actions link together, that there is a network of interlinked groups and relations.

Another approach is to view society as the largest social system or the largest social group organized by a people, of which all other social systems and groups are subsystems and subgroups. The value of this has been to treat society as a single entity, therefore as an object for study.

But there has been a flaw in such an approach. Society as the largest group containing all other groups is often regarded as a self-sufficient system with well-marked boundaries and well-defined memberships, occupying a specific territory. The definition offered by sociologist Talcott Parsons is typical: "A social system . . . which meets all the essential functional prerequisites of long-term persistence from within its own resources will be called a society."[1]

But throughout history there are too many cases that violate such a definition. Boundaries have often been ill-defined, if they were defined at all. People were involved in interactions that overlapped and cut across established territorial boundaries and group memberships. Reality, in short, has never been that neat. Furthermore, in the world today, societies, even the largest of them, are not independent but are interdependently involved in the world as an ecological system, as a political community, and as a world market.

It is increasingly difficult to locate all social groups as subgroups of a particular society. The Catholic Church has long existed as a large entity which is not a total society but which is not contained in any other society. It has a membership, but its members are the populations of other societies. The new multinational (or transnational) corporations are becoming more like the Catholic Church: organizations which penetrate national boundaries and "belong" to no particular one.[2] Science is becoming increasingly international, linked by international organizations. Now, there is also a World Council of Churches.

That suggests something else, that the concept of society today often means in fact the social order maintained by a nation-state, which does claim boundaries to a specific territory and the population within it. But the nation-state as we know it now is an historically emergent phenomenon; it did not always exist and perhaps it may not exist again.[3] A sociological conception of society must be more encompassing.

The Definition of Society

Basic to the concept of society is that of a population, for a society is sustained by a population. Following sociologist Leon Mayhew, we define a *societal population* as consisting "in the self-perpetuating inhabitants of a territorial area."[4] For this purpose, "self-perpetuating" means mating and "inhabitant" means relatively permanent residence. The boundaries of a population that sustains a society, then, are established by the limits of the largest ter-

[1] Talcott Parsons, *The Social System* (New York: The Free Press, 1951), p. 19.

[2] *See* our discussion of world capitalism and the multinational corporation in Chapter 14.

[3] *See* Karl Polanyi, *The Great Transformation: The Political and Economic Origins of Our Time* (Boston: The Beacon Press, 1957).

[4] Leon Mayhew, *Society: Institutions and Activity* (Glenview, Ill.: Scott, Foresman and Company, 1971), p. 21.

ritorial area within which mating is common and residence is relatively permanent. But this *societal population* is not itself the society; it sustains a society, which may then be defined as *"all of the systems of action sustained by a given societal population."*[5]

Societies Large and Small

Such a definition of society does not signify any given size; societies can be large or small. In the modern world the trend for some time has been to large national societies politically organized and controlled by a nation-state, which monopolizes power and authority over a given territory. American society is such a politically organized society. But prior to the growth of the nation, societies were smaller entities in which a population and its territory were not organized as a nation. A tribe, for example, with a population of a few hundred or a few thousand at best, is such a society.

In Africa, former European colonies have become independent nations. Their political boundaries were originally shaped by the way in which colonizers seized territory, not by the way in which the indigenous population defined *its* territory. Even now they often do not constitute any definition of territory identified culturally and historically with tribal societies. National territory often includes a number of tribes; sometimes it cuts across and splits traditional tribal territories. In Nigeria, for example, different ethnic (tribal) groups dominate different federal regions. In the North, the Hausa-Fulani are powerful in a largely Muslim area; the Yoruba are the predominant group in the western region,

and the Ibo people are a majority in the eastern region.

While these new nations exist as political units, the concept of nationhood has only begun to find cultural roots in the politically organized population; tribal loyalties and identities are still alive and often serve as a basis for intense struggles for power within the political structure. In short, new national societies are still taking shape, still emerging out of old tribal societies. The tribe as society is slowly, and sometimes very grudgingly, giving way to a national society that encompasses a much larger population. Inevitably, a great deal of social conflict accompanies such a social process.

THE DEVELOPMENT OF SOCIETY

As we know them now, human societies are typically large structures controlled by nation-states as has been said. Human society has developed in form and structure thousands upon thousands of years. It is not our task to record that long history here, but it is useful to have some conceptions of what that process was.

To understand how human societies have evolved over time, it is necessary to put emphasis on two basic factors: *technology* and *levels of social integration*. In the absence of any technology human society is only a small, wandering *band* of people who gather and hunt in order to live. Change comes with the development of technology.[6]

Improvements in technology give man a

[5] Mayhew, *op. cit.,* p. 21.

[6] *See* Leslie White, *The Science of Culture* (New York: Grove Press, Inc., 1958); William Ogburn, *Social Change* (New York: The Viking Press, Inc., 1922); and Fred Cottrell, *Energy and Society* (New York: McGraw-Hill, Inc., 1955).

Figure 6.1 A Hausa villager with his daughter, one of three major groups of tribesmen from Nigeria. *(Wide World Photos.)*

greater capacity to harness energy, making possible increased production and a greater control over the environment. This is followed by *ecological* expansion, a process of absorbing once unrelated populations extending over wider territory into a single society.[7] By the migration of population, by conquest, subjugation, and political consolidation, and by economic penetration and control over local markets small independent societies become incorporated into larger ones.

Integration

Such expansion creates problems in the *integration* of the enlarged population, requiring greater specialization of roles and

new associations and institutions. Political and military processes for control and administration emerge, as do traders and merchants to exchange goods among distant producers. Administrative centers in towns or cities become focal points for ruling elites and new, dominant social groups. By *differentiation* and *centralization,* then, a new and more complex form of society comes into being.

The integration of society that accompanies ecological expansion is both normative and functional.

Functional Integration

Human cooperation is difficult enough when it involves only a small set of individual actors organized in a *division of labor*. When it involves social groups as well, coordinating interlinked activities so as to avoid both chaos and conflict puts

---

[7] For a discussion of the ecology of expansion, *see* Amos Hawley, *Human Ecology* (The Ronald Press Company, 1950), Chs. 18–20.

additional demand on human cooperation. Now some constraints and controls appear, some necessary accommodation; there must be a *functional integration* so that the total pattern of human activity meshes into an interdependent process. From the farmer who grows wheat to a loaf of bread on the dining table is not only work and labor divided, it is also labor coordinated, or else the wheat has no market, the baker gets no flour, the customer gets no bread.

In modern society particularly a great deal of specialization occurs—by occupational and other roles, as well as by organizations—such as factories, farms, armies, churches, and schools—carrying out varied activities. None of these can function by themselves; each depends on the activities of others. This interdependency requires that they be connected by transportation, communication, and administrative processes. Goods must be moved and information must be exchanged. All these varied activities must be integrated by scheduling and coordination. Unless this is done, the specialized activities will not fit into an overall integrated pattern.

A great urban metropolis, for example, depends on the rural sector for food and fiber, and there must be a marketing process to connect farmers with urban consumers. The farmer, in turn, depends on the manufacturing sectors for his farm machinery, and on business firms for seeds, pesticides, and the like; on the local bank or cooperative for a loan; and perhaps on the county agent for the latest in scientific knowledge developed at the land-grant state university.

Communities may be specialized too. A small town may be a trading center for a farming area and an administrative center for county government; a larger city may be a center for certain kinds of manufacturing, as Pittsburgh is for steel produc-

tion. A very large city, like New York City, may be a financial, commercial, and communication center for the entire nation. These centers integrate activity over a wide area, local or national.

Normative Integration

But integration is never simply functional; it requires agreement about who has what rights, what obligations, where there is authority to decide issues at stake, who is entitled to what shares of the material resources, who has access to what opportunities.[8] Integration is *normative* as well as functional.

Normative integration implies a *political* process by which legitimate rule-making and rule-enforcing occurs, so that coordination and control can be legitimized. But it is much more than that; it is sharing through symbols a common set of values and myths. Through such sharing a population becomes a *people*. Common life styles and honored customs; rituals of birth, death, and marriage shared weld a people together and create social *solidarity*. Actions and symbols that enhance solidarity promote stability in a society, constrain actors to stay within accepted limits, leash the potential for disruption and discord. Thus, *social institutions* appear to mark the greater solidarity and integration of a society.

The Institutions of Society

There are two different ways to speak of institutions. Probably the more frequent one begins with the idea of an *institutional norm* and defines an institution as a complex of such norms. Institutional norms are

[8] The legitimate access of blacks and women, for example, to job opportunities once held exclusively by white males is an example of a challenge to and change in the integrating norms of American society.

supported by strong group consensus, and sanctions for violation are imposed by enforcing agencies, for they are also *obligatory*. They are, indeed, what Sumner meant by the mores (*see* Chapter 4, pp. 64-5). A second conception of institution stresses the social acts which the norms govern, thus suggesting *institutional roles and relations.*

These two ways to define institutions are not incompatible. One calls institution the norms that govern action; the other calls institution the action itself; an institution is clearly composed of norms and roles. But we still need to know something else: why some activities are institutionally normative and some are not.

Some activities are more important than others for the maintenance of society; getting married is more important than going to a party, and raising a child is more important than playing bridge. These are probably more important for most individuals, too. It is important that these activities are carried out, but it is also important *how* they are carried out. Out of its historic experiences, including conflict and struggle among contending groups, each society develops an institutional pattern which for that society becomes sanctioned and supported. This gives us a definition of institution as *a normative order defining and governing patterns of social action deemed morally and socially crucial for the existence of society.*

The institutions of society are:

1. *Family* Every society develops a social arrangement to legitimize mating and the care and socializing of the young.
2. *Education* The young must also be inducted into the culture and trained in necessary values and skills. In preindustrial societies this is accomplished largely within the kinship system, but in modern societies a separate education system develops.
3. *Economy* Every society organizes its population to work, to produce, and distribute material goods in some manner deemed legitimate that assigns rights and obligations to people as participants, such as property rights. Again, in technologically simple societies economic activity may be embedded in kinship groups.
4. *Polity* Every society develops a system of power and authority, which insures social control within a system of rules, protects and guarantees established interests, makes decisions, and mediates among conflicting groups.
5. *Religion* Every people develop a sense of sacredness about its life ways, which then is a powerful integrating force when it provides support for social action in society. In modern societies competing religious groups weaken this integrative function. More secular ideologies, however, often serve to legitimize social practices in modern society.

These are basic to all societies. But the greater specialization of modern societies also elaborates an integrative pattern for *law, medicine,* and *science*—all of which are of sufficient importance to such societies to warrant calling them institutions.

Because social institutions are actions supported by strong normative sanctions, they are the most stable elements of a society, most resistant to change. Yet they are sometimes slowly altered over long periods of time, accompanying other changes in society, as for three centuries the Industrial Revolution slowly but radically altered the basic institutions of Western societies. Sometimes change comes swiftly and violently as in a political revolution.

Society: Institutions and Coercion

Institutions designate stable patterns of relations among roles and groups, as well as integrating processes that constrain action and pressure against change from established ways. On the other side, adaptive processes pressure for innovation and change, for new actions, and even normative violation in order to move in new directions and respond to new opportunities and new issues.

Human societies as we know them from historical record are the end points of long development within which conflict and struggle have been decisive. A society is shaped in struggles through which social groups have imposed their culture on others. If the integration of society signifies institutionalized consensus on values and norms, it also signifies power and coercion. There are in any society shared values but also interests in conflict. There is consensus; there is domination. Societies "hang together" as working systems, but this integration is as much a matter of force and constraint as it is of values and moral consensus.[9]

Types of Societies

Scholars seeking to understand how technology and social integration relate often group together societies that represent roughly equivalent levels. Just how to do this is a matter of considerable debate among specialists, who offer us various versions of societal types. Major developments in technology are usually the basis for characterizing these societal types. From nomadic to settled hunting and food-gathering societies, for example, is a transition made possible because such technological advances as the development of the bow-and-arrow considerably increased con-

trol over the food supply. In such a process the *tribe* replaced the *band* as the form of social integration. A tribe is unified by common language and shared customs, but has no overarching government or centralized political organization. Instead, local kinship groups are the major political units. A later development is a *chiefdom*, where political offices unite kinship groups and thus institute a centralized political authority.

Development in domestication of animals and cultivation of crops brought about larger, settled populations and eventually agriculturally-based states. By virtue of the Industrial Revolution, agricultural states in Europe became industrial societies organized as nation-states.

As had always happened with each major technological development, the Industrial Revolution harnessed still more energy, vastly increased material production, and extended control over human populations. The new nation-state that succeeded the once smaller principalities of Europe was a new level of ecological expansion. Many people were aware that a radically new development in human society was underway, and (as we noted in Chapter 1) sociology emerged from that concern. With great cities replacing villages and great nation-states replacing traditional communities, a new order led many to try to contrast what was coming into being to what was passing away. There was not then the more sophisticated evolutionary theory that now exists, so that "pre-industrial" often was a category for lumping together many different forms of society.

Furthermore, understanding the transition of human society through an evolutionary pattern was not the major concern; instead, it was to understand how

[9] For an influential discussion of this idea, *see* Ralf Dahrendorf, *Class and Class Conflict in Industrial Society* (Stanford, Calif.: Stanford University Press, 1959).

Figure 6.2 The 35 people attending this reunion in the Middle West make up an unusually large family for modern times. *(UPI Photo)*

the quality of life had necessarily changed through industrialization, particularly in the transition from small-scale communities to large societies.

Folk and *urban* are the terms that the American anthropologist, Robert Redfield, developed;[10] but there have been many others, including *status* and *contract* by Henry Maine, and *mechanical* and *organic* by Émile Durkheim.[11] Ferdinand Töennies' *Gemeinschaft* and *Gesellschaft* gave wide prominence to this typology and its intended contrast, and probably remains the most classic expression of it in the litera-ture.[12] We shall say *folk* and *modern* in this book.

Folk and Modern Societies

The contrasting types of folk and modern are concepts intended to analyze as precisely as possible the essential elements that differentiate modern societies from older ones. The terms are not to be taken as exact descriptions of any particular society; rather, in each case they are a selection of elements found in a number of similar societies. These are the basic elements — and notice how they effect the social organization of the societies:

1. *Size* Folk societies are typically small; the

[10] Robert Redfield, ''The Folk Society,'' *American Journal of Sociology*, 52 (January 1947), pp. 293–308.

[11] Henry Maine, *Ancient Law*, original edition, 1861 (New York: E. P. Dutton & Co., Inc., 1960). Émile Durkheim, *The Division of Labor in Society*, George Simpson, trans., original French edition, 1893. (New York: The Macmillan Company, 1933; The Free Press, 1947).

[12] Ferdinand Töennies, *Community and Society*, Charles Loomis, trans. and ed. (East Lansing, Mich.: Michigan State University Press, 1957).

primitive or peasant village compared to the huge, sprawling metropolis is the relevant contrast. The social groups that are its constituent parts are small, too; family and kinship and the small primary groups of peers are the significant networks of social relations for the individual. Interaction is thus more frequently on a face-to-face basis, in contrast to the impersonal interactions of the large-scale organizations that dominate modern life.

2. *Kinship* Kinship is the basis of social organization in folk society. It is a cooperative group for meeting most needs and functions, including the economic. Kinship obligations are binding and family ties are close and secure. In modern society kinship declines in functional importance, as do its obligations, and other, more specialized agencies assume functions once carried out by kin groups: schools, welfare agencies, business firms, old-age homes, and the like.

3. *Division of Labor* The folk society lacks mechanization and science and consequently has little specialization in occupations or economic functions. Tasks may be divided among men, women, and children — a differentiation by sex and age — but there is only a limited number of tasks to perform, and most members know and understand these and share in the skills and competencies. Modern society, in contrast, offers an extensive and complex division of labor. There is a separate organization for almost any particular function or activity, and *within* large organizations there is extensive specialization. Furthermore, there has been so marked a specialization of occupations that the United States government lists 21,741 separate occupations.[13]

4. *Homogeneous Culture* Since there is a limited division of labor, the people in a folk society share a common body of practical knowledge, as well as common standards of conduct. Their culture is homogeneous; that is, one common to all its carriers, for it is constructed from interaction within a limited scope of shared activities. Modern society is highly differentiated into a large number of varied subgroups, and displays a more diverse, less consistent culture. Folk culture is more cohesive and integrated; there is more adherence to established custom. What one person does is what all persons do; just as what one person knows and believes, all others do also. In modern society, people engage in many different activities, resulting in diverse beliefs, skills, and knowledge.

5. *The Sacred* A sense of the sacred is pervasive throughout folk society and affects much of its activity. Long-established and uncritically accepted traditions produce a deep sense of reverence for the ways of the group. Many objects are invested with sacredness in folk society and are kept away from the ordinary and profane, often by ceremony and ritual. Among the villagers in Yucatan, for example, the field in which maize is grown is *zuhuy*. "Everything that is protected from or is not exposed to the contamination of the ordinary, the earthly, the profane, is zuhuy."[14] Maize growing in the field is *zuhuy*, guarded over by unseen gods, including the Virgin. It is even called "by the same word, *gracia*, used to denote the spiritual essence of offering made to the gods."[15] Only when prepared for eating or when sold in the market is it called by the ordinary word for maize (*ixim*).

In modern society the realm of the sacred shrinks. Modern society maximizes the instrumental and pragmatic, making a sharp distinction between ends and means. Furthermore, the rationality of science and technology encourages skepticism about practices not based on tested procedures,

---

[13] U.S. Employment Service, *Dictionary of Occupational Titles,* 3rd ed. (Washington, D.C.: Government Printing Office, 1965).

[14] Redfield, *Folk Culture of Yucatan,* p. 120.
[15] Redfield, *op. cit.,* p. 121.

and develops attitudes that welcome new ideas and new knowledge.

Limitations of the Folk-modern Comparison

Comparing folk and modern as societal types has provided some perspective on what industrialization has wrought, but this particular comparison has some very real limitations. Perhaps the most significant is that modern society is defined negatively in terms only of the loss of valued attributes of folk society, such as kinship and sacredness.

Whether intended or not, this perspective has romanticized folk society, presenting it as being secure, harmonious, integrated with nature, cooperative, with a deep reverence for life.[16] This idyllic image is rooted in the old notion of primitives as noble savages—even though here the primitives were peasants—and civilization as the loss of the dignity and serenity which presumably comes so naturally to simple, "uncivilized" people. It is an exaggerated contrast drawn to provide criticism of modern life as cold and impersonal, manipulative in its orientation to people, lacking deep roots and a sense of belonging.

But a great deal of field work tells us that real primitives and peasants are not the noble creatures they have been made to appear in so much romanticized literature. From an anthropological point of view, primitive man is neither noble nor debased, neither a savage nor nature's ideal human uncorrupted by civilization. He is simply human in his own particular way.

So, too, are peasants. Oscar Lewis, for example, restudied, seventeen years after Robert Redfield had done so, the same three villages in the Yucatan. He found them to contain discord; criminal behavior; politically generated violence; poverty; oppression; and interpersonal relations marked by fear, envy, and distrust.[17]

The romanticized image of the folk utopia, then, is often quite unlike the real communities that social scientists discover in field work. Folk society is often authoritarian, impoverished, parochial, suspicious of the stranger, and intolerant. If it offers a deeply rooted life, it binds the person to it without options or much individual choice. If it provides a sense of belonging and a clearly established identity, it may also demand uncritical adherence to established ways of life. The "other face" of folk society is a denial of the individualism, freedom, and personal choice so prized and at least partially realized in modern society.

The concept of the folk society groups food-gathering, hunting, pastoral, and agricultural peoples together, without any distinctions. It is, thus, an inclusive category for all pre-industrial societies, intended to emphasize the social characteristics lost when man made the transition to industrial-urban society. Yet Oscar Lewis and others have demonstrated that characteristics attributed to modern society—role conflict, for example, or impersonal monetary exchange processes—occur in some folk societies, and that such folk attributes as strong kinship networks still exist in modern societies.[18]

[16] It should be noted that Émile Durkheim is an important exception to this. *See* at various points his comparison of *mechanical and organic* solidarity in *Division of Labor in Society*, George Simpson, trans. (New York: The Free Press, 1947).

[17] Oscar Lewis, "Tepoztlan Restudied: A Critique of the Folk-urban Conceptualization of Social Change," *Rural Sociology*, 18 (1953), pp. 121–134.

[18] *See* essays by Lewis and Hauser in Philip M. Hauser and Leo F. Schnore, eds., *The Study of Urbanization* (New York: John Wiley & Sons, Inc., 1965).

DISCOVERING THE REAL NATIVE

Figure 6.3 A Yąnomamö male in an hallucinogenic trance. *(Napoleon A. Chagnon)*

Even well-trained anthropologists, at least prior to direct field experience, may have some romantic notions of primitive peoples. They may then undergo culture shock, the unsettling exposure to the culturally different. Witness, for example, the experience of anthropologist Napoleon A. Chagnon on first encountering the Yąnomamö, a fierce Indian tribe in tropical South America:

I looked up and gasped when I saw a dozen burly, naked filthy, hideous men staring at us down the shaft of their drawn arrows! Immense wads of green tobacco were stuck between their lower teeth and lips making them look even more hideous, and strands of dark green slime dripped or hung from their noses. We arrived at the village while the men were blowing a hallucinogenic drug up their noses. One of the side effects of the drug is a runny nose. The mucus is always saturated with the green powder and Indians usually let it run freely from their nostrils. . . . Then the stench of the decaying vegetation and filth struck me and I almost got sick . . .

So much for my discovery that primitive man is not the picture of nobility and sanitation I had conceived him to be.

Chagnon also had difficulty adjusting to the social nature of the Yąnomamö. They begged, for example, incessantly and aggressively, and combined this with threats of reprisal such as chopping a hole in his canoe, if he did not give them something. "I was bombarded by such demands, day after day, months on end, until I could not bear to see an Indian." But giving in only made matters worse, for next time the demand was bigger:

I soon learned that I had to become very much like the Yąnomamö to be able to get along with them on their terms: sly, aggressive, and intimidating.

Despite the fact of his initial harsh treatment, Chagnon was able to develop a number of warm and lasting friendships with members of the tribe. Still, his personal feeling is that "The Fierce People" do not exemplify the noble savage of either romantic literature or many textbooks on primitive culture.

From Napoleon A. Chagnon, *Yąnomamö: The Fierce People* (New York: Holt, Rinehart and Winston, Inc., 1968), pp. 4–8.

Peasants and the Agricultural Society

Long before the Industrial Revolution there were towns and cities and there were societies with large populations covering a large geographical area. Though relatively isolated peasant villages may have seemed like small folk societies, the peasant village was not in fact a separate society but was part of a much larger one. Often present in the peasant village were people who were not peasants, though they may have come from peasant stock; priests, for example, who provided an important link between the village and the larger society.

The peasant village, then, was tied into a larger society, religiously, politically, and economically. But the seat of government was in a distant city, and the lives of peasants were governed by decisions made in remote towns by distant officials. They were forced to turn over much of what they produced to support the urban population; thus, they lived in an enforced poverty, despised by urban elites.[19]

Contrary to the image of the harmonious society, such societies were often wracked by war and internal revolt. Peasant uprisings were a persistent part of the history of such societies, usually ruthlessly suppressed before they spread beyond a given locality. Yet in England a peasant revolt in 1381 did spread, and there was a German Peasants' War in 1524–1525.

Though peasants were by far the majority in agrarian societies, there was nonetheless a substantial urban population with a considerable differentiation of occupational specialties. Besides a wide array of various craftsmen, there were merchants, clergymen, and military men. At the top in power was a small ruling elite, a governing class which concentrated power in its own hands and used its power for self-aggrandizement. This created enormous disparities of wealth between the impoverished level of the peasant and the luxurious living styles of the elite class.

In these societies the city was the point of contact between the society and other societies beyond its borders. It sat astride the major transportation routes that linked the urban elite to the peasants and to the lesser provincial elites. The city made possible an urban, even urbane, mode of life which contrasted sharply with the culture of the illiterate peasantry.

MODERN SOCIETY

Contemporary society is sometimes called *industrial* society, sometimes *urban* society, and sometimes industrial-urban. These terms symbolize what is basic in the historic transition in Europe, which we have come to call the Industrial Revolution, and they signify what is basic to the form which society has taken in its most recent development. It is also then *modern* society.

Much of classical sociology from the nineteenth century to now has been an intellectual effort to discover what modern means, especially how modern society differs from premodern. The contrast of folk and modern was one such effort. It was neither a balanced view, nor did it state what was basic to making a society modern.

Modern society is the outcome of a number of master trends of the last three hundred years, which includes the following:

[19] For the significant place of the city in preindustrial societies *see* Gideon Sjoberg, *The Preindustrial City: Past and Present* (New York: The Free Press, 1960); *see also* Max Weber, *The City*, Don Martindale and Gertrude Neuwirth, trans. and eds. (New York: Collier Books, 1962).

1. *Industrial technology* The development of mechanized processes for vastly increased production of goods shifts the base of work and occupations from agriculture to industry, raises the material level of most of the population, and also vastly extends the system of markets for acquiring raw materials and disposing of manufactured goods.

2. *Urbanization* This industrialization then shifts the population from predominantly rural to predominantly urban locations. While cities are not new, only in modern society has most of the population lived in urban places.

3. *The nation-state* The ecological expansion created by industrialism has brought into being the nation-state as the politically integrative unit, extending national loyalties among more diverse human populations than had ever occurred before.

4. *Bureaucracy* The compelling need to administer rationally larger units of population, particularly people from diverse tribal and other cultural identities, brought into being the social pattern called bureaucracy, particularly in the economic and political spheres.

5. *Science* Scientific knowledge is the most valued knowledge in modern society; it is the knowledge on which modern society's powerful mastery of nature and its harnessing of energy is based, and on which technological advance is assured. It requires highly logical reasoning based on empirical observation, reducing human reliance on magical and other nonrational modes of knowledge for encountering and adjusting to the environment. Science is the basis for a modern secular mentality, a state of mind highly logical and rational in all relevant matters.

6. *Mass education* Modern society requires, minimally, the literacy of almost all its population. Beyond that, it requires mass education to train the population in industrial techniques and skills, to build commitment and loyalty to the nation-state, to be assured of highly trained scientific and technological manpower, to instill the secular mentality, and to train and socialize people to be mobile. From the modern societal perspective, a population needs to be *mobilized,* to be brought out of its smaller localized groups and involved in the larger economic and political processes of society.

No existing society today is completely modern; within it still survive traditional modes of life, which can become incorporated into modern society.[20] In Japanese factories, for example, traditional feudal relations are successfully adapted to the industrial structure.[21] Caste associations have become modernized political units in India.[22] Such adaptation is necessary, or else modernization would be too disruptive. Furthermore, such traditional elements are not mere vestiges of the past; they remain functional components of modern society.

Modernization

The more traditional, premodern societies of man's long past still abound in the world. Africa, Asia, and Latin America are great land areas with large human populations made up mostly of such societies. But now these societies are undergoing radical and often disruptive change. If they are not yet modern, they are *modernizing.*

Modernization requires radical changes in the economic and political institutions, the development of a modern bureaucracy,

[20] *See* Joseph Gusfield, "Tradition and Modernity: Misplaced Polarities in the Study of Social Change," *American Journal of Sociology,* 72 (January 1967), pp. 351–362.

[21] James C. Abegglen, *The Japanese Factory* (New York: The Free Press, 1958).

[22] *See* M. N. Srinivas, *Caste in Modern India* (Bombay: Asia Publishing House, 1962).

Figure 6.4 Small-town life, like folk society, tends to be homogeneous. Almost a whole town population turns out for games at a Fourth of July celebration. *(Louis S. Davidson, Monkmeyer)*

and a system of mass education. It requires urbanization and an urban-based labor force. When a modernizing change is underway, large, secular groups—such as political parties, labor unions, and professional associations—emerge; these in turn compete for the loyalty and commitment of youth with more traditional groups—such as tribes and villages, clans and kinship groups, and even religious groups. This breaking of ties with local groups is the mobilization process without which there could not be modernization.

As societies modernize, new systems of human recruitment and social control are created, and new modes of socialization and education come into being. Formal and deliberately created social groups—factories and schools, for example, and political parties and labor unions—replace those traditional ones by which people had been linked to one another. The new groups are

larger, for under modernization the scale of organization increases sharply. In Africa, for example, large numbers of people in the new, modernizing nations are leaving their tribal villages for new occupations and sometimes entirely new life styles in rapidly growing cities.

Modernization is also a process of the "Westernization" of the non-Western world, for modern society originated in Europe and thus became interwoven with Western culture. Early exploration first brought contact and exchange with the non-Western world; but when the industrialization of Europe was accompanied by an extension of markets abroad, modern European societies took control of the premodern societies elsewhere in the world and in many cases made them colonies. The military, commercial, political, linguistic, and educational patterns of a European nation are often still indelibly marked on a former colony that is now independent.

Society and Empire

The territorial control of other societies by more powerful ones is *imperialism*, the building of empire. Empire-building is no new phenomenon; Europe, for example, was moved more rapidly along the path of societal development by its subjugation to the Roman empire, and empires existed long before that. Modern imperialism, however, has been the acquisition of great land areas in Asia, Africa, and Latin America by European industrial nations. These areas became colonies and furnished raw material for the industry of the dominant nation; in turn, they were a market for some of its cheaply produced goods.

The independence of former colonies from colonial status, and the breakup of such empires as those of Germany, Belgium, France, and Britain is a prominent element of recent history. Many of these former colonies have now emerged as nations actively undertaking modernization. Imperialism has not, however, disappeared because of that; it has simply changed. (*see* Chapters 14 and 15) It no longer depends on territorial control. It remains a process whereby large, national societies, including the United States, undertake systematic economic exploitation and political control of other, usually smaller, underdeveloped societies.

BEYOND MODERN SOCIETY

While much of the world is struggling to become modern, some societies, such as that of the United States, have been modern long enough to be disenchanted with it and long enough also to see emerging changes that promise to move modern society into a new form. In the first instance, the critical, disenchanted view sees modern society becoming *mass society*, a development that levels out society into an undifferentiated cultural sameness; modern man is a little cog in a big machine. In the second instance, modern society has been developing beyond the patterns now known as modern into something not yet experienced, a post-modern society only barely discernible to those who would dare to look beyond modern society.

Mass Society

The basic idea of mass society is the presumed failure of modern society to provide *community*, the integrated context for human living in which people can find meaning and value in their shared existence. Industrialism and modern capitalism and the market economy, it is asserted, have burst forever the small, closely-knit folk communities of the past and have left people unattached and rootless in a large and impersonal society that cannot command a deep sense of loyalty. The bureaucratized social life of mass society presumably reduces all social relations to an impersonal, manipulative interaction in which others are treated as objects to be used instrumentally, as means to a calculated end. The result is a population easily manipulable by the organs of mass communication.

Although the modernization of society does erode the primary and communal ties of traditional societies, it does not follow from this that modern society has become the wholly negative entity called mass society. It does not follow that the erosion of some traditional forms never leads to the creation of new ones; to assume so is to deny to modern people the age-old capacity to create new groups and new social structures as a way of meeting change.

If folk society is an idealization which ignores the harsher realities of life in primitive and peasant societies, so too mass society is a one-sided view that points out the negative aspects but ignores the positive ones in modern society. Thus, Daniel Bell says:

If it is granted that mass society is compartmentalized, superficial in personal relations, anonymous, transitory, specialized, utilitarian, competitive, acquisitive, mobile, and status-hungry, the obverse side of the coin must be shown, too—the right to privacy, to free choice of friends and occupation, status on the basis of achievement rather than of ascription, a plurality of norms and standards, rather than the exclusive and monopolistic social controls of a single dominant group.[23]

Similarly, Edward Shils views mass society as integrated through the complex web of social ties which give it a vibrant if often discordant existence:

It is held together by an infinity of personal attachments, moral obligations in concrete contexts, professional and creative pride, individual ambition, primordial affinities, and a civil sense which is low in many, high in some, and moderate in most persons.[24]

To interpret modern society as mass society, then, is to use a selective frame of reference that depends for its historic referent on a conservative, idealized, and historically inaccurate image of folk society. Such an interpretation ignores the fact that the individualism it worries about is also a creation of modern society, as is opportunity and mobility. Both scientific analysis and critical intellectual inquiry require a more balanced view of modern society than the concept of mass society gives us. (At the same time, we must recognize that those who have so vigorously criticized the concept of mass society, such as Bell and Shils, have a selective frame of reference of their own, one which seem to uphold modern society against criticism that people in modern society suffer alienation and loss of community.)

The Post-modern Society

Modern society is not the last phase in the development of human society; it is only the most recent. The folk-modern contrast, which originated in classical sociology in the nineteenth century, provided a critical perspective by looking at modern society in Europe in relation to its traditional past.

But now we can view modern society from the perspective of the modernization of traditional societies in the non-Western world and also from the perspective of continued development of modern society in its most advanced forms, of which the United States is the prime example. What is significant about contemporary society is not merely the characteristics of modern, which were true fifty years ago. Changes over time point to a still further development of society beyond modern, a *post-modern* society.[25]

As yet this is but a perspective, in no sense a sociological theory. There is not yet even a settled vocabulary; "post-modern" is one term; "post-industrial" is another. As perspective, it constitutes an

---

[23] Daniel Bell, *The End of Ideology* (New York: The Free Press, 1960), p. 29.

[24] Edward Shils, "Primordial, Personal, Sacred and Civil Ties," *The British Journal of Sociology*, 8 (June 1957), p. 131.

[25] *See* Daniel Bell, *The Coming of Post-industrial Society* (New York: Basic Books, Inc., 1973); and *also* M. Donald Hancock and Gideon Sjoberg, eds., *Politics in the Post-welfare State* (New York: Columbia University Press, 1972).

effort to take stock of some few visible indicators of changes now occurring which suggest how different the world will be by the end of this century.

What the post-modern society will look like in major outline is suggested by these basic points:

1. *Beyond the nation-state* No longer can the world be defined even with partial adequacy as an array of independent, boundary-maintaining, self-enclosed states. More and more the political units are *interdependent*; supra-national political units, such as the alliance of European Common Market nations, impose processes on individual nations as terms for sharing in international cooperative structures. Thus, Britain has to accept the value-added tax to join the Common Market. The "free world," the "Communist bloc," and the "Third World" indicate political blocs and alignments of the present; some may persist, others not, but those which do not will be replaced by new ones.

   In economic affairs the powerful World Bank influences trade and development by its lending policies, and multinational corporations operate across national boundaries in a world market. There is a world economy emerging which is much more than the age-old process of trade and exchange among societies. In his economic role, each person is an actor in a world economy, not any longer merely a local or even national one. The individual's economic interests are thus affected by world developments.

2. *From production to service* Economically and technologically, the post-modern society is post-industrial; it is based on *service*, in contrast to the production of *goods* that defined industrial society.[26] An enormous shift in occupations from production to service, a growth in white-collar occupations requiring more education continues an already discernible trend. This also means rising income, rising levels of consumption, and new demands and expectations from the populations of post-modern societies. In the post-industrial society of service, the "central person is the professional, for he is equipped by his education and training to provide the kinds of skills increasingly in demand."[27]

3. *Political economy* A post-modern society will no longer continue the myth of separate economic and political sectors. The rising demands of a more educated and affluent population will enlarge the public sector. Increasing investment in health and education will be necessary; but so will many other public services. Public decision-making will thus become more important; it will increase the self-conscious participation of more people in the making of public decisions.

4. *Science, technology, and education* In a post-modern society innovation comes more from "the intellectual institutions, principally the universities and research organizations, rather than the older, industrial corporations."[28] Thus, the "knowledge industry" becomes the principal source of change and innovation, and also therefore a major source of power. Men of knowledge, an intelligentsia, are crucially important in society, and exercise a decisive influence.[29]

5. *Social change* In modern society change is viewed primarily as a linear extension of the present into a predictable future. Thus, determining rates of growth or decline up to the present, and then extending that into

---

[26] This is the thesis of Bell's *The Coming of Post-industrial Society;* for a briefer treatment, *see* his "Labor in the Post-industrial Society," *Dissent,* 19 (Winter 1972), pp. 163–189. *See also* Daniel Bell, ed., *Toward the Year 2000* (Boston: Houghton Mifflin Company, 1968).

[27] *See* Bell, "Labor in the Post-industrial Society," p. 166.

[28] Daniel Bell, "The Year 2000—The Trajectory of an Idea," *Daedalus,* 96 (Summer 1967), p. 644.

[29] John Kenneth Galbraith makes a similar point for what he calls the "educational and scientific estate." *See* his *The New Industrial State* (New York: Houghton Mifflin Company, 1967; paperback ed., New American Library, 1968), Ch. XXV.

Figure 6.5 Directors of the powerful World Bank meet in Washington, D.C. (*Monkmeyer*)

an indefinite future has been a principal way to predict what is going to happen. No longer will that suffice.

In the post-modern society change will be linear only in the short run. Instead, it will often be protean, taking off in new directions that could not be predicted on the basis of linear patterns. Furthermore, change will more frequently be deliberately planned and intended, rather than the unintended, unanticipated, and often uncontrolled consequence of other actions. Making the future in some rational manner, but building in options and diversity, suggests a potentiality for developing a society consistent with human intentions and desires, though not without risks and problems.[30]

6. *Culture* Critics of modern society predict a mass culture to accompany mass society, a culture which is shallow and exploits mass

fears and anxieties. But post-modern culture is likely to be quite different. Subcultural variation will not disappear but proliferate, particularly in the effort to create new life styles that provide meaning and value for individuals. There will be a neo-traditionalism which uses past life styles in the present in the way that antique-users adapt old objects into their current life styles. The pursuit of identity will result in the self-conscious creation of new life styles, leading to still newer forms of counter-culture not now imagined. Much of this will be a selective adapting and borrowing from the historic past, particularly by youth.

Post-modern society is not a utopia. The changes which bring it about will create new problems and new sources of tension and conflict. The struggle for power, for example, will take new forms; control over resources has always meant power, and when knowledge becomes a resource, new bases for power, such as professionalism, are created. Thus, Bell anticipates that

[30] There is already a considerable literature on making the future. For a representative selection of ideas and conceptions *see* Alvin Toffler, *The Futurists* (New York: Random House, Inc., 1972).

professionalism will clash with popular demand for more rights and greater participation; "the clash between the professional and the populace, in the organization and in the community, is the hallmark of conflict in the post-industrial society."[31]

There are other sources of conflict, too. For minorities, for the poor, and for sections of the working class, finding a worthy place in an increasingly professionalized society, outside of welfare, may prove difficult. Unneeded people are not assured of more than bare subsistence living. Clashes among life styles, particularly with newer countercultural ones, are as likely as the present conflict between "straights" and "hippies."

In the world as a whole post-modern societies will be in conflict with modernizing societies. Modernizing nations will not try slavishly to imitate the United States but to leap over such models into even newer ones based in part on the most advanced technology, in part on what of their traditional cultures can be incorporated into their new structures.

There will be cultural and intellectual conflict over the model of *modernity*; there will be political and economic conflict over sharing the world's resources and opportunities.

With 6 percent of the world's population, the United States consumes about 52 percent of the world's resources. Struggles between the post-modern rich and the modernizing poor are likely to be intense and difficult. And not least, within post-modern societies the struggle for control and use of a highly technologized industry may very well create a new form of capitalism, or something else.

[31] Bell, "Labor in the Post-industrial Society," p. 167.

SUMMARY

A *society* is all the systems of action sustained by a given societal population, which, in turn, is the self-perpetuating inhabitants of a territorial area.

The *institutions* of society are a normative order defining and governing patterns of action deemed morally and socially crucial for the existence of society. These are the family, the economy, the polity, education, and religion.

Societies develop when new technology produces ecological expansion, requiring new levels of integration, both functional and normative. This leads to further differentiation of groups and associations and centralization of ruling elites.

The *folk* society is an idealized type based on traditional forms preceding industrialization of society, characterized by small size, little division of labor, kinship, a homogeneous culture, and a sense of sacredness pervading much of social life. But the image of folk society romanticizes peasant life and puts too many different preindustrial peoples in a single category.

Modern society is defined in terms of advanced industrial technology, urbanization of the population, control by a nation-state, rational bureaucratic administration, and a central place for science and mass education.

Mass society is a negative perspective on modern society, emphasizing its individualism carried to the point of rootlessness, with a loss of meaning and values. Like folk society, it is a one-sided perspective.

Post-modern society is the emerging society of the future. It will develop beyond the nation-state, will shift from production to service, will integrate political and economic processes, and will give a central place to science, technology, and education. Its social change will be more protean than linear, and its culture will be highly varied, with a self-conscious creation of new life styles.

Suggested Readings

Daniel Bell, *The Coming of Post-industrial Society: A Venture in Social Forecasting* (New York: Basic Books, Inc., 1973). The culmination of Bell's efforts of many years to see the coming shape of society.

James S. Coleman, Amitai Etzioni, and John Porter, *Macrosociology: Research and Theory* (Boston: Allyn and Bacon, Inc., 1970). Three eminent sociologists discuss how to do research at the macrosociological level of society and its major units.

Amitai Etzioni, *The Active Society* (New York: The Free Press, 1968). A sociologically imaginative effort to grasp the idea of post-modern as a societal type that contrasts favorably with both the contemporary totalitarian and the Democratic-Capitalist.

John Kenneth Galbraith, *The New Industrial State* (New York: Houghton Mifflin Company, 1968; paperback edition, New American Library, 1968). A famous economist-critic analyzes how economic and technological change has already reshaped our society.

Bertram Gross, ed., *A Great Society?* (New York: Basic Books, Inc., 1968). A number of capable scholars examine the demands and needs of becoming post-modern.

Claude Lévi-Strauss, *The Savage Mind* (Chicago: University of Chicago Press, 1966). A remarkable effort to compare how modern and primitive thought differs, suggesting caution in making folk-modern comparisons.

Oscar Lewis, *Tepoztlan: Village in Mexico* (Holt, Rinehart and Winston, Inc., 1960). A version of folk society that seriously challenges the idyllic version offered by Redfield.

Leon Mayhew, *Society: Institutions and Activity* (Glenview, Ill.: Scott, Foresman and Company, 1971). A brief but highly instructive effort to update sociology's central but often neglected concept, society.

Philip Olson, ed., *America as a Mass Society* (New York: The Free Press, 1963). A still useful set of readings delineating the idea that America is a mass society.

Talcott Parsons, *Societies: Comparative and Evolutionary Perspectives* (Englewood Cliffs, N.J.: Prentice-Hall, Inc., 1966). A foremost theorist examines society from a renewed evolutionary perspective.

Karl Polanyi, *The Great Transformation: The Political and Economic Origins of Our Time* (Holt, Rinehart and Winston, Inc., 1944; paperback, Boston: The Beacon Press, 1957). A classic analysis of the origins of modern society in Europe.

Robert Redfield, *The Folk Culture of Yucatan* (Chicago: University of Chicago Press, 1941). The most influential study of folk society in recent social science.

Ferdinand Töennies, *Community and Society*, Charles Loomis, trans. and ed. (East Lansing, Mich.: Michigan State University Press, 1957). The great classic of folk society, *gemeinshaft* and *gesellschaft*.

Alvin Toffler, ed., *The Futurists* (New York: Random House, Inc., 1972). A series of fascinating essays about the future beyond modern society.

Colin M. Turnbull, *The Mountain People* (New York: Simon and Schuster, 1972). The author describes the negative effects on tribal social structure brought about by a forced change from a wandering life style to a fixed one.

These [primary] groups, then, are springs of life,
not only for the individual but for social institutions.
—*Charles Horton Cooley*

Chapter 7

Small Groups

A society is a wondrously interwoven pattern of social groups of all sizes, organized for all possible human purposes, through which individuals carry on all the activities by which a social life is sustained. The study of society, therefore, is the study of social groups, from small primary groups to large organizations.

It is common to define a group as two or more persons in interaction, but this includes too much. An aggregate of people waiting to cross the street, barely aware of one another, is not, for sociological purposes, a group. Nor is a group a social category, like all taxpayers, parents, or baseball fans. All taxpayers do not interact with one another, nor do all parents. Some parents, however, might form a PTA, and some taxpayers might organize a group to do something about taxes. Baseball fans are an unorganized collectivity of people who share an interest; they, too, can be the basis for a group, as a fan club, and they can become a public.

What this suggests, then, is that the fleeting and ephemeral interaction of people passing each other in public places is not sufficient to be a group, but the absence of interaction, as among a category of people, also means there is not a group. People in groups interact with some frequency, and their interaction is patterned to carry on activities. The kinds of useful activities individuals can engage in by and for themselves is always severely limited.

A group can be defined, then, as *a plurality of persons sharing in a common pattern of social interaction.*

Belonging to a Group

People in social groups are conscious of belonging together in common membership. In formally organized groups who belongs is indicated by membership rosters and appropriate insignia (cards, badges, pins, even uniforms or dress). Even in small, informal groups, conferring recognition on one person as belonging and another as not may be done by forms of address and by obvious ways of inclusion and exclusion in the group. No human group has any difficulty in letting an individual know whether he is "one of the group."

Integration and Unity

Social groups, from the smallest to the largest, persist over time only when members feel bound to the group and have reasons to belong. There is nothing to guarantee a group will go on forever. When an ethnic group worries that the marriage of its youth to outsiders will weaken the group, when a church worries that it is not reaching youth and it is not recruiting enough young people into the ranks of the clergy, when a civil rights group is warned that talk of "black power" will scare off white members—these are instances in which group leaders are conscious that the persistence of the group is not assured.

Yet, there are situations in life in which

the demise of social groups is accepted as natural and inevitable, as, for example, the high-school cliques that break up after graduation, and the peer groups in the army that break up with demobilization. Every family group breaks up eventually; the maturity of children and the death of parents are inevitable. In some cases, divorce does it more quickly.

Groups persist, then, if they have activities to carry on which people value and need. When that is so, sharing membership in a group and sharing in its activities can develop a strong sense of group unity. A "consciousness of kind" may arise among those who share valued experiences within a group.[1]

But the unity of a group is not an automatic consequence of there being a group; it is present to a lesser or to a greater degree. Since the members of one group belong to other groups, no one group may claim a total loyalty or a full commitment from an individual. Also, the heterogeneity of large groups reduces the group's consciousness of kind and makes a common sense of unity and purpose harder to achieve. Large groups often suffer a weak sense of belonging among their members if they place only a utilitarian value on membership in the group. They may belong only as long as it serves a personal purpose, as when highly mobile and ambitious professionals accept employment for a time in a particular university or corporation to advance their personal careers.

The study of large groups, such as organizations, then, offers some problems different from the study of small groups. Yet small groups and large groups are in

---

[1] A term first coined by Franklin Giddings in his *Principles of Sociology* (New York: The Macmillan Company, 1896).

both cases essential to modern society. In this chapter we will examine small groups, before we turn to the larger ones.

THE PRIMARY GROUP

As Charles Horton Cooley first defined it, the primary group is a small, intimate group within which is found the kind of social relationship that permits socialization to occur. The family and the peer group of children are the obvious examples. The concept of primary group, then, gets at two things: a type of social relationship and the type of group within which this relationship is sustained.

The Primary Relation

The primary relation between human beings is probably best exemplified as that idealized one between mother and child, between lovers, between the closest of friends. It is a relationship of love, of close affectional attachment, of emotional involvement, and it is never viewed instrumentally, as something useful and a means to some other end; rather, it is valued as an end in itself.

It is also a relationship that is *personal*, not impersonal; it is a relationship between particular persons, and each person is interested in the other *as a person*, not as an agent of or role-player in social organization. Such a relationship involves the whole person in all his human concreteness, not merely a segmented aspect of the self with whom another has to interact in order to carry out certain necessary functions.

One consequence of this is that the affectional primary relation is *diffuse*—it is not explicitly limited to specific obligations that each has for the other. What a parent

or friend is obligated to do for one is not specified beforehand. In this sense it differs from the *contractual* relationship that governs, say, the well-understood (even legally specified) obligations of employer and employee to one another.

What is the kind of group that makes possible and best sustains the primary relation? There are three basic conditions for a group to be primary: small size, face-to-face interaction, and reasonably long duration.

Size

A primary group must be small enough for each person to be a unique personality to the other. As a group increases in size, interaction ceases to be between total persons but is between agents and role-players, thus involving only limited aspects of the self. Being small, then, is a necessary element of a primary group, but it alone is not sufficient to produce the primary relationship. There are many small groups that are not primary, such as committees in large organizations.

Face-to-Face Interaction

It is only very rarely that primary relations do not depend on the close physical proximity of face-to-face interaction. Yet such physical proximity does not guarantee the relationship will be primary. Face-to-face interaction occurs every day when people ride a bus or shop in a store, yet these interactions are passing and ephemeral and will have little meaning for either party. Neither is likely to respond to the other as a unique person. Like size, then, face-to-face interaction is a necessary element of a primary group but is not in itself sufficient.

Duration

The development of a primary relationship cannot occur when interaction is infrequent and sporadic; it must be frequent and durable. People need to interact frequently over an extended period of time. The longer people interact face-to-face, the more intimately do they become related to one another; the better they know one another as whole persons, the more they become attached and emotionally involved with one another.

Specific Primary Groups

These three basic conditions for the primary group are most frequently met in the family and in friendship groups. They may also be met in the stable neighborhood and the small community, though in modern society they frequently are not.

Primary groups at best but imperfectly embody the pure primary relationship, which has no intent or goal other than the relationship itself. Therefore, they are best realized in spontaneous, freely chosen, and informally organized groups. But the family is an institutionalized group as well as a primary group, embodying societally sanctioned authority and legal responsibility for the care of children. Furthermore, not all families successfully maintain primary relations among their members; thus, not all families are primary groups.

Primary groups in the work situation cannot freely choose their members; rather, they must accept whoever is assigned to work at a given place or on a particular job. These primary groups, then, do not escape the intrusion of the demands and restraints of society into the primary relationship.

Peer Groups

Another kind of primary group found in adolescent cliques and friendship groups is often called a peer group. Unlike the family, the peer group is not institutionalized by society. Instead, it emerges spontaneously from among social equals, who are thus likely to share the same life conditions. Unlike the family also the peer group does not have differences of status and authority, but it does have leaders. "Peer" means equal in status. Adolescents form peer groups, for they are equal in an age-defined status; workers in a factory form a peer group, for they are equal in a work-defined status.

Peer groups can be examined from a number of different perspectives, but in the study of modern society the interest is in their significance for society. Cooley and George Herbert Mead stated one significance when they pointed out the importance of peer groups among children for socialization. The peer group, we saw earlier, is also a powerful agent of social control.

But in modern society peer groups develop most frequently within large organizations: among adolescents in school, soldiers in the army, workers in a factory, and the like. Studies of peer groups within such organizations have focused on two related problems: (1.) that of social control and group power, and (2.) integration.[2]

Social Control and Group Power

The reality of primary group influence in the work situation was first discovered in

[2] See Peter M. Blau and Marshall W. Meyer, *Bureaucracy in Modern Society,* 2nd ed. (New York: Random House, Inc., 1971).

Figure 7.1 A relationship of close affection is an end in itself, not something useful for another purpose. *(Wide World Photos.)*

a pioneering study by Elton Mayo and his associates at the Hawthorne plant of Western Electric.[3] These studies explored every possible influence on worker productivity and job satisfaction. It was only toward the end of years of careful research that Mayo, a psychologist, discovered that small networks of interpersonal relations among workers who interacted in face-to-face situations had a great deal to do with their work behavior. Prior to that he had been defining his problem as one of *individual* behavior, and thus had been looking for various physical and psychological influences on the individual. The discovery of a hitherto unrecognized peer group was a revealing finding.

Social Control

One of the more influential of the Hawthorne studies was that of the Bank Wiring Room, where the ability of the peer group to control individual work behavior was impressively evident.[4] Fourteen workers were engaged in an interrelated production task—they were a functionally integrated group—for which management had specified how work was assigned, how it was to be done, and at what rate. But the work group developed a spontaneous pattern of interaction, including its own norms to govern work.

[3] A detailed accounting of the study is by Fritz Roethlisberger and William J. Dickson, *Management and the Worker* (Cambridge, Mass.: Harvard University Press, 1947). For a critique of Roethlisberger and Dickson's sociological analysis of small groups, *see* Sheman Krupp, *Pattern in Organizational Analysis* (Philadelphia: Chilton Company, 1961).

[4] Roethlisberger and Dickson, *op. cit.,* Part IV.

Workers helped one another and exchanged work assignments, even though this was forbidden. They altered the pattern of functional integration first imposed by management.

Most important of all, the peer group developed a normative integration, achieving a consensus about output of work; and each worker was governed by the group's norms, not management's. These norms allowed less output than management wanted; from management's point of view, therefore, the peer group was responsible for restricting output.

Furthermore, the group was very effective in handling the individual who was tempted to stray from the norms of the group and increase his output. In this study, as in many other factory studies, the recalcitrant worker meets the opposition of the group to his "rate-busting" performance. The sanctions imposed on him can take the form of ridicule, harassment, ostracism, and even physical violence.

A large number of factory studies have since documented the principle that workers will, on their own group initiative, restrict output by setting production norms of their own and will also quite effectively control one another.[5] Nor can such group restrictions be easily seduced by managerial efforts to provide individual inducements and rewards for maximizing individual effort. Such inducements as piecework, bonus payments, and the like have encountered serious resistance among workers, who will not allow production standards to exceed what they regard as a "fair day's work," if they can help it.

Group Power

These factory studies have focused primarily on the demonstrated power of the peer group to impose group norms on its members in the face of and contrary to the official norms and regulations of the factory. But to see it only as restriction of output is to invoke a managerial not a sociological perspective. Equal emphasis must be given to the fact that these work groups emerge naturally and spontaneously among those who share the same life situation and environmental conditions—in this case, workers in a factory—and that work restriction is a collective and cooperative effort to achieve a level of control over the circumstances of the job that cannot be done by the individual alone.

When workers impose their own group standards they are seeking some small expression of group power in behalf of their interests, as they conceive them. Their peer group, then, is an emergent adaptation to the circumstances of being fully controlled and otherwise powerless in the job situation. Without the intervening group, the individual stands alone within the large organization; isolated individuals are unable to resist organizational demands.

Integration

An extended series of studies carried out on enlisted men during World War II provided evidence that the peer group does not necessarily operate *against* the large organization but may function to support it.[6] The emergence of a set of pri-

[5] For a review of many such studies *see* Morris S. Viteles, *Motivation and Morale in Industry* (New York: W. W. Norton & Company, Inc., 1953).

[6] Samuel A. Stouffer and others, *The American Soldier: Combat and Its Aftermath*, Studies in Social Psychology in World War II (Princeton, N.J.: Princeton University Press, 1949), vol. II. *See also* Edward A. Shils,

Figure 7.2 Employees exercise peer-group control over the individual factory worker. *(Monkmeyer.)*

mary relations among soldierly peers served, however unintentionally, to tie the individual soldier into the large military structure and to sustain him in the face of difficult demands for soldierly performance. For civilians conscripted into the army, the existence of satisfactory primary relations was basic to their being able to act effectively in combat situations and to withstand the strains and stresses, the fatigue and danger of combat.

In combat situations both American and German soldiers were influenced less by

propaganda about the aims of the war, the meaning of the conflict, and the concept of great causes at stake, than they were by a sense of loyalty and obligation to a few others with whom they shared hardship and danger. Thus, the primary relationship of comradeship was more important for individual morale than all the efforts to convince conscripted soldiers about the national or even international importance of what they were doing.

The German Army during World War II fought effectively and seemed to maintain morale until the very end, despite some sustained efforts at psychological warfare intended to weaken their resolve to fight on, particularly when there were serious reverses and the war was going against them. Propaganda, apparently, had little effect on the German soldier; like his American counterpart he was bound into primary ties of enduring comradeship, and

"Primary Groups in the American Army," in Robert K. Merton and Paul F. Lazarsfeld, eds., *Continuities in Social Research: Studies in the Scope and Method of "The American Soldier"* (New York: The Free Press, 1950), pp. 16–39. A different interpretation, based on direct observation of combat soldiers in Vietnam, by sociologist Charles C. Moskos, Jr., stresses a less dominant function for primary groups. *See* his "Why Men Fight," *Transaction*, 7 (November 1969), pp. 13–23.

his loyalty held him to the task of combat and sustained his morale.[7]

These primary ties enabled the German Army to resist disintegration and remain relatively cohesive until the last days of combat. If the rate of desertion is taken as an indicator of social disintegration, then the German Army resisted disintegration until the very last, for it had few deserters until then. Among those who did desert, a failure to assimilate into a primary group was the most important factor in their desertion, more so than any political dissent. In fact, anti-Nazi political dissenters did not desert, and when captured, justified this by reference to their sense of comradely solidarity.

In another study Edward Shils found that Soviet soldiers were much the same as the Germans; their ability to endure combat "drew relatively little sustenance from any attachment to the central political and ideological symbols of the society in which they lived."[8] Instead, support came from other sources, of which one was "the morale of the small unit, i.e., the mutual support given by members of the group to each other . . ."[9]

These studies of men in combat are striking examples of the importance of the primary group for sustaining the individual and giving him emotional support and security.

But the lesson holds true in all large organizations and in circumstances less personally threatening than those of com-bat. When first becoming part of a large organization, the individual often feels alone and insecure—a stranger, uncertain about everything. College freshmen and newly drafted soldiers, for example, can feel homesick even when surrounded by many others. Being lonely is a *social* and *psychic,* not a physical state of affairs.

But if a peer group takes him in and "shows him the ropes," the entrant learns his way around and soon feels more "at home," and his transition to new roles in a new group is eased. For the college freshman or the new soldier the feeling of homesickness abates as new primary relations integrate him into the organization.

But if such primary relations do not develop, if the individual, by choice or not, is a "loner," then his performance is likely to be lessened and his personal well-being hampered. Such persons often suffer a sense of personal disorientation that may very well produce neuroses and emotional disturbances. It may also lead to his withdrawal from the organization, to quitting college, or to going AWOL in the army. At worst, it can lead to violent conduct against others or against self—suicide.

This is what Durkheim told us about integration in his great study, *Suicide.* When people are integrated into a group, it sustains them against life's vicissitudes. When not, they suffer in some way. What additional point needs to be made here is that in modern society—where most groups are large, impersonal, and poorly integrated in any normative sense—peer and other primary groups perform much of this essential integrating and sustaining function.

Peer Groups and Subcultures

When small peer groups develop among enlisted men in the army, among workers

---

[7] Edward A. Shils and Morris Janowitz, "Cohesion and Disintegration of the Wehrmacht in World War II," *Public Opinion Quarterly,* 12 (1948), pp. 280–315.

[8] Edward Shils, "Primordial, Personal, Sacred, and Civil Ties," *The British Journal of Sociology,* 8 (June 1957), p. 141.

[9] Shils, *op. cit.,* p. 141.

Figure 7.3 German soldiers during World War II were bound together by the primacy ties of comradeship. *(UPI Photo.)*

in a factory, among blacks in the urban ghetto, or among students in the university (to take a few examples from many possibilities), the larger aggregate of peers becomes an extended network among whom there is a sense of sympathy for shared status and a "grapevine," a communication network that allows for a wider sharing of norms. Thus, peer groups are an important unit in the emergence of subcultures that challenge the power and official norms of the more institutionalized groups and the great impersonal organizations of modern society. At the same time subcultures provide the cultural context from which peer groups can develop.

The sense of "we" that so closely identifies one with another, and which Cooley regarded as an indicator of the primary group, flows out from the smaller and more intimate peer group to the larger network of peer relations. If the relationships of this larger network are not so intimate and are not always face-to-face, they are developed, nevertheless, in a perspective of sympathy and identification ("he's one of us") that enables individuals to view them as extensions of their primary relations, as interactions with others who share the same fate and life circumstances. Cooley thought that neighborhoods and communities were just such larger and somewhat more extended "we-groups," more primary than secondary, even though all in it cannot engage in face-to-face interaction.

Neighborhoods and communities in modern society are not often extended we-groups. But they can be in some instances, and the stable ethnic neighborhood is a good example. One such was the "urban villagers" that Herbert Gans described: an Italian neighborhood of second-generation Italian working-class people.[10] Within this physical area a subculture that is both working class and ethnic provides a context for interaction from which peer groups emerge. Each peer group, however, is formed from the same kind of people who share the same values. Social class and ethnicity as major sources of identity-formation, then, are often also the subcultural base for peer groups.

Where other people do not find sufficient cultural homogeneity in the neighborhood or community, they may find it in shared status in large organizations—soldiers, students, workers, and the like. In the same way the sense of having "brothers" and "sisters" develops among members of social movements.

Peer Groups and Adolescents

Understanding the significance of the peer group for the emergence of subcultures is necessary for understanding the relation of the peer group to the adolescent in modern society. Adolescence is an uncertain and insecure status found only in modern society, where preparing for adulthood is lengthened, partly by the demand for longer years of education, partly because an advanced technology does not need the young coming into the labor force at an early age.

The adolescent is neither a child nor an adult. In this extended and uneasy transition to adulthood, primary relations among peers provide a sympathetic context for ready acceptance by others and for a sympathetic sharing of the problems of grow-

ing up. Interaction among peers produces groups that become highly valued by the individual. Such peer groups, as we saw earlier, are agents for a continuing socialization, modifying and sometimes contradicting socialization by the family.

Through peer groups, then, the adolescent discovers a way to come to grips with a larger society, to resist and challenge it, even rebel against it, which would not be possible for the individual alone. The sustaining support of peers and the emotional ties of primary groups are necessary elements in generating an adolescent subculture.[11]

Peer Groups and Subcultures of Resistance

There is comparability between adolescent peer groups in school and peer groups of workers in the factory: Each is evidence of a subculture of resistance to the official authority and work standards of the organization in which they are lowest in status and power. In each case the peer group is the core element in generating a perspective and orientation that expresses the meaning of being in subordinate status in a situation over which the individual formally has little control.

The network of group relations which emerge around primary group interests and the control over individual conduct then permits these subordinate persons to take back some control over their own life circumstances. Workers impose their own production norms and restrict output

---

[10] Herbert Gans, *The Urban Villagers: Group and Class in the Life of Italian-Americans* (New York: The Free Press, 1962).

[11] For a study of the importance of cliques in high school in governing action and affecting values and goals *see* James S. Coleman, *The Adolescent Society* (New York: The Free Press, 1961).

Figure 7.4 Adolescent peer groups develop and live by values of their own creation. *(Paul Conklin, Monkmeyer.)*

to less than management wants, as we have seen. Adolescents, in turn, find means for having adult-forbidden experiences (sex, alcohol, and smoking, for example), for resisting the work and study values that are official for the school, and for developing a set of their own values that center around personality development and identity-seeking, often in the process creating styles and fads that repel and bewilder adults.

It should not be thought, however, that because the peer group can be an instrument of subcultural resistance to power, that all peer groups are created only under such conditions of subordination and resistance. Peer groups also exist among those who are powerful and dominant. And peer groups would exist among students and workers even if a culture of resistance did not develop.

THE STUDY OF SMALL GROUPS

Studies of peer groups are almost always about groups in their natural habitat, but there is also the study of small groups under controlled laboratory conditions. In varied experimental ways social scientists have observed social action as an outcome of the face-to-face interaction of a small number of persons. Their primary interest is in the *forms* rather than the *content* of interaction; that is, in *how* the group interacts, not in *what* it interacts about. Though such study of small groups is recent—practically all research comes after 1950 —George Simmel first suggested its value more than fifty years ago.

Small Groups in the Laboratory

Research on small groups under carefully controlled laboratory conditions is usually the study of *task* groups; that is, groups which have some specifically assigned goal or function. A committee in almost any organization is an obvious example, but other task groups are work groups in industry, a team to fly a large plane on a bombing mission or to ferry passengers, or a research team to undertake a scientific project.

Analyzing Interaction in Groups

In 1947 Robert Bales and his associates at Harvard University began an influential series of experiments on how people interact in small group situations.[12] Each group was given a task to carry out, consisting of a set of facts about a problematic situation and a request to review the facts and make a recommendation for action. The observers ignored what the discussion was about and concentrated instead on the forms of interaction as the group discussed, agreed, disagreed, and sought consensus.

Bales and his associates worked out a set of categories for observing the interaction, distinguishing between remarks that elicited responses, responses to those remarks, whether they were positive or negative, or whether they were questions or suggestions. A further breakdown of these produced twelve interaction categories:

A. Positive reactions	Shows solidarity
	Shows tension release
	Shows agreement
B. Problem-solving attempts	Gives suggestion
	Gives opinion
	Gives orientation
C. Questions	Asks orientation
	Asks opinion
	Asks suggestion
D. Negative reactions	Shows disagreement
	Shows tension increase
	Shows antagonism

A major finding from these studies seriously challenged the common idea that a small group consists of a leader and several followers, and that the leader is the best-liked and most active member of the group and is regarded by the others as the best performer in whatever tasks the group undertakes. Instead, Bales and his associates developed the conception of two complementary leaders, an *"idea* man," who initiates problem-solving attempts but who also disagrees more with others and shows more antagonism to others, and a *"best-liked* man," who offers responses that are positive—he agrees, is supportive, and makes humorous remarks that releases group tension. He also asks more questions. These are two complementary roles, "with the idea man concentrating on the task and playing a more aggressive role, while the best-liked man concentrates more on social-emotional problems, giving rewards and playing a more passive role."[13]

A further important finding was that *high* (frequent) participators were more likely to be the specialists in problem-solving, whereas *low* participators specialized in positive or negative responses or questions. Those who make many problem-solving attempts necessarily talk a lot; while those who are liked best provide positive responses to others, including letting them talk more. Apparently, leaders

---

[12] Robert F. Bales, *Interaction Process Analysis: A Method for the Study of Small Groups* (Cambridge, Mass.: Addison-Wesley Publishing Co., Inc., 1950). For a summary of subsequent research, on which the following discussion is based, *see* Robert F. Bales, "Task roles and Social Roles in Problem-solving Groups," in Eleanor Maccoby, Theodore Newcomb, and Eugene Hartley, eds., *Readings in Social Psychology*, 3rd ed. (New York: Holt, Rinehart and Winston, Inc., 1958), pp. 437–447.

[13] Bales, "Task Roles and Social Roles in Problem-solving Groups," p. 442.

must choose between task effectiveness and popularity.

But should we not distinguish between sheer amount of activity—talking a lot—and the value placed on it by the group? Bales suggests that three factors emerge when group members rate each other or are rated by observers: *activity, task ability,* and *likeability.* In effect, task ability is distinguished from activity, the effort to stand out from others and achieve prominence in the group. Although both mean high participation, the group recognizes the difference.

On the basis of these three factors, Bales suggests five types of roles in small groups:

1. The *good leader,* or "great man," a rare type who is high on all three factors.
2. The *task specialist* who is high on activity and task-ability, but is less well-liked.
3. The *social specialist* who is well-liked, but ranked less high on activity and task ability.
4. The *overactive deviant* who is high on activity, but relatively low on task ability and likeability.
5. The *underactive deviant* who is simply low on all three factors.

The Range and Limits of Small Group Studies

This example of an important, innovative study in small groups can barely suggest the many different studies of small groups which illuminate the nature and consequences of social interaction.[14] Some

---

[14] For a recent review of small group studies *see* Theodore Mills, *The Sociology of the Small Group* (Englewood Cliffs, N.J.: Prentice-Hall, Inc., 1967). For a collection of representative research articles *see* A. Paul Hare, Edgar Borgatta, and Robert F. Bales, eds., *Small Groups: Studies in Social Interaction,* 2nd ed. (New York: Alfred A. Knopf, 1965).

studies have observed the emergence of group norms as a consequence of social interaction and the function of these norms in patterning behavior. These studies have also observed the exercise of social control by the group over the individual, sometimes in quite ingenious experimental situations. Other studies have been concerned with problem-solving alternatives, democratic and authoritarian leadership, differences in communication network, morale and cohesion, and problems of group size.

However valuable these studies have been, and however rich and suggestive in findings, there are still some apparent limitations on the controlled study of small groups under experimental conditions. In many task-oriented group studies the groups are not enduring, having come together for only the research purpose, and the task itself is of no consequence to the individuals. There is no set of shared understanding built up over time, and there are no binding commitments and ties. Thus, artificial and real groups differ in ways which limit the scope and significance of small-group research.

THE VALUE PROBLEM OF SMALL GROUPS

Small towns are supposed to be warm and friendly, big cities cold and impersonal. No less today within the younger generation than with the theorists of folk society, the growth of large and impersonal organizations is viewed as dwarfing the individual and denying him his individuality. The widely expressed fear of sameness and uniformity, as well as conformity and the stifling of creativity, are viewed as the inevitable outcome of the eventual dominance of society by bureaucratic structures.

Yet such a perspective distorts what we know sociologically about the significance of size in social groups for the individual and for society. To speak of the warmth and personal relations of the small community is to stress but one side of the coin. The small community or any other small human group also exerts greater social control and "invades" the personality to a much greater extent. The small group exposes the private individual to the others; the more intimate the relationship, the less there is that is secret or entirely a private matter. The more people know about what we think and feel, the greater is the pressure to think and feel as they do.

The greater formality and impersonality

GEORGE SIMMEL

(The Granger Collection.)

It was George Simmel (1858–1918) who first drew sociological attention to the importance of studying social interaction in the small group. Simmel wanted sociology to become the science of *forms* of interaction. The unique historical and cultural content could be left to other sciences; it was the underlying uniformities that should concern sociologists he felt. His basic position was that if society is conceived as interaction among individuals, the task of the science of society is the description of the forms of this interaction.

While sociologists have not followed his advice and restricted sociology only to being *formal sociology*—that is, a sociology of forms of interaction—they have made such analysis central to the sociological enterprise. Earlier, American sociologists—such as Robert Park and Ernest Burgess—adopted Simmel's concern for interaction as social process: conflict and cooperation, centralization and decentralization, subordination and superordination.

of secondary (that is, not primary) relations protect the person against an invasion of his privacy of feelings and thoughts by others. Role-playing in a complex society may very well mean that we don "masks" behind which our genuine selves are concealed — a frequent criticism about modern society — but this also serves to protect these intimate feelings from an exposure that might bring attack if they are deviant from the group's perspective. The problem of human freedom and group size, then, is much more complicated than the oversimplified generalization that bigness in organization thwarts individuality.

Furthermore, personal preference for relationships that are primary confuses personal desirability with social function. An increase in the scope of organization promotes other social values, among which

---

Simmel was also the first sociologist to suggest that qualitative changes were introduced in social interaction as a consequence of a change in the numbers of the group, such as an increase of two (a dyad) to three (a triad). The dyad differs from all other social groups in that the two members have to confront, not a collectivity, but each other. There can be no collective majority arrayed against the individual and he cannot, therefore, be subject to the control and restraint that the group can exercise over one of its members.

But the addition of one member achieves a qualitative change; the triad is the smallest group that can attain some control over each member. Simmel's imaginative and creative mind demonstrated the many new relationships possible when one person was added to the dyad, a consequence of the nature of interaction that was independent of the psychological attributes of the participants.

Simmel also explored some implications of the increase in group size. In small groups the members interact directly with one another, but this is less possible as the group increases in size. The larger group develops various mechanisms for patterning interaction, such as role differentiation. The small group allows for intense interaction and close involvement of the person, but a larger group cannot sustain this mode of interaction. Therefore, a weaker and more segmented attachment of the person to the group occurs. Yet Simmel also recognized the more coercive and closer scrutiny of the small group over its members and the liberation from this made possible by an increase in group size.

For a further study of Simmel see:

Lewis Coser, ed., George Simmel (Englewood Cliffs, N.J.: Prentice-Hall, Inc., 1965).

Nicholas J. Spykman, The Social Theory of George Simmel (New York: Atherton, 1965).

Kurt Wolff, George Simmel, 1859–1918: A Collection of Essays (Columbus: Ohio State University Press, 1959).

Kurt Wolff, ed. and trans., The Sociology of George Simmel (New York: The Free Press, 1950).

Kurt Wolff and Reinhard Bendix, trans., Conflict and the Web of Group Affiliations (New York: The Free Press, 1956).

are diversity, greater choice, and opportunity, as well as organizational efficiency and effectiveness on which greater productivity and high standards of living are based. Even impersonality has its functional value; for a larger number of people to interact efficiently in accomplishing some useful task requires some degree of impersonality.

There is a paradox, then, in the contrast between the small and the large in human groups, between the primary and the secondary. Although a world without the primary would be cold and humanly unbearable, a world that is only primary could seem small and confining to those persons expecting to exercise the individual choice and personal freedom so prized in modern society. It is part of the historic record that we became freer and more of an individual when societal development "liberated" some individuals from the small and confining context of kinship and village. The very context of the individual person as something separate from his social groups—both as a fact of life and as a social value—emerged strongly in human consciousness only in the larger network of relationships in complex and segmented societies.

SUMMARY

A *group* is a plurality of persons sharing in a common pattern of social interaction. Members of groups are conscious of who belongs and who does not. A group persists successfully when it achieves a degree of unity and integration of its members around shared activities.

The *primary* group is small, with face-to-face interaction, and of reasonably long duration. It makes possible primary relations, which have no purpose other than the relationship. Family and peer groups are the most notable cases of primary groups.

The *peer* group is significant for effectively controlling individual conduct. It either integrates the person into the larger group by providing him with a sustaining set of relations, or it enables him to resist official standards and controls.

Peer groups are basic to developing subcultures among those who share a common life situation, and they are basic to the development of the adolescent as a person, helping to detach him from family and socialize him to other situations, particularly in generating resistance to established authority.

The study of small task groups under controlled circumstances has focused largely on how people interact to solve problems and accomplish tasks, dividing labor between task specialists and social specialists.

Small groups are idealized over large ones, which distorts a complex value problem. Small groups tend to be warm and personal, yet often more controlling; large groups tend to be more impersonal, yet may create the conditions for greater personal freedom and individuality.

Suggested Readings

Robert F. Bales, *Interaction Process Analysis: A Method for the Study of Small Groups* (Cambridge, Mass.: Addison-Wesley Publishing Co., Inc., 1950). Ground-breaking sociological studies in interaction in the small group.

Albert K. Cohen, *Delinquent Boys* (New York: The Free Press, 1955). A pioneering study of delinquency as peer-group phenomena.

James S. Coleman, *The Adolescent Society* (New York: The Free Press, 1961). A study of cliques in high school and their significance as peer groups.

Herbert Gans, *The Urban Villagers: Group and Class in the Life of Italian-Americans* (New York: The Free Press, 1962). How a community of working-class Italians organize their life through peer groups is superbly analyzed by Gans.

A. Paul Hare, Edgar F. Borgatta, and Robert F. Bales, eds., *Small Groups: Studies in Social Interaction,* 2nd ed. (New York: Alfred A. Knopf, 1965). A series of empirical studies of small-group interaction.

George Homans, *The Human Group* (New York: Harcourt Brace Jovanovich, 1950). An outstanding theorist of small-group interaction here develops an influential statement about the small human group.

Theodore M. Mills, *The Sociology of Small Groups* (Englewood Cliffs, N.J.: Prentice-Hall, Inc., 1967). A short, useful introduction to the study of small groups.

James F. Short, Jr., and Fred L. Strodtheck, *Group Process and Gang Delinquency* (Chicago: University of Chicago Press, 1965). An empirical study of a large number of delinquent groups.

William F. Whyte, *Street-corner Society: Structure of an Italian Slum,* rev. ed. (Chicago: University of Chicago Press, 1955). A superb study of peer groups among young adults in an ethnic community.

"... the great modern state is absolutely dependent upon a bureaucratic basis."
—*Max Weber*

Chapter 8

The Formal Organization

In the modern world ever larger organizations rise to dominate the social landscape, commanding a greater share of the social resources, ever greater social power, and proving to be effective mechanisms for organizing large aggregates of people in the pursuit of social goals.

Large organizations differ among themselves in many ways. Political parties, business firms, voluntary civic groups, governmental agencies, hospitals, prisons, universities, and armies are all large organizations; yet all are different from one another in the goals they pursue and in the kind and amount of resources they command. If they are all large, however, they are not equally so, for what is large can be defined as anything from a department store or a social service agency to the General Motors Corporation or the U.S. Department of Defense.

The effort in sociology to understand the nature of these large and dominating organizations has produced theories of bureaucratic structure. Although variations in size and in purpose distinguish large organizations from one another, what is probably most common to them is a tendency to move toward *formalization* and then *bureaucratization*; these terms will be defined later on. It is these developments in modern organizations which will be the concern of this chapter.

Goal Specificity

Formal organizations are constructed for the pursuit of relatively specific objectives. It is goal specificity that makes it possible for organizations to build a *rational* structure; that is, one in which activities are organized so as to lead efficiently to a previously defined goal. The more clearly and precisely an organization defines its goals, the more able it is to construct a rational structure.

Goal specificity is a matter of degree, not an all-or-nothing matter. Some organizations are more specific than others about what their goals are. Universities, for example, are often less specific than a business firm or a governmental agency. Undergraduate education, graduate training, and research are three valued activities in a university, but which should have precedence over the others, or what balance should be sought among them, is often an unsettled matter. Thus, where to put resources, what kind of teaching load to assign to the faculty, and how large a class size should typically be in the undergraduate school may be matters of dispute within the university.

If the goals of formal organizations are specific, however, they are not unchangeable. Even in such organizations as business firms, specific goals first established are subject to change over time, as circumstances change and as different groups within the organization reshape goals to suit their particular interests.

Goals, too, may become too costly or even unattainable, or full success in attaining a goal may no longer justify putting so much of the organizational resources into it. When Dr. Jonas Salk developed a successful vaccine for polio, for example, the nationwide organization devoted to raising funds for the fight against polio—the National Foundation for Infantile Paralysis—was no longer justified. But organizations do not disappear for these reasons; the self-interest that many people have in an organization produces new goals and activities to enable it to continue. The National Foundation, for example, took up other childhood diseases and birth defects to which it could easily adapt an already existing medical services program and its nationwide "March of Dimes" fund-raising program.[1]

Formalization

The structure of an organization is "formal" when its positions and relations among them are officially and explicitly designated, independently of the characteristics of the persons who might occupy the positions. It is possible to draw a diagram of a formal structure, to picture it as a series of *offices* which rank above and below one another on a chart of the organization. Like goal specificity, formalization is a matter of degree; some organizations have formalized their structures more thoroughly than others have. (Every organization also has an "informal" organization, too, which we shall examine later in the chapter.)

Bureaucratization

Formalization makes the rules, the authority, and the functions of office explicit.

[1] *See* David L. Sills, "Voluntary Associations: Instruments and Objects of Change," *Human Organization,* vol. 18 (Spring 1959), pp. 17–21; reprinted in John N. Edwards and Alan Booth, *Social Participation in Urban Society* (Cambridge, Mass.: Schenkman Publishing, 1973), pp. 173–179. *See also* David Sills, *The Volunteers* (New York: The Free Press, 1957).

Bureaucratization carries this one step further; it is the development of a specialized administrative staff whose task is the control and coordination of the other participants in the organization. What the owner-manager of an enterprise once did himself (and still does in small organizations) is now subdivided among a number

THE RATIONALIZATION OF SOCIAL LIFE

Max Weber (1864–1920) analyzes bureaucracy as sociologically significant not only because it is increasingly dominant in modern life but also because its very dominance signifies the increasing *rationalization* of modern life. For Weber, a world grown more rational is the most significant development in the history of Western culture. A rationalized world is one less spontaneous, less mysterious, more subject to rule and procedure. It is a world moving away from custom and emotion, disregarding these to base action on criteria related to the efficient attainment of objectives.

As Weber made clear, the rationalization of life proceeds in a number of different directions, but bureaucratic rationalization constitutes a major one. This is by no means the only one; science, for example, is another. It may be that science and bureaucracy are the most significant of the rationalizing forces at work altering the world.

Science strips the world of much of its mystery and sometimes, unintentionally, of much of its charm. It contributes significantly to a "disenchantment with the world"—here Weber was quoting Friedrich Schiller. It treats the world as a natural process that proceeds by rules of nature. The more man-as-scientist penetrates into nature, the more nature becomes known and unmysterious, and much of the workings of natural process become quite matter-of-fact.

Bureaucracy is a rationalizing force because it seeks to order its own world in a systematic fashion, within a clearly defined set of rules and procedures applying to all possible situations. In short, it seeks to reduce the world to a calculated and predictable pattern, controlled by criteria that logically relate means to ends.

Bureaucracy proceeds in the most efficient manner, not, therefore, necessarily in a customary manner. It is ever ready to discard tradition; it tries to repress the claims of sentiment; it abhors passion; and it ignores esthetics. It has a place for the engineer but not the poet. Bureaucracy encourages matter-of-factness in thinking, seeing the world as a set of facts and things to be handled, manipulated, and treated.

When bureaucracy proceeds so rationally, it contributes significantly to rationalizing the world. Increasingly, this literal attitude, the treatment of the world as an environment of objects and things which behave according to natural rules, and are thus manipulable and controllable, constitutes a secular rationality that is now an inherent part of modern thinking, not merely scientific thinking. We are all living in a rationalized world.

of specified functions, such as personnel, sales, production, research, advertising, and the like. Thus, when organizations grow in size, administering them requires a separate staff:

In an organization that has been formally established, a special administrative staff usually exists *that is responsible for maintaining the organization as a going concern and for coordinating the activities of its members.*[2]

THE ORIGINS OF BUREAUCRACY

If we were to ask why bureaucracy is so pervasive in the modern world, an adequate answer can be either *historical* or *functional*.

The Emergence of Bureaucracy

Bureaucracy is not a new thing; some degree of bureaucracy was characteristic of great empires of the past. When control of long frontiers for defense or of waterways for subsistence was necessary in an empire, the complex administrative task generally brought into being a body of administrative officials and some methods for administering the set up in a routine and stable fashion, so that there was an accountability of these officials to the emperor.[3] For this reason, bureaucratic structures existed during the Roman Empire and in civilizations such as the Chinese, the Byzantine, and the Egyptian.

Though bureaucracy in some ancient forms has existed outside of a money economy (where payment was in kind),

Max Weber showed that the emergence of a money economy facilitated the development of bureaucracy; it permitted the payment of salaried officials who could count on the security of their position and thus on an opportunity for a career.[4] Such officials were dependent on the organization and on their superiors, yet were independent enough to carry out assigned functions and to exercise judgment and expertise in doing so.

Yet, while bureaucracy existed in many pre-modern societies, it was seldom the dominant mode of organization it has become in modern society. The development of capitalism and the modern state, two major components in the emergence of modern society, stimulated the growth of bureaucratic organization. The rational calculation of economic risks required not only a money system and a rational system of accounting but also a political system that was not arbitrary and disruptive. Stable control of the economic and political conditions under which business flourished, then, demanded a rule of stable and accountable law, and a system of officials who could be counted on to enforce law and to insure stability. According to Weber, "the great modern state is absolutely dependent upon a bureaucratic basis. The larger the state, and the more it is or the more it becomes a great power state, the more unconditionally is this the case."[5]

The Functional Meaning of Bureaucracy

According to this historical view, the bureaucratic form of social organization

---

[2] Peter M. Blau and Richard W. Scott, *Formal Organizations: A Comparative Approach* (San Francisco: Chandler Publishing, 1962), p. 7. Emphasis in original.

[3] *See* Karl Wittfogel, *Oriental Despotism* (New Haven, Conn.: Yale University Press, 1957).

[4] Hans Gerth and C. Wright Mills, eds. and trans., *From Max Weber: Essays in Sociology* (New York: Oxford University Press, 1946), Ch. VIII, "Bureaucracy," pp. 196–244, particularly pp. 204–209.

[5] Gerth and Mills, *op. cit.,* p. 211.

grew as certain social conditions encouraged its development. It thus provides historical evidence for the functional argument; namely, that bureaucracy is a response to a problem in social organization. Whether the bureaucracy is a factory, an army, or any process of organizing and administering the work of a fairly large and diversified number of people, those who seek to carry it out have to face a basic problem: What is the organizational form by which the efforts of so many people can be effectively coordinated into a common, productive effort? Bureaucracy is an indispensable aspect of modern society because growth in size and in complexity and differentiation of organization requires some processes whereby a stable and routinized administering process permits effective control and operation of the entire structure.

According to Max Weber, bureaucratic organization has grown because of its purely technical superiority over any other form of organization. He goes on to note that bureaucracy compares with any other form of organization "exactly as does the machine with the nonmechanical mode of production."[6] Bureaucracy develops because a society's culture places a foremost value on efficiency and effectiveness of administration.

But not all societies give priority to efficiency and effectiveness. In societies where other, more traditional values are emphasized, a rational model of organization cannot easily develop.[7]

[6] Gerth and Mills, op. cit., p. 214.
[7] Monroe Berger, for example, found that over 40 percent of Egyptian civil service officials believed that family connections, wealth, and social background should count in the selection of civil servants. See his Bureaucracy and Society in Modern Egypt (Princeton, N.J.: Princeton University Press, 1957).

FORMAL STRUCTURE

The effort to efficiently coordinate the actions of many people toward a single objective leads to the development of *formal* structure. We call it formal, following Weber, whose classic formulation of the components of bureaucracy is still the basic one. Weber specified these components:

1. Each person in a bureaucratic organization occupies an *office*, which exists as an explicit definition of duties and functions, separate from the person who holds the office. The office, therefore, does not belong to any person; no one has a special claim on it by virtue of inherited position, special rank, or privilege. Rather, claimants for the office are those who possess explicit qualifications based on defined duties and functions. This separation of office from person frees the organization from dependence on any particular person, and provides a condition whereby individuals become dispensable and replaceable actors in the organization.

2. The relationships in a formal structure are relations among offices, not among persons, hence are *impersonal*. This insures cooperation among persons who must interact to carry out their assigned duties; their personal feelings for one another can be subordinated to the demands of the office. The spirit of impersonality is one of detachment and distance, enhancing the capacity to render rational and objective judgments, uninfluenced by likes and dislikes of particular persons.

3. In a bureaucracy the norms are spelled out, generally in written and codified form, in quite explicit sets of *rules* and *regulations*. The rules are specific, in that they apply to quite definite situations and circumstances, but are also general, in that they formally apply to all (or at least all office-holders within the scope of the rule) in an impersonal manner.

4. Bureaucracy develops a high degree of *specialization* of function and areas of *tech-*

Figure 8.1 A huge factory complex, such as the General Motors Technical Center in Michigan, cannot function unless it is bureaucratically organized—right down to who parks his car in what lot. *(A. Devany, Inc., N.Y.)*

nical competence. The selection of personnel for office then comes to be made in terms of technical and professional qualifications. This makes important the development of tests and other measures of technical achievement by which the qualified can be certified. Any college student is aware of how much his life is governed by various kinds of tests.

5. A bureaucracy has a hierarchy of offices, with a chain of command and a centralization of authority and major decision-making within a management or administration. Thus, bureaucracy makes explicit the location of authority and the range and limits of the exercise of authority for any office. Each person in a bureaucracy is responsible *to* someone above him and is responsible *for* the actions of those under his authority.

The Formalization of Organization

These several points provide a conception of the formalization of organization. It is rendered explicit and unambiguous and thus highly rational; indeed, it can be put down on paper by reducing it to a chart of organization that defines offices, codifies rules, specifies the flow of authority and the extent of responsibility, and indicates the technical competences that provide qualification for office.

Such an organization has distinct advantages over a more traditional one. For one thing, a formal organization does not depend on the sentiments that the members hold toward one another, as Weber stated; it even discourages those positive sentiments that might interfere with professional discipline and objective judgment. The organization becomes independent of any particular person and can replace anyone and continue to function. A large formal organization is unlikely to be disrupted by the loss of even its top-ranking officer.

Authority, Rewards, and Communication

The analysis of formal structure in large organizations has often focused particularly on three issues: authority, rewards, and communication.

Authority

Formal organizations are designed so that, consistent with the hierarchy of positions, some positions have authority over others. In order that the occupant of each position will be able to carry out his tasks, sufficient power is provided in the form of control over resources—an adequate budget, access to personnel—and also control over people in subordinate positions by the capacity to reward or sanction. Weber notes that hierarchy in office and "graded authority means a firmly ordered system of super- and subordination" by which lower offices are supervised by the higher ones.[8]

But this "firmly ordered system" of graded authority needs to be viewed as legitimate by participants in the system, else the exercise of decision-making at any given point will be challenged and orders will not be obeyed. Authority is always *delegated* downward in formal organization, so that each position operates with the authority allocated to it from above. But there has to be an ultimate source of legitimation of authority. That lies in charters, articles of incorporation, constitutions, by-laws, and legal statutes. The president of a corporation has his authority delegated by the board of directors, which draws its authority from the incorporation papers and the legal statutes governing corporation structure and the rights of private property. Universities differ from corporations and

other bureaucracies in that the faculty, which nominally ranks low on the chart of organization of the university, claims and exercises authority independently of the president and the chain of command, an authority over curriculum and other academic matters, usually delegated directly by the trustees. The president of a university has authority delegated by the board of trustees, which in turn derives its authority from a corporate charter or, in the case of public universities, by some constitutional authority.

Rewards

One consequence of ranked positions in formal organizations is an unequal distribution of rewards. Salaries range upward from that of the night watchman to the president's. Other rewards—designated parking spaces, private offices, a window, private secretaries, executive bonuses—may be available only to some upper level of rank.

When judiciously used, this differential distribution of rewards functions to recruit new members and to serve as an incentive to people to be productive. But the intricately complex differentiation within formal organization often makes the reward system a source of discontent. It is not easy to get agreement on the criteria by which rewards should be distributed.

Sometimes this may be because non-rational criteria enter in; women, for example, may be paid less because they are women, not because they are less productive. (At the same time, note that it may be efficient—thus rational—for a corporation to take advantage of the weaker, more vulnerable position of women in the labor market in order to

[8] Gerth and Mills, *op. cit.*, p. 197.

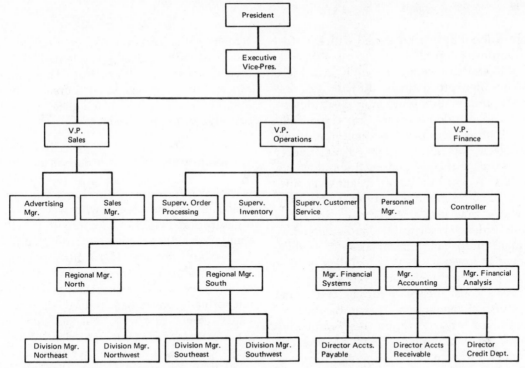

Figure 8.2 A typical business organization chart.

buy competent service more cheaply. Such efficiency may be rational from one perspective, but is hardly based on a rational conception of reward by merit.) In other cases, it is because credentials, such as a college degree, are judged to be indicative of greater capacity to perform with more ability or skill, when to many without the college degree it may not be obvious that the "college boys" are doing more, only that they get more money because they went to college.

Finally, an organization does not necessarily attempt to provide equity in distributing rewards; it may only pay what it needs to get trained people and keep them in the system. This may mean that at one time it will be able to get secretaries and production workers cheaply, but pay dearly for engineers or research chemists, for example.

Communication

No complex organization can function effectively—or indeed at all—unless it has assured channels of communication. A pioneering student of organization, Chester Barnard, has made the existence of formal communication networks the central focus of his conception of organization.[9] Channels of communication, he says, must be known to all participants; each member should have access to the formal channel of communication; the lines should be as short and direct as possible; and those communicating should make use of the appropriate line of communication, not bypassing any link. Ideally, each member will have access to what he needs to know

[9] Chester Barnard, *The Functions of the Executive* (Cambridge, Mass.: Harvard University Press, 1938).

but will not be overburdened with extraneous information.

But effective communication in a hierarchy often proves to be difficult. For one thing, information flows more easily downward than it does upward, and the middle levels often block or distort communication between top and bottom. Furthermore, Barnard's principle that each should have access to what he needs to know is subject to interpretation; upper levels may believe that lower levels need to know only orders—what to do—and some occasional propaganda from the top, while those in lower levels may feel they need—and have a right—to know more.

As a consequence, informal and extra-legitimate channels of communication in organizations—"grapevines," "scuttlebutt," "rumor mills"—operate in the absence of effective formal communication. Someone calls a strategically placed friend to find out "what is going on," or a secretary tells another secretary who tells someone else, and so on. In some cases these informal channels may contribute to the effectiveness of the organization by making possible quick and efficient communication not possible with formal means, or by encouraging a sharing of information among those who have similar tasks and responsibilities. But when these channels transmit inaccurate information, particularly at times of change and tension, they inhibit the effectiveness of the organization.

INFORMAL STRUCTURE

In his pioneering studies Max Weber focused on the formal processes that make bureaucracy a rational system, leaving relatively unexamined the spontaneous and unplanned actions that can also be observed in any large organization. What actually goes on in large organizations, then, is only partially explained by a theory about formal structure. This other aspect of organization—"bureaucracy's other face"—is what sociologists conventionally call *informal structure*.

The Emergence of Informal Structure

However impersonal bureaucracy is supposed to be, the people who work in an organization interact frequently with some others; they come to know each other as persons, not merely as office-holders. As a consequence, they build a complex network of social relationships that are not formally prescribed; indeed, they may violate some of the formal sanctions of the organization. Thus, as friends, they may "cover" for one another when they take time off that is not allowed; or they may provide one another with information about what is going on, creating informal gossip channels that circumvent the slower and less informative official channels. They invoke friendship as a way to get favors from others or to get information or material resources they need to do their jobs; or they use these primary relationships to violate the bureaucratic rules for personal benefit.

Through informal interaction, then, people turn the rational organization into a complex, nonrational network of cliques, primary groups, and informal communication networks, as well as informal channels of influence and advantage. If bureaucracy means a rational use of human beings as instruments of organization, informal structure means these very same human beings struggle to master and control the organization, or at least segments of it, to provide job security and to humanize it as a working environment.

Figure 8.3 "Bureaucracy's other face"—informal interaction at the water fountain. *(Featherkill Studios.)*

This last point is basic; there is a very human resistance to being treated as a replaceable unit, a standard human item in an organization. No amount of favorable or competitively advantageous personnel policies—better wages and salaries, a retirement system, or generous vacations—can offset the resentment at being a faceless cog in a vast machine. In a thousand and one little ways people actively humanize the presumably impersonal environment of the organization. A pattern of primary relationships running across the formal roles and relations is one way; numerous small ways not to conform to all the regulations is another.

The peer groups we have previously described (*see* Chapter 7) fit into the informal structure. As we saw, they assert their own norms of production, exercise control over individual members, and impose informal and unofficial standards and regulations on the work situation. In this fashion formal standards for work and formal authority are challenged and possibly subverted by a quite informal but nonetheless real and effective structure of social relationships within small groups.

Informal Groups as Problem Solving

An informal structure may also arise from an almost opposite circumstance, in which by informal means people try to get problems solved and activities carried on when the formally prescribed processes move too slowly; are too complicated; or are adapted to an earlier situation, whereas conditions have in fact changed. The intended efficiency of bureaucracy sometimes has its own inefficiency, "red tape," a too-complex process for getting things done—clearing with too many offices or filling out too many forms. In particular, this may make it difficult to act quickly in sudden emergencies. Shortcuts are devised, such as getting informal approval *first,* then doing the formal paperwork *after* the activity is finished.

These informal procedures are not intended to subvert the goals of the organization but instead to carry them out when the formal procedures are inadequate. Informal structure, then, may often represent the effort of office-holders to get around rules and procedures that hamper effective performance and to devise less formal ways of achieving their assigned goals.

BUREAUCRATS AND PROFESSIONALS

The original conception of the hierarchical structure of bureaucracy did not anticipate some developments that have become significant in this century. The place of the professional in bureaucratic structure is a major one. Increasingly, professional people do not practice independently, but are employed in large organizations. Physicians join clinics;[10] lawyers are employed by large corporations or by government agencies, or even by large law firms; engineers and scientists work in laboratories and research units in large corporations.

A professional's work is based on considerable advanced training and is marked by a special competence based on scientific or technical knowledge. As an expert the professional needs and demands a large degree of autonomy from lay control. Who else can judge the work of a surgeon or a scientist but other surgeons and scientists? As more occupations in modern life become professionalized, the organization of work must allow room for expert judgment. Thus, autonomy of activity marks the advanced professions, even within large organizations. Most autonomous are those professionals whose work is necessarily least routinized—physicians, for example, and the scientists and researchers on the frontiers of knowledge, seeking and testing new theories.[11]

As a consequence, professionals create problems for the authority system of a large corporation, and a frequent struggle goes on between professionals and administrators. In hospitals there is a conflict in authority between the control exercised by the hospital administrator and the authority of the physicians. In industry, it is between management and the research scientists.[12]

Management has found scientists difficult to manage, and their morale suffers from conventional managerial practices, for most of all they want to be left alone to do their work as they see fit. Professional authority enables them to exercise their expert judgments on technical matters, but bureaucratic authority is still necessary to provide coordination with the work of others in attaining the objectives of the organization as a whole. There is often tension between professional and bureaucratic authority. However, too much control hampers the scientist's work; but too

[10] For a discussion of colleague control in group medical practice, *see* Eliot Friedson, *Professional Dominance: The Social Structure of Medical Care* (New York: Atherton Press, 1970).

[11] According to sociologist Roger Krohn, scientists are more closely regulated and less autonomous than physicians; *see* his *The Social Shaping of Science: Institutions, Ideology, and Careers in Science* (Westport, Conn.: Greenwood Publishing, 1970).

[12] *See* William Kornhauser, *Scientists in Industry: Conflict and Accommodation* (Berkeley, Cal.: University of California Press, 1962); *also,* Simon Marcson, *The Scientist in American Industry* (New York: Harper and Row, 1960).

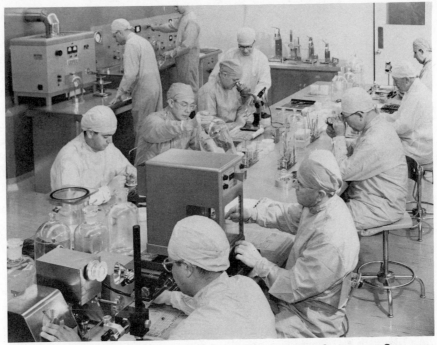

Figure 8.4 Professionals, like these scientists at Sperry Gyroscope Company, increasingly affiliate with large organizations. *(A. Devaney, Inc., N.Y.)*

little threatens to make him less useful to the organization.

Line and Staff Conflict

Sometimes organizations have tried to accommodate professionals by giving them a staff status, separate from the line authority of the organizational hierarchy. Staff organization consists of research and advisory functions for professional experts; line organization is the vertical hierarchy which has authority over routinized production or service processes. Often this intended solution turns out to be a source of conflict.

Melville Dalton has described such a staff-line conflict in an industrial firm.[13]

[13] Melville Dalton, "Conflicts between Staff and Line Managerial Officers," *American Sociological Review*, vol. 15 (June 1950), pp. 342–351.

Line officers regarded their authority as "something sacred" and resented the implication that they needed the assistance of less-experienced newcomers. Staff officers, in turn, thought of themselves as agents of top management, experts and managerial consultants who tended to approach middle- and lower-line officers with an air of condescension.

These differences of function were aggravated by social differences between the two groups. Staff officers, as research specialists, were better educated and younger than the line officers; and they were ambitious and anxious to win rapid promotion. In their effort to develop new techniques and get them accepted, they were impatient with line officers; and this only confirmed the latter's suspicion that staff personnel would, if allowed, usurp their authority.

Professional Goals versus Organizational Goals

Dalton's study suggests that professionally trained people may bring professional goals into organizations; and these may influence the goals and activities of the organization itself. Charles Perrow discovered such a case in his study of voluntary general hospitals, organized first and once controlled by unpaid trustees, who were civic leaders and community representatives.[14] But the medical staff gradually took control of the hospital, bringing about a shift from *official* to *operative* goals; that is, from the publicly proclaimed goals of the organization, on which community support was mobilized, to a set of professionally defined goals. These operative goals "are likely to be defined in strictly medical terms and the organization may achieve high technical standards of care, promote exemplary research, and provide sound training."[15] But when this occurs, resources may be used for the benefit of private (paying) patients with less attention to such community problems as the medically indigent. So, too, there may be less emphasis on preventive care or on innovating new forms of patient care.

When professional goals become the operative goals of the organizations, then professional interests alone shape the organization. Professionals "may develop an identity and ethic which cuts them off from the needs of the community and favors specialized, narrow, and—to critics—self-serving goals."[16] In the universities,

says Perrow, criticism of emphasis on research and overspecialization in graduate training at the expense of undergraduate education is a case in point.

Professionals are not, however, the only subgroups within organizations that seek to shape or at least strongly influence organizational goals. Even top administrators may have self-serving not organization-serving goals. So may other subgroups at practically every level.

BUREAUCRACY AND SOCIAL POWER

Bureaucracy by design and intent is not democratic. To say that is not to criticize but to observe that a significant issue in modern society is the relationship of bureaucratic structure to the distribution and exercise of power.

The hierarchical nature of bureaucracy has always concentrated authority at the top. This is so even when, for reasons of efficiency, considerable authority may be decentralized to subordinate units of the organization, and when the professional expert may enjoy considerable autonomy in the performance of his functions. Accordingly, a complex and efficient organizational apparatus is controlled by its top administrators, who are in a position to exercise power relatively independently of those to whom they are nominally responsible—such as trustees, directors, or elected cabinet officers.

When bureaucrats are full-time career officials of government agencies and their superiors are elected or appointed cabinet officials, the cabinet members are often at a severe disadvantage in carrying out policy that the career officers oppose. The control of the organization by career officials enables them to offer considerable resistance to new policies. When a Socialist party in

[14] Charles Perrow, "The Analysis of Goals in Complex Organizations," *American Sociological Review,* vol. 26 (December 1961), pp. 854–855.
[15] Perrow, *op. cit.,* p. 859.
[16] Perrow, *op. cit.,* p. 862.

an agrarian province of Canada came to power, conservative career officials effectively subverted the efforts of the newly appointed cabinet members to carry out a reform program.[17] The cabinet officers depended so much on the bureaucratic machinery, as well as the knowledge and skills of the bureaucrats, that they were vulnerable to the resistance of the bureaucrats to political innovations.

This suggests that bureaucracy is often a conservative force in resisting social change, because a combination of power, based on control and competency, and an ideological orientation may lead bureaucrats to favor a particular social policy. However, the opposite effect can also be achieved. By appointing new officials who have a different political ideology but the same professional competence, bureaucracy can be a powerful force for social change.

Bureaucracy and Totalitarian Power

Historical scholarship has provided evidence of the importance of bureaucratic structures in the rise to power of totalitarian groups. Stalin, for example, used his strategic position as Secretary of the Central Committee of the Bolshevik Party, and the control of party machinery that this position gave him, to ascend to power within the party structure and to defeat and destroy his opponents.

Communists have long recognized the importance of organizational bureaucracy as an instrument of power. Philip Selznick, for example, documented the Bolshevik technique of capturing power within an organization to use it as a weapon in the struggle for power.[18] In this process, the offices of secretary and treasurer are more useful to hold than that of president, since through these positions the money and the appointed staff positions of the organization can be controlled.

Bureaucracy and Democracy

Those who control large bureaucratic organizations constitute an elite of power, for large and efficient organizations are significant instruments of power, whether they are labor unions, political parties, corporations, trade associations, civic organizations, or governmental agencies. According to Peter Blau and Marshall Meyer:

... bureaucracies create profound inequalities of power. They enable a few individuals, those in control of bureaucratic machinery to exercise much more influence than others in society in general and on the government in particular.[19]

In modern society bureaucracy and democracy at best live in tension with one another, for they are two very different human systems. Bureaucracy is a system for the efficient organization of human action for explicit goals; and it uses human beings as experts who know better than anyone else how to carry out specialized tasks. Democracy, in turn, is a system for governing by the participation and consent

[17] Seymour M. Lipset, *Agrarian Socialism* (Berkeley, Cal.: University of California Press, 1949).

[18] Philip Selznick, *The Organizational Weapon* (New York: McGraw-Hill, Inc., 1952). The relationship between bureaucracy and the consolidation of totalitarian power is examined in detail in Franz Neumann, *Behemoth: The Structure and Practice of National Socialism* (New York: Oxford University Press, 1942).

[19] Peter M. Blau and Marshall W. Meyer, *Bureaucracy in Modern Society,* 2nd ed. (New York: Random House, Inc., 1971), p. 166. This is one of the few studies of bureaucracy that contains any discussion of its relation to democracy. *See* Ch. 8.

of the governed; achieving the consent of the governed requires that dissent be allowed and indeed freely expressed in order that consent by a majority be freely attained.

The unintended but nonetheless real effect of the proliferation of bureaucracies in modern society, then, is to contribute to the creation of a social world of large organizations. Each is hierarchical, authoritative, highly organized, and rationally planned; and each manned by administrative and technical experts with professional qualifications for what they do, for the judgments they render, and for the decisions they make or at least strongly influence. Such a world, however unintentionally, is not democratic. This concentration of power in bureaucratic organization has far-ranging implications that were not anticipated in democratic theory, the basic ideas and values of which have their roots in the small-scale world of the eighteenth century.

Yet bureaucracies are not entirely antidemocratic (and antiequalitarian) in their influence. For one thing, they make use of rational employment policies which accept all who qualify, regardless of such ascribed status as sex or race.[20] Furthermore, equal treatment under the law (or rule or regulation), and disinterested and equal treatment of all according to some objective criteria are values that bureaucracies readily accept in principle.

To be sure, large organizations by no means always practice these values. But attainment of such values is not contrary to rational bureaucratic functioning. If public bureaucracies, like the police and the schools, were to treat all citizens equally, regardless of class or race, such neutral practice would strengthen democracy. This does not happen because influential groups in the community maintain their privileged positions within organizations against the rational criteria of the bureaucratic process.

Furthermore, formal organization is an instrument by which modern society undertakes tasks of large dimension and accomplishes them efficiently. The gathering of human skills and technical resources into a single highly rationalized organization permits the effective exploitation of opportunities for technological development, for scientific advance, and for the mass production and distribution of resources that create an affluent society.

The abolition of large-scale organization would require a return to small communities, to a simpler and less productive technology, to lowered standards of living, and indeed to many of the conditions that prevailed in the nineteenth century. It is unlikely that the moral deficiencies and human problems of bureaucracy—real and compelling as these are—are going to induce a modern people to forego the obvious advantages of organization for a return to some romanticized version of a simpler life. Thus—the dilemma of bureaucracy and democracy. A concluding comment by Blau and Meyer makes a worthy point:

Even if we could turn back the clock of history and abolish bureaucracies, we would be reluctant to do so because of having to surrender the benefits we derive from them. Some authors have concluded that modern society's need for bureaucratic methods spells the doom of democracy. But why interpret a historical dilemma as a sign of an inescapable fate? Why not consider it a challenge to find ways to avert the impending threat? If we want to utilize efficient bureaucracies, we must find democratic methods of controlling them lest they enslave us.[21]

---

[20] Blau and Mayer, *op. cit.*, pp. 164–165.

[21] Blau and Meyer, *op. cit.*, pp. 167–168.

Figure 8.5 Organization Man—robot or independent? *(Featherkill Studios.)*

BUREAUCRACY IN A POST-MODERN SOCIETY

Whatever may be the moral stance we take toward it, the fact remains that we live in an "organizational society." The working lives of most of us are absorbed in large, bureaucratized organizations. The significant economic, political, and civic activities that shape decisions for the future are made largely by and through modern organizations. The theory of formal organization that began with the work of Max Weber stressed the hierarchical control of routinized work processes in highly centralized organizations. The moral response to that was to see pervasive bureaucracy as a threat to the freedom of the individual, and bureaucratic conformity as producing "organization men" in gray flannel suits.

But as is so often the case, reality moves ahead of theory. In recent years a number of innovations and developments in organizational structure have challenged ex-isting theory. It seems that bureaucracy in post-modern society will not be what we now know bureaucracy to be, though post-modern society will not decrease the range and scope of bureaucratic organizations.

Some of the changes are readily apparent now. Professional autonomy and expertise, for example, force modification in hierarchical controls and achieve greater freedom of movement and decision-making on the job. We can expect this trend to increase. Greater technical competence on the part of people in bureaucratic structures will require greater modification to accommodate to their professional work patterns. More and more, people will be recognized as competent, self-regulating individuals who can be entrusted to do a job without close supervision.

Furthermore, technological developments move large organizations away from the model of the routinized production line, whether in factory or office; routine work is increasingly mechanized, requiring fewer but better trained people on the job who can and must assume greater personal responsibility for what goes on at the point of production. Automation only maximizes this process. (*See* the discussion of automation in Chapter 14.)

If the authoritarian and hierarchical patterns of conventional bureaucracy are no longer functional for all organizational tasks, this means that *decentralization*, rather than continuing centralization, is likely in the future. Bureaucracy of necessity becomes a flexible process, adjusting rapidly to new demands and opportunities. Sociologist George Berkley has described the new form of bureaucracy as "a loose, amorphous, and sprawling affair."[22] He sees it as a more-or-less stationary center connected by lines to its units, many of which are task forces that dissolve when tasks are completed. Furthermore, management's function is less that of authority and control, more one of coordination and support.

Not the least factor in the new form of organization is the resistance of more educated people to being treated like "organization men." Michel Crozier, one of Europe's foremost students of organization, insists that a more "sophisticated" people in a more "complex culture" are a basic factor in the evolution of organization in modern society.[23] From his perspective this

has another consequence: the power of experts is to be reduced, not strengthened. Managerial power will be less a technical power—that of the expert—and more a political and judicial power; administrative success will depend more on the human qualities of leadership than on scientific know-how or on being the "boss."

These predictions about bureaucracy in post-modern society are about changes in the internal structure of formal organization. They herald new forms that will be more livable for a better educated, more professionalized work force. If this is to be so, then bureaucracy may more successfully integrate individuals into the organization, individuals who can build strong commitments to a career in the organization and to its objectives.

But in a society more, not less bureaucratized the problems of the relation of bureaucracy to democracy remain difficult. The view of the future from the perspective of emerging organizational theory does not yet tell us where to look for change in that matter.

Furthermore, these changes are developments to be found in organizations around the world, not merely in the United States. They herald a new period in the history of organization.

Whether, as George Berkley says, this truly marks the "passing of organization man," or merely his metamorphosis into an as yet unperceived new type of organization member functioning in a new type of organization, posing new problems and threats to the concept of a free people in a free society, remains yet to be decided.

[22] George E. Berkley, *The Administrative Revolution: Notes on the Passing of Organization Man* (Englewood Cliffs, N.J.: Prentice-Hall, Inc., 1971), p. 24.

[23] Michel Crozier, *The Bureaucratic Phenomenon* (Chicago: University of Chicago Press, 1964).

SUMMARY

Formal organization is characterized by *goal specificity*, by *formalization*, and by *bureaucratization*.

A formal structure has these components: (1.) positions are explicitly defined as offices; (2.) social relationships are impersonal; (3.) norms are explicit rules and regulations; (4.) a high degree of specialization of function is present, with utilization of criteria of technical competence; and (5.) a formalized hierarchy of offices and a centralization of authority exists.

Authority in organization is delegated downward, but is always ultimately legitimated.

A system of *rewards* is used to assure adequate recruitment and to encourage productivity, but disagreements over criteria can make rewards a source of discontent.

Clear channels of *communication* are essential for effective organization. Where formal communication is inadequate, informal "grapevines" provide needed information.

Formal organizations also have an *informal* structure. Interaction among peers leads people to know each other as persons and so to act in ways other than those officially prescribed. They help one another to get around "red-tape," and they resist being mere agents of the organization.

Professionals create problems for organizational authority by demands for *autonomy* in work and by efforts to promote *professional* goals at the expense of organizational goals.

Bureaucracy is a source of power in society; and power accrues to officials who manage bureaucratic organizations. Yet they also contribute to democracy, even as they threaten it.

Bureaucracy in the future is likely to be as common as now, but also to change; it will be more flexible, more decentralized, less authoritarian.

Suggested Readings

Chester I. Barnard, *The Functions of the Executive* (Cambridge, Mass.: Harvard University Press, 1938). A pioneering study by an experienced executive that stresses communication.

Morroe Berger, *Bureaucracy and Society in Modern Egypt* (Princeton, N.J.: Princeton University Press, 1957). A study of the problems of bureaucracy in a society still traditional in many ways.

George E. Berkley, *The Administration Revolution: Notes on the Passing of Organization Man* (Englewood-Cliffs, N.J.: Prentice-Hall, 1971). A review of changes in organizational theory and practice presumably heralding a post-bureaucratic era.

Peter M. Blau, *Bureaucracy in Modern Society*, 2nd ed. (New York: Random House, Inc., 1965). A brief survey of the study of bureaucracy by a foremost student, including a chapter on democracy and bureaucracy.

Peter M. Blau, *The Dynamics of Bureaucracy* (Chicago: University of Chicago Press, 1955). Blau's renowned study of bureaucracy in social service agencies.

Peter M. Blau and W. Richard Scott, *Formal Organizations* (San Francisco: Chandler Publishing Co., 1962). A thorough review and analysis by two of sociology's best students of formal organization.

Michel Crozier, *The Bureaucratic Phenomenon* (Chicago: University of Chicago Press, 1964). An influential French study that predicts the transformation of bureaucracy to less authoritarian forms.

Amitai Etzioni, *Modern Organizations* (Englewood Cliffs, N.J.: Prentice-Hall, Inc., 1964). A short introduction to the study of organizations by a foremost student.

Hans Gerth and C. Wright Mills, eds. and trans., *From Max Weber: Essays in Sociology* (New York: Oxford University Press, 1946). Weber's famous pioneering essay on bureaucracy is included.

Alvin Gouldner, *Patterns of Industrial Bureaucracy* (Glencoe, Ill.: The Free Press, 1954). An oft-quoted study of bureaucratization processes in a mine and a factory.

Seymour Lipset, *Agrarian Socialism* (Berkeley, Cal.: University of California Press, 1950). A study of how entrenched bureaucracy can resist political change.

Franz Neumann, *Behemoth: The Structure and Practice of National Socialism* (New York: Oxford University Press, 1942). Still a superb study of the political and economic bureaucratization of Germany under the Nazis.

Max Weber, *The Theory of Social and Economic Organization,* A. M. Henderson and Talcott Parsons, trans. (New York: Oxford University Press, 1947). Another source of Weber's writings on bureaucracy.

All cities are mad: but the madness is gallant. All
cities are beautiful: but the beauty is grim.
—*Christopher Morley*

Chapter 9

Community

One of the oldest forms of social group is that created by human aggregates
clustering within a geographical area, a social arrangement that varies from
the most remote village to the gigantic metropolis. This conception of *community* as a social group with a territorial base has been a central one for
sociologists, and it is this type of social group which will be the concern
of this chapter.

Community as Locality Organization

When a population resides in a geographical area, that fact requires some
forms of social organization to insure that social life is sustained. Roland
Warren defines community from this perspective as: "the organization of
social activities to afford people daily local access to those broad areas of
activities which are necessary in day-to-day living."[1]

A community is not a formal organization; it does not have the explicit
and specific objectives that bureaucracies do, nor is it centralized in the
same way. Nor does a modern community have the close ties of intimacy

[1] Roland Warren, *The Community in America* (Chicago, Ill.: Rand McNally & Company, 1963), p. 9.

and belonging, the intense we-feeling that marked the small folk societies of the historic past.

Nonetheless, people are still grouped in localities, and there is social organization that develops in response to the problems of providing common residence and sustenance for a population sharing a limited territorial space. People in localities develop sentiments about community, an attachment and a sense of unity and belonging together that formal organizations rarely do. That, most basically, is what community is all about.

URBANIZATION

For most of humanity's social existence a predominantly agrarian life put many people into small communities within which they lived out the span of their lives and within which they found the total range of their social world. A social life so confined was a little society, and not in any significant sense a part of any larger form of social organization.

However, the Industrial Revolution broke through this predominant pattern, and community in this *folk* sense no longer provided the social context within which people lived. In Europe this began some three centuries ago, with the movement of vast numbers of peasants to cities and factory towns, where they became urban workers. This was a tremendous uprooting process, in which former peasants lost any sense of being located in a stable and traditional community, organized around kinship, religion, and a common life.

In the United States the rapid pace of industrialization after the Civil War converted the nation into an industrial society in a few decades, and set in motion a rapid urbanizing process. Americans became city people in large numbers in a short period. By now, about three Americans out of four are urban and more than half live in metropolitan areas of over 100,000 population. The trend continues to run strongly in that direction. The continued industrial and technological transformation of modern society promises only further urbanization of its population.

The Rise of Cities

Cities are not anything new. According to historical records, as well as archeological evidence, people have lived in cities for three or four thousand years, but usually only a small part of a society's population inhabited the city; the majority lived an agrarian life in the surrounding countryside.[2]

Cities could not emerge, however, until certain specified conditions made it possible. For one thing, there had to be a sufficient surplus of food and other resources to enable some small segment of the population not to engage in direct, food-producing activities. At first, this segment was probably a priesthood, which became in time an administrative and political elite. But secondly, there also had to be a level of technology and of social organization that enabled the city to have sufficient control over the countryside in order to insure its own existence. Armies and bureaucracies, then, came to be essential units in the social organization that made the city possible. Peasants, it should be understood, did not willingly yield up any surplus; cities were built by forcefully

[2] See Gideon Sjoberg, *The Preindustrial City: Past and Present* (New York: The Free Press, 1960); *see also* R. M. Adams, *The Evolution of Urban Society* (Chicago: Aldine Publishing Co., 1966).

expropriating a surplus from the country-side.

Medieval Cities

The growth of cities never occurred at an unbroken pace. In Europe, for example, the fall of Rome brought an urban decline for several centuries. Cities did not become significant again in Europe until the restoration of trade and commerce in about the tenth century. Then, cities grew up around the walled towns that served as administrative centers and defensive strongholds for the feudal aristocracy. Gradually an urban population of artisans and merchants built the great medieval cities that produced a distinctly urban culture and way of life.[3]

Throughout the Middle Ages, however, these cities were small by present standards, and grew slowly. For example, Florence in 1388 had a population of 90,000 and Venice in 1422 had 190,000. London in 1377 had only 30,000, but by 1801, as the major city of the most industrialized nation in the world, it had 865,000 inhabitants.

The Urbanized Society

Prior to 1850 there were large industrial cities in the Western world, yet no society had so concentrated its population in cities to an extent sufficient that the society could be called an *urbanized* one. Even in 1900 probably only Great Britain was an urbanized society. But now all industrial socie-ties are urbanized, and there is an accelerating world trend toward global urbanization.

The growth of an urban population in the world is greater than population growth in general, even though the world's population has grown rapidly since 1800. The world's population living in cities of 20,000 or more has increased in this manner:[4]

1800	2.4 percent
1900	9.2 percent
1950	20.9 percent

Comparably, the world's population in cities over 100,000 has increased as well:

1800	1.7 percent
1900	5.5 percent
1950	13.1 percent

Urbanization in the United States

The United States has been an urbanized society for only a few decades. According to the first census in 1790 only one person in twenty (5.1 percent) lived in an urban place. From the Civil War on, however, the urban population grew steadily:[5]

1860	19.8 percent
1870	28.2 percent
1900	39.7 percent
1920	51.2 percent
1950	59.0 percent

The turning point had arrived in 1920;

[3] For a classic analysis of medieval cities *see* Henri Pirenne, *Medieval Cities: Their Origins and the Revival of Trade* (Princeton, N.J.: Princeton University Press, 1925; Anchor paperback edition, 1956). *See also* Max Weber, *The City*, Don Martindale and Gertrud Neuwirth, trans. and eds. (New York: The Free Press, 1958; paperback edition, Collier Books, 1962).

[4] Kingsley Davis, "The Origin and Growth of Urbanization in the World," *American Journal of Sociology*, vol. 60 (March 1955), pp. 432–433.
[5] For a discussion of urban growth in the United States, with this and additional data, *see* Donald J. Bogue, "Urbanism in the United States, 1950," *American Journal of Sociology*, vol. 60, (March 1955), pp. 471–486.

MEASURING THE URBAN POPULATION

Until 1950 the U.S. Bureau of the Census defined *urban* as all places of 2,500 or more incorporated as municipalities. But this had become an inadequate definition. Because of the growth of an urban fringe around central cities that remained unincorporated, yet had the density and social characteristics of an urban place, the urban population was underenumerated.

A new definition of urban, then, includes all incorporated places of 2,500 or more, as before, but adds two new categories: (1.) the densely settled urban fringe around cities of 50,000 or more, and (2.) unincorporated places of 2,500 or more people outside of the urban fringe.

The *urban fringe* is defined as continuously built-up areas outside of major cities which have a density of about 2,000 persons per square mile.

As a consequence of this new definition, the 59.0 percent considered urban in 1950 by the old definition became 63.7 percent. Seven and a half million people were added to the urban category—and subtracted from the rural one—by this redefining process.

---

by then more than half the population of the United States lived in urban places. As it turned out, the census figure of 59.0 urban population in 1950 was an undermeasurement. By redefining urban the Census Bureau increased the 59.0 to 63.7 percent (*see* "Measuring the Urban Population"). By 1960, under the new definition of urban, the proportion reached 69.9 percent, and by 1970 it was 75 percent.

World Urbanization

This rapid urbanization is hardly unique to the United States; several nations, in fact, are even more urbanized. In 1951 the following nations had the highest percent of urban population:[6]

Scotland	82.9
England and Wales	80.7

Israel	77.5
Australia	68.7

Another measure of urbanization is the percent of population living in cities of 100,000 and over:[7]

England and Wales	51.9
Australia	51.4
Scotland	50.7
United States	43.7
Israel	39.9

The Metropolitan Area

The movement of people from rural to urban areas is continuing, but today it is accompanied by a shift from city to suburb. The urban population now spreads out from the city into a hinterland, formerly but no longer rural, frequently larger in physical area than the central city, and

[6] The source of these data is Donald J. Bogue, *The Population of the United States* (New York: The Free Press, 1959), p. 34.

[7] Bogue, *op. cit.*, p. 34.

Figure 9.1 Walled medieval cities grew up as trade centers and defensible areas to house the local aristocracy. *(The Bettmann Archive.)*

sometimes equal to or even surpassing the central city in population.

The term, *metropolitan,* refers to a concentration of urban population distributed among a central city and a complex of smaller satellite cities and villages surrounding it. This is the metropolitan area

measured by the Census Bureau as *standard metropolitan statistical area (SMSA)* (*see* Boxed Material on p. 172).

Data since only the 1950s give us graphic evidence of what has been happening. The data in Table 9.1 tells us that the largest gain in population since 1950 has

TABLE 9.1 Population in Metropolitan and Nonmetropolitan Areas, United States, 1950–1970

	1950		*1960*		*1970*	
	Number (millions)	*Percent of total*	*Number (millions)*	*Percent of total*	*Number (millions)*	*Percent of total*
Metropolitan	86	57	120	66.7	140	68.6
Central Cities	50	33	60	33.4	64	31.4
Suburbs	36	24	60	33.3	76	37.2
Nonmetropolitan	65	43	60	33.3	64	31.4
Total Population	151	100	180	100	204	100

Source: For 1950: Conrad and Irene B. Taeuber, *The Changing Population of the United States* (New York: John Wiley & Sons, Inc., 1958), p. 140; for 1960 and 1970: U.S. Bureau of the Census, Census of Population, 1970, vol. I, *Characteristics of the Population,* Part A, Number of Inhabitants, Section 1, p. 34.

TABLE 9.2   Population Decline in Selected Cities, 1950–1970

City	1950 Population	1960 Population	Percent Decrease	1970 Population	Percent Decrease
Boston	801,444	697,197	13.0	641,071	08.1
Buffalo	580,132	532,790	09.8	462,768	13.1
Chicago	3,620,942	3,550,404	01.9	3,366,957	05.2
Cincinnati	503,998	502,550	00.3	452,524	10.0
Cleveland	914,808	876,050	04.1	750,902	14.3
Detroit	1,849,568	1,670,144	09.5	1,511,482	09.5
Philadelphia	2,071,605	2,002,512	03.3	1,948,609	02.7
Pittsburgh	676,806	604,332	10.2	520,117	13.9
St. Louis	856,796	750,026	12.4	622,236	17.0

Source: U.S. Bureau of the Census, Census of Population, 1970, vol. I, *Characteristics of the Population,* Part A, Number of Inhabitants, Section 1, Table 20.

occurred *in* metropolitan areas but *outside* central cities; that is, in the suburbs. In 1950, 36 million people, almost one-fourth of the population, lived in the suburbs; while 50 million, or one in three, lived in a central city. By 1970, the suburbs had 12 million more people than the central cities; and more than one-third of all Americans lived in a suburb.

Even this is deceiving, for many of the larger and older central cities of the United States, particularly in the North and East, lost population in the decade, but newer cities in the Southwest gained considerably. Table 9.2 reports this decline in the population of older cities. Note, too, that nonmetropolitan America also declined proportionately, and only gained 3 million people in a time when the total population was increasing by 41 million.

The 1960 census recorded for the first time that in some metropolitan areas more people now reside in the suburbs than in the central city itself. This included these larger cities: Detroit, Los Angeles, Philadelphia, San Francisco, Boston, Pittsburgh,

DEFINING THE METROPOLITAN AREA

In 1950 the redefinition of urban residence led the U.S. Bureau of the Census to create several new categories by which to measure the urban concentration of the population:

1. *Urban area* includes the central city plus all the contiguous areas with densities of about 2,000 inhabitants per square mile.
2. The *standard metropolitan statistical area* includes one or more cities of 50,000 or more, the one or more counties in which they are located, and any adjoining counties that by certain social and economic criteria are dependent on the central city (or cities).
3. The *standard consolidated area* is composed of contiguous standard metropolitan statistical areas. At present, two are designated: one for "New York-Northeastern New Jersey" and one for "Chicago-Northwestern Indiana."

TABLE 9.3   United States Cities with More than 250,000 Nonwhite Residents: 1960 and 1970

	1960		1970	
City	Nonwhite Residents (in thousands)	Percentage of City's Population	Nonwhite Residents (in thousands)	Percentage of City's Population
New York	1,141	14.7	1,688	23.8
Chicago	838	23.6	1,103	32.7
Philadelphia	535	26.7	654	32.7
Detroit	487	29.2	660	43.6
Washington	419	54.8	538	71.1
Los Angeles	417	16.8	504	17.9
Baltimore	328	35.0	420	46.2
Cleveland	253	28.9	289	38.3
St. Louis	—	—	254	40.8

Source: U.S. Bureau of the Census, Census of Housing, 1960 and 1970, vol. I, *Housing Characteristics for States, Cities, and Counties*, Parts 2–52.

St. Louis, Washington, D.C., Cleveland, Newark, Buffalo, Cincinnati, and Kansas City. In some of these areas the suburban population had become as high as three out of every four persons in the metropolitan area. Here are the metropolitan areas with the highest proportion of people living outside the central city in 1970:

Newark	79.4 percent
Boston	75.8 percent
Miami	72.5 percent
Pittsburgh	71.8 percent
St. Louis	67.0 percent
Detroit	61.9 percent

Data such as these suggest how powerful the current of migration from central city to suburb is, while at the same time Americans are becoming increasingly urban.

Race in the Metropolitan Area

Not everyone gets to move to suburbia; it has been overwhelmingly a white community. In fact, by 1960 more whites lived in suburbs than in central cities. As a consequence, blacks are becoming an ever-larger proportion of the central city, and in one city, Washington, D.C., they were a majority by 1960. (Table 9.3 records the proportion of blacks in those American cities in which nonwhites number more than a quarter of a million.) Since Washington is a federal city without home rule and largely controlled by a Congressional committee, blacks becoming a majority in the city went largely unnoticed, for it had no political impact. But in 1967 the election of black mayors in Gary, Indiana, and in Cleveland, Ohio, pointed up a significant political implication of white exodus from and black increase in the central city. Black voting majorities in central cities brings a new and untried dimension to urban politics.

THE DECLINE OF LOCAL AUTONOMY

One significant consequence of urbanization—concomitant with the rise of the modern nation-state, the market economy, and bureaucratic associations—is the decline of local autonomy. The extent of local autonomy in the eighteenth and nineteenth centuries has probably been overstated, but nevertheless the rural community approximated in some ways a localized society. Few modern communities can do so. The modern nation moves increasingly toward centralized political controls, and modern government penetrates into even the smallest of communities in many ways. Local independence of action is increasingly limited, and local resources are increasingly inadequate compared to the richer resources of the nation-state.

As a result, local government has only circumscribed powers and increasingly assumes responsibility for only a small range of services—streets, sewers, garbage collection, and zoning, for example. It does more than this only when the local situation is desperate—as when the closing of a local factory results in a vigorous industrial development program—or where federal or state government prods and encourages and assists—as in school consolidation and urban renewal.

Any illusion that the small town in modern society could be a contemporary *folk* community was probably dispelled forever by Vidich and Bensman's provocative study of a small community in upstate New York.[8] In Springdale people believed in the moral superiority of their community and believed also that they maintained a cherished life style not to be found in larger places. But in reality Springdale was thoroughly dependent on and influenced by the larger society, and it had lost any significant capacity it might ever have had

to make decisions about its own destiny. The small community in modern society has no autonomous existence of its own, even though its local ideology may continue to maintain such an illusion.

Furthermore, Springdale was not an equalitarian and democratic community. Vidich and Bensman demonstrated how the community was differentiated along lines of both status and power. In effect, *Small Town in Mass Society* made it difficult to continue to hold to the romantic illusion about small towns as autonomous communities and as grass-roots democracies.

Politically, local communities in the United States are not, and never have been, separate and independent governments; their powers are granted by state governments. Local school systems have increasingly been subject to the controls and standards of state boards of education. The local economy is absorbed into a national market; and its local enterprises are frequently the branch plants of large firms whose headquarters are elsewhere. Even the political life of the community may function through the local units of the Democratic and Republican parties. In addition, local units of the NAM (National Association of Manufacturers), of the AFL-CIO, of particular national unions, and of various trade associations may be involved in both economic and political activities in the community. In each case these local units operate within a framework of policy set down from state and national headquarters.

There are numerous such examples: local churches affiliated with the large denominations; local Boy Scout and Girl Scout organizations; local YMCA and YWCA organizations; local Red Cross chapters; local chapters of Moose and Eagles, of the

[8] Arthur Vidich and Joseph Bensman, *Small Town in Mass Society* (Princeton, N.J.: Princeton University Press, 1958).

American Legion and Veterans of Foreign Wars, and of Rotary and Kiwanis. Each of these may be conceived of as a "community" organization, and although its orientation may be toward local action, its basic policy and goals are not determined within the local community.[9]

What we can conclude from this, then, is that many people now find their community roles less significant for their life chances than are their roles in the nation, in large-scale associations, and in occupational and economic organizations. In the face of this, community recedes in its meaning to the individual. One measure of this recession is the decline of community ceremonials and celebrations, such as Memorial Day and the Fourth of July, which once expressed and so reinforced community integration.[10] Yet, more and more people continue to reside and work in great urban aggregates, and that fact alone makes the urban community a phenomenon of sociological significance.

URBAN ECOLOGY

Of all the forms of social organization, community by definition is locality-based; accordingly, the shape and form of community is influenced by the physical environment and by existing technology. The location of communities as well as the dis-

tribution of people, functions, and services in its physical space are both matters of the *ecology* of the community. (Ecology, as we saw in Chapter 4, studies the relationship between organisms and environment.)

Towns and cities have grown from small villages when their strategic location linked them into larger systems of trade and exchange. Thus, communities located at seaports or on navigable rivers grew into cities, while villages in the hinterland remained small. The coming of steam power and railroads opened up further opportunities for locating urban sites, but even here water routes still played an important part.[11]

In the Middle Ages fortified castles ringed by walls were built on high land; such a location was more defensible from military attack. When trade was renewed and flourished again, by the tenth century, merchants found it safer to locate close to the protective walls of these castles, and from such locations many medieval cities grew.[12]

The Uses of Urban Space

Every community, no matter how small, locates different activities and functions somewhere within its available space. How that process occurs is what urban ecology is largely about. For example, in earlier industrial cities, when workers walked to and from work, residential and industrial areas could not be far apart. As a consequence, workers lived in close-in neighbor-

[9] For a discussion of this issue *see* Roland Warren, "Toward a Typology of Extra-community Controls Limiting Local Community Autonomy," *Social Forces,* vol. 34 (May 1956), pp. 338–341; reprinted in Roland Warren, ed., *Perspectives on the American Community* (Chicago: Rand-McNally & Company, 1966), pp. 221–226.

[10] For an analysis of community integration through a Memorial Day ceremony *see* W. Lloyd Warner, *The Living and the Dead* (New Haven: Yale University Press, 1959), Ch. 8.

[11] For a discussion of how industry and technology determine the location of community *see* William H. Form and Delbert C. Miller, *Industry, Labor and Community* (New York: Harper and Row, 1960), Ch. 2.

[12] *See* Henri Pirenne, *Medieval Cities: Their Origins and the Revival of Trade.*

hoods which suffered all the possible pollutional consequences of early industry; only the middle class was able to reside further from industrial complexes.

Commuting by railroad and later the development of the electric streetcar freed people from close-in residence and in time permitted a greater separation of residence and work. The advent of the automobile accelerated this process of residential patterning and made possible an even greater separation of work and residence.

Observing these processes a half-century ago led sociologists to develop an urban ecological model for understanding how urban space was used. According to this model, the competition for space in the city produces a segregation of people and facilities. At the center of the city is the principal business district (frequently called "downtown"), which centralizes in a relatively small space major commercial and financial functions. These processes of *segregation* and *centralization* produce areas inhabited by specific categories of people—the poor, the wealthy, the immigrants, the minorities—as well as areas used for specific functions: factory districts, shopping areas, theater districts, and the like.

The Concentric Zone Model

In 1925 Ernest Burgess advanced the idea that the city could be visualized abstractly as a series of concentric circles, each circle being a different zone for the functional use of space in the city (*see* Figure 9.2).[13]

[13] Ernest W. Burgess, "The Growth of a City: An Introduction to a Research Project," in Robert Park, Ernest W. Burgess, and Roderick D. Mackenzie, eds., *The City* (Chicago, Ill.: University of Chicago Press, 1925), pp. 47–62.

Burgess' *concentric zone* theory was built on analysis of Chicago, and was criticized by other sociologists for not adequately describing other cities. In addition, cities in other cultures are so constructed that they do not develop along the concentric zone pattern. In cities in Latin America, for example, middle-class residential areas are close to the center of the city and the worst slums are much farther out.

Other American sociologists have developed other theories, though Burgess' has remained the best known. Homer Hoyt suggested *sectors* instead of zones; a more complicated *multiple nuclei* model has been developed by Chauncey D. Harris and Edward L. Ullman. Neither of these models challenges the basic assumptions that undergird Burgess' theory, but they see the working out of competition for space being too simply represented by a concentric zone model.

The Growth of the City

Whatever its deficiencies, the value of Burgess' theory was its effort to explain the *growth* of the city. According to Burgess, the city grew out from its centers, pushing out to its periphery as population grew and demands for space increased. The theory implicitly recognized that areas and neighborhoods aged, leading to physical deterioration. As a result, original residents or business users of the area moved out to newer places where land was not yet used up and often was cheaper. Left behind were old and worn out areas and also those groups of people who could not successfully compete for the newer areas.

As time goes on, a middle-class area of fine, large homes ages, and the economic value of the location declines. At some

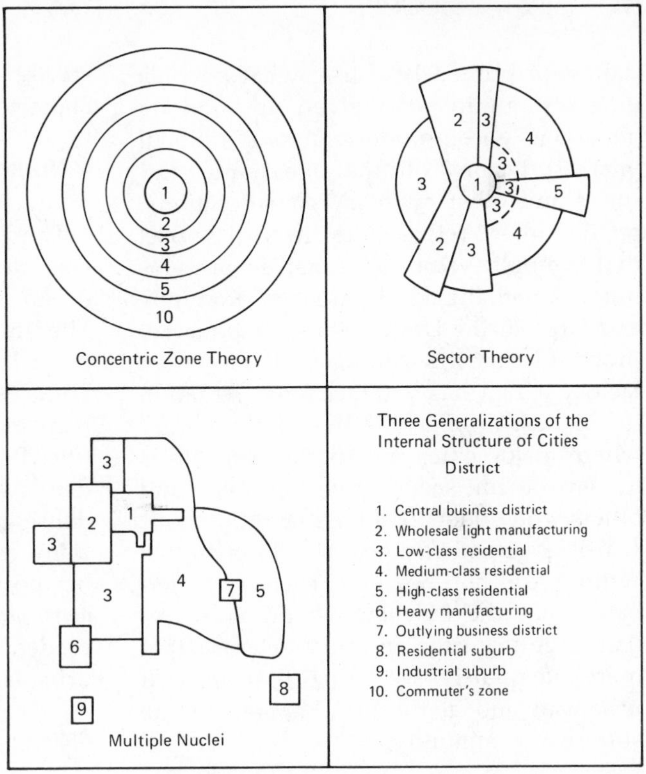

Figure 9.2 Three generalizations of the internal structure of cities.

Adapted from Chauncy D. Harris and Edward L. Ullman, "The Nature of Cities," *The Annals of the American Academy of Political and Social Science*, vol. CCXLII (November 1945), p. 13.

Concentric Zone Theory

Sector Theory

Three Generalizations of the Internal Structure of Cities

District

1. Central business district
2. Wholesale light manufacturing
3. Low-class residential
4. Medium-class residential
5. High-class residential
6. Heavy manufacturing
7. Outlying business district
8. Residential suburb
9. Industrial suburb
10. Commuter's zone

Multiple Nuclei

point a social group of lesser economic status begins to move in—"invasion"—and when they have become the dominant residential group, *succession* has occurred. In this way an area may change from white to black, or from an older immigrant group to a newer but economically poorer one.

Those who move in the face of "invasion" form new areas farther out; the movement to the suburbs is one index of "invasion" and succession having gone to the point where the central city has used all its available land space. The search for new space, particularly by the economically affluent, now goes on largely beyond the city limits.

But competitive processes in the market, where economic value is set by supply and demand, are never decisive alone for ecological patterning. In a study of Boston, for example, Walter Firey found that high-status families chose to remain in such older residential areas as Beacon Hill; thus, nonrational values can also influence the use of land in the city.[14] Such considerations as, for example, a desirable view, scenery, an elevated or commanding site, a spacious area, or a comfortable distance from "nuisance" activities are mentioned by Alvin Boskoff as some of the major reasons for retaining land use that defies market criteria.[15] Upper-middle-class residents of Chicago, for instance, have maintained residence in a particularly desirable lake-front area, replacing old large homes over time with high-rise apartments.

The ecology of an urban community, then, is a dynamic process of adjustment and accommodation among competing

[14] Walter Firey, *Land Use in Central Boston* (Cambridge, Mass.: Harvard University Press, 1947).
[15] Alvin Boskoff, *The Sociology of Urban Regions* (New York: Appleton-Century-Crofts, 1962), p. 108.

claims for limited land use; what prevails in a community at a given point in its history is a compromise among rational (market) factors, on the one hand, and status and other symbolic considerations, on the other. Yet, despite the real impact that symbolic values have had in preserving and revitalizing old areas of a city, by and large in the United States it is market processes that are dominant. It is market factors which has produced the situation in this last third of the twentieth century where major cities are dying and efforts to save them seem futile. Burgess and others who understood the market process, which governed city growth earlier in this century, did not, however, seem to anticipate what the outcome would look like half a century later. In order to assess that more adequately we must first look at urbanism and at the development of the suburban community.

URBANISM

The decline of the small, relatively autonomous community and the growth of large cities as the common mode of life for most people in modern society thrust into public consciousness the issue of what life was like in cities. The sociological view on *urbanism* until very recently was quite consistent with the view held both in popular and academic literature, in folklore and in intellectual analysis.[16] The city was viewed negatively, while the small town of the past was romanticized. Rural life, it was thought, maintained

sturdy virtues; city life eroded moral character.

Urbanism as a Way of Life

The sociological version of urbanism was developed over several decades of urban studies most notably of Chicago. The image of the urban community implicit in these studies was made plain by Louis Wirth in an influential essay, "Urbanism as a Way of Life," whose very title became a common phrase.[17] Wirth defined the city as "a relatively large, dense, and permanent settlement of socially heterogeneous individuals."[18] Thus, he postulated three characteristics: *size, density,* and *heterogeneity,* and then proceeded to derive the characteristics of urbanism from them.[19]

Size

The relatively large *size* of the modern city, according to Wirth, produces a wide range of social differences, and such diversity weakens the bonds of kinship and neighborliness, as well as the sentiments generated within a folk tradition. Most daily relationships become impersonal, superficial, transitory, and segmental.

Density

The city, also according to Wirth, concentrates large numbers in a limited space,

16 For a fine summary and analysis of this antiurban tradition in American life, including sociology, *see* Morton and Lucia White, *The Intellectual versus the City* (Cambridge, Mass.: Harvard University Press and M.I.T. Press, 1962; paperback edition, New York: Mentor Books, 1964).

17 Louis Wirth, "Urbanism as a Way of Life," *American Journal of Sociology,* vol. 44 (July 1938), pp. 1–24.
18 Wirth, *op. cit.,* p. 1.
19 For a contemporary sociological analysis of the state of society due to population explosion (size), implosion (increasing density), and heterogeneity *see* Philip M. Hauser, "The Chaotic Society: Product of the Social Morphological Revolution," *American Sociological Review,* vol. 34 (February 1969), pp. 1–19.

and the resulting *density* produces diversification and complexity. The physical closeness of people who are not tied by bonds of sentiment produces competition, aggrandizement, and mutual exploitation. Movement throughout the congested city brings frictions and irritation; and close contact among unrelated people brings about reserve and increases the likelihood of loneliness.

Heterogeneity

The *heterogeneity* of the city is its diverse population, different each from the other in so many ways. Wirth credits this difference with fragmenting memberships and loyalties, since each individual associates with a number of groups, but each group is related to only a segment of the individual's personality (as parent, worker, taxpayer). City people are transitory, even within the city; group membership changes, and organization is hard to maintain. The typical city dweller is not a stable, long-residing neighbor.

Reassessing Urbanism

This overwhelmingly negative view of the city assumes as ideal the small folk community of the past; the characteristics of urbanism are derived by measuring the city against that model. The social diversity and contrasting life styles of the city are deplored. An appreciative conception of the city as freer than the village, with a wider range of social choices for the individual, is lost when the reference point is the traditional, tightly integrated folk community.

Wirth's essay summarized a tradition of sociological observations made largely during a period of very rapid growth in Chicago, when an incessant flow of mi-

grants into the city brought together people without families and not yet into occupations and more stable life styles. Even then, however, there were areas of stable family residence. But it was the residential *instability* of in-migrant areas, says Herbert Gans, which produced heterogeneity, not the other way around.[20] From instability, not size and density, came those negative aspects of urban life.

The imagery that Wirth and others gave us, then, is historically specific; when the city is viewed at a later period, and when the most stable as well as the least stable areas of city life are included in the analysis, it appears as a less disorganized context for human experience. Recent sociological research on the city has even more thoroughly reassessed and challenged this negative description of the city, particularly on the issues of primary relations and the urban neighborhood.[21]

Primary Relations

While it is true that a large proportion of any person's social relations in the city are necessarily impersonal, nonetheless, urban people do find satisfying primary relations in the city.[22] If the neighborhood

---

[20] Herbert Gans, "Urbanism and Suburbanism as Ways of Life: A Re-evaluation of Definitions," in Arnold Rose, ed., *Human Behavior and Social Processes* (New York: Houghton Mifflin Company, 1962), pp. 306–323.

[21] For a cogent discussion of these issues *see* Scott Greer, *The Emerging City: Myth and Reality* (New York: The Free Press, 1962).

[22] *See,* for example, Morris Axelrod, "Urban Structure and Social Participation," *American Sociological Review,* vol. 21 (February 1956), pp. 13–18; and Nicholas Babchuk, "Primary Friends and Kin: A Study of the Associations of Middle Class Couples," *Social Forces,* vol. 43 (May 1965), pp. 483–493. Both papers are reprinted in John N. Edwards and Alan Booth, *Social Participation in Urban Society* (Cambridge, Mass.: Schenkman Publishing, 1973).

no longer seems a significant basis, they find other sources. They develop friendships out of acquaintances made within their profession or occupation; their place of work; their membership in church, labor union, fraternal lodge, business organization, or political party. Interest groups provide the context within which some urban people sort out those congenial few who form a small circle of primary relations.

The Urban Neighborhood

The urban neighborhood, however, is still a source of primary relations for many, particularly where stability of residence prevails. There some residents develop closer and more intimate relations with other neighbors. This occurs more in neighborhoods of single-family homes than in apartment house areas, and more in home owner neighborhoods than in rental areas. It is also more characteristic of working-class and lower-middle-class neighborhoods than of upper middle class ones. It is most evident in ethnic neighborhoods.

The Ethnic Neighborhood

Established ethnic neighborhoods often constitute small social worlds of culturally homogeneous people; they are *urban villages*, such as Herbert Gans found in an Italian working-class area of Boston.[23] Their way of life is based on primary groups and kinship within the structure of the ethnic group; it lacks the anonymity and secondary-group relations which Wirth emphasized; and it is weak in the frequency and influence of formal organiza-

tions. Its members possess an in-group outlook that makes them suspicious of people and activities outside their own groups. Thus, their lives are characterized by a great deal of isolation from others, even though they live in close physical proximity. This pattern of urban villagers prevailed in American cities in Wirth's day even more than now. While the pattern is in significant decline, it nonetheless persists.

More recently, Gerald Suttles has studied a poor area of Chicago and outlined the strategies by which residents of slum and near-slum neighborhoods order their relations in such a way as to preserve peace and maintain some decent order.[24] Four different ethnic groups, each with its own internal structure and life style, share the same area. The neighborhood street-corner groups and social clubs protect group interests and keep boundaries intact. People rarely cross these boundaries, which are based on ethnic solidarity, on sexual and territorial segregation, and on age-grading.

Order in the City

But such a moral order cannot always be successfully maintained under conditions of change and deterioration in the central city. James Q. Wilson argues that "it is the breakdown of neighborhood controls (neighborhood self-government, if you will) that accounts for the principal concerns of urban citizens."[25] And it is this same concern, he says, that leads a majority of Americans (except blacks) to prefer

[23] Herbert Gans, *The Urban Villagers* (New York: The Free Press, 1962).

[24] Gerald D. Suttles, *The Social Order of the Slum: Ethnicity and Territory in the Inner City* (Chicago: University of Chicago Press, 1968).

[25] James Q. Wilson, "The Urban Unease: Community vs. City," *The Public Interest,* vol. 12 (Summer 1968), p. 28.

Figure 9.3 Ghetto areas and protected high-rise apartments exist side by side in the central city. *(A. Devaney, Inc., N.Y.)*

small towns and suburbs, where there is greater social homogeneity and where local government can reinforce the informal neighborhood sanctions.

More and more, cities are places where people are unable to maintain the sense of community, defined by Wilson as:

...a desire for the observance of standards of right and seemly conduct in the public places in which one lives and moves, those standards to be consistent with—and supportive of—the values and life-styles of the particular individual.[26]

This inability to maintain community in the city is particularly true for affluent white people, who retreat into well-protected high-rise apartments; for poor white people, often elderly, who cannot escape to the suburbs; and for blacks. In this latter case, says Wilson, the growth of "black

power" has positive implications for "a growing pride in self and in community, and these are prerequisites for the creation and maintenance of communal order."[27]

THE SUBURBAN COMMUNITY

Suburban residential development is not new; in the early 1800s English industrialists moved their family residences out of such industrial cities as Manchester and Liverpool in order to escape the filth and fetid air. Residence beyond the city limits for the more prosperous of the city's industrial and financial leaders was a well-developed pattern in the United States before the turn of the century.

At first, suburban residence was limited to upper-income people who could afford the private transportation and the time

[26] Wilson, *op. cit.*, p. 27.

[27] Wilson, *op. cit.*, p. 37.

spent in travel. With the growth of railroads, suburban communities sprang up along railroad lines. Probably through the 1920s most suburban residents commuted by train to the city. With the growth of motor transportation and the mass consumption of automobiles, suburban communities were no longer confined to railroad lines, and a much larger space around the periphery of the city became potentially available for residential development. With car and bus available to a much broader stratum of people, so was the opportunity for suburban residence.

In the United States suburban development accelerated rapidly after World War II. There were a number of economic factors to account for this: (1.) a depression decade followed by war produced little new housing; (2.) then, postwar prosperity and delayed marriage for servicemen produced a pent-up demand for new housing. These circumstances were propitious for a great increase in the construction of new housing.

But why did this occur in suburban areas? Why not in the city?

By the end of World War II most larger American cities had exhausted their available land space and population potential. Additional population and housing growth had no alternative but to spill into the areas surrounding the city. Then, too, the construction industry was now ready to change from individual, handcraft construction to the mass construction of homes. Only outside the central city was there sufficient land available for this.

Thus, we can explain the growth of suburbs at this point in time by such factors as: (1.) the development of modes of transportation, (2.) the demand for and supply of new housing, and (3.) the exhaustion of land space in the central city. These constitute the social conditions,

primarily economic and ecological, which account for the growth of suburban residential communities at a greatly accelerated rate in the United States since World War II. But this does not tell us who can and who does move to the suburbs.

Who Goes Suburban?

Who does go suburban, then? The young, the more economically secure, the socially mobile—these find suburban living most accessible and most congenial to their interests and values. Obversely, suburbia excludes the poor, the older, and the social minorities; and these people constitute in turn a significant segment of those left behind in the movement out of the city. This tells us in objective terms what the selective process which sorts out the urban population for suburban residence is.

The mass construction of housing in suburban developments means that the suburb is no longer a symbol of upper-class status. Yet, this "democratization" of suburbia has not gone so far as to make it equally accessible to all economic levels. Although blue-collar workers have joined white-collar workers in moving to the suburbs, and large metropolitan areas now possess working-class suburbs, suburban residence nevertheless remains most economically accessible to middle-income people. It is also less accessible to people who are not white, as we have previously noted. Blacks have been blocked in efforts to find suburban housing even when their incomes, education, and occupational levels were the same as those of whites residing in the community.

Suburbia as Anti-city

Suburbia pulls people to it because of what it has to offer, but also the city frequently pushes them out. They flee the city to escape its noise and congestion, its dirt and untidiness, its crowdedness and decaying housing. But the city is more than physically unattractive to many people; it is often socially unattractive as well. It possesses slums and slum dwellers; poor whites and blacks recently arrived from the rural South, whose less-educated children are viewed as threatening the academic levels of the city's public schools. Poor schools and slums, racial conflict and large relief roles, juvenile gangs and criminal violence—these are some of the negative symbols of the city which lead people to seek the suburban life.

Much of the movement to the suburb, then, is an effort—individual by individual, family by family—to escape urban blight and to shed social responsibility for the larger and more difficult problems of American cities. It is an attempt to create small enclaves isolated from the problems of urban-industrial existence, while enjoying its amenities and advantages.

Family Life and the Suburb

For two decades now social observers have noted a seeming connection between the new suburbs and a renewed emphasis on family life. In an earlier study, for example, Wendell Bell argued that a child-centered family life is chosen by suburbanites as a value over other possible alternatives.[28] In the suburbs, then, higher than average economic status, a decline of ethnic identification and clusterings, and a strong familistic orientation mark a distinctive suburban life style.

More recently, Richard Sennett has argued that family closeness is *the* basic factor explaining the existence of suburbs as homogeneous communities, more important than the economic and ecological factors which made the suburbs possible. According to Sennett, ". . . people who now live in suburbs value their home settings because they feel that closer family ties are more possible there than in the city center."[29] This leads, he says, to a *simplification* of the social environment; wide swatches of houses of the same socioeconomic level are separated from wide swatches of commercial development, particularly the suburban shopping center. "People desire this simplification because it permits the intensity of family relations to gather full force."[30] The assumption behind this, Sennett notes, is that the family might be weakened if its members were exposed to a richer, more diverse social condition.

Sennett finds in this a basic malaise of modern life, a fear of the richness of urban society, stemming from the fact that "suburbanites are people who are afraid to live in a world they cannot control."[31]—thus, the impulse to simplify life by living in relatively more isolated, homogeneous environments for family life.

Suburbia: Myth or Reality?

There has been a pervasive myth about suburbia, an unflattering image of affluent, status-conscious America in its new resi-

---

[28] Wendell Bell, "Social Choice, Life Styles, and Suburban Residence," in William Dobriner, ed., *The Suburban Community* (New York: G. P. Putnam's Sons, 1958), pp. 225–247.

[29] Richard Sennett, *The Uses of Disorder: Personal Identity and City Life* (New York: Alfred A. Knopf, 1970; paperback edition, Vintage Books, 1971), pp. 69–70.

[30] Sennett, *op. cit.*, p. 70.

[31] Sennett, *op. cit.*, p. 72.

dential life style. Suburbia, so goes the myth, has developed a hyperactive social life, which includes both intensive neighboring, with a loss of personal and family privacy, and an active organizational life that reflects every conceivable kind of shared interest in the community.

All of this is possible, the myth says, because the suburbanites are a very homogeneous people: (1.) They are about the same age; (2.) they are at about the same point in family cycle with children about the same age; (3.) they have similar education and jobs, and (4.) their social aspirations and values are the same. Such a pervasive similarity then produces a "classless" community—really a one-class community. It also results in a similar life style' that suggests conformity in values and behavior.

Yet all this may be more myth than reality.[32] Perhaps the starting point is the discovery that the suburban community is not exclusively middle class. There are now numerous blue-collar suburbs; and many large middle-income suburban developments attract a range of social classes. In a study of one of these, Herbert Gans carefully documented the variation from working class to lower-middle class to upper-middle class among residents of the same suburban community; as well as the variation in aspirations, life styles, family styles, political orientations, and degrees of community involvement to be found within this suburb.[33] The apparent excessive homogeneity of people in any one suburb is more likely in the early years of its existence, and less so as time goes on and there is more movement in and out.

That suburbia presumably exacts conformity and a common life style from its inhabitants once promoted the idea that it turns Democrats into Republicans. But Bennet Berger found that automobile workers who had moved to a new suburb continued to vote Democratic.[34] Gans has documented in even greater detail the fact that politics, family patterns, and life style were not thoroughly altered by the movement to Levittown, one of the first mass-produced suburban communities.

The workers and lower-middle class of suburbia are not mobile; they know it, and do not absorb the life styles of rising, better-educated executives and professionals. Berger found that most of his workers did not belong to any organization other than a union, though Gans found a large number of civic organizations operating in Levittown.

Furthermore, the presumably *suburban* life style turns out on close inspection to be a *middle-class* life style, evident among middle-class people whether they reside in the suburb or in the city. In one recent study, for example, H. Lawrence Ross compared the life styles of upper-middle-class white apartment dwellers, differing only in central city and suburban residence.[35] He found no significant differences between the two. What differences there are between city and suburb are more likely to be explained by class and ethnicity than place of residence.

---

[32] *See* Bennet M. Berger, "The Myth of Suburbia," *Journal of Social Issues,* vol. 17 (1961), pp. 38–49. *See also* William Dobriner, *The Suburban Community* (New York: G. P. Putnam's Sons, 1958), pp. xxi–xxiv.

[33] Herbert J. Gans, *The Levittowners: Way of Life and Politics in a New Suburban Community* (New York: Pantheon Books, Inc., 1967).

[34] Bennet M. Berger, *Working-class Suburb* (Berkeley, Cal.: University of California Press, 1960).

[35] H. Lawrence Ross, "Uptown and Downtown: A Study of Middle-class Residential Areas," *American Sociological Review,* vol. 30 (April 1965), pp. 255–259.

Figure 9.4 The sameness of urban housing tends to produce a one-class community. *(Monkmeyer, Zimbel.)*

METROPOLIS AND CITY

The steady movement of population, particularly white and affluent, to the suburbs now brings into being a large metropolitan area, which is not an integrated community yet is more than simply a geographical area. The city keeps losing population, particularly white and affluent, with a consequent deterioration as we have seen. Its functional position, then, as the *central* city in the metropolis becomes a problematic issue.

As a consequence there are two struggles going on. One of these is over the further unifying of the metropolis to create metropolitan government, a supercity, uniting suburbs and city and also taking away what autonomy suburban communities now have. The other is the struggle to renew the city, to halt deterioration and decay and middle-class flight to the sub-

urbs, and thus to restore the central city to its centrality. The outcome of these struggles is not self-evident at the present.

The Unity of the Metropolis

For some purposes the metropolitan area can be (and is) treated as a functionally integrated community. It is a single trading area: One or more daily newspapers serve its population; large department stores deliver to the suburbs and establish branch stores there; supermarkets, drug stores, and banks operate a chain of branches throughout the area. The services basic to an interacting and interdependent population are also provided on an area basis: water and sewage, electric power, gas, public transportation, and telephone. So also are cultural activities, hospitals, and various social services. For many significant purposes, then, the metropolitan area is organized as an interdependent system.

Politically, however, the metropolitan area is not one community but many. It is fragmented into numerous small political subdivisions that make difficult any common effort to handle metropolitan-wide problems—water, sewage, expressways, and similar services.

But the effort to promote political unification is a cause which attracts as yet only a small though influential number of civic leaders and urban professionals. To these proponents of metropolitan unification, the political subdivisions of the metropolitan area are an irrational structure based only on petty jealousies and parochial interests. Political scientist Robert Wood expressed their opinion as:

A theory of community and a theory of local government are at odds with the prerequisites of contemporary life and, so far theory has been the crucial force that preserves the suburb. There is no economic reason for its existence and there is no technological basis for its support.[36]

The heavy value on "community" and on "local" government, says Wood, prevents rational metropolitan organization. "If these values were not dominant, it would be quite possible to conceive of a single gigantic metropolitan region under one government and socially conscious of itself as one community."[37]

Yet despite what Wood says, there is reason for the persistence of small suburban communities. The ideology (or theory) that suburbanites hold utilizes some hallowed American traditions about local independence and grass-roots of democracy which defend the existence of independent suburban communities, however inefficient they may be. Undoubtedly, suburbanites take seriously their own myth about independence and grass roots.

But this ideology, if taken at face value, conceals group interests. At the present time, for example, suburbs are selective about who gets in; they have managed to erect quite firm barriers against racial minorities. The more economically advantaged suburbs now maintain the best public school systems, and their academically excellent high schools offer the best access to the more preferred colleges and universities.

For these and other reasons, the suburbanite feels that he has a stake in the existence of his suburb. The myth he perpetuates rings the bell on some hallowed *values,* but his *interests* are in the economic and social advantages that the selectivity of a suburb makes possible. When Robert Wood says: "There is only the stubborn conviction of the majority of suburbanites that it ought to exist, even though it plays havoc with the life and government of our urban age," he ignores the real social interests of suburbanites that are served by not having political unification to the metropolis.[38] For some time to come there is not going to be a single metropolitan government.

But that fact should not obscure the forces that press toward unification. For one thing, the proponents of unification are influential in the professions having to do with government and public service; and they have significant allies in certain corporate executives, foundation officials, and federal government executives—all of whom are committed to the rational and efficient organization of the large American metropolis. Secondly, the effort to

[36] Robert C. Wood, *Suburbia: Its People and Their Politics* (New York: Houghton Mifflin Company, 1958), p. 18.

[37] Wood, *op. cit.,* p. 18.

shift taxes from local property to state and federal sources will further weaken local government and, among other things, indirectly contribute to metropolitan unification.

One possible consequence, therefore, is a compromise that will allow the fiction of local independence and identity to remain, with perhaps some power retained over local schools and over decisions about who gets to live in the suburb; while relinquishing effective control over necessary services to metropolitan authorities, such as a water and sewage authority, a road authority, a metropolitan park authority, and the like. In time, there may be a suburban version of the myth that Vidich and Bensman found in Springdale, a myth of being an independent community preserving a preferred life style but contradicted by the facts about societal and bureaucratic penetration into the small community.[39]

The Renewal of the City

For about two decades now federally funded urban renewal has been a means by which cities have attempted ambitious projects of urban renewal. Slum areas close to the central business district have been cleared away, and the recaptured area has been used as a new commercial location or as new residences planned to entice upper-middle-class professional and managerial people back to the center of the city. But as yet, there is no strong evidence that these efforts are going to succeed.[40]

The Inner City

The renewal of the city is primarily a renewal of the *inner* city, the area beyond the central business district that includes transient residential areas, slums, and racial ghettoes. In many cities the inner city now extends for miles, and its present development suggests that it may someday envelop the entire central city and perhaps even the older suburbs. What is not inner city—the outer city—is much like the suburbs in social character, so that, as Herbert Gans observed, the real distinction in urban life is not between the central city and the suburbs but between the inner city and the outer city, regardless of where corporate boundaries may fall.[41]

In the contrast of inner and outer cities are two social worlds, two collections of compatible life styles. Gans sees several types of people who are inner-city dwellers. One of these is the *cosmopolites,* those students, intellectuals, writers, musicians, and artists, and some other professionals, who find in the city a compatible cultural atmosphere. They are usually childless. Another inner-city resident is the "ethnic villager." There are also two groups of disadvantaged who cannot escape the city: the *deprived,* the very poor and the nonwhites; and the *trapped,* those usually older or otherwise disadvantaged people who are left behind when a neighborhood is invaded by a lower-status group.

The Black Inner City

To a considerable extent, then, the growing inner city contains many people who lack the organization and power to represent their own interests effectively. Perhaps

[39] Vidich and Bensman, *Small Town in Mass Society.*
[40] For sociological analysis of urban renewal *see* Scott Greer, *Urban Renewal and American Cities* (Indianapolis: The Bobbs-Merrill Company, Inc., 1965); *see also* Peter H. Rossi and Robert Dentler, *The Politics of Urban Renewal* (New York: The Free Press, 1961).

[41] Herbert Gans, "Urbanism and Suburbanism as Ways of Life: A Re-evaluation of Definitions," pp. 635 ff.

only in the rapidly increasing concentration of black people in the inner city is there a potential for powerful political organization. But this may come to mean that the inner city will signify *black* and the outer city *white*.

The taking of political control of the central city by blacks, then, will pose new difficulties. There may be greater resistance to even mild forms of suburb-city cooperation; and there may be a political effort to wrest control of the city from blacks—or at least to wrest control from blacks of basic, center-city-based public services by some form of metropolitan organization. In a very real sense the future prospects of the city are inextricably interwoven with the future prospects of race relations in urban America.

Death by Decentralization

A basic assumption behind much of the effort to revitalize the city is that it constitutes a basic core of the metropolitan area. The centrality of the city gives it organizing functions in coordinating a large urban complex that is viewed in roughly a circular pattern. However, new trends in urbanization, evident to anyone who studies census statistics and maps, call such an assumption into question. The central city may no longer be central, either geographically or functionally.

Urban sprawl has reached the point where one metropolitan area merges into another, and large metropolitan belts and corridors are now growing rapidly. Furthermore, the movement of residence to the suburbs has been followed first by shopping centers and other services and now by business. New office buildings and factories are locating in the suburbs, while those in the city are increasingly abandoned. Modern technology no longer requires the degree of centralization that once gave the central city such dominance.

A powerful process of decentralization, then, threatens the future of the city and may render futile all urban-renewal efforts. While it is unlikely to be a conscious and deliberate public policy, or at least one not openly acknowledged, one real prospect is for a persistent neglect of the city. Within its boundaries the poor and unemployed, the people on welfare, the poorly educated, the racial minorities, the neglected elderly will reside. The city's educational efforts will suffer and its community resources will steadily decline.

Around it will flourish a spreading metropolitan area, uneasy about the city but not anxious to do anything for it, and trying hard to insulate itself from the central city. More and more, suburban residents will have less reason than ever to travel into the center city for jobs, shopping, services, or entertainment; it will become a no-man's land for the middle class.

To be sure, there is still an enormous investment in the central city to be protected and maintained: office buildings and department stores, banks, and theaters. There are also museums, libraries, civic centers, and universities in the central city—and little likelihood that any suburb could marshall the resources to replace these. For financial and cultural reasons, then, there is reason to try to rebuild and renew the city. Henry Ford, for example, is investing many millions in downtown, river-front Detroit, and inducing other large investors to do likewise. There are still those who yet believe that the city can be rescued. Whether the gamble of their investments will pay off, however, is difficult to predict.

THE FUTURE OF COMMUNITY

Increasingly, as we have seen, modern society is urban society, its population concentrated in huge metropolitan areas. The small communities of the past are probably forever in the past; the urbanization of modern society is not something to be set aside for small, communal arrangements, even if this were desirable.

If this is so, what are the prospects for community? The question is not asked simply about locality; the trends in urbanization and metropolitanization tell us about how people are to be distributed in space. Rather, the question is asked about *community*, that historic sense of common identification that makes a place always more than a place on a map, that makes it a social group that arouses a strong sense of personal identification.

Suburbs as Community

The movement from city to suburb has taken people out of large cities into smaller ones. There were fewer Americans in 1970 in cities of over a million people than there were in 1920, as has been said. The greatest increase, in turn, has come in the suburban cities of 10,000 to 100,000 population. Many proponents of suburban life have seen in this a useful reduction in urban scale, and a revitalized political life, with the increasingly active involvement of local citizens. People in suburbs want independent local government in order to maintain and protect the way of life they have found there among people who, in some rough fashion at least, are like themselves.

Suburbs, however, are changing as time goes on. Not only are they more varied in social class, they are no longer so overwhelmingly the communities of single family homes. Apartments are now built extensively in suburbs, bringing in many more families without children and more unmarried people. In addition, new technology also brings more industry to the suburb and more office buildings. Increasingly, suburbs look like cities. Increasingly also, suburbs are more built up, more crowded, more traffic-jammed, and more beset with social problems and rising taxes. The suburb's exclusiveness and homogeneity, which some prize and others criticize, is threatened by these recent developments. It remains to be seen whether the desire for community can be sustained in changing suburbs.

The Ethnic Neighborhood

The ethnic neighborhood, as we saw, still exists in many larger cities, and there has been a renewed appreciation of what it represents in the way of community. Yet it, too, is threatened. For one thing, its residents are the least educated and least skilled — the occupationally non-mobile — members of their ethnic group. They usually have no effective political organization to protect and maintain the neighborhood against encroachment by urban renewal programs which want the area for other uses; nor can they act effectively against the general deterioration that besets all old urban areas. Whether they will remain for more than another generation is uncertain.

Neighborhood Government

A sense of community in the city would seem to depend on some reasonable stability of the residential neighborhood, some limit on the heterogeneous variations found within it, as well as a capacity for effective social controls to maintain its social character.[42] Poverty and racial tension undoubtedly threaten this stability, and steady physical deterioration make it unlikely that such communities can be maintained indefinitely. The diversity of urbanism is not incompatible with a sense of community in the city but it clearly requires an understanding of how communal order can be built in the diverse and heterogeneous city, a perspective that is largely absent as yet from most images of the city.

But there is another perspective that views large urban neighborhoods not as homogeneous social units, such as ethnic communities, but as political units, the basic unit of political life.[43] Milton Kotler argues persuasively that many still identifiable urban neighborhoods were once separate and independent communities: Germantown in Philadelphia, for example, was a separate community for 171 years before it was annexed without the consent of its residents in 1854.[44] In Boston the neighborhood of Roxbury now has an organization, The Roxbury United Front, demanding independence from Boston. The boundaries it claims coincide with those of the township of Roxbury established in 1630, which remained politically independent until it was annexed by Boston in 1868.[45]

The issue of urban decentralization, creating smaller self-governing units in the city, is a cause given considerable impetus by the issue of school decentralization, first in New York City, later in other places like Detroit. It is an effort to reverse the trend toward centralized political control in large cities, accompanied by increased bureaucratic and professional control. It is just this absence of neighborhood government, James Q. Wilson observed, that makes white Americans look elsewhere for community. It is an issue, then, that may offer one direction for renewing the city.

At the present time the central issues for neighborhood organization seem to be maintaining local schools, keeping down taxes, providing health and other necessary services, improving relations with police, and controlling zoning, as well as improving the economic base of the area. Different urban neighborhoods stress different issues, depending on their own social conditions and relations to the larger city.

Nonetheless, there is much opposition to decentralization, often including the civil service bureaucracy, teachers' organizations, and major business interests. Effective neighborhood government is not going to be achieved easily.

Communes as Community

In more recent years communes have developed rapidly in the United States. They have often been heralded as alternate communities, in which a true sense of belonging can be established and maintained. In practice the vast majority have been too small to be communities in any viable sense, and it is here that they con-

---

[42] For another discussion of the importance of community in the city *see* Jane Jacobs, *The Death and Life of Great American Cities* (New York: Random House, Inc., 1961).

[43] Milton Kotler, *Neighborhood Government: The Local Foundations of Political Life* (Indianapolis, Ind.: The Bobbs-Merrill Company, Inc., 1969).

[44] Kotler, *op. cit.,* p. 3.

[45] Kotler, *op. cit.,* p. 4.

Figure 9.5 The modern commune constitutes an alternate social community. *(Wide World Photos.)*

trast sharply with the utopian communities of the nineteenth century.[46] As Rosabeth Kanter notes, nineteenth-century utopias often called themselves *societies*, while present communes are more likely to call themselves *families*.

The new communes have their own distinctive characteristics, three basic ones being: a rejection of *hierarchy* in status in favor of egalitarian arrangements, a belief in the value of *small* communities over larger ones, and a consciously *antibureaucratic* structure.[47] Yet any commune is a form of social organization, a social group however different it seems from conventional ones. It faces, therefore, the same basic problems of maintaining the group: that "of ensuring control over certain resources (food, shelter, and the like) and the cooperation of the individuals within the group."[48] Neither of these problems proves to be easy.

While there are always difficulties for most communes in economic survival, internal problems also threaten them. The egalitarian atmosphere, for example, often prevents many communes from achieving even the minimal level of effective cooperation necessary for survival. And almost all communes have been beset, particularly in summer, with parasitical free-loaders.

[46] For a useful discussion of past utopian communities and present communes *see* Rosabeth Moss Kanter, *Commitment and Community: Communes and Utopias in Sociological Perspective* (Cambridge, Mass.: Harvard University Press, 1972).

[47] Ron Roberts, *The New Communes: Coming Together in America* (Englewood Cliffs, N.J.: Prentice-Hall, Inc., 1971), pp. 10–14.

[48] Roberts, *op. cit.*, p. 17.

Communes try to be egalitarian communities of free persons, cooperative rather than competitive. To be so, they need to balance individual freedom with cooperative organization, for an unrestrained individualism is incompatible with the needs of social organization. However free and tolerant its members want to be, however free of rules and restrictions, they still need some cooperative basis for organization. And if there is not to be hierarchy and authority there must be some other basis for achieving group control of behavior. A commune, to be a community, must achieve effective organization.

In most cases communes have been short-lived; the problems for white, middle-class people in organizing these alternate communities, or families, have proved to be much more difficult than is usually anticipated. Furthermore, it is hard to draw from them any significant lesson about restoring or rebuilding community in the modern world. To say that is not to dismiss them as without point or meaning. For one thing, the difficulties of creating community in rural retreat is itself a useful lesson. For many young people today the commune is a *temporary* retreat from modern life, one that some of them experience more than once; but it does not seem, in itself, to be a more permanent unit of social organization for very many people.

Is Community Possible?

The movement to the suburbs and the establishment of communes have one thing in common: both are flights from the dense, disorderly city to a community made up of people of similar interests, values, and life styles. It is in both cases a search for unity built on sameness, on homogeneity. For a long time that is what community has meant. Besides communes and suburbs, student "ghettoes" near large universities and large retirement complexes for elderly people are other examples of community constructed from the segregation of particular categories of similar people.

But there have always been those who have seen in the city the value inherent in the new, the changing, the different, in the diversity of life. Thus, Kotler's interest in neighborhood government is to revitalize the city by revitalizing its neighborhoods politically. It is an effort, then, to restore localism without destroying the city.

A different if compatible view is that of Richard Sennett. He regards it as desirable that the city be dense and disorderly, for this makes possible mature personal growth. He undertakes a sustained attack on the communal solidarity that affluence makes possible in the suburb. Among the consequences of such solidarity, he says, is, first, "the loss of actual participation in community life, the loss of situations of confrontation and exploration between individual groups of men."[49] This encompasses the belief that if all are alike, it does not matter who takes care of community business. Secondly, the coherence of community represses deviance. Thirdly, when the basis of community order is community sameness, there is a greater readiness for violence in confronting that which cannot be bureaucratically handled, as the invasion of a black family into suburban residence.

[49] Richard Sennett, *The Uses of Disorder: Personal Identity and City Life,* p. 41.

They feel that the very survival of the community is at stake, and in a sense they are right. Individuals in the community have achieved a coherent sense of themselves precisely by avoiding painful experiences, disordered confrontations and experiences, in their own identity formation. Having therefore, so little tolerance for disorder in their own lives, and having shut themselves off so that they have little experience of disorder as well, the eruption of social tension becomes a situation in which the ultimate methods of aggression, violent force and reprisal, seem to become not only justified, but life preserving.[50]

Too much orderliness, too much social control, too much bureaucracy is a basic disease of modern life, Sennett feels, so that reducing this considerably, and forcing people to confront one another in the urban situation, introduces a healthy dose of anarchy into urban life and becomes a significant antidote to the overorganized sameness of suburban existence. Sennett argues for greater density of population and more points of necessary contact among people as a basis for creating a vital, freer, more diverse urban existence, and for the mature growth and identity of the human being. Falling back on one's own kind for identity and association, he equates with adolescence—a condition, he feels, that is common for much of the presumably adult population in modern society.

The Future of Community?

There is, then, no common conception of what the future of community in the United States at the present time can be. Different people want different things. Yet locality, as place of residence and work and of family life, remains a basic fact of human

50 Sennett, *op. cit.,* pp. 43–44.

existence. In that sense there will continue to be some kind of community.

But what is not obvious or clear as yet is what forms community will take. One powerful trend in the shaping of community is the segregation of homogeneous populations. The suburban development manifests that best, but so does the ethnic neighborhood, the black ghetto, the student ghetto around a university, the retirement communities of older people, the huge apartment complexes with childless families. It is this which Richard Sennett objects to so strenuously.

There is also the effort to renew the city, to create local government and thus vital local political life there. It seeks to combine the diversity and challenge of the large city with a smaller, more controllable scale of organization. In addition, people like Sennett seek to renew the urban experience of daily confrontation with the diversity of city life.

Each of these experiences of community in the urban complex—suburb, ghetto, commune, ethnic neighborhood—provides some measure of the problem of achieving community in modern society. They are each an experience from which to learn. None seems to provide the fully satisfactory model for community in a society moving rapidly from modern to postmodern. Perhaps, indeed, no one form of community can meet the needs of all modern people. After all, some people even find their sense of community in groups that have no locality base.

Perhaps there is one generalization that can safely be drawn from the urban experience in the twentieth century: That the search for community is an effort to find some localized dimension of manageable social and political size without also dismantling the large-scale (and often bureau-

cratized) organization that is the hallmark of modern society; and that such a
confrontation between the possibilities,
values, and disabilities of small and large

is most likely to occur in the urban metropolis. Here is where community will be
created for the many, not the few, if it can
be created at all.

SUMMARY

Urbanization is a worldwide process correlated with industrialization. It
has brought about the decline of the autonomous local community.

Wirth saw "urbanism as a way of life" as a consequence of *size, density,*
and *heterogeneity,* and from this produced a negative image of the city.
This image has been somewhat redressed by recent sociological work.

Urban *ecology* relates people to land in a competitive process. Burgess'
concentric circles represent zones of differing land use to explain city
growth. Competition for space is a rational-functional process of market
values, modified somewhat by symbolic values, such as status.

The *suburbs* have been more accessible for the young, the economically
secure, and the mobile, while less available for the poor, the elderly, and
minorities. Suburbia has been explained as an escape from the city and an
effort to create a secure, homogeneous environment in which to raise
children.

Metropolitan areas are a single entity for many service functions, but are
politically fragmented. The rational appeal to unite for efficiency is rejected by suburbanites who see in their separate localities the preservation
of their interests.

Efforts to renew the city may not succeed. The *inner city* and the *outer
city* (not always the same as city and suburb) are two contrasting social
worlds. The concentration of blacks in the central city means that inner
city and outer city may in time signify black and white, posing new political problems. Furthermore, the decentralization of population, services, and
industry makes possible the future abandonment of the central city.

The future of community in an urbanized society is as yet unclear, but it
will probably be the outcome of an effort to provide small, localized communities without abandoning the large-scale, functional organization of
modern society.

Suggested Readings

Bennet Berger, *Working-Class Suburb* (Berkeley, Cal.: University of California
Press, 1960). A careful study of blue-collar suburbanites.

Herbert Gans, *The Levittowners: Way of Life and Politics in a New Suburban Community* (New York: Pantheon Books, Inc., 1967). Perhaps the best study yet made
of the suburban community.

Scott Greer, *The Emerging City: Myth and Reality* (New York: The Free Press, 1962).

A foremost urban sociologist explores most of the topics, as well as others, raised in this chapter.

Rosabeth Moss Kanter, *Commitment and Community: Communes and Utopias in Sociological Perspective* (Cambridge, Mass.: Harvard University Press, 1972). A fine comparison of present-day communes with nineteenth-century utopian societies.

Milton Kotler, *Neighborhood Government: The Local Foundations of Political Life* (Indianapolis, Ind.: The Bobbs-Merrill Company, Inc., 1969). A provocative case is made for neighborhood government in the city as the basis for political liberty.

Robert and Helen Lynd, *Middletown* (New York: Harcourt Brace Jovanovich, 1929). The most famous community study in sociology.

Henri Pirenne, *Medieval Cities: Their Origin and the Revival of Trade* (Princeton, N.J.: Princeton University Press, 1925). A classic, scholarly analysis of the emergence of the city in medieval Europe.

Ron Roberts, *The New Communes: Coming Together in America* (Englewood Cliffs, N.J.: Prentice-Hall, Inc., 1971). A sociologist's sympathetic analysis of communes as a new effort at creating community.

Richard Sennett, *The Uses of Disorder: Personal Identity and City Life* (New York: Alfred A. Knopf, 1970; paperback edition, Vintage Books, 1971). A stimulating plea for the density and disorder of the city as a maturing atmosphere for achieving personal identity.

Maurice Stein, *The Eclipse of Community* (Princeton, N.J.: Princeton University Press, 1960). A compelling analysis of the decline of the American community.

Gerald D. Suttles, *The Social Order of the Slum: Ethnicity and Territory in the Inner City* (Chicago: University of Chicago Press, 1968). A recent study of how diverse social groups occupying the same urban territory organize their social relations.

Arthur Vidich and Joseph Bensman, *Small Town in Mass Society* (Princeton, N.J.: Princeton University Press, 1958). A convincing portrait of a small town's false image of its own autonomy.

Roland Warren, ed., *Perspectives on the American Community* (Chicago, Ill.: Rand-McNally & Company, 1966). A collection of sociological essays analyzing the community in the United States.

Max Weber, *The City*, Don Martindale and Gertrud Neuwirth, trans. and eds. (New York: The Free Press, 1958; paperback edition, Collier Books, 1962). Weber analyzes historically the place and function of the city in Western civilization.

Morton and Lucia White, *The Intellectual versus the City* (Cambridge, Mass.: Harvard University Press and M.I.T. Press, 1962; paperback edition, New York: Mentor Books, 1964). Two intellectual historians analyze the anticity bias that has been prevalent for so long in American thought.

PART IV

STRATIFICATION

The golf links lie so near the mill
That almost every day
The laboring children can look out
And see the men at play.
            —*Sarah N. Cleghorn*

Chapter 10

Class and Status

In any human society people rarely, if ever, accept all others as social equals. Instead, they build into the very structure of society inequalities of material goods and social opportunities that set off from others in persistent distinctions of higher and lower ranks. Some are rich and some are poor, some are privileged and others are not; a few are admired, most are not—and some are even despised.   *Based on needs of society*

In the most basic sense, then, the *stratification* of society means its division into a series of levels, or strata, ranking one above the other by virtue of the unequal distribution of certain social assets, such as material rewards, privilege, opportunity, and power. However much modern people may profess a belief in equality, inequality is built into the structure of modern society.

It has always proved difficult to discuss stratification without either justifying or attacking it. Down through the centuries most theories of stratification have been, in effect, explanations of why there must be inequality, or explanations of why the injustice of inequality ever occurs. Sociologists have similarly theorized in ways that, intentionally or not, seemed either to justify the inequality found in society or to attack and criticize. Most sociologists would assert, however, that the intention of their analysis is not to justify or condemn stratification but to examine the conditions under which various forms of stratification occur.

The Inequalitarian View ✓

There are a number of different ways by which stratification has been justified, but they tend to fall into two main perspectives: those that base their argument on inherent differences in human nature; and those that base it, instead, on the requirements of society.

Inherent Inequality

In ancient Greece Aristocracy defended slavery on the ground that some people are naturally free and others are not. Many times since then the defense of social inequality has been rooted in conceptions of natural human differences—a *biological inferiority and superiority*—that presumably justify *socially* established differences of power and privilege. Thus, inequality in social position presumably reflects inequality in human nature.

The argument had wide currency in American society throughout the first decades of this century. It was used to assert the superiority of whites over blacks and Anglo-Saxons over more recent immigrant groups from southern and eastern Europe, and thus to justify various modes of segregation and discrimination.

Inequality by Merit

Today such biologically based arguments have generally been rejected as scientifically invalid and politically reactionary. Instead, the most influential argument now is that which first endorses equality of opportunity and then argues that the more technically and professionally *qualified* people should occupy the "better" positions in society and thus get more reward than the less qualified. A society based on assignment of position and greater social reward for those presumed to be more qualified is a *meritocracy*, a term first coined by British sociologist Michael Young.[1]   *inequality by merit.*

The proponents of meritocracy agree that in fact equal opportunity is not yet true of any industrial society. But they advocate social measures to make it possible, including various testing measures to sort out the more able from the less so, and to allow the more able to obtain higher education.

The basic theme of meritocracy is inequalitarian for two reasons. First, it accepts the unequal rewarding of social positions as justified. Secondly, it assumes that, even after equal opportunity is achieved, there will still be differences in demonstrated ability; that is, there will be the qualified, the less qualified, and the unqualified. What the advocates of meritocracy want to achieve is a close fit between rankings of unequally rewarded positions and unequally qualified persons.

The Functional View

A recent sociological version of the inequalitarian argument asserts that in every society there are some positions that are of the greatest importance for society and that require the greatest amount of

[1] *See* Michael Young, *The Rise of the Meritocracy, 1870–2033* (London: Thames and Hudson, 1958; paperback edition, Baltimore, Md.: Penguin Books, Inc., 1961).

training or talent.[2] To insure that these important positions are filled by qualified persons, there must be inequalities in the distribution of such social rewards as income, status, and power. According to this functionalist perspective, stratification is the "unconsciously evolved device by which societies insure that the most important positions are conscientiously filled by the most qualified persons."[3]

Unavoidably, such a sociological defense of inequality aroused controversy. Some sociologists, for example, pointed out that it is difficult to prove that the greatest reward goes to the most qualified who perform the most needed functions. This led to a modification of the functionalist argument stressing only that there had to be sufficient inequality in reward to insure that people would undertake the longer and more arduous training required of the more demanding positions.

This modified argument obviously does not explain such things as similar rewards for different levels of skill, or differential rewards for similar skills, nor does it explain low reward jobs—like garbage collecting—which are essential functions in the community. Like the meritocracy argument, the functional theory supports greater reward for the professionally qualified in societies in which the professions are expanding. Both arguments are justifications for inequality particularly appealing to professional strata.

The Equalitarian View

A contrary thesis—that inequality is neither just nor necessary—has persisted

as a counter-argument over the centuries. In the transition from medieval to modern society the scholarly work of such men as John Locke and Jean-Jacques Rosseau undercut such ideas as the divine right of kings (which declared that kings ruled because God sanctioned them to do so) and made more acceptable the democratic principle that sovereignty rests in the people. Much of the social effort of the eighteenth century was to destroy the justification for legal inequality. Equality before the law became a hallmark of democratic society.

The Marxian View   *never defined social class.*

In the nineteenth century a powerful critique of inequality was offered by Karl Marx. For Marx, the private ownership of the means of production—land, tools, and machinery—created an oppressive class system, divided between exploitative owners and exploited workers. Human freedom and equality were not possible, then, until the control and direction of the means of production was shared among all who did the productive work. Only then could exploitative class relations be abolished. By sharing in goods and participating in necessary work, Marx believed, "from each according to his ability, to each according to his need."[4]

A Conflict Perspective

In contemporary sociology, partly in opposition to the functional conception of stratification, a *conflict* perspective has emerged, deriving impetus from the writings of C. Wright Mills and the German

---

[2] *See* Kingsley Davis and Wilbert Moore, "Some Principles of Stratification," *American Sociological Review,* vol. 10 (April 1945), pp. 242–249.

[3] *See* Kingsley Davis, *Human Society* (New York: The Macmillan Company, 1949), p. 367.

[4] *See* Karl Marx, *Selected Writings in Sociology and Social Philosophy,* T. B. Bottomore and Maximilien Rubel, eds. (New York: McGraw-Hill Book Company, Inc., 1964), p. 258.

sociologist Ralf Dahrendorf, and, more basically, from Karl Marx.[5] Conflict theorists see society as an arena of combating groups struggling over the distribution of scarce goods, a struggle in which social power is the significant key to their distribution. These theorists emphasize the significance of conflicts over group interests, as well as the coercion of one group by another. It is power and conflict, then, which decides who gets how much of the scarce goods—and the associated privileges and opportunities—and justifications are but rationalizations by those who get the most.

A Synthesis of Perspectives

Some sociologists have sought a synthesis of functional and conflict perspectives on stratification. The most ambitious of these efforts has been Gerhard Lenski's distributive theory, based on assumptions about human nature and society.[6]

Lenski conceives man to be a social being who must live in society with others, but who, when faced with decisions, will always choose his own or his group's interests over others. Since most of the things (material and nonmaterial) people strive for are in short supply, there is always a struggle in every society. Furthermore, says Lenski, people are always unequally endowed by nature for this struggle and anyway tend to be creatures of habit and custom.

[5] See C. Wright Mills, The Power Elite (New York: Oxford University Press, 1956); Ralf Dahrendorf, Class and Class Conflict in Industrial Society (Stanford, Calif.: Stanford University Press, 1959).
[6] See Gerhard Lenski, Power and Privilege: A Theory of Stratification (New York: McGraw-Hill Book Company, Inc., 1966). For the following discussion see particularly Chs. 2 and 3.

The Two Laws of Distribution

These assumptions provide Lenski with a basis for what he calls the two laws of distribution. First, people will share the product of their labors to an extent required to insure the survival and continued productivity of those others whose actions are necessary or beneficial to themselves. Human survival requires human cooperation. Cooperation and sharing dominate in those technologically simple societies with little or no surplus of goods; in such societies we find no well-developed social stratification, though there may be a simple division of labor, such as by sex and age, and some moderate distinctions in prestige and power, based largely on personal skills and abilities.[7]

But when technology and the division of labor produce a surplus, then the second law of distribution applies: Power will determine the distribution of nearly all of the surplus possessed by the society—"nearly all" because altruism plays a small part. A struggle will occur over the surplus, and those with power will obtain the largest share. Furthermore, Lenski says, the greater the surplus, the more will be distributed by social power.

Might and Right

To make power the key concept in explaining stratification should not give the impression that force or coercion is all that is involved. To be sure, the capacity to use force is fundamental to the ability to use power, but what happens is that the distributive system becomes legitimized. The unequal distribution that power has made possible comes to be defended as right; legitimating myths about superiority in skills, or about greater ability, or about

[7] See Lenski, op. cit., Ch. 5.

greater risks or investment are used to justify the inequalities of distribution. Even people of modest positions are likely to believe that natural and social differences warrant social inequalities. Nonetheless, the acceptance of the legitimizing myth is almost always greater among those who have more than among those who have less.

Lenski's effort to develop a theory of stratification marks a major step for American sociology in recognizing the basic relationship of stratification to power. Marx had always recognized this relationship, and so had Max Weber (as we shall see later). Despite this, the study of stratification for many American sociologists had been the measurement of *prestige*, particularly occupational prestige. For Lenski, prestige is largely a function of power and privilege in societies of substantial surplus; most of the prestige of an occupation, for example, can be accounted for by the income accruing to the occupation and the education required for it.[8]

THE FORMS OF STRATIFICATION

Two issues persistently occur in discussing stratification as a general feature of all human societies. One of these is the extent to which the system of stratification in a society is relatively open or closed; that is, whether people must remain in the stratum into which they were born or not. The other is the issue of whether there is a single basis for stratification, or instead a multiplicity of dimensions by which social ranking occurs.

Open and Closed Systems

A comparison of class in modern society with such systems as *castes* and *estates* is

[8] *See* Lenski, *op. cit.*, pp. 430–431.

usually made to contrast *closed* systems in the historic past or in still preindustrial societies with the presumed *open* system of modern society.

Caste

The concept of *caste* refers to the permanent, very rigid form of social stratification developed over long centuries in India.[9] Each caste is usually an occupational category, closed to one another so that an individual cannot in principle change his caste designation (though in practice the principle is sometimes violated). Since the castes are *endogamous* (marriage occurs only within the caste) intermarriage is not available as a way of changing caste position. The individual is born into his caste; this alone determines his membership.

Neither economic nor political organization alone could provide the almost complete separation of the castes from one another. But the Hindu religion provides a supernatural explanation and thus sanctifies and justifies the order of castes. Caste imposes duties and obligations on each person. No matter how lowly and menial such duties are, the Hinduism provides a sacred basis for observing caste patterns and for not violating the provision and rules of caste order. Industrialization in India has put a severe strain on the ancient caste system, though it has not yet eliminated it. Though new occupations and professions require new sets of relations, the caste system has shown a remarkable capacity to adapt to social changes of considerable scope. As

[9] *See* Edmund R. Leach, ed., *Aspects of Caste in South India, Ceylon, and North-west Pakistan* (Cambridge, Eng.: Cambridge University Press, 1960); and M. N. Srinivas, *Caste in Modern India and Other Essays* (Bombay, India: Asia Publishing House, 1962).

(handwritten notes at top left:)

major
Types of caste levels in
India:

1. Braha = preists, kings
2. Kshatryaa = police-civil servants, soldiers.
3. Basya - small merchants, clerks, business, artisens.
4. Sudra - manual labor, servants

Figure 10.1 An hereditary aristocracy still controls the upper class of Great Britain. Here, Queen Elizabeth II knights Sir Francis Blam of eastern Nigeria. *(Wide World Photos.)*

modernization continues in India, a modified system of caste may yet survive, at least for a long time, as an adaptation to a more modern society.

Estate

In contrast to caste, the *estate* was a series of social strata in medieval Europe rigidly set off from one another and supported by custom and law, but not, like caste, sanctified by religion.[10] A hereditary, landed aristocracy was the upper class of the estate system, with the clergy closely associated with this class. Below them were merchants and craftsmen, then free peasants, and at the bottom were serfs, when serfdom existed.

Though upward movement in status was never forbidden by religion, both custom

---

[10] *See* Henri Pirenne, *An Economic and Social History of the Middle Ages* (New York: Harcourt Brace Jovanovich, 1937).

(handwritten:)
1. Nobility
2. Cleary
3. Peasantry

(handwritten at top of right column:) cl

and law tended to keep people in their estates of birth. This was based on a technologically simple agricultural economy. An agrarian system with a large number of peasants and a relatively low level of productivity did not permit much expansion of occupation or much opportunity for individuals to move from one social level to another. The class system was reinforced by customs associated with inheritance of status and property and with laws that established the particular rights and privileges of each social level.

Class

In contrast to caste and estate, a class system is *open* in that its social strata are not reinforced and made rigid or fixed by religion or law, or even to the same extent by custom. Furthermore, moving up in class position is valued and encouraged. Yet the contrast with castes and estates often leads

203

Class based on achievement.

to exaggerations of the openness of class systems. Inheritance of property and class differences in educational opportunities signifies that class systems are only relatively open.

From Caste and Estate to Class

Contrasting class with caste and estate points up the fact that each form of stratification has emerged in and is a significant part of the social structure of historically quite different types of society. As the world modernizes, such older systems of stratification as caste change radically or even disappear, as the estate system has; a modern class system comes to be the dominant form of stratification. To this point, we have only linked class to industrialization and to the occupational structure. We must now examine more closely the concept of social class.

Social Class

The fact that class is somehow related to economic organization leads some people, particularly Americans, to define class simply in terms of income. However, income alone does not adequately define class. Often skilled workers and even unionized, semiskilled workers in the large, mass-production industries earn as much if not more than many people in white-collar occupations. Many white-collar and blue-collar incomes overlap. Income does not sufficiently differentiate people whose relation to the productive process is quite different.

Many social scientists have specified the *source* of income as a criterion of class: The combination of what people do in the division of labor (occupation) or of what they own (property), as well as what they

earn (income), can provide an adequate and revealing conception of stratification in economic terms. This concern constantly takes sociologists back to the writings of Karl Marx and Max Weber in order to understand what social class is.

Karl Marx on Class   *Political*

Marx's analysis of class begins with the recognition that the members of society are divided into economic strata, each stratum being made up of those who share a similar function in the organization of economic production. The division of labor at any time in the history of a society, based on the existing technology, creates what he calls the "mode of production"; that is, the set of social relationships among people as workers. This necessary cooperation in the division of labor separates people into different functions—such as peasant and landlord, worker and owner-employer—and provides the basis for the existence of social classes.

Marx believed that each person's participation in the productive process provides him with a crucial life experience, one that shapes his beliefs and strongly influences his actions. At the same time those who share similar positions have similar experiences, and so come to have similar attitudes and beliefs, a process fostered by frequent communication and interaction with one another. Furthermore, they share in time an awareness of economic interests and of conflict and disagreement with other strata over the distribution of wealth. One of Marx's definitions of class says much of this:

Insofar as millions of families live under economic conditions of existence that divide their mode of life, their interests and their culture from those of other classes, and put them into hostile contrast to the latter, they form a class.[11]

This "hostile contrast" is, for Marx, a necessary aspect of social class. In uniting to do "common battle" against another class, a stratum of workers or peasants becomes a social class. Otherwise, as Marx saw it, they are in individual competition with one another. While it is common to assert that Marx viewed economic factors as determining how people act, this conception of class is *political*. A social class, in his conception, exists only insofar as an economic stratum is aware of and is prepared to struggle for its economic interests against another class: ". . . the struggle of class against class is a political struggle."[12]

Max Weber on Class

Max Weber, like Marx, asserts that the economic organization of society is the basis of social class. People are in the same *class situation,* Weber says, when their occupations or ownership of property under the conditions of the commodity or labor market gives them a similar chance, however large or small, to obtain some of the things valued in a society: material goods, physical health, education, travel, leisure, and exposure to a wide range of highly prized social experiences. Some people have goods to sell to others, and it is this which determines their *life chances.* Other people sell their skills or labor on a labor market to available employers. Still others, such as professionals, offer highly valued and relatively scarce services to a clientele. Each of these constitutes a different "class situation." For Weber, class is a collectivity of people who share a common set of life chances as these are determined by property, occupation, and income. His specific definition is:

We may speak of a "class" when (1) a number of people have in common a specific casual component of their life-chances, in so far as (2) this component is represented exclusively by economic interests in the possession of goods and the opportunities for income, and (3) is represented under the conditions of the commodity or labor markets.[13]

Weber recognized the varied ways in which the possession of property and of goods by those who "do not necessarily have to exchange them" gave them an advantage in the market over those who have to sell their goods to survive or who have no goods but only their "services in native form." Weber sounded not too different than Marx when he said: " 'Property' and 'lack of property' are, therefore, the basic categories of all class situations."[14]

For both Marx and Weber social classes are outcomes of the differentials in social power that insure that unequal social rewards will accrue to various economic strata for their participation in the productive processes of the society.

The Multidimensionality of Stratification

Social class as economically-based stratification does not exhaust the forms which stratification takes, though it is the most

---

[11] See Karl Marx, *The Eighteenth Brumaire of Louis Bonaparte* (New York: International Publishers Company, Inc., n.d.), p. 109.

[12] See Karl Marx, *The Poverty of Philosophy* (New York: International Publishers Company, Inc., n.d.), pp. 145–146.

[13] See Max Weber, "Class, Status, and Party," in Hans Gerth and C. Wright Mills, eds., *From Max Weber: Essays in Sociology* (New York: Oxford University Press, 1946), p. 181.

[14] See Weber, *op. cit.,* p. 182.

important. Of all major students of stratification, Weber best took account of the complexity of stratification in suggesting such forms as *class, status,* and *party.*[15]

Status Groups

As distinct from class, according to Weber, status refers to the ranking of social groups by *prestige* and *honor*. A *status group* may be said to exist when a number of individuals occupy a similar position in the prestige ranking of their community, and when they recognize each other as equals and interact regularly with one another. They form friendship circles, dine together, belong to the same organizations, encourage the intermarrying of their children, and otherwise exhibit a common *style of life.*

Religious and Ethnic Status

Religion and ethnicity provide criteria not only for status in the community but also in society. The Jews, for example, are a people whose ancestry and traditions go far back in time; they have a specific identity, and they are more culturally homogeneous than many ethnic groups. Jews develop an organizational and community life that parallels that of other middle-class groups. They create their own associations and clubs, their own welfare organizations, indeed, all the forms of social life in a typical community. This not only gives them a sharp sense of separate identity and status it also gives others a conception of the Jews as a separate status group.

While higher status frequently goes to those who have established a community, or at least are long settled there, low status

equally frequently goes to those people who are the most recent arrivals, especially if they enter at a low economic level. This was usually the case with the great mass of immigrants who came to the United States from eastern and southern Europe after 1880. Relatively unskilled at first; largely from rural, peasant backgrounds; speaking little, if any, English—they clustered in immigrant colonies in America's rapidly growing industrial cities and soon constituted ethnic status groups that ranked low in the community.

Racial Status

When we speak of Jews and European immigrants we have reference to *cultural* criteria for distinguishing one status group from another. But *racial* criteria for status also enters into the issue. Race is a biological factor, and when race becomes a criterion for status, whether scientifically valid or not, the members of the society *evaluate the biological differences in terms of superior or inferior*. This may mean that they impute to race social differences (such as mental ability or moral character) that are not in fact empirically verifiable by scientific standards. But if people *believe* that such differences exist, they act accordingly; thus, the social consequence is to create a ranking of racial groups.

When criteria of status are racial, religious, and ethnic, and when those who rank low by such criteria are disesteemed by others and are denied the life chances accorded to others, we have *minority status* and *minority groups* with associated *prejudice* and *discrimination*. Obversely, those who rank high by such criteria—such as white, Anglo-Saxon Protestants (WASPs)—are advantaged. In either case, a common

[15] *See* Weber, *op. cit.,* p. 181.

status situation, like a common class situation, affects people's life chances.

Status and Class

Though it is useful to distinguish status from class, the two are always interlinked; status is never independent of class. Low status is usually associated with lower-class position, and high-status groups usually hold higher-class positions, though the relation may not be perfect. On the other hand, people in the same social class may be in different status groups: middle-class whites and blacks; Jews, Protestants, and Catholics, for example. In the upper class established families of old, inherited wealth often constitute a "high society" status group which is closed to less "cultured" new money—the *nouveaux riches*. However, the latter's children may be able to achieve social acceptance in high society, because they can be educated to the life style of an upper-status group, and because, unlike their self-made fathers, they did not have to work themselves up from a lower social level.

In preindustrial societies the distinction between class and status is less evident. Where there is little mobility from one social class to another, and thus where the same set of families occupies a particular class level from one generation to the next, the social interaction among them develops a commonly shared style of life. Peasants, artisans, merchants, and aristocrats in medieval society not only existed in different class situations, each also exhibited a common style of life quite different from other classes. In such cases, then, class and status merge into a single pattern of stratification.

Under conditions of relatively rapid so-cial mobility class and status diverge, and people in the same class situation may belong to different status groups. Weber recognized this when he observed:

> When the bases of the acquisition and distribution of goods are relatively stable, stratification by status is favored. Every technological repercussion and economic transformation threatens stratification by status and pushes the class situation into the foreground.[16]

Furthermore, focusing on both class and status as different dimensions of stratification makes more sense in understanding stratification in some societies than in others. Thus, Frank Parkin, a British sociologist, claims that:

> This "multi-dimensional" view of the reward system is perhaps useful in analyzing societies like the United States which are highly differentiated in terms of race or ethnicity, religious affiliation, and sharp regional variations (especially between north and south) as well as by social classes. But in societies like Britain and many other European countries, multiple cleavages of this kind tend to be rather less marked, so that the multi-dimensional model would seem to be less applicable.[17]

Party

Why does Weber put party with class and status in his forms of stratification? For Weber the three phenomena are linked by virtue of their being various aspects of social power. Parties, Weber observed, are structures organized to acquire power and thus to achieve domination, whatever their historic form. They may recruit followers

---

[16] *See* Weber, *op. cit.,* p. 194.

[17] Frank Parkin, *Class Inequality and Political Order: Social Stratification in Capitalist and Communist Societies* (New York: Frederick A. Praeger, Inc., 1971), p. 17.

from either classes or status groups, and thus be concerned with representing class or status interests in political struggles, or they may become neither class nor status parties exclusively, which is usually the case. Nonetheless, sociologists rarely deal with parties as an aspect of stratification. Instead, Weber's distinction between class and status has been incorporated into sociological analysis.

Community Status and Social Class

In the United States the work of a social anthropologist, W. Lloyd Warner, has greatly influenced the American study of social stratification, particularly his study of Newburyport, Massachusetts (Yankee City).[18] Warner and his associates studied how prestige was distributed in small communities, combining both economic and non-economic criteria in defining a series of "classes."

Warner developed a six-fold classification by taking the familiar terms—upper, middle, and lower—and dividing each into an upper and a lower. Thus, there is an upper-upper class, composed of the community's elite of long-standing, its old ruling families of high prestige; and a lower-upper class of rising families with newly-won wealth, eager to achieve social acceptance. (In some of the small Mid-

western towns studied, there was only a single upper, thus a five-class system.) The upper-middle class constitutes the established business and professional people; and the lower-middle class is made up of varied white-collar occupations, small businessmen, and skilled workers. The upper-lower is composed of skilled and other workers who are "respectable," though poor and who are hard-working; whereas the lower-lower includes the most economically depressed, whose way of life is generally not respected by other members of the community.

While this set of concepts was devised to characterize social class in small communities outside metropolitan areas, some of them nonetheless—particularly upper-middle and lower-middle—have entered the American vocabulary to designate approximately the same kinds of people that Warner did.

SOCIAL CLASS IN INDUSTRIAL SOCIETY

As a consequence of the Industrial Revolution in Europe two distinctly new class roles emerged. One was that of the Capitalist *entrepreneur*, who put up the capital for an enterprise; he thus had ownership of the machinery and materials that went into the production of goods, and so, too, of the finished commodities. These he sold for profit on the market. He combined in his person the functions of managing and owning a business.

The contrasting role was that of the *worker*. He was employed to operate machinery by which goods were produced; and he was paid a wage for his work. He did not own the machinery he operated. He was an employee, and was property-less in the sense that the tools of produc-

[18] The several volumes of the *Yankee City* series (New Haven, Conn.: Yale University Press) are: W. L. Warner and P. S. Lunt, *The Social Life of a Modern Community* (1941); W. L. Warner and Leo Srole, *The Social System of American Ethnic Groups* (1945); W. L. Warner and J. O. Low, *The Social System of the Modern Factory* (1947); W. Lloyd Warner, *The Living and the Dead* (1959). Warner summarized these studies in a single volume, *American Life, Dream and Reality* (Chicago, Ill.: University of Chicago Press, 1962).

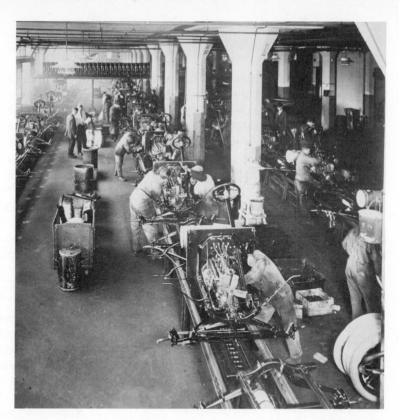

Figure 10.2 The worker does not own the machinery he operates and in that sense, as an employee, is propertyless. *(Courtesy of the Ford Archives, Henry Ford Museum, Dearborn, Michigan.)*

tion belonged not to him but to the *entrepreneur*.

The industrial process under capitalism with its private ownership of property, then, created two basic social classes, a *middle class* and a *working class*. Under early industrialism these classes were rather clearly separated. One earned profits, the other wages; one class was self-employed and employed others, the other was employed. Wages were relatively low, and a considerable difference in standard of living separated the two classes. The ownership of property, specifically the tools of production, and the independent status of self-employment, as well as the authority inherent in being an employer, became the symbols of middle-class prestige and respectability.

But as industrialism advanced, as large industrial organizations replaced the many smaller family enterprises; as the indi-

vidualistic, competitive capitalism of the eighteenth century became twentieth-century corporate capitalism, a modification of class structure occurred.

The Middle Classes

With the growth of large-scale enterprise over the last eighty years, a wide range of new, white-collar positions were created. These technical and administrative positions are salaried; and the individuals are employees. Thus, they are not middle-class in the nineteenth-century sense of the term; they do not derive income from profit nor own the business. Yet they are not in the same stratum as wage-earners. Their positions often require a great deal of training; and as highly specialized persons, they work with less supervision or direction than do workers. In their managerial capacities they exercise authority over others. Furthermore, their compensation exceeds that of workers, often several times over. Consequently, sociologists have found it useful to recognize an *old* middle class and a *new* middle class.[19]

The Old Middle Class

The old middle class is made up of those whose relation to property is one of ownership, who operate their own individual or family enterprises, and whose income is derived as profits from the ownership and operation of such a business. In addition, the old middle class includes the "free" (self-employed) professionals, who "hang out their shingles," and conduct a private practice in law, medicine, dentistry, and the like. Their incomes are derived from the fees paid them by their clients.

The New Middle Class

The new middle class, in turn, covers a wide range of salaried, white-collar positions. The salaried manager or executive, the technical specialist, and the salaried professional make up this class. A combination of skills and specialized knowledge are necessary for these middle-class occupations, some of which are professionalized, most of which are specialized and skilled. There is also the development of the office staff, those routine, subordinate clerical positions in large organizations. These have been filled mainly by women.

Class and Occupation

Occupation alone does not distinguish between the old and new middle class. For example, two different persons might

be accountants. But if one operates his own accounting business he is a small businessman of the old middle class; whereas the other, who is employed at a salary, is not. The occupation is the same, but the class position is different. Similarly, a lawyer with an independent practice is old middle class, but a salaried lawyer working for a corporation or a large law firm is a salaried professional of the new middle class.

The old middle class has been declining throughout this century, while the new middle class has been expanding relatively rapidly. In 1971 only about 12 percent of employed persons in the United States were self-employed.[20] (Table 10.1 provides recent data on incomes of both the old and new middle classes in the United States in 1971.)

Upper and Lower Middle Class

If we can make a distinction between old and new middle classes, we can also make a distinction between upper- and lower-middle classes, though perhaps not as precisely. It is not difficult to perceive an upper-middle class of salaried professionals, managerial executives, and other college-educated professionals on the one hand, and independent professionals and owner-operators of larger businesses on the other. The large white-collar army of sales and clerical personnel make up a lower-middle class, as do those small merchants, businessmen, and small farmers who own and operate numerous small enterprises.

---

[19] *See* C. Wright Mills, *White Collar* (New York: Oxford University Press, 1953).

[20] U.S. Bureau of the Census, *Current Population Reports,* Series P-60, no. 85, "Money Income in 1971 of Families and Persons in the United States" (Washington, D.C.: Government Printing Office, 1972), p. 88.

THE VOCABULARY OF CLASS IN THE UNITED STATES

The United States has never developed any stable vocabulary of class, any agreed-upon set of terms by which Americans can identify themselves and others. When asked what class they belong in, most Americans use terms like average, moderate, and the like—anything but upper and lower. And many cannot think of any appropriate term.*

The most frequently cited evidence for this "middling" view of class by Americans is a Gallup poll, which asked a national sample of Americans if they thought they were upper, middle, or lower class. The results.**

Upper class	6 percent
Middle class	88 percent
Lower class	6 percent

However, when psychologist Richard Centers added *working class* to the other three terms, the results were:†

Upper class	3 percent
Middle class	43 percent
Working class	51 percent
Lower class	1 percent
Don't know	1 percent
Don't believe in classes	1 percent

These data from national polls go back almost three decades. Has there been any change since then? A recent study, done in 1964, showed the following:††

Upper class	2.2 percent
Upper-middle class	16.6 percent
Middle class	44.0 percent
Working class	34.3 percent
Lower class	2.3 percent
No classes exist	0.6 percent

Some decline in working-class identification and some increase in middle-class identification seems to have occurred since the 1940s, perhaps reflecting actual shifts in occupational patterns since that time.

---

* *See,* for example, the *Fortune* survey, *Fortune Magazine,* February 1940.

** George Gallup and S. F. Rae, *The Pulse of Democracy* (New York: Simon and Schuster, Inc., 1940), p. 169.

† Richard Centers, *The Psychology of Social Classes* (Princeton, N.J.: Princeton University Press, 1949), p. 77.

†† Robert W. Hodges and Donald Tremain, "Class Identification in the United States," *American Journal of Sociology,* vol. 73 (March 1968), pp. 535–547.

TABLE 10.1   Total Money Income for Males in White-collar Occupations, 1971

	Self-employed Professional and Technical Workers	Self-employed Managers and Administrators	Salaried Professionals and Technical Workers	Salaried Managers and Administrators	Clerical Workers
Under $7,000	19.9	34.4	19.7	13.3	35.8
$7,000– 9,999	8.7	19.1	20.1	18.7	19.6
$10,000–14,999	16.6	22.1	32.7	29.7	29.1
$15,000–24,999	21.9	16.0	22.2	26.7	4.7
$25,000 and over	32.9	8.4	5.4	11.6	0.8
Mean income	$21,674	$11,687	$12,366	$15,002	$8,321

Source: U.S. Bureau of the Census, *Current Population Reports*, Series P-60, no. 85, "Money Income in 1971 of Families and Persons in the United States" (Washington, D.C.: Government Printing Office, 1972), Table 50, p. 120.

In any modern society the upper-middle class has an importance out of all proportion to its numbers, for it is the standard-bearer of what modern is. Its members provide organizational and institutional leadership; they control the development of ideas and imagery in the media, in the universities, and in the intellectual and scholarly communities. They are the educated people, the modernizing ones, who set the standards and norms for the whole society. They travel widely, read extensively, and are well-informed; and they are oriented not to local culture but to national and international networks of like-minded people. They define the problems and issues that get national attention. Their beliefs and sympathies have important consequences in action and policy; so do their blind spots and prejudices.

The Working Classes

Since the worker in modern industry never was self-employed, the distinction between old and new, as in the middle class, does not apply to the working class. There is, however, a plurality of working classes. Broad spectrum.

Perhaps the basic working class, under industrial conditions, has been that of semiskilled individuals directly involved in operating the machinery of industrial production. This broad stratum of blue-collar workers has been organized in mass unions in the United States since the 1930s, in Europe even earlier.

But there is also a class of workers, such as those in the tool and die industry and skilled craftsmen in the construction trades, whose high skills bring good wages and working conditions. They are the "cream" of the working class. Often they are organized in craft unions.

Below these classes there is a class of unskilled laborers, employed in factories and in service industries, whose training and experience count for little and whose wages and security of employment are both low. There is also a shrinking class of domestic servants, still a form of employment for a large number of women, mostly black. In the agricultural area farm laborers, including migratory workers, constitute another kind of lower working class.

The unskilled and underemployed—in whose ranks are what is now called *the working poor*—suffer by comparison with the working classes in social power (they are not usually organized), in income, and in job security. Their ranks are now increased by the addition of many of those dispossessed by mechanized agriculture (and mechanized mining in Appalachia) in rural America; a disproportionate number of them are black.

Class Consciousness and Embourgeoisement

Studies of workers in Europe, as well as in the United States, give support to the idea that industrial workers no longer possess the militant class consciousness so evident in the nineteenth century and even in the decade of the 1930s. Certainly, violent class struggles have declined in the Western industrial nations, and have been replaced by unions and collective bargaining. This, in turn, has suggested an *embourgeoisement*—becoming middle class —of the workers as they have shared in society's affluence. One sociologist, for example, says:

The time honored invidious distinctions between the style of life of middle class employees and manual workers have become blurred to a considerable extent. The rising standard of living has made many elements of a middle class style of life, such as home ownership, suburban living, paid vacations, and highly valued consumer goods, available not only to white collar employees but also to large numbers of manual wage earners.[21]

Sociologist James Rinehart has taken a hard look at all available data and studies and has come to the conclusion that "the extent of working class embourgeoisement

[21] *See* Kurt B. Mayer, "The Changing Shape of the American Class Structure," in Jack Roach, Llewellyn Gross, and Orville Gursslin, eds., *Social Stratification in the United States* (Englewood Cliffs, N.J.: Prentice-Hall, Inc., 1969), p. 584.

has been exaggerated. The middle-class manual worker is more a mythical figure than a reality."[22] Rinehart describes the economic situation of blue-collar workers as not yet equal to that of white-collar workers in earnings. He cites 1969 data on median income of white-collar males as evidence:

Sales workers	$9,233
Clerical and kindred occupations	$7,942

Blue-collar workers earned median incomes as follows:[23]

Craftsmen and foremen	$8,741
Operatives and kindred workers	$7,324
Laborers	$6,024

Furthermore, blue-collar workers lack the job security of white-collar workers and do not share equally in mobility opportunities. (Table 10.2 provides data on the income of blue-collar workers in the United States in 1971.)

Any discussion of "affluent" American families must recognize that in two families out of five in 1971, both husband and wife worked. The difference between the two mean incomes reported in Table 10.3 suggests that an employed wife adds, on the average, about 20 percent to the family income.

Is There an Upper Class?

The assertion that the working class and the middle class were the two basic classes

[22] *See* James W. Rinehart, "Affluence and the Embourgeoisement of the Working Class: A Critical Look," *Social Problems,* vol. 19 (Fall 1971), p. 159.

[23] Rinehart's source: U.S. Bureau of the Census, Current Population Reports, Series P-60, no. 75, "Income in 1969 of Families and Persons in the United States" (Washington, D.C.: Government Printing Office, 1970).

TABLE 10.2   Total Money Income for Males in Blue-collar Occupations, 1971

	Craftsmen	Operatives	Service Workers	Laborers
Under $7,000	29.7	46.9	62.5	68.4
$7,000–9,999	29.7	30.3	19.4	21.3
$10,000–14,999	31.6	20.6	15.3	8.6
$15,000–24,999	8.7	2.2	2.6	1.4
$25,000 and over	0.5	0.2	0.2	0.2
Mean income	$9,177	$7,247	$5,987	$5,173

Source: U.S. Bureau of the Census, *Current Population Reports*, Series P-60, no. 85, "Money Income in 1971 of Families and Persons in the United States" (Washington, D.C.: Government Printing Office, 1972), Table 50, p. 120.

to emerge from industrialization seems to imply that no upper class now exists. The term originally applied to a landed aristocracy, a ruling class whose wealth was derived from the ownership of large agricultural estates in an agrarian society, and whose power enabled it to monopolize the functions of political management and decision-making. Industrialization seriously undercut the privileged position and entrenched class power of the aristocracy. Land became subordinate to industry as a source of wealth, and democratic revolutions overthrew the ruling aristocracy.

Since then the term upper class has had no consistent meaning. Some would argue

that historically the upper class passed out of existence. Others apply the term to those who are simply the wealthiest. An upper class, if one exists, ought to be distinguished from upper-middle class by income, by power, privilege, style of life, and by function in the division of labor. Does such a class exist in the United States?

Sociologists divide between two perspectives. One sees an old upper class of families of great wealth, usually with income derived from extensive investments and property holdings, not from occupation. Upper-class families are characterized by a distinctive and exclusive life style, based

Table 10.3   Income of Families with Male Head by Employment of Wife in 1971

Percent Earning	Wife in Paid Labor Force	Wife Not in Paid Labor Force
Under $10,000	30.6	51.7
$10,000–14,999	32.9	26.5
$15,000–24,999	29.7	16.1
Over $25,000	6.6	5.6
Mean income	$13,882	$11,307

Source: U.S. Bureau of the Census, *Current Population Reports*, Series P-60, no. 85, "Money Income in 1971 of Families and Persons in the United States" (Washington, D.C.: Government Printing Office, 1972), Table 17, p. 43.

on family wealth, family lineage, and unique patterns of socialization.[24]

The other perspective focuses on a widely proclaimed distinction between ownership and control in private industry as the basis for defining a new *managerial class*, which takes on the corporate decision-making function without possessing ownership. More than thirty years ago James Burnham predicted the emergence of the managerial class as the ruling class of industrial society, the makers of a non-Marxian revolution in which a managerial elite replaced a propertied elite.[25] (For a discussion of the social-scientific debate on this issue, *see* Chapter 14.)

But C. Wright Mills argued that the considerable incomes of the new managerial class permitted them not to displace the propertied elite but to merge with them "into the more or less unified stratum of the corporate rich."[26] More recently, sociologist C. William Domhoff, followed up on Mills, culminating several years of research on high status and social power in sketching out a portrait of a national upper class, cohesive on the basis of in-group interaction and common life style:

...I believe it can be argued that the upper class is more cohesive than any other level of the American social hierarchy. Its smaller size, greater wealth, different sources of income (stocks and bonds), different schooling, different leisure activities, and different occupations, not to mention its complicated web of intermarriages, are evidence for this statement.[27]

Social Class under Communism and Capitalism

The most familiar sociological analyses of class emphasize the nature of class structure under *industrialism*, largely ignoring any differences that might occur between Communist and Capitalist societies, both types of which are industrial. Usually the point is made that, despite the ideological claims of Marxism, there have developed structured inequalities in Communist societies much like those in Capitalist societies.

Such a broad similarity, however, may obscure some differences between the two types of societies that are worth noting. Frank Parkin, a British sociologist who has examined this issue, begins with laying out what he believes to be the basic reward system of advanced Western capitalist societies:[28]

Professional, managerial and administrative
Semi-professional and lower administrative
Routine white collar
Skilled manual
Semi-skilled manual
Unskilled manual

Parkin then looked for a significant "break" in the reward hierarchy and argued that "...in Western capitalist societies this line of cleavage falls between the manual and non-manual occupational categories."[29] This is so, Parkin insisted, even though there is an overlap in the *incomes* of the lesser white-collar occupations with the more skilled manual workers. But the overlap obscures other differences; reward is always more than income.

[24] *See* E. Digby Baltzell, *Philadelphia Gentlemen: The Making of a National Upper Class* (New York: The Free Press, 1958).

[25] James Burnham, *The Managerial Revolution* (New York: The John Day Company, Inc., 1941).

[26] C. Wright Mills, *The Power Elite* (New York: Oxford University Press, 1956), p. 147.

[27] *See* G. William Domhoff, *The Higher Circles: The Governing Class in America* (New York: Random House, Inc., 1970), p. 97.

[28] *See* Frank Parkin, *Class Inequality and Political Order: Social Stratification in Capitalist and Communist Societies* (New York: Frederick A. Praeger, Inc., 1971), p. 19.

[29] *See* Parkin, *op. cit.*, p. 25.

Figure 10.3 The managerial class has developed out of corporate growth. Its members—like (*left to right*) Alan Greenspan of the National Association of Business Economists, B.W. Sprinkel of the Harris Trust and Savings Bank, A.J. Karchers of IBM, and T.C. Gaines of Manufacturers Hanover Trust—often make decisions for owners but are not owners themselves. (*Wide World Photos.*)

Class Inequality in the Soviet Union

The Soviet Union has not maintained a consistent position on the matter of class and equality. The Revolution in 1917 brought about a period of greater equalization of rewards, as well as of social opportunities. But in the early 1930s Stalin attacked "equality-mongering" and declared greater material incentives and privileges had to be offered as a stimulus to get people to learn skills and assume responsibilities in building an industrial society. From this development the Soviet Union built a complex and highly differentiated reward structure; in the 1940s further changes in taxes favored the better paid and further increased inequality.

After Stalin's death, however, some of the trends to greater inequality were reversed. The minimum wage level was raised; a variety of workers were granted raises so as to reduce differentials among various skilled categories. The income tax became more progressive, easing the burden on lower income groups.

Inequality in Eastern Europe

In the Communist societies of eastern Europe the fluctuations between equalitarian and inequalitarian trends have not been as sharp as they have been in the Soviet Union, but similar reactions have occurred. After an early period of socializing property and reducing class differentials of reward, similar campaigns against "equality-mongering" appeared in the 1950s, producing greater inequality among the range of occupations so that Parkin could say: "It is certainly the case that in eastern, as in western, Europe the occupational reward hierarchy tends to correspond to the hierarchy of skill and expertise."[30]

[30] *See* Parkin, *op. cit.,* p. 147.

However, here, too, increasing inequality was halted by government action, and in the 1960s blue-collar workers had been put into a more favorable position.

Blue-collar and White-collar in Communist Societies

In these Communist societies "highly skilled or craft manual workers enjoy a higher position in the scale of material and status rewards than do lower white-collar employees."[31] In Yugoslavia, for example, in 1961 skilled workers on the average earned about 25 percent more than office staff, while the latter earned about 35 percent more than unskilled laborers. Indeed, by 1964, manual workers averaged better incomes than did lower white-collar workers in Bulgaria, Hungary, Czechoslovakia, and the Soviet Union; only Poland was an exception.[32] Such differences have affected the distribution of occupational prestige. Skilled workers have a higher social standing in these countries than do the routine white-collar positions. The overall reward hierarchy, according to Parkin, in contrast to the Capitalist societies, runs as follows:[33]

White-collar intelligentsia (professional, managerial, and administrative positions)
Skilled manual positions
Lower or unqualified white-collar positions
Unskilled manual positions.

On the basis of this hierarchy, Parkin claims that the reward structure of these societies does not break between manual and non-manual as clearly as it does in Western societies. Instead, "... the most obvious break in the reward hierarchy oc-curs along the line separating the qualified professional, managerial, and technical positions from the rest of the occupational order."[34]

SOCIAL MOBILITY — movement in stratification structure.

How people are recruited for the class positions of society opens up a complex and often controversial issue, that of social mobility. If each social class transmits its property and position to the next generation within its own ranks, then each social strata is *closed* and there is no mobility. If, instead, there is no such transmission by mechanisms of inheritance, then the system is *open* and there is social mobility.

Industrial societies are usually categorized as open, in contrast to the caste and estate systems. But such openness is relative, and the contrast with caste and estate systems may unwittingly be exaggerated. What becomes crucial about open systems is that expectations and aspirations of mobility are developed, and a claim is made, at least in the United States, about *equality of opportunity;* namely, the equal chance to be mobile. *But, there is not and never has been an equal chance for individuals in all social classes to be mobile.*

horizontal — moving but retaining same class.

Structural Mobility

What makes mobility a reality is a change in occupational structure, enlarging the range and proportion of middle and upper-level occupations while reducing the proportion of lower-level ones. By first moving peasants into urban occupations and later increasing white-collar occupations, the transition from an agrarian to an industrial economy provides social mobility not imagined before. Mobility created by changes

---

[31] *See* Parkin, *op. cit.,* p. 146.
[32] *See* Parkin, *op. cit.,* p. 144. His source of data is the United Nations *Economic Survey of Europe in 1965,* Part II.
[33] *See* Parkin, *op. cit.,* p. 147.

[34] *See* Parkin, *op. cit.,* p. 149.

in the occupational structure of the society is *structural* mobility (sometimes called *forced* mobility).

But social change does not stop at the transition from agricultural to industrial society. Rather, advanced industrial countries move beyond the predominance of manufacturing occupations to develop the *tertiary* branch of the economy: trade, transportation, communication, and personal and professional services. At the same time agricultural employment declines both proportionately and absolutely, while manufacturing declines proportionately. This change increases white-collar and middle-class occupations.

An advanced industrial society, then, expands the proportion of middle-level occupations through technological and commercial development and reduces physical and unskilled labor. These developments, rather than individual effort primarily account for social mobility. This is true of any industrial society, whether that society is Capitalist or Socialist.

The Soviet Union, for example, has undergone rapid industrialization since the Russian Revolution of 1917. In the process millions of peasants have been shifted to urban occupations, and higher education has increased considerably as a necessary means of training large numbers of people for varied technical and professional fields. The industrialization of the Soviet Union simply created a great middle stratum where it had not existed before.

Mobility and the Family

The family is the social unit through which an individual is placed into the class structure. Through the family the child inherits property, occupation, educational opportunity, life style, family connections, even titles and legal privileges. In non-industrial societies this may constitute the major process for locating individuals in the social structure. In industrial societies inheritance processes do not guarantee transmission of social status by kinship to nearly the same extent, but such societies do not eliminate inheritance as a significant process.

Family and Education

Even where the family cannot transmit property to the next generation, it nonetheless seeks to maximize the social chances of its children. Middle-class people seek preferred educational opportunities for their children, to teach them what they believe to be the attributes of successful people, to provide them with the necessary credentials, and in other ways to increase their children's chances of being mobile.

For the nonpropertied classes particularly, education is a necessity in the mobility process. Educational opportunities have never been equally open to all economic levels, though the growth of public education to the university level has widened the chances for an education and made it no longer the narrow class privilege it once was. In the nineteenth century individuals gained entrance into the middle class by accumulating some modest capital; in the twentieth century a college education more and more becomes the "social capital" necessary to make one's way into the middle class. Differences in the ability of families to make a college education possible, financially and culturally, are now as crucial as accumulating and transmitting property once was.

Family and Life Style

In other ways, too, families of higher social status improve the mobility chances of their children. Having fewer children, for example, increases the chances of a family to do more for the children it does have; in all industrial societies the upper economic levels have fewer children than do those of the lower economic levels.

But perhaps more importantly, upper-status families improve the mobility chances of their children by their very life style. A child of a professional person is exposed to the cultural atmosphere and a pattern of attitudes and values appropriate to and expected of someone at that class level. In subtle ways they are prepared for a professional or equivalent occupation by their childhood socialization. Such a child has a distinct advantage over the offspring of a factory worker.

Inheriting Occupation

Studies of social mobility seem to indicate that most people are not mobile, and that what mobility does occur is not usually from bottom to top but instead a small movement from one level to the next. In one of the recent studies, for example, the authors report that 30 percent of the men in the sample had "inherited" their fathers' occupational levels. Most of the others usually moved only to an adjacent or near-adjacent category.[35] Furthermore, they note, such occupational inheritance is especially marked for sons of professionals; 40.4 percent of the professionals in their national sample were the sons of professionals.[36]

Perhaps more revealing evidence comes when the authors collapse their urban occupational distinctions into manual and nonmanual. Then:

. . . the data show that almost one third of the sons of nonmanual workers fall into the manual stratum and the same proportion of manual sons rise into nonmanual jobs; about two-thirds of the sons from both origins are stable . . .[37]

The available facts tell us that social mobility is real enough, but that there is undoubtedly much less than the myths about equal opportunity would have one believe.

Social Mobility in Europe and America

Americans readily believe that the chance to be mobile is greater in the United States—"the land of opportunity" —than in any European society. Furthermore, Europeans seem also to believe this. Does such a view rest on solid evidence? What is accepted as a widespread impression is not necessarily a fact.

It is not easy to decide this, for data that allow accurate comparisons are hard to come by. But in the 1950s a study by sociologists Seymour Lipset and Reinhard Bendix undertook such an effort, and more studies have followed.[38]   *cross-cultural studies*

Lipset and Bendix divided their data into a simple manual-nonmanual distinction for a number of industrial countries— existing data did not permit a more refined breakdown. They computed the *upward* mobility of manual workers' sons into nonmanual occupations, the downward mobility of nonmanual workers' sons into manual occupations, and from this computed an index of total vertical mobility, expressing this as a percentage of the total

[35] *See* Elton F. Jackson and Harry J. Crockett, Jr., "Occupational Mobility in the United States: A Point Estimate and Trend Comparison," *American Sociological Review,* vol. 29 (February 1964), p. 6.

[36] *See* Jackson and Crockett, *op. cit.,* Table 1, p. 7.

[37] *See* Jackson and Crockett, *op. cit.,* p. 9.

[38] *See* Seymour M. Lipset and Reinhard Bendix, *Social Mobility in Industrial Society* (Berkeley, Calif.: University of California Press, 1959).

number of sons in each national sample. The resulting index varied only a little from one industrial society to another, from a high of 31 percent for Germany to a low of 23 percent for Switzerland.

More recently, Lenski has computed a similar manual-nonmanual index based on data from a variety of sources; he lists the United States as first with a mobility rate of 34 percent.[39] But five other countries— Sweden, Great Britain, Denmark, Norway, and France—are only a few percentages below that. The consistency in such data leads to the conclusion that mobility is fairly similar in all industrial societies. Perhaps the most basic finding is that upward mobility for manual workers' sons is largely into the more modest white-collar positions, and mobility into the upper, elitist levels of occupations is most possible for those who start halfway up the scale.

Social Mobility in Communist Europe

How does social mobility in the Western industrial (and Capitalist) societies compare with that of Eastern Europe? Because of difficulties in getting comparable data, few sociologists have dared to make any comparisons. But Frank Parkin has sought out data from Communist societies and attempted some comparison.[40] From a quite subtle discussion we can abstract two basic points. One is that the dominant class of managers and professionals, like such classes in Capitalist societies, is able to transmit competitive advantage to their own children.

Evidence from Eastern Europe does in fact suggest that those born into the white-collar

intelligentsia tend to do well in the competition for academic honors. As a result they enter occupations similar to those of their parents; very few become manual workers or lower white-collar employees.[41]

The other point is that, though privileged classes assure high position for their children, there is nonetheless much social mobility for peasants and manual workers in Eastern Europe. The increase in white-collar positions as a consequence of industrial expansion has provided a level of mobility for those lower in occupational rank that exceeds that level of mobility in the United States and Western Europe. Parkin cited a 1963 study of Hungary, for example, that showed that 77 percent of managerial, administrative, and professional positions were filled by men and women of peasant and worker origin; and that 53 percent of doctors, scientists, and engineers were from such families.[42]

Furthermore, argues Parkin, this *fact* of social mobility has encouraged high aspirations among the working classes: "... parents' ambitions for their children are pitched much higher in socialist than in capitalist society."[43] This is true to such an extent that the numbers of aspiring young people is greater than the number of higher positions available.

It does not follow that such mobility will continue indefinitely into the future. Once a new, dominant class comes into being and its own children have distinct advantages in the recruitment for higher positions, and once the period of rapid change in the occupational structure is over, what then? Parkin acknowledges that whether the openness of the Socialist sys-

[39] *See* Lenski, *Power and Privilege*, p. 411.
[40] *See* Parkin, "The Problem of Classes in Socialist Society," Ch. V, pp. 137–159.

[41] *See* Parkin, *op. cit.*, p. 154.
[42] *See* Parkin, *op. cit.*, p. 155.
[43] *See* Parkin, *op. cit.*, p. 156.

upper lower class — determined children get ed.

Figure 10.4 Professional athletes like Hank Aaron have found alternate routes to a higher status in American society. *(Wide World Photos.)*

tem can be maintained over the long run is a crucial issue for which no answer is now available.

Coping with Limits on Mobility

If most people are not mobile, or are only modestly so, the question of how they cope with this reality in a society like the United States, which upholds mobility and claims there is opportunity for all, becomes an important issue.

The Immobiles

What do people in a modern society do when they cannot be mobile? One possibility is to define oneself as a failure, as lacking in what is required for success. But this is highly self-punishing; most people hedge in assuming that it is entirely a matter of their own deficiencies, though

conceptions of low self-esteem may be internalized.

Alternatively, a person can alter his aspirations by expecting and being satisfied with much less than he once hoped for. Individuals lower their aspirations over time to fit the modest gains in status they can realistically accomplish. Some people also come to believe that chance plays an important part in their mobility. The only difference between themselves and a more mobile person, they believe, is a "lucky break."

Other people recognize their own non-mobility as fact, but transfer their unrealized aspirations to their children. Sociologist Eli Chinoy found this phenomenon among automobile workers, who knew they were not going to escape from factory work or move up in the factory hierarchy but who maintained strong hopes that their children would make it into middle-class occupations.[44] In this way, they were able to keep alive in themselves a belief in opportunity in America.

Alternate Routes to Mobility

Between those who are mobile and those who are not there is a quite different category: Those who are mobile but not by moving up within the typical structure of business and professional occupations. A movie or television star, a recording and concert rock music performer, or a professional baseball or football star are successes, too, for they are mobile. A person who has achieved high political office is also a success. So is a high-ranking labor leader.

Popular entertainment, professional athletics, politics, and labor, then, are each an avenue for career mobility in American society. A successful entertainer or athlete can attain wealth and public fame. Through labor and politics power can be attained. Popular entertainment, professional athletics, and politics may lead to social acceptance from the more conventional high-status people and so insure middle or upper-class status for the children of such a person. Labor leaders often transfer middle-class status to their children.

Social mobility through these avenues does not require the usual certificates of education and professional training, though it may require long years of hard work, practice, and accumulated experience. For those who have ability and ambition but lack formal training, a career in one of these ways can provide mobility not otherwise possible. This explains why so many people in these fields come from lower-status backgrounds, particularly from minority groups.

THE FUTURE OF SOCIAL CLASS

The transition from an agricultural to an industrial society radically altered the class structure of modern society. But what of the future? A post-modern society will clearly affect occupations and also social classes, though just how is obviously difficult to perceive. There are two major trends, however, that are basic to any conception of the direction which stratification will take in even the near future: a trend in the occupational base of social classes and trends in the distribution of wealth.

Trends in Class Structure

Since the class structure of industrial society is a direct product of its division of labor, anything that is likely to alter the division of labor will influence social class. Technological developments that eliminate occupations and create new ones change the division of labor and thus the class structure. In part, the emergence of new middle-class positions, for example, arises from the development of new professional and technical fields; these are most likely to be salaried positions, requiring considerable training, and will probably be in large public and private organizations.

Throughout this century in the United States, from 1900 to 1969, there has been a dramatic shift away from farm occupations to urban ones, and from blue-collar to white-collar occupations (*see* Table 10.4). In 1900 only 17.6 percent of all workers were white-collar; but in 1956 the percentage had surpassed those in blue-collar jobs,

---

[44] Eli Chinoy, *Automobile Workers and the American Dream* (New York: Random House, Inc., 1955).

Figure 10.5 Labor Leader Walter Reuther, here addressing the CIO Auto Workers Union heads, typifies the man from a working-class background who wins a higher social place by means of his career. *(Wide World Photos.)*

and the proportion increases steadily. By now, almost half of the employed are in white-collar jobs, while blue-collar jobs have remained a fairly stable proportion of all jobs.

The greatest change has occurred in farming. In 1900 more people were in farm jobs than in any other category. By 1950 this figure was down to 12.4 percent. Since

then it has continued to decline rapidly, so that by 1969 only 4 percent of the labor force was in farming.

There seems to be no reason to assume any change in this basic trend in at least the near future. Sociologist Daniel Bell, for example, has computed projections for 1980 in the basic four work categories given in Table 10.4. Look at the 1969 fig-

TABLE 10.4 Percentages in Major Occupational Groups, 1900–1969, in the United States

	1900	1950	1969
White-collar workers	17.6	37.5	47.6
Blue-collar workers	35.8	39.1	35.7
Service workers	9.0	10.9	12.6
Farmworkers	37.5	12.4	4.0

Source: For 1900 data: Bureau of the Census, *Historical Statistics of the United States, Colonial Times to 1959,* p. 74; for 1950 and 1969 data, *Statistical Abstracts of the United States, 1969,* p. 222.

ures and compare them to these estimates for 1960.[45]

White collar workers	50.8
Blue-collar workers	32.7
Service workers	13.8
Farm workers	2.7

If the trend continues indefinitely, there will be a substantial decline in the working class as it has been historically defined.

At the same time many social scientists have been speaking of a "new" working class, white-collar rather than blue-collar, performing technical functions in an even more technologized society, employed in large organizations but not possessing managerial prerogatives and powers. According to social critic Michael Harrington, "the new technology is calling into life a new class structure."[46]

Harrington sees the new class as coming to be a significant force in American social life:

The new stratum on which we focus is not based upon property or employment in the private corporation. Its members work, for the most part, in public, or semipublic sectors—education, health, social services, defense and defense-related industries, aerospace—and are therefore dependent on federal political decisions for their economic well-being. They also tend to be employed by large organizations and often, for all their educational attainments, they are subordinate participants in a hierarchical system.[47]

It is this publicly-based position that orients them to white-collar unionism and to politics, according to Harrington—and

white-collar unions have been the fastest growing unions in recent years.[48]

There is much debate and disagreement among both European and American scholars over this new working class, and about whether it will be a progressive political force or not. But the emergence of a large and steadily growing white-collar aggregate of technically trained people in administratively subordinate positions now seems to be a basic trend. Combined with the decline of farmers and farm laborers, as well as blue-collar workers, this trend suggests a major change in the society's occupational structure, into new patterns in life changes for most people, and in the occupational and class basis of democratic politics.

Trends in the Distribution of Wealth

The trends in occupation and rising productivity in the United States, accompanied by social reforms instituted in the 1930s, created a widely shared conception of a more equitable distribution of wealth than was true in the years before the Depression. But research by Robert Lampman and others, the consumer surveys of the University of Michigan, and government data all refute such an impression.[49] There is

---

[48] The fastest-growing union is the American Federation of State, County, and Municipal Employees; 40 percent of its membership is white-collar, including engineers, scientists, and medical technicians. The second fastest-growing union is the American Federation of Teachers.

[49] For a summary and evaluation of these several sources of data see Ferdinand Lundberg, *The Rich and the Super-Rich* (New York: Bantam Books, 1969). *See also* Gabriel Kolko, *Wealth and Power in America* (New York: Frederick A. Praeger, Inc., 1962).

[45] *See* Daniel Bell, "Labor in the Post-industrial Society," *Dissent* (Winter 1972), Table 5, p. 172.

[46] *See* Michael Harrington, "Old Working Class, New Working Class," *Dissent* (Winter 1972), p. 159.

[47] *See* Harrington, *op. cit.,* pp. 159–160.

as great an inequality in the distribution of wealth now, if not a greater one, than was true in the 1920s.

Take, as examples, some few items from a rich body of data. The wealthiest 1 percent of the population own:[50]

About 80 percent of all publicly-held corporate stocks
About all (tax-exempt) state and local government bonds
About 40 percent of all federal bonds
36 percent of all mortgages and notes
About 30 percent of the nation's cash.

If one looks at total wealth from all sources, one-half of 1 percent (0.5 percent) of the adult population have at least one-third of the nation's private-sector wealth.[51]

In terms of personal money income (including money-in-kind expense accounts) the top 20 percent of families has received over 40 percent of such income since World War II. The bottom 20 percent of families, in turn, has received but 5 percent of the total (see Table 10.5).

Nor does the federal income tax serve to redistribute wealth. In general, poor peo-ple pay out a higher proportion of their income in taxes than do wealthy people. For example, persons with incomes of less than $2,000 are the heaviest taxed—19 percent of their income in federal taxes, 25 percent in state and local taxes, for a total of 44 percent of their incomes.[52] In contrast, persons with incomes from $2,000 to $15,000 pay out around 27 percent of income in taxes. For persons over $15,000, the total tax rate is 38 percent. The top 1 percent in income pay only 26 percent in federal tax rates (excluding capital gains and dividends), which is less than those who earn under $2,000.

These data—and more—document the enormous disparity in material rewards. A more progressive tax structure does have an effect on income redistribution in some (but not all) European countries, but considerable disparity remains. Even in the Soviet Union and other Communist countries there are those who earn much higher than average incomes, plus receiving such privileges as access to automobiles and country homes comparable to the expense-account benefits of Capitalist societies.

[50] See Robert Lampman, The Share of Top Wealth-holders in National Wealth (Princeton, N.J.: Princeton University Press, 1962), p. 8 ff.
[51] See Ferdinand Lundberg, op. cit., p. 11.

[52] See Joseph Pechman, "The Rich, the Poor, and the Taxes They Pay," Public Interest, vol. 17 (Fall 1968), pp. 21–43.

TABLE 10.5   Percentage Share of Aggregate Income by Each Fifth of Families, 1947–1971

Percent	1971	1968	1965	1960	1950	1947
Lowest fifth	5.5	5.7	5.3	4.9	4.5	5.0
Second fifth	11.9	12.4	12.1	12.0	12.0	11.8
Third fifth	17.4	17.7	17.7	17.6	17.4	17.0
Fourth fifth	23.7	23.7	23.7	23.6	23.5	23.1
Highest fifth	41.6	40.6	41.3	42.0	42.6	43.0

Source: U.S. Bureau of the Census, Current Population Reports, Series P-60, no. 85, "Money Income in 1971 of Families and Persons in the United States" (Washington, D.C.: U.S. Government Printing Office, 1972), Table 14, p. 38.

In several Western European Capitalist countries, Socialist parties control the government. But, according to Frank Parkin, while leading to a strong system of social welfare, this has not produced any major pressure to equalize income. "After thirty-five years of socialist rule in Sweden, income differentials between working-class and middle-class occupational groups are no narrower than in western societies ruled by *bourgeois* governments."[53]

More significantly, according to Parkin, these Socialist parties in Western Europe have since the 1950s abandoned their long-standing commitment to *egalitarian* socialism in favor of *meritocratic* socialism; that is, a commitment to equality of opportunity for the individual and competitive pursuit of unequally rewarded positions. Meritocratic socialism would not eliminate rich and poor. There is, therefore, in both the Western Capitalist and Eastern Euro-

pean Communist societies no political party any longer committed to equality among the social classes.

There has been underway for some time, as we've said, a growth of white-collar occupations and a decline of blue-collar ones, as well as a continued inequality in the distribution of rewards. These changes, based upon technological developments, suggest further political changes in the consciousness and ideology of social classes. We have, however, as yet said little about this matter; that awaits examination of class and politics in Chapter 15. There are some other developments, such as the rise of a world market and the exporting of manufacturing jobs from the United States to countries with cheaper wage structures, that suggest potentially new, hostile relations between corporate capital and the unions of the working class in the near future.

Now that we have sketched in a basic mapping of class structure, we can examine these other issues in subsequent chapters.

[53] *See* Parkin, *op. cit.*, p. 121.

SUMMARY

Social stratification is the inequality of status found throughout social structure, though it varies in form from one society to another. An inequalitarian view accepts stratification as right and natural, even necessary. An equalitarian view believes stratification is both unjust and unnecessary.

In explaining stratification Lenski asserts *two laws of distribution:* first, that people will share the product of their labors when necessary to insure the survival of the group, a process of human cooperation; second, that power will determine the distribution of nearly all the surplus possessed by a society.

Though power and privilege are always basic to stratification, the inequalities of distribution are always *legitimized*.

Caste is a rigid form of stratification sanctioned by religion; while *estates* are rigid forms of stratification enforced by law and custom but not by religion. *Classes* are relatively open strata, not fixed by law, custom, or religion.

Marx saw classes as economic strata politically organized, engaged in struggle against the oppression of dominant classes.

Weber saw stratification as multi-dimensional: *class* as economic strata, *status* groups as noneconomic bases for prestige, and *parties* as groups contesting for power.

Warner called classes the prestige rankings of the community's status groups.

Status, in contrast to class, is evident in such things as the status of old, settled families; the glamour status of "star" performers; and status based on a person's religion, ethnicity, and race. In times of economic stability stratification by status is pre-eminent and class and status tend to merge. But in situations of change, class becomes prominent again.

Under capitalism two basic classes emerged: a *middle* class of owner-operators and a *working* class of employees. In time a *new* middle class of salaried employees developed and became more numerous. With the demise of aristocracy the existence of an upper class has been argued pro and con, though recent sociological work has provided some documentation for a class of very wealthy families of inherited income and extensive property ownership.

Working-class people are being viewed as becoming less class conscious now, due to an *embourgeoisement* caused by affluence. But class consciousness rises with unemployment and insecurity, and the embourgeoisement of workers has been exaggerated. They are still behind white-collar workers in income, job security, and chances for mobility.

Social mobility is less a matter of individual aspiration, and is more a matter of change in occupational structure that increases middle-class positions. The family affects mobility by its process of social inheritance and by providing better social chances for its children.

There is only a small difference in the degree of mobility between the United States and European nations, despite common belief to the contrary. Even *immobiles* often believe in opportunity, taking satisfaction in very modest gains and transferring their aspirations to their children. For those who aspire but cannot make it conventionally, there are alternate routes: athletics, entertainment, politics, and labor unions.

The growth of white-collar, salaried classes is the major trend in class structure.

There has not been any reduction in the discrepancy of wealth between the richest and the poorest in the United States. A very small group at the top still possesses most of the nation's wealth.

Selected Readings

E. Digby Baltzell, *Philadelphia Gentlemen: The Making of a National Upper Class* (New York: The Free Press, 1958). A sociologist who is upper class describes what the upper class is like.

T. B. Bottomore, *Classes in Modern Society* (New York: Pantheon Books, Inc., 1966). A short, critical review of the literature on social classes in modern society.

G. William Domhoff, *The Higher Circles: The Governing Class in America* (New York: Random House, Inc., 1970). Domhoff pulls together varied data to prove the existence of an American upper class.

R.J. Herrnstein, *IQ in the Meritocracy* (Boston, Mass.: Little, Brown and Company, 1973). A Harvard professor argues that the meritocratic tendency produces a trend that puts the genetically superior on top.

Gabriel Kolko, *Wealth and Power in America: An Analysis of Social Class and Income Distribution,* rev. ed. (New York: Frederick A. Praeger, Inc., 1964). A strong critique of the idea that there is a trend toward equalization of wealth in the United States.

John C. Legget, *Race, Class, and Labor: Working-Class Consciousness in Detroit* (New York: Oxford University Press, 1968). A study of potential and real class consciousness among black and white auto workers in Detroit.

Gerhard Lenski, *Power and Privilege: A Theory of Stratification* (New York: McGraw-Hill Book Company, Inc., 1966). The foremost effort in American sociology to examine stratification in terms of power and privilege.

Seymour M. Lipset and Reinhard Bendix, *Social Mobility in Industrial Society* (Berkeley, Calif.: University of California Press, 1959). An effort to compare social mobility in the United States with social mobility in Europe.

Gaetano Mosca, *The Ruling Class* (New York: McGraw-Hill Book Company, Inc., 1969). A classic work claiming that human society is always divided between the rulers and the ruled.

Stanley Ossowski, *Class Structure in the Social Consciousness,* Sheila Patterson, trans. (New York: The Free Press, 1963). A Polish sociologist explores class and class consciousness in Marxian and non-Marxian sociological theory.

Frank Parkin, *Class Inequality and Political Order: Social Stratification in Capitalist and Communist Societies* (New York: Frederick A. Praeger, Inc., 1971). A British sociologist examines and compares the inequality of class in both Capitalist and Communist societies — and finds both basically committed to inequality.

John Porter, *The Vertical Mosaic: An Analysis of Social Class and Power in Canada* (Toronto: University of Toronto Press, 1965). A fine study of how class and ethnicity combine in forming national elites in Canada.

Richard Sennett and Jonathan Cobb, *The Hidden Injuries of Class* (New York: Alfred A. Knopf, 1972). A sensitive, penetrating exploration of the psychic and moral injuries of loss of dignity and feelings of unworthiness experienced by ordinary workers in a status-conscious society.

E. P. Thompson, *The Making of the English Working Class* (New York: Pantheon Books, Inc., 1964). A fine piece of historical scholarship on the shaping of a working class in an industrializing society.

Melvin M. Tumin, *Social Stratification* (Englewood Cliffs, N.J.: Prentice-Hall, Inc., 1967). A brief, readable analysis of the issues and a good review of the most commonly accepted findings.

Laws grind the poor, and rich men rule the law.
— *Oliver Goldsmith*

Chapter 11

Minority Groups and the Poor

Inequality in society takes many forms, but none has commanded more public attention nor aroused more social controversy in the United States in recent years than the inequality signified by *race* and *ethnic* status and by *poverty*. That the poor and the minorities are overlapping categories only compounds the issue.

While understanding of minorities overlaps with understanding poverty, the issues are not identical, and in this chapter we give separate consideration to each.

RACIAL AND ETHNIC MINORITIES

Some members of society, by virtue of their racial or ethnic status, are blocked from full and equal participation in all phases of social life—and this makes them a *minority*. Minority as a status, then, must be distinguished from minority as a numerical proportion. It is true that in the United States whites are the numerical majority and blacks the numerical minority. But in the Republic of South Africa, dominant whites are fewer in number than the subordinate blacks. The numerical minority can thus be dominant and

minority group - object of prejudice + who think of themselves as a minority group.

ARE THERE OTHER MINORITIES?

Louis Wirth's definition of minority can include more than racial and ethnic groups. Religion has been a not infrequent basis for minority status. In recent years feminism has made vocal the charge that women are denied equal rights with men, just because they are women.

A recent work has argued that there is a whole set of groups in the United States who fit the definition of minority, even though there may be little public recognition of them.* It offers essays with this interpretation for:

Women	The Physically Disabled
Homosexuals	The Mentally Retarded
Adolescents	Lepers
Hippies	Ex-convicts
The Aged	The Radical Right
The Cripple	The Police
The Dwarf	The Intellectuals

*Edward Sagarin, ed., *The Other Minorities* (Waltham, Mass.: Ginn & Company, 1971).

in control, while the numerical majority can be in a subordinate status. Sociologically, a minority group is *not* primarily defined by its number. Louis Wirth provided a useful definition:

We may define a minority as a group of people who, because of their physical or cultural characteristics, are singled out from the others in the society in which they live for differential and unequal treatment and who therefore regard themselves as objects of collective discrimination.[1]

Prejudice and Discrimination

Explanations of why minorities exist usually invoke such concepts as *prejudice* and *discrimination*. Yet this often clouds the issue as much as it clarifies it. For one

[1] See Louis Wirth, "The Problem of Minority Groups," in Ralph Linton, ed., *The Science of Man in the World Crisis* (New York: Columbia University Press, 1945), p. 347.

thing these are negative terms, and most people deny that they are themselves prejudiced or that they discriminate. In addition, these are emotionally-loaded terms, so that their use in objective discussion becomes confused. Lastly, the two terms are often used interchangeably, though in fact they have different meanings.

Basically, prejudice refers to attitudes and feelings, while discrimination has reference to behavior, specifically, to differential treatment of persons by virtue of their race or ethnicity. Thus, to refuse a person a job or admission to a college because of his race, even when he has the ordinarily required qualifications, is to discriminate.

Does Prejudice Cause Discrimination?

The folklore and common sense of our culture tells us that prejudice causes discrimination. This is an argument so basic to an American perspective, and seemingly so obvious to many, that too few have ever questioned it. Yet, to the social scientist it does not follow that every act of discrimination is a consequence of a prejudicial attitude.

To say that prejudice causes discrimination is to say that *attitude causes behavior*.[2] But a prejudicial attitude can cause discriminatory behavior only if the prejudiced person is free to act solely as he would wish. This is only rarely the case for anyone. In any organized society each person must on most occasions act in ways that are expected, even demanded, and he does not have the choice of acting out his prejudice. Does this mean there can be prejudice without discrimination and discrimination without prejudice? The answer is yes.

Prejudice without discrimination occurs when the prejudiced person cannot discriminate even if he would want to. An employer who cannot refuse to hire because of race, an admissions director who cannot deny admission to a student because of race, a restaurant owner or manager who cannot refuse to serve anyone because of race—these are all instances where an individual's prejudice does not lead him to discriminate. Law or custom or official policy may prevent such behavior on his part.

Furthermore, the opposite can be true as well. Much discrimination, when it does occur, is not so much the behavior of individuals with prejudicial attitudes as it is behavior determined by policy or law or even long-established custom. Thus, it is equally true that an act of discrimination

may be less the result of a person's own attitudes and more a consequence of prevailing local policy or law, informal pressure, cultural expectations, and longstanding customs.

In short, discrimination has to be explained in terms of group processes and structure, as well as the culture of the group, rather than solely, or even primarily, in terms of individual attitudes. Whether people do or do not discriminate is more a matter of acting consistent with expectations of the situation than of acting out their own attitudes.[3] Nor can we overlook the use of social power to support or countervail law, policy, or custom.

Minority Status and Social Power

To explain discrimination in terms of law and social policy, even of custom, requires that one social group be able to control and define law and custom and social policy in order to dominate the other. And this requires that it have *social power*. To be a majority group and to confine a minority group to a subordinate position within the social structure—"to keep them in their places"—requires the majority group to have the instruments and mechanisms of power necessary to sustain its dominant position. Whites can discriminate against blacks in employment, for example, only if whites control the distribution of jobs.

It is this process of discrimination that creates a minority group. The very act of discriminating—in jobs, housing, income, social services, and education—is the social process by which a racial or ethnic

---

[2] The outstanding work on prejudice is still Gordon Allport, *The Nature of Prejudice* (Cambridge, Mass.: Addison-Wesley Publishing Company, Inc., 1954; paperback edition, New York: Anchor Books, 1958).

[3] *See* Melvin L. Kohn and Robin M. Williams, Jr., "Situational Patterning in Intergroup Relations," *American Sociological Review*, vol. 21 (April 1956), pp. 164–174.

group is converted into a minority group. The mere holding of prejudicial attitudes by one group toward another does not make a minority of the recipient group; that merely indicates the existence of group hostility. Thus, blacks develop attitudes of resentment and hostility toward whites, but whites do not become a minority because of this.

The Function of Prejudice

If prejudice does not cause discrimination, what (if anything) does it do? One function of prejudice is to provide a rationale or justification for discriminatory behavior. The late anthropologist Ruth Benedict, for example, argued that racial beliefs and prejudices came *after* the onset of the slave trade, specifically in response to the attacks upon it as inhuman and un-Christian.[4] Racist beliefs emerged, she argues in effect, to justify already existing behavior.[5]

When the difference between a dominant and a subordinate group is racial, myths about racial inferiority and superiority will constitute the core of the justifying prejudice. Then prejudice is more than attitude, it is a set of culturally developed beliefs about how one group is superior to another and thus deserving of its advantaged position. Furthermore, it makes use of *stereotypes* of both the dominant and subordinate groups. Stereotypes are culturally-based images of a category of people, attributing to them uniformly a common set of characteristics; for subordinate categories, the stereotypes are negative and

deny positive characteristics. Thus, when whites hold a stereotype of blacks as lazy, less intelligent, and given to criminal behavior, they also hold a stereotype of whites as ambitious, intelligent, and law-abiding. A negative image of the subordinate group is accompanied by a flattering self-image by the dominant group of itself, one that justifies it as being dominant, indeed, makes it seem natural that it should be.

When this constitutes a firm social belief it provides a perfectly logical basis for its discriminatory behavior for the majority group. It feels justified in sustaining inequalities in educational opportunity, for why extend equal educational chances to people who are unequal in ability? It feels justified in denying voting rights, for why extend the franchise to people who do not have the intelligence to understand the political process? It feels justified in discriminating in employment, for why extend job opportunities to people who do not have the ability to hold a job demanding skill and ability?

The Function of Discrimination

If the function of prejudice is to justify discriminatory behavior, what, then, is the function of discrimination? What does discrimination *do?* What a group does when it discriminates against another group is to set up social mechanisms by which it allows unequal access to the rewards of society. It makes race or ethnicity a major determinant in the distribution of life chances.

The Structure of Discrimination

The crux of minority status, we have seen, is the capacity of one group to impose discrimination upon another. Though discrimination can and does take many

[4] *See* Ruth Benedict, *Race: Science and Politics* (New York: The Viking Press, Inc., 1940), Ch. VII, "A Natural History of Racism."

[5] On the emergence of racist beliefs to justify a gradually developing chattel slavery, *see* Oscar Handlin, *Race and Nationality in American Life* (Boston, Mass.: Little, Brown & Company, 1948), Ch. 1.

forms, there are a few modes of discrimination that are significant, even crucial, because the entire structural arrangement of majority-minority relations depends on them. They are the key to the advantages and domination which discrimination gives to the majority.

Economic

Discrimination in the economic sphere is primary; by such means a dominant group controls jobs, land, credit, and investment. Discrimination in *employment* has understandably received most attention in a society like ours, in which most people are employees rather than self-employed.

Economic discrimination is the crucial process in allocating whites and blacks unequally throughout the occupational structure, and thus also throughout the class structure. If discrimination did not operate in the allocation of jobs, then one could expect that racial groups would be distributed proportionately throughout the occupational structure. But in the United States we find that nonwhites are underrepresented in the better-paying occupations, and overrepresented in the others. Based on census data for 1968, Norval Glenn has computed the actual representation of nonwhites in occupations as a proportion of an expected representation, if there were equal chances (and measured as 1.00):[6]

Professional and technical workers	.59
Managers, officials, and proprietors	.28
Clerical workers	.67
Sales workers	.30
Craftsmen and foremen	.60

[6] See Norval D. Glenn, "Changes in the Social and Economic Conditions of Blacks during the 1960s," in Norval D. Glenn and Charles M. Bonjean, eds., *Blacks in the United States* (San Francisco, Calif.: Chandler Publishing Company, 1969).

In contrast, nonwhites are overrepresented in other, less-rewarding occupations:

Operatives (semiskilled)	1.27
Private household workers	4.22
Service workers	1.81
Laborers	2.00

Education

In an industrial society the quality of an individual's education is increasingly significant for his life chances. Perhaps nowhere has equal opportunity come to be asserted more than in the sphere of education. Effective discrimination in education, then, relegates any minority to inferior positions in the class structure. It makes easier the practice of economic discrimination; indeed, little if any overt discrimination need be practiced in assigning jobs, for example, if the educational process has consistently prepared the dominant group well and the subordinate group poorly. In short, education, probably more than any other factor, affects people's chances to compete for occupational status. (In Chapter 13 we shall look at this in the context of the institution of education in modern society.)

Politics

Denial of political rights to a minority is a denial of political power. As long as free elections exist, minority groups can translate their grievances and demands into political goals. Nor do they need to possess great numbers to do so. Rather, they can make a difference in otherwise close elections, providing the margin by which one party or the other, one candidate or the other wins. Given freedom to vote, therefore, a minority group can mobilize its members behind a determined leadership and learn to exercise genuine political power. The elimination of other forms of discrimination—jobs, schools, housing—can then become significant goals toward which such political power is effectively exercised.

In societies such as the Republic of South Africa the dominant but numerical minority of whites has written a constitution that gives full citizenship only to whites, and denies it to blacks. In the United States the passage of the Fifteenth Amendment to the Constitution in 1870 guarantees the political rights of citizenship to all regardless of race. Thus, white control of the political process has had to resort to more devious devices, especially in counties in the South where blacks were a numerical majority.

To prevent blacks from voting a wide range of techniques have been used. One was the white primary—restricting the Democratic Party's primary to whites on the supposition that parties were not actually governments but were private clubs. In the once one-party South, the primaries were the real election. There was also a poll tax (a tax to vote) which discouraged the poor, both white and black, from voting. A more sophisticated and even more dishonest technique has been a literacy requirement, or a requirement to demonstrate some familiarity with the Constitution and the American system of government. By employing very rigorous standards for blacks and very relaxed standards for whites, white election officials could then fail even educated blacks while passing semi-educated poor whites. By court decisions and legislation, and by vigorous federal enforcement under President John Kennedy, which was a response, in turn, to rising black militancy and civil rights action, these practices were severely reduced, and the participation of blacks in the electoral process in the South has increased rapidly, changing the Southern political process considerably.[7]

Housing

Discrimination in housing is primarily a matter of residential segregation. The restriction of blacks to specific residential areas, and their exclusion from most of the residential neighborhoods of the community, particularly the more desired ones, is a pattern of segregation not legitimized in law since the Supreme Court in 1947 ruled as unconstitutional the practice of *restricted covenants*. (These were clauses in deeds to property restricting sale to whites only, sometimes to gentiles only.)

Nonetheless, residential segregation has been effectively carried on by a series of practices worked out by realtors, home-financing institutions, property-owners associations, and political officials.[8] Within large Northern cities in the last two decades, however, white movement to the suburbs has broken some of the resistance, making a wider range of housing available to blacks. In turn suburban communities have sought to exercise the racial restrictions once so successfully practiced within the central city.

Perhaps the most significant consequence of racially segregated housing is segregated schooling. Once segregation in schooling was regarded as *de facto*; that is, not legally required but the unplanned

[7] For a detailed analysis of black voting in the South, and its impact on Southern politics, *see* Donald R. Mathews and James W. Prothro, *Negroes and the New Southern Politics* (New York: Harcourt Brace Jovanovich, 1966).

[8] For an excellent analysis of how this has been done in one city (Chicago), *see* Rose Helper, *Racial Policies and Practices of Real Estate Brokers* (Minneapolis, Minn.: University of Minnesota Press, 1969).

Figure 11.1 Although the white population of the Republic of South Africa is in a numerical minority, it holds enough political power to deny equality to blacks. Here, Johannesburg Africans wait for a bus that will take them to their homes outside of the city. *(Paul Conklin, Monkmeyer.)*

consequence of other restrictive practices. But in recent court cases the National Association for the Advancement of Colored People (NAACP) has sought to demonstrate that there have been deliberate efforts to draw neighborhood boundaries in such a way as to preserve all-white schools. School bussing, the most controversial attempt to end segregation in schooling, is an effort to assign pupils on a basis other than residence, on the assumption that residential segregation, particularly between white suburbs and black inner cities, is a pattern that will remain for some time, especially if it sustains segregated schooling.

Each of these major patterns of discrimination relates to the others. Segregation in schooling is associated with differential quality in education, and with differential bases of financial support for the education of white and black children. Residential segregation makes that possible. Differences in education provide quite different capabilities in the competition for jobs as we have seen.

None of these forms of discrimination can be practiced except as whites possess the power to do so: to control property and land values and access to housing, to control political office, to control jobs and credit—in short, to control the economic, political, and educational resources of the society.

Institutional Racism

This control of the several institutions of American society by whites to the disadvantage of nonwhites has been called *institutional racism.* Black activist Stokely Carmichael and political scientist Charles Hamilton gave this concept prominence in their widely read book, *Black Power;* and then social activist Louis L. Knowles and political scientist Kenneth Prewitt explored it in some detail.[9]

Carmichael and Hamilton note that most whites would not do anything as savage as bombing a black church and killing five black children, as was done in Birmingham, Alabama. But when in that same city "five hundred black babies die each year because of lack of proper food, shelter and medical facilities," they claim, "that is a function of institutional racism."[10]

Basically, whites assume a white superiority and a set of prerogatives that go with it. Some whites base their assumption on notions of racial (genetic) superiority; more enlightened ones base it on assumptions of cultural superiority. What they do not often recognize, however, is the subtle workings of advantage for whites when such assumptions and the prerogative they justify are built into the very functioning of the institutions.

Getting a job or getting admitted to college, for example, depends on meeting some job requirements. Even if race is consciously banned as a requirement an equal competition between blacks and whites is not immediately created. Past workings of other institutions, such as education, have produced differences in the quality of learning, of job training, of opportunities for various significant experiences. All this will give whites an advantage over blacks. (In the same manner males get an advantage over females, and middle class over working class.)

The practices of social institutions are

never equal toward those they serve, and so the distribution of benefits is not either. When such differences affect whites and blacks to the advantage of whites, this is institutional racism. When the differences are of sex, the term is *sexism*. When they are those of social class, there seems to be no term as yet to point up that fact.

Types of Minority Groups

What are the types of groups that most frequently become organized into majority-minority relations? An examination of the historical record tells us that dominant social groups have defined minority groups in terms of a very few criteria, of which the two most important ones have been *racial* and *ethnic*.

Race

Historically, in the United States, *race* has referred almost exclusively to black people, for they are not only the largest racial minority their particular status, originating in slavery, has been a morally and politically crucial issue throughout all the days of the nation. But more recently there has been a widening recognition of two other nonwhite minorities: the *American Indians* and the Spanish-speaking *Mexican-Americans* (Chicanos).[11] Both groups have followed the blacks in pressing for rights long denied, in developing pride in their separate cultural and racial identities. Unlike blacks, Indians were never slaves (though efforts were made,

[9] *See* Stokely Carmichael and Charles V. Hamilton, *Black Power: The Politics of Liberation in America* (New York: Random House, Inc., 1967); and Louis L. Knowles and Kenneth Prewitt, eds., *Institutional Racism in America* (Englewood Cliffs, N.J.: Prentice-Hall, Inc., 1969).

[10] *See* Carmichael and Hamilton, *op. cit.*, p. 4.

[11] For brief yet comprehensive reviews *see* Murray L. Wax, *Indian Americans: Unity and Diversity* (Englewood Cliffs, N.J.: Prentice-Hall, Inc., 1971); and Joan W. Moore with Alfredo Cuéllar, *Mexican Americans* (Englewood Cliffs, N.J.: Prentice-Hall, Inc., 1970).

Figure 11.2 Ever since the early nineteenth century American Indians have been shut up in reservations under conditions of extreme poverty. *(Paul Conklin, Monkmeyer.)*

unsuccessfully, to enslave them), but in the nineteenth century they were forcefully expelled from their lands, killed off in large numbers, and penned up in reservations under conditions of extreme poverty and deprivation.

The Spanish-speaking Chicanos have long been concentrated in the southwestern United States, where they have provided a reservoir of poor, unskilled labor. Few of them have been successful in achieving middle-class status. They have also been the source of much of the migratory farm labor working from California all the way to the Midwest. That is why the movement to organize migrant workers, led by Caesar Chavez, is so much a Chicano movement.

The Chicano people possess a culturally distinct heritage, much different from those of the Europeans who migrated directly to the United States. Racially, they are a mixture of the Spanish invaders and the more numerous indigenous population.

The Chinese and Japanese are also racial minorities with a long experience of prejudice and discrimination in the United States, including a ban on immigration for many years.[12]

Ethnic Groups

The historically significant ethnic groups in the United States have been those nineteenth- and early twentieth-century immigrant groups from Europe, particularly those from Eastern and Southern Europe, who were visibly different by virtue of their cultural patterns and life

[12] *See* Rose Hum Lee, *The Chinese in the United States* (Hong Kong: Hong Kong University Press, 1960); and Harry H.L. Kitano, *Japanese-Americans: The Evolution of a Subculture* (Englewood Cliffs, N.J.: Prentice-Hall, Inc., 1969).

styles.[13] They spoke a language other than English; they dressed differently; and their customs and ways of life contrasted sharply with dominant customs and life styles. When they clustered together in ethnic ghettoes, they perpetuated for several generations a life style that made them culturally visible. Even when their use of English, as in the next or later generations, was not noticeably different, their names were identifiably ethnic—whether Irish, Polish, or Italian.

Simply being culturally different, however, does not make an ethnic group a minority. But poor immigrants who worked at low-paying jobs and who were the object of extensive discriminatory practices, as well as much prejudice toward "foreigners," became minority groups. They also became the major source of cheap, unskilled labor in a rapidly expanding industrial economy. "By 1912, some 60 percent of the miners and some 58 percent of the iron and steel workers were foreign-born, and an additional 15 to 20 percent were their native-born children."[14]

The status of ethnic groups changed, however, with industrial and occupational change. As a group they took advantage of changes in the division of labor to move into more rewarding occupations and to increase their standards of living. Unions helped, too, by providing higher wages and greater job security.

There were other factors inducing this group mobility. Political organization and the expansion of municipal government opened a civil-service spectrum of jobs—

you've heard about the legendary Irish cop? After World War II the expansion of education brought members of these groups into school teaching, other professions, and into expanding corporate and governmental bureaucracies.[15]

From the days of political bosses and machines ethnic groups have used the political process to accumulate wealth and position and then to use it for the benefit of group members: municipal contracts let to one of their own group, choice political and judicial appointments, and the like. The criminal rackets, too, were often a source of illicit wealth, which could then become a source for capitalizing legitimate businesses.[16]

This group mobility has been viewed by historians and sociologists as hastening the process of assimilation and acculturation, and thus of causing a gradual decline in ethnic identity.[17]

The idea of America as a "melting pot" has long had strong support as a major value in American society, with the goal of gradual absorption of varied ethnic groups into the major cultural pattern. What has been a goal to many has seemed also to be an historical fact: The old ghettoes disappeared and the younger generation seemed to lose much of their ethnic identification.

---

[13] A Pulitzer Prize-winning history of these immigrants to American society, including an excellent study of the development of ethnic communities, is Oscar Handlin, *The Uprooted* (Boston: Little, Brown & Company, 1951).

[14] Oscar Handlin, *America: A History* (New York: Holt, Rinehart and Winston, Inc., 1968), p. 696.

[15] For a detailed review of such changes in one city (New York), *see* Nathan Glazer and Daniel Moynihan, *Beyond the Melting Pot* (Cambridge, Mass.: The M.I.T. Press and Harvard University Press, 1963).

[16] *See* Daniel Bell, "Crime as an American Way of Life: A Queer Ladder of Social Mobility," in his *The End of Ideology* (New York: The Free Press, 1960), pp. 115–136.

[17] For a discussion of how sociologists and others have used the concept of assimilation *see* Milton M. Gordon, *Assimilation in American Life: The Role of Race, Religion, and National Origins* (New York: Oxford University Press, 1964), especially Chs. 3 through 6.

But sociologists may have been too ready to write off ethnic groups as no longer a significant part of American social life. Sociologist Nathan Glazer and Daniel Moynihan studied ethnic groups in New York City and concluded that they were very much "alive," that an identification with ethnic groups was still quite meaningful to many, and that ethnic groups were significant units of the political structure of the city.[18]

The Jewish Minority

The Jews are one of the Western world's most persistently minority groups. They have existed for centuries in various societies, taking on some of the characteristics of the host society, yet always remaining a group apart as much by choice as by the prejudices of the dominant group. They have maintained over centuries a culture which has sustained them through the vicissitudes of mistreatment and persecution.[19]

In Europe, in the Middle Ages, the Jews were often restricted to a limited set of occupations; and their presence in cities was often tolerated only on condition that they lived separately. This frequently meant in a walled-off part of the city—the first meaning of *ghetto*.[20] If the ghetto described segregation enforced by gentiles, it was also a form of protection; Jews were safe from molestation behind the walls.

In the smaller towns and cities of East-ern Europe Jews were often the target of violence, the scapegoats of others' class and group frustrations. Often they were the victims of a *pogrom*, literally being driven out and forced to move on. These *pogroms* were responsible for the emigration of Russian Jews to the United States in the nineteenth century.

What is historically significant about Jews in both Europe and the United States is their refusal to give up their identity. They have persistently resisted being assimilated, or even accepting the goal of assimilation. Instead, they have always taken a position in favor of *pluralism*—a situation in which culturally distinct groups can maintain their separate identities and pursue their group interests without suffering from discrimination—in short, to be an *ethnic* group but not a *minority*.

The idea of cultural pluralism is not new; it was worked out by philosopher Horace Kallen over a half-century ago, challenging the idea that ethnic groups should be pressed to assimilate into a homogeneous "melting pot."[21] This position did not become the nation's dominant philosophy or social policy, however, but recent events have made it more attractive. Now, blacks, Indians, and Chicanos, as well as Jews and traditional European ethnic groups all seem to strive to retain their group identities while not being denied their equal rights in a democratic society.

Rediscovering Ethnic Groups

The idea that the end of immigration meant the *acculturation* of ethics—their absorption into the dominant culture—has been a powerful belief for several decades.

[18] *See* Glazer and Moynihan, *op. cit.*

[19] For a study of Jews in American society *see* Nathan Glazer, *American Judaism* (Chicago, Ill.: University of Chicago Press, 1957); and Marshall Sklare, ed., *The Jews: Social Patterns of an American Group* (New York: The Free Press, 1958).

[20] For an understanding of the ghetto's origins, and a detailed study of the Chicago ghetto of the 1920s, *see* Louis Wirth, *The Ghetto* (Chicago, Ill.: University of Chicago Press, 1928).

[21] *See* Horace Kallen, *Culture and Democracy in the United States* (New York: Boni & Liveright, 1924).

It was sustained throughout the 1950s and 1960s despite evidence to the contrary from social scientists. Sociologist Gerhard Lenski first challenged this idea in his study of racial and religious affiliation in Detroit.[22] Though not explicitly concerned with ethnicity, he found significant cultural and political differences among blacks, white Protestants, Catholics, and Jews. Then came the Glazer and Moynihan study of the continuity of ethnicity (and race) in New York City. It made a strong case for the idea that the "melting pot" had not yet eliminated ethnic groups as viable bases for political action.

The more theoretical work of sociologist Milton Gordon helped clarify the issue.[23] Gordon distinguished among variants of assimilation. _Acculturation_ — absorbing the dominant Anglo-Saxon culture — was the first form of assimilation and clearly the one most in evidence. But this did not necessarily mean the readiness of Anglo-Saxon groups to allow the acculturated ethnics into the institutional positions they controlled, so that there was little _structural_ assimilation.

Furthermore, acculturation did not imply a conscious _identification_ with the majority group and a rejection of ethnic origins. As Michael Parenti points out, the sharing of a common residential neighborhood is not necessary for ethnic cohesion and identity, nor does the movement to the suburbs prevent such identity.[24] As a result, though many (but far from all) ethnics have been occupationally mobile and relatively affluent, "rather than the expected structural

assimilation, parallel social structures flourish among the more affluent ethnics."[25] Among ethnics of whatever social class, movement from the original ethnic neighborhood and the emergence of American-born generations does not lead to the disintegration of the group but to new adjustments in minority organization.

Even when most of the life-styles assume an American middle-class stamp, these in-group social patterns reinforce ethnic identifications and seem to give them an enduring nature. Today identifiable groups remain not as survivals from the age of immigration but with new attributes many of which were unknown to the immigrants. In short, changes are taking place in ethnic social patterns, but the direction does not seem to be toward greater assimilation into the dominant Anglo-American social structure.[26]

Now, in the 1970s, the persistence of ethnicity is widely recognized. There is even some sympathy for the working-class ethnics who remain in the central city, caught in the midst of racial conflict and struggling to preserve their way of life against any and all encroachments, including that of blacks. Many of these white ethnics left behind in an old section of the central city are poor and share in all the disadvantages that low income always brings.[27] They lack education and their children are being poorly educated in inner-city schools. They are, economically and socially, little, if at all, better off than blacks — and feel threatened by black gains and forgotten and ignored by middle-class whites, who seem to them to be concerned exclusively with the problems of black people.

---

[22] Gerhard Lenski, _The Religious Factor_ (New York: Doubleday & Company, Inc., 1961).

[23] See Gordon, _Assimilation in American Life._

[24] See Michael Parenti, "Ethnic Politics and the Persistence of Ethnic Identification," _American Political Science Review,_ vol. 61 (September 1967), pp. 717–726.

[25] See Parenti, _op. cit.,_ p. 722.

[26] See Parenti, _op. cit.,_ p. 721.

[27] For a highly readable account of the social life and problems of one such area (Kensington in Philadelphia) see Peter Binzen, _Whitetown: U.S.A._ (New York: Random House, Inc., 1970).

Figure 11.3 Despite dispersal throughout Europe and elsewhere, Jews have nevertheless refused to give up their separate identities and have maintained their distinction as an ethnic group. *(Library of Congress.)*

Yet, by and large, the persistence of ethnicity has less to do with minority status and more to do with the search for a distinctive group identity in American society. Undoubtedly some patterns of prejudice and discrimination remain, and the descendants of the Eastern and Southern European immigrants are not even today equally represented in the upper middle-class levels of the class structure.

But it is the distinction between white and nonwhite that is most fundamental to minority status in the United States, as it is in many other places in the world. Ethnics are no longer minorities in any way comparable to racial groups.

RACE AND RACISM

Even though the collapse of European colonialism has lessened (though not eliminated) white domination of nonwhite peoples in Africa and Asia,[28] the fact of race has become strikingly significant in the structure of world affairs in the twentieth century, and a source of internal conflict of major proportions throughout the world, including some major industrial societies, such as in the United States.

Beliefs about racial superiority are not an invention of Western peoples; they have appeared from time to time elsewhere, even in Africa prior to the coming of white colonialists. Nonetheless, there is a pattern of racist belief peculiar to the Western world, perhaps the most pervasive and powerful racist ideology the world has known. Although its roots go back to the slave trade, according to sociologist Pierre

---

[28] The Republic of South Africa and Rhodesia, for example, have emerged as white-controlled nations, while Portugal still maintains a large colony in East Africa within which a bitter guerrilla war for liberation goes on.

241

L. van den Berghe, Western racism emerged as a distinct ideology only around the 1830s and 1840s and reached its peak between 1880 and 1920.[29] It has since entered a period of decline, but it remains alive and cannot be expected to disappear for three or four more decades.

The emergence of Western racism, says Van den Berghe, requires the presence of racially distinct groups, different enough so that at least some of their members can be readily classifiable.[30] But these visible group differences must overlap with differences in status and culture and a situation of established inequality. These conditions most likely occur when groups come into contact through migration, when one group invades another people's territory and enslaves them, or when one group "imports" another as slaves or as an indentured alien group. Yet, even then, the prevailing ideology is not always racist; it may only proclaim the cultural superiority of the dominant group.

Explaining the origins of Western racism, according to Van den Berghe, must take into account three main factors:

1. Racism provided a rationalization for Capitalist exploitation of the New World and of colonial expansion in Africa, in particular the exploitation of non-European, nonwhite people, including systems of slavery.
2. Racism fitted with the new Darwinian theories in the biological sciences, which made notions of the racial superiority of white people over nonwhite people *seem* scientific.
3. Ideas of equality and freedom could only be violated (and they were) to justify slavery

and the exploitation of colonial peoples if some distinction were drawn between *humans* (who were entitled to be free and equal) and *subhumans* (who were not).

The end of slavery as a legal institution did not end racist ideology; indeed, in the United States, as Van den Berghe noted, its peak was from 1880 to 1920. It was only after the 1920s that scientists came to reject racist theories and that social scientists developed explanations of race relations that were not based on presumed racial differences.

Political action for civil rights in the United States had been directed toward providing equal rights and equal treatment for blacks, as for all minorities; to end various discriminatory practices; to eliminate racial segregation; and to achieve racial integration in politics, in jobs, in education, and, eventually, in housing. Probably most blacks accepted these goals, too, though even before the end of slavery a tradition of black thought offered other alternatives, including a cultural nationalism that would maintain a black version of cultural and social pluralism.[31] In the twentieth century black intellectuals thought through the race issue to arrive at conclusions quite different than those of white intellectuals about the future of black people in the United States.[32] This literature, however, received but scant attention from white intellectuals and social scientists until the black revolt in the 1960s

[29] Pierre L. van den Berghe, *Race and Racism: A Comparative Perspective* (New York: John Wiley & Sons, Inc., 1967), p. 15.
[30] The next three paragraphs draw from Van den Berghe, pp. 13–18.
[31] *See* John H. Bracey, Jr., August Meier, and Elliot Rudwich, eds., *Black Nationalism in America* (Indianapolis, Ind.: The Bobbs-Merrill Company, Inc., 1970).
[32] *See* Francis L. Broderick and August Meier, eds., *Negro Protest Thought in the Twentieth Century* (Indianapolis, Ind.: The Bobbs-Merrill Company, Inc., 1965); *see also* Harold Cruse, *The Crisis of the Negro Intellectual* (New York: William Morrow & Company, Inc., 1967).

made it apparent that there was no longer a taken-for-granted agreement between blacks and liberal whites on the future of race relations in the United States.

The rejection of the goal of integration in a new mood of militancy and separatism by some blacks, particularly youthful ones, confronted sociologists in the 1960s with a major sociological problem: How do we explain race relations in the United States? It seemed that the events in the real world of racial conflict might no longer fit the prevailing model of explanation that had dominated sociological thought for several decades—the *assimilation* model. From this crisis of theory alternate models emerged. Let us examine some of them briefly.

The Assimilation Model

The experience of most European immigrants in gradually assimilating themselves into American life provides the model that explains the gradual change in the status of blacks and other nonwhite minorities. Immigrants first clustered in urban ghettoes, experienced destitution and discrimination, and were controlled in various ways—politically and economically—by other groups. In time, they built up communities, gained a political base, and reduced the disadvantages that beset them. They experienced some mobility and a great deal of acculturation.

Applying the assimilation model to blacks means looking upon them as an ethnic group, and, like other ethnics, as immigrants—though in this case their migration was not from Europe but from the rural South. As the most recent immigrants they are therefore the group lowest in status, and they suffer most in treatment of them in society. But presumably they too will create communities out of their

ghettoes, gaining enough political power in time to reduce the discriminatory power of dominant groups. Life chances will improve for many of them, and social mobility will then move many blacks into the middle class.

There has, however, been serious disagreement, not over thinking of blacks as ethnics but over the comparability of their experience with earlier generations of European immigrants. The *Report of the National Advisory Commission on Civil Disorders* (known as the Kerner Report) suggested that there were several factors that made it impossible for blacks to follow the path of earlier immigrants.[33] For one thing, the maturing corporate economy no longer needs the unskilled labor that immigrants once offered. Hence, it no longer needs the lower-class black. Sociologist Sidney M. Willhelm has explored this point in considerable depth.[34]

Further, the *Report* argues that racial discrimination—the racism of white Americans—far exceeds the discrimination experienced by European immigrants—"a bar to advancement, unlike any other."[35]

The *Report* cites other reasons, such as the decline of political machines that once gave immigrants economic help in exchange for political support. Basically, the *Report* is arguing that the 1960s and 1970s do not offer blacks the opportunity for a long, hard climb out of ethnic poverty and discrimination:

The immigrant who labored long hours at hard and often menial work had the hope of a better future, if not for himself then for his

---

[33] (New York: Bantam Books, 1968).

[34] Sidney M. Willhelm, *Who Needs the Negro?* (New York: Schenkman, 1970; paperback version, Anchor Books, 1971), Ch. 6, "Economic Racism."

[35] See *Report, op. cit.,* p. 279.

children. This was the promise of the "American dream"—the society offered to all a future that was open-ended; with hard work and perseverance, a man and his family could in time achieve not only material well-being but "position" and status . . .

What the American economy of the late 19th and early 20th century was able to do to help the European immigrants escape from poverty is now largely impossible.[36]

The Economic-class Model

That more and more blacks are economically obsolescent is the premise of the economic-class model; and so economic deprivation is seen as the basis of race relations. Because of changing economic circumstances—increasing technology and reduction of less-skilled jobs—many blacks have become an *underclass* of impoverished and unusable labor. The future promises only an increase in this state of affairs, as automation and other technological developments further reduce the need for unskilled labor. (Remember the projections given at the end of Chapter 10.)

From this perspective any hope of social and economic advancement for black people would seem to lie in social change brought about by a political coalition of depressed classes.[37] A politics of economic interest would unite blacks with poor whites, Puerto Ricans, and Mexican-Americans for the purpose of advancing their *class* interests. Established labor unions might also join in such a coalition.

The Colonial Model

The idea that blacks could be viewed as a colonized people, instead of an immi-

grant group or an underclass, came originally from the writings of several black scholars. It got wider recognition when Stokely Carmichael and Charles Hamilton publicized the concept of *internal colonialism*.[38] Then sociologist Robert Blauner took the idea up as a serious sociological argument.[39]

It violates common understanding for most Americans to speak of colonialism except in terms of establishing domination by a colonizing nation over the geographical territory of a conquered people typically different in race and culture. The land and labor of the colonized people are exploited and the colony is made subordinate, economically and politically, to the colonizing nation. Obviously, this does not seem to fit the American case. As Blauner notes: "Classic colonialism involved the control and exploitation of the majority by a minority of outsiders. Whereas in America the people who were oppressed were themselves originally outsiders and are a numerical minority."[40]

But this argument, Blauner insists, misses the major point: that the concept of *colonization* captures the common experiences of racially subjugated people in America and elsewhere and is applicable even when there is not a *colonial system*. There are four basic aspects to colonization. First, it begins with the *forced* entry of the colonized people into the dominant society, in contrast to the *voluntary* entry of immigrants. Second, the colonizing power seeks to control, transform, even destroy the values and life style of the colonized people. American slaveholders, for example, separated tribal members in order to

[36] *See Report, op. cit.,* p. 282.
[37] For advocacy of such an approach *see* Bayard Rustin, "From Protest to Politics," *Commentary,* (February 1965), pp. 25–31.
[38] *See* Carmichael and Hamilton, *op. cit.,* Ch. 1.
[39] *See* Robert Blauner, "Internal Colonialism and Ghetto Revolts," *Social Problems,* vol. 16 (Spring 1969), pp. 393–408.
[40] *See* Blauner, *op. cit.,* p. 395.

Figure 11.4 Without the social mobility that marked the experience of Europeans who came to the United States voluntarily, blacks must deal with the frustrations of being "the most recent immigrants" without the power to move into other classes. The frustrations sometimes erupt in riots and looting. *(United Press International Photo.)*

weaken all cultural and organizational ties among the slaves. Thirdly, the colonizers closely administer and control the colonized people, giving them the experience of being constantly managed and manipulated by outsiders. Finally, colonization employs racism to justify the domination and control of one people by another.

The colonial model points out some crucial differences between blacks and the white immigrants from Europe in the United States. First, unlike blacks, European immigrants came voluntarily. Secondly, their ghettoes tended to be one- or two-generation phenomena, whereas the black ghetto persists. Though some few individuals escape it, most do not. Thirdly, and perhaps more crucially, white ethnics in a generation or less were able to develop ownership of their own stores and residences and also to enter the social structure so that much local control was exercised by people from their own groups.

But for blacks this has never been so. Their segregated communities have remained under white control and ownership. Whites own most of the residences and stores, and whites control the jobs. The schools have been run by whites, as have the social work agencies and political parties—and white police patrol the segregated streets. Blacks are thus relatively powerless because they control no significant resources, economic or otherwise.

To sociologists like Blauner the colonial model makes more understandable the black demand for community control, as well as the movement to black nationalism, neither of which makes sense if one assumes that assimilation is proceeding for blacks as it did for white immigrants. Community control and black nationalism are but particular aspects of a politics of liberation from colonial status. Liberation may take several forms, one of which could be the creation of an independent ethnic group, participating as one organized political group in a plurality of such groups. Another is *cultural,* asserting the separate collective identity of black people with a history and traditions, and a cultural integrity of their own.

So far we have been concerned with the status of racial and ethnic minorities. Most minorities are poor, but poverty afflicts many in industrial societies who are by race and ethnicity a part of the majority. Let us now turn to that other dimension of inequality—poor people.

THE STRUCTURE OF POVERTY

In a time of relative affluence it is not necessarily apparent that large numbers of people are poor. To a considerable extent the poor are not as visible to the middle classes as they once were. They are confined to ghettoes or to rural pockets hidden from view beyond the great expressways. It is this lack of easy visibility, for example, that sustained the widely shared myth during the 1950s that there were no longer any substantial number of Americans who were poor. As distinguished an economist as John Kenneth Galbraith, for example, helped support that myth. But

in the early 1960s Michael Harrington's *The Other America* pointed out the reality of poverty and led to its rediscovery.[41]

How Many Are Poor?

Those who insist that poverty is on the decline in the United States point to a considerable change since 1947. Using the 1962 poverty figure of $3,000, "... we find that between 1947 and 1963 the proportion of families in poverty dropped from 32 percent to 19 percent (in 1962 dollars)."[42] Since then, the number of Americans in poverty has continued to decline, although since the late 1960s the figure has remained between 12 and 13 percent (see Table 11.1). At the outset of the 1970s one out of every eight Americans is still poor.

A Profile of the Poor

The designation of poverty today fits a constellation of people quite different from

[41] *See* John Kenneth Galbraith, *The Affluent Society* (Boston: Houghton Mifflin Company, 1958); and Michael Harrington, *The Other America* (New York: The Macmillan Company, 1962).
[42] *See* Henry P. Miller, *Poverty: American Style* (Belmont, Calif.: Wadsworth Publishing, 1966), p. 115.

TABLE 11.1   **Number and Percent of Persons Below Low-income Level, 1959, 1964, and 1969 to 1971, by Race**

| Years | Number Below Low-income Level (thousands) | | | Percent Below Low-income Level | | |
	Total	White	Black	Total	White	Black
1971	25,559	17,780	7,396	12.5	9.9	32.5
1970	25,420	17,484	7,548	12.6	9.9	33.5
1969	24,147	16,659	7,095	12.1	9.5	32.2
1964	36,055	24,957	11,098*	19.0	14.9	49.6*
1959	39,490	28,484	10,475	22.0	18.1	55.1

* Blacks and other races not separated this year.
Source: U.S. Bureau of the Census, *Current Population Reports*, P-60, no. 86, "Characteristics of the Low-income Population, 1971," U.S. Government Printing Office (Washington, D.C., 1972), Table A, p. 1.

HOW POOR IS POOR?

Throughout the 1960s there has been both confusion and controversy about how many Americans are poor. What level of income defines anyone as poor is clearly a relative matter, both because of a persistently increasing cost of living and because of variable situations: What an elderly couple can get by on would be inadequate for a family of five with three school-age children.

In 1964 the federal government adopted a poverty index developed by the Social Security Administration. This index of low income was based on a nutritionally adequate food plan designed by the Department of Agriculture, and it took account of such factors as family size, sex of the family head, number of children under eighteen years old, and farm-nonfarm residence. Annual revision of the index was based on price changes of the items in the economy food budget.

This poverty index was modified in 1969. Annual adjustments in the levels of income were based on changes in the Consumer Price Index rather than merely on the cost of food in the economy food plan. In 1964, the farm level had been established as 70 percent of the nonfarm level on the assumption that farm families produced for their own use about 30 percent of their food budgets. This came to be regarded as an inadequate measurement, and thus the farm level was redefined to 85 percent of the nonfarm level.

For 1971 the poverty level for a nonfarm family of four with a male head was $4,139. For a family of seven or more, it was $6,771. For a couple over age 65 it was $2,450.

For a more detailed discussion *see* the following publications of the Bureau of the Census:

Current Population Reports, Series P-23, no. 28, "Revision in Poverty Statistics, 1959 to 1968," or *Current Population Reports*, Series P-60, no. 86 (December 1972) "Characteristics of the Low-income Population, 1972," p. 1 and pp. 17–18.

those so designated for the first half of this century. The structure of poverty has undergone considerable change.

Any analysis begins with the fact that changing conditions in the American economy make for poverty as well as affluence. The advance of technological change, for example, for which the term *automation* often serves as a symbol, results in the *displacement* of workers, and this happens in both rural and urban jobs. Farm workers are displaced by mechanization and the growth of large farms, many

of whom then move into urban slums. There are also urban factory workers, whose unskilled and more probably semi-skilled jobs have been eliminated by technological changes. Thus, one major category for the creation of poverty is the continuing displacement of workers by technological changes.

But who are the poor whom structural changes put at such a disadvantage? Although displacement by technological change can strike at random across American society, there is nonetheless a discernible pattern of who are most likely to be affected and who least so. The chances of getting access to the opportunity structure are *least* for certain categories of people: the nonwhite, the uneducated and untrained, those families with a female head, the elderly, families headed by youthful untrained males, and people on farms (*see* "A Profile of the Poor").

Poor Whites and Blacks

In absolute numbers there are a lot more poor whites than blacks, some 17.8 million compared to 7.4 million; this is a ratio of about 7 to 3 (*see* Table 11.2). As a result, almost seven in ten of the poor were white (69.6 percent) in 1971, while three in ten of the poor (28.9 percent) were black. (One and a half percent were of other races.)

But whites outnumber blacks in America almost 9 to 1, which means that the *proportion* of blacks who are poor is much higher than it is for whites. Thus, the almost 70 percent of the poor who are white is less than 10 percent of all whites; while the almost 30 percent of the poor who are black makes up one of every three blacks. The chance of being poor is obviously much greater for a black than for a white.

Age and Poverty

Age is related to poverty in two ways. Older people, particularly those over 65 years of age, are often without adequate savings to keep pace with rising living costs; and they are at a severe disadvantage in finding employment in a labor market that uses age as a criterion for employment—the older you are, the more difficult it is to obtain employment. Although increases in Social Security and

now Medicare have lifted many aged people from the very bottom levels of poverty, it has still left a large number who fall short of levels of adequacy and comfort.

But it is not merely older people who suffer disproportionately from poverty. Children, too, comprise a disproportionate share of the poor. And young families headed by males up to the age of 25 are a disproportionate segment of the poor. This is even more true if the head is a female, as we will see in the next section. In these cases youth who have left school and married early are without sufficient skills to find regular employment or to find employment outside of the lowest-paying fields.

These categories, then, are the beginning of a profile of the poor. Also concentrated among the poor are the functionally illiterate, those whose education has been so meager that for all practical purposes they *are* illiterate. Others lack marketable skills.

The Changing Poor

Since 1959 poverty, as measured by the federal government, has declined from 22.0 percent to the 1971 percentage of 12.5 (*see* Table 11.2). That overall decline, however, obscures several changes within the subgroups who are poor, which has considerably altered the 1959 profile of the poor. For one thing, whites in poverty have decreased more rapidly since 1959 than have blacks; while the poor have declined by 35 percent, the decline for whites is 38 percent, for blacks 29 percent. One important factor is that since 1959 the number and proportion of families in poverty headed by males, both black and white, decreased in number by about 50 percent, while poor families headed by white females have increased slightly, and

A PROFILE OF THE POOR: 1971

One out of every eight Americans (12.5 percent) is poor.

Race

One out of every ten whites (9.9 percent) is poor.
One out of every three blacks (32.5 percent) is poor.

Education

Almost half of the poor (49.2 percent) have only an elementary education or less.
Almost seven in ten (68.8 percent) have not finished high school.

Age

Better than one in five (21.6 percent) of persons 65 years and over are poor.
Almost four in ten (39.3 percent) of black persons 65 years and over are poor.
Almost one in five (18.0) of families headed by a person under 25 years of age is poor.

Sex

Almost four in ten (38.7 percent) of families headed by a female are poor.
Over half (56.1 percent) of families headed by a black female are poor.

Family Size

While one in every ten families is poor, almost one-fourth (23.9 percent) of families with seven or more persons is poor.

Farms

While less than one in twenty Americans (4.6 percent) is in farming, one in five (20.9 percent) of all persons on farms is poor.
Almost two in three (62.9 percent) of all black persons on farms are poor.

Work and Welfare

Two out of three (64.0 percent) of poor families earned some income by work.
One in four (26.5 percent) poor families received Social Security.
One in three (33.9 percent) poor families received public assistance.

Source: U.S. Bureau of the Census, *Current Population Reports*, P-60, no. 86, "Characteristics of the Low-income Population, 1971" (Washington, D.C.: U.S. Government Printing Office, 1972).

those headed by black females have increased by about one-third. As a consequence, almost two out of five poor families are now headed by a woman; these were less than one-fourth of the poor in 1959.[43]

While the aged are a disproportionate component of the poor, they are now a smaller proportion of families in poverty than are young families with heads under 35 years. These young family heads are now approximately 35 percent of all poor family heads, compared to 27 percent in 1959.[44]

These internal shifts in the poverty group, then, suggest that increasingly whites will escape poverty more readily than blacks, and that young families, particularly those headed by females, will become a larger part of the total poor population. Such shifts suggest that what is emerging is a "hard-core" of poor people, harder to assist with politically viable poli-

cies, a group that will receive less public sympathy or even understanding for their poverty.

The poor people who find themselves in one or another of these categories are not there by choice. But they are not able to choose to be anywhere else.

The Near-poor

It should not be assumed that all those above the government's poverty level are affluent. The level set by the government is so low that many families not officially in poverty are nonetheless quite poor. There is a large near-poor for which there is little specific measurement. The U.S. Government Census Bureau has defined a larger group of poor by using a poverty measurement of 125 percent of the official level. Whereas an income of $4,137 per year is the official poverty level for a nonfarm family of four, at the Census Bureau's 125 percent that income figure becomes $5,171 per year. Table 11.2 shows how the number who are poor increases by using this alternate measure. Note particularly the high proportion of female-headed families in poverty by this measurement.

[43] U.S. Bureau of the Census, *Current Population Reports*, P-60, no. 86, "Characteristics of the Low-income Population, 1971" (Washington, D.C.: Government Printing Office, 1972), pp. 2–3.
[44] "Characteristics of the Low-income Population," p. 3.

TABLE 11.2   Percentage of Persons in Poverty by Official Standard and by 125 Percent of Official Standard, 1971

	Official Low-income Level	"Near-poor": 125 Percent of Official Level
All persons	12.5	17.8
Whites	9.9	14.6
Blacks	32.5	42.7
Families with female head	38.7	48.4
Families with black female head	56.1	67.7

Source: U.S. Bureau of the Census, *Current Population Reports*, P-60, no. 86, "Characteristics of the Low-income Population, 1971" (Washington, D.C.: U.S. Government Printing Office, 1972), Table 2, pp. 30–34.

The Poverty Trap

The poverty in which several million American families find themselves is sustained and reinforced by a set of conditions that are beyond the scope of the individual to alter. Obviously, the poor are poor because they have little money; but they also have few prospects for significantly increasing their supply of money. They are unemployed or underemployed, or they are employed in low-paying jobs; there are both welfare poor and working poor. But a changing labor market needs less and less the relatively unskilled or low-skilled labor which the poor can provide. They are in effect marginal to the needs of the economy.

Nor are the poor organized or otherwise able to exercise power. They are in no position to force a redistribution of income that would eliminate their poverty. Without power they are unable to change the circumstances of their lives, or to fight effectively the landlords, merchants, politicians, social workers, educators, and others whose practices only insure a continuation of their poverty.

Housing is one of the major expenses that raises particularly difficult problems for the poor. Slums by definition are areas of inadequate housing, and the United States Census records that substandard housing still exists in substantial numbers in American cities. The numerous "inner cities" are large areas of deteriorated and still deteriorating housing. The poor either accept inadequate housing, or else they pay comparably more for housing than anyone else; as much as a third of their income may be paid to exploiting slum landlords. To make these payments they sacrifice clothing, medicine, or important consumer items.

While the poor can purchase adequate housing only at a serious sacrifice of life's other necessities, most of their consumer purchasing is also done at a disadvantage. Slum merchants also exploit the poor. Sociologist David Caplovitz has documented the fact that the poor pay more for goods of poorer quality than do any other group of people in the cities.[45] They are victims, in the first place, of an inability to travel around enough to do comparison shopping. More to the point, they have little cash on hand, and their credit is nonexistent in most stores in the community. But there are merchants who specialize in selling on credit to the poor and manage to make this a profitable enterprise. The poor are as hungry as other Americans for such durable goods as furniture, television sets, and radios; and this creates a set of circumstances in which their effort to share in the affluent society's consumption patterns makes them vulnerable to effective economic exploitation. Their desire for consumer goods only increases their entrapment in the world of poverty.

The poor must accept the quality of schooling that the community makes available to their children. And that schooling is inferior. This is strongly denied by public-school authorities, but sociologist Patricia Cayo Sexton documented how the level of parental income paralleled the quality of education in one large city. The quality of educational facilities provided for students from the lowest-income families in the community was inferior to that provided for the upper-income families, even though this was a single school system with a single tax base.[46]

The children of the poor perpetuate the

[45] *See* David Caplovitz, *The Poor Pay More* (New York: The Free Press, 1963).

[46] *See* Patricia Cayo Sexton, *Education and Income* (New York: The Viking Press, Inc., 1961).

lack of education of their parents and, in a technological and affluent society, this in turn perpetuates poverty. To say that the poor fail to complete an education is not to criticize them. It is simply to state a fact of great importance. Put another way, a body of professional educators consistently fails to educate the children of the poor in a satisfactory fashion. (We shall return to this issue in Chapter 13.)

The structure of poverty does something to the poor besides compounding a network of disadvantages in housing, consumption, and schooling; it constitutes a pattern of life that takes a personal toll in physical and mental health. Chronic ill health plagues the poor, and they are more susceptible to contagious diseases; a slum environment inevitably threatens health standards. Yet medical care is provided only grudgingly.[47]

Furthermore, the poor suffer a great deal from emotional difficulties. However, they get little attention from psychiatric facilities until they reach that serious point where they are disruptive in their relations with others and must be hospitalized.[48]

On Understanding Poverty

The poor have rarely been viewed favorably by other social classes; most of the time they have been looked down on unsympathetically and blamed for their own plight. Throughout the long development of industrial society, and even before, the dominant middle-class image of the poor was a morally critical one. The rapid

pace of industrialization within the past 150 years did little to change the perspective expressed originally in the Elizabethan Poor Laws, adopted during the reign of Queen Elizabeth in England (1558–1603). These laws were based on the assumption that any condition of personal dependency was the fault of the individual and an indication of a morally defective character.[49]

In the nineteenth century scientific explanations joined moral ones in condemning the poor and dependent as inherently inferior. Thus, the poor were given a double stigma: They were genetically inferior and morally unfit. Such definitions of why the poor were poor were easily attached to blacks, given the persistence of racist ideologies in the United States.

But these interpretations of genetic and moral unfitness were also attached to immigrants from Eastern and Southern Europe at the turn of the century, defining them in racial rather than cultural terms. A halt to immigration was hastened by dire warnings of the danger of allowing such "inferior" people to come into the United States in large numbers.

Although details may vary slightly over time, this middle-class perspective on poverty has changed but little over the last several centuries. The claim that the poor lack qualities of moral responsibility and individual initiative, as well as personal pride and independence, allows the middle class self-satisfaction about its own primary virtues. Therefore, so goes the ideology, the plight of poor people is their own fault, a consequence of genetic and moral defects. That is why much remains

---

[47] See Anselm Strauss, "Medical Ghettoes," *Transaction* (May 1967), pp. 7–15.

[48] See Frank Riessman, Jerome Cohen, and Arthur Pearl, eds., *Mental Health of the Poor* (New York: The Free Press, 1964).

[49] For a review of the origins and development of welfare as one aspect of the development of industrial society *see* Harold Wilensky and Charles N. Lebeaux, *Social Welfare and Industrial Society* (New York: Russell Sage Foundation, 1958).

Figure 11.5 When Governor Nelson Rockefeller of New York proposed a cut in welfare spending in 1969 about 3,000 demonstrators massed on the Capitol Building steps to protest. *(United Press International Photo.)*

of this perspective even today.[50] Now it is likely to be directed specifically at those on welfare, particularly at blacks. Many Americans seem to believe that people on welfare are lazy, prefer charity to working, are uneducated because they are stupid, are given to criminal behavior, and have loose morals so that they produce illegitimate children. In particular, many whites believe that this is true of blacks, and they also feel that welfare money supports such immorality.

But this historically conservative view now has competition. There is another perspective, one which rejects all racist and genetic arguments as unscientific and reactionary. Instead, it is asserted, poverty is a consequence of social and cultural conditions. The poor are made that way by conditions in the society. Yet, the new, liberal ideology, according to psychologist William Ryan, still blames the victim for his condition, though much more subtly:

> The new ideology attributes defect and inadequacy to the malignant nature of poverty, injustice, slum life, and racial difficulties. The stigma that marks the victim and accounts for his victimization is an acquired stigma, a stigma of social, rather than genetic, origin. But the stigma, the defect, the fatal difference—though derived in the past from environmental forces—is still located *within* the victim, inside his skin.[51]

Ryan's thesis is that middle-class liberals, backed by social-scientific research,

---

[50] Social scientist Edward C. Banfield has given wide currency to a contemporary version of this argument; *see* his *The Unheavenly City* (Boston: Little, Brown & Company, 1968).

[51] William Ryan, *Blaming the Victim* (New York: Random House, Inc., 1971; paperback edition, Vantage Books, 1972, p. 7).

still see the poor person as basically inadequate and incompetent, though not at fault. He is thought of as uneducated or "culturally deprived" or unmotivated for achievement or lacking in occupational skills. These defects, then, must be corrected by changing the victim.

He is to be changed by being made more like the middle class: presumably educated, responsible, hard-working, skilled, or whatever other flattering attributes the middle class assigns to itself and regards as the basis for its "success." This is arrived at, Ryan notes, by first identifying a social problem, then determining how the victims differ from the middle class, and then defining the differences as the cause of the social problem.[52] By that logic, the poor are poor because they are uneducated. There is no grasp of the idea that the poor are uneducated because they are poor. There is a vast difference between these two concepts.

Changing the victim becomes a program of action that shifts the target from the basic causes of the problem — racism, unemployment, low income, poor schools — to the victims themselves. We are asked, says Ryan, to ignore continued discrimination against black people, the gross deprivation of services to the poor, the heavy stresses endemic in their lives. "And almost all our make-believe liberal programs aimed at correcting our urban problems are off target; they are designed either to change the poor man or to cool him out."[53]

The Culture of Poverty Myth

The liberal mythology for blaming the victim has been supported by social scien-

tists through the theory of a *culture of poverty,* a term first developed by anthropologist Oscar Lewis on the basis of his sympathetic portraits of poor people in Mexico. He characterized such a culture as:

. . . a strong present time orientation, with relatively little ability to defer gratification and plan for the future, a sense of resignation and fatalism based upon the realities of their difficult life situation, a belief in male superiority which reaches its crystallization in *machismo* or the cult of masculinity, a corresponding martyr complex among women, and finally, a high tolerance for psychological pathology of all sorts.[54]

The culture of poverty theory makes much of childhood socialization, and indeed, tends to overemphasize the profound effects of the early years, which is consistent with an older psychological theory. Thus, Lewis again:

Once the culture of poverty has come into existence it tends to perpetuate itself. By the time slum children are six or seven they have usually absorbed the basic attitudes and values of their subculture. Thereafter they are psychologically unready to take full advantage of changing conditions or improving opportunities that may develop in their lifetime.[55]

Deferred Gratification

The poor are often accused of being spendthrift, of squandering any resources that might come to them, and of not postponing pleasure for the sake of saving. In the language of the psychologist, they do not *defer gratification,* a presumed inability

---

[52] *See* Ryan, *op. cit.,* p. 8.
[53] *See* Ryan, *op. cit.,* p. 25.

[54] Oscar Lewis, *The Children of Sanchez* (New York: Random House, Inc., 1961), pp. xxvi–xxvii. For a telling critique of the idea of a culture of poverty *see* Charles A. Valentine, *Culture and Poverty* (Chicago: University of Chicago Press, 1968).
[55] Oscar Lewis, "The Culture of Poverty," *Scientific American,* vol. CCXV, (October 1966), p. 7.

that for many social scientists makes the poor so very unlike the middle class.

But perhaps too much emphasis has been put on this one characteristic—or so some social scientists now believe.[56] For one thing, the ability to defer gratification until some future time, to plan for a future and save for it, to forego pleasure in the present for the sake of one's future is hardly an accurate description any longer of the middle class, which now buys on time, goes into debt, complains of not havin‑
lights
enter
secor
style

A
the
catio
that
ued,
or s
is tl
fica
plac
whi
the
a c
and
con
goal.

In similar fashion, presumed differences between middle-class culture and a lower-class culture of poverty on such matters as sexual behavior, child-rearing, aspirations for children, and attitudes toward law-abiding behavior do not differentiate the

poor from others sharply. Sociologist Hylan Lewis, for example, found that lower-class parents differed little in values and attitudes from the middle-class parents, but were less able than middle-class parents to act consistent with those values.[57]

All those who are poor cannot and should not be forced into a single cultural model; even Oscar Lewis, who invented the concept, claimed that only a minority of the poor fitted the culture of poverty. There is enormous psychological and cultural variation among people who happen to be poor.

This is not to say that the poor are simply like other people. Poverty is a destructive condition with a strong impact. Sociologist Hyman Rodman has suggested that members of the lower class share the dominant values of society but that circumstances do not permit them to live by all these values, so they *stretch* them to take account of the severe limits a life of poverty imposes on them.

They do not maintain a strong commitment to middle-class values that they cannot attain, and they do not continue to respond to others in a rewarding or punishing way simply on the basis of whether these others are living up to the middle-class values. A change takes place. They come to tolerate and eventually to evaluate favorably certain deviations from the middle-class values. In this way they need not be continually frustrated by their failure to live up to unattainable values. The resultant is a stretched value system with a low degree of commitment to all the values within the range, including the dominant, middle-class values.[58]

What Rodman and others have argued is

---

[56] *See* S.M. Miller, Frank Riessman, and Arthur Seagull, "Poverty and Self-Indulgence: A Critique of the Nondeferred Gratification Pattern," in Louis A. Ferman, Joyce L. Kornbluh, and Alan Haber, eds., *Poverty in America* (Ann Arbor, Mich.: University of Michigan Press, 1965), pp. 285–302.

[57] Hylan Lewis, "Child Rearing among Low-income Families," in Ferman, Kornbluh, and Haber, pp. 342–353.

[58] *See* Hyman Rodman, "The Lower-class Value Stretch, *Social Forces* (December 1963), p. 209.

that poor people must of necessity adapt to the unrewarding, even threatening conditions of poverty, and much of their behavior can be accounted for in this way. What those who have defined the very poor as a culturally different lower class have done is, first observe these differences in behavior and then infer values and norms that would make them logical. In that way they seem to be a culturally different people. But often they have behaved as they have not from a radically divergent cultural perspective but out of force of circumstances and lack of alternatives. In that sense much of their behavior is *adaptive* to the circumstances of poverty, deprivation, and powerlessness.

Sociologist Lee Rainwater makes this observation and then adds:

If lower class culture is to be changed and lower class people are eventually to be enabled to take advantage of "opportunities" to participate in conventional society and to earn their own way in it, this change can only come about through a change in the social and ecological situation to which lower class people must adapt.[59]

Any anti-poverty strategy, according to Rainwater, must be a "resource equalization strategy," and equalization of resources must include as a key factor an equalization of income.

The Welfare Poor

One of the significant discoveries coming from new concerns about poverty includes how little welfare has done to alter

[59] *See* Lee Rainwater, "The Problem of Lower Class Culture and Poverty-war Strategy," in Daniel P. Moynihan, ed., *On Understanding Poverty* (New York: Basic Books, Inc., 1969), p. 251.

the depressed status of the poor. The present structure of welfare was created in the 1930s and has changed little since then, even though the prevailing assumption of the Depression—that people were only in temporary need of help until the Depression ended—no longer fits the reality of poverty in the 1970s.

All the poor do not benefit from welfare. The permanently unemployed have exhausted unemployment benefits, and, being jobless, are not paying into Social Security. The millions who are employed at low wages—the working poor—do not qualify for any welfare benefits, except eligibility for public housing. Perhaps the major source of welfare assistance has become ADC (Aid to Dependent Children), which provides minimum support for families lacking a male head and breadwinner. The local public welfare rolls constitute the last resort for those who qualify for nothing else.

Welfare is immensely unpopular as social policy among both the working and middle classes. The poor, we noted earlier, are blamed for their own plight—today, even as they were in the past. With so many black people on welfare it is even more unpopular with whites. However inaccurate, the prevailing white American stereotype of a welfare existence is the black ADC mother raising several illegitimate children.

Yet those in power who so dislike welfare seem to be unable to do away with it. In a significant study Frances Fox Pliven and sociologist Richard A. Cloward demonstrate that relief performs two important functions: (1.) it prevents or at least moderates disruption and rebellion on the part of the poor, and (2.) it maintains a pool of cheap labor by periodically pushing people off relief into low-paying jobs and by making relief as demeaning and unpleasant as possible to its recipients.[60]

Public welfare is a vast, bureaucratic, controlling apparatus operated by middle-class professionals. If the poor become dependent on it, the apparatus does nothing to remove that dependency. And many poor people have no alternative but to be dependent on it for food, clothing, shelter, and medical care. None of these necessities is offered without red tape and an invasion of people's lives — a demeaning experience — and none is offered in any quantity or quality comparable to what middle-class people can readily buy. Welfare is not a *solution* to poverty — it was never intended to be — but is a custodial process that discourages independence, self-reliance, and self-respect — those attributes that the poor are so often accused of not possessing.

THE FUTURE OF INEQUALITY

The protest movements of the 1960s focused on inequality in the class and race structure of the United States, and also in the status of women. But these movements did something else; they raised the issue of whether or not any significant effort to reduce inequality was underway. It was during the 1960s that research disputing earlier claims to changes in the disparities of shares of wealth held by various income groupings gained wider recognition.

But in the 1970s the protest movements seem weaker, and an attack on the efforts to achieve greater equality, particularly for racial minorities and poor people, is occur-

ring. The attack has taken several directions, none new.[61] First is a return to the argument about genetic differences among the races. The work of psychologist Arthur Jensen in particular has given credence to the once-discredited idea that blacks are mentally inferior to whites (*see* our discussion in Chapter 13). Second, the poor and the blacks, it is asserted, are marked by a culture and a set of attitudes that make them incapable of taking advantage of any opportunities they might have. The presumed inability of poor people to defer gratification is the common argument — one we have already shown to be dubious. Third, it is asserted that the importance of personal and family stability — the values of steady work and strong family ties — are values, as Nathan Glazer claims, that are weakened by the practices of welfare.[62] For those who accept them, these arguments justify reducing governmental action to remedy inequalities and widen social opportunities for racial minorities, for poor people, for women.

The belief in equality has always been tempered in philosophy and moderated in practice. Though equal opportunity is a widely acknowledged right, the effort to make it real — to reduce inequalities in life chances between races, classes, and sexes — still lacks an effective politics of equality in the United States.

One reason for this is that the dominant value system of American society does

[60] *See* Frances Fox Pliven and Richard A. Cloward, *Regulating the Poor: The Function of Public Welfare* (New York: Pantheon Books, Inc., 1971).

[61] *See* S. M. Miller and Ronnie Steinberg Ratner, "The American Resignation: The New Assault on Equality," *Social Policy,* vol. 3 (May/June, 1972), pp. 5–15; and subsequent articles in the same issue.

[62] *See* Nathan Glazer, "The Limits of Social Policy," *Commentary,* vol. 52 (September 1971). For criticism of this position *see* Miller and Ratner, pp. 9–10; and Pliven and Cloward, "Nathan Glazer's Retroactive Wisdom on Welfare," *Social Policy,* vol. 3 (May/June, 1972), pp. 26–27.

not—verbal pretensions aside—proclaim belief in the principle of human equality. Rather, there are specific beliefs in *equality of opportunity* and *equality before the law.* Neither of these values is systematically practiced, so that reality violates even these beliefs.

It seems unlikely that equality of opportunity and equality before the law can be made real in a society where property, income, and education are unequally distributed.[63] The advantaged classes and groups protect and justify their advantages. An emerging meritocracy in both Communist and Capitalist societies, as we noted in Chapter 10, may in fact herald the new form that stratification will take, and with it a new rationalization for inequality.

If that is the case the struggles among groups and classes with unequal shares in the rewards of society will go on, though in new forms. Inequality is a basic patterning of human societies, a basic source of ideologies about how life should be organized and how people differ from one another. It is also a basic source of group and class struggle; thus it is fundamental to the politics of any society.

However inevitable inequality may seem to be, the ideal of equality as a perspective on what society might become and as a source of criticism for the institutional inequalities of any society remains. If a post-modern society generates a new form of inequality, such as meritocracy, it will also generate new dreams of human equality.

---

[63] Sidney Willhelm argues that, this being so, equality for blacks becomes meaningless in the face of white economic domination and advantage. *See* his *Who Needs the Negro?*, pp. 229–243.

SUMMARY

Minority designates a *status,* not a quantity—a status of domination and control by a majority (dominant) group. The power to discriminate by one group over another creates a minority.

Prejudice is the attitudinal aspect of minority status, *discrimination* the behavioral. The relation of prejudice to discrimination is complex; it is not simply true that prejudice causes discrimination. Instead, prejudice justifies discrimination.

Institutional racism refers to the discriminatory practices of institutions—particularly the educational, economic, and political.

Minorities are racial and ethnic groups. Ethnicity, thought to be disappearing by virtue of assimilation, is now rediscovered as a still meaningful identity for many. While there has been cultural assimilation—acculturation—there has been less *structural* assimilation, and so parallel structures for ethnics continue to exist.

Explaining race relations in the face of rejection of integration by some blacks has led to doubts about the value of the *assimilation* model, which was based on comparing blacks with immigrants. By contrast, the *economic-class* model interprets blacks as an economically obsolescent underclass and a *colonial* model based on the nature of the colonizing process: forced entry, as by slavery; the destruction of the original culture; close control; and racism.

The major forms of discrimination are in employment, education, politics, and housing.

Millions of Americans are still poor, despite the country's affluence. The poor disproportionately include: the nonwhite, the poorly educated; the elderly; the young, untrained worker; and families headed by females.

The poor are trapped in a set of structural conditions beyond individual control: poor housing, poor schooling, slum landlords, and exploiting merchants, with a consequent physical and mental toll.

Middle-class explanations of poverty still blame the poor for being poor—blaming the victim—but while some employ older ideas of inherent inferiority, others utilize a *culture of poverty* theory.

The attack on inequality of the 1960s has abated and there is now a renewed attack on ideas of equality, particularly in terms of racial and cultural inferiority. Many Americans believe not in equality but specifically in equality of opportunity and equality before the law, even though both are violated in practice.

Suggested Reading

Robert Blauner, *Racial Oppression in America* (New York: Harper & Row, 1972). A series of critical essays on the sociological effort to understand racism.

Stokely Carmichael and Charles Hamilton, *Black Power: The Politics of Liberation in America* (New York: Random House, Inc., 1967). A compelling analysis of the problems blacks face, by a militant black activist and a black social scientist.

Harold Cruse, *The Crisis of the Negro Intellectual* (New York: William Morrow & Company, Inc., 1967). The crises of black intellectuals in assessing America is analyzed historically by a black intellectual.

Vine Deloria, Jr., *Custer Died for Your Sins: An Indian Manifesto* (New York: The Macmillan Company, 1969). A mordantly witty analysis of the condition of the American Indian and his relations with white Americans.

Eugene D. Genovese, *In Red and Black: Marxian Explorations in Southern and Afro-American History* (New York: Vintage Books, 1972). A brilliant young American historian, a Marxist, ranges over a set of issues, from slavery to contemporary black issues, to identify ideological issues in the struggle for equality.

Nathan Glazer and Daniel Moynihan, *Beyond the Melting Pot* (Cambridge, Mass.: The M.I.T. Press and Harvard University Press, 1963). An important study making it clear that ethnicity still survives.

Milton Gordon, *Assimilation in American Life: The Role of Race, Religion, and National Origins* (New York: Oxford University Press, 1964). A fine analysis of assimilation and cultural pluralism in American life.

Michael Harrington, *The Other America* (New York: The Macmillan Company, 1962). The still relevant study that "rediscovered" poverty.

Louis L. Knowles and Kenneth Prewitt, eds., *Institutional Racism in America*

(Englewood Cliffs, N.J.: Prentice-Hall, Inc., 1969). A documentation of racism as an institutional process.

Hyman Lumer, *Poverty: Its Roots and Its Future* (New York: International Publishers Company, Inc., 1965). One of the better radical critiques of the welfare program and its relationship to "hard-core" poverty.

S. M. Miller and Pamela Roby, *The Future of Inequality* (New York: Basic Books, Inc., 1970). A thorough sociological examination of the sources of inequality in American society, with suggestions for tentative goals for the near future.

National Advisory Commission, *Report of the National Advisory Commission on Civil Disorders* (New York: Bantam Books, 1968). A study of racism as the basic cause of racial disorder.

Michael Novak, *The Rise of the Unmeltable Ethnics* (New York: The Macmillan Company, 1971; paperback edition, 1973). A provocative, sympathetic study that suggests that white ethnics will be increasingly important politically during the 1970s.

Francis Fox Pliven and Richard A. Cloward, *Regulating the Poor: The Function of Public Welfare* (New York: Pantheon Books, Inc., 1971). A brilliant, prize-winning study of how relief programs function to control the poor in American society.

William Ryan, *Blaming the Victim* (New York: Vintage Books, 1972). A searing, provocative critique on how the middle class blames the poor for their poverty.

Charles A. Valentine, *Culture and Poverty* (Chicago: University of Chicago Press, 1968). A critique of the idea that there is a culture of poverty.

Sidney M. Willhelm, *Who Needs the Negro?* (New York: Schenkman, 1970; paperback version, Anchor Books, 1971). Documents the economic obsolescence of lower-class blacks.

Pierre L. van den Berghe, *Race and Racism: A Comparative Perspective* (New York: John Wiley & Sons, Inc., 1967). An influential work in carrying the study of racism beyond the analysis of individual attitudes.

PART V

PART V

INSTITUTIONS
AND SOCIAL
STRUCTURE

Women are not altogether in the wrong when they refuse the rules of life prescribed to the world, for men only have established them and without their consent.
— *Montaigne*

Chapter 12

The Family

Through the ages the family has been a fundamental social institution at the very core of society. Family values have long been regarded as fundamental—a source of morality and decent conduct—so much so as to warrant strong measures against any behavior that violated them. The family has also been defined as a primary force for controlling behavior and civilizing the human animal.

But when people talk loftily about the family, they really often mean the Western family and perhaps only the middle-class Western family. Yet this is only one form, for anthropologists tell us that what may properly be called *family* is arranged in a much wider and more varied set of social patterns worldwide.

Sociologists, in turn, have always regarded the family as a significant social group. Yet the family received little direct attention in early analyses of society. In fact, the study of the family around the turn of the century was largely carried on by anthropologists and archaeologists, who examined it in preliterate and ancient times. Perhaps Edward A. Westermack's *The History of Human Marriage* was the climax to the relatively objective, historical, and anthropological approach to the family which recognized the differences in family life in many places and at a variety of times. By the time American sociologists gave serious attention to the subject, particularly after 1920, a strong basis for a comparative look at the family as a social institution had already been established.

THE UNIVERSALITY OF THE FAMILY

The family can be found in all known human societies, although not in the same form. According to anthropologist George P. Murdock, a basic kinship group can be empirically observed in all societies which provides for:

1. Permission of sexual access between adults.
2. Legitimate reproduction.
3. Responsibility for the care and upbringing of children.
4. Cooperation as an economic unit, at least in consumption.[1]

Apparently most social scientists agree that these four activities are of great importance in all human societies; they regulate and control in some institutionalized manner the relationships of the sexes and provide for mating in order to reproduce. This is true even among so-called "primitives." But they strongly disagree that it is always the same group which carries out these activities, or even in all cases that it is a kinship group.

The Family as a Group

Social scientists disagree also with Murdock's further claim that the *nuclear* family of husband, wife, and children is *universally* the kinship unit by which these basic activities are carried out. There are

well-known examples of societies in which at least some activities are carried out by other groups, some kinship-based but some not. In an Israeli *kibbutz,* for example, the mother-father unit does not raise and train the children; this is a communal responsibility. The *kibbutz,* according to anthropologist Melford Spiro, "can function without the family because it functions as if it, itself, were a family; and it can so function because its members perceive each other as kin, in the psychological implications of that term."[2] In China (at least prior to 1949) and in many traditional, preindustrial societies, cooperation as an economic unit and the care of children have been carried on within an *extended* family group (one that includes more than the nuclear family).

Although the nuclear family is widespread, it is not, apparently, universal; among the Nayar of India, for example, the resident family group consists of brother, sister, and the sister's children. The father of the children resides elsewhere and is not part of the family as a group, though he is part of the institutional arrangement for mating and procreation.

Anthropological research shows us, in short, that no *one* form of human group must exist to carry out family activities, therefore no *one* of them is universal.

The Family as Institution

To understand what is universal about the family we need to make a theoretical distinction between the family as an *institution* and the family as a *social group*. Societies which survive work out culturally

[1] *See* George P. Murdock, *Social Structures* (New York: The Macmillan Company, 1949).

[2] *See* Melford Spiro, "Is the Family Universal?," *American Anthropologist,* vol. 56 (5: 1954), p. 844.

approved ways of assuring the reproduction, maintenance, socialization, and placement of the young.

1. *Reproduction:* Marriage sanctions a sexual union that leads to procreation and to a legitimate status for the new member of society.
2. *Maintenance:* In whatever way, there must be someone assigned to provide care for the human young, who is dependent for a longer period of time than any other animal.
3. *Socialization:* Also, someone (or several) must teach the young both the skills and norms essential for participation in society. Even though much learning does occur outside of any family group, particularly in modern society, socialization remains a primary family function.
4. *Placement:* Legitimacy of birth provides for a stable process of placement in society, by *inheritance* of property, *succession* of status, and *descent,* that is, placement at birth in ethnic, kinship, or even religious groups.

It is this *institutional* process which is *universal.* There is a range of group structures by which this can be done and to which the label, *family,* can be attached. As a social group, the family is a small, kinship-based, interacting unit (nuclear or extended), within which at least some of these familial functions are carried out.

Variations in the Family

An appreciation of just how varied in form the family can be is an essential element in a sociological perspective on the family, even if one's concern is only with the American nuclear family. What follows is a brief notation of some of the variations.

Mate Selection

In any society mate selection is never a chance procedure, but only in some socie-

ties is there a notion of romantic love as a basis for a *free* choice of mates by the individuals themselves. In a large number of traditional, agrarian societies, mate selection has been a prerogative of the family. These are often crucial and complex decisions for families, involving many economic and status interests, since inheritance of position and property may be associated with marriage.

In addition, the selection process in most societies is also governed by rules of *endogamy* and *exogamy* (See "The Terminology of Kinship"). In traditional societies such rules are formally prescribed. In modern societies there are few formal requirements, yet there are powerful informal expectations of endogamy and exogamy that often influence how young people make their choices. Race and religion are the most obvious examples of these, particularly race, for interracial marriages had long been forbidden by law in some states of the United States. (Recently, these laws were invalidated by the Supreme Court.) Yet the strength of these endogamous rules does not rely on law but on widely diffused cultural expectations.

Forms of Marriage

While the Western form of marriage is *monogamy,* many societies in the world have practiced *polygamy.* In polygamous societies to marry several women means to be able to support them and their children and, consequently, can serve as an index of status and wealth. The lot of the common man is to be able to afford but one wife.

In the United States and some other Western societies, marriage, divorce, and remarriage (sometimes several times) is now so common that many observers have

THE TERMINOLOGY OF KINSHIP

Choice of Partners

Endogamy: marriage partners chosen from *within* a group: tribe, community, religious group, and so on.
Exogamy: marriage partner chosen from *without* a group—clan, tribe, kinship group, and so on.

Forms of Marriage

Monogamy: one man to one woman.
Polygamy: a plurality of mates.
 Polygyny: a man has several wives.
 Polyandry: a woman has several husbands.

Rules of Authority, Descent, and Residence

Patriarchal: authority held by the father.
 Patrilineal: descent (names, property) through father's line.
 Patrilocal: newly married couple reside with husband's parents.
Matriarchal: authority held by the mother.
 Matrilineal: descent through mother's line.
 Matrilocal: newly married couple reside with wife's parents.
Other:
 Bilineal: descent follows both lines.
 Neolocal: newly married couple resides separately.

---

noted this is a departure from traditional monogamy—"until death do us part"—and might be labeled *serial polygamy.*

Rules of Authority and Descent

Wherever the male is dominant and holds the authority of the family, the family is *patriarchal.* This is the Western tradition. Usually closely associated with a patriarchy is a *patrilineal* tracing of descent through the male side of the family. Inheritance of name and property, for example, is frequently patrilineal.

But there are also rules of descent which are neither matrilineal nor patrilineal. The tracing of descent may be *bilateral,* as it is, though imperfectly, in American society—imperfectly, because we are patrilineal in such things as transmitting names. But we do relate the child equally to each line of his descent; one set of grandparents is not favored over the other.

Authority in our system is still formally (and therefore legally) patriarchal, but in practice the trend has been steadily in the direction of an equal relationship, concomitant with gains in the status of women.

The Family as a Primary Group

When sociological analysis focuses on the contemporary American family, there is an additional concern for what has been called the "affectional function." The argument is that the intense and close interaction of children and parents in a separate household creates a small, primary unit that is the major source of sustaining affection for both parents and children. The modern American family frequently lives away from other relatives, and this intensifies the interaction among mother, father, and children occupying a common household.

The frequent and intimate interaction of parents and children *universally* creates within some circumscribed circle of kin a basic *primary* group that can generate the deepest of human feelings of love and affection (and possibly also the opposite). But now, among most American families there is a very conscious *expectation* of happiness to be derived from the intimate and primary character of family relationships. In a study of 900 Detroit families, for instance, *companionship* was the aspect of marriage most valued.[3]

Apparently adults increasingly see in the family a fundamental source of primary response to a world more and more impersonal in its relationships. It is just when the individual is no longer so *economically* dependent on the family that such expectations of happiness become so important to people.

In a study of the wives of young corporate executives William H. Whyte pointed to devastating effects on those marriages where the woman showed reluctance or an inability to live up to corporate expectations about her role.[4] Yet, the corporation also recognized the primary nature of the family when it expected it to function as a "refueling station," providing the love and warmth that resuscitated the exhausted executive and readied him once more in energy and spirits for the daily business struggle.

Divorce

1970 - 1 out 3.5 marriages

This increasing expectation of happiness and companionship to be derived from marriage makes understandable the fact of a rising divorce rate in the United States. in 1900 the divorce rate was 4.0 per 1,000 existing marriages; by 1956 it was 9.3.

All analyses of divorce have emphasized that most divorces are of young couples married only one or two years and having no children. Given this fact, divorce seemed less damaging to the structure of the family.

However, more recently the proportion of divorces involving children has increased sharply. In 1953 less than half involved children, but in ten years almost two thirds of the divorcing couples had children.[5] In part, this is because there is an increase in the age of couples getting divorced; it is no longer so overwhelmingly the very young who are shortly married.

INDUSTRIALIZATION AND THE FAMILY

A generation ago many people, sociologists included, viewed with alarm the

---

[3] See Robert O. Blood, Jr., and Donald M. Wolfe, *Husbands and Wives: The Dynamics of Married Living* (New York: The Free Press, 1960), p. 172.

[4] See William H. Whyte, *Is Anybody Listening?* (New York: Simon and Schuster, Inc., 1952), Chs. 8 and 9.

[5] See *Divorce Statistics Analysis, United States 1963,* Public Health Service Publication No. 1000, Series 21, no. 13.

changes in the family that seemed to accompany the industrialization of society. The common theme in this bleak outlook was to predict the decline of the family as a consequence of a decline of its social functions. One influential such formulation was that the family was passing "from institution to companionship."[6] According to this interpretation, the agrarian family (even in the nineteenth century) was necessarily the center of life for the individual. It possessed major economic functions, for the agrarian family was a *productive* unit, organized by a division of labor to operate a farm. Except for a few who went into religious institutions or into the cities, the individual was tied to his family status and his economic role was found in the family as a work group.

In preindustrial societies the family performed many functions that have since become community or societal responsibilities. It not only socialized the young, it provided much other training of the child as well. Among European peasants, and even later among American farmers, a boy learned his occupation by working with his father at a young age.

Furthermore, in an agrarian society the kinship group maintained the aged, nursed the sick, buried the dead, and provided for the mentally ill or physically crippled. It also insured support for widows and orphans and made a place for the occasionally unmarried woman.

As a result one can understand the growth of a moral outlook that made kinship a most binding and obligatory relationship, regardless of personal feelings, and requiring family interests to take

[6] *See* Ernest Burgess and Harvey J. Locke, *The Family: From Institution to Companionship* (New York: American Book Company, 1953).

precedence over individual ones. The individual was locked into a demanding structure of kinship obligations and duties that extended beyond the nuclear family to a wider network of kin.

The Consequence of Industrialization

The transformation of society by industrialization thoroughly altered this set of institutional arrangements. Some of the major changes were:

1. *Separation of work and home.* A developing machine technology took work out of the home and put it into a factory; as a consequence, the family ceased to be a productive unit. Work, located elsewhere, became in time the almost sole responsibility of the father.

2. *Decline in family size.* Children were no longer economically necessary, unlike agrarian society where a father without sons might not be able to maintain himself. Now they were mouths to feed, and the reward for having sons was no longer in economic values. Birth rates declined as society industrialized—as did family size, particularly in the middle class, where children were viewed as competitive with other values.

3. *Decline of extended family system.* There was the decline of the extended family system of kinship obligation and an increase in the small, nuclear family maintaining a separate and independent household.

4. *Separation of family and education.* The need for new kinds of occupational training and more advanced education led to the emergence of a mass educational structure separate from the family.

5. *Loss of occupational succession.* As society industrialized, parents could less and less transmit an occupational status to their children, except where there was a family business; and family-owned businesses (including farms) have declined rapidly. Children may pursue careers not even known or available to their parents.

1970 - 3.62 persons in a family

How much industrialization can be assigned responsibility for the decline of extended kinship units and the increase of the more isolated nuclear family is a matter of considerable scholarly argument. Sociologist Morris Zelditch summarizes a complex set of issues and comparative data by pointing out that industrialization can produce these changes, but so can other economic forms such as commercial export agriculture, as long as these forms effectively divorce economic and occupational structures from the kinship structure.[7]

When occupational and kinship structures are separated, says Zelditch:

> ... the power and patronage on which the corporate descent group and extended family depend for their authority erode; after which their authority, in turn, erodes; and what is left is a primarily expressive kindred in which relatives continue to find personal reasons for liking each other and helping each other but without the same compelling subordination to a common goal and common authority.[8]

There is a danger, however, that this radical transformation of the family under industrialization will lead us to overlook the significance the family still plays in the lives of its members. The ties of kinship remain meaningful, and the family has remained a source of help to its members. Sociologist Marvin Sussman, for example, found in a study of middle-class families in New Haven, Connecticut, that many middle-class parents provided partially concealed subsidies for a child at marriage in order to establish the child at the same class level as the parents.[9] The

following discussion of stratification and the family will further document the continuing importance of family.

STRATIFICATION AND THE FAMILY

By and large, even in mobile societies the family acts as a stabilizing factor in the class structure, for it is through the family that most individuals are placed in the class structure. In part this is done because the family has the resources, the knowledge, the "contacts" and influence to locate their children in class positions similar to their own. An upper-class family, even a middle-class family, knows how to choose educational lines of greatest advantage, or how to gain entry into the corporate structure through personal contacts. Skilled workers sometimes manage to get their own sons preferential entry into an occupation, where access depends on getting into an apprenticeship program or a union.

These are the factors that have made family more important in small towns than in big cities, more important for those of higher social status, and more important in the past than it is now or is likely to be in the future.

Social Class and Socialization

By socialization of the child the family naturally and unconsciously transmits the attitudes and values, modes of individual action, and life styles typical of the parent's social class. The child, therefore, becomes a person whose very approach to life makes him an appropriate member of a given social class.

---

[7] See Morris Zelditch, Jr., "Marriage, Family, and Kinship," in Robert E. L. Faris, *Handbook of Modern Sociology* (Chicago: Rand-McNally, 1964), pp. 723–728.

[8] See Zelditch, *op. cit.,* p. 725.

[9] See Marvin B. Sussman, "The Help Pattern in the

Middle-class Family," *American Sociological Review,* vol. 18 (February 1953), pp. 22–28.

Figure 12.1 The size of the American family has declined, particularly where a middle-class couple may regard children as competitive with other values. *(Magnum Photos.)*

Because of this, sociologists have concentrated on studying variation by social class in the family's socialization of the young, and particularly in its child-rearing practices. But classes are often wide and internally varied strata, and the assumption, for example, that there is *a* middle-class family may give insufficient attention to differences in family patterns *within* the middle class. A study in the Detroit area, for example, deliberately sought to compare self-employed, "entrepreneurial," and salaried "bureaucratic" families in their orientation to child training.[10] In effect this was a comparison of the old and the new middle class.

The new middle-class ("bureaucratic") parents taught their children the impor-

tance of adjustment to society, security, getting along with peers, an orientation consistent with the newer child-training literature and fitting in with an "organization-man" perspective of the world. The old middle-class ("entrepreneurial") parents, on the other hand, instilled in their children a more active and manipulative approach to life in which the child learns the necessity of strong aspirations and hard striving toward his goals. These are the familiar historic values of the Protestant Ethic; and they are also the child-training values found in the professional literature of twenty and thirty years ago.

Class and Ethnicity

Within the United States the peasant origin of many ethnic families has meant a tradition of a strong and cohesive family, with meaningful interaction along lines of

[10] *See* Daniel R. Miller and Guy E. Swanson, *The Changing American Parent* (New York: John Wiley & Sons, Inc., 1958).

extended kin. Where class and ethnic culture meet in the same families, they modify one another. Perhaps one of the best expositions of this has been Herbert Gans' study of working-class Italians in Boston, mentioned earlier. Gans described this family type as one between the modern, and particularly middle-class, *nuclear* family and the *extended* family typical of peasant societies.[11] The *households* are nuclear, in that a single nuclear family lives separately, but the family maintains a rich and meaningful set of relationships with kin, particularly among adult brothers and sisters and their spouses.

There is, however, less interaction across the generations, with the important exception of the mother-daughter relationship, which remains close even after the daughter's marriage. She usually locates her new home close to that of the mother's. The extended family pattern provides much of the social interaction for the adults; and they also depend upon one another for advice and help. Thus, interaction outside the family is limited by the high degree of interaction within it.

The relationship (in Gans' study) between the sexes, however, contrasts sharply with that of the middle class. First of all, there is no easy interaction between the sexes, and men much prefer to interact only with men. Even within the same house, or within the same room, the men will speak to men and the women to women. Communication across sex lines, therefore, is limited, and men particularly are ill at ease in such a situation, feeling that women talk faster and are more skillful at it; women, in turn,

depend on their ability to talk their husbands into things they want.

In husband-wife relations there is what Gans called a *segregated* relationship, in that there is a clear differentiation between the tasks and duties of husband and wife, and thus much less, if any, of the joint relationship that characterizes many middle-class marriages. Husbands rarely assist in household duties, and women did not even feel it would be right to ask them to do so. Women assume entirely the very large task of caring for children, leaving perhaps only the most severe punishment to the father.

This family pattern is both ethnic and working class. Gans feels that the class dimension is the more important, and he compares this family pattern with the working-class family elsewhere, such as in England, to emphasize how much of the type he studied is a consequence of social class.

The Lower-class Family

Of all the issues relating family to stratification, none has been more controversial than the issue of the lower-class family in the urban slum. That proportionately more of these families are black than white brings a racial note to an already complicated issue. That many of these families are on welfare and characterized by higher-than-average illegitimacy rates makes any effort at an objective understanding particularly difficult.

Actually, the controversy is not the families of lower-class people, nor those of lower-class blacks—it is lower-class families headed by a female. While the female-headed family occurs at any class level, the policy-oriented and sociological inter-

[11] *See* Herbert J. Gans, *The Urban Villagers: Group and Class in the Life of Italian-Americans* (New York: The Free Press, 1962).

est has focused on the mother-headed family in the lower class, where it is most frequent and where it shows characteristics responsive to the poverty and deprivation of this class level.

One basic fact about this family pattern is generally agreed on: the severe difficulty in earning a regular and adequate family-sustaining income by the male destroys his capacity to function as a breadwinner and head of the family, and so to meet cultural expectations. As a consequence, women by default come to head the family. By work and by welfare they provide income, but in both instances it is a low income.

Here are some basic facts for 1971:[12]

56 percent of all black families with incomes below the poverty line were headed by a female.

61 percent of poor black children under 14 years lived in families headed by a woman.

In the United States a woman can receive AFDC (Aid to the Families of Dependent Children) if she has no male support. This policy encourages unemployed males to "disappear" in order that their families can be supported. (When he is able to earn a living the black male readily supports his family; in 1971, 80 percent of black families headed by a male were above the poverty line.[13])

The most familiar interpretation of this pattern by sociologists (and others) is that it produces a *disorganization* of family life, with a set of harmful consequences for all the members: illegitimate children, low

educational ambitions, criminal and delinquent behavior, mental and emotional disturbances in greater proportion than in other classes.[14]

In addition, the effect of the female-headed family on the roles and relationships of males and females has been the focus of much attention. A great deal of social-scientific literature makes one central point: that the black male suffers from this family arrangement by an impairment of his masculinity; he lacks an adequate male model, such as the one a father usually provides for his sons.[15]

The Matriarchal Black Family: Disorganized or Adaptive?

Drawing on a wide range of available data about black lower-class families, the social scientist, Daniel P. Moynihan, Assistant Secretary of Labor under President Lyndon Johnson, in 1965 issued a controversial report arguing, first, that the lower-class black family was a consequence of poverty and racism, but secondly — and here was what made it controversial — that the "tangle of pathology" so created had in itself become a factor inhibiting further progress for blacks.[16] In short, the black lower-class family, Moynihan argued, now produced people who simply could not

[12] *See* U.S. Bureau of the Census, *Current Population Reports,* P-60, no. 86, "Characteristics of the Low-income Population, 1971" (U.S. Government Printing Office, 1972), pp. 4 and 31.

[13] U.S. Bureau of the Census, *Current Population Reports,* P-60, no. 86, p. 31.

[14] For a review of the research *see* Thomas F. Pettigrew, *A Profile of the Negro American* (Princeton, N.J.: Van Nostrand Reinhold Company, 1964), pp. 150–154.

[15] *See* Lee Rainwater, "Crucible of Identity: The Negro Lower-class Family," in Talcott Parsons and Kenneth B. Clark, eds., *The Negro American* (Boston: Houghton Mifflin Company, 1966), pp. 167–181.

[16] *See* Office of Policy Planning and Research, U.S. Department of Labor, *The Negro Family: The Case for National Action* (Washington, D.C.: U.S. Government Printing Office, 1965).

succeed, could not take advantage of economic opportunities when and where — and
if — they were offered:

> Three centuries of injustice have brought
> about deep-seated structural distortions in the
> life of the Negro American. At this point, the
> present tangle of pathology is capable of per-
> petuating itself without assistance from the
> white world. The cycle can be broken only if
> these distortions are set right.
>
> In a word, a national effort towards the prob-
> lems of Negro Americans must be directed
> toward the question of family structure.[17]

What was the controversy about? None
of Moynihan's critics disputed the evidence he cited about economic disadvantage and racial discrimination. Nor did
they in large part deny the apparent outcome of this disadvantage: the lowered
performance and achievement of blacks, as
measured by tests, by educational attainment, by income, and by jobs.

What was in serious dispute, however,
was Moynihan's interpretation of such
facts. He had extended the frequent argument about the harmful effects of disadvantage by arguing that the black family
in the ghetto, itself a consequence of such
causal factors as poverty and discrimination, had now become a further cause of
the plight of black people. No improvement could occur, Moynihan asserted, unless governmental programs were designed
to restore stability to the black family.

Moynihan's argument was supported not
only by the array of statistics about the
condition of life in the ghetto but by the
familiar and comfortable assumption that
family *disorganization* always occurred under circumstances of poverty and racial
discrimination, an assumption that had a

long ancestry in the sociological literature.
Families without male heads are almost
automatically defined as "broken" or "disorganized." Illegitimate births in such families were taken as further evidence of
disorganization.

Most social scientists and civil rights
leaders focused criticism on one matter in
particular: that Moynihan's arguments had
the effect of detracting from what they
took to be the fundamental issue — providing black males with regular employment
at decent wages. This, they argued, should
be the concern of social policy. If this were
done, the plight of the black family would
remedy itself. No tinkering with the family
as a policy of the federal government would
be either helpful or desirable. As sociologist Herbert Gans has stated:

> "... however difficult it may be to improve and
> desegregate the schools and to provide jobs, it
> is easier, more desirable and more likely to
> help Negro family life than attempts to alter
> the structure of the family or the personality of
> its members through programs of "cultural en-
> richment" or therapy, not to mention irrespon-
> sible demands for Negro self-improvement.[18]

Gans was but one of a number of social
scientists who subjected Moynihan's
analysis to a further more severe theoretical critique. He argued that, in contrast
to data offered by Moynihan, other data
show "no relationship between school
performance and broken families," and
that a study of mental health in Manhattan
"demonstrated that among whites at least,
growing up in a broken family did not
increase the likelihood of mental illness as

[17] See The Negro Family, op. cit., p. 47.

[18] Herbert J. Gans, "The Negro Family: Reflections on
the Moynihan Report," in Lee Rainwater and William L. Yancey, eds., The Moynihan Report and the
Politics of Controversy (Cambridge, Mass.: The M.I.T.
Press, 1967), p. 450.

Figure 12.2 Does the black male always suffer in the development of his masculinity by being brought up in a female-headed family? *(Magnum Photos.)*

much as did poverty and being of low status."[19]

Nor was it felt that the matriarchal family in itself was the cause of social pathology:

Likewise, the matriarchal family structure and the absence of a father has not yet been proven pathological, even for the boys who grow up in it. Sociological studies of the Negro family have demonstrated the existence of an extended kinship system of mothers, grandmothers, aunts and other female relatives that is surprisingly stable, at least on the female side. Moreover, many matriarchal families raise boys who do adapt successfully and themselves make stable marriages. The immediate cause of pathology may be the absence of a set of emotional strengths and cultural skills in the mothers, rather than the instability or departure of the fathers.[19]

[19] *See* Gans, *op. cit.,* p. 451.

Gans also suggested that "similar skepticism" can be applied to illegitimacy. It does not, he insisted, have the same moral significance in the lower class, and thus neither the mother nor the child suffer the stigma that would have to be borne in the middle classes. Furthermore, "since illegitimacy is not punished in the lower class as it is in the middle class, and illegitimate children and grandchildren are as welcome as legitimate ones, they may not suffer the pathological consequences that accompany illegitimacy in the middle class."[20]

In short, according to Gans, the building up of a bleak picture of the black, lower-class family may be exaggerated:

"... we do not even know whether the lower-class Negro family structure is actually patho-

[20] *See* Gans, *op. cit.,* p. 451.

275

logical as the Moynihan Report suggests. However much the picture of family life painted in that report may grate on middle-class sensibilities, it may well be that instability, illegitimacy, and matriarchy are the most positive adaptations possible to the conditions which Negroes must endure.[21]

Gans' use of the term *adaptation* is instructive. The mother-centered family is a mode of coping with an environment in which the culturally preferred nuclear family headed by a male is difficult of achievement because of poverty and unemployment. And this is the basic issue: The lower-class matriarchal family is sociologically understood not as family disorganization but as an alternate type of family structure developed under circumstances in which the conventional nuclear family is unattainable.

Nor is such a family pattern peculiar to the lower-class ghettoes of urban America. A number of social scientists have observed similar matriarchal family patterns elsewhere in the world. Among these, Hyman Rodman, who studied a village in Trinidad, asked the question of whether the marginal role of the male and the consequent mother-centered family were universal for the lower class.[22] They were not, he asserted. Rather, they occur only in the "stratified, achievement-oriented society in which the occupational role is differentiated from family roles and in which the man is expected to be the family provider."[23] This does not hold in a homogeneous peasant society, for example, in which the family (not the male head) works the land as a group. In any society in which

manhood is not defined primarily by earning capacity—by the male occupational role as the source of family income—males suffer no loss of esteem even if economic deprivation strikes.

However, the stratified, achievement-oriented society is likely to be more and more the society of the future in most of the world, for peasant social structures are losing out to industrial modernization. Accordingly, we can expect to find a lower-class family pattern that is matriarchal and possesses a relatively high rate of illegitimacy in such societies, as long as unemployment, irregular employment, and even employment at low wages in deadend jobs is all that is offered the lower-class male.

THE CHANGING AMERICAN FAMILY

The once pessimistic forecast about the future of the family, so common a generation ago, has now given way to a perspective which acknowledges that the family remains a significant institution. But there are changes underway, and possibly more to come, that have produced a whole new discussion about the meaning of the family for the individual and for American society, now and in the future.

Women: Family Role and Social Status

Throughout history the basic organization of the Western family has rested on a sexual division of labor and a differential of power, justified by an ideology overtly claiming the superiority of males. Although there has been gradual change over the centuries, the significant transition in the status of women has come since and as a consequence of the Industrial Revolution. Its impact on the structure of the family

---

[21] *See* Gans, *op. cit.,* p. 450.

[22] *See* Hyman Rodman, *Lower-class Families: The Culture of Poverty in Negro Trinidad* (New York: Oxford University Press, 1971).

[23] *See* Rodman, *op. cit.,* p. 178.

could not help but affect the role of women in society. Nonetheless, these changes did not fundamentally alter the fact that the status of women has still been defined primarily by her female capacity for childbearing and her principal task of keeping the home—in short, her family roles of *wife* and *mother*.

Rationalizations about the inferiority of women no longer have the same credence they once did. A long struggle, going back over a century, has brought women the vote, property rights, and an equality in civil status before the courts of the United States. Yet women are still far from equal to men in every phase of social life. Job discrimination still exists, both in terms of access to jobs, pay, and promotions. Women still do not find it easy to gain access,

educationally and occupationally, into the historically male professions, such as engineering, architecture, and medicine (*see* Table 14.1).

In a recent study, for example, sociologist Larry E. Suter and economist Herman P. Miller compared a national sample of men and women 30–44 years old. Women's earnings were only 39 percent of men's.[24] The authors then undertook an analysis that showed that if women had the same occupational status as men, had worked all their lives, and had the same education and year-round full-time employment as

[24] *See* Larry E. Suter and Herman P. Miller, "Income Differences between Men and Career Women," *American Journal of Sociology*, vol. 78 (January 1973), pp. 962–974.

TABLE 12.1   Numbers and Total Earnings of Males and Females in Selected Occupations, 1971

| | Professional and Technical | | | | | |
| | Total | | Self-employed | | Salaried | |
	Male	Female	Male	Female	Male	Female
Number with income in thousands	6,859	4,530	741	225	6,118	4,305
Percent earning over $10,000	61.4	20.7	71.4	9.6	60.3	21.3
Percent earning over $25,000	8.3	0.5	32.9	2.7	5.4	0.4
Mean income full-time year-round workers	14,631	6,142	23,845		13,641	8,757

| | Clerical | | Managers and Administrators (salaried) | | Sales Workers | |
	Male	Female	Male	Female	Male	Female
Number with income in thousands	3,352	10,045	5,099	1,062	3,203	1,880
Percent earning over $10,000	34.6	3.2	68.0	21.4	43.5	2.6
Percent earning over $25,000	0.8	0.1	11.6	0.8	5.5	0.1
Mean income full-time year-round workers	9,754	8,439	15,718	8,439	12,513	5,218

Source: U.S. Bureau of the Census, *Current Population Reports*, Series P-60, no. 85, "Money Income in 1971 of Families and Persons in the United States" (Washington, D.C.: U.S. Government Printing Office, 1972).

* Base less than 75,000.

men, their incomes would still be only 62 percent of the men's. Furthermore, Suter and Miller found that women's pay is commensurate with effort and education, but incomes tend to cluster around the average rather than varying widely around the regression line. The absence of marked variation means that most women were receiving "just average" wages, regardless of training, job status, or experience. The income distributions of men, on the other hand, tend to be skewed toward the higher income levels.[25]

Is Sexual Equality Near?

It seems to be a common assumption today that women are approaching equality with men, and that this has been gradually occurring over a long period of time. In fact, women both gain and lose with social and economic changes, and their improvement in social status has by no means been steady. Page Smith, for example, points out that women lost ground in status from the Puritan era to the nineteenth century, particularly at the end of the eighteenth century (which was the period of the American Revolution).[26] Perhaps more significantly, sociologist Dean Knudsen has shown that—as measured by income, education, and occupation—women's status relative to men's has *declined* in the last twenty-five years.[27] Furthermore, a study of women in underdeveloped countries has shown that as industrialization increases the position of women declines.[28]

Equal within the Home? Yes and No

But what is true within the economy may not be true within the home. Here the received wisdom is that men's roles as fathers and husbands have declined radically in power over both wives and children. The man's absence from the home, presumably, has given the wife, even if by default, more responsibility and consequently more authority. One sociologist argues that: "Based on the data on hand one has to conclude that the dominant-father model is neither practical nor functional in contemporary society and is tending to disappear."[29]

So, it is widely claimed, wives have become the equal of their husbands. Thus, in their Detroit study, Blood and Wolfe argued that power relations in a marriage are an individual matter, an interpersonal relation testing the competency of two persons; therefore, the partner with more education, more organizational experience, and a higher status background is the one who makes the decisions.[30]

But this is strongly challenged by sociologist Dair Gillespie's argument that the "distribution of power is not an interpersonal affair but a class affair."[31] Women are in an inferior class position to men,

[25] *See* Suter and Miller, *op. cit.,* p. 973.

[26] *See* Page Smith, *Daughters of the Promised Land* (Boston: Little, Brown & Company, 1970).

[27] *See* Dean Knudsen, "The Declining Status of Women: Popular Myths and the Failure of Functionalist Thought," *Social Forces,* vol. 48, (December 1970), pp. 183–193.

[28] *See* Ester Roserup, *Woman's Role in Economic Development* (New York: St. Martin's Press, 1970).

[29] *See* Ersel E. LeMasters, "The Passing of the Dominant Husband-father," in Hans Peter Dreitzel, ed., *Family, Marriage, and the Struggle of the Sexes* (New York: The Macmillan Company, 1972), pp. 110–111.

[30] *See* Blood and Wolfe, *op. cit.,* p. 37.

[31] *See* Dair L. Gillespie, "Who Has the Power? The Marital Struggle," *Journal of Marriage and the Family,* vol. 33 (August 1971), pp. 445–458.

Figure 12.3 The traditional class position of the suburban wife may not be due to her competency but to the class advantage which gives her husband power in the marriage. *(Hays, Monkmeyer.)*

therefore differences in individual competency will not offset the class advantages that men have. Gillespie points out that Blood and Wolfe's own data show that since higher-status men are usually better educated than their wives, middle-class, white-collar suburban-residing males have more power over their wives—contrary. to common myth—than do blue-collar, less-educated, city-dwelling males. To this, Gillespie adds the argument that women acquire their status from their husbands, that they are socialized to think of themselves as inferior, and that they are psychologically conditioned—*programmed* is today's term—to be wives and mothers, noncompetitive with men because they are less able to compete. (Academic achievement suggests that little girls do not realize this until high school; before that they do as well or better than boys in school. An increasingly larger number are getting a different message.)

Furthermore, women earn less than men and have less access to the more prestigeful, better-paying occupations, even when equally prepared. The laws still favor men; a wife has no legal claim to her husband's salary, but he is entitled to her services, can legally decide where they will reside, and need not pay her any income. (The Equal Rights Amendment to the Constitution, if adopted, could change this.)

Having children increases the husband's power, for the wife becomes more dependent. In summary:

Thus, it is clear that for a wife to gain even a modicum of power in the marital relationship, she must gain it from external sources, i.e., she must participate in the work force, her education must be superior to her husband's, and her participation in organizations must excel his. Equality of resources leaves the power in the hands of the husband. However, access to these resources of power are structurally blocked for women.[32]

These disputes over the changing status of men and women tend to counter most claims about the gains in status made by women in recent decades, while not denying that change has occurred, change that also affects the family.

Working Wives

While women in the labor force are not a new phenomenon, a more recent one is the growing number of working married women, particularly those with children. (See "Women in the Labor Force.") Once people believed that working women would necessarily neglect their children. But sociologist Valerie Oppenheimer points out "that continued economic development in our society has increased the demand for female labor."[33] Other factors that lead women to work are the increased standard of living possible when both partners work, and the increasing proportion of women who work to support children.

What effect does a working wife and mother have on the family? According to Robert Blood: "Employment emancipates women from domination by their husbands and, secondarily, raises their daughters from inferiority to their brothers (echoing the rising status of their mothers)."[34] He

cites other studies which found that sons become more dependent and more obedient, reflecting their observations of their father's lessened status, while daughters become more independent, more self-reliant, more aggressive, more dominant, even more disobedient.

In such ways, the shape of the American family is being altered by the exodus of women into the labor market. The roles of men and women are converging for both adults and children. As a result, the family will be far less segregated internally, far less stratified into different age generations and different sexes. This will enable family members to share more of the activities of life together, both work activities and play activities.

The old assymmetry of male-dominated, female-serviced family life is being replaced by a new symmetry, both between husbands and wives and between brothers and sisters. To this emerging symmetry, the dual employment of mothers as well as fathers is a major contributor.[35]

Marital Happiness

Does the fact of the wife working have any consequences for the happiness of the marriage? Most research has been inconclusive on this matter, but a recent study provided support for the idea that employment of the wife need not harm the marriage, that, in fact, when women have the freedom to choose to work there is less tension in the marriage; but this gain is not apparent if the wife is working out of necessity.[36]

---

[32] See Gillespie, op. cit., p. 457.

[33] See Valerie Kincaide Oppenheimer, "Demographic Influence on Female Employment and the Status of Women," American Journal of Sociology, vol. 78 (January 1973), p. 948.

[34] See Robert O. Blood, Jr., "Long-range Causes and Consequences of the Employment of Married Women," Journal of Marriage and Family Living, vol. 27 (February 1965), pp. 43–47.

[35] See Blood, op. cit., p. 47.

[36] See Susan R. Orden and Norman M. Bradburn, "Working Wives and Marriage Happiness," American Journal of Sociology, vol. 74 (January 1969), pp. 392–407.

WOMEN IN THE LABOR FORCE

Over the past seventy years there has been a considerable change in women's labor-force participation:

1. *Increasingly, more and more women work.* Women age 18–64 in the labor force numbered:

> 20 percent in 1920
> 30 percent in 1940
> 50 percent in 1970.

2. *Working women are no longer only young women. Before* 1940 most women worked only before marriage and children; the proportion of employed women declined with age. *After* 1940 women past 35 entered or re-entered the labor force at a sharply increasing rate. In 1970 between 49 and 54 percent of women 35–59 were in the labor force.

3. *More young married women with children now work. Before* 1950 few young married women with preschool children worked. This number has increased sharply, particularly since 1960. The proportion of working married women 20–24 (husbands present) with preschool children numbered:

> 13 percent in 1951
> 18 percent in 1960
> 33 percent in 1970.

Source: U.S. Bureau of Labor Statistics, *Marital and Family Characteristics of Workers, March 1970,* Special Labor Force Reports, no. 130 (Washington, D.C.: Government Printing Office, 1971).

The Sexual Revolution

These changes in the roles and status of women, induced largely by economic changes, are one basic feature of the *sexual revolution.* Another has to do with changing attitudes about sex itself. Whether changing attitudes are accompanied by changed behavior is a matter of dispute among students of family and sex behavior. Some, such as sociologist Ira Reiss, assert there has been no sexual revolution. This is because, according to Reiss, there always has been much sex outside of marriage; now a greater attitudinal permissiveness accepts it.[37] Furthermore, he asserts, attitudes and behavior are now closer than they ever were before, and we can expect them to become closer still, and to proceed together into a period of greater permissiveness and even greater frankness.

[37] *See* Ira A. Reiss, "How and Why America's Sex Standards are Changing," in Joann S. Delora and Jack R. Delora, eds., *Intimate Life Styles: Marriage and Its Alternatives* (Pacific Palisades, Calif.: Goodyear Publishing Company, Inc., 1972), pp. 104–112.

In support of this thesis a study by Kaats and Davis found that college students were moving toward a converging sexual equalitarianism, but that a double-standard which allowed greater sexual freedom for the male still existed, and was perceived by these students to be strong as yet among peers, family, and friends.[38]

An additional aspect of the sexual revolution is the continued development of a social value that constantly undermines the older puritanical viewpoint that sex is "dirty"; it becomes defined as "natural" for healthy human beings. The major change is that open value can now be placed on a healthy sex life, and its purpose is no longer to be restricted to procreation. It is only a step from there to separating sexual activity from the expectation that it should occur only in marriage. Thus, sexuality may be in the process of "becoming institutionalized autonomously, that is, in its own right, rather than primarily within the institutional contexts of reproduction and child-rearing."[39]

The relatively greater ease with which contraception is now available, and indeed widely encouraged, contributes to this separation of sex from family life. Contraception is no longer an issue of serious moral controversy in much of American society, though there are still well-defined positions of opposition. Instead, the conflict over abortion has taken precedence over the contraceptive issue.

THE FUTURE OF THE FAMILY

On a worldwide basis the family is changing from old patterns and adapting to the kind of society that is coming into being everywhere. The industrialization of the world is accompanied by the emergence of the nuclear family on a world basis, with a decline of the extended kinship so predominant in more traditional family forms. Sociologist William J. Goode emphasizes that this conjugal family pattern is in itself a world revolution, but that it is also one factor in a larger, more encompassing world revolution—the transition to the modern industrial society.[40]

As a part of the revolution the conjugal family emphasizes the freedom of the individual to choose his own life and control his own destiny, released in good part from the once-rigid controls of extended kinship structures. At the same time there is an obvious price: The shrinking of ties among kin reduces the sense of responsibility that family members have for one another.

Do We Need the Family?

Goode's argument proceeds on the generally accepted premise that the family in some modified pattern has survived the major social changes into industrialization and has a future in modern society. Once the only significant contrary voice had been that of sociologist Barrington Moore, who has suggested that the family may not survive as an institution.[41] He follows the

---

[38] See Gilbert R. Kaats and Keith E. Davis, "The Dynamics of Sexual Behavior of College Students," *Journal of Marriage and the Family*, vol. 32 (August 1970), pp. 390–399.

[39] See Jetse Sprey, "On the Institutionalization of Sexuality," in Joan S. Delora and Jack R. Delora, *op. cit.*, p. 80.

[40] See William J. Goode, *World Revolution and Family Patterns* (New York: The Free Press, 1963).

[41] See Barrrington Moore, "Thoughts on the Future of the Family," in his *Political Power and Social Theory* (Cambridge, Mass.: Harvard University Press, 1958), pp. 160–178.

Figure 12.4 The roles of men and women are no longer as distinct as they once were, particularly where wives and mothers have entered the labor market. *(Magnum Photos.)*

British philosopher Bertrand Russell in viewing the family from an evolutionary perspective that raises the possibility that it may be an obsolete institution or become so before long. Moore argues that there are conditions which "make it possible for the advanced industrial societies of the world to do away with the family and substitute other social arrangements that impose fewer unnecessary and painful restrictions on humanity."[42]

His basic argument is that there is no need for the family today, and that many of its basic features are outmoded if not useless. The obligation of affection among kin, for example, is characterized as a relic of barbarism. Moore regards the contemporary role of the wife and mother as one which makes demands that are impossible to meet, children as often a burden to parents, the troubles of adolescence as evidence of the family's inadequacy in stabilizing the human personality, and motherhood as frequently a degrading experience. He does not even believe that the necessity of affection and love for the infant requires family, though he acknowledges that the present bureaucratized hospital nursery lacks the necessary warm and affectionate structure.

But Moore again follows Russell in regarding this as a soluble problem, suggesting radical and perhaps as yet unacceptable arrangements for child-rearing that would free most people from what may have become burdensome if also rewarding relationships. Moore's conception of a world revolution toward the freedom of the individual goes much

[42] *See* Moore, *op. cit.*, p. 162.

further than does Goode's idea of the conjugal family pattern.

Now Moore's voice has been joined to others. Marriage as a desired and idealized relationship has been challenged by those whose argument is basically quite simple: Wedlock "until death do us part" made sense in earlier times in which the family was necessarily a basic institution of society and dependence on the kinship structure was unavoidable for the individual. People change in interests and values, in aspirations and life styles throughout life—changing careers in midlife is now more frequent, for example— and thus, it is pointed out, a close, intimate relationship with the same person cannot reasonably be expected to persist over an adult lifetime. The pattern of divorce in middle-class life is cited as testimony to that fact.

If this is so, assert the new critics of marriage, then new marital relations should be developed, relations that persist only so long as a mutually satisfying shared life is possible. No undue sacrifice by either partner for the other, it is felt, makes any sense; for both men and women are entitled to equal consideration from each other. Each is equally an individual, with equal rights and a separate life to live.

Alternatives to Traditional Marriage and Family

Throughout the United States, as well as in Europe, particularly Scandinavia and Germany—and to some extent in all advanced industrial societies—many young people are trying out various alternatives of having human and sexual relationships,

sometimes even of raising children.[43] Here are some of them.

Androgynous Marriage

An androgynous marriage is more than an equalitarian one; it is a marriage in which there is no sex-role differentiation; that is, no tasks done to the woman that are not also assumed by the man. There are no stereotyped behavioral differences between the roles of male and female simply on the basis of sex. The marriage is sexually monogamous and closed, however, unlike these next two.

Comarital Adultery

Comarital adultery, or "swinging," occurs when both the husband and wife, with each other's consent, engage in sexual relations with other persons—often one other couple. Social-scientific observers have found "swingers" to be typically white suburbanites, middle class, bored with marriage, but not otherwise deviant in behavior. Mate-swapping is compatible with monogamy and is in fact a strategy to revitalize and thus maintain a marital relationship.

Open Marriage

An open marriage is again equalitarian, with an emphasis on eliminating the sense

[43] For a discussion of some of these alternatives *see* Delora and Delora, *op. cit.*, Part 6, "Current Alternatives to Traditional Marriage," and Part 7, "Future Intimate Life-styles," pp. 288–412. For a more detailed discussion of alternatives *see* the paper by Swedish sociologist Erik Grønseth, "The Familial Institution: The Alienated Labor-producing Appendage," in Larry T. Reynolds and James M. Henslin, eds., *American Society: A Critical Analysis* (New York: David McKay Company, Inc., 1973).

Figure 12.5 A commune, such as this one in Seattle, is one alternative to the traditional family. *(Wide World Photos.)*

of possessiveness of one partner about the other. Thus, there is an easy interaction and involvement of each partner with other persons, including sexual relationships.[44]

Living Together

There seems to have been a considerable increase in recent years in people living together without marriage. Among the very young this is sometimes a trial marriage or a prelude to marriage, ending in either legal marriage or dissolution of the relationship. Among older adults, who have been previously married, living together is usually an alternative to marriage.

[44] *See* Nena O'Neill and George O'Neill, *Open Marriage: A New Life Style for Couples* (New York: Avon Books, 1973).

Communes

Living in a communal family system is more than an alternative to the traditional family; it is an alternate way of life encompassing more than marriage or family. Most people who choose a commune are seeking a person-oriented group, an absence of hierarchy organized to make the emotional needs of individuals an end in itself. Since this is difficult to achieve, most communes are short-lived. Because they are, how children fare in communes over time is as yet little known.[45]

[45] For a rare, serious study of children in communes *see* Bennett M. Berger, Bruce M. Hackett, and R. Mervyn Millar, "Child-raising Practices in the Communal Family," in Dreitzel, *op. cit.*, pp. 271–300.

Celibacy

Given the new permissiveness about sex, and the effectiveness of contraceptives, it is possible to remain single while yet finding acceptable ways to find intimacy, companionship, and sexual fulfillment. Sociologist Jessie Bernard points out, however, that a number of radical women have arrived at the revolutionary position that "celibacy is not a fate worse than death, but an honorable status."[46]

If sexual reproduction is going to be only a very minor part of some women's lives in the future, Bernard notes, then radical women are "helping us to catch up with revolutions that have already occurred or are in process, with revolutions which the technologists have precipitated and which we must come to terms with."[47] Bernard is referring to radical changes which reduce the frequency of child-bearing and the drudgery of housekeeping.

Group Marriage

If life without marriage is a radical innovation, so would group or multilateral marriage be. It is radical because it rejects the ancient Western sanctity of monogamy.[48] The felt need of some people to find community with others has led to innovations in multilateral marriages. What is basic is that the single, propertied possession of one person by another, but particularly the woman by the man, with accompanying jealousy, rights, and demands for fidelity are set aside in favor of a new pattern of relationships.

The Family in the Future

Not even the most ardent advocate of new forms of marriage and family maintains that any mass transformation in the family will occur in the near future. (On the basis of the 1970 U.S. Census it seems that about 8 percent of the population is now experimenting with marriage.) In the short run there will be a powerful trend to equalizing—but not necessarily *achieving* true equality in—the conventional conjugal relations. Other people, though a minority, will experiment with new forms.

But in the long run we can anticipate that there are forces pressing for more revolutionary changes, without being sure what these will be. Certainly, sexual freedom and an equality of the sexes are trends that have the most revolutionary implications for the family as we have traditionally known it, since a fundamental inequality of the sexes and a powerful control of sexual behavior have been basic to family structure in the past. Alter these, and a radical transformation of human relations having to do with sex, reproduction, and family are inevitable.

Women's status has been changing radically, especially in reference to their newly found awareness of that change. That means, most of all, a change in their relations to men; which, in turn, means an unavoidable change in men. The liberation of women from their lesser status and its historic version of what is feminine will also "liberate" men, whether they like it or not, from their historic conceptions of manhood; in each case, what it means to be a man or a woman is rooted funda-

---

[46] *See* Jessie Bernard, "Woman, Marriage, and the Future," in Delora and Delora, *op. cit.*, p. 373.

[47] *See* Bernard, *op. cit.*, p. 372.

[48] *See* Rustum Roy and Della Roy, "Is Monogamy Outdated?" in Dreitzel, *op. cit.*, pp. 332–350; also in Delora and Delora, *op. cit.*, pp. 358–369.

mentally in the relations of the sexes to each other.

The State and the Family

Undoubtedly also the state and social policy will play an ever more important part in guaranteeing sexual rights; in seeking to limit birth in order to control population; in providing more services for children, such as day-care centers, and so on; perhaps even in deciding who can have children and when. Indeed, the state may come decisively to control whatever new social arrangement is devised for procreation and the socializing of children.

Many people for a long time have condemned the family as a conservative institution, because it socializes the young to old patterns and tends to reproduce each generation on older models. But socialization of each generation by the family also prevents a society-wide, common programming; all the cultural and psychological variations in society are reproduced. It does not follow that this is inferior to programmed socialization by the state. It all depends on what kind of human beings are wanted.

SUMMARY

The *universality* of family means the existence of a basic unit responsible for legitimate procreation, for the care and maintenance of children, and for their socialization and placement in society. However, the form of the group by which these functions are carried out is not always that of the *nuclear* family of father, mother, and children. To these universal functions can be added for modern society a renewed emphasis on an *affectional* function, which then emphasizes the family as a primary group.

Variation in family structure includes variations in accepted modes of mate selection (endogamy and exogamy), in forms of marriage (monogamy and polygamy), in rules of authority (patriarchal or matriarchal), in rules of descent and inheritance (patrilineal or matrilineal and sometimes bilateral), in rules of residence (patrilocal and matrilocal and neolocal usually in modern society).

Industrialization brought about these changes in the family: separation of work and home, decline in family size, decline of extended family systems, separation of family and education, loss of occupational succession.

The family in modern society varies considerably by class and status in the way it socializes children. Working-class and ethnic status merge in shaping a family structure: in child-rearing, in marital functions and relations between the sexes, and in sustaining kinship patterns over the generations.

The *lower-class family headed by a female* has long been defined as family disorganization by social scientists. But a better sociological conception of it is as a family type developed in response to the fact that poverty,

discrimination, and unemployment make unattainable the culturally preferred, male-headed nuclear family.

The family has changed radically over time, consistent with other structural changes in society, particularly economic ones. Changes in *sexual
values* and relations and in *women's status* continue to affect the family.
Indeed, there is a world revolution away from traditional family types
toward new forms reflecting a smaller, more equalitarian family.

Criticism of the conventional family has brought about innovations and
experiments in new marital and family patterns: androgynous marriage,
comarital adultery, open marriage, living together, communes, celibacy,
and group marriage.

Suggested Readings

Jesse Bernard, *The Future of Marriage* (Cleveland, Ohio: The World Publishing
Company, 1972). A long-experienced sociologist writes knowingly—and sympathetically—of the radical challenges to the institution of marriage.

Andrew Billingsley, *Black Families in White America* (Englewood Cliffs, N.J.:
Prentice-Hall, Inc., 1968). A black sociologist writes on the struggle of blacks, in
slavery and after, to maintain stable family patterns.

Robert Blood, Jr., and Donald Wolfe, *Husbands and Wives: The Dynamics of Married
Living* (New York: The Free Press, 1960). A study in support of the possibility of
more nearly equal marriage in modern America.

Joann S. Delora and Jack R. Delora, *Intimate Life Styles: Marriage and Its Alternatives* (Pacific Palisades, Calif.: Goodyear Publishing Company, Inc., 1972). A wide
range of challenging articles on sexual and marital changes still going on.

Hans Peter Dreitzel, *Family, Marriage, and the Struggle of the Sexes* (New York:
The Macmillan Company, 1972). An interesting collection of articles on the effect
on the family of changes in women's status.

Herbert Gans, *The Urban Villagers: Group and Class in the Life of Italian-Americans*
(New York: The Free Press, 1962). How class and ethnicity interact in shaping a
distinctive family pattern.

William J. Goode, *World Revolution and Family Patterns* (New York: The Free
Press, 1963). A world revolution toward the conjugal family is mapped out.

Joan Huber, ed., *Changing Women in a Changing Society* (Chicago, Ill.: University
of Chicago Press, 1973). A group of sociologists, mostly women, analyze woman's
changing status, including its implications for the family.

Mirra Komarovsky, *Blue Collar Marriage* (New York: Random House, Inc., 1964).
A study of marriage in the working class, contrasted at a number of points with
marriage in the middle class.

Daniel Miller and Guy E. Swanson, *The Changing American Parent* (New York:
John Wiley & Sons, Inc., 1958). A comparison of old and new middle-class child-
rearing practices and family styles.

Lee Rainwater and William L. Yancey, *The Moynihan Report and the Politics of
Controversy* (Cambridge, Mass.: The M.I.T. Press, 1967). Includes Moynihan's paper

on the black, lower-class family, the history of the controversy, and critical papers by Gans and others.

Hyman Rodman, *Lower-Class Families: The Culture of Poverty in Negro Trinidad* (New York: Oxford University Press, 1971). An empirical analysis of an alternate family type, with discussion of its meaning and significance.

Ester Roserup, *Woman's Role in Economic Development* (New York: St. Martin's Press, 1970). The consequence of economic development to women is not necessarily steady progress toward improved status.

Only the educated are free.
— *Epictetus*

Chapter 13

Education

Prominent among the dominant trends of this century is the growth of a complex and bewildering web of institutional arrangements called education. It commands an ever-larger share of the resources of society and affects in varied ways more and more persons for longer and longer periods of their lives. It interlocks with economic and technological structures, with political structures and elites, and with economic development and world affairs in a manner never dreamed of a few decades ago. Education, apparently, is one of the central activities of modern society.

It has to be. The process of educating people is one of the major tasks in modern society; and it has now become a rapidly changing and profoundly complicated one. It becomes necessary, therefore, for sociology to examine education as one of society's institutions.

THE FUNCTIONS OF EDUCATION

The *universal* functions of education are to help socialize the young and to transmit the culture to the next generation. Transmitting the culture means to teach norms and values, to teach knowledge, and to train the young in applicable skills. Any society does this, but preindustrial societies did so without schools and teachers, at least for the majority of people.

In traditional, preliterate societies learning took place within the pattern of association between adults and children in the routine of daily activities, particularly within kinship structures. If some conscious training took place—as it necessarily did—still no full-time teachers were needed. Teaching was a task adults assumed as a regular part of their rearing of the young.

Even when literacy was a developed skill in preindustrial societies, the peasant majority of the population remained illiterate; there seemed to be no functional need for them to be able to read. Education became a prerogative of particular groups: (1.) the priests and others who were the learned men of society; (2.) the aristocratic and ruling stratum; and, later, (3.) merchants and others involved in commercial transactions.

But a modern, industrial society simply cannot function with widespread illiteracy. Increasingly, it required people to have higher levels of literacy and of professional or technical training. Thus, education as a mass process became a prerequisite for the functioning of modern society.

The Transmission of Culture

Education indoctrinates the young in the established ideologies of the culture and thus has been a conservative force in society. Even when education is less consciously concerned with teaching prevailing values, it still does so. Values, for example, may play a large part in selecting both the kind of knowledge to be taught and the perspective from which it is taught. For instance, teaching history often be-

comes a process of inculcating a national self-image, and of indoctrinating the young into nationalistic and patriotic perspectives.

The School as Moral Authority

The school has long been assigned the task of moral training. This was a highly pronounced emphasis in American education from elementary school through college in the nineteenth century, and continued well into the twentieth. Émile Durkheim, perhaps the only one of the great founders of sociology to be much concerned with education, depicted the *(used to be)* teacher as primarily a moral authority, both by virtue of experience and as a recognized authority on the culture.[1]

But in modern technological and mobility-oriented societies, such traditional moral authority dissolves. In an educated society teachers are no longer the unique symbols of moral authority and intellectual competence they once were, and so no longer speak authoritatively about the culture.

One consequence of this change is fairly evident—what sociologist Burton Clark calls "a crisis of authority" as "a fair characterization of the role of the teacher in much American education."[2]

Many parents, apparently, still want teachers to be an authoritative moral force. In a Gallup Poll conducted in 1972 to measure the attitudes of the public to education, "lack of discipline" emerged as the top issue, ahead of problems of school finance or racial integration.[3] On the ques-

[1] See Émile Durkheim, *Education and Society* (New York: The Free Press, 1956).

[2] See Burton Clark, "Sociology of Education," in Robert E. L. Faris, ed., *Handbook of Modern Sociology* (Chicago, Ill.: Rand-McNally & Company, 1964), p. 765.

[3] See the New York *Times*, September 3, 1972.

tion of specific educational goals for secondary schools the public gave first choice to "teaching students to respect law and order." But there is a serious question as to whether teachers can teach respect for law and order simply because an older generation wants them to do so.

Education and the Economy

The development of a modern economy by the process of industrialization has had a radical effect on education. As work shifts from primarily manual skills, traditionally acquired within the family, to mental work that requires nonfamily training, new and demanding educational requirements emerge. Education and occupation become closely tied together, for educational achievement provides the major mode of access to preferred occupational roles. What people can do is increasingly defined by what education they have, and educational certification becomes necessary for improving one's life chances. (For the increasing level of education in the United States *see* Table 13.1.)

TABLE 13.1   Level of School Completed by Persons 25 Years Old and Over, 1940–1972

	Not High-school Graduate	4 Years of High School or More	4 Years of College or More
1940	75.5	24.5	4.6
1952	61.2	38.8	7.0
1959	56.3	43.7	8.1
1965	51.0	49.0	9.4
1970	44.8	55.2	11.0
1972	41.8	58.2	12.0

Source: U.S. Bureau of the Census, *Current Population Reports*, Series P-20, no. 243, "Educational Attainment: March 1972" (Washington, D.C.: U.S. Government Printing Office, 1972), p. 1.

If the lack of education severely limits anyone's life chances, and if getting an education is necessary for social mobility, then the *level* of education attained is a crucial matter to everyone—education is no longer the concern or privilege of the few.

The demands of the economy have a profound effect on the structure of education. Changes in curriculum, efforts to upgrade academic and technical performance, struggle to provide functional literacy for the most educationally disadvantaged, responses to the demand for more scientifically trained people—all these and other changes are indexes of education's sensitive response to the changes in the occupational requirements of a modern economy.

STRATIFICATION AND EDUCATION

Those who constantly urge young people to continue their education are fond of quoting statistics to prove the economic value of education. Certainly preparing people for an occupation is one of the significant functions of education, and one indication of the relationship between education and social stratification.

Sociologists have seen this relationship around the hypothesis that stratification serves to distribute educational opportunity unequally—the children of the poor and uneducated get a poorer education; the children of the affluent and educated get a better education.

An increasingly technological society will not merely stabilize the generations. Rather, the transformation of the occupational structure puts education to the task of developing the mass training of middle- and high-status persons. Thus, consciously or not, education becomes an instrument for selecting, training, and placing persons in occupations higher than those of their parents. This suggests a different hypothesis: that the educational process is the major mechanism for social mobility.

The Opportunity to Be Educated

When sociologist August Hollingshead described the pervasive influence of a community class structure on the educational process of the local high school in 1949, it came as a shock to many.[4] Hollingshead showed how the school's teachers and administrators acted toward students in ways determined more by the students' social class positions than by their qualities or abilities, even to the point of the distribution of grades and scholarships. In such a community the school was subservient to the community's dominant status groups. For the adolescent the school experience differed in no significant way from experience outside of school: the children of the lowest stratum were as disadvantaged in school as they were in the community.

Is inequality of educational opportunity due to Hollingshead's finding, namely, that the advantages of high status include preferential experiences in school? Or do the children of low status fail to take advantage of educational opportunities available to them because of lack of aspiration or little ability, or perhaps both?

A number of studies have shown—what is hardly surprising—that the higher the social status, the more likely one is to go to college. Several studies have also demonstrated that family position considerably influences the *aspiration to go to college*, though none of these studies agreed on how much relative weight to give to family position and how much to the ability of the student.[5]

But family is not the only relevant dimension. Robert Havighurst and his associates found that children tend to reflect the educational values of the neighborhood.[6] These different neighborhoods constitute what sociologist Alan B. Wilson called a "climate of aspiration";[7] they are a result of the educational segregation created by building schools in neighborhoods of varying social status.

The aspiration climate is lower in low-status neighborhoods and higher in high-status ones. Although most neighborhoods are homogeneous in terms of class, there is sometimes variation. Thus, working-class boys in a predominantly middle-class school are likely to raise their aspirations, but these same aspirations will usually be depressed in a slum-located school.

In a series of research studies that go back to the 1950s, sociologist William H. Sewell and various associates (but particularly Archibald O. Haller) have worked out a model for relating education to occupa-

---

[4] *See* August H. Hollingshead, *Elmtown's Youth* (New York: John Wiley & Sons, Inc., 1949).

[5] Examples of such studies are J. A. Kahl, "Educational and Occupational Aspirations of 'Common Man' Boys," *Harvard Educational Review*, vol. 23 (1953), pp. 186–203; William H. Sewell, A.O. Haller, and Murray A. Strauss, "Social Status and Educational and Occupational Aspiration," *American Sociological Review* (February 1957), pp. 67–73; and Natalie Rogoff, "Local Social Structure and Educational Selection," in A.H. Halsey, Jean Floud, and C.A. Anderson, eds., *Education, Economy, and Society* (New York: The Free Press, 1961), pp. 241–251.

[6] *See* Robert J. Havighurst, Paul H. Bowman, Gordon P. Liddle, Charles V. Matthews, and James V. Pierce, *Growing Up in River City* (New York: John Wiley & Sons, Inc., 1962).

[7] *See* Alan B. Wilson, "Residential Segregation of Social Classes and Aspirations of High School Boys," *American Sociological Review*, vol. 24 (December 1959), pp. 836–845.

tional attainment.[8] The focus of their research was to measure the influence of

significant others. They determined whether there was parental encouragement to go to college; whether there was similar encouragement by teachers; and what college plans the student's friends had.

In testing this model in empirical re-

[8] See William H. Sewell, Archibald O. Haller, and Alejandro Portes, "The Educational and Early Occupational Attainment Process," American Sociological Review, vol. 34 (February 1969), pp. 82–92.

JENSEN AND THE IQ PROBLEM

In the United States no idea has been more tenaciously defended by many whites than that which asserts that blacks (and other nonwhites, also) are naturally inferior in intelligence, and so white children are more educable than black children.

But what was taken for granted by white Americans for a very long time has been seriously challenged and rejected by the vast majority of scientists concerned with the issue—sociologists, psychologists, geneticists, and anthropologists—for close to half a century now.

Nonetheless, the issue has remained stubbornly alive, and the results of thousands of IQ tests, used almost every day on school children, provide evidence that those who insist on the superiority of whites over blacks continually point to. What do IQ tests show? They show that:

1. In the United States the average IQ score of black children is 10 to 15 points below that of white children.
2. Black and white children are found in all IQ categories, from the highest to lowest, though disproportionately more white children are in the higher categories, disproportionately more black children in the lower categories.

Scientists do not dispute these differences in scores; they are demonstrated facts. What is in dispute is how to interpret them.

Most scientists believe that these test results would prove that blacks are innately inferior only if the IQ test adequately measures an inherited intelligence independent of other, environmental factors; that is, if they are culturally unbiased tests, and if their application in test situations takes adequate account of environmental differences in the test population. Few scientists believe these special qualifications are taken into account. Most IQ tests, according to the weight of scientific judgment, favor the socially and educationally advantaged.

In short, as long as black and white are social categories with significantly different life chances and life experiences, there will be differences in average IQ scores.

Jensen's Thesis

The IQ controversy received new stimulus when a respected educational psychologist, Arthur Jensen, wrote a long article arguing the probability of different kinds of intelligence being unequally distributed among racial groups.* While acknowledging that environment does influence IQ, Jensen argued that .80 of

search conducted on high-school seniors in the state of Wisconsin, Sewell and his associates found that the central importance they gave to the influence of significant others was borne out in whether the student entered college. So was the fact of direct influence due to socioeconomic status — meaning that such influence was strongest on higher-status boys — and to academic achievement — meaning that encouragement was centered on those already doing well in school.

IQ is inherited, and that discrimination and inequalities in education cannot account for the differences in achievement and in IQ scores for black and white children.

On that basis Jensen argued for "differential educational treatment" based on these differences in measured capacities, even though, as a result, there would not be an equal distribution of races and classes in each grouping.

Jensen's critics have argued in response that he has not proved his case,** that:

1. He too uncritically accepts IQ tests as valid measurements of intelligence.
2. He does not adequately account for the great overlap in the genetic pools of blacks and whites in the United States — 90 percent of blacks have some degree of white ancestry.
3. He draws together different test results and studies with different and often uneven controls and checks, many inadequate.
4. He does not adequately account for the problem of controlling for the effects of socioeconomic environment.
5. He does not specify how much the expected differences in IQ scores are caused by different environmental opportunities.

This last point views inherited ability as a potential differently developed in different environments.

Judging by Jensen's responses to his critics, he is not moved by their criticism.

Some of Jensen's critics are less disturbed by his scientific arguments than by his suggestions for educational policy; namely, from a young age treating differently children who first measure differently. His advice emphasizes developing such cognitive abilities as abstract reasoning in children who score higher on the IQ, but turning to other abilities in children who first score lower. Many feel that this would fasten on some young children a stigmatized status as incapable of learning, with consequent differential educational opportunities for classes and races. Though Jensen himself does not seem to want this outcome — he seems to want only the chance for each child to develop his inherent capacities — the consequences of such a policy, when widely used, would probably have the negative result of different educational opportunity.

---

* See Arthur R. Jensen, "How Much Can We Boost IQ and Scholastic Achievement?" *Harvard Educational Review*, vol. 39 (Winter 1969), pp. 1–123.

** See the *Harvard Educational Review*, vol. 39 (Spring 1969) and vol. 39 (Fall 1969), for a number of telling critiques of Jensen's work.

For further discussion of this issue of IQ see Melvin Tumin, ed., *Race and Intelligence: A Scientific Evaluation* (New York: Anti-Defamation League, 1963).

The Assumption of Educability

Research such as that reported by Sewell makes it clear that teachers' views of students are important factors in the educational process. Many white teachers seem to believe that lower-class and black children are less able to learn than middle-class and white children are, either because they believe there are genetic differences or because they believe "cultural deprivation" cannot be overcome in their classrooms (see "Jensen and the IQ Problem"). When that happens, there is a pattern of nonlearning in classrooms where teachers do not teach; students do not learn; and the education process does not educate anyone.

How teachers act on their beliefs in the way they treat their students is hard to measure in any scientific way. Some dramatic evidence has been supplied by the first-hand experiences of young teachers who did not share the prevailing feeling that children in their schools were poor learners—these teachers generally got into trouble for that reason.[9]

Nor is it a matter of indifference what teachers expect of their students. The now renowned "Pygmalion" experiment of psychologist Robert Rosenthal and educator Lenore Jacobson documented just how much expectation can make a difference.[10] They gave IQ tests to 650 students in an elementary school in a working-class neighborhood; then told the teachers they would use the results to predict which students were about to take off intellectually. But the names they gave the teachers were drawn randomly from the class. The teachers were led to expect more from a group of children no different by IQ test results from the others.

Did it make any difference? It did, according to retests up to two years after the first one. For children in the first and second grades IQ scores improved beyond the level of chance, though their "expectancy advantage" faded away after another year. But for older children it increased still more in the second year.

"Cooling Them Out"

American public education rarely recognizes or admits there is educational discrimination by class and race. Claims to equality of educational opportunity must be symbolically upheld. According to the 1972 Gallup Poll cited before, 57 percent of the total sample and 67 percent of educators blamed the child's home life for educational failure; only 6 percent blamed the school. The disadvantage of home background that poor children bring to school is now being used to let the school off the hook and to cover up the pervasive and compelling fact of unequal education.

In higher education this claim to equal opportunity is achieved by the *open door* policy of community colleges.[11] In addition, some state universities grant admission to almost any graduate of a high school within the state. But they use the freshman year as a screening process, eliminating large numbers by academic failure. These stu-

---

[9] See, for example, Jonathon Kozol, *Death at an Early Age* (Boston: Houghton Mifflin Company, 1967); and Herbert R. Kohl, *36 Children* (New York: New American Library, 1967). *See also* Kenneth B. Clark, *Dark Ghetto: Dilemmas of Social Power* (New York: Harper and Row, 1965); and Robert Coles, *Children of Crisis* (Boston: Little, Brown & Company, 1967).

[10] See Robert Rosenthal and Lenore Jacobson, *Pygmalion in the Classroom* (New York: Holt, Rinehart and Winston, Inc., 1968).

[11] See Burton Clark, *The Open Door College* (New York: McGraw-Hill Book Company, Inc., 1960).

Figure 13.1 How teachers act toward their students—and what they believe the children are capable of learning—may have widespread repercussions on the students' ability to learn. *(Ford Foundation, William Simmons.)*

dents do not recognize the class basis of their academic failure, for they have been led to believe that they were indeed "given a chance." Their academic failure is seen by them, by their families, and by educators as evidence of the students' inadequacies. It looks as if they were *individually* eliminated by low grades and by counseling them out. This is what Burton Clark calls *cooling them out*. He means that public educational institutions confer legitimacy on social inequality by making academic failure seem to be an individual responsibility, an inadequacy of the person not of the educational process.

The same thing can be accomplished by high-school tracking. In about half the high schools in the United States today, students are sorted into different tracks, one being college preparatory; the others vocational, technical, industrial, business, general, and the like.

Though sorting into tracks is presumably done on the basis of ability, a recent study found that class and racial background strongly influenced which track a student took, quite apart from his IQ or achievement in junior high.[12] Furthermore, track position had an effect on academic achievement greater than social class background, IQ, or past performance. The effect was to lower the academic performance of non-college prep students and raise that of the college prep ones. Not being in the college prep program hurt a student's self-esteem; led to a deterioration of academic performance; and encouraged less participation in school activities, a greater likelihood of

[12] *See* Walter E. Schafer, Carol Olexa, and Kenneth Polk, "Programmed for Social Class: Tracking in High School," *Trans-action*, vol. 7 (October 1970), pp. 39–46; reprinted in William Feigelman, *Sociology Full Circle: Contemporary Readings on Society* (Frederick A. Praeger, Inc., 1972), pp. 145–158.

dropping out, and more frequent involvement in behavior problems in school and out.

Schooling and Inequality: the Jencks Report

A careful and detailed review of all American studies on the relationship of class and race to educational and occupational achievement, known as the Jencks Report after its principal author, achieved widespread public recognition and discussion even before its publication in 1972.[13] Some of the discussion in the press distorted the findings and their policy implications.

The basic findings of the Jencks Report can be summarized as:

1. Though educational inequality has been reduced in the United States, educational opportunity is still very unequally distributed.
2. The distribution of cognitive skills, as measured by test scores, is unequal among the social classes and between black and white children. This inequality is largely a function of both genetic and environmental inequality, and could be reduced but not eliminated if educational inequality were eliminated and everyone's economic status were equalized. Also, eliminating racial and class segregation would reduce inequality further.
3. Family background has more influence than any other factor on educational achievement. This means that a school's "output" depends largely on a single "input"—the background characteristics the children bring with them.
4. People's occupational statuses are closely tied to their educational attainment.

5. But family background, cognitive skill, educational attainment, and occupational status do not explain much of the variation in *income*. Either there are other factors that do explain it—Jencks speculatively suggested "luck" and personality—or there has not been adequate measurement as yet.

Sociologists long experienced in this area, like James Coleman and William Sewell, believe that serious measurement problems still beset this research. Sewell says: "We have been more successful in explaining educational attainment than in explaining occupational attainment and much more successful in explaining occupational attainment than in explaining earnings."[14] (For recent data on the relationship of income and education, *see* Table 13.2.)

From this analysis Jencks came to the conclusion that schools can do little toward making adults more equal. This particular finding has been widely disseminated, and one of its consequences was to use Jencks' work to argue for a lessening of effort to improve education, thus relieving the schools of much responsibility for the academic failure of children.

But Jencks did not intend to give aid and comfort either to complacent educators or anti-reform political groups. He argues for a diversity of reforms in education, even though their outcomes would not make us all equal. But making us all equal is exactly what Christopher Jencks does believe in, and for this he advocates a program of *income equality*. He ends his book with this statement:

As long as egalitarians assume that public policy cannot contribute to economic equality

[13] *See* Christopher Jencks and others, *Inequality: A Reassessment of the Effect of Family and Schooling in America* (New York: Basic Books, Inc., 1972).

[14] *See* William Sewell in "Review Symposium," *American Journal of Sociology,* vol. 78 (May 1973), p. 1537. *See* contributions by James Coleman and Thomas Pettigrew to this same review of the Jencks Report.

Destroyed idea that education will solve all our problems.

TABLE 13.2   Level of School Completed by Employed Males 25–64 Years Old, by Income in 1971

	Not High-school Graduate	High-school Graduate		
		No Years of College	1–3 Years of College	4 Years of College or More
Under $10,000	72.8	53.7	42.0	27.7
$10,000–14,999	21.6	33.9	36.5	29.0
$15,000 and over	5.6	12.5	21.4	43.3

Source: U.S. Bureau of the Census, *Current Population Reports*, Series P-20, no. 243, "Educational Attainment: March 1972" (Washington, D.C.: U.S. Government Printing Office, 1972), p. 6.

directly but must proceed by ingenious manipulations of marginal institutions like the schools, progress will remain glacial. If we want to move beyond this tradition, we will have to establish political control over the economic institutions that shape our society. This is what other countries usually call socialism. Anything else will end in the same disappointment as the reforms of the 1960s.[15]

Education and Social Mobility

In a changing and mobile society education cannot continue to define the educational chances of children solely by reference to the status of their parents. Social mobility, as we tried to make evident in Chapter 10, is also a process of selectively moving large numbers of people upward in status in order to fill the social positions created by the rapid expansion of the middle class. Determining who moves up from the lower ranks rests largely with education, which has two tasks in this changing structure of increased mobility:

1. It must locate and educate more people from lower status levels for higher status positions.
2. It must increase the general level of education at practically all class levels in the society.

[15] *See* Jencks, *op. cit.*, p. 265.

But this is a task for which schools and universities were not historically designed, and as yet they do not do it well.

Schools and universities were not designed for the selection processes thrust upon them in a modern economy by the tightening bond of schooling with occupation, and hence with social class, nor were they designed to act as agencies of social justice, distributing "life-chances" according to some meritocratic principle in face of the social claims of parents for their children. . . . The distribution of educational facilities in all countries is but loosely related to the distribution of ability.[16]

Going to College

At the turn of the century only 4 percent of those aged 18 to 21 were in college; this figure has doubled about every 20 years, so that it was 16 percent in 1940. In October 1972, 38 percent of males aged 18 and 19 were in college, and 34 percent of females. Of the age group 20 and 21 years, 36 percent males and 26 percent females were in college.[17] However, the peak of

[16] *See* Jean Floud and A.H. Halsey, "Introduction," in Halsey, Floud, and Anderson, *op. cit.*, pp. 5 and 7. In this same work *see* essays by T.H. Marshall and H. Schelsky.
[17] *See* U.S. Bureau of the Census, *Current Population Reports*, P-20, no. 247, "School Enrollment in the United States: 1972" (Washington, D.C.: U.S. Government Printing Office, 1973), p. 4.

college attendance for men was in 1969, when it was up over 44 percent. From 1969 to 1972 the college enrollment rate for men declined by 8 percentage points, while for women it increased by 5 percentage points.[18]

This expansion does not necessarily do away with unequal chances. Data by Dael Wolfle indicate that the proportion of those entering college by occupational categories of parents ranges from 67 percent for professional and semiprofessional; 50 percent for managerial; 48 percent for sales, clerical, and service; and 26 percent for manual occupations.[19]

Education for a Meritocracy

It should be apparent that one significant change in education in the United States is from a bastion of class privilege to a democratization that claims to select on the basis of ability and aspiration. To be sure, as yet the children of the affluent have the advantage even here, for they come from homes where the importance of education is usually understood and appreciated, and where the young are strongly socialized to expectations of educational achievement. A strong belief in discovering and educating the talented and the more intelligent is a major rationale for programs that test and rank students (witness the National Merit Scholars) and for awarding scholarships and admitting students to academically prestigious schools.

Also, it has become a major rationalization of the modern, bureaucratic middle class that they hold their positions by virtue of achievement, and that they have risen by their own merit not by the advantages of race or class. Furthermore, it is now a prevailing belief that this is exactly how the high and responsible positions in a modern society are to be filled, for then merit demonstrated by education and occupational success will give society the best leadership.

The concept of meritocracy, then, suggests a society in which people earn their social positions on merit and in which advancement through a hierarchy of social positions is based on "objective" criteria, such as test scores, grades, degrees, and other forms of earned credentials. Presumably, the elite of such a society will be its most qualified people. And there will be elites, for meritocracy is a way of stratifying society from top to bottom; it is not a program for equality.

There is no actual meritocratic society today anywhere in the world, but there is powerful pressure in this direction in most modern and modernizing societies, regardless of ideological orientation. The idea is most attractive within the new middle class — those professionalized strata that have succeeded in the process of becoming educationally qualified. And education is the basic process of sorting out and sifting among the pools of human talent, for grading and classifying people as to measurable quality.[20]

It is within bureaucratic structures that meritocracy is most proclaimed as the basis for selecting the qualified. But the selection of people for advancement is never wholly a matter of their education-

[18] See "School Enrollment in the United States: 1972," p. 1.

[19] See Dael Wolfle, "Educational Opportunity, Measured Intelligence, and Social Background," in Halsey, Floud, and Anderson, op. cit., p. 230.

[20] For a sophisticated discussion of the larger implications of this see Alvin W. Gouldner, The Coming Crisis of Western Sociology (New York: Basic Books, Inc., 1970; paperback edition, Equinox Books, 1971), Ch. 3, "Utilitarian Culture and Sociology."

Figure 13.2 Who goes to college? The answer determines in great part the life chances of both those who earn a college degree and those who don't. *(Magnum Photos.)*

ally-certified merit. Political and ideological criteria are always important, however much they may be formally denied. Technical merit alone will not bring promotion if the individual's relations with colleagues and fellow workers are difficult—one must "relate" well to others—or if his social and political attitudes are too deviant from conventional views.

But a more basic issue is that the opportunity to qualify for advancement is still very unequally distributed. Discrimination by social class, as well as by race and sex, begins so early in life that inevitably the successful meritocrats are drawn disproportionately from the middle and upper levels of society. Furthermore, we have no scientific capacity to provide a genuinely equal process for determining merit. None of the objective criteria escape cultural limitations, particularly those of class. The qualified in present-day meritocracy win out mostly because of a head start in life, one that enables them to succeed in earlier grades in order to qualify for later education and the winning of the best credentials.

What is more important is that the meritocratic viewpoint may come to dominate more and more. Various testing processes from earliest childhood on not only rank people they stigmatize many as average or mediocre. Once such tags are firmly fixed, they are acted upon, so that in time they produce the reality of the academically mediocre. The children of the meritocrats will escape this fate more often than not, while the children of others will most often be its victims.

RACE AND EDUCATION

In both quantity and quality of education black people lag behind whites, as Table 13.3 shows. It has never been other-

**TABLE 13.3 Level of School Completed by Persons 20 Years Old and Over,
by Age and Race, March 1972**

| | | High-school Graduate | | |
Age and Race	Not High-school Graduate	No Years of College	1–3 Years of College	4 Years of College or More
White				
20–24 years	15.1	43.7	29.5	11.6
25 years and over	39.6	36.4	11.4	12.6
Black				
20–24 years	34.0	42.9	19.7	3.5
25 years and over	63.5	24.9	6.5	5.1

Source: U.S. Bureau of the Census, Current Population Reports, Series P-20, no. 243, "Educational Attainment: March 1972" (Washington, D.C.: U.S. Government Printing Office, 1972), p. 7.

wise in the United States, but in the last two decades, since the Supreme Court decision of 1954, the differences in educational opportunities and educational achievement between the races has been a major concern of legislative policy and court decisions.

Segregated Schooling

Segregation of the races in public facilities, including schooling, had been held to be constitutional since the Supreme Court ruled that separate facilities did not violate the Fourteenth Amendment to the Constitution guaranteeing equal protection under the laws, *if* those facilities were otherwise equal. This was the famous *Plessy vs. Ferguson* decision of 1896, the "separate but equal" ruling that remained basic federal policy until 1954, when the Supreme Court overturned the earlier decision and ruled that children, when required on the basis of race to attend separate schools, were deprived of the equal protection assured by the Fourteenth Amendment.

Racially separate schools, the Court said in its written opinion, have "a tendency to retard the educational and mental development of Negro children and to deprive them of some of the benefits they would receive in a racially integrated school." They also ruled that separation of children solely because of race "generates a feeling of inferiority as to their status in the community that may affect their hearts and minds in a way unlikely ever to be undone."

Desegregating Schools

Though this decision became the law of the land, it did not lead to any rapid change in the segregation of the races in public schools, North or South. Only slowly and grudgingly did change come. Indeed, as late as 1965, 80 percent of all white children were attending schools that were from 90 to 100 percent white, and 65 percent of black children were in schools that were at least 90 percent black.

What is more significant is that during the 1960s a trend for *increased racial separation* became evident. This is a consequence of increasing white concentration in the suburbs and conversely increasing black concentration in the central cities. In fifteen large metropolitan areas in 1960,

79 percent of the nonwhite enrollment was in central city schools and 68 percent of the white students attended suburban schools; the trend through the 1960s and into the 1970s has done nothing to alter that, but has increased it.[21]

In the central cities, however, racial segregation is still maintained, even when black students outnumber whites. In 75 American cities surveyed for the 1965–1966 school year, three-fourths of the black students were in elementary schools that were 90 percent or more black; 83 percent of the white students were in all-white schools.[22] By the middle sixties, racial isolation did not differ greatly from the North to the South.[23]

An additional contributing factor in central cities is the increasing enrollment of white students in private schools. In 1965, 40 percent of the total white elementary-school population in St. Louis attended nonpublic schools; in Boston, 41 percent, and in Philadelphia, more than 60 percent. These patterns only increase the isolation of white and black children from one another in school.[24]

The paradox of this pattern is that it comes when all opinion surveys reveal increasingly more positive attitudes about blacks by whites, a presumed decline in the level of expressed prejudice.[25] Yet, attitudinal change of this general kind does not translate itself into a readiness by white parents to desegregate. Why not? According to *Racial Isolation in the Public Schools* there are three reasons why white parents fear desegregation in the schools:

1. They fear the loss of the neighborhood school.
2. They fear a lowering of educational standards.
3. They fear that contact with black children will be harmful to their children.

The Coleman Report: Equal Educational Opportunity

A massive national study by sociologist James Coleman tried to account for the differences in the quality of education attained by white and black (and other minority) students in the United States.[26] Differences are substantial. Black students in the twelfth grade in the urban Northeast, for example, were reading at a ninth-grade level and doing math at a seventh-grade level. Eighty-five percent of black students were below the white average.

In a massive collection of tables and statistical analyses, the Coleman Report found that such things as the physical quality of the school and its resources seemed to have little to do with the academic achievement of black students. In its conclusion, the Report said:

Taking all these results together, one implication stands out above all: that schools bring little influence to bear on a child's achievement that is independent of his background and general social context; that this very lack of an inde-

[21] See U.S. Commission on Civil Rights, *Racial Isolation in the Public Schools*, vol. I (Washington, D.C.: Government Printing Office, 1967), p. 3.
[22] See *Racial Isolation in the Public Schools*, vol. I, p. 3.
[23] See *Racial Isolation in the Public Schools*, vol. I, pp. 38–39.
[24] See *Racial Isolation in the Public Schools*, vol. I, pp. 39–39.
[25] See, for example, Herbert H. Hyman and Paul B. Sheatsley, "Attitudes toward Desegregation," *Scientific American*, vol. 211 (1964), pp. 16–23. For a review of ambiguity and inconsistency in such attitudes see John Brigham and Theodore Weiss-

bach, "The Current Racial Climate in the United States," in their edited *Racial Attitudes in America* (New York: Harper and Row, 1972), pp. 1–8.
[26] See James S. Coleman, and others, *Equality of Educational Opportunity* (Washington, D.C.: Government Printing Office, 1966).

pendent effect means that the inequalities imposed on children by their home, neighborhood, and peer environment are carried along to become the inequalities with which they confront adult life at the end of school.[27]

As a result, notes the Report, in order for there to be equality of educational opportunity, schools must have a strong effect that is independent of the child's immediate social environment, and "that strong independent effect is not present in American schools."[28]

What the Coleman Report did find, consistent with its overall result, was that when children from a disadvantaged background were in a class with less disadvantaged children, they did better than if their fellow students were all adversely affected like themselves. Even when black disadvantaged students were in classes with similarly disadvantaged white students, they did better—this is a finding made much of by the supporters of school integration.

In a separate analysis of the Coleman Report data, it was reported that:

> The combined effects of social class integration and racial desegregation are substantial. When disadvantaged Negro students are in class with similarly situated whites, their average performance is improved by more than a full grade. When they are in class with more advantaged white students, their performance is improved by more than two grade levels.[29]

A Cautionary Note

The Coleman Report is a very large, ambitious, and influential study, but it is not a definitive one. Critics have pointed out some weaknesses, including alleged flaws in research design, a weak set of attitude questions, and the refusal of a

substantial number of schools to participate in the study. It relies heavily on self-reporting by teachers and administrators. Experts on research have offered more technical disagreements about the Report's statistical analysis.

Implications for Policy

It is important to remember that the Coleman Report falls short of being a definitive study, especially when it is cited as the basis for social policy. There are perhaps two important conclusions that have been drawn from the study:

1. That disadvantaged black students do better when placed in classes with more advantaged students leads many (including Coleman himself) to argue that educational integration is the necessary answer to the problem of educating the disadvantaged minority.
2. Many school officials have drawn the conclusion from the study that the failure to educate black children is not a failure of the school but a failure of the children's background. They do not want to be held responsible for the considerable differences in achievement between white and black students.

For many social scientists and black intellectuals, however, the Coleman Report, assessed in the context of white parental opposition to integration by bussing and white political control of public schools, has led to thinking out some alternate ways in which improved educational achievement for the disadvantaged child can be attained—for no one overtly opposes this.[30]

[27] *See* Coleman, *op. cit.*, p. 325.
[28] *See* Coleman, *op. cit.*, p. 325.
[29] *See Racial Isolation in the Public Schools*, vol. I, p. 91.

[30] For a series of thoughtful essays on the implications of the Coleman Report *see* Harvard Educational Review, *Equal Educational Opportunity* (Cambridge, Mass.: Harvard University Press, 1969). This is an expansion of the Winter 1968 Special Issue of the *Review.*

Figure 13.3 Despite the Supreme Court ruling of 1954, which desegregated schools, racial integration is being challenged by real-life situations such as housing and education budgets. *(A. Devaney, Inc., N.Y.)*

Even Kenneth Clark, a black social psychologist long associated with the effort to achieve desegregation and an outstanding opponent of racially separate schools, argues for a more diverse attack on the problem of equality of education, including seeking improved quality in racially segregated schools while keeping desegregation as the main goal.[31] He argues for two kinds of reforms:

1. Reorganizing the public school system "away from the presently inefficient and uneconomic neighborhood schools to more modern and viable systems or organizations such as educational parks, campuses, or clusters . . ."[32]
2. Breaking the monopoly of the rigid and bureaucratized public school systems in large cities by providing competitive high schools run by states, by the federal government, by industry, by labor unions, even by the army.

Others have read the Coleman Report as evidence that only all black schools will educate black children adequately.

A more basic critique of the Coleman Report has been made by an economist, Samuel Bowles, who contends, first of all, that the Report's finding that the physical and economic resources going into education have no effect on outcome (achievement) is open to serious challenge.[33] Bowles argues that educational equality in outcome can only be achieved if the expenditure for black students and for poor white students is greater than that for more affluent students.

[31] *See* Kenneth Clark, "Alternative Public School Systems," in *Equal Educational Opportunity*, pp. 173–186.

[32] *See* Clark, *op. cit.*, p. 180.

[33] *See* Samuel Bowles, "Toward Equality of Educational Opportunity?" in *Equal Educational Opportunity*, pp. 115–125.

But Bowles makes two other basic arguments. One is that the school system alone cannot bear the burden of achieving equality of educational opportunity. As long as racial discrimination and poverty exist, education alone will not equalize life chances, as these are measured by jobs and incomes. (This is the same point made in the Jencks Report.) Racial discrimination in the job market must be attacked directly, Bowles feels. Blacks earn less than whites even when their education is the same, and the greater the gap in education, the greater the difference in earning power.[34]

Bowles' third point is a basic challenge; namely, that whites gain competitively by the under-education of blacks, so that achieving equality of educational opportunity puts whites and blacks into a real conflict of interests. Therefore, according to Bowles, blacks must attain greater political power—a greater involvement of the black community in educational decision-making—before education can be changed enough to provide an equal opportunity for all.

These suggestions do not exhaust the proposed remedies. School bussing, for example, one of the more recent controversial issues, is an attempt to achieve the placement of black children in the schools of more advantaged white children in the face of suburban and central city concentrations of white and black students, respectively. Numerous efforts at compensatory programs have been attempted, with varied but not usually impressive results. Community control by the parents of the disadvantaged is another suggested remedy.[35]

HIGHER EDUCATION

The changes in American higher education throughout this century have paralleled the changes going on throughout the whole of our society. The small, private liberal arts colleges and local normal schools for preparing local teachers have been overshadowed by the rise of large universities. These have come to dominate higher education by their standards and criteria of what is academically excellent. As a result:

. . . higher education has ceased to be a marginal, backward-looking enterprise shunned by the bulk of the citizenry. Today it is a major growth industry, consuming about 2 per cent of GNP, directly touching the lives of perhaps 4 per cent of the population, and exercising an indirect effect on the whole of society.[36]

The Origins of the Modern Western University

The university is an ancient and prestigious structure, which has survived over centuries of radical transformation of society, from medieval to industrial. Yet rarely has it led in that transformation; instead, it typically has followed changes originating elsewhere in the society, and often only after considerable resistance. Medieval universities were closely tied to the religious structure. But even after they had freed themselves from close religious control, they were slow to adapt to the emerging industrial society. Most of all, they were resistant to democratizing higher edu-

---

[34] See Bowles, op. cit., pp. 122–124.

[35] For a review of these and other efforts see George Eaton Simpson and J. Milton Yinger, Racial and

Cultural Minorities: An Analysis of Prejudice and Discrimination, 4th ed. (New York: Harper and Row, 1972), pp. 566–570.

[36] Christopher Jencks and David Riesman, The Academic Revolution (Garden City, N.Y.: Doubleday and Company, Inc., 1968), p. 13.

cation and making access to it more available to non-elites.

But when Wilhelm von Humboldt established a new university in Berlin in 1810 a new type of institution emerged. Others soon followed and within a decade or so they became centers of *scientific* learning in which the laboratory turned out to be as important as the lecture hall. This German model of the university, with its emphasis on scientific training, in time influenced universities in the United States. The graduate school, for example, developed as a parallel to the German institute. According to Jencks and Riesman, "it was not until the 1880s that anything like a modern university took shape in America," and by World War I, "two dozen major universities had emerged."[37] Thus, within a space of forty years, a major transition in higher education had taken place.

Higher education is not what it was even two decades ago, and colleges and universities have undergone enormous changes. What are those changes? Two recent incisive analyses have argued that the *univer*sity has been replaced by the *multiver*sity, and that this is but one component of an *academic revolution*.

The Multiversity

When Clark Kerr, a social scientist and former president of the University of California, coined the term *multiversity* he meant that there was no longer a single center of values and tasks to which the organization was dedicated.[38] The varied functions and responsibilities of the university gave it multiple goals and a highly diversified academic effort. For one thing, the large public universities have expanded to accommodate increased enrollments in their undergraduate divisions. But they have also grown as the major centers for training graduate students and thus for producing professionals, scientists, and scholars in greater numbers than before. And the university is the major source of scientific research.

There has been a vast increase in students at American universities; campuses that contain 25,000 or more are no longer uncommon. This makes difficult the maintaining of a single, cohesive sense of student life—and perhaps no desire among many that there even be one. But thousands of students on any large campus face a problem of being a nameless face in a huge student body, unknown but to a few friends, and seemingly unable to find means for more personalized interaction with faculty. It is this alienated condition that most observers credit for so much of the student rebellion that first broke out at the University of California at Berkeley.[39]

However, it is not merely numbers that render the relationship of the student to the faculty so impersonal and frequently bureaucratized. In the large American university the student is by no means the only concern of the faculty and sometimes not the primary one. The vast research enterprise that large universities carry on now creates a different type of role for the professor that competes with his teaching role.

[37] *See* Jencks and Riesman, *op. cit.*, p. 13.
[38] *See* Clark Kerr, *The Uses of the University* (Cambridge, Mass.: Harvard University Press, 1963).

[39] *See* Seymour M. Lipset and Sheldon S. Wolin, eds., *The Berkeley Student Revolt* (Garden City: Anchor Books, 1965); and Richard Flacks, *Youth and Social Change* (Chicago, Ill.: Markham Publishing Company, 1971).

For most professors, the rewards of his occupation—recognition in his profession, publication of his work, offices in professional societies, and awards and honors—come, not from teaching but from research and the publication of research. A great teacher is great only on his campus, but an outstanding researcher can have a national—even an international—reputation. He may travel to conferences on an expense account, and his well-funded research may provide him with assistants, a second office, secretarial help, and a light teaching load, or even no teaching at all; none of this may be available to the teacher-professor.

Many college professors have become less preoccupied with educating young people and more preoccupied with educating one another by doing scholarly research which advances their disciplines. Many faculty would defend such work on the grounds that the maintenance and creation of knowledge is the primary function of the true "university," while the four-year "college" has as its primary task the education of students. Undergraduate education has become less a terminal enterprise and more a preparation for graduate school.[40]

The Academic Revolution

The basic changes in American higher education—which Jencks and Riesman have called an academic revolution—besides the transition to a multiversity, include something more fundamental: the rise to unprecedented power of professional scholars and scientists within the university and in time within the society.

[40] *See* Jencks and Riesman, *op. cit.*, p. 13.

The Professionalization of Faculty

The *professionalization* of university professors and their assumption of greater power within the university are two related processes. Over the years professors in modern universities have been able to establish their right to choose their own colleagues, to control the curriculum, and even to determine criteria for choosing students. They have successfully imposed a professional claim to competency to make these decisions—a professional expertise that others as *laymen* presumably do not have. Furthermore, the professors, organized in departments, control graduate instruction. "They turn out Ph.D.s who, despite conspicuous exceptions, mostly have quite similar ideas about what their discipline covers, how it should be taught, and how its frontiers should be advanced."[41] And, "they have established machinery for remaining like-minded," including national and regional meetings, national journals for publishing their research, and an informal network for job placement.[42]

The powerful graduate schools, expanding rapidly since World War II, have become pacesetters in the promotion of meritocratic values. They choose their candidates by their demonstrated ability to do good academic work, ignoring other "particularistic" claims, such as class background. (Despite this, universities have not proved to be easily accessible to women and blacks.)

The graduate schools have led the way in extending meritocratic values to the professions themselves. The leading law firms and the most prestigious hospitals

[41] *See* Jencks and Riesman, *op. cit.*, p. 14.
[42] *See* Jencks and Riesman, *op. cit.*, p. 14.

Figure 13.4 Alienation of students, especially on large campuses like that of the University of California at Berkeley, was one factor in causing the student rebellion of the sixties. *(Wide World Photos.)*

try to hire the best graduates of the leading professional schools, and colleges and universities seek after the most recommended graduates of the best graduate departments in their disciplines. Since graduate education and professional training within universities increasingly finds an outlet in the best job opportunities, the training in values and outlook provided by graduate-school professors has an increasing effect upon how the professions function. And professors are the reform-minded intellectuals of any profession, even in the business school.

The increasing expansion of university enrollments gave university professors the opportunity to press for *selectivity;* that is, choosing competitively those students who had scored well by various academic measurements (grades, test scores, and so on). In this way they have not only extended meritocracy to undergraduate edu-

cation, they have created what Jencks and Riesman call the *university college,* one which puts most of its effort into preparing its graduates for admittance to professional schools and graduate departments in the best universities.

While professional schools; the small number of large, graduate-training universities; and the university colleges undoubtedly involve only a minority of those who seek a higher education, their influence is nonetheless dominant. They have the prestige, set the standards for others, and attract the best students and faculty (as "best" is measured in conventional academic criteria). They train the faculty for most other colleges, and few academics going through graduate school escape socialization into the predominant values. As a result, these faculty often want to imitate the most prestigious universities. While there are persistent exceptions to this, they "do little to shape the future. The model for the future is the university college, and the result is likely to be a continuing trend toward the meritocracy."[43] This makes of higher education an instrument for "meritocratic sorting and grading" of the future middle-class work force of modern society.

This *training* of individuals for professional and technical labor markets, as well as providing various forms of service to state and society, is not easily made compatible with higher education's historic claim of *educating* people to a capacity for critical, objective thought. The former process produces technically qualified individuals who fit readily into corporate and governmental bureaucracies, while the latter equips people to think independently, to pose critical questions, and to challenge comfortable assumptions. The meritocratic emphasis on training has an unintended but nevertheless real stultifying effect on educating the independent mind.[44] The emphasis on obtaining credentials to get a good job creates in universities an atmosphere in which education of the mind loses out to a competitive scramble for grades, credits, and degrees.

Change and Dissent in Higher Education

However powerful and pervasive are the professional and meritocratic processes we have outlined above, there are other significant changes occurring that are not

entirely caught within this pattern. For one thing, since the ferment of the 1960s there has emerged a new, younger faculty more committed to undergraduate education. They are critical of pervasive undemocratic and discriminatory processes at work in society, even in the university. And they criticize the increasingly elitist orientation that is inherent in meritocracy. They have subjected their professionalized and often tamed disciplines to highly critical scrutiny.[45] Beneath much of the verbal and ideological confusion stands one fundamental issue: What kind of a university is it to be in what kind of a society? The close tie of some universities to the Department of Defense, the heavy dependency on the federal government for research funds, and the dominance of research and graduate teaching over undergraduate education are issues that have motivated efforts for change.

It is evident that the university now constitutes a community in which there is centered much of the criticism of modern society: (1.) its bureaucratization, (2.) its patterns of inequality, and (3.) the vulgar, opportunistic quality of much of modern culture. There is also criticism of the university itself and of how it relates itself to the larger society, of the *irrelevance* of much teaching and research for the lives of students and the critical events of the society. The new dissent within the academy asks that universities redefine their conception of public responsibility, and that they become centers of social change,

[43] *See* Jencks and Riesman, *op. cit.*, p. 27.

[44] *See* Ted Vaughn, "The Educational Institution: The Indoctrinating Appendage," in Larry T. Reynolds and James T. Henslin, eds., *American Society: A Critical Analysis* (New York: David McKay Company, Inc., 1973), pp. 225–247.

[45] *See*, for example, Theodore Roszak, ed., *The Dissenting Academy* (New York: Pantheon Books, Inc., 1968). For a more inclusive survey of academic people today *see* Charles H. Anderson and John D. Murray, eds., *The Professors* (Cambridge, Mass.: Schenkman Publishing Company, Inc., 1971).

even radical change. These dissenters press for the independence of the university from other power centers and established institutions of the society.

By the 1970s some of this criticism has receded. There have been some changes: increased admissions of minorities and programs geared particularly to their needs, efforts at opening admissions to many others once left out, and the participation of students with faculty in academic government.

But modern universities, and especially public ones, are now such integral parts of modern society and perform such critical functions for it that they cannot simply cease to perform the many teaching and research that make "multiversities" of them. Thus, universities are beset by conflicting and competing demands from within and without, and their academic leadership is struggling to balance them in such a way as to satisfy those groups too powerful to ignore. These powerful social groups within and without the university are also the groups which will shape it in the time ahead.

Blacks in Higher Education

One of the significant changes that has occurred in higher education in recent years is the substantial increase in the number and percentage of black students. College enrollment of blacks increased 211 percent from 1964 to 1972; in 1964 they were 5 percent of all college students, compared to 9 percent in 1972.[46] However,

much of this enrollment is still in black colleges in the South. In 1950 an estimated 60 percent of black students were so enrolled; by the mid-sixties, slightly more than half of all black college students were still in black colleges, though by 1968 this figure was down to 36 percent.[47]

An increase in the admission of black students in predominantly white universities and colleges in the North, particularly the public ones, has come about during criticism that these colleges had for too long been indifferent to the educational needs of blacks. The effort to recruit more black students included allocating more funds for scholarships, in recognition of the greater proportion of these students who were from low-income families, and in easing some admission standards in consideration of the larger number of these students whose high-school education was too poor to win regular admission. These actions proved to be controversial; criticisms included, first, the lowering of standards, and second, discriminating against white students.

One answer to easing admission standards was "open admissions"—admitting any student with a high-school diploma. Though widely discussed, only one major experiment has been made—at the City University of New York, which has nine four-year colleges and seven two-year community colleges. The major effect of open admissions was to increase the enrollment of white Catholic students from working-class families; previously, Jewish students had been in the majority. No definitive

[46] See U.S. Bureau of the Census, *Current Population Reports,* Series P-20, no. 247, "School Enrollment in the United States, 1972" (Washington, D.C.: Government Printing Office, 1973), p. 1.

[47] See U.S. Bureau of the Census, *Current Population Reports,* Series P-23, no. 29, "The Social and Economic Status of Negroes in the United States, 1969" (Washington, D.C.: Government Printing Office, 1970), p. 53.

decision can yet be made on this experiment; so far, both students and faculty are apparently divided on its value, as is the public.

Accommodating the New Black Student

An increase in the proportion of black students on many campuses produced new, unanticipated problems for white faculty and administrators. The new generation of black students on campus was different from those who had been present in the past. They made new demands about admissions, financial aid and scholarships, counseling, and living units. They displayed more negative feelings about white people.[48] What liberal faculty least expected was the demand for separate meeting and residential quarters, something that looked to many of the white faculty like a form of segregation. If black students want to be separate, why go to a predominantly white school in the first place? There are, according to black sociologist Harry Edwards, four reasons:[49]

1. The predominantly white universities have the best equipment and facilities.
2. The white authorities who control these colleges will not shut them down to stop black political activism—something done in black colleges in the South. Thus, the administrators must negotiate over demands or face disruptions and confrontations.
3. A black student can be "blacker" at such colleges than at Southern black colleges, where conservative administrators are responsible to conservative, if not racist white boards.

4. Finally, the black student knows he will always be surrounded by whites in the United States, so that at a predominantly white college he is in a situation "more closely representative of that which awaits him in the society at large—a minority of blacks engulfed by a majority of whites who are often hostile, seldom understanding, and almost always racist."[50]

Black Studies

No less controversial on many campuses has been the effort to create programs in black studies. Part of the controversy has been over a black separatist dimension: demands for a black faculty, black student control over the programs, and exclusion of whites from the programs. Another has been over black studies as a curriculum for blacks instead of more occupationally-oriented, skill-achieving programs intended to provide mobility into a white-dominated middle-class society.[51] Other defenders of black studies argue that black students need programs to teach them about their own culture, to build favorable self-images, to strengthen identification with the black community, and to enable blacks to analyze social problems from a black perspective.[52]

Black students in significant numbers at formerly almost all-white universities have changed the campus situation, though relations among these black students, white students, the faculty, and the administration are still being worked out. But few American universities will ever be as lily-white again as in the past, and for that reason they will never be the same.

[48] See William M. Banks, "The Changing Attitudes of Black Students," in Brigham and Weissbach, op. cit., pp. 176–182.
[49] See Harry Edwards, Black Students (New York: The Free Press, 1970), pp. 71–73.

[50] See Edwards, op. cit., p. 73.
[51] For a summary of the black studies controversy see Simpson and Yinger, op. cit., pp. 603–606.
[52] See Simpson and Yinger, op. cit., p. 603.

Figure 13.5 Open admissions have not favored the black student as fully as was anticipated, although the lily-white university is a phenomenon of the past. *(Hugh Rogers, The City University of New York.)*

THE CONTROL OF EDUCATION

Whether public or private, the school system (or systems) of a society are subject to controls exerted from outside the educational process itself. To a considerable extent education has been a process of preparing young people to meet the requirements set down by other institutions of the society, and the changes in educational standards are a response to changing demands within the society.

But the educational structure is not equally responsive to the demands and interests of all the various status groups and classes. Historically, the established elites and privileged groups have exerted control over education in two ways. First, they have usually established separate schools for their own offspring, such as the English public schools (which are really private schools), the German law faculties,

the Ivy League universities, and the elite prep schools. Second, they have exerted a strong ideological control over the content and subject matter of the education of other social classes, once these other social classes gained voting rights.

Public education for most people began only in the nineteenth century, partly in response to the demands of such people for an education for their children. Labor unions and workingmen's parties and the voting power of a newly enfranchised working class put power behind such a demand. But, business classes and propertied elites, once working people got the vote, pressed for universal education to accompany universal suffrage. They wanted working-class children in school in order to indoctrinate them with such values as respect for property and for law and order, hard work, frugality and savings, competition and achievement, and belief in

America as the unequaled land of opportunity and freedom.[53] What began historically as a democratic movement for *free* education became in time *compulsory* schooling for all social classes in schools controlled by the economic elite.

Since then, schools have never ceased to be uncritical instructors in political and moral orthodoxy, and they are in trouble when they try to do otherwise. Though there is frequent lip service to the ideal of teaching the young to think critically, schools in fact are organized too authoritatively and teach too uncritically to accomplish that. A distinguished American political scientist put it:

In modern societies the school system, in particular, functions as a formidable instrument of political power in its role as a transmitter of the goals, values, and attitudes of the polity. In the selection of values and attitudes to be inculcated, it chooses those cherished by the dominant elements in the political order. By and large the impact of widely accepted goals, mores, and social values fixes the programs of American schools. When schools diverge from this vaguely defined directive and collide with potent groups in the political system, they feel a pressure to conform.[54]

What Is Not Taught

As important as what is taught is what is *not* taught in the schools. American public schools have taught very little about

[53] *See* Samuel Bowles, "Unequal Education and the Reproduction of the Social Division of Labor," in Martin Carnoy, ed., *Schooling in a Corporate Society* (New York: David McKay Company, Inc., 1972), particularly pp. 37–46. For a fuller development *see* B. Bailyn, *Education in the Forming of American Society* (Chapel Hill: University of North Carolina Press, 1960).

[54] *See* V.O. Key, Jr., *Politics, Parties, and Pressure Groups* (New York: Thomas Y. Crowell Company, 1964), pp. 12–13.

racial issues, particularly the expulsion from their land holdings and decimation of Indians and the enslavement of blacks. They have not taught black children anything about their own history, and, as sociologist-historian George Rawick points out, schools have failed to teach that black history is an integral part of American history.[55] Nor have they allowed Indian children to learn of the Indian heritage in their schools. In both cases, schooling has been a means of *not* teaching their own heritage, history, and collective identity to subordinate groups. They have not even taught them enough of the dominant culture to allow them to succeed within it.

This is no less true of working people and European immigrants. Their children have learned nothing about the lives and struggles of immigrants, or of the history of labor violence that occurred so frequently until the 1930s.

In both these instances, the schools have treated American society as if there were no unequal groups and classes, when in fact such stratification is a fundamental key to the inequality that besets education today.

From Local to National Control

In the United States education has been primarily a local enterprise, in contrast to Europe, where education has been under national control. This localistic pattern developed when the United States was primarily locally focused or at best regional in its economic structure.

But now, local markets are superseded by a national (and even international) market. Occupational opportunities are

[55] George Rawick, *From Sundown to Sunup* (Westport, Conn.: Greenwood Press, Inc., 1972).

viewed increasingly in terms of national trends. Accordingly, the demands on the local schools are to prepare young people to enter college and then enter job markets, neither of which are any longer a strictly local enterprise.

Education has become a matter of national policy and is receiving a steadily increasing share of national resources. The rapid growth of the U.S. Department of Education into a position of leadership in education, with resources for the support of varied types of programs for the development of education, is less than two decades old. The National Science Foundation has undertaken a national program for upgrading science training, as well as extensive support of scientific research in universities.

There are other forces working against localism. Private foundations, for example, throughout this century have undertaken various projects intended to improve quality or to innovate in the area of curriculum. Increasingly, state governments have acted to minimize local differences through state certification of teachers, some common course requirements, and also through allocation of tax funds for education. Thus, state departments of education have long been a major force for removing local differences in education.

Professionalization

A highly significant development, consistent with the emergence of a more professionalized middle class, has been the _professionalization_ of education on a national level, introducing national standards that put pressure on local school boards and protect both teachers and administrators from local pressures. More and more local systems must conform to nationally accepted standards in order to compete successfully for available good teachers, to remain accredited, and to place their graduates in decent colleges and universities.

This also means a proliferation of significant control agencies, including accrediting agencies. This leads to control over substantive curriculum matters by groups outside the local school system or university. Frequently a board of education or a board of trustees has no choice but to meet such requirements or have its programs disaccredited and its degrees devalued.

Another development, the growth of professional power over the day-to-day educational process by teachers and administrators, the professionals of education, has occurred. This increased professional power has developed "teacher power" and has been accompanied by economic action, including strikes, a behavior once defined as unprofessional. Now professors, too, are organizing into faculty collective-bargaining organizations.

All of this movement away from local control has occurred without a great national debate over the issue of local versus national control. Yet local control takes on renewed meaning for citizens when they see its significance for influencing processes and decisions vital to their interests. School bussing and community control of schools are two such recent issues.

Bussing: Local versus Centralized Control

Bussing children to integrate schooling touches on racial attitudes, but on other issues as well. New programs to bus children around and across a large metropolitan area (such as in and around Detroit, Michigan, and Richmond, Virginia) had other implications. One was to reduce the power of the local school district and local citizen control. Citizen involvement in schools was threatened when school attendance was assigned across community boundaries. Local boards lose real power when the citizens who elect them and pay the taxes do not send their children to those schools. Parental participation is discouraged when children attend schools in distant districts. School bussing is a complicated issue, but its effect on local control of education is to reduce that control.

Community Control of Schools

That fact is not lost on those who have advocated that black people gain control of their own communities, particularly of the local schools that seem unable to educate their children well.[56] Community control is then an effort to give black children the same ability to pass tests, earn credentials, and get jobs that white children get.

Decentralizing large urban school districts (as has been done in New York City and Detroit) into several local boards has become a political goal. Making it a political reality, however, is more difficult. To restore real power, not merely a semblance of power, to local districts within a large city—and thus to blacks and white ethnics and working-class people in their own neighborhoods—is an idea not readily accepted by established political leaders or by professional educators. It has not been appealing to many middle-class people whose professional experience and training lead them to put their confidence in

trained professional "expertise," and in the dominance of the more educated over the less educated. The professional organizations of teachers also have generally opposed community control in big cities.

The drift toward national control, which coalesced around professional and governmental structures beyond the influence of local people, is a trend so far along that any reversal meets enormous entrenched resistance. But these two issues, bussing and community control of schools, call attention to how much centralized control has occurred in education without any clear national decision to legitimize it.

EDUCATION IN CONFLICT AND CHANGE

From a varied set of perspectives, education is under constant criticism. Few, whatever their expectations and views of education, are satisfied with the status quo. Basically, education has the task of fitting children into a modern society—a technological, highly differentiated, and stratified society. It is not an instrument for reforming society; rather, it has always been shaped and formed by other forces and groups within society, producing demands on education not always consistent, sometimes contradictory.

Preparing People for Jobs

The belief that the school has the task of preparing people for jobs and for getting ahead is widespread, held as tenaciously among the poor and disadvantaged as among the affluent. Here is where much intended reform fails to meet the issue. Schools have no independent power to transform themselves into educational processes that do other than fit people

[56] See Alan A. Altschuler, *Community Control: The Black Demand for Participation in Large American Cities* (New York: Pegasus, 1970); *see also* Henry M. Levin, "The Case for Community Control of the Schools," in James W. Guthrie and Edward Wynne, eds., *New Models for American Education* (Englewood Cliffs, N.J.: Prentice-Hall, Inc., 1971).

into the existing society. Variations in ways of educating children compete for attention and support, but all must finally meet the same tests—and these are the credential-winning tests imposed on the schools, which cannot retain credibility if they fail to teach children to take exams and achievement tests and do well on them.

The schools, in short, will carry out the tasks of preparing the young for society, but the schools do not on their own decide what the preparation is to be. In an increasingly meritocratic society, schooling is a process of teaching and testing for the skills and values that make for success in other institutions, on terms set down by other elites. (Note, though, that professional educators may come to believe thoroughly in these same skills and values as the essential curriculum.) Schools provide instruction and then sort and sift to stamp best grade on some, only good to average on others, and mark some as rejects.

Liberating Children

Some middle-class whites seek to reform education by creating *free schools*.[57] To these people, school is too often oppressive and joyless, and learning is a dull chore. They seek liberation from authoritarian classrooms and want new, unstructured learning environments. They want joy restored to learning, but they want learning that is not primarily organized around acquiring skills for the sake of passing tests.

This is an educational goal of high-

status people, whose own success and security allows them the freedom to experiment with the new, liberating forms of education. Most blacks, and also working-class and lower middle-class whites, cannot afford the luxury of thinking of schools in such terms. For them, acquiring skills and credentials, even through college, is the route to a better job and thus to a better life, an escape from the inadequate income and insecurity that besets those who do not have an education.

Deschooling Society

Perhaps the most radical idea for reforming education has been advanced by a Latin-American intellectual, Ivan Illich, whose book, *Deschooling Society*, has been widely read in the United States. Illich argues that *schooling* and *learning* are not to be equated. Yet schools seek a monopoly of learning experiences, with a consequent enforced dependency of individuals on the schools.

Rich and poor alike depend upon schools and hospitals which guide their lives, form their world view, and define for them what is legitimate and what is not. Both view doctoring oneself as irresponsible, learning on one's own as unreliable, and community organization, when not paid for by those in authority, as a form of aggression or subversion. For both groups the reliance on institutional treatment renders independent accomplishment suspect. The progressive underdevelopment of self- and community-reliance is even more typical in Westchester than it is in the northeast of Brazil. Everywhere not only education but society as a whole needs "deschooling."[58]

---

[57] For a brief review *see* Bonnie Barrett Stretch, "The Rise of the Free Schools," in Carnoy, *op. cit.,* pp. 211–223.

[58] *See* Ivan Illich, *Deschooling Society* (New York: Harper and Row, 1970; paperback edition, 1972), pp. 3–4.

What Illich advocates is creating alternate ways to promote learning on an equal basis. He emphasizes the wide range of human possibilities, including self-learning and learning from one's peers. He also advocates giving people access to learning centers on an equal basis, without regard to previous certification. His concerns are with the failure of obligatory schooling to do its assigned task adequately, with its failure to provide equal educational opportunity, and with its making people dependent on elites and elite-controlled institutions. Therefore, if we deschool society, he argues, "our reliance on specialized, full-time instruction through school will now decrease and we must find more ways to learn and teach: the educational quality of all institutions must increase again."[59]

It could also mean that men will shield themselves less behind certificates acquired in school and thus gain in courage to "talk back" and thereby gain control and instruct the institutions in which they participate.[60]

Illich's notion of deschooling society is probably too revolutionary to be a serious basis for educational reform in this so-ciety, and probably in most societies in the world. Yet his contribution is significant. He provides us with a highly penetrating critique of the place of school in contemporary society the world over, and the emphasis given to what he regards as its negative outcomes: supporting inequality, making people too dependent and docile, making the less educated feel inferior to the more educated, institutionalizing and legitimizing the values of elites. These make more difficult the construction of a world in which we can discover how to use technology "to create institutions which serve personal, creative, and autonomous interaction and the emergence of values which cannot be substantially controlled by technocrats."[61]

Illich's critique points up the basic principle we have dealt with earlier in this chapter: Education is not an independent institution but is responsive to the demands of other institutions for training and certifying people for a hierarchical structure and for socializing them to the established values. If education is to do anything else, it requires a basic reform that is part of a basic reform of society.

[59] See Illich, *op. cit.*, pp. 33.
[60] See Illich, *op. cit.*, p. 34.

[61] See Illich, *op. cit.*, p. 2.

SUMMARY

The *function* of education is to *socialize* the young and to *transmit the culture*, functions which necessarily support the established order.

Education relates to *stratification* in two ways. First, educational opportunity is distributed unequally, reflecting existing differences in class and status. *Family* and *neighborhood* re-enforce quite different educational aspirations for youth of different social classes. Teachers often assume that children are not equally educable, with the result that less effort is made in teaching the children of the poor and minorities. But this is never acknowledged. Rather, *cooling them out* leads such youth to believe that their lower achievement is their own fault. The Jencks Report emphasized that family background has a greater effect than anything else on educational achievement.

Second, since unskilled positions are being eliminated and newer positions require more skill, education contributes to mobility by providing a new generation with more education, so that some people from lower-status origins can move up to higher-status positions.

Meritocracy is a process in which educationally-established merit will determine how individuals are placed in the class structure. It appeals most to the professionally educated, but merit is hard to measure, and other factors, political and ideological, always intrude to affect how people are selected.

Despite legal efforts, *racial segregation* in schools has increased in the present. The Coleman Report found a child's achievement depends more on his background than his school, but that disadvantaged black children improved in classrooms shared with more advantaged students.

Modern universities have become *multiversities,* organizations to train scientists and professionals, do research, and educate undergraduates. These several goals create tensions; for example, teaching suffers if research is maximized.

But this is only one aspect of an *academic revolution;* the emergence of a relatively autonomous and professionalized body of scholars and scientists, who reproduce themselves in graduate training, promote meritocratic values, and altogether dominate and reshape higher education is its central feature.

Controlling education is important to dominant elites, for they see it as a way of indoctrinating the young of all social classes with the values necessary to maintain the institutional structure.

Education in the United States has gone from a locally controlled system to a nationally coordinated one, influenced by national needs and concerns. Recent efforts to restore community control encounter a powerful drift to centralized and professional control.

Today, education is in conflict. No reform in teaching children can escape being measured by performance criteria: how well children learn the skills necessary to compete in a hierarchical society. The affluent want to restore joy to learning, thus liberating children from oppressively dull classrooms, but the poorer classes are primarily concerned with their children learning marketable skills.

If education is to do more than socialize children to established values and train and certify them for a hierarchical structure, society must be basically reformed.

Suggested Readings

Alan A. Altschuler, *Community Control: The Black Demand for Participation in Large American Cities* (New York: Pegasus, 1970). An exploration of a powerful idea about changing communities and education.

Martin Carnoy, ed., *Schooling in a Corporate Society* (New York: David McKay Company, Inc., 1972). A series of essays offering a radical critique of education in contemporary Capitalist society.

Burton Clark, *The Open Door College* (New York: McGraw-Hill Book Company, Inc., 1960). A study of the community college as an open door to education for those once not admitted to college.

James Coleman, and others, *Equality of Educational Opportunity* (Washington, D.C.: Government Printing Office, 1966). The "Coleman Report," now an influential source of information on the problems of educating poor black children.

Harry Edwards, *Black Students* (New York: The Free Press, 1970). A black sociologist provides an understanding of the conduct and commitment of today's black college students.

Beatrice and Ronald Gross, *Radical School Reform* (New York: Simon and Schuster, Inc., 1969). A collection of essays that offers a sampling of radical ideas about how to reform education.

Harvard Educational Review, *Equal Educational Opportunity* (Cambridge, Mass.: Harvard University Press, 1969). A series of provocative essays on the meaning of the Coleman Report.

Ivan Illich, *Deschooling Society* (New York: Harper and Row, 1970; paperback edition, 1972). A penetrating critique of an educational system that insists on ending obligatory schooling.

Christopher Jencks and David Riesman, *The Academic Revolution* (New York, Doubleday and Company, Inc., 1968). An impressive analysis of the transformation of the University into a meritocratic institution.

Clark Kerr, *The Uses of the University* (Cambridge, Mass.: Harvard University Press, 1963). The influential work defining and describing the multiversity.

Herbert Kohl, *36 Children* (New York: New American Library, 1967). A white teacher in a black school in Harlem has a depressing experience, but learns much about how to teach these children.

Jonathon Kozol, *Death at an Early Age* (Boston: Houghton Mifflin Company, 1967). As a new, young teacher, Kozol witnessed the crushing of spirit and mind in black children at a public school.

Robert Rosenthal and Lenore Jacobson, *Pygmalion in the Classroom* (New York: Holt, Rinehart and Winston, Inc., 1968). The revealing study of the importance of teachers' expectations on school performance.

Theodore Roszak, ed., *The Dissenting Academy* (New York: Pantheon Books, Inc., 1968). A series of essays by dissenting scholars criticizing the university and its professors.

U.S. Commission on Civil Rights, *Racial Isolation in the Schools,* vol. I (Washington, D.C.: Government Printing Office, 1967). A thorough, official analysis of increasing racial separation in schools, and its consequences.

Robert Paul Wolff, *The Ideal of the University* (Boston: The Beacon Press, 1969). A subtle, radical philosopher-intellectual subjects the modern university to a penetrating critique.

To a greater extent than any other phase of culture, modern Christendom takes its complexion from its economic organization.
— *Thorstein Veblen*

Chapter 14

Economy and Society

Without sustenance and shelter no other human activity is possible. It is only a step beyond that truism to recognizing that this necessary economic activity has an enormously shaping impact on all other aspects of social life. One is neither "Marxian" nor an "economic determinist" to recognize that fact.

Yet sociology has been slow to develop an understanding of the place of the economy in the total fabric of society. It has largely treated economic and political institutions as separate and differentiated, consistent with a classical liberal theory which assumed that in fact economics and politics were quite separate spheres of human activity. *Economics* and *political science* were regarded as separate modes of study.

In fact economics and politics are not fully separate spheres and never have been. Now, more than ever, *political economy* is important in modern societies. In this chapter and the next we will deal separately with economic and political institutions, but our analysis will give full recognition to the close involvement of each with the other.

THE ECONOMY AS
SOCIAL ORGANIZATION

In any society there is social organization for satisfying those material wants—food, shelter, and clothing—without which life could not be sustained. In a cooperative and interdependent process many different persons contribute in some manner to the total task of producing and distributing goods.

Production

The productive factors—land, capital, labor, and organization—are combined in cooperative efforts at producing goods, and these efforts in turn bring about a division of labor and a system of occupations, however rudimentary. Work is always done in social groups, whether that is the family, the small household unit, or the large modern factory. The existing state of technology determines how labor can be divided and what type and size of work units are possible. The large modern factory with assembly-line production of masses of goods, for example, is only possible with an advanced machine technology.

Distribution

Distributive processes are organized around the claims of each person to a share of the goods produced by the collective efforts of the group. Goods have always been relatively *scarce*; that is, demand exceeds supply, and distribution has always been unequal beyond (as Lenski pointed out in Chapter 10) the minimum necessary to sustain life in the group. Distribution, then, becomes a problem focused on *surplus*; that is, on the supply beyond that minimum.

At this point economy intersects with both the political structure and the class structure. Differences in power permit some to gain a larger share of the economic surplus, and these social strata always control the political process by which unequal distribution is both insured and legitimized. In all known societies such political control has been one factor in the allocation of surplus.

Only when there is a surplus beyond a subsistence minimum can there be economic growth and development.

Surplus alone is not enough to insure development; it is necessary that there be some form of social organization for concentrating surplus and committing it to the tools of production and the equipment of civilization. Hence the intimate connection between systems of economic distribution and social stratification. The distribution and concentration of surplus defines the social strata that can control wealth and power and make the crucial allocative decisions.[1]

Property

Property, too, rests on the conception of scarce resources, for if resources were unlimited and inexhaustible, no one would need to claim ownership of anything. The most common confusion about property is to conceive of it as a material object—land or tools—when property is *ownership* of an object, not the object itself. Ownership means the right to use, consume, or have access to and control of an object.

A further distinction is necessary. Private ownership of *consumer* goods—automobiles and television sets—does not dis-

[1] *See* Leon Mayhew, *Society: Institutions and Activity* (Glenview, Ill.: Scott, Foresman and Company, 1971), p. 106.

tinguish one social system from another; even Socialist systems permit much private ownership of these goods. But _ownership of the means of production_—of land and natural resources, of tools, machinery, and factories—is the crucial factor in defining a society as one of private or socialized property.

Whatever their forms, property rights are sustained by collective agreement within the society and backed by legitimate forms of power and authority. This is no less true of private property than of any other kind. A person has private property rights only because the laws and courts of the state will protect and enforce such rights.   _corporation – imp._

If property rights are socially defined and enforced, it follows that such rights are always limited. Laws regulate the use of property, and in the modern world there is a whole set of restrictions on private owners: fire and health regulations, zoning ordinances, and safety regulations, are examples. Property may be confiscated for public use, under specified circumstances, as when buildings are taken in order to build highways. Lastly, taxes are levied and if they are not paid, property rights are forfeited.

Types of Property

In traditional societies property has often been _communal_, in that land for tilling and hunting was regarded as belonging to the group—tribe or village—as a whole. _Public_ ownership has meant that rights to resources are claimed in the name of a political collectivity—the state or some subgrouping of the state. Public or private ownership of the "means of production" has been the key principle and perhaps

the basic issue in the great ideological debate of the nineteenth century between the proponents of capitalism and socialism.

From the Marxian perspective two assumptions were made: first, that the right of private property created two basic classes, those who owned productive property and those who did not; and the owners had power as a consequence of having property. On this issue the Marxian position is sociologically sound: The right of property does create power for its possessors over those who are propertyless. Control of scarce resources necessary for human subsistence has always created a powerful social class in any human society, whether agrarian or industrial.

A second assumption was that ownership meant actual control and operation. From a nineteenth-century perspective property owners were also the operating entrepreneurs, the "bosses," who ran businesses on a daily basis. But it was just this assumption that was called into question in the twentieth century by the development of the modern corporation.

The Separation of Ownership and Control

The invention of the legal corporation was significant in the development of capitalism in that many people could invest in a single enterprise, instead of relying on the capitalizing abilities of the rich few, while still protecting these many investors by limiting the liability of ownership they incurred. But corporations brought about an unanticipated consequence: Dispersing ownership among a large body of stockholders separated ownership from the actual, operating control of the enterprise. Increasingly, actual decision-making rested with _management_, which not only directed and supervised the employees in internal daily operations but also made fundamental policy decisions for the firm.[2]

Not all economists and social scientists agree fully with this analysis. However, none disagree that a professional management intent on maximizing profits is now the typical decision-making group in American corporations, particularly the larger ones. Some analysts feel that this does not remove ownership from the control of the stockholders, at least not the large owners. While over 30 million Americans own stock, according to the New York Stock Exchange, there is nonetheless a high concentration of ownership in the hands of a relatively small group. Economist Robert Lampmann, for example, found that some 75,000 adults, each with total assets of $500,000 or more, owned at least 40 percent of all the corporate stock in the United States, and that this stock represented over 55 percent of their personal wealth.[3] A larger group of the top 1 percent of wealth-holders, about 1.5 million people, owned at least 80 percent of all stock. Corporate managers are themselves substantial owners of stock, often earning from stock more than they earn in salaries.[4]

ECONOMY AND SOCIAL STRUCTURE

An analysis of the relationships between the economy and the social structure hinges

on one basic idea: that the modern trend is toward an increasing *differentiation* of economic processes into separate institutional arrangements and economic groups, relatively uncontrolled by the social values of other institutions. In traditional societies the communal outlook does not permit the pursuit of economic gain at the price of other values, and it relates economic activity more closely to religious conduct and family activities.

Anthropologists studying "simple" societies often cannot even clearly distinguish an economic activity from a religious or political one. One of the first anthropologists to study primitive economies, Bronislaw Malinowski (1884–1942), found that the economic processes of Melanesian tribes were thoroughly interwoven with the entire social life of the society.[5] Kinship was crucial in the organization of work, and there was communal labor based on the obligations of kinship. Furthermore, assistance in building a canoe, for example, was a communal enterprise without economic motives and with no wage payments. Magic provided an integrative force by giving psychological confidence to the craftsmanship that went into the construction of the canoe.

The principles of modern analytic economics, however, have been developed to explain an economy that is a highly differentiated social structure, operating with a monetary system of exchange, an elaborate credit system, and a market organized around a price structure. This is very different from the economies of traditional

[2] The first full statement of this change was made in A.A. Berle and Gardner Means, *The Modern Corporation and Private Property* (New York: The Macmillan Company, 1933).
[3] See Robert Lampmann, *The Share of Top Wealthholders in Personal Wealth, 1922–1956* (Princeton, N.J.: Princeton University Press, 1962), Tables 75–80.
[4] For a discussion of the several factors involved in this issue *see* Michael Tanzer, *The Sick Society: An Economic Examination* (New York: Holt, Rinehart and Winston, Inc., 1971), Ch. 1.

[5] Malinowski's work on primitive economics is to be found in *Argonauts of the Western Pacific* (London, Eng.: Routledge & Kegan Paul, Ltd., 1922) and *Coral Gardens and Their Magic* (London, Eng.: G. Allen & Son, Ltd., 1935).

Figure 14.1 Private ownership of such a complicated piece of machinery as this reactor control center at the Oak Ridge National Laboratory would be beyond the means of an individual Capitalist. *(Oak Ridge National Laboratory operated by Union Carbide Corporation, Nuclean Division, for U.S. Atomic Energy Commission.)*

societies. It is even different from the small-scale economy of a century ago, where a small shop owner often did much of his own work, aided by members of his family, and also was his own salesman. Now these functions have been differentiated into separate organizations for production, wholesale distribution, and retail selling. It is only a further step to separation of ownership from control.

The Autonomy of the Economy

In the long transition to modern society there has been an extensive differentiation of specific societal functions, including a gradual freeing of economic groups and activities from the network of customs, obligations, and religious values that once tied them closely to other institutions.

Economic activity has now been rationalized by establishing criteria that maximizes efficiency and, from this, economic productivity.

The rationalization was accomplished by defining land and labor as _commodities_— objects which could be valued _monetarily_ in terms of supply and demand. Considerations of custom and sentiment, morality and belonging gave way to the norms of the market and the impersonal and rational criteria that governed production and distribution of goods.

This not only made possible a reshaping of society around the rational standards of the market and the status to be derived from making money, it also lessened the control of other institutions, such as religion, which had long been the source of moral guidance in business. It also gave powerful dominance to economic institutions.

Kinship and the Economy

The impact of an industrializing economy on the structure of the family, as we saw in Chapter 12, is considerable. In the first place work is removed from the home to the factory and the kinship group ceases to be a unit of production. Many functions once assigned to the family unit become communal or societal responsibilities. Some of the major changes we enumerated were: decline in family size, decline of extended family system, separation of family and education, and loss of occupational succession as a family function. These changes also brought about the freedom of the individual from the compelling obligations of the kinship structure.

Religion in the Economy

Max Weber undertook what is still the most extensive and penetrating study of the relationship between religion and economy. He wanted to show that religion was one significant factor (though by no means the only one) in explaining economic behavior. To do so, he studied religion and economy in several non-Western societies and in Western Europe, specifically to test the proposition that religious values either generated support for or hindered the emergence of capitalism.[6]

In *The Protestant Ethic and the Spirit of Capitalism* Weber's basic thesis was that

early Protestantism independently generated an ethical outlook and a religious orientation to the world that encouraged economic behavior which permitted a break with feudal economic patterns and the subsequent development of modern rational capitalism. This he called the Protestant Ethic.

Early Protestantism encouraged self-discipline and hard work, initiative and material acquisition, and an individualism that favored competitive practices. The early bourgeois Protestant was encouraged to work hard at the occupation to which God had called him, and to live ascetically. His asceticism generated the famous Puritan virtues of frugality and self-denial; the pleasures of the flesh were taboo. Such hard work and self-discipline led to economic success, yet asceticism would not permit the Protestant to spend material gain for his own worldly enjoyment. So his wealth became capital accumulation that was reinvested, leading to expansion and development. Thus, religious motives underlie the economic behavior that led to the development of capitalism.

The early Protestant theologians, such as John Calvin, had no idea of encouraging any particular economic order. What Protestant asceticism encouraged most of all was a profoundly rational view of the world, and particularly of the economic sphere, in which the mastery and control of the physical environment and the social world became a dominant motivation.

Religion in a Secular World

As the world became more consistent with the Protestant ethic, the ethic itself became detached from religion, and became increasingly a secular view of the world. The descendants of its originators

---

[6] Translations of Weber's comparative study of religion are primarily these: *The Protestant Ethic and the Spirit of Capitalism* (London: Edward G. Allen & Son, Ltd., 1930; New York: Charles Scribner's Sons, 1958); *The Religion of China: Confucianism and Taoism* (New York: The Free Press, 1951); and *The Religion of India: The Sociology of Hinduism and Buddhism* (New York: The Free Press, 1958).

were hard-working businessmen, less ascetic in nature and less given to rejecting the world. The "spirit" of capitalism that Protestantism helped stimulate and develop tended in the most Capitalist and Protestant of countries to develop a church whose teachings were supportive of the middle class and business, and whose message was less and less comprehensible to the working classes. Nor was this development confined only to Protestant countries. In Catholic nations, such as France and Italy, where industrialization and modern capitalism also developed, the Catholic church strongly supported the system of private property and the Capitalist pattern of economic activity.

Even more basic, perhaps, has been the development under rational capitalism of an economic order that is guided by its own normative system and is no longer under the moral guidance of religion. The economic order of modern society has been a most rational and secularized sphere, detached from the traditional moral values of the culture that find their most profound expression in religion.

Politics and the Economy

The term *laissez faire* once suggested that a free society was best promoted by the separation of the religious, economic, and political institutions from one another. Specifically, it admonished the government to let the economic order alone, except for the enforcement of laws against criminal and fraudulent behavior.

But now the concept of laissez faire no longer has any reference to economic reality. Government regulation of various forms of economic activity is well-established. There is, on the one hand, a complex *welfare state* that includes some effort to reduce the impact of the market on those subject to low income and unemployment, and an equivalent welfare for business in the form of *tax breaks* and *subsidies*. On the other hand, there is governmental power to regulate money, credit, and interest in order to limit any radical swings of the business cycle.

Business never did stay far removed from the political process. The economically powerful have always managed to exercise political power as well, for economic resources can be translated into political power. In the United States the development of a political economy makes it impossible to pretend any longer that politics and economics are distinct enterprises unrelated to one another.

The federal government now tries to protect the dollar, improve the balance of trade, reduce inflation, increase sources of energy, reduce unemployment, protect natural resources and the environment, reduce pollution, mediate among conflicting economic interests, and regulate a wide sphere of economic activities in the interest of public health and welfare. Economic policy is a central concern of government, perhaps its most important activity.

INDUSTRIALISM AND CAPITALISM

In the Western world industrialism and capitalism developed together, yet they are distinct economic phenomena.

Industrialism is an organization of the productive technology, a system of social relationships adapted to the logic of technology and machine production, including a technologically determined division of labor and such organized units as factories. A society can be both industrial and Capitalist, but it need not be. The Soviet Union is industrial without being Capitalist, and much of the industrialization that is proceeding among the new nations in Asia and Africa is non-Capitalist. Socialism shares with capitalism a positive value of technology and industrial production.

Capitalism is an organization of the processes for producing and distributing goods. It includes such things as legally free labor, commodity and labor markets, private ownership of the means of production, and production for maximization of profit. (*Socialism,* in turn, would substitute public for private ownership and would not allow profit maximization to be the primary determinant of what is to be produced.)

Looking at each separately focuses on some different aspects of the economy; in the first instance, technology and the division of labor; in the second instance, the changing forms of capitalism.

Technology and the Division of Labor

Industrialization brought about a social reorganization of work impelled by the introduction of new and complex machinery, before which all other historically known technologies seem primitive and crude. Vast social consequences flow from this change from simple to highly productive technology.

Perhaps the most significant consequence is the creation of an intricate division of labor, for technology requires numerous specialized tasks. The days of the old craftsman who made a total object with a few tools and his remarkable skills are gone. Now, the man-made object is the end product of a vast system of production that involves many skills, specializations, and complex machinery; each

person contributes but one small part to the finished product.

These technological changes have not merely replaced the craftsman with the machine-tending worker. Gradually but irrevocably the worker has lost control over tools, skills, quality of work, hours of work, and the like. The alienation of the worker, as Karl Marx fully recognized, is rooted in this development, as we shall see later.

Technology and Occupations

Probably more than any other factor, technology shapes and reshapes the occupational structure. Every change in technology modifies occupations, even eliminates some and creates new ones. Early industrialization created a small elite of technically skilled occupations and a large number of unskilled ones. Then, technological changes created more and more semiskilled occupations found in mass production. Now, the most advanced technology is eliminating these positions and creating a smaller number of more technically demanding jobs.[7]

Automation

The social consequences of technology have been made vividly apparent in recent years by the development of automation, which is not merely more advanced mechanization. It involves two principles: a continuous process of production, whereby machine-controlled parts move from one point to another without being touched by human hands; and self-control by means of a feedback process, in which machines

---

[7] The most thorough analysis of the occupational structure in the United States is in Peter Blau and Otis D. Duncan, *The American Occupational Structure* (New York: John Wiley & Sons, Inc., 1967).

Figure 14.2 Automation has brought about job losses for unskilled and semiskilled workers, but has increased the demand for highly skilled technicians. *(Wide World Photos.)*

provide information on which decisions can be made, such as the decisions ordinarily made by inspectors or maintenance men.

Automation eliminates many of the machine-operative positions that once provided most of the jobs on an assembly line. Its long-run consequences on the need for labor are not yet quite clear and are still subject to contradictory interpretations. But it is quite evident that automation reduces the need for lesser skills and increases the need for more technically skilled people. Within the factory, technicians replace unskilled and semiskilled positions. Furthermore, the automating of the industrial process lessens the amount of physical labor and shortens the work day and work week.[8]

Perhaps one of the most significant consequences has to do with the degree of control over the job exercised by workers. Sociologist William Faunce's study of automation suggests that one of the profoundest effects will be on the nature of social interaction on the job.[9] In an automated automobile factory he found that there was little interaction among work groups and that they were smaller than in nonautomated factories. Automated work also seemed to require more interaction with superiors, reducing interaction with peers.

Since machines are controlled automatically, work groups will have less control over output, and even worker morale will have less influence on productivity. Thus, peer-group interaction, which industrial

[8] For a discussion of these and other consequences *see* Daniel Bell's comments in his essay "Work and Its Discontents," in his *The End of Ideology* (New York: The Free Press, 1960), pp. 255–261.

[9] *See* William Faunce, "Automation in the Automobile Industry: Some Consequences for In-plant Social Structure," *American Sociological Review,* vol. 23 (August 1958), pp. 403–406.

sociologists have taken to be a powerful influence on the level of productivity, may cease to be so influential and a reassessment of the work group in industry may be in order.

Industrial Societies: More Alike?

The powerful impact of industrialization on human society, sweeping away old occupations and economic processes and instituting an intense division of labor and intricate specialization, has led a number of social scientists to argue that eventually there will be a convergence of development among the world's societies. Under common industrialization they will grow increasingly alike.[10]

There is, according to this argument, a logic of industrialization whereby the rational application of science and technology requires specific forms of social organization: a highly skilled work force, for example, which in turn requires an ever-increasing level of education. There will also be large-scale organization, urban dominance, strong government, and a modern pattern of occupations. A typical judgment is: "There is no place for the extended family in industrial society; it is on balance an impediment to requisite mobility."[11]

But the evidence on industrialization outside of Europe and the United States suggests that these generalizations may be too sweeping. Japan, for example, built an industrial society while maintaining many traditional elements, including the central position of the extended family. Economist Bert Hoselitz found no reason for incompatibility between the family and industrialism.[12]

Perhaps a more basic argument is that industrialism has come at a different time under different historical conditions for developing societies, and these may learn from history and develop in different ways, particularly with a new technology. Their conscious intention to retain cultural distinctiveness may lead to differences of some significance, avoiding that thoroughgoing convergence so confidently predicted by social scientists some years ago.

Capitalism

Capitalism, perhaps once in fact and for longer in myth and ideology, was an economic system of small, competitive, individual producers, each one taking his chances in a free market, where there was no political or other interference with the competitive market's ability to set prices for goods and for labor solely on the basis of demand and supply. This was *laissez-faire* capitalism.

Laissez-faire capitalism has been succeeded by *corporate* capitalism. The modern corporation has been an effective means of concentrating ever-larger investments and gaining control over larger concentrations of technology and highly skilled manpower. This concentration gives to fewer but larger corporations greater power over economic processes. Competition declines when a few firms dominate a large industry.

While many small businesses remain in such an economy, small business no longer sets the economic pattern. It does not control the direction of investment or affect the level of prices. Indeed, much small

---

[10] *See* Clark Kerr, and others, *Industrialization and Industrial Man* (Cambridge, Mass.: Harvard University Press, 1960).

[11] Kerr, *op. cit.*, p. 35.

[12] Bert F. Hoselitz, *Sociological Aspects of Economic Growth* (New York: The Free Press, 1960), p. 228.

business is in fact controlled by large business, as small retail outlets are dependent on the large firms that produce the goods they sell; and an increasing number are local, franchised outlets for national brands or services—automobile dealers, service stations, fast-food outlets, and the like.

There is nothing new in this. The growth of monopolistic corporations was recognized publicly at the beginning of the century, and "trust-busting" (anti-monopoly) legislation had strong public support. Yet over time stopping the growth of large corporations has proved ineffective. Economic concentration has gone on; larger firms have grown still larger; and merger has reduced the number of competing firms in most big industries to a powerful few.

The Corporate Concentration

Most efforts to analyze the concentration of business size in American capitalism concentrates on the top 500 corporations, which are listed each year in *Fortune* magazine. But this obscures as much as it reveals, as economist Robert Heilbroner points out, for the top 50 industrials have an aggregate of sales as large as the bottom 450, and the profits of the top 10 companies are equal to almost half the profits of the rest.[13] A more useful measure, Heilbroner says, would be the top 150 supercorporations, each of which owns a billion dollars' worth of assets or sells a billion dollars' worth of goods and services. This "tiny group of immense corporations constitutes a bastion of formidable economic strength within the sprawling expanse of the American economy . . ."[14]

Large corporations are professionally managed concerns, but there are among them also some dominant families with large stock-holdings. "Among the 150 supercorporations, there are perhaps as many as 1,500 or 2,000 operational top managers, but as few as 200 to 300 families own blocks of stock that ultimately control these corporations."[15]

The power of such corporations in the society is enormous, but not infinite. Corporate business does not have the unchallenged capacity to exploit its workers and its consumers quite to the extent it did before the 1930s, nor is government so ready to do everything corporations ask. Yet the basic power of corporate capitalism is enormously enhanced by its ideological domination in American society. For some time now there has been no competitive ideology with any degree of broad support.[16] Across the social classes, millions of Americans seem to have faith in an idealized "free enterprise."

Empires and Colonies

When capitalism developed in European societies, so did colonialism. By the seventeenth century major European nations were interested in a secure hold on raw materials from sources outside Europe. Once economic penetration occurred, interest in a trade monopoly and in a secure political structure to develop production and trade led Western nations to assume political control over their economic satellites. Furthermore, profits from trade with colonies, according to some historians, pro-

---

[13] *See* Robert L. Heilbroner, *The Limits of American Capitalism* (New York: Harper and Row, 1966), p. 10.

[14] *See* Heilbroner, *op. cit.,* p. 14.

[15] *See* Heilbroner, *op. cit.,* p. 26.

[16] *See* James Weinstein, *The Decline of Socialism in America 1912–1925* (New York: Vintage Books, 1969).

vided much of the capital for expansion of the European economy.[17] Thus, colonialism from the outset was a political as well as an economic phenomenon.

The classic pattern of colonialism was an international division of labor in which the colony provided raw materials and was a market for finished goods, while the dominant Western nation used the raw materials to manufacture goods for both domestic and foreign markets. It was a political structure of domination and subordination, evident in political controls, in the enormous differences in the standards of living between the two societies, and in the ideologies that were developed to justify conceptions of racist and cultural superiority, the consequences of which are still a source of conflict and hostility in the world.

Since imperialism has conventionally meant outright political control of colonies, this helped create the idea that the United States, though a major industrial society, was not imperialist. But there are few outright colonies in the world today, and so this may not be the most useful criterion. Nor does political control require outright possession.

A number of major nations in the world are twentieth-century imperialists. They wield enormous political control over other nations, maintain a flow of raw materials from former colonies that are now underdeveloped nations, and compete with one another for control over sources of raw materials and markets for finished goods. These are rich nations producing 60 percent of the world's wealth with only 20 percent of its people.[18] The United States

is one of these nations. Japan and the larger nations of Western Europe are others.

After World War II the United States moved rapidly to establish itself as the dominant military power of the "free world" and to acquire thousands of military bases around the world. American firms extensively increased their investments abroad, seeking new outlets for American capital. Foreign investments by American firms increased more than seven times from 1946 to 1966. In the decade and a half after 1950 sales of American goods in foreign markets tripled. By 1965 the size of the foreign market of U.S. firms equaled approximately 40 percent of the domestic production by farms, factories, and mines. So much did the international business of American corporations grow that it now constitutes the third largest economic unit after the U.S. and Soviet domestic economies.[19]

Until recently little of the social scientific literature acknowledged that the United States could be regarded as an imperialist society, with all the exploitative relations long associated with this term. It has remained for a group of radical critics of American society to insist that the evidence of domination and control in world markets and in relations with other, particularly poorer nations, warranted such a position.[20]

While some deny that America is in any

[17] See Mayhew, op. cit., p. 103.
[18] Gustav Lagos, *International Stratification and Underdeveloped Countries* (Chapel Hill, N.C.: The University of North Carolina Press, 1963), p. 4.

[19] See David Horowitz, in his edited volume, *Radical Sociology: An Introduction* (San Francisco, Calif.: Canfield Press, 1971), p. 288.
[20] See David Horowitz, *Empire and Revolution* (New York: Random House, Inc., 1969); Harry Magdoff, *The Age of Imperialism* (New York: Monthly Review Press, 1969); Gabriel Kolko, *The Roots of American Foreign Policy* (Boston: Beacon Press, 1969); and Felix Greene, *The Enemy: What Every American Should Know about Imperialism* (New York: Vintage Books, 1970).

way imperialist, there are others who acknowledge it, but maintain it is accidental and benign:

. . . the American empire came into being by accident and has been maintained from a sense of benevolence. Nobody planned our empire. In fact, nobody even wanted it.[21]

Such thinkers also claim that our empire-building activities were intended as a means of containing communism.

"Containing communism" can mean different things. To many Americans it means to protect the "American way of life," of democracy and individual freedom. But the international threat of communism was the ideological basis for the Cold War, for a fearful nuclear arms race, for a high defense budget, and for military involvement in Korea and Vietnam. The more negative consequences of this policy for American democracy have included the severe internal dissension over Vietnam, an increasing centralization of power in the executive branch of the government, a greater emphasis on secrecy in governmental action, and the building of a costly military-industrial complex, including a defense industry removed from the usual process of producing for a market.[22]

Furthermore, containing communism also means maintaining political access to economic markets by keeping them— through economic aid, military assistance, and outright intervention—from moving into the political orbit of the Soviet bloc or from nationalizing their foreign-owned (meaning American-owned) industry at great loss to American corporations.

The political and military support for American economic investment abroad provides convincing enough evidence that there is a political economy.

CONFLICT AND CONTROL IN THE ECONOMY

One does not have to be a Marxist to recognize an economic basis for social conflict. Many scholars with no Marxian assumptions have observed peasants struggling against rich landowners, workers against employers, the poor against the rich, and nations fighting over (1.) access to markets and raw materials, (2.) land, (3.) trade routes, and (4.) sources of food for their populations.

From a Marxian perspective, the basic struggle in life is always a *class struggle,* in which the *interests* of a subordinate class (peasants or workers) are pitted against a dominant class (landowners or employers) in an irreconcilable conflict. These class struggles shape quite different kinds of societies, and through these struggles societies are changed. "The history of all hitherto existing societies is the history of the class struggle."[23] Thus, for Marx, conflict is the significant source for historical change; to deplore conflict is to argue for the dominance of established patterns and to fail to understand how society changes.

In one way or another, however, the propertied and dominant—landowners, Capitalist employers, and the like—have looked for ways to insure a stable supply of labor that can be effectively controlled. This has involved efforts at ideological

[21] Ronald Steel, *Pax Americana* (New York: The Viking Press, Inc., 1967), p. 15.

[22] *See* Seymour Melman, *Pentagon Capitalism: The Political Economy of War* (New York: McGraw-Hill Book Company, Inc., 1970).

[23] A famous quotation from *The Communist Manifesto* written by Karl Marx and Frederick Engels.

control, then legitimization of unions, and human relations.

Ideology in Conflict and Control

Early Capitalists and modern management have not hesitated to develop ideological claims to rights and authority over the worker.[24] At one time in the United States, up until the 1930s, most American industry espoused an "open-shop" position, rejecting the right of workers to organize unions and bitterly opposing every such effort. Extensive labor violence was often the result.

This class position of dominance was maintained by force, including the police power of the state, which invariably intervened on behalf of the employers.

In response, Socialist politics and militant unions put forth counterideologies. Unions challenged the authority of management, at least in those aspects affecting workers, and developed an ideology to justify the right of workers to act collectively on their own behalf. It projected a view of the union as struggling for social justice for otherwise powerless workers, and of labor as a social movement of the working class seeking to revolutionize or at least reform society.

A second level of ideological counterattack was a sweeping rejection not only of managerial authority but of the entire social structure on which it rested. Communism and socialism have attacked the institutions of private property and of capitalism, and have called for a new social order in which the worker would no longer be subject to the control of his employer.

Labor Unions

Labor unions are organizations which represent the class interests of workers, but this function does not necessarily make them revolutionary. Historically, in fact, unions have tended to be pragmatic and reformist. Even in periods of violent conflict and forceful repression, when they are usually militant, unions' ultimate goals are not usually revolutionary.[25]

In the United States labor unions won legitimate status as collective-bargaining agents through the Wagner Act of 1935. Their transition from a struggling, class-based social movement to stable social organizations with a legitimate function in society, defined and protected by legislation, reduced their commitment to class-based ideologies.

Long and difficult as was the struggle by labor unions and some allied middle-class reformers, the victory was not simply a conquest of an unregenerate Capitalist class forced to come to terms despite itself, even though this could accurately be said of many individual corporate leaders. But from the turn of the century on, a more sophisticated group of business leaders saw the need to accept many reforms which would stabilize the continued expansion of the economy, insure continued influence over government, and yet undercut the growing threat of socialism. This was done by accepting, indeed promoting, many liberal reforms, including, first, workmen's compensation for work-related injuries

---

[24] For a comparative study in different societies at different times *see* Reinhard Bendix, *Work and Authority in Industry* (New York: John Wiley & Sons, Inc., 1956).

[25] For an insightful analysis of American unions *see* Daniel Bell, "The Capitalism of the Proletariat," in his *The End of Ideology,* pp. 208–221.

Figure 14.3 Labor violence in the 1930s and earlier often erupted over the opposition of the bosses to the organization of unions. *(Wide World Photos.)*

and finally the recognition of unions as the legitimate representative of workers in collective bargaining.[26]

Today, both management and labor accept a new legal order that insists both parties bargain in good faith and enter into contractual relations. Social mechanisms—such as bargaining elections, federal mediation of prolonged disputes, and union-management contracts as the legal basis for worker-management relations—have become institutionalized.

As a consequence, labor unions have accepted capitalism and in turn have been accepted as the legitimate representatives of workers' interests. Through collective bargaining they seek to get "more and more" for workers while not altering the basic pattern of property relations under capitalism.[27]

But if unions now represent workers *within* the Capitalist system, rather than organize them to oppose capitalism, then they become agencies for *integrating* workers into Capitalist society. (A more critical perspective would say that unions have been used to coopt the workers.)

Labor unions have never accepted an unregulated, laissez-faire capitalism. They have been an active and decisive element in a political coalition of reformist groups —including representatives of corporate capitalism—steadily building a welfare

[26] For studies on these historical changes by dominant groups within American capitalism's leadership *see* Gabriel Kolko, *The Triumph of Conservatism: A Reinterpretation of American History, 1900–1916* (New York: The Free Press, 1963); and James Weinstein, *The Corporate Ideal in the Liberal State: 1900–1918* (Boston: The Beacon Press, 1968).

[27] On the state of American unions in the 1970s *see* Wilfrid Sheed, "What Ever Happened to the Labor Movement: A Report on the State of the Unions," *Atlantic Monthly*, vol. 232 (July 1973), pp. 42–69.

state by putting political force behind legislation for social security, unemployment compensation, civil rights, housing, welfare, and education.

Human Relations in Industry

The emergence of stable unions and socially supported mechanisms for managing tensions in industry has been accompanied by a new and powerful ideology of "human relations." It has developed most extensively in the United States, supported by numerous in-plant studies by sociologists and psychologists. Human relations, as ideology and theory, originated in the work of Elton Mayo and his associates in the famous Hawthorne study of the 1920s (discussed in Chapter 7). A shift from a concern with the individual worker to a concern for the work group and its relationship to the immediate work environment brought into being an analytical approach, which accepts the existing framework of institutional arrangements, or at least takes them for granted, and focuses on the interaction of workers and managers in the work situation.

It looks for the conditions that generate cooperation, good morale, rewarding social relations on the job, and then high productivity as a consequence of these. Furthermore, it tries to link informal work groups to the goals of production, largely through supervisory leadership trained in "human relations," thus hopefully reducing friction between group norms and official goals.

Despite its widespread acceptance by management, or perhaps just because of that, human relations has been regarded by many others as an ideological tool of management—of seeking to maximize production (a managerial goal), of favoring harmony and cooperation over conflict and change, and of being a "managerial sociology."[28] Yet, despite all such efforts, industrial workers, if they are not revolutionary, seem to be alienated.

Work and Alienation

According to Max Weber the Puritan viewed work as his "calling," as we have seen. Hard and methodical labor came to be regarded as doing God's will. From the perspective of the Protestant ethic, then, work should be the central life interest of industrial man; it is his dominant and rewarding role, and other roles and relationships are subordinate to it.

But do workers actually find factory work to be so central to their lives? Do they find it more rewarding than other activities? There is much evidence to suggest they do not. For the working classes, work has always been a necessity, not a joy.

Robert Dubin, an industrial sociologist, for example, attempted to determine the "central life-interests" of industrial workers.[29] He discovered that these were not in work but in human associations outside of the job. Less than 10 percent of the workers preferred the informal relationships on the job to other possibilities. Dubin also found that workers place higher values on the work organization than they do on other organizations in which they have membership.

[28] See Harold Sheppard, "The Treatment of Unionism in 'Managerial Sociology,'" *American Sociological Review,* vol. 14 (April 1949), pp. 310–313.

[29] See Robert Dubin, "Industrial Workers' World: A Study of the 'Central Life-Interests' of Industrial Workers," *Social Problems,* vol. 3 (Winter 1956), pp. 131–142.

MARX ON ALIENATION

Under the conditions imposed by capitalism, according to Marx, the worker is required to sell his labor for a wage in order to live; work becomes a commodity, for sale like any object; work is divided up to suit technological efficiency; and since property is private, neither the machines nor the product belongs to the worker. The result is alienation.

Marx's own words:

What, then, constitutes the alienation of labor? First, the fact that labor is *external* to the worker, i.e., it does not belong to his essential being; that in his work, therefore, he does not affirm himself but denies himself, does not feel content but unhappy, does not develop freely his physical and mental energy but mortifies his body and ruins his mind. The worker therefore only feels himself outside his work, and in his work feels outside himself. He is at home when he is not working, and when he is working he is not at home. His labor is therefore not voluntary, but coerced; it is *forced labor*. It is therefore not the satisfaction of a need; it is merely a *means* to satisfy needs external to it. Its alien character emerges clearly in the fact that as soon as no physical or other compulsion exists, labor is shunned like the plague. External labor, labor in which man alienates himself, is a labor of self-sacrifice. Lastly, the external character of labor for the worker appears in the fact that it is not his own, but someone else's, that it does not belong to him, that in it he belongs, not to himself, but to another.

From *Economic and Philosophic Manuscripts of 1844*, Martin Milligan, trans., with an introduction by Dirk J. Struik, ed. (New York: International Publishers Company, Inc., 1964), pp. 110–111.

The Alienated Worker

Ever since Karl Marx spoke of the *alienation* of the worker critics of modern industry under capitalism have maintained that the worker typically feels his work is only for the purpose of earning a living, and that he is not in any way fulfilled by work itself, that it is not a rewarding activity. Marx was concerned with a *social process* of alienation occurring under certain conditions, which affected workers more than any other social class. (*See* "Marx on Alienation.") Contemporary sociologists have focused on alienation as a *social-psychological* state of feeling, most typically like that described by sociologist Melvin Seeman: experiences of powerlessness, of meaninglessness, of isolation, of normlessness, and of self-estrangement.[30]

Using Seeman's categories, sociologist Robert Blauner undertook an ambitious sociological effort to study alienation in work. His major innovation was to make *type of work* a significant variable. To do that he contrasted craft work with machine-tending and then with assembly work, and lastly with a continuous process industry, such as the chemical industry, where work is highly automated.

Blauner discovered a regular progression

[30] Melvin Seeman, "On the Meaning of Alienation," *American Sociological Review*, vol. 24 (December 1959), pp. 783–791. For a review of these categories *see* Ch. 5, pp. 104–105.

of feelings of greater alienation, particularly powerlessness and meaninglessness, from craft work, where it was low, to automobile assembly work, where it was highest, with a reversal under the newer circumstances of automated continuous production. Both craft workers and those operating automated processes felt they had control over their jobs, were freer from close supervision, and were not merely appendages to the technological processes.

What Blauner's research optimistically suggests is that the apex of alienation from work may have been reached in the mass, assembly-line production process; and that its eventual replacement by automated processes may produce work environments less conducive to feelings of powerlessness and meaninglessness in work, less isolating and estranging. But this may actually hold true only for a technical elite of highly skilled workers and not for others.

Blue-collar Blues

It has been fashionable to say that intellectuals have made much of alienation because they think factory jobs are dull and boring, but that workers do not necessarily find them so and that they are really fairly content. But now greater worker absenteeism and turnover, especially among younger workers, have provided separate evidence that most factory workers do not like their jobs or conditions under which they work and find them demeaning, yet do not (at least as yet) put much blame on anyone or anything besides themselves.[31]

As a consequence, there is much talk of *job enrichment* as a solution to the problem — something which management does not like but then neither does most union leadership. For both, such changes would disrupt their established ways, and unions want only those changes they bargain for as the workers' legitimate spokesmen.

Despite this coolness of both management and unions there is increased interest by workers, some union leaders, and students of industrial organization in various possibilities for job enrichment, the most intriguing of which is *group assembly;* that is, assigning a group of workers the task of assembly and allowing them to make the product as a group project. This is an innovation borrowed from Europe, particularly from Sweden and Yugoslavia. How extensively it will be adopted in the United States, and whether it will alter in any significant way the deep estrangement of many blue-collar workers from the conditions of their work life are not now evident.

Is Work Valued?

Discussions of alienated workers imply that people in other occupations do like their work and find rewards in it. There is not as yet any systematic evidence, but sensitive observers of American life, such as sociologist David Riesman, have sensed a perceptible shift from the older, religiously sanctified values on work to leisure pursuits as the sphere of life which provides a significant meaning for living.[32] Certainly, mass culture, which does not

[31] *See* Harold L. Sheppard and Neal Q. Herrick, *Where Have All the Robots Gone?: Worker Dissatisfaction in the 70s* (New York: The Free Press, 1973); and Richard Sennett and Jonathan Cobb, *The Hidden Injuries of Class* (New York: Alfred A. Knopf, 1972).

[32] *See both* David Riesman, *Individualism Reconsidered* (New York: The Free Press, 1956) and *Abundance for What? And Other Essays* (Garden City, N.Y.: Doubleday & Company, Inc., 1964).

Figure 14.4 Blue-collar factory workers may show their dissatisfactions with their work through absenteeism and turnover. *(A. Devaney, Inc., N.Y.)*

celebrate the world of work, is oriented to rewards and meaning found in nonwork activities. The bureaucraticized and rationalized nature of work in modern industry, while maximizing production and profits, treats employees as commodities and as dispensible costs of production. This has led people to search for a meaningful life in a variety of human activities and relations other than those found in the corporation. But the matter has not yet been systematically studied.

MODERNIZATION AND ECONOMIC DEVELOPMENT

Throughout the existing non-Western world the modernization of traditional societies is underway, and the central process by which this occurs is economic development. For economists, economic growth in any society is determined by four variables: natural resources, capital for investment, labor, and entrepreneurial talent. These in turn are related to several other variables: savings, inflation, balance of payments, foreign aid, size of population, and rate of population growth.

Sociologists have stressed how each of these economic variables is affected in part by noneconomic variables, particularly traditional values, kinship systems, attachment to land, and religious values. To some extent, these sociological analyses have been used to explain why underdeveloped nations remain underdeveloped, in that a commitment to traditional cultural ways impedes economic development.

The emergence of a highly motivated, actively innovating entrepreneur, for example, breaking with traditions and established customs, is called the single most decisive factor in economic development

339

by Everett H. Hagen.[33] Sociologist Wilbur Moore asserts that:

. . . some degree of "achievement orientation," of ambition for personal betterment and the acquisition of the education and skills to further that ambition, must exist in some groups and spread rather widely, if sustained growth is to be accomplished.[34]

However, social scientists such as Hagen and Moore work with a conception of economic development modeled closely — perhaps too closely — after the Western Capitalist experience, where the free-wheeling entrepreneur was for a long time unchecked by any kind of social regulation. Even though Moore recognizes that structural changes are necessary, he still asserts that "extensive value changes are the most fundamental conditions for economic transformation."[35]

Economic development is not simply a matter of underdeveloped societies not having the right values, anymore than poor Americans are poor because they lack ambition as we saw in Chapter 11. What is most important is that economic growth everywhere is occurring in the context of a world economy. The historical circumstances that initiated economic development in the Western world three centuries ago have only limited relevance for development in the non-Western world in the twentieth century. As sociologist Leon Mayhew notes, "backward systems are deeply penetrated by the economies of the richer societies," making it impossible to treat each society today as an independent instance of a repeating sequence of societal evolution.[36] It cannot happen now as it once did. "The heritage of colonialism and the continuing international organization of trade make almost all underdeveloped economies heavily dependent on the export of a few basic products, either minerals or the products of tropical agriculture."[37]

Modernizing Elites

In underdeveloped societies a key factor in the program of development is the emergence of new elites committed to modernization and capable of mobilizing people and resources. Most modernizing societies were colonies of European nations until recently; therefore, their newly independent status produces indigenous elites for whom racial sensitivities and nationalist ideologies are paramount in providing leadership. Both *nationalism* and *socialism* become attractive ideologies.

Modernizing elites are *political* elites, for underdeveloped nations have such large problems of acquiring capital and investing efficiently for national growth that they depend heavily on government to increase capital and decide how it is to be invested. For this reason the Soviet record of controlled yet rapid development is a model to admire and emulate more than the American model is.

The political structures of developing societies concentrate power in the hands of a political elite, often within only one political party. Western social scientists seem divided on the merits of this historical process.

The sweeping power of national identification in new societies often serves to

---

[33] *See* Everett H. Hagen, *On the Theory of Social Change* (Homewood, Ill.: Dorsey Press, 1962).

[34] *See* Wilbert Moore, *Social Change* (Englewood Cliffs, N.J.: Prentice-Hall, Inc., 1963), p. 96.

[35] *See* Moore, *op. cit.*, p. 93.

[36] *See* Mayhew, *op. cit.*, p. 96.

[37] *See* Mayhew, *op. cit.*, p. 115.

legitimize new political authority sufficient to challenge and disrupt their traditional order. Socialism legitimizes the centralizing of control over basic resources and the introduction of social planning, thus providing the power to control all relevant factors for development.

Typical of those who view this process with alarm is sociologist William McCord, who offers a reasoned argument against authoritarian rule in developing societies.[38] Authoritarian regimes, McCord argues, are not more likely than democratic ones to enhance economic growth. Being authoritarian is no guarantee of wisdom, and resources can be expended unwisely without any effective opposition, while coercive power can breed suspicion and sabotage by disaffected elements, stifling the spirit of inventiveness and innovation.[39]

In contrast, British sociologist Peter Worsley argues that these emerging nations are *solidarist* societies—they are homogeneous in terms of class or have used political centralization to override ethnic division, or both. "The latter is likely to be a particularly highly integrated society. The archetype is Guinea, where society is undifferentiated, and bitter struggle against France has further consolidated the population under a militant and solidary political party."[40] Particularly when there is military struggle, Worsley suggests, the one-party state is the norm, and even in free competition, when it exists, minor parties disappear.

Where there are pluralist societies (more than one party), the basic division is likely to be *ethnic*. Even here, within each ethnic region, a single party dominates. What results, therefore, is *party tribalism*, a contest for power that in some cases can degenerate into fratricidal conflict.[41]

But in the more developed countries, such as India and Indonesia, once dominant parties that held the loyalty of all since independence and in the earlier years of development are now being challenged by new parties based particularly on social classes, from the Communist Party, representing urban workers and sometimes peasants, to parties representing propertied and business interests.[42] A multi-party system is emerging.

These political elites believe that the nations of the world should be equal. They know that their power depends on the industrial and economic capacity of their societies. For that reason, they strive to modernize their countries by mobilizing their populations for economic growth and by giving political direction to the economy. All this occurs in the context of the development of an emerging world economy.

THE NEW WORLD ECONOMY

It is conventional to conceive of an economy as bound by the limits of a society—thus, the American economy or the Soviet economy—though always engaging in some trade beyond the society's borders. But economic systems are never effectively contained within societal boundaries, less so than with any other social process.

Now, the growth and change of any national economy seems to depend less on national concerns and objectives, more on

---

[38] See William McCord, *The Springtime of Freedom* (New York: Oxford University Press, 1965).

[39] See McCord, *op. cit.*, pp. 240–246.

[40] See Peter Worsley, *The Third World* (Chicago: University of Chicago Press, 1964), p. 177.

[41] See Worsley, *op. cit.*, pp. 209–212.

[42] Worsley, *op. cit.*, pp. 209–217.

how that economy fits into an international pattern. The markets for most goods are worldwide; rich economies penetrate poor ones; and almost everyone of us is caught up in a market structure beyond national political controls. In speaking of the fate of traditional peasant economies and their markets, Mayhew noted that "remote events in the larger world alter the fate of peasants in the village."[43]

What is true for Asian peasants is no less true for American farmers, whose economic fates may rest on the world grain market and on political deals to sell grain to China and the Soviet Union as much as on the domestic market. So, too, it is true for the American worker, whose job may be eliminated as production is shifted by a multinational corporation from the United States to a nation with a cheaper wage scale.

There are two dimensions that need to be noted: that there is an international system of economic stratification, and that world capitalism is moving toward domination by multinational corporations.

International Stratification

If there is, increasingly, a world market and a world economy, there is still within it much differentiation. First of all, there are rich nations and poor nations, and the gap between the rich and the poor is widening. But there is also a tripartite division that reflects both historical differences in development and differences in social organization and ideology.

The *First World* is made up of the Capitalist nations of North America and Europe, among which the United States has been the most powerful and influential.

[43] *See* Mayhew, *op. cit.*, p. 108.

The *Second World* is the Communist bloc of nations dominated by the Soviet Union.

The *Third World* is the complex of nonaligned nations still in the process of developing, though generally moving toward some form of socialism. Located mostly in Asia, Africa, and Latin America, many are former European colonies and neither by culture nor race are they tied directly to Anglo-American societies.

Among these blocs and nations there is much jockeying and struggle for development and gain. While the Third World borrows from both the other models of economic and political structure, its elites are increasingly intent on building societies that are *not* sheerly imitative of either the United States or the Soviet Union. The future they wish to shape for themselves is rooted in their own distinctive history and culture, and they do not intend to obliterate that by modernization.

World Capitalism and the Multinational Corporation

Corporations have become bigger and bigger, but mere growth is not the only change. Once a corporation was intent on becoming the dominating firm in a single industry, as was General Motors in automobiles and United States Steel in steel. But now corporations diversify by buying up a controlling interest in corporations in other industries. The rapid growth of these diversified, multi-firm *conglomerates* in recent decades has not been seriously impeded by the anti-trust policy of the United States government. The effect is further economic concentration and also economic power.

Most conglomerates are still national concerns; they diversify within the American economy. But the *multinational* corporation is now coming on the scene. Some

Figure 14.5 This giant extrusion-dryer of the Firestone Tire & Rubber Company in Harbel, Liberia, is one of a number of plants owned by this multinational corporation throughout the world. *(Firestone News Service.)*

conglomerates go abroad, investing in European, Asian, and Latin American markets, buying up firms or creating their own subsidiaries.

Such a development is too recent to command any definitive analysis. There are a few aspects, however, that are evident even now:

1. There are 187 giant American firms which are multinationals (according to economist Raymond Vernon[44]), and these are most of the multinational corporations of the world so far. They are "supergiants" and in a class by themselves when measured against *Fortune's* list of America's 500 largest firms. They account for about a third of all sales in the United States; and they perform a dominant role in U.S. exports, so that their activities are important for the balance of trade, the value of the dollar, and, in general, America's national trade policy.

2. Multinational concerns move in a sphere that cannot be effectively controlled by national governments; the new multinational corporate leadership regards the nation as a politically constraining entity. It seeks a new international system of political controls to regulate the world market and to reduce the impact of nationalistic self-interest (tariffs, for instance, and even nationalization of industry). This leadership can be expected to rationalize its position by an ideology of free enterprise, free markets, free trade, and internationalism, with a possible case made for if not world government at least international political controls.

3. American multinational firms are resented and feared abroad, where they are sometimes seen as an extension of American power and control, thus, as evidence of the growth of an American empire. Their sheer size and power easily matches if not ex-

[44] Raymond Vernon, *Sovereignty at Bay: The Multinational Spread of U.S. Enterprises* (New York: Basic Books, Inc., 1971), p. 11.

1. anti-Americanism
2. Jobs

ceeds that of small nations, nations which control fewer resources than do many American corporations. ("General Motors' $25 billion in sales is, it is noted with concern, larger than the Gross National Product of about 130 countries."⁴⁵) The threat to the multinational firms, in turn, is the nationalization of all business controlled by foreign (read American) investors.

4. Multinational firms are increasingly viewed as a threat by American labor unions.⁴⁶ First, they are larger and management has more options, so that pinning them down to a contractual agreement in an American high-wage industry is harder than with corporations. As labor unions see it, multinational firms *export jobs* as well as capital investments.

The economic changes induced by the emergence of the giant multinationals suggest two sources of tension and conflict for the future. One lies in the fact that most multinationals are American, so that resistance to their domination also becomes a worldwide anti-Americanism. Such resistance, furthermore, sparks both nationalism and socialism as ways of creating alternatives to domination by this new pattern of world capitalism.

But perhaps an equally severe strain lies within the United States. Exporting jobs threatens much of the American working class and also a sizable section of its technically skilled personnel. While the United States might receive vast amounts of money through the profits of multinationals, that fact does not promise to offset lost jobs for individuals, since it is the owners who will profit and the top 1 percent of shareholders own about 75 percent of personally held corporate stocks and about 85 percent of corporate bonds.⁴⁷ Such wealth is not shared sufficiently to insure the welfare of the nation as a whole.

But even more basic is a potential clash between the logic of multinational corporate growth and operation on a global scale and the interests and values of nations. Raymond Vernon symbolizes this issue by calling his book *Sovereignty at Bay*. He opens his study with these words:

Suddenly, it seems, the sovereign states are feeling naked. Concepts such as national sovereignty and national economic strength appear curiously drained of meaning . . .⁴⁸ [multinational corporations] sit uncomfortably in the structure of long-established political and social institutions. They sprawl across national boundaries, linking the assets and activities of different national jurisdictions with an intimacy that seems to threaten the concept of the nation as an integral unit.⁴⁹

These new patterns of economic development suggest significant changes in capitalism; specifically, a new tension between capitalism and nationalism. On the world scene and within nations, this change in capitalism promises to produce new, exacerbating forms of economic conflict.

A FINAL NOTE ON ECONOMY AND SOCIETY

Throughout history it has always been necessary for people to work, and the resources that sustained life have always been scarce. Although industrialization

---

⁴⁵ *See* Vernon, *op. cit.*, p. 7. Gross National Product (GNP) is the total of goods and services produced by a nation in a given year.

⁴⁶ *See* Gus Tyler, "Multinational Corporations vs. Nations," *Current* (September 1972), pp. 52–63. Originally published as "Multinationals: A Global Menace," *The American Federationist* (July 1972).

⁴⁷ *See* Tyler, *op. cit.*, p. 58.
⁴⁸ *See* Vernon, *op. cit.*, p. 3.
⁴⁹ *See* Vernon, *op. cit.*, p. 5.

vastly increased the capacity to exploit and master the natural environment, it did not make goods so abundant as to negate economic theories based on the assumption of scarcity.

But the future holds a promise that such a world of abundance and plenty may be coming into being, and the compulsions of labor and the organization of work may no longer dominate the time, interests, and values of people as they have in the past. Increasingly more rationalized and mechanized, demanding greater technical and professional skills, and thus greater education, the new technology may nonetheless be producing a world in which the eco-nomic order itself is a less dominant and compelling institution.

It may also produce a society governed by a technocratic elite, where the rational and efficient control of human beings, justified in the name of science, is as thorough and remorseless as in any contemporary dictatorship. Relative affluence promises to liberate us from the constraints once imposed by scarcity. But it does not guarantee a free society. That remains as a political task.[50]

[50] For a radical challenge to both capitalism and social-ism in presenting a vision of the future *see* Murray Bookchin, *Post-scarcity Anarchism* (Berkeley, Calif.: Ramparts Press, 1971).

SUMMARY

From a sociological perspective the economy is a system of productive and distributive processes for meeting material wants. It requires co-operative organization for production and an institutionalized system of power and values for distribution of goods.

Property consists of rights in objects, not the objects themselves. It is ownership of the means of production that distinguishes private-property systems from socialized ones.

In modern industrial society the separation of ownership and control means that actual control of the means of production may be located in managerial elites rather than in private owners (investors) or in publics. Yet a small number of very wealthy families still maintain controlling interests.

In modern societies the economy is increasingly differentiated from religion, kinship, and community, in contrast to traditional societies, where economic activity always had other meanings and was always controlled by noneconomic values and norms. Thus, rational capitalism is an economy able to maximize productive efficiency at the expense of other customs and values.

Industrialism is an organization of the productive technology, creating an intricate division of labor and shaping the occupational structure. Automation has profound effects on occupations and on how work is organized.

Capitalism has changed from competitive, laissez faire to corporate form. By dominating the poor, undeveloped nations the Capitalist nations have become imperialist.

The economy always produces problems of conflict and integration. Labor unions under capitalism have become representative of workers' interests, accepting capitalism but seeking social reforms. Industry, in turn, has used *human relations* to integrate workers at the place of work.

Alienation of workers occurs when work becomes a thing apart from the worker, an alien force beyond his control. Modern workers do not make work their central life interest, and their degree of alienation varies with the type of work—crafts less so, assembly work more so.

Economic development transforms emerging traditional societies into industrial ones. Modernizing elites seek to do this more rapidly, using nationalistic and socialist ideologies, with a concentration of political power.

There is now a world economy, characterized by *international stratification* into three worlds, and a world capitalism dominated by *multinational* corporations, the actions of which threaten to conflict with national interests.

Suggested Readings

Robert Blauner, *Alienation and Freedom: The Factory Worker and His Industry* (Chicago: University of Chicago Press, 1964). A comparison of alienation as a consequence of types of work.

William Faunce, *Problems of an Industrial Society* (New York: McGraw-Hill Book Company, Inc., 1968). An industrial sociologist explores the problems generated by basic features in industrial society.

Felix Greene, *The Enemy: What Every American Should Know about Imperialism* (New York: Vintage Books, 1970). A particularly informative work for the uninitiated by a severe critic of American capitalism.

Robert Heilbroner, *The Limits of American Capitalism* (New York: Harper and Row, 1966). A provocative examination of the future prospects of the corporate sector of the American economy.

David Horowitz, ed., *Radical Sociology: An Introduction* (San Francisco, Calif.: Canfield Press, 1971). Selections on economy and society and on society and empire address themselves to issues raised in this chapter.

Irving Louis Horowitz, *The Three Worlds of Development: The Theory and Practice of International Stratification* (New York: Oxford University Press, 1966). A leading American sociologist provides a detailed analysis of relations among the developed and underdeveloped worlds.

Joachim Israel, *Alienation from Marx to Modern Sociology: A Macrosociological Analysis* (Boston, Mass.: Allyn and Bacon, Inc., 1971). A thorough and absorbing study of the difficult concept of alienation.

Clark Kerr, John T. Dunlop, Frederick Harbison, and Charles A. Myers, *Industrialism and Industrial Man* (Cambridge, Mass.: Harvard University Press, 1964). A major effort to explore the consequences of the logic of industrialism.

Harry Magdoff, *The Age of Imperialism* (New York: Monthly Review Press, 1969). An example of a penetrating analysis by a capable Marxian scholar.

Karl Marx, *Selected Writings in Sociology and Social Philosophy*, T.B. Bottomore, trans. (New York: McGraw-Hill Book Company, Inc., 1956). A good set of briefer selections from Marx's discussion of Capitalist and pre-Capitalist society.

Seymour Melman, *Pentagon Capitalism: The Political Economy of War* (New York: McGraw-Hill Book Company, Inc., 1970). An analysis of a "second" political economy combining the Pentagon and the defense industry.

Neil J. Smelser, *The Sociology of Economic Life* (Englewood Cliffs, N.J.: Prentice-Hall, Inc., 1963). A brief introduction to a sociological analysis of the economy.

Michael Tanzer, *The Sick Society: An Economic Interpretation* (New York: Holt, Rinehart and Winston, Inc., 1971). An economist relates capitalism and its imperialist programs to America's domestic problems.

Raymond Vernon, *Sovereignty at Bay: The Multinational Spread of U.S. Enterprises* (New York: Basic Books, Inc., 1971). A look at a new stage in capitalism: the multinational corporation.

W. Lloyd Warner and J.O. Low, *The Social System of the Modern Factory* (New Haven, Conn.: Yale University Press, 1947). Warner provides a detailed analysis of how changes in the shoe industry from the days of skilled craftsmen to modern factory production in firms now owned outside the community radically transforms family life, the occupational and class structure, and the community.

Max Weber, *The Protestant Ethic and the Spirit of Capitalism* (New York: Charles Scribner's Sons, 1958). Weber's world-famous study of the relationship of religion to capitalism.

Peter Worsley, *The Third World* (Chicago: University of Chicago Press, 1964). A British sociologist provides a sympathetic analysis of development in the Third World.

Power is always gradually stealing away from the
many to the few, because the few are more vigilant
and consistent.
                                        —*Samuel Johnson*

Chapter 15

Politics
and Society

In all human societies people engage in some form of political activity.
In modern society they vote; they run for office; they lobby; they get peti-
tions signed; they attend political rallies. Whatever the activity, it has to
do with *power, authority,* and *decision-making,* for that is what the political
process is all about.

In traditional, preindustrial societies the political process often is only
partially differentiated from the religious and economic processes, and
political authority is embedded in customs and traditions of ancient origin.
But in modern society the political process has developed specialized structures and roles, and authority is legally specified in charters, constitutions,
and by-laws.

SOCIAL POWER AND POLITICAL STRUCTURE

The central concept of political sociology is *power.* Social scientists have
used the concept of power in different ways, but there is an increasing
tendency to define power in terms of decision-making. Power is then conceived of as a social process, not an object or "thing" divided among power-

holders. To have power is to participate in a decision-making process. To be powerful is to effectively control decision-making or at least have a very strong influence on what decisions are made. To be powerless is to be excluded from decision-making.

Authority

Power cannot be understood apart from authority. When a president of the United States vetoes a bill, he exercises the authority of his office, as does the legislature when it votes on a bill. City councilmen and mayors, governors and senators are all political roles in which some authority is vested. Authority is *legitimate* power, the right to make a decision that is based on an acceptance of the claims of decision-makers that their decisions are legally binding on all members of the social organization involved.

The sources of legitimation are diverse. Max Weber has indicated that in stable social orders the legitimacy of authority may be *traditional,* as in the authority of a tribal chief, rooted in custom and cultural tradition; or it may be *legal-rational,* as in modern societies, derived from documents (laws, charters, and constitutions). In situations of instability and change, authority is often *charismatic;* that is, based on the personal devotion of the followers of a leader, who attribute to him great qualities.[1] When this happens, masses of people have withdrawn legitimacy from whatever traditional or legal-rational system of authority prevails.

Yet others besides those with authority

do exercise power. In a complex process of reaching decisions other actors participate when they have *access* to those who have authority. Those who have such access are *influentials.*

Influence and Authority

Some influentials—such as party bosses, lobbyists, and businessmen—are often credited with having more to say about decisions than those who possess authority. "Real" power, it is claimed, rests with dominant influentials, an elite possibly not even known to the larger public.[2] Officials are then regarded as mere puppets who respond to the order of party bosses, the requests of lobbyists or large party contributors, or the demands of economic influentials.

However weak the system of authority may be and however dominant a structure of influence, nonetheless, the exercise of power still cannot dispense with legitimate authority. For if it does, then decision-making by powerful people can only be regarded as a system of naked coercion, as well as one of corruption and fraud. Authoritarian systems in the past have always claimed legitimacy, as by divine right of kings. Modern totalitarian systems also develop and propagate a rationalizing ideology to justify the monopoly of power by the party in power. Decisions, then, must always seem to be the acts of those who hold the symbols of authority.

This suggests that the definition of power is the distribution of influence, pressure, and authority within a social system for

---

[1] *See* Max Weber, *The Theory of Social and Economic Organization,* A.M. Henderson and Talcott Parsons, trans. (New York: Oxford University Press, 1947), p. 328.

[2] Such an assertion was made by Floyd Hunter in his *Community Power Structure* (Chapel Hill, N.C.: University of North Carolina Press, 1953).

the making, legitimizing, and executing of decisions.[3]

This last point is basic: A decision is not a decision until it has been carried out. Perhaps only in the literature of bureaucracies has there been recognition of the problems involved in the execution of decisions. In the middle level of bureaucracies officials can significantly modify or even subvert a decision taken at higher echelons, so that a decisive outcome is not what was intended when the decision was made. Presidents of the United States, at least since Harry Truman, have acknowledged their frustration in seeking to carry out decisions against subtle but effective sabotage by permanent civil-service bureaucrats.

Inclusion and Exclusion

If all members of the society had equal access to authority, influence and pressure would be no issue. But in fact this is not so. Some sizable segment of people even in democratic societies are excluded from decision-making. In general, the higher the social status, the more effectively are people included and able to influence de-

[3] While probably most social scientists view power in some such way as this, noted ones such as Talcott Parsons and Amos Hawley insist on a conception of power as a *facility* by which a social system accomplishes the general goals of the system. *See* Talcott Parsons, *Structure and Process in Modern Society* (New York: The Free Press, 1960), Ch. 6, "The Distribution of Power in American Society," reprinted in G. William Domhoff and Hoyt B. Ballard, eds., *C. Wright Mills and the Power Elite* (Boston: The Beacon Press, 1968), pp. 60–88.

See also Amos H. Hawley, "Community Power and Urban Renewal Success," *American Journal of Sociology*, vol. 68 (January 1963), pp. 422–431.

For an effort to integrate these different perspectives on power *see* William A. Gamson, *Power and Discontent* (Homewood, Ill.: Dorsey Press, 1968).

cisions; the lower in status, the more effectively they are excluded, despite formal rights of inclusion.

Sometimes people are legally excluded: slaves in a slave society, aliens without the rights of citizenship, for example. Convicted criminals may lose the right to vote or hold office. Once, women had no legal rights, but in time most industrial societies (as in the United States in 1920) extended the franchise to women. Earlier in history the working class did not have legal rights, either, but property restrictions were abolished to bring workers into political society.

Even when legal exclusion has been eliminated, an effective, informal exclusion may still be practiced. Though the fifteenth amendment was adopted in 1870, insuring political rights for black people, such rights were still denied in practice in much of the South for almost a hundred years later. It took federal marshals under direct orders from President John Kennedy, intervening in some Southern counties, to get county registrars to register blacks.

Inclusion in the political process through voting is the formal right most widely extended, it provides a very limited way of participating in decision-making. It may come down to merely endorsing decisions made elsewhere. In 1972 the Democratic Party made procedural changes in its convention in order to include representative numbers of women, racial minorities, and youth. Yet even this process did not change the domination of the Party's convention by people of middle- and upper-class position, whether measured by occupation, education, or income. (This domination is even more true of the Republican Party.)

One projected solution to the student unrest on campuses in the late 1960s was to give students some representation in

Figure 15.1 The 1972 Democratic convention in Miami Beach, Florida, included representative numbers of women and youth. *(Wide World Photos.)*

academic government, which presumably made sit-ins and the taking over of buildings unnecessary. In an earlier time accepting labor unions as legitimate by management gave workers participation through collective bargaining in decisions about wages and working conditions.

What this tells us is that, historically, there has been a gradual extension of the legal right to participate, as in voting and holding office, to ever larger numbers of people; but that more extensive participation in decision-making, or even influential access to such, has continued to be restricted to those who control economic resources and possess higher status: men over women, whites over blacks, middle-aged over youth, affluent over poor, employers over employees, the propertied over the nonpropertied, middle class over working class, the educated over the less educated.

The distribution of power in a system is usually organized in such a way as to reflect the system's stratification structure and subgroup control of resources. There is, almost always, then, a structure of power in a community or a society.

Decision and Consensus

When decisions are made about controversial issues in complex societies or even in large groups a good deal of compromise may be necessary in order to take account of the claims of all the groups with interests affected in some way and able to exert some influence or pressure. Such a decision, when finally hammered out, may not be the ideal one for any group. Decisions, in short, are not usually a matter of *consensus,* if that means an agreement in values and opinion. In such complex processes people do not reach consensus; they reach a workable, acceptable agreement.

What may be a matter of consensus, however, is the process for arriving at decisions and the acceptance of those decisions as legitimate. Democratic processes imply consensus on such matters as majority vote and rule, so that such decisions are legitimately binding on both winners and losers.

The Nation-State

In the modern world almost everyone is a citizen of a nation, and so everyone has a nationality. Yet the process of creating nations is still recent history in Europe and America—note that Germany and Italy only became nations within the last century. Nation-building, furthermore, is a central component of the modernizing process throughout the non-Western world.[4] So, while the advocates of world capitalism and multinational corporations look beyond the nation for a new form of political organization, political elites in the still modernizing economies, as in Africa, are struggling to construct nations out of territories once divided among tribes diverse in language and culture.

That is the significance of nation for the modern world: It unites populations larger than the tribal and village structures of the past, breaks down local barriers to trade and commercial development (industrialism and capitalism, then, encouraged nation-building), and integrates a population under a central government. In the process it turns that population into a *people*, sharing a common language and a common heritage. (To be sure, there often remain old cultural groupings, loyalties, and languages within nations; for example, the cultural and linguistic divisions in Belgium, Yugoslavia, and India.) National identity and loyalty generally supersede the former restricted and localized identities that were once so central to people's lives: village, tribe, kinship, and church.

Nations unavoidably bring into being a more powerful government, one controlling a larger population and governing a wider territory than did earlier forms of government.

The *state* governs the nation. Max Weber defined the state as a political organization that claims binding authority and a legitimate monopoly of force within a territory.[5] In the modern nation, then, the state is an inclusive group from which there is no escape. A stateless person belongs nowhere and is, in terms of rights and status, a nonperson. All other social groups are subordinate to the authority and power of the state.

The Function of the State

The organization and exercise of power in modern society is very largely a function of the nation-state. Social scientists conventionally credit it with carrying out these basic political functions:[6]

1. Limiting internal power struggles to maintain internal peace.
2. Bringing power to bear on other societies in defense of national interests or in expanding and building empire.

---

[4] *See* Clifford Geertz, ed., *Old Societies and New Nations* (New York: The Free Press, 1963); *see also*, Reinhard Bendix, *Nation Building and Citizenship* (New York: John Wiley & Sons, Inc., 1964).

[5] Hans Gerth and C. Wright Mills, *From Max Weber: Essays in Sociology* (New York: Oxford University Press, 1946), p. 78.

[6] *See* Leon Mayhew, *Society: Institutions and Activity* (Glenview, Ill.: Scott, Foresman and Company, 1971), p. 127.

3. Controlling the members of society so as to bind them to the pursuit of collective goals.
4. Recognizing and implementing the interests and demands of various groups; thus, by combination and compromise, aligning interests in the making of public policy.

In contrast to this conventional view of the state, the Marxian does not see it as a political structure for maintaining social order and adjusting competitive claims for goods and services. Instead, it is a necessary mechanism in a society with class antagonisms, used to maintain the structure of domination by which some classes control and exploit others.

The Political Party middle, upper-class males.

Since the state is the politically dominant and controlling force, with binding authority, political struggles in a nation are struggles for control of the state. Of the kinds of groups that organize for this struggle, the *political party* is the most significant. As Weber said, parties "live in a house of 'power,'" and "are always structures struggling for domination."[7]

The political party originated in political clubs that organized to support candidates who, once in office, could reflect the interests and concerns of some citizens more than others. The existence of parties, then, testifies to differences in class and group interests—the propertied and nonpropertied groups, the richer and the poorer, who want different kinds of political action and different kinds of social policies from the state.

The relationship of the party to the state is varied, ranging from one-party states to multiple-party states. In one-party states,

one powerful political group, committed to a dominant ideology and program, completely controls the state and allows no alternative choice of program and policy. The forms of party and electoral process are retained, but are not used to make political choices. Instead, they are used to provide symbolic expressions of support by loyal citizens.

Democratic states are, theoretically and constitutionally, multiple-party states, for its citizens have the right to form any party they choose. But among democratic nations there are in fact some varied patterns. One is found in nations like France and Italy, where the citizens divide among a number of parties from right to left, and only rarely does one party have a majority. A coalition among several parties to control the state is then necessary. The weakness of such a system lies in the fragility of these coalitions, so that an instability of rule produces frequent elections. Also, it is in these democratic nations that strong parties of the right and left emerge. The Communist parties of France and Italy, for example, are among the larger parties of those nations.

A second pattern is found in the nations of the British Commonwealth—Britain, Canada, New Zealand, and Australia—and those of northwestern Europe.[8] Here two parties usually dominate, but for the most part they offer sharper ideological alternatives to the voter, based as they are on social classes. One of them is either called the Labor Party (as in the British Commonwealth nations, except Canada) or the Social Democratic Party. These working-class based parties have in some cases intro-

---

[7] *See* Hans Gerth and C. Wright Mills, *op. cit.*, pp. 194–195.

[8] For a comparison of political parties in Great Britain, Australia, Canada, and the United States *see* Robert Alford, *Party and Society* (Chicago: Rand-McNally & Company, 1963).

duced elements of socialism into national life.

In the United States a still different situation prevails. While, constitutionally, multiple parties are always possible, and many small parties always exist, there is nonetheless a powerful two-party ideology that severely restricts the chances of other parties becoming seriously contending forces. Furthermore, the two American parties are not primarily *ideological* parties, but have liberal and conservative wings, and so overlap. American politicians are rarely spokesmen for clearly defined ideologies, or for the specific groups and classes such ideologies speak for. They are primarily political brokers who seek to create winning coalitions of groups and classes within the parties before the election instead of among several parties after an election.

The American Party System

What is distinctive about the politics of the United States is the failure to develop a party of the left, based solidly on the working class and espousing Socialist programs. In that way the American party structure differs from practically all other industrial Capitalist nations. According to sociologist Richard Hamilton, this accounts for the inadequacy of social welfare and for the relatively unlimited growth of the military complex in the United States.[9]

Given the American two-party system, what are the consequences for control and direction of the state? When both parties strive to be political canopies that stretch widely over a diverse range of social groups and classes, they come into competition for at least some of the same ones, thus tending to push the parties nearer to a purported ideological center. They become more alike in program and purpose. Indeed, for purposes of winning elections, the parties must exaggerate their differences, relying increasingly on the political personality of candidates, rather than issues and programs, to bring victory. They constantly risk being seen as Tweedledum and Tweedledee.

Despite that, some perception of ideological differences between the parties persists in the American population. A majority of adults perceive the Democratic Party as the party of the poor and the working man, and the Republican Party as that of the rich and of business.[10] Furthermore, if all American workers do not vote Democratic, *most* do, and that fact is significant in determining the character of both the Democratic and Republican parties. So is the fact that *most* businessmen and wealthy people are Republicans, even if all are not.

The American two-party system operates within a pervasive political culture that demands that the parties and their major candidates stray not too far from some presumed ideological center, and then defines a fairly sizable deviation as unacceptably "radical" or "extremist" and calls for a "landslide" defeat of a candidate. The defeat of Republican candidate Barry Goldwater in 1964 and Democratic candidate George McGovern in 1972 occurred at least in part out of such circumstances.

Perhaps the basic point is now apparent: In the United States party politics operate

[9] Richard Hamilton, *Class and Politics in the United States* (New York: John Wiley & Sons, Inc., 1972), p. 541.

[10] *See* Alford, *op. cit.,* p. 100.

within a political culture that works to *restrict* issues and programs for elective choice.[11] This is possible only because both parties accept as given and beyond political discussion the main structural features of the society, particularly the economic: the distribution of property and wealth, the class structure, corporate control and organization of the economy, and both party leaderships drawn overwhelmingly from upper middle-class levels.

Money and Votes

Political parties in democratic societies are the organizations by which an electorate is mobilized. To do that, parties must appeal to masses of people, promising programs that will solve problems, ease burdens, or protect their interests. But elections cost money and since little money comes from the voters, the parties turn elsewhere. In the United States, at least, various interest groups provide financial support to make campaigns possible.

Thus, the political party links two separate and sometimes incompatible forces: masses of ordinary citizens, who supply votes, and powerful economic and social interests, who supply money. There is corruption inherent in such a process. To make it work, interest-serving activity is concealed from voters. While such concealing can be successful in specific cases, over the long run it is not. The result is a widespread contempt for politics and politicians on the part of citizens, a situation that discourages political participation and weakens confidence in the democratic process.

The Future of the American Parties

The American two-party system has been so long and so well established that most Americans assume its indefinite continuity. Yet, changes may be coming. Richard Hamilton's assessment of political poll data suggests to him that the United States may develop a party and a half, because much of the Republican base in the population (older people, rural, and small-town people) is shrinking and that of the Democratic Party is increasing.[12] If the Democratic Party were to be the dominant one, then, he predicts, the dominant groups will join it in order not to be left out of the permanent ruling party.

But another development is taking place —more and more voters are detaching themselves from parties. According to political analyst David Broder, this is true of the electorate as a whole throughout the United States, and as a consequence many more voters split their tickets.[13] A Gallup Poll in 1968 reported that 84 percent of the voters said they voted for the man, not the party. The party—and the party politicians—are not held in high esteem.

Under these circumstances, there is some possibility of a new, third party developing, though the old parties have long put extremely difficult obstacles in the way of any new party movement. But George Wallace's successful attack on both parties as unresponsive to the common man's desires showed that a third party was still possible.

Another interpretation has been that the

---

[11]For an analysis of how the two-party system can thwart and block majority desires *see* Hamilton, *op. cit.*, pp. 3–15.

[12] *See* Hamilton, *op. cit.*, pp. 534–537.
[13] *See* David Broder, *The Party's Over* (New York: Harper and Row, 1972).

Republican Party could become a new majority by capturing the South, the suburbs, the Wallace vote, and frightened ethnics to add to their traditional constituencies.[14]

It may be that none of these possibilities will occur in the near future. But shifting party allegiances and the independence of an increasingly larger segment of the electorate suggests that some kind of change in the two-party system is likely.

Parapolitical Groups

Political parties are not the only political groups that operate in the house of power. In the United States the right of assembly makes legitimate the organization of private citizens into groups that can seek ways to influence government and change social policy. (Political parties exist under this same right.)

This makes *political* many private and voluntary associations that are not ordinarily so defined: chambers of commerce, labor unions, manufacturers' associations, civic groups, taxpayers' associations, veterans' associations, and almost any other organized interest in the society. These are parapolitical groups.[15]

These groups can and do operate in different ways, aiming their efforts at different targets. Some groups concentrate primarily on the legislative and executive branches of government. They lobby; that is, they try to influence policy and legislation to suit their own interests. Powerful groups, especially economic ones (includ-

ing corporations) lobby on a permanent basis, with a consequent advantage in affecting policy. Other groups emerge temporarily around new and controversial issues, and their lobbying is limited and sporadic. The purpose of lobbying, particularly in its regular aspects, is usually to protect group *interests*.

Other groups concentrate on *issues*, formulating programs and policies for change and seeking to "educate" people to their desirability. These groups publicize problems and projected solutions outside of party structure, and in time mobilize sufficient support to command serious attention from governmental agencies and political parties. (To be sure, they may also do some limited lobbying, and they may testify before legislative committees.) The case for ecological reform, anti-pollution measures, conservation of natural resources, as well as the case for birth control and abortion, and for constraints on population growth are all issues that were first developed through the activities of voluntary, parapolitical groups.

Bureaucracy and Politics

None of the political structures we have been speaking of—states, parties, even parapolitical groups—escape bureaucratization. Modern government, in fact, is a paramount example of bureaucratic structure. Yet, few sociological studies have sought to determine the significance of bureaucratization for the political process, and particularly for democratic processes.

One can argue, as sociologist Seymour M. Lipset does, that bureaucracy provides a neutral function that reduces political conflict, for the bureaucrat is an impartial

[14] *See* Kevin Phillops, *The Emerging Republican Majority* (New Rochelle, N.Y.: Arlington House, 1969).

[15] *See* Scott Greer and Peter Orleans, "The Mass Society and the Parapolitical Structure," *American Sociological Review,* vol. 27 (October 1962), pp. 634–646.

Figure 15.2 Voter participation has declined in the seventies, while the number of voters who split their tickets has increased. *(Monkmeyer, Sybil Shelton.)*

expert, not a partisan.[16] Impartial experts in government can perform two integrative functions for a democratic society. First, they can provide a stable and routine administration of established political functions, rendering less disruptive the change of power from one party to another. Second, they can reduce conflict to administrative decisions and expert judgments, thus making sources of conflict more manageable and less disturbing within the social order.

Perhaps the outstanding American example of this function of bureaucracy is the complex social mechanism of federal mediation for resolving labor-management conflicts and insisting on a resolution that embodies a workable agreement in a bind-

ing contract. This requires a body of experts—both within and without government—who can be called upon to provide technical skill for resolving a dispute and finding the grounds for agreement. By this process issues that are always a source of conflict are removed from the political arena and cease to be the basis for conflicting ideological positions taken by political parties. A possibly disruptive issue within the political process is then minimized.

But, as Lipset also notes, this stabilizing effect of bureaucracy can also be viewed as conservative in its significance for the political process, and so it will be viewed by those interested in social change. In his *Agrarian Socialism,* Lipset described how a Socialist party in Canada, after having won office, was thwarted in carrying out its program by the resistance of the permanent bureaucracy of civil ser-

[16] Seymour Martin Lipset, "Political Sociology," in Robert K. Merton, Leonard Broom, and Leonard S. Cottrell, Jr., eds., *Sociology Today* (New York: Basic Books, Inc., 1959), p. 102.

vants.[17] Weber recognized that control over the administrative implementation of decision-making was decisive for political power; and he felt negatively about the chances of democratic politicians to keep such control from the permanent bureaucrats. Although bureaucracy may be stabilizing and a mechanism for reducing conflict, this, in Weber's view, did not make it supportive of democracy. His ultimate view of the impact of bureaucracy on democracy was pessimistic, and he thought it essential to prevent a bureaucratic domination of all social life.[18]

Besides governments, political parties, too, become bureaucratized. This is more likely to occur when parties maintain large, permanent organizations, which is more true of European parties than of American ones.

ELITES AND POWER

In the long record of known human societies, so it has seemed, the select few, however chosen, appear always to rule over the many. Not even the emergence of political democracy has seriously weakened the idea that political power always rests in the hands of an *elite*. Though by no means new, this somewhat dispiriting idea was systematically developed in the late nineteenth and early twentieth centuries in the face of rising power by mass-based Socialist parties in Europe. For a while it seemed that masses of ordinary people, through such working-class parties, would take power by democratic means in a

number of European nations. To show this was not humanly possible was the intent of three influential sociologists: Gaetano Mosca, Vilfredo Pareto, and Robert Michels.

The Rulers and the Ruled

In his *The Ruling Class*, Gaetano Mosca (1858–1941) asserted that all human societies were always and everywhere ruled by a controlling social class, and thus human society always divided between the rulers and the ruled.[19] Every ruling class, furthermore, to *legitimate* its power, uses the dominant values prevailing in the culture, as when kings presume to rule by the will of God and elected presidents by the mandate of the people.

Mosca is hardly original in arguing that there is always a ruling class—that had been taken for granted by many scholars for centuries. However, his detailed documentation amassed an impressive range of supporting historical data, and the timing of his study coincided with serious intellectual concerns about new forms of political power and the potentialities for democratic order.

Vilfredo Pareto (1848–1923), in turn, taking the existence of a ruling class for granted, concentrated his study on "the circulation of elites."[20] He was basically concerned with the consequence of "open" and "closed" elites; they were open when access to elite position was possible for persons of non-elite origin, and closed when an elite class monopolized its position for those born into it, as an hereditary

[17] Seymour Martin Lipset, *Agrarian Socialism* (Berkeley, Calif.: University of California Press, 1950).

[18] For a fuller discussion of Weber's views on bureaucracy and politics *see* Reinhard Bendix, *Max Weber: An Intellectual Portrait* (Garden City, N.Y.: Doubleday & Company, Inc., 1960), pp. 432–459.

[19] *See* Gaetano Mosca, *The Ruling Class* (New York: McGraw-Hill Book Company, Inc., 1939).

[20] *See* Vilfredo Pareto, *Mind and Society* (New York: Harcourt Brace Jovanovich, 1935).

aristocracy. Since no elite has an inherited monopoly of brains and skills, a stable political process required that the ruling elite co-opt into its own ranks the best talent from the ranks of the non-elite.

Yet the tendencies to closure are always strong in elites, says Pareto, for they often impute superiority to themselves and inferiority to subordinate classes. When the inevitable decay of a closed aristocracy produces cleavage and dissension within its own ranks, new elites emerge from other classes to give leadership to revolutionary change. Then, a new ruling class will take over from a deposed one.

The Iron Law of Oligarchy

"Who says organization, says oligarchy." With these words, Robert Michels expressed in modern language an ancient pessimism about the human capacity to achieve freedom and democratic order within social organization.[21] Oligarchy, the rule of the few over the many, he considered to be an *inevitable* outcome of social organization, and his "iron law of oligarchy" was a sociological formulation of this idea.

Michel's argument has two aspects. First, he argues for the necessity of leadership; and second, he tries to show how such leadership becomes an oligarchy. Leadership, Michels argues, is necessary in any group that organizes for collective action, for this requires a division of labor and an assignment of specialized and skilled functions on behalf of the group to some of its membership. Leadership *roles* necessarily emerge from this solution.

But why does this necessarily result in oligarchy? First of all, because the delegation of tasks and authority to a leadership places in its hands a concentration of skills and prerogatives that the members do not have. Leaders become specialized in carrying out tasks that others know little about, and the experience of being a leader sets these members apart from the others.

Leadership also makes possible an internal power. It affords the opportunity to build a staff of people who are loyal; it gives control over the channels of communication; and it can practically monopolize access to the members. Only the leaders control the membership files, the official records, and the treasury, and without in any way being dishonest or illegal, they can use these to their own advantage.

Any theory about oligarchy, however, must also account for the followers. According to Michels, the membership of any large social organization contributes to the emergence of oligarchy because of their indifference to running the organization and their unwillingness to become greatly involved. Furthermore, Michels argued, the members appreciate the greater skills and ability of leaders and they feel beholden to them. Thus they have no inclination to prevent their leaders' growing power.

The manner in which a leadership becomes self-perpetuating has consequences for the organization. An oligarchic leadership becomes conservative and cautious; and it develops interests of its own that may be quite different from the formally stated objectives of the organization. The more these organizations grow and prosper, the more do they become stable and bureaucratic organizations. Michels had studied the great Socialist parties of Western Europe and observed that their original

[21] *See* Robert Michels, *Political Parties* (New York: The Free Press, 1949), p. 401. This book was first published in German in 1911, in English in 1915.

goals to effect radical change in society diminished as they became more oligarchic.

Social organization creates a set of conditions that makes oligarchy possible. Michels' formulations did not require psychological explanations, such as a lust for power or a desire to dominate, though he did sometimes talk in this manner. Instead, his perspective is basically sociological, for he interprets oligarchy as an inevitable outcome of a set of structural conditions that begins with the division of labor. Nor does this theory require any moral charge against leadership. Oligarchy is not the intent of leaders; nor did Michels doubt their personal integrity.

But Is It Inevitable?

Michels' thesis of the inevitability of oligarchy is an impressive if dismaying argument. And it takes only a little astute observation of political parties, labor unions, and civic organizations to see how well presumably democratic leadership can effectively perpetuate itself, seemingly indefinitely. But does it have to be that way?

One important sociological study sought to test that out by studying a union that seemed to be the exception to the usual oligarchic process, the International Typographers Union (ITU).[22] The major finding of the study was that the ITU had remained democratic by institutionalizing a two-party system within the union, creating *effective* opposition to any incumbent leadership—effective because they had access to necessary information, resources, and to the membership. There

---

[22] *See* Seymour M. Lipset, Martin A. Trow, and James S. Coleman, *Union Democracy: The Internal Politics of the International Typographical Union* (New York: The Free Press, 1956).

could be, then, structural conditions of opposition and contest that would reduce the likelihood of oligarchy.

Community Power Elites

In studying power in the community some sociologists have claimed the existence of an elite, but other social scientists have projected instead a more pluralistic model of the community, one in which varied groups compete to influence the outcome of social issues.

In *Community Power Structure,* sociologist Floyd Hunter described in detail an economic elite—mostly corporation executives and bankers—who by informal communication and because of a similar social point of view agree on the major decisions affecting the lives of all the citizens of the community. This is an elite not known to the community, for its members do not usually hold official positions and its decision-making activities are not publicly visible.

Power, then, seems to be centered at the very top of the social structure in the hands of the community's "economic dominants." They exercise social power because they control the community's economic resources: the banks and credit, the corporations and jobs. The elite decides, but others, whom the community identifies as leaders, then go about the task of carrying out the decision, including mobilizing community support.

These community leaders, including elected public officials and the heads of the well-known large organizations of the community, are not, according to Hunter, decision-makers in their own right. They are men of second and third rank in the power structure, whose function is to carry

Figure 15.3 "Hard Hats" and business executives attend a lunchtime political rally on Wall Street. *(A. Devaney, Inc., N.Y.)*

out decisions, not make them. So are the organizations they run: the Chamber of Commerce, for example, and numerous civic organizations. This leads to the inference that these organizations are not controlled by their membership but are used to control that membership; their support is mobilized for decisions made by the elite.

Robert Dahl, a political scientist, has quarreled seriously with Hunter's study as a generalized model for all American communities.[23] He criticized Hunter for centering on who the decision-makers are but not on how decisions are made. In turn Dahl has insisted on the importance of observing the issues in the community over which decisions are made and of

observing the decision-making process that occurs. The same people, he notes, are not necessarily involved in the different areas of decision-making—education, city government, and community welfare, for example. This perspective gives a different image of community power structure, one much less monolithic, with a less close relation between power and status and a wider citizen participation in decision-making.

It occurred to more than one critic of Hunter's work that the concentration of community power in an economic elite was not necessarily true of all communities, and that differences in the attributes of communities could account for a concentration of power in one community, a dispersion of power in another.

With that in mind, sociologist Michael Aiken reviewed fifty-seven studies of community decision-making undertaken by

[23] *See* Robert A. Dahl, *Who Governs? Democracy and Power in an American City* (New Haven, Conn.: Yale University Press, 1961).

sociologists and political scientists.[24] He found a number of important structural characteristics related to variations in the diffusion of power. Perhaps the most interesting of his findings was that decentralized community power was more characteristic of communities that *economically* were dominated by absentee-owned firms (rather than locally-owned ones), were more industrialized, and were more industrially diverse.

In *political* terms reform municipal government, marked by city managers and small city councils elected at large, are likely to be more concentrated in power, while old-fashioned, unreformed political structures — mayor-council form of government, direct election of mayors, and large councils elected by ward or district — are associated with a decentralized power structure. Given the familiar imagery of machines and bosses, this may be a surprising finding. Reform governments that promised to clean up corrupt politics also put more control in the hands of the city manager and often, by reducing city councils in size and eliminating local districts, made it easier for the economic elite to succeed in citywide elections. The representation of many diverse groups, particularly ethnic and working-class ones, is increased by large councils elected by districts. In short, the reform of civic government earlier in this century restored community power to the economically dominant elements and reduced participation in decision-making by those with less status.

[24] *See* Michael Aiken, "The Distribution of Community Power: Structural Bases and Social Consequences," in Michael Aiken and Paul Mott, eds., *The Structure of Community Power* (New York: Random House, Inc., 1970), pp. 487–525.

There were other related political characteristics. Cities with concentrated power, for example, have strong executives and have more bureaucratized city governments — though they are likely to be more efficient. Cities with decentralized power are more likely to have a liberal electorate.

When Aiken examined communities in terms of *social structure,* he found that decentralized power and nonreformed government was more likely to be found in cities with a large working-class population, many Catholics, and a high degree of ethnicity. (Interestingly, Aiken could find no relation between the proportion of the nonwhite population and the degree of diffusion of power.)

Cities with a higher proportion of white-collar workers, and a higher proportion of high-school graduates, as well as a higher than average median income are more likely to have concentrated power structures. In short, the more heterogeneous a city, the more diffused in power; while homogeneous, middle-class communities are more concentrated in power.

All of the relations that Aiken found, as summarized above, were measured statistically, and the measurements were all moderate; some were even weak. Therefore, there were many exceptions to what has been said and the findings are not to be taken as hard and fast generalizations that apply in all cases.

One thing can be noted. Cities with concentrated power are more likely to be those whose political structure has been reshaped by the business community to be more efficient, which they are, and to be run like a business, which requires a strong executive. This does not encourage a wider sharing in community decision-making.

National Power Elites

Until recently, most studies of power in the United States have been community studies. However, the late C. Wright Mills undertook a sociologically bold and imaginative effort to delineate the national power structure of American society, describing an elite of the very rich and of top leaders in industry, government, and the military united by a common ideological outlook.[25]

In contrast, other social scientists view social power as more pluralistic. They perceive a wide and diversified array of interest groups, each with access to authority and each managing to bring pressure on official decision-makers. The complexity of the decision-making process and the fact of social change, it is felt, makes it unlikely that a single elite can control all decisions.

This was the argument of sociologist Arnold Rose, who deliberately challenged Mills' argument and offered instead a pluralistic model of power.[26] Rose did not deny there were elites. He simply saw many instead of a single one, and furthermore claimed that "the top business elite are far from having an all-powerful position; that power is so complicated in the United States that the top businessmen scarcely understand it, much less control it; and that since 1933 the power position of businessmen has been declining rather than growing."[27] The political elite, Rose believes, in the political arena, at least, is not subordinate to the economic elite.

Sociologist G. William Domhoff took basic issue with Rose and sought to detail how a national power elite, protecting and advancing the interests of an upper class, was able to shape social legislation by working through universities and their scholarly experts, through foundations funding research, and through nonpartisan civic groups.[28] Such an elite, said Domhoff, controlled, not by resisting change but by developing a moderate program of social reform. They more clearly controlled foreign policy—even Rose conceded that a power elite did in fact control foreign policy. Both Domhoff and Rose point out the power of secret groups, such as the CIA, and the influence of organizations such as the Foreign Policy Association and the Council on Foreign Relations in making foreign policy. Domhoff had sketched in upper-class control of these influential organizations.

Who Rules—and How?

Subsequent literature arguing the issue of an American Capitalist elite controlling the major decisions of the society pro and con has revealed, more than anything else, how little such a basic issue has been studied by American social scientists—a revealing point in itself. But there would seem to be two questions that need to be answered:[29]

[25] See C. Wright Mills, *The Power Elite* (New York: Oxford University Press, 1956).

[26] See Arnold M. Rose, *The Power Structure: Political Processes in American Society* (New York: Oxford University Press, 1967).

[27] See Rose, *op. cit.*, p. 490.

[28] See G. William Domhoff, *The Higher Circles: Governing Class in America* (New York: Random House, Inc., 1970).

[29] A good review of these issues, arguing that there is such a ruling elite, is by Milton Mankoff, "Power in Advanced Capitalist Society: A Review Essay on Recent Elitist and Marxist Criticism of Pluralist Theory," *Social Problems*, vol. 17 (Winter 1970), pp. 418–430.

1. Has an ideological domination been obtained, ruling out serious alternatives to the economic and political structures now prevailing? Corporate capitalism destroyed its small-scale business and farmer opposition in the "critical" election of 1896, according to political scientist Walter Dean Burnham who describes the election as critical because: "this brought to a close the 'Civil War' party system and inaugurated a political alignment congenial to the dominance of industrial capitalism over the American political economy."[30] Subsequently, according to historian James Weinstein, by World War I significant liberal social reforms led by a segment of the corporate leadership had won out over what had been a serious conflict between capital and labor, wherein an anti-Capitalist perspective had made inroads into organized labor and the working class.[31] In more recent decades, a strong anti-communism among almost all social classes has associated socialism with totalitarianism and "free enterprise" with liberty and democracy.

Corporate capitalism, then, seems to have achieved an ideological legitimacy among the non-elite classes, one which restricts public discussion and competitive party platforms to choice among alternatives not threatening to elite domination.[32]

2. Is there class-consciousness and a cohesive sense of purpose and unity in the economic elite? Arnold Rose says no, that business has not effectively articulated its own interests. As a consequence, he argues that the economic elite has given way to the political elite in the making of decisions.[33] But Domhoff, Weinstein, and historian Gabriel Kolko[34] argue that the disunity of the business class is more apparent than real, and that there has been a highly articulate segment of the business elite who have been able to shape government policy through a structure of influence that backs reforms and changes in such a way as to protect basic class interests. Sometimes this put them into outright opposition to such "unenlightened" members of their own class as the Chamber of Commerce and the National Association of Manufacturers (NAM).

This argument does not claim any complete unity in an economic elite in either political action or ideological outlook. Indeed, Domhoff insists there is both a more liberal and a more conservative segment of this class; they differ, not on fundamental interests but on the means by which their interests can best be advanced in American society.

There is a host of other questions to ask and answer before a ruling class can be clearly identified: how it manages to control important decisions, for example, and what decisions are important and acted upon, what are unimportant and left to others. Very little is known about upper-class consciousness, except inferentially, for the economic elite does not usually submit to interviews or make frank comments on their world views.

A few years ago C. Wright Mills provided the only evidence for a ruling elite; almost all other social scientists were on the pluralist side, believing in many elites. But in

[30] See Walter Dean Burnham, "The End of American Party Politics," *Trans-action* (December 1969), p. 13.

[31] See James Weinstein, *The Corporate Ideal in the Liberal State: 1900–1918* (Boston, Mass.: The Beacon Press, 1969).

[32] For a sophisticated discussion of the legitimacy of capitalism in Western industrial societies *see* Norman Birnbaum, *The Crisis of Industrial Society* (New York: Oxford University Press, 1969); and Ralph Miliband, *The State in Capitalist Society: An Analysis of the Western System of Power* (New York: Basic Books, Inc., 1969).

[33] See Rose, *op. cit.*, pp. 89–92. Richard Hamilton also supports this position; *see* his *Class and Politics in the United States*, p. 516.

[34] See Gabriel Kolko, *The Roots of American Foreign Policy: An Analysis of Power and Purpose* (Boston, Mass.: The Beacon Press, 1969).

recent years the works already cited and others have discovered more empirical evidence for making the case for a ruling elite in American society. We can expect more evidence—and more theoretical debate—from both camps in the future.

CENTRALIZING AND DECENTRALIZING POWER

The dominant trends of modern society—industrialization, bureaucratization, and nationalism—are powerful organizing forces that tend to concentrate power. Even without any plans or schemes by anti-democratic groups, democracy is threatened by the possibility of total power concentrated in the central organs of the state.

De Tocqueville and Pluralist Society

One of the great classics of political sociology is _Democracy in America_ by Alexis de Tocqueville, a Frenchman of aristocratic origin who visited the United States in the 1830s, intent on observing the democratic process as it functioned in this new nation.[35] While accepting the democratization of society accomplished by the French Revolution, De Tocqueville was yet concerned with the potentiality for amassing total power in the governments of the new, industrial nations.

De Tocqueville's solution to the danger of concentrated power was the _pluralist society_—one in which there are several sources of power other than the state, and in which there is a potentiality for engaging in conflict and struggling for goals against other groups. Thus, political (but

[35] _See_ Alexis de Tocqueville, _Democracy in America,_ vols. I and II (New York: Vintage Books, 1954).

peaceful) conflict is insurance against the domination of society by a single center of power.

In the United States, De Tocqueville thought, the _local, self-governing community_ and the _voluntary association_ could be the significant sources for a pluralism of power. As active sources of political engagement, experience, and training for citizens, they would be an independent source of politically capable leadership. They would also generate new centers of power to contest both among each other and with the state for a basis for democratic consensus.

What concerned De Tocqueville was the existence of centers of power intermediate between the individual citizen and the nation-state. As an unorganized mass, aggregates of individual citizens could not oppose the centralized power of the state. Intermediate political organizations that had free access to masses of citizens and opportunity to organize them to engage in political contest, whether in competition for office or in conflict over policy, was a guarantee of a democratic society.

However, local self-government has become less and less significant as a source of independent social power. It has clearly declined as an autonomous unit in society (as we saw in Chapter 9). Furthermore, local government is often mostly responsive to local dominant majorities and the local elites based on them, which often choose _not_ to act upon major issues, such as race, housing for the poor, and the like. In the metropolitan areas of the United States the shared powers of a pluralistic society produce a proliferation of local governments that are too small to act effectively on metropolitan problems (see this discussion in Chapter 9).

Perhaps more than Europeans have, Americans have made a virtue of the voluntary association.[36] These have been the parapolitical groups that have organized citizens to seek and demand rights and services, to advance causes, and to enlarge the political choices available to a democratic electorate.[37]

But the theorists of pluralism also make an assumption about voluntary associations as intermediate organizations—that they are reasonably equal to one another in the capacity to influence decisions, and this is unlikely to be so. The pluralistic conception of society has often ignored the vast differences in size, in material resources, public prestige, access to authority and decision-making, and in ideological advantage that accrues to some. Pluralism is then no guarantee against a preponderant domination by powerful groups over decisions that affect the lives of all members of the society.

Decentralizing Power

The undeniable trend toward the concentration of power at the top of hierarchies of decision-making is a common theme that runs through discussions about the future prospects of democracy and individual liberty from quite varied perspectives: liberal, conservative, and radical. A cynical acceptance of power located beyond the reach of ordinary citizens has been a component of American political culture for generations now. Our grand-

fathers were likely to say: "You can't fight city hall." Today, people are just as likely to say that, as well as: "You can't fight the corporation."

"Power to the People"

Radical critics of American society—and President Richard Nixon—have called for more power to the people to reverse the trend toward centralizing power. President Nixon said it to justify revenue-sharing with the state and local governments, giving them more resources in order to perform more services for their own constituencies. Such governments, he asserted, were closer to the people and they knew better both what people wanted and what was needed. This ignores the historical fact that federal programs grew because state and local governments lacked resources and because they were often controlled by groups that had no intentions of being responsive to social needs and providing needed social services.

Radical critics, however, mean something else, such as including people not previously included in decision-making: students, racial minorities, women, and the poor. Extension of voting rights once denied—enfranchising the disenfranchised—is an example of this, but so is an extension of representation for groups once not considered legitimately due any representation—such as students in academic government. A still further development is the organization of the previously unorganized. An early example was Saul Alinsky's organization of a multi-ethnic, working-class area of Chicago near the stockyards—the now renowned "Back-of-the-Yards" Movement.[38] The organizations of tenants and

---

[36] An Association of Voluntary Action Scholars (AVAS) has recently been formed. It has now produced two annual reviews, *Voluntary Action Research: 1972* and *Voluntary Action Research: 1973* (Lexington, Mass.: Lexington Books, 1972 and 1973).

[37] For studies of voluntary associations in contemporary urban life *see* John N. Edwards and Alan Booth, *Social Participation in Urban Society* (Cambridge, Mass.: Schenkman Publishing Company, 1973).

[38] *See* Saul D. Alinsky, *Reveille for Radicals* (Chicago, Ill.: University of Chicago Press, 1946).

Figure 15.4 Welfare mothers and their children organized a march on the White House to protest the President's 1972 welfare reform program. *(United Press International Photo.)*

renters is another example, as is the organization of welfare mothers, and the organization of migrant workers under Caesar Chavez.[39]

Such groups as these then move into the political arena, taking their places alongside already established groups and competing with them to affect decision-making. Organizing the unorganized, then, integrates into the political system people once left out or at best only marginally involved. It extends further the right of democratic participation, and as a social reform strengthens the existing political structure.

[39] *See* Robert K. Binstock and Katherine Ely, *The Politics of the Powerless* (Cambridge, Mass.: Winthrop Publishers, 1971); and Gilbert Y. Steiner, *The State of Welfare* (Washington, D.C.: Brookings Institution, 1971), Ch. 8. *See also* Michael Lipsky, "Rent Strikes: Poor Man's Weapon," in August Meier, ed., *The Transformation of Activism* (Chicago, Ill.: Aldine-Atherton, Inc., 1970), pp. 29–45.

But radical critics want more than merely integrating people into the existing system. Richard Flacks, a sociologist and advocate of participatory democracy,[40] calls for the development of community-based, self-determining organizations. He sees them as carrying out these functions:

1. Achieving community control over previously centralized functions, through local election of school and police administrators; by forming community-run cooperatives in housing, social services, retail distribution, and the like; by establishing community-run foundations and corporations.

2. Maintaining close control over elected representatives; running and electing poor

[40] Participatory democracy, according to its proponents, would provide more direct participation in and control of decisions by the people affected by them than present representative democracy does. Self-management in work organizations, decentralization, and local community organizations are among the changes advocated.

people to public office; insuring direct participation of the community in framing political platforms and in shaping the behavior of representatives.

3. Acting like a trade union in protecting the poor against exploitative and callous practices of public and private bureaucracies, landlords, businessmen, and so on.[41]

Much of this program is an effort to restore local control and so to make community once again a viable location of decision-making. (Relevant here is our earlier reference in Chapter 9 to Milton Kotler's thesis about neighborhood government, and in Chapter 13 to the effort to develop community control of schools and other functions in large cities.[42]) But there are problems with such efforts.

Local, grass-roots decision-making, for one thing, is meaningless unless there is also local control over resources. Thus, local power implies local economies. But the economy has long since been integrated into national and international markets. Control of economic resources—of property, jobs, and capital—now lies in corporate structures that are neither controlled by nor dependent on local communities or groups.

Restoring power to the people may require more than decentralizing political structures. It requires coping with the fact that economic resources are concentrated in great corporate organizations which, by virtue of the right of private property, are

difficult to hold *accountable* for decisions that can so drastically affect people's lives.

That such a possibility is at least technologically feasible, given the development of a cybernated technology, one operated by self-regulating control mechanisms rather than human labor (which does not require either the huge factory or the large corporation to be economical) is an argument carefully reasoned out by anarchist Murray Bookchin.[43] He says:

I do not profess to claim that all of man's economic activities can be completely decentralized, but the majority surely can be scaled to human and communitarian dimensions. *It is enough to say that we can shift the overwhelming weight of the economy from national to communitarian bodies, from centralized bureaucratic forms to local, popular assemblies in order to secure the sovereignty of the free community on solid industrial foundations*. This shift would comprise a historic change of qualitative proportions, a revolutionary social change of vast proportions, unprecedented in man's technological and social development.[44]

---

[41] *See* Richard Flacks, "On the Uses of Participatory Democracy," in Matthew F. Stolz, ed., *Politics of the New Left* (Berkeley, Calif.: Glencoe Press, 1971), p. 30.

[42] Two useful works cited in those chapters and relevant here are Milton Kotler, *Neighborhood Government: The Local Foundations of Political Life* (Indianapolis, Ind.: The Bobbs-Merrill Company, Inc., 1969); and Alvin A. Altschuler, *Community Control: The Black Demand for Participation in Large American Cities* (New York: Pegasus, 1970).

[43] Anarchism is an antipolitical doctrine which opposes the state and all centralized political authority and seeks to replace them with new forms of human association. Anarchists share with liberals a high valuation on individualism and with socialists an opposition to private ownership of the means of production, yet anarchy stands in basic opposition to both. "In a sense too socialist for the liberals and too liberal for the socialists, the anarchists found capitalism and Marxism equally distasteful." Marshall S. Shatz, ed., *The Essential Works of Anarchism* (New York: Bantam Books, 1971), p. xvi. *See also* David Apter and James Joll, eds., *Anarchism Today* (Garden City: Anchor Books, 1972).

[44] *See* Murray Bookchin, "Toward a Liberatory Technology," in C. George Benello and Dimitrios Roussopoulos, *The Case for Participatory Democracy: Some Prospects for a Radical Society* (New York: The Viking Press, Inc., 1971), pp. 96–139. Italics in the original. *See* this volume for other relevant articles on the issue of participatory democracy.

Accountability

Decentralizing power into the hands of ordinary citizens, including the poorer and lesser educated, encounters another source of opposition: The claimed authority and autonomy of professionals and experts, a claim that implicitly asserts the incompetency of ordinary citizens. Technical and professional competence does exist, but many times these experts have been "servants of power," using their very real technical expertise for the benefit of the corporate or governmental organization that employs them, and so for the specific class and group interests these organizations serve, rather than for some larger public interest.[45] Decentralizing power may require holding accountable both corporations and government agencies, and the professionally qualified experts employed by them. This is one of the most difficult problems of a highly complex and differentiated society: How to prevent private and public groups from serving their own or other special interests rather than the interests of citizens, customers, clients, or some version of a public interest.[46]

Who Watches the Watchman?

But there is a further aspect. Public agencies are supposed to protect and advance public interests, while private groups are expected to pursue their own interests, though within limits. But when private interests and public agencies are in collusion, public interests are unguarded.

Thus, the United States Department of Agriculture (USDA) presumably looks after the interests of farmers, as well as the larger public interest concerning the production and distribution of agricultural products. But for some time now USDA has been charged with being part and parcel of an *agri-business complex*, composed of land-grant universities and their agricultural extension services and experiment stations, the Farm Bureau, the large food-processing firms, the farm machinery and chemical companies, and the major food-distributing chains. USDA has been accused of fostering corporate farming at the expense of family farming, of benefiting big farmers over small farmers, of helping the processors at the expense of consumers, of hindering ecological efforts to protect the environment, and of doing research to displace farm laborers by machinery but doing nothing to help such displaced farm labor get back into the labor force.[47]

But if public agencies fail to look out for public interests, who does? *Who watches the watchman?* Public interest research groups, modeled after Ralph Nader's efforts, have partially filled the gap. Small resources, limited access to records, and no legitimate public status of their own hinder them, though the credibility of Ralph Nader has given enormous impetus to this effort to cope with power by holding it accountable.

More to the point, Nader has created a now widely copied model of independent research and investigative organizations that probe into any situation where private power and public authority combine to

[45] Daniel Bell claims that this conflict between "professional and populace" is the hallmark of the postindustrial society. *See* his "Labor in the Post-Industrial Society," *Dissent* (Winter 1972), p. 167.

[46] As an example, *see* James R. Hudson, "Police Review Boards and Police Accountability," *Law and Contemporary Problems* (August 1971).

[47] *See* Jim Hightower, *Hard Tomatoes, Hard Times: The Failure of the Land Grant College Complex* (Washington, D.C.: Agribusiness Accountability Project, 1972). On the role of the Farm Bureau in the agri-business complex *see* Samuel R. Berger, *Dollar Harvest* (Lexington, Mass.: Heath Lexington Books, 1971).

THE NADER REPORTS

Action for a Change: A Student's Guide to Public Interest Organizing by Ralph Nader and Donald Ross.

Bitter Wages: Ralph Nader's Study Group Report on Disease and Injury on the Job by Joseph A. Page and Mary-Win O'Brien.

The Chemical Feast: Ralph Nader's Study Group on the Food and Drug Administration by James S. Turner.

The Closed Enterprise System: Ralph Nader's Study Group Report on Antitrust Enforcement by Mark J. Green with Beverly C. Moore, Jr., and Bruce Wasserstein.

The Company State: Ralph Nader's Study Group Report on Dupont in Delaware by James Phelan and Robert Pozen.

Corporate Power in America: Ralph Nader's Conference on Corporate Accountability edited by Ralph Nader and Mark J. Green.

Damming the West: Ralph Nader's Study Group Report on the Bureau of Reclamation by Richard L. Berkman and W. Kip Viscusi.

The Interstate Commerce Commission: Ralph Nader's Study Group Report on the Interstate Commerce Commission and Transportation by Robert C. Fellmeth.

The Monopoly Makers: Ralph Nader's Study Group Report on Regulation and Competition edited by Mark J. Green.

Old Age: The Last Segregation: Ralph Nader's Study Group Report on Nursing Homes, Claire Townsend, Project Director.

Politics of Land: Ralph Nader's Study Group Report on Land Use in California, Robert C. Fellmuth, Project Director.

A Public Citizen's Action Manual by Donald K. Ross.

Small—On Safety: The Designed-in Dangers of the Volkswagen by the Center for Auto Safety.

Sowing the Wind: A Report for Ralph Nader's Center for Study of Responsive Law on Food Safety and the Chemical Harvest by Harrison Wellford.

Unsafe at Any Speed: The Designed-in Dangers of the American Automobile (expanded and updated, 1972) by Ralph Nader.

Vanishing Air: Ralph Nader's Study Group Report on Air Pollution by John C. Esposito.

The Water Lords: Ralph Nader's Study Group Report on Industrial and Environmental Crisis in Savannah, Georgia by James M. Fallows.

Water Wasteland: Ralph Nader's Study Group Report on Water Pollution by David Zwick with Marcy Benstock.

What to Do with Your Bad Car: An Action Manual for Lemon Owners by Ralph Nader, Lowell Dodge, and Ralf Hotchkiss.

Whistle Blowing: The Report of the Conference on Professional Responsibility edited by Ralph Nader, Peter Petkas, and Kate Blackwell.

The Workers: Portraits of Nine American Jobholders by Kenneth Lasson.

You and Your Pension: Why You May Never Get a Penny/What You Can Do About It by Ralph Nader and Kate Blackwell.

All of the Nader Reports are published by Grossman Publishers, Inc.

Figure 15.5 Political influence and power can be exercized by other than elected officials when technical and professional expertise is needed at such a meeting as this budget hearing in Albany, New York. *(Monkmeyer, Mimi Forsyth.)*

thwart public interest. He began by publishing a report critical of the safety of American-made automobiles.[48] When General Motors was found to have hired a private detective to spy on him, his successful suit brought him funds for developing his model of investigation, and the resulting publicity made him a national figure—and a hero to many.

Since then, he has challenged a wide range of industries and governmental agencies with revealing investigations. (*See* "The Nader Reports.") By probing and publicizing, he has made facts public that often force government to correct problems thus revealed.

Beyond that, he has tried to encourage—perhaps revive would be a better term—a pattern of independent citizen action on

[48] *See* Ralph Nader, *Unsafe at Any Speed: The Designed-in Dangers of the American Automobile,* expanded and updated edition (New York: Grossman Publishers, 1972).

behalf of consumer, citizen, and taxpayer interests without depending on political office-holders. Indeed, these office-holders are often part of the problem, rather than part of the solution. Nader-inspired Citizen Action Groups and John Gardner's Common Cause, as well as a wide range of independent local groups in many urban communities, have sparked a renewed spirit of independent citizen investigation that has increased considerably the prospects of holding government and business accountable for the consequences of their actions on the interests of others.

POLITICAL PARTICIPATION

All politicians know that there are differences among the social classes in both interest in and participation in politics. It is a truism, for example, that a heavy vote favors the Democrats, since it is the workers and the poor who vote less consistently, and they are more likely to vote for the Democrats.

Much research on political participation seems to confirm what politicians instinctively know: that people higher in class position are more likely to participate in politics than people in lower class position are.[49] Whether status is measured by income, education, or occupation, the result is the same. Furthermore, in the United States blacks participate in politics much less than whites.[50]

The selection of candidates and political leadership in general also manifests the fact of class. In the United States the Democratic Party, even with a large working-class base, tends to select candidates from the middle class. Even in labor unions, leadership comes mostly from the ranks of the more skilled; and within most civic organizations the leaders are generally of higher social status than the average member.[51]

This relationship of status to participation seems to hold also outside the United States, though not to the same extent. Where political parties are more clearly class-based, the way is open for those of lower status to achieve positions of leadership.

Participation in politics is studied overwhelmingly in the social-science literature as a matter for individuals. But, in fact,

little participation aside from voting and shopping occurs outside of a group context. Many studies by both sociologists and political scientists have portrayed the politics of medicine, agriculture, veterans' benefits, and the like as the process by which some organized groups manage to carry their demands through the decision-making process. These organizations sometimes become involved in electoral campaigns, but more frequently they are politically active between elections, often on issues on which the electorate is unheard or on which they have no developed opinion—possibly because there has been little public opportunity to develop one.

This does not mean that interest groups always work against popular opinion. Rather, they frequently base themselves on an articulate constituency; and they often exploit grass roots sentiments and prejudices, as well as the frequent indeterminacy and indecisiveness of the electorate.

Voting

In democratic societies voting becomes the resolution of conflict among contesting political parties. Elections and campaigns are a basic social mechanism for resolving conflict and for reaffirming social consensus.

In emphasizing democratic elections as a means of maintaining consensus, American social scientists have been particularly concerned with avoiding the conflict that produces serious cleavage along class or group lines. Thus, consensus is defined as essential for democracy, serious and persistent cleavage as subverting it. Note the basic value choice that is embedded in this position: a preference for a consensus that makes for stability over the conflict

[49] See Lester W. Milbrath, *Political Participation: How and Why Do People Get Involved in Politics* (Chicago: Rand-McNally & Company, 1965), Ch. V, pp. 110–141.

[50] See Milbrath, *op. cit.,* p. 138. For a detailed analysis of black participation in Southern politics *see* Donald R. Matthews and James W. Prothro, *Negroes and the New Southern Politics* (New York: Harcourt Brace Jovanovich, 1966).

[51] See Wendell Bell, Richard J. Hill, and Charles R. Wright, *Public Leadership* (San Francisco, Calif.: Chandler Publishing Company, 1961).

and cleavage that mandates change. It is not that the consensus-oriented thinkers are opposed to change, so much as that they are fearful for the prospects of democracy in the face of serious conflict.

Their fear is based on two things: doubts about the commitment among ordinary people to the tolerance and moderation these social scientists feel democracy requires, and a concern that cleavage along class and group lines may create more conflict than the society can manage successfully.

This consensus theory of democracy holds that democracy is more viable under three sets of conditions:

1. Democracy is more viable when there is a wide-ranging agreement on the essential components of the social order, such as on property, the distribution of wealth, social opportunities, and the like. When this is so, and these institutional features are set and unarguable, then conflict is over lesser issues. Though it may still generate strong feeling, it can be more easily contained.

   In the history of democratic societies, however, there have been issues so lacking in consensus that politics spilled into the streets instead of the ballot box or legislative hall. In the United States, race has been such an issue. Violent racial conflict has broken out persistently in the United States throughout the twentieth century. In decades past, conflict between workers and employers also regularly erupted into violence. Our industrial history was largely dominated by violent conflict until the rise of labor unions among hitherto unorganized workers in the 1930s. No such comparable agreement has as yet been worked out for the racial conflict. Note also, that widespread conflict over our participation in the Vietnam War was fought out in militant and sometimes violent demonstrations, until seeking peace became the avowed policy of those domi-

nant groups that had earlier supported the conflict.

Such examples as these suggest — as consensus theorists argue — that democratic societies may not be able to settle deep and lasting conflicts by the ballot box. Yet, the rise and successful assumption of office by socialist parties in several European societies also suggests that radical differences on major issues more seriously in dispute than those the United States has faced, can, in fact, be successfully accommodated to the democratic process. Britain, for example, has democratically fought out such basic issues as the socialization of medical services and the nationalization of such a basic industry as coal without resorting to violent conflict. If one took the consensus argument wholly seriously, no one would be able to raise any fundamental issue lest it threaten the democratic process.

2. Democracy is also viewed as more viable when there is consensus on the rules and norms of the political process itself: on parties and elections, for instance, with the losers in these battles losing only the spoils of office (patronage and influence), not their liberties or their lives. Civil liberties accompany these processes, in order to insure that there is freedom of political action. Also, there is a secret ballot, and votes are presumably counted accurately, meaning honestly.

3. Democracy is presumably more viable if the political parties are each able to garner some support from all social classes and groups, even when a majority votes for one party. Sociologist William Kornhauser has argued that if the members of the working class are organized into labor unions, vote Democratic, belong predominantly to the same ethnic and civic groups, and are mostly Catholic; while, on the other hand, the middle class votes Republican, belongs to completely different ethnic and civic organizations, and is mostly Protestant, the cleavage of class so coincides with other affiliations that conflict is exacerbated and

consensus is difficult to achieve.[52] This returns to the argument for a pluralist society, but one in which the political parties (and other voluntary associations) develop memberships that cut across group identities, so that no one party or other group would have too strong a hold on the loyalties of the individual.

But again, the experience of European parties, in contrast to those in the United States, suggests that parties reflecting the basic cleavages of class (and sometimes of religion) do not necessarily generate a conflict beyond the scope of the electoral process to contain.

As Seymour Martin Lipset points out, the study of voting, one of the major research activities of political sociologists, has rarely been designed to investigate the problem of conflict and consensus.[53] Instead, most studies of voting have been studies of individual voting behavior, a social-psychological investigation of how the individual makes up his mind about voting. Such studies have explored the context of family and peer groups within which the individual engages in an interpersonal exchange about politics, leading to a gradual crystallization of voting preferences generally consistent with these. Many such studies have been of natural small groups, and they have been studies of the *voter* rather than of voting as a social process.[54]

Lipset also points out that these studies have emphasized cleavage along class, ethnic, and religious lines, and how the family and peer group socialize the person to commitments that reinforce that cleavage. Where persons are caught on cross-cleavage memberships—as workers who are Republicans, Protestants who are Democrats, Catholics who are Republicans—the cross-pressures they are subject to when class, religion, and ethnicity pull them in different directions more often than not result in their not voting; in effect, they opt not to choose and thus not to alienate themselves from their most intimate groups.[55]

Apathy and Alienation

In American elections two parties compete for votes within the same groups and classes, and only in national elections does even 60 percent of the electorate bother to vote. This fact is often both noted and lamented; there is perhaps no more frequently expressed value in American society than that everyone should vote.

But during the 1950s a different perspective emerged in American social science, one that argued that relative apathy was functional for democratic process, and that, conversely, very high levels of participation were not. According to Lipset, "an increase in the level of participation may reflect the *decline* of social cohesion and the breakdown of the democratic process, whereas a stable democracy may rest on the general belief that the outcome of an election will not make too great a difference in society.[56]

[52] See William Kornhauser, *The Politics of Mass Society* (New York: The Free Press, 1959), pp. 80–81.

[53] See Lipset, "Political Sociology," p. 92.

[54] The major voting studies are Bernard R. Berelson, Paul F. Lazarsfeld, and William N. McPhee, *Voting* (Chicago, Ill.: University of Chicago Press, 1954); Eugene Burdick and A.J. Brodbeck, eds., *American Voting Behavior* (New York: The Free Press, 1959); and Angus Campbell, Phillip E. Converse, Warren E. Miller, and D.E. Stokes, *The American Voter* (New York: John Wiley & Sons, Inc., 1960).

[55] This persistent observation was reported in the earliest of the voting studies. Compare Paul H. Lazarsfeld, Bernard Berelson, and Hazel Gaudet, *The People's Choice* (New York: Columbia University Press, 1948).

[56] See Seymour M. Lipset, "Political Sociology," p. 95.

We have then two apparently contrasting if not contradictory views. One view interprets low voting as an apathy that threatens the democratic process. The other view is that high voting is evidence of intense conflict, a threat to the democratic process. Each proceeds from a different assessment, not only of voting apathy but of the character of the politically apathetic.

The position that low voting and relative apathy is no threat, but very high voting is, makes two arguments. The first is that low voter turnout in an election may be evidence of no *intense* dissatisfaction with things as they are. But the more important argument defends moderate participation by projecting a negative view of those who participate but little in democratic elections. It distinguishes between regular voters and nonvoters, those who rarely if ever vote.

Nonvoters, it is asserted, are more likely than voters to be authoritarian in their outlook, to be indifferent to if not opposed to democratic values, to prefer "strong" (meaning authoritarian) leadership, and to oppose civil liberties for radicals and political dissidents. Nonvoters, then, are viewed as politically alienated, not only from the political process but from the democratic values that underlie it. To induce such people to vote may represent no actual gain in those conditions that make for a democratic order.

Studies of local elections, where voting normally runs quite low, are cited as evidence that any high turnout is the result of participation by those least committed to the local community. Thus, a high vote is also likely to be a negative vote, and evidence for this seems to come from the analysis of voting on such issues as school bonds and fluoridation, where a high turn-

out increases the negative vote and defeats the measure.[57]

The Powerless Apathetics

But other social scientists define the apathetic differently. They see the apathetic as alienated voters who cannot find in elections a solution to the problems that most concern them. For them, the two-party system offers too little choice, too little change from the status quo. Thus, the politically alienated are likely to be the socially and economically disadvantaged.

Electoral data support this argument in that participation in elections is lowest by the poorest and least educated. They do not see their interests, however they conceive them, as served by existing political parties and groups and by elections as contests for power and resolution of issues. They feel they are without power.[58]

Recently a number of social scientists have challenged this conventional view of so many social scientists that those voters of higher status are relatively more liberal and tolerant and those of lower status are illiberal and intolerant, a thesis about working-class authoritarianism first advanced by Lipset and long a source of controversy.[59]

A careful examination of Lipset's thesis of working-class authoritarianism raises three critical questions:

[57] For a brief review of such studies *see* Greer and Orleans, "Political Sociology," pp. 819–820; *see also* James S. Coleman, *Community Conflict* (New York: The Free Press, 1957).

[58] For an empirical study of the sense of powerlessness among municipal voters *see* Murray Levin, *The Alienated Voter: Politics in Boston* (New York: Holt, Rinehart and Winston, Inc., 1960).

[59] *See* Seymour M. Lipset, *Political Man* (Garden City, N.Y.: Doubleday & Company, Inc., 1960), Ch. IV, "Working-class Authoritarianism."

1. The argument is based on survey data from opinion polls, in which lower-class people always seem to answer questions in such a way as to appear more non-liberal and intolerant than the middle class. The educated strata are sophisticated enough to give the "right" answers to these questions and do not acknowledge any racial or religious bias. Lipset acknowledges, for example, that British workers admit to anti-Semitism and the middle class does not. However, it is the Labor Party that elected several Jewish members to Parliament—and from non-Jewish, working-class districts—whereas the middle class has elected no Jews. The evidence from social surveys on such highly intense matters as prejudice and related attitudes may often be unreliable.

2. Lipset lumps together working class, lower class, and lower strata and fails to make any rigorous distinction between a stable and integrated working class and an unintegrated lower class; the latter group has historically provided the source of the "know-nothings" who have often acted violently in situations of political and social stress.

3. A considerable amount of research seeking to test Lipset's thesis of working-class authoritarianism has failed to provide adequate documentation. At best, empirical results have been inconclusive. For example, assuming that a supportive position on the Vietnam War calling for escalation of military combat is consistent with a more authoritarian or non-liberal approach to politics, we find that in 1964 escalation was advocated more by whites than by blacks, by males than by females, by the young than by the old, by those in high-status occupations than by those in low-status ones, and by the better educated than by the less educated.[60] In 1968 the same differences held except that those of

high status had become more dove-ish.[61]

Locating authoritarian politics in the working class is not borne out adequately by data. One of Lipset's critics points out that his thesis assumes more of a liberalizing of attitudes through education than in fact occurs, and that he also underestimates middle- and upper-class authoritarianism.[62]

Apathy, then, is a concept that does not do justice to the problem of political participation. Full participation and high voter turnout may mean that the issue at stake strains the existing consensus in the community, producing high levels of negative voting, but, at the same time, such an election serves as a rough measure of the extent of the uncommitted and alienated, who normally find no reason for electoral participation.

This suggests an important question: Can a democratic order survive the alienation from politics of a large segment of its citizens? Although nonvoting by the alienated may conveniently contribute to the stability of the democratic process, this apathy is indicative of sources of dissension that the political process may be failing to resolve. As tensions grow and the number of alienated voters increase, a serious conflict may occur, fought out in other, possibly violent ways until a new basis for social order is achieved.

The New Alienated

Recent examination of both electoral and survey data suggests that an increasing

---

[60] See Richard Hamilton, "A Research Note on the Mass Support for Tough Military Initiatives," *American Sociological Review*, vol. 33 (June 1968), pp. 439–445.

[61] See James D. Wright, "The Working Class, Authoritarianism, and the War in Vietnam," *Social Problems*, vol. 20 (Fall 1972), pp. 133–150.

[62] See Wright, *op. cit.*, pp. 146–147. Richard Hamilton has undertaken a very detailed review of a vast amount of survey data and finds Lipset's thesis unsupported. *See* his *Class and Politics in the United States*, Ch. 11, pp. 399–506.

number of citizens are detaching themselves from the parties, are splitting their tickets, or are not bothering to vote. A Gallup poll in 1971, for example, reported that these percentages of Americans responded in this manner when asked their party affiliation:

Democratic	44 percent
Republican	25 percent
Independents	31 percent

An increasingly larger number of voters split their tickets. More than 50 percent of the ballots cast are now split. In 1968 a Gallup Poll reported that 84 percent of the voters said they voted for the man, not the party.

Nor are these independents the same as those formerly identified as the alienated: low in social status and less educated or politically uninvolved. They are the more educated, increasingly a larger segment of the middle class.

Voting as one form of political participation never has been a major activity of American adults, except for presidential elections once every four years. In the post-World War II years, the turnout has been less than two out of three adults:

1952	62.7 percent
1956	60.4 percent
1960	63.5 percent
1964	62.0 percent
1968	60.8 percent
1972	53.7 percent

The 1972 election shows a striking decline in voter participation, not yet explained by a systematic study. About 72 percent of the eligible were registered, so that one of four of these (in contrast to the usual one in five) did not vote. President Nixon's "landslide" victory was gained by winning just under 61 percent of the votes cast. That means that no more than one adult in three gave President Nixon what his supporters have called a mandate.

In the 1972 election, as in past ones, women voted less than men did, and blacks less than whites. Furthermore, despite the great emphasis on the new youth vote, young voters, as in past elections, voted to a lesser extent than did others. Less than half of the new voter group, ages 18–20, claimed to have voted; and the age group 18–24 had the largest proportion not registered—about 41 percent (*see* Table 15.1).

TABLE 15.1   Reported Registration and Voting by Age and Race: November 1972

Age and Race	Percent Reported Registered	Percent Reported Voted
All voters		
18–24 years old	58.9	49.6
25 years old and over	75.3	65.9
White voters		
18–24 years old	60.6	51.9
25 years old and over	76.1	67.2
Black voters		
18–24 years old	47.7	34.7
25 years old and over	70.5	57.1

Note: These are inflated figures, for they represent what people said about their registration and voting. If the figures for all voters were accurate, then 63 percent voted in November 1972. But only 53.7 voted in the presidential election. What is important about these figures (assuming all are inflated) are the *differences* by race and age.

Source: U.S. Bureau of the Census, Series P-20, no. 244, "Voter Registration in November, 1972." (Washington, D.C.: Government Printing Office, 1972).

ON POLITICAL ECONOMY: A FINAL NOTE

To study society the sociologist must study politics, for a society, as Max Weber told us, is a delicate balance among conflicting forces, an arena of groups contending for dominance in status and power. Conflict is always present in society.

Social scientists once studied politics as a process separate to a large extent from other processes, especially the economic. The liberal ideal of capitalism and democracy, the economic and the political, as two structures that touched each other but very little was always more an ideal than a reality. But this no longer applies in any Capitalist society. The economy and the polity are thoroughly interwoven with one another. We made this point at the outset as we examined the economic structure in Chapter 14. It is useful to stress it again in ending this brief examination of the political.

The dominance of the economic and political in human life surely needs no emphasizing. But the lesson for students of society should be clear: No understanding of modern society can be carried out without starting with the structures of domination that originate in the economic and political processes, as well as the modes of stratification that accompany them.

SUMMARY

Power is *decision-making* and *authority* is the right to make decisions; that is, *legitimate* power. However, other actors, by influence and pressure, participate in decisions; still others, mostly of low status, are excluded.

The *nation-state* organizes a large population into a modern society; it claims binding authority and a legitimate monopoly of force within a territory. A conventional view of the state sees it as carrying out four *functions*: (1.) maintaining internal peace, (2.) promoting the national interest among other nations, (3.) controlling its members in pursuit of collective goals, and (4.) compromising among various interests in making public policy. A *Marxian* view, however, sees the state as an instrument for maintaining class domination.

Political parties are organizations which mobilize citizens to get control of the state. There are one-party states and multiple-party states. The American two-party system manages to restrict ideological competition; it is the only party system in Western nations not to develop a party of the left.

Parapolitical groups are citizen groups that lobby on behalf of interests and promote various issues.

Rule by *elites*, even in democratic societies, is the claim of an influential body of literature which insists *oligarchy* is inevitable — an "iron law" — in all organizations. Recent sociological literature has presented both elite and non-elite (*pluralist*) versions of power in American communities and, more recently, in American society.

Alexis de Tocqueville thought that in the United States *decentralized* power was possible in a *pluralist* society, one in which such organizations as the *local, self-governing community* and the *voluntary association* could mediate between the unorganized citizen and the powerful state. But local government is no longer a source of much power and voluntary associations are not equally influential. Consequently, new ideas for decentralization include *participatory democracy,* a *decentralized* economy, and citizen action groups to hold *accountable* those in authority.

Political participation in a democratic society varies with class: Those higher in class generally participate more. *Voting* is, according to one version, a means to settle issues and achieve consensus. There is, however, a theoretical issue over whether *apathy* promotes or hinders democracy. Some social scientists argue for only moderate participation, on the ground that high participation by the lower class and the alienated threatens democracy. Others have disputed the evidence behind this claim.

New trends show less commitment to American parties and more ticket-splitting among voters.

The combination of closely related political and economic processes — the political economy — and the associated system of stratification are basic to an understanding of modern society.

Suggested Readings

Michael Aiken and Paul Mott, eds., *The Structure of Community Power* (New York: Random House, Inc., 1970). A collection of articles assessing what we now know about community power.

Robert Alford, *Party and Society* (Chicago: Rand-McNally & Company, 1963). A study of the party system in the four Anglo-American democracies: Britain, Australia, Canada, and the United States.

C. George Benello and Dimitrios Roussopoulos, eds., *The Case for Participatory Democracy: Some Prospects for a Radical Society* (New York: The Viking Press, Inc., 1971). A collection of challenging essays on the possibilities of participatory democracy.

Murray Bookchin, *Post-scarcity Anarchism* (Berkeley, Calif.: The Ramparts Press, 1971). A radical, but anarchist and libertarian (not Marxian) approach to reorganizing society.

Angus Campbell, Phillip E. Converse, Warren E. Miller, and D.E. Stokes, *The American Voter* (New York: John Wiley & Sons, Inc., 1960). An analysis of what we know about how the voter makes up his mind.

Robert A. Dahl, *Who Governs? Democracy and Power in an American City* (New Haven, Conn.: Yale University Press, 1961). The influential work that challenged Hunter's study and insisted community power was not concentrated in an elite.

G. William Domhoff, *The Higher Circles: Governing Class in America* (New York: Random House, Inc., 1970). The most recent sociological work to provide empirical evidence for the existence of a national ruling class.

Richard Hamilton, *Class and Politics in the United States* (New York: John Wiley & Sons, Inc., 1972). A thorough analysis of survey data on political attitudes, which challenges some sociological received wisdom.

Floyd Hunter, *Community Power Structure* (Chapel Hill, N.C.: University of North

Carolina Press, 1953). The first and most influential of the studies on community power, asserting there is a community power elite.

Seymour M. Lipset, *Political Man* (Garden City, N.Y.: Doubleday & Company, Inc., 1960). A series of essays by an influential political sociologist, concerned with the conditions for democracy, authoritarianism, consensus, and other issues.

Donald R. Matthews and James W. Prothro, *Negroes and the New Southern Politics* (New York: Harcourt Brace Jovanovich, 1966). A thorough analysis of how blacks have begun to participate in politics in the South.

Robert Michels, *Political Parties* (New York: The Free Press, 1949). The work that advanced the famous thesis of the "iron law of oligarchy."

Ralph Miliband, *The State in Capitalist Society: An Analysis of the Western System of Power* (New York: Basic Books, Inc., 1969). A penetrating analysis of the relationship between capitalism and the democratic state.

C. Wright Mills, *The Power Elite* (New York: Oxford University Press, 1956). The first work to describe the outlines of a national power elite in America.

Gaetano Mosca, *The Ruling Class* (New York: McGraw-Hill Book Company, Inc., 1939). A classic study proclaiming the inevitability of a ruling class in human society.

Arnold M. Rose, *The Power Structure: Political Processes in American Society* (New York: Oxford University Press, 1967). The most influential work from the pluralist perspective, challenging Mills' thesis of a power elite.

Alexis de Tocqueville, *Democracy in America,* vols. I and II (New York: Vintage Books, 1954). The great, unsurpassed classic on the problems and prospects for democracy in the United States.

James Weinstein, *The Corporate Ideal in the Liberal State: 1900–1918* (Boston, Mass.: The Beacon Press, 1969). An historical documentation of the relation between the liberal, reforming state and a dominant Capitalist class.

. . . the tension between the value-spheres of
"science" and the sphere of the "holy" is un-
bridgeable.
— *Max Weber*

Chapter 16

Religion
and Science

Religion and science can be viewed as different ways—sometimes competing and even in conflict, sometimes complementary—to interpret the
natural order of things and to explain and come to terms with the events
of our lives. Since both are viewed as major institutional structures in
modern society, and since they provide important ways to look at life,
both must be examined by the student of society.

At one time it seemed that science had emerged triumphant in a "war"
with religion, and that religion would eventually fade away as scientific
thinking was inculcated into modern populations. Then there seemed to
be a new accommodation in which religion acknowledged the domain of
science in explaining all natural things; it occupied a more restricted
sphere of its own, primarily concerned with finding a larger set of meanings for human existence, meanings that an empirical science did not even
claim to supply.

Yet this never became a fully dominant position. Many people still felt
that religion was unnecessary and archaic. In turn, fundamentalists—those
who make a literal interpretation of the Bible—never conceded the validity
of scientific explanations over biblical ones, as evidenced by the renewal

of the debate over evolution (based on Darwin's theory) and creation (based on the Book of Genesis in the Bible) in the education of children.

Even this accommodation now seems unsettled. The prestige of science has been damaged, particularly among younger generations, in the light of concern over a potentially imminent nuclear holocaust, as well as other doubts relating to population growth and ecological devastation. The triumph of science has made these things possible, as it has the dominance of the technological over the human—or so it seems to many people today. The emergence of counter cultures is one expression of this declining respect for science, including, as it does, a renewed interest in Eastern wisdom and the occult. In this context religion, too, becomes newly meaningful for many, albeit often in nontraditional forms.

In this chapter we will look first at religion, for there was religion before there was science. Then, after viewing what the sociologist sees when he examines science, we will undertake an effort at assessing the changing status of science and religion in contemporary society.

RELIGION AND SOCIETY
vast diff. in Rel. & Christianity.

How to explain or even define the phenomenon of religion has probably yielded less scholarly agreement than almost any other matter studied. Religion is so diverse in historical development, so culturally varied, that definitions developed from our own Western experience often fail to encompass it adequately.

What comes out of these scholarly efforts, however, is the recognition that religion emerges from common experience in society and offers explanations that transcend

whatever ordinary, factual knowledge is available. These are explanations expressed in symbolic forms and acts which relate a people to the ultimate conditions of their existence.

We have no historical or archaeological reason to believe that religion began full blown. Instead, it developed slowly along with the evolution of human society, and in its more primitive forms—itself an evolutionary development beyond the earliest pre-religious people—possessed no organization or special roles (no church or clergy), only a communal sharing in rituals that gave expression to religious symbols.[1]

As religion and society evolve, a sense of sacredness takes concrete form in objects and images that become sacred, whether these are persons, animals, or natural objects, human artifacts or symbolic expressions. The sacred also becomes expressed for the living in *ritual*, where behavior gives objective form to mood and feeling. A division between the sacred and the *profane* eventually marks off religious from nonreligious activity.[2]

The Functions of Religion

Of all possible ways to understand the connection between religion and society the *functional* interpretation has been the dominant one. It asserts that every society has a number of necessary conditions that it must successfully meet in order to survive, and one of these is the cohesion or solidarity of its members. Religion, it is asserted, provides this function for society.

According to the functionalists, two

---

[1] *See* Robert Bellah, "Religious Evolution," *American Sociological Review*, vol. 29 (June 1964), pp. 358–374.

[2] *See* Peter Berger, *The Sacred Canopy: Elements of a Sociological Theory of Religion* (Garden City, N.Y.: Doubleday & Company, Inc., 1967), p. 26.

things occur. First, sharing the same religious interpretation of the meaning of life unites a people in a cohesive and binding moral order. But these people are also members of the same society; the religious order and the social order have the same members. Therefore, secondly, the integration of society is sustained when a society is supported by a moral order, the ultimate values of which are ritualistically expressed in a religion shared in common by the members of that society.

Just such a notion was stressed by Émile Durkheim in his classic study of religion. He defined religion as:

. . . a unified system of beliefs and practices relative to sacred things, that is to say, things set apart and forbidden—beliefs and practices which unite into one single moral community called a Church, all those who adhere to them.[3]

When the *moral* community of believers is identical with the social community, as was common in more traditional societies, then the symbolism of the sacred supports the more mundane aspects of social life. Religion then *legitimizes* society; it provides sacred sanction for the social order and for its basic values and meanings.

In traditional societies the religious and nonreligious spheres of life are not sharply differentiated. But in complex, highly differentiated societies, religion and society are not synonymous. The emergence of different modes of life experience leads to different meanings of life, producing a religious differentiation. The all-encompassing church gives way to competing religious groups. Religion may still provide cohesion, but now only for the subgroups in society.

[3] See Émile Durkheim, *The Elementary Forms of Religious Life,* Joseph Ward Swain, trans. (New York: The Free Press, 1948), p. 47.

Religion can also be a source of and contributor to conflict. The history of Christianity in Europe, and of other religions in Asia, testifies to religious strife. Religious wars are invariably brutal and bloody contests, for the commitment to a religion can lead to a struggle to the death with others not of the same faith. Recently, the tragic events in Ireland testify to some extent to the degree to which religious hatred can add fuel to seemingly irreconcilable conflicts.

Religion as Social Control

Whether it is fear of fire and brimstone, so long prevalent among Christians, or the injunction to do good works, religious belief can influence the conduct of those who believe. The recognition that religions can control human action and keep people "in line" makes it a useful instrument for a ruling class. Throughout history these classes have consciously recognized this particular value. Frank E. Manuel said that in the eighteenth century even skeptics and atheists recognized that "religion was a mechanism which inspired terror, but terror useful for the preservation of society . . ."[4]

This recognition was carried into the twentieth century. Such prominent Protestants as industrialist Mark Hanna, railroad baron James Hill, and President William Howard Taft found in the Catholicism of millions of immigrant workers a strong bulwark against socialism and "anarchy."[5] Hill explained his donation of

[4] See Frank E. Manuel, *The Eighteenth Century Confronts the Gods* (Cambridge, Mass.: Harvard University Press, 1959), p. 240.

[5] See Louis Schneider, "Problems in the Sociology of Religion," in Robert E.L. Faris, ed., *Handbook of Modern Sociology* (Chicago, Ill.: Rand-McNally & Company, 1964), p. 784.

a million dollars for the establishment of a Catholic seminary on the grounds that, with "millions of foreigners pouring into this country" the Catholic Church is "the only authority they fear or respect."[6]

While conservatives have valued religion for this protective function, radicals have countered with a strong reason for defining religion as a bulwark of the established order. Marx's life-long associate, Frederick Engels, for example, once noted that the bourgeoisie in England discovered that religion could make the masses "submissive to the behests of the masters it had pleased God to place over them."[7] And Marx once called religion the opium of the people.

Religion as Psychotherapy

In twentieth-century America there is another way in which religion is viewed instrumentally; it becomes a supporting psychology, a form of psychotherapy. Religion is viewed in upbeat terms, and God is conceived of as a humane and considerate God; such a hopeful perspectives turn away from the older Christian conception of a stern and demanding God.

This "psychologizing" of religion has created an "Americanized religion" (as sociologists Louis Schneider and Sanford M. Dornbusch have called it), for which someone like Norman Vincent Peale, a prominent Protestant clergyman, with his "power of positive thinking," serves as a typical example.[8] "Americanized religion" provides peace of mind, and promises prosperity and success in life, as well as effective and happy human relations. It is thus a source of security and confidence, of happiness and success *in this world*.

But it does not stop there. Pastoral counseling—for which clergymen get psychological training—is apparently a more significant function of American clergy than it is of the European. According to one careful observer:

The more routine but flourishing engagement of religion in the affairs of a very large proportion of Americans consists in their submitting hurts and hopes to the care and help of pastors. Gauged by both consumer demand and by clergymen's self-evaluation, the chief business of religion in the United States is now—as it has probably long been—the cure of souls.[9]

The religious practitioner has moved into a relevant place in the mental-health field as a helping professional. Consequently, pastoral counseling has become so much a specialty that a national organization, the American Association of Pastoral Counselors, has been formed to set professional standards, regulate practice, and certify practitioners.

The Organization of Religion

To the Western mind religion is always socially organized, and thus faith and creed become institutionalized in social structures. But religious structures vary considerably in size, form, and in their relation to society.

Church and Sect

The German scholar Ernst Troeltsch distinguished between *church* and *sect* as two

[6] *See* E. Digby Baltzell, *Philadelphia Gentlemen* (New York: The Free Press, 1958), p. 224.

[7] *See* Karl Marx and Frederick Engels, *On Religion* (Moscow: Foreign Language Publishing House, 1955), p. 303.

[8] *See* Louis Schneider and Sanford M. Dornbusch, *Popular Religion* (Chicago, Ill.: University of Chicago Press, 1958).

[9] *See* William A. Clebsch, "American Religion and the Cure of Souls," in Donald R. Cutler, ed., *The Religious Situation: 1969* (Boston, Mass.: The Beacon Press, 1969), p. 993.

basic types of religious organization.[10] (Since by *church*, Troeltsch meant something more limited than the general meaning usually conveyed by that term, we will follow the lead of other sociologists and substitute for it the Latin word, *ecclesia*.)

The ecclesia is defined, fundamentally, by its acceptance of society with all its imperfections. It does not fight society, nor does it withdraw. It is both *in* and *of* the world and seeks to be a power within the world. This leads the ecclesia to engage in a close set of relationships with the secular institutions of the society, particularly the government.

As a universal church the ecclesia defines as members all those born within a given territory from all social classes. This inclusiveness—of a large and diverse religious community—requires large-scale organization, formal and hierarchical, a religious bureaucracy with a chain of command from top to bottom.

By definition, the ecclesia is a universal world church. But this is an ideal type which is only approximated by historical cases. The Roman Catholic Church in the Middle Ages is perhaps nearest to the type, at least in the Western world. The Anglican Church in England and the Lutheran Church in Germany are examples of national ecclesia, contrasting with the international scope of the Roman Catholic Church.

The *sect* is typically a small and exclusive religious group whose members are not born into it but voluntarily join it. Those who choose to belong to a sect must be accepted on its rigorous terms. (To be sure, the children of sect members are often thoroughly socialized to a commitment early in life, particularly when the

sect's way of life isolates them from other contacts.) Its discipline extends into personal lives. What it lacks in controlling organization (and sects develop only a rudimentary formal structure), it more than makes up for in fervent commitment to a belief.

Typically, sects are *in* but not *of* society, for they reject worldliness. Some sects take a radical stance toward secular government by refusing to pay taxes, to serve in any civil or political capacity, or even to take oaths. (Jehovah's Witnesses are a contemporary sect often in difficulty with government for such reasons.)

While some sects have taken a militant posture toward the world, seeking to change it, others have been passive and withdrawing, seeking to remain as removed from society as possible. The Old Order Amish in Pennsylvania and the Hutterites in the Midwestern states and Canada, for example, reject and withdraw from the world.[11]

Denomination and Cult

Sociologists of religion have found it useful to add two other types of religious organization, *denomination* and *cult*. The *denomination* falls between ecclesia and sect; it is a stable church that does not fight or withdraw from the world but, unlike the ecclesia, does not seek to control it either and does not monopolize a territory. It is often a former sect that has made peace with the world, frequently when its members are no longer disadvantaged or of marginal status in society.

The *cult* is a small and almost formless religious organization, grouped around a charismatic leader. It appears most fre-

---

[10] *See* Ernst Troeltsch, *The Social Teachings of the Christian Churches* (New York: The Macmillan Company, 1950).

[11] For an examination of sects in modern society *see* Bryan Wilson, *Sects and Society* (London: William Heinemann, Ltd., 1961).

quently in urban centers, where its appeal is often to those who feel lost and without a sense of belonging in an impersonal and anonymous city life. Cults flourish in slums and among minorities, and can be found, for example, among the "storefront" churches in ghetto areas. The Black Muslims began in this way in Detroit in the 1930s. But cults also appeal to middle-class people, who experience loneliness and frustration just as readily as the poor.

Religion in Society

These distinctions between ecclesia and sect, and between denomination and cult, are intended to draw attention to the inherent tension between the sacred concerns of religion and the secular interests of society. Religion constantly draws closer to society and then draws away. Religion accepts society, ignores it, or rejects it.

Sects, for example, draw their members mostly from the less attached and more disadvantaged; in this way, religion gives expression to the social experiences of groups and strata within society. As sects become denominations, dissident religious groups come to terms with society, and tensions lessen as the worldly status of its members improves. But new sects and cults constantly appear among those whom society materially and socially disadvantages, or among those who find no rewarding sense of meaning in life. There is thus constant religious *movement*, an increasing or lessening of tension between the sacred and the secular, between religion and society. Religion never completely embraces society, nor does it completely reject it.

Religion and Stratification

Churches cannot avoid the simple fact that stratification separates the population into higher and lower statuses; and reli-

gious organization undeniably mirrors the class structure of society. Whatever their doctrinal position may be, churches usually develop a membership drawn disproportionately from one social class or another. Membership in church, like membership in a voluntary association, varies directly with social class: higher status, higher membership; lower status, lower membership.[12]

For reasons that have less to do with doctrine and more to do with historical origins such denominations as the Episcopalians have been high-status churches in America. The Presbyterians have been middle-class churches; and such large denominations as the Baptists have been lower-middle and working-class churches. But this statement must be qualified. Though the Episcopal Church is a high-status church, it enrolls many middle- and working-class members. A report of the National Council of Churches, for example, showed that about 42 percent of the Episcopal membership was in the working class, despite its strong appeal to high-status people.[13] The major, large denominations always draw membership from all social classes; they only differ from one another in the proportions drawn from each class.

The Suburban Church

When the middle class moves to the suburbs, the churches follow their most consistent parishioners. In many instances congregations move—lock, stock, and barrel—from the city to the suburb, selling their former church buildings to those left behind, which often means to black people.

This movement to the suburbs often re-

[12] *See* Nicholas J. Demerath III, *Social Class in American Protestantism* (Chicago, Ill.: Rand-McNally & Company, 1965), p. 4.

[13] *See* Demerath, *op. cit.,* p. 2.

Figure 16.1 Mennonites, like these Pennsylvanians, favor plain living and are opposed to serving in public office or doing military service. *(Monkmeyer, Mark Chester.)*

moves the middle class from the harsher problems that beset those who remain within the city—those of race and poverty, for example. The church that follows them also turns from such problems, organizing itself around the central interests of the middle-class congregation: family and teen-agers, leisure, and the concerns of morality and values typical of the affluent. The church is captive to the suburban interests and perspectives of its memberships.[14]

The Church and the Working Class

The greatest failure of the Christian mission has been its inability to hold the industrial working classes within the church. The estrangement of the working class from the Christian churches has been greater in Europe than in the United States,

but religious data from Great Britain, France, Italy, Germany, Belgium, *and* Latin America provide detailed support of the idea that the working class has largely abandoned any significant attachment to or involvement in the church, Catholic or Protestant.

There have been two basic reasons given for the inability of organized religion to attract the working classes in industrial society. The first of these—stressed by American sociologists—sees a cultural affinity between church atmosphere and middle-class life style, an atmosphere in which people of lower social status feel strange and out of place, even unwanted.[15]

[14] Such is the theme of G. Winter's study, *The Suburban Captivity of the Churches* (Garden City, N.Y.: Doubleday & Company, Inc., 1961).

[15] *See* James West, *Plainville, U.S.A.* (New York: Columbia University Press, 1945); W. Lloyd Warner and Associates, *Democracy in Jonesville* (New York: Harper and Row, 1949); and Robert J. Havighurst and H. Gerton Morgan, *The Social History of a Warboom Community* (New York: Longman's, Green & Company., Inc., 1951).

These studies have stressed how much the liturgy, sermon, the pattern of Sunday School, women's guilds, youth groups, and the like reflect the tastes and standards, as well as the interests and concerns, of the middle class.

Religion and Radical Politics

European sociologists give a second reason for the inability of the church to hold the working class, based on the observation that where radical politics flourish among workers church membership declines. French sociologists E. Pin and A. Dansette, for example, assert that the French worker is not integrated into modern society, that he suffers from a sense of an unjust world, and that his political orientation is still the anti-Capitalist ideology of the nineteenth century. French workers vote Communist in large numbers, and in equally large numbers stay away from the Catholic Church. Pin argues that French workers are estranged from the church precisely because it gives no promise of pursuing justice *in this world*.[16]

A similar pattern comes from other European societies. Surveys from Britain and the Netherlands, for example, reveal that the working class is less likely to attend church or even hold religious views than are members of other social classes, and that those who are supporters of Socialist and Communist parties are less religious than supporters of conservative parties.[17] Sociologist Rodney Stark has examined British data and asserts that "the

strength of lower-class radicalism in Britain partly accounts for lower-class religious apathy."[18]

In some other countries, the United States in particular, the estrangement of workers from religion is not so pronounced. Indeed, the Catholic Church in the United States has managed to hold its immigrant, working-class members very well. This may be because, for the European immigrant, the church was a haven and source of both spiritual and material assistance when so little else was available. These immigrants were very largely from rural, peasant backgrounds, among whom religion had always been strong. Nonetheless, though there is considerable variation from one society to another, the general pattern remains clear and is supported consistently by statistics: Those of lower social status are least attracted to the Christian churches.

Working-class Sects

In the United States, Great Britain, and some few other countries where Protestantism has been dominant there is another response of the working class and others of low social status—they break off and regroup in newly created small churches of their own. Each time this happens, another sect is born. Such sects are often hostile to the dominant churches and reject the world as essentially corrupt. Yet, their energies go into apolitical activities, and they find their hope not in justice in this world but in a just heaven or in a milennium to be brought about by the second coming of Christ. As a consequence they drain off

---

[16] For a review of the work of these French sociologists *see* Louis Schneider, "Problems in the Sociology of Religion," pp. 796–799.

[17] *See* Charles Glock and Rodney Stark, *Religion and Society in Tension* (Chicago, Ill.: Rand-McNally & Company, 1965), Chs. 10 and 11.

[18] *See* Rodney Stark, "Class, Radicalism, and Religious Involvement in Great Britain," *American Sociological Review*, vol. 29 (October 1964), p. 706.

potential radical commitment by alienated workers. They are therefore viewed by radical parties as competitive.

An influential English historian, E.P. Thompson, has suggested that one important reason for much less revolutionary action in England, compared with that in other European nations, was the English workers' attraction to Nonconformist religion, especially Methodism.[19] Sociologist Robert Blauner accounts for the failure of labor unions and labor-oriented politics among Southern white workers by pointing to the growth of evangelical sects in that region.[20]

Religion among the Oppressed

Sects and cults have more often than not appeared first among social groups subject to conditions of oppression and cultural destruction. Frequently these are racial and cultural minorities overrun by powerful industrial and military powers, unable to continue their traditional way of life yet not able or even permitted to share fully in the life of their conquerors.

Religious responses to such conditions are often *nativistic* and *revivalistic,* proclaiming the restoration of the traditional, native ways and the invaders to be driven from the land. The "Cargo cults" among the natives of Melanesia, which began in the late nineteenth century as a mode of resistance to white control, is a notable example of such a movement.[21]

As the native saw it, the white men did not manufacture any of the goods they needed but received abundant supplies by ship; in return they merely sent back scraps of paper. According to the legend which grew up, these cargoes were made by the natives' own ancestors and were stolen from them by the whites according to some secret. Prophets of the new cults appeared and propounded a system of belief and ritual by which this secret could be learned, the cargoes secured, native independence re-established, and the white man defeated.

In the 1870s and again in the 1890s a Ghost Dance spread among such Indian tribes as the Cheyenne, the Arapaho, the Pawnee, and the Sioux, promising to restore the buffalo and the old ways of life. The movement ended once and for all at the Battle of Wounded Knee. Among the Utes and Shoshones of the Rocky Mountain area a Sun Dance cult emerged, with a ceremony from which these Indians obtained a sense of power and redemption despite their oppression by whites.[22]

While such religious protest sects among the powerless do not succeed in overthrowing their conquerors, and are usually impermanent, they nevertheless have an impact. At their beginnings they provide a sense of dignity and personal integrity

[19] E.P. Thompson, *The Making of the English Working Class* (New York: Vintage Books, 1966).

[20] *See* Robert Blauner, "Industrialization and Labor Response: The Case of the American South," *Berkeley Publications in Society and Institutions* (Summer 1958). *See also* Liston Pope's *Millhands and Preachers* (New Haven, Conn.: Yale University Press), which remains a useful American study examining the formation of sects by working-class people in the South.

[21] The foremost study of the "Cargo" cults is by Peter Worsley, *The Trumpet Shall Sound: A Study of the "Cargo" Cults in Melanesia* (London: MacGibbon & Kee, 1957).

[22] *See* James Mooney, *The Ghost-dance Religion and the Sioux Outbreak of 1890* (Chicago, Ill.: University of Chicago Press, 1965); and Joseph G. Jorgensen, *The Sun Dance Religion: Power for the Powerless* (Chicago, Ill.: University of Chicago Press, 1972). *See also* Vittorio Lanternari, Lisa Sergio, trans., *The Religions of the Oppressed: A Study of Modern Messianic Cults* (New York: Alfred A. Knopf, 1963).

for people oppressed and often treated without respect. They enable these people better to survive as persons, thus escaping the personal despair that invites personal disorganization, so often evident in alcoholism, suicide, and the like.[23]

In time, according to sociologist Milton Yinger, these sects produce other types of movements. One is a more accommodative kind, accepting the impossibility of restoring traditional ways and often calling for peace, reform, and personal morality. The original protest sect, then, has shaped new values and has served a "bridging function" by contributing "to the breaking of ties to a crumbling old order and to orienting to the new order in a way that helps individuals and groups to maintain a sense of control and of dignity."[24]

Religion and Race in the United States

When revolt and protest by native peoples took religious form, as we have seen, religion could be radical rather than conservative in its implications. In North America the overall effect has to be seen as largely conservative, even though radicalism is also present.

When slavery began in the American South, slaveholders came to view religion as an effective means of social control, and so slaves were Christianized. According to a noted historian:

Through religious instruction the bondsmen learned that slavery had divine sanction, that insolence was as much an offense against God as against the temporal master. They received

the Biblical command that servants should obey their masters, and they heard of the punishments awaiting the disobedient slave in the hereafter.[25]

When slavery ended, the black church became central to black life, the one unique organization usually safe from white invasion, the nearest thing to an untouchable sanctity.[26] Consequently, and since few opportunities for leadership existed, capable blacks were disproportionately attracted to the ministry; and black clergy were leaders of black society to an extent never attained by their white counterparts. The historic record of black churches for a century has been one of being largely accommodative, yet also invariably central to black protest and militancy.

The black church sought to turn its parishioners into black puritans, rigorous upholders of the puritanic virtues of abstention from sex, liquor, and gambling. It has been basic in the construction of life styles of sobriety and respectable behavior, particularly for middle-class blacks. Thus, one significant effect of the Christian religion on blacks has been to promote traditional Protestant morality and so to make an underprivileged group more amenable and conforming to the dominant culture.

At the same time religious faith made it possible for black people to sustain a sense of personal dignity and worth. It sustained a capacity to endure indignities and hardships by taking seriously the Christian belief that "the meek shall inherit the earth." Reward in an afterlife became a reward for people that otherwise could have found no

[23] This is the interpretation offered by Milton Yinger, *Sociology Looks at Religion* (New York: The Macmillan Company, 1961), Ch. 2.

[24] *See* Yinger, *op. cit.*, p. 43.

[25] *See* Kenneth Stampp, *The Peculiar Institution* (New York: Alfred A. Knopf, 1956), p. 158.

[26] *See* E. Franklin Frazier, *The Negro Church in America* (New York: Schocken Books, Inc., 1964).

legitimacy or even sense in the conditions of their existence, for there was certainly no reward in this life.

Yet such Christian dignity could produce political passivity. Sociologist Gary Marx found that many black Christians avoided demonstrations, even though they wanted integration to take place.[27] They believed that, since God was on their side, they did not need to do anything on their own. Marx found that the more religious blacks were less militant, and that the more militant ones were less religious.

Nonetheless, many religious blacks have been militant. The black church was central to the civil rights action during the 1960s. It was the meeting place for protest; and black ministers were major figures among the civil-rights leadership, particularly in the South. Many of the protest songs, such as "We Shall Overcome," are secularized versions of hymns; and their very mood and style is that of the spiritual. It is no accident that such a major civil-rights leader as Martin Luther King was a minister.

Religion: Radical and Conservative

Religion, now and in the past, obeys the biblical injunction: "Render unto Caesar the things that are Caesar's." Even when a religious sect rejects the world, it may yet endure hardships patiently, believing that "the meek shall inherit the earth," as we have seen.

Yet we have said that there is always a basic tension between religion and the secular world, and a reforming and even revolutionary impulse in religion never seems to be extinguished. However buried

under conformity to secular order, reform manages to break out and seek again to change the world.

Religion as a Culture

Max Weber always understood religion to be a set of meanings by which people interpreted their social lives and their societies, and sought to alter or adjust to religion or even reject it. Religion not only interpreted the world it provided an orientation toward ethical conduct; it helped shape the world, even as it, too, was fashioned by its encounter with the world. Whatever its organizational features may be, religion is primarily belief and perspective and value.[28]

Weber undertook a monumental effort to demonstrate that ideas were not merely a reflection of human behavior and organization but that they *interacted* with what Marx called the "material forces" to be *a* (but never the only) determinative force in shaping human society. For his demonstration Weber chose religion in the realm of ideas; for the realm of action he chose the economic.

The Protestant Ethic and the Spirit of Capitalism is but one of several works that Weber wrote pertaining to a specific problem, the emergence of rational capitalism.[29] His studies of religion in Europe, China, and in India explored the reasons why capitalism emerged or was blocked from

[27] *See* Gary T. Marx, *Protest and Prejudice: A Study of Belief in the Black Community* (New York: Harper and Row, 1967).

[28] *See* Max Weber, *The Sociology of Religion* (Boston, Mass.: The Beacon Press, 1963).

[29] *See* Max Weber, *The Protestant Ethic and the Spirit of Capitalism* (New York: Charles Scribner's Sons, 1958). Other works are *The Religion of China* (New York: The Free Press, 1951); *Ancient Judaism* (New York: The Free Press, 1952); *The Religion of India* (New York: The Free Press, 1958).

development. In each case he found reasons in the character of religion as a set of fundamental meanings that led people to favor or disfavor certain modes of action, such as the type of economic conduct that produced capitalism. In each society the religious outlook on life produced an economic ethic, a religiously sanctioned standard of economic conduct. The emergence of Protestantism in Christian Europe led to an ethic that encouraged the kind of economic behavior which supported the emergence of rational capitalism. But in China and India religion discouraged this same kind of economic behavior.

The Protestant Ethic

The religious revolt generally known as Protestantism ushered in a period of significant breaks from the hitherto secure unity of Christendom. Some of the new sects that broke away were both socially and religiously radical.

To these people revolutionary preachings by such men as John Calvin and John Knox provided a new religious perspective. Calvin's teachings were religiously radical in their central challenge to a basic tenet of Catholic doctrine: that the church, as the valid Christian ecclesiastical system, was the duly authorized administrator of sacraments.

Calvin argued that the granting of sacraments could not influence whether or not a person would lead an eternal life in heaven. The Catholic faithfuls' reliance on Mary and on saints was disputed—and criticized. Only God, said Calvin, knew who was saved and who was eternally damned, and the intervention of no others, mortal or immortal—priests and bishops, Mary, Jesus, or saints—would change it. This God of Calvinism was a stern and ter-

rible God who had *predestined* men to either heaven, if they were the *elect*, or hell, and neither their individual good works nor sacramental grace would save them.

Belief in predestination created for the Calvinist an anxious concern about his own unchangeable eternal fate. He possessed a terrible fear of hell and eternal damnation; and he was saddled with the frightening necessity of facing God alone, without the intervention of the church. In the face of this fear he understandably sought some evidence of his predestined fate. But instead of being frozen into inactivity, Calvinists engaged in an active campaign against the external world, warning the powerful that they were in danger of eternal doom.

Although Calvinists believed that people were predestined to a given eternal fate, and could not change it, yet it mattered to them how one lived one's life. They insisted that each person should act as if he were one of the elect and live his life for the greater glory of God.

Central to their belief was the Protestant conception of a religious theory of signs. Calvinists came to argue that one's earthly fate was a sign of one's eternal fate. Accordingly, prosperity in the world signified election or salvation, whereas poverty and worldly failure signified an eternal damnation.

The consequences of this belief were revolutionary. Calvinists practiced industry, self-denial, and thrift. They considered it sinful to indulge themselves in worldly goods or to lust after pleasures. They became what Weber called "inner-worldly ascetics" by exercising virtue in their occupations as a calling. Their hard work and ascetically harnessed energy resulted in savings and surplus, and led to investment

Figure 16.2 The middle-class congregation is often oriented toward the politically conservative and the economically successful and away from such urban problems as poverty, crowding, and racism. *(Monkmeyer, Frinly.)*

that made an expanding capitalism possible.

Over time the belief in predestination diminished and ceased to be significant in religious belief, but the economic ethic that developed out of Calvinism stood independent, detached from any particular religious faith. What Weber had called the Protestant Ethic came to be the dominant ethical orientation to work for the middle classes of Western industrial societies. It culminated in secular versions of the ethic that placed a central value on work and made of economic success a this-worldly goal that needed no relation to anything beyond this life.

Secularization

The decline of religious influence on other social institutions is *secularization*. For a long time secular has meant "worldly," contrasted to "religious" or "sacred." Fundamentally, secularization means "the process by which sectors of society are removed from the domination of religious institutions and symbols."[30] Secularization, then, is a *desacralization* of the world, one in which there is no over-arching religious symbolism bearing on the integration of society, and in which an understanding of human beings and their society is no longer stated primarily in religious terms.

The Sources of Secularization

Secularization is hardly a new or even a modern process. Its origins in the Western world lie in the Christian religion, even though the process is interpreted as a loss of the power and effectiveness of religion.

[30] *See* Berger, *op. cit.,* p. 107.

The religion of ancient Israel, for instance, divorced God from the "natural" processes of the world, with the significant consequences that God was not manipulable by magic; He did not confer divinity upon humans, even kings; and His divinity was not expressed in nature worship.

Max Weber credited Calvinism and the emergence of the Protestant Ethic as being a major development in the rationalization of the world—and secularization is part of that rationalization. Protestantism divested the world of much of the magic and the miracles of medieval Catholicism. It reduced the number of sacraments and eliminated all the intermediaries between God and man: saints, the Virgin, angels, miracles, and the sacraments through which grace could be dispensed. "At the risk of some simplification, it can be said that Protestantism divested itself as much as possible from the three most ancient and most powerful concomitants of the sacred —mystery, miracle, and magic."[31]

Yet no one would claim that secularization has driven religiosity entirely from modern life. Rather, religion has been remained more closely associated with the institution of the family, and is not yet entirely divorced from education. Yet it has been most thoroughly removed from the economy and the state, probably most of all from the economy, for industrial capitalism has long been a dynamic force for secularization.

Secularization has not affected modern societies uniformly. Its impact has been stronger on men than on women, on the middle-aged than on the young or the old, on Protestants and Jews than on Catholics, and on those social classes directly linked to modern industrial production than on

such more traditional occupations as artisans and small shopkeepers. It has had a deeper impact on those in the cities than on rural people. Political and economic institutions have developed their own independent symbolic systems, and thus secular ideologies have emerged.

The loss of religion's capacity to be the integrating symbol system for society means that religion has lost that basic function which once defined it sociologically as an institution. Secularization, therefore, has been *deinstitutionalizing* for religion. In such a world the rational perspective of science becomes a major organizing belief for a secular and increasingly rationalized world.

Secularization as Modernizing and Being Relevant

Secularization induces a response in the modern church that encourages greater acceptance of the secular world by the church, and presses for new ways to get religion back into social life to make it relevant again. In the Catholic Church Pope John XXIII coined the term *aggiornamento* (Italian for "bringing up to date"), which became a powerful symbol of the reform and modernizing movement within the church itself.

Changes in liturgy have been accompanied by other developments, such as the shedding of traditional, distinctive garments by nuns and priests—one symbol of moving from cloister to street and of redefining their relationship to the congregation and even to the larger body of the nonreligious. A strong plea for release from celibacy comes from young priests, and many young nuns seek new ways to express their vocation, ways that bring them into closer contact with a secular world

[31] *See* Berger, *op. cit.*, p. 111.

Figure 16.3 The new Mass—one of the reforms instituted as a result of Pope John XXIII's *aggiornamento.* *(Monkmeyer.)*

and protect them less from its more everyday aspects.

Another way of being modern and relevant is through political action. Both Catholics and Protestants, black and white, plunged into the civil-rights movement in the 1960s. Perhaps Father Groppi and the Reverend Martin Luther King were the best known of the dedicated civil-rights leaders among the clergy—and the most controversial. Today, men like Daniel and Phillip Berrigan, brothers and Catholic priests, take active political stands, opposing the Vietnam war by destroying draft records and consequently being imprisoned. This activism is testimony to the power of the religious vision to sustain a radical stand against the secular state.

Beyond the borders of the United States a more radical political stance comes from a once-conservative Catholic Church. In Spain the Church, which once backed Franco's holy crusade to restore Christendom, has become a powerful force in modernizing society. Even more dramatically, Catholic priests in a number of Latin American countries have joined the radical political struggle against dictatorial regimes and for democracy, and even socialism, in some instances with the backing of their bishops. They have been jailed and like other political prisoners in such regimes tortured.

The churches have made a great effort to attract youth who seem to find little meaning in religion. Young clergy in particular, in campus-based parishes, have looked for ways to connect with college students. Coffee houses and folk singers in church basements are part of the program of a youth-oriented and less conventional church.

In all these efforts the religious have gone forth into the secular world and joined movements and developments stemming from alienated young and from the poor and dispossessed. Such political action while of the secular world seeks always to be more than secular, to find a deeper religious significance and sanction for taking sides in political disputes between the dispossessed and powerless and the powerful elites and established institutions. That religion can be, and has from time to time been, a radically moral critic of worldly institutions and practices should be evident from such contemporary examples.

Yet established churches and their conservative, middle-class constituency have reacted against this secular involvement in political and social action. The National Council of Churches, for example, has had to cut its social programs back drastically, for funding has been withheld by member churches.

Whether established religion gains or loses over the long run by maintaining its conservatism is not yet evident. It alienates many in the younger generation of committed clergy who want to see their church, Protestant or Catholic, actively seeking to change this world. It also suggests that the practice of staying away from "good works" which threaten the status quo confirms what many youth have come to believe, that the established churches are part of an established society from which these youth have withdrawn legitimacy.

A Secular Theology

Recently a perspective in theology that welcomes secularization has emerged, perhaps most effectively expressed in theologian Harvey Cox's The Secular City.[32]

Cox calls secularization "the *liberation* of man from religious and metaphysical tutelage, the turning of his attention away from other worlds and toward this one."[33] He also refers to it as an "emancipation."

Cox's work is a theologically radical effort to shed the religious perspectives of presecular eras and to find a new grounding for religion in the unmistakably secular world of the twentieth century. He seeks to present in theological terms what religion can be like in a secular society. Few sociologists have attempted any similar effort, nor would they be likely to regard this as a sociological task. Yet, in attempting to assess the consequences of secularization for religion, several social scientists have predicted something of the religious future. Both sociologists Peter Berger and Robert Bellah, for example, suggest that religion as it becomes more subjective, becomes, as Bellah notes, less orthodox, and established belief gives way to personal interpretation.[34] He observes that "for many churchgoers, the obligation of doctrinal orthodoxy sits lightly indeed, and the idea that all creedal statements must receive a personal reinterpretation is widely accepted."[35]

Sociologist Thomas Luckmann suggests that in the modern world different social institutions are each autonomous within their own sphere; this leaves a private sphere for the individual in which he may develop a private world view that may or may not be congruent with an official model of religion. Thus, there emerges the basis for a noninstitutionalized, *privatized*

---

[32] *See* Harvey Cox, *The Secular City*, rev. ed. (New York: The Macmillan Company, 1966). For a brief discussion of the sources of secular theology *see* Berger, *op. cit.*, pp. 163–169.

[33] *See* Cox, *op. cit.*, p. 15.

[34] *See* Peter L. Berger, "A Sociological View of the Secularization of Theology," *Journal for the Scientific Study of Religion*, vol. 5 (Fall 1966), pp. 3–16; and Robert Bellah, "Religious Evolution," *American Sociological Review*, vol. 29 (June 1964), p. 364.

[35] *See* Bellah, *op. cit.*, p. 372.

model of religion.[36] When this happens, religion recedes from the public stage and becomes socially and politically innocuous. "The gods of traditional religions live on as private fetishes or the patrons of congenial groups, but they play no significant role in the public life of the secular metropolis."[37]

SCIENCE IN SOCIETY

It would be unimaginable to try to understand today's society without taking into account the influence of modern science. This is a highly rational activity with immense practical consequences for almost every phase of social life.

When the natural scientist talks about science, he does so primarily in terms of theory and method, though he sometimes acknowledges that science is committed to certain values. He is less likely to recognize that modern science is socially organized, and, indeed, is now an institutionalized sector of society. Yet it is this fact which makes science important to the student of society. Science is a complex and extraordinarily influential process in modern society, and the role of the scientist is now one of the more important ones in the organization of that society.

The Growth of Science

Science as we know it in our time is the historic outcome of several centuries of significant social development in the Western world and is inextricably interwoven with Western culture and history. In a rudimentary manner science is found in all cultures, even "primitive" ones. All people have made empirical observations about nature, generally related to practical considerations, and have developed arts and skills from these. There is thus some continuity in the development of science. Yet science has taken major developmental steps forward at particular times and in particular cultures. Over a thousand-year span, for example, the Greeks developed an impressive science with a large number of significant achievements to their credit.[38] But knowledge of this science was lost to Europe after the fall of Rome, and not until well into the Middle Ages did renewed trade and commerce bring Greek and Islamic science back into a Europe in which technology was already well developed.

During the sixteenth and seventeenth centuries, usually defined as the period of the rise of modern science, a major breakthrough occurred in scientific discovery and achievement. A complex set of processes produced an atmosphere that was congenial to scientific creativity, and one of the truly great periods in the history of science developed.[39]

Perhaps most significantly, René Descartes provided a new rational philosophy for science that stressed the need to make precise observations and rigorous logical and mathematical calculations in order to establish necessary relations among events. There was also a refinement of experimental techniques, enhanced by the invention of new instruments of observation and measurement: the telescope, the microscope, the thermometer, the barometer, the pendulum clock, and the air pump. A new mathematical ration-

[36] See Thomas Luckmann, *The Invisible Religion* (New York: The Macmillan Company, 1967).
[37] See Cox, *op. cit.*, p. 2.
[38] Brian Tierney, *et al., Ancient Science* (New York: Random House, Inc., 1968).
[39] The following discussion is drawn from Bernard Barber, *Science and the Social Order* (New York: The Free Press, 1952; Collier Books edition, 1962), Ch. 2.

THE SEPARATE SPHERES OF RELIGION AND SCIENCE

Sacred symbols are largely non-logical, evocative, and expressive. They speak of feelings and mythic beliefs, not necessarily true or false, which lie deeply embedded in the ongoing emotional life of the species. The words and concepts of a religion may be logically organized and systematically arranged according to the tenets of some of the greatest of the logicians, yet all such sacred systems are ultimately based on the non-logical feelings of man. Ultimately, proof and validity are not to be found in any kind of empirical testing, for the ultimate meaning of such mythic symbols lies beyond ordinary experience.

Attempts to prove or disprove mythic beliefs as true or false by the methods of empiricism are foolish and unjustified. The truth of such symbol systems has nothing to do with the thinking and methods of empirical verification. Their truths are to be found in the larger experiences of man and his species. To be valid they do not need the support, or criticism, of rational thought. Mythic symbols and their truth or falsity are not dependent, nor can they be, on the methods of science. They represent a different order of reality. They tell of older and more fundamental facts of man's poor existence. Science is not equipped to test the truth of their meanings. The basic "truths" our species has learned and transmitted through living millions of years on earth, expressed in an infinite variety of sacred signs and deified symbols, belong to an order of reality beyond the concepts and methods of contemporary science. Science can only know them in its own terms and imperfectly translate them into a symbol system often contrary to their nature. But for the scientist their natural meanings can be discovered only in what they represent, what they evoke, and how they function in the social and species life of man.

W. Lloyd Warner

From W. Lloyd Warner, *The Living and the Dead: A Study of the Symbolic Life of Americans* (New Haven, Conn.: Yale University Press, 1959), pp. 484–485.

ality combined with new emphasis on empirical observation to create a powerful modern science. The concern for practical inventions useful in mining and other industries also led to technological innovations that in turn made possible new scientific tools of observation and experimentation. At this point in history, technology was better developed than science and did not depend on science; actually, science gained from technology. In the background of these developments were the Western explorations of the newly mapped world and a mercantile capitalism that sought wider markets.

This period also saw religious changes and developments; and the emergence of Calvinism provided a new strong impetus to science. Max Weber claimed that Western society was more congenial to the development of science than was any other, in particular because its religious view presumed a rational God revealed in nature and discoverable by the rationality of man.

These several factors, then, coming together at a particular time in history, brought into existence a social climate in which science flourished and grew. A great panorama of giants of science came upon the scene in a relatively short period—Newton, Leibnitz, Copernicus, Kepler, Galileo, and Boyle among them.

Nonetheless, the number of persons who were scientists remained but a tiny fraction of the human community; literally, a handful of people. In the twentieth century, science has grown to enormous proportions. According to a distinguished historian of science, Derek J. de Solla Price, "Whereas in the mid-seventeenth century there were a few scientific men—a denumerable few who were countable and namable—there is now in the United States alone a population on the order of a million with scientific and technical degrees."[40]

The growth of scientific manpower over the past 250 years, according to Price, has been at an exponential rate whereby it doubles about every fifteen years. But we have reached the point where such growth cannot continue. If it did, says Price, ". . . we should have two scientists for every man, woman, child, and dog in the population, and we should spend on them twice as much money as we had."[41]

There is another development that may be of even more social significance: The enormous lead in scientific development once held by such scientifically developed nations as Great Britain, the United States, and Germany is now lost in the face of rapid gains from other nations, such as Japan and the Soviet Union, and even the less well-developed societies—the Chinese

scientific population, for example, is doubling every three years.[42] Science is diffusing rapidly throughout the world, and the scientifically underdeveloped nations are quickly catching up.

Developing Science in Underdeveloped Nations

Weber said that Protestantism encouraged the development of capitalism and science in the Western world as we've seen; and that the lack of such a rational world view was a barrier to developing science in other parts of the world. This argument has been liberally applied in explaining the lesser development of science in Asia and Africa. But what may have been significant in explaining an historical development two or three centuries ago may be less relevant today.

Indian scientists, for example, in examining the very real problems of developing science in their own society, point out that other-worldly attitudes, in contrast to the this-worldly Protestant Ethic, does not suffice as an explanation for lack of scientific growth, for it does not accord with the reality of contemporary Indian life. Inadequate technological development, a scarcity of resources for science, and a weak educational base in the population are the basic factors inhibiting the development of science in India.[43]

The Scientific Community: Ethos and Autonomy

Though science has more than its share of creative talent, it has always been more

[40] See Derek M. de Solla Price, *Little Science Big Science* (New York: Columbia University Press, 1963; paperback edition, 1965), p. 8.

[41] See Price, *op. cit.*, p. 19. Price's Ch. 1 is a good discussion of the exponential growth of science and its implications.

[42] See Price, *op. cit.*, p. 101.

[43] See Surajit Sinha, "Indian Scientists: The Sociocultural and Organizational Context of Their Professional Environment," pp. 105–153; and Purnima Sinha, "Social Constraints on Science in India" in Surajit Sinha, ed., *Science, Technology and Culture* (New Delhi: India International Center, 1970), pp. 154–160.

than a collection of bright, rational minds; it is also a communal effort. Every separate science has one or more scientific organizations, but there is also a scientific community, a widely shared sense of a common enterprise that is different in a basic way from the other enterprises found in modern society—or at least, so scientists confidently think. In effect, scientists share a common *ethos*, characteristic and distinguishing attitudes and actions that set science apart from other occupational groups.

Scientists, for example, have always proclaimed the free dissemination of knowledge, so that all scientific claims can be publicly scrutinized by other scientists, as a basic principle. Scientists claim not to recognize national, racial, or religious boundaries. Nothing was more offensive to scientists than the Nazis' effort to discredit Albert Einstein's work because he was a Jew.

Another principle that scientists claim is the freedom to choose their own problems, so that they can follow new leads and hypotheses on the frontiers of knowledge, unrestrained by the practical interests of nonscientists. On the basis of these values, scientists have long stressed independence from political and economic interests—an *autonomy* seen as essential for science.

Basic and Applied Science

Within the scientific community there has long been a fundamental distinction made between basic and applied scientific research. Logically and historically, the distinction is one between "pure" research—concerned with advancing fundamental, theoretical knowledge—and "practical" research—applying already existing scientific knowledge to the solution of everyday problems.

Among scientists, basic research has more prestige than applied, and some theoretical scientists are disdainful of applied scientists and engineers. Their assumption is that applied scientists depend completely on basic science, and thus that technology rests exclusively on pure science, so that advances in technology are only possible after theoretical advances.

But this is an incomplete and inaccurate reading of the historical and contemporary record. Technology and science mutually interact and influence one another; one is not wholly dependent on the other. Although technology does in fact advance by applying pure scientific principles to practical problems, its own successes often contribute in unanticipated ways to the advancement of basic science.

Distinctions between science and technology, as between basic and applied science, once seemed simple and clear to scientists and nonscientists alike. This is no longer true. Contemporary scientific journals are replete with efforts to redefine each type of science and re-establish clear distinctions between them, but no consensus is achieved. To many others, the very effort seems an academic exercise of no value in understanding the nature of a complexly interdependent process.

The Autonomy of Science

Historically, the scientific community has enjoyed a relatively high degree of autonomy from the economic and political power structures of society. There have been a number of reasons for this. First of all, until perhaps World War II, science was small science, not influential in the society, marginal but respected. This autonomy also benefited by the fact that science was primarily housed within the university with which it shared many values. If the university has, at least in part, been an "ivory tower," somewhat detached from the rest of society, this has served the scientific and scholarly communities well. It enabled them to pursue rational inquiry and intellectual life somewhat away from the impassioned scrutiny of partisan interests and from ideological (and sometimes antiintellectual) perspectives. (To be sure, government and business did not subsidize and use the university then as they do now, and few academic people saw any problem in carrying on an intellectual life in universities still primarily organized to serve privileged classes.)

In the last half-century, however, science has become useful; and modern, industrial society has had a major payoff for its investment in modern science. Science has become indispensable to the modern world, so that even totalitarian societies have had to concede some autonomy to science. To be sure, they have done this more for physical science than for the biological, and least of all for social science.

There have been, nonetheless, some noted instances in which government—particularly authoritarian government—has interfered severely with scientific autonomy. Hitler's Germany and Stalin's Russia are the two most noted examples. In those two cases scientists were subjected to political controls and direction and forced to make their scientific theory compatible with the ruling ideology.[44]

In democratic societies, such as the United States, there has been no such crude political subjugation of science to party and ideology, but no less effectively, as we shall see, the autonomy of science has been seriously breached.

Science has also benefited by its own success. The enormous fruits of natural science have given to it an unchallenged prestige, superior to that of any other kind of scholarship. This has worked to keep science well supported and, more importantly, relatively free from interference by others. The scientist has become a major authority figure in the modern world, and the scientific method has become the major standard for determining what to believe.

Yet two related developments now suggest that the relationship of the scientific community to modern society is undergoing—if it has not already completed—a significant transformation. There is, first of all, the emergence of what a number of observers have come to call big science; and second, there is the closer involvement with and control by the national government of science, which threatens its prized autonomy.

Big Science

Since 1940 there has been an enormous change within the scientific community. We have discussed the growth in the number of scientists, but change is also reflected in the vastly increased flow of funds for the support of scientific research, and in the importance that government and

---

[44] On Germany *see* Joseph Needham, *The Nazi Attack on International Science* (London, England: Watts and Cox, 1941); and Sir Richard Gregory, *Science in Chains* (London, England: Macmillan & Co., Ltd., 1941). There is also a fine discussion in Joseph Haberer, *Politics and the Community of Science* (New York: Van Nostrand Reinhold, 1969).

On Russia, see Julian Huxley, *Heredity East and*

West: *Lysenko and World Science* (New York: Henry Schuman, 1949) and Conway Zirkle, ed., *Death of a Science in Russia* (Philadelphia: University of Pennsylvania Press, 1949).

For a brief review of both cases, see Bernard Barber, *Science and the Social Order*, Chapter 3.

the military now attach to scientific activity. Science has become big science.

As a consequence of its enormous growth science is no longer housed entirely within the university, though this still remains its primary home. Private research institutes, industrial laboratories for applied work, and governmental laboratories now employ a large part of the scientific population of the United States. Many basic researchers—not to mention applied researchers—are neither students nor teachers in universities. Yet, as recently as 1940, "perhaps 90 percent of all basic scientific research in the United States was done by professors, or by students working under their direction."[45] There have been a number of other important changes in science as a consequence of its changed size and status:

1. A newly found affluence has created a scientific elite who enjoy high status and rewards; who commute among visiting appointments, conferences, and the like; and by such "commuting" are able personally to exchange ideas, as well as to constitute a select list for mailing preprints and otherwise unpublished material. These scientists make up an *invisible college* of creative and productive elites, whose significance cannot be observed only by consulting published journals.[46]

2. The way in which research is carried out has changed from the single, creative scientist, working alone or with a few students, to team work and an organization reminiscent of large-scale business operations.

Just as the modern corporation has supplanted free partnership and apprenticeship in industry, so a more complex form of organization may be supplanting free collaboration and the professor-student association in science. Both changes involve the development of a more complex division of labor, the separation of the worker from the tools of production, and the greater centralization of authority.[47]

Team work occurs within large research organizations, which have sources of support usually far superior to those which scientists can get elsewhere—this being one of their attractions. The scientific community seems divided as yet on whether or not the team work of big science is superior to the individual project typical of little science. Proponents of both are still to be found in the scientific community.[48]

3. Applied research has grown far more rapidly than has basic research, both in large government laboratories and in the industrial laboratories of corporations. Some of this research is still basic—at least from the scientist's perspective—but from the organization's viewpoint it is supported because it is likely to have useful (and for corporations, profitable) applications.[49]

Scientists in Politics

Two significant developments have altered the older pattern of a highly autonomous and politically remote science. One is that scientific knowledge and technology are so closely involved in military and political decisions that scientists now assume new roles as administrators and ad-

[45] *See* Spencer Klaw, *The New Brahmins: Scientific Life in America* (New York: William Morrow & Company, Inc., 1968), p. 155. *See especially* Ch. VI, "Scientists without Students," pp. 155–167.

[46] *See* Price, *op. cit.*, Ch. 3, "Invisible Colleges and the Affluent Scientific Commuter,"; *see also* Diane Crane, *Invisible Colleges: Diffusion of Knowledge in Scientific Communities* (Chicago, Ill.: University of Chicago Press, 1972).

[47] *See* Warren Hagstrom, "Traditional and Modern Forms of Scientific Teamwork," *Administrative Science Quarterly*, vol. IX (December 1964), p. 251.

[48] For the flavor of the large research institution *see* Klaw, Ch. V, "The Styles of Big Science," pp. 134–154.

[49] *See* Klaw, *op. cit.*, Ch. VII, "The Vineyards of Utility," and Ch. VIII, "The Industrial Labyrinth."

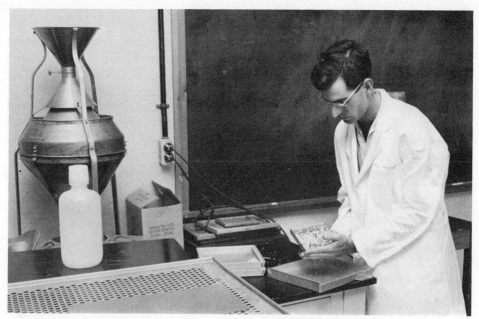

Figure 16.4 The detachment of the university scientist in his "ivory tower" has been broken down to a great extent, forcing the scientist to participate in political and military governmental decisions. *(The Ford Foundation, Sheldon M. Machler.)*

visors in which they must make judgments that are not only technical but also political and moral. The other is that modern society sees in science a major instrumentality for solving problems of military power, food production, physical disease, and the like; and thus has attempted to harness science more closely than ever before to national policy.

The new place of science in modern society has imposed upon many scientists, and particularly the leadership of science, advisory roles that are essentially political. The creation of numerous advisory boards and committees to governmental agencies and offices is an official acknowledgment of scientific consultation. During the 1950s a Special Assistant to the President for Science and Technology was appointed; this was followed by the creation of the President's Science Advisory Committee.

Ideally, scientists are presumed to advise on matters that are within their technical competence, but experience with the hydrogen bomb, nuclear power, and the radiation fallout and testing controversy in the 1950s suggests that these technical matters are often inseparable from political and moral issues. In addition, some scientists have not hesitated to speak out in moral terms, with the result that they have often been in the position of publicizing quite contradictory advice.

There is another kind of role that may very well have as much influence on science as the political one: the role of the scientific advisor on those decisions about how government can advance science. A modern government that wants to use science extensively knows it also has to support science. It is here that the scientific advisor becomes a political emissary from the scientific community to the government, explaining the position of scientists to the government about what should be done and what is needed in strengthening science: science education, recruitment of scientists, participation in international conferences, and investment in various new areas of scientific exploration.[50]

Increasing involvement in the political process has rarely turned scientists into social and political critics of the government. Their ideological outlook seems to be little different from that of the military and political leaders whom they advise. Donald N. Michael characterizes a "new breed" of scientist, a science entrepreneur, deeply involved in the politics and power of Washington:

The science entrepreneurs are supported by and in turn support big business, big publicity, big military, sometimes big academia and parts of big government. They are both the captives and the kings of these powerful coalitions —kings for obvious reasons, captives because in reaping the benefits of affiliation they capitulate in some degree to the operating principles of these institutions. They have climbed to power through conservative hierarchies and tend to hold conservative values.[51]

Politics in Science

No modern society can do without a national policy on science. Congress, for example, established the National Science Foundation as an agency to support scientific education and also to provide funds

[50] See Klaw, *The New Brahmins,* Ch. IX, "Movers and Shakers," for a discussion of scientific advisors in Washington. *See also* Daniel A. Greenberg, *The Politics of Pure Science* (New York: New American Library, 1966); and Don K. Price, *The Scientific Estate* (New York: Oxford University Press, 1968).

[51] See Donald N. Michael, "Science, Scientists, and Politics," in John G. Burke, ed., *The New Technology and Human Values* (Belmont, Calif.: Wadsworth Publishing Company, Inc., 1966), p. 359.

for scientific research. Governmental support of research, however, comes from a whole variety of agencies, including the military establishment.

But the support that government so generously gives science is not without its costs. What is lost is some of the autonomy and independence scientists have long prized and judged so necessary. Here are some of the consequences:

1. Others besides scientists have an impact on the direction of scientific research. When a government amply funds one kind of scientific research and not another it affects the disposition of scientific talent and thus the development of science. Sociologist Norman Kaplan puts it this way: ". . . the 'market place of ideas' determining the choice of scientific problems is rapidly being replaced by a deliberate attempt to link the goals of society with the research goals of science."[52]

Scientists are not compelled to study what political leaders think important, but they find it easier to fund a project—and remember that research in physical science is very expensive—if they choose to work in those areas of scientific endeavor that are in agreement with national policy. From the scientific point of view nonscientists frequently fail to appreciate the importance of basic research designed only to advance scientific theory without regard for any immediate application.

Scientist Barry Commoner, for example, argues that because about one-third of government funds for basic research comes from the National Aeronautics and Space Administration (NASA), which concentrates on the space program—particularly throughout the 1960s on the task of getting a man on the moon—there is a distortion of scientific research. The space program, Commoner

[52] See Norman Kaplan, "Sociology of Science," in *Handbook of Modern Sociology* (Chicago, Ill.: Rand-McNally & Company, 1964), p. 871.

argues, has not been created in the interests of science.[53]

2. Scientists have always opposed *secrecy;* all scientific research, they believe, should be publicly available for scrutiny. But, Commoner notes, "now even *basic* scientific work is often controlled by military and profit incentives that impose secrecy on the dissemination of fundamental results."[54]

3. The technology that scientific advances make possible often puts these to military or other uses before scientists have had a chance to measure the consequences fully, particularly the hazardous impact on life itself. Scientists have been unable to stop this usage — and some have aided and abetted it — with the results that the integrity of science has been seriously eroded, according to a report of a major scientific organization.[55]

This report and the critical comments by Barry Commoner are evidence of another significant development: In recent years the scientific elite, and through them the whole scientific community, have been subject to widespread and often severe criticism for their uncritical participation in governmental policy-making. Such an organization as the Federation of Atomic Scientists illustrates the possibilities for an independent and critical function carried on by qualified scientists. The Federation originated in the moral concerns of atomic scientists engaged in research at atomic energy research laboratories during World War II. The terribly destructive potential of nuclear energy, when harnessed

to war uses, disturbed these scientists, more so when the first atom bomb fell on Hiroshima.

Since then the Federation has published the influential *Science and Public Affairs,* a monthly periodical that is an intellectual forum for a wide range of issues having to do with the responsible and humane uses of scientific knowledge. It provides an intellectual bridge between scientists and other scholars concerned about the control and use of science in the modern world and such problems as radiation, disarmament, pollution, and the relationship of science to government and the military.

More recently, new groups of scientists concerned with ecology and population have emerged to widen the range of qualified scientists expressing positions on policy matters independent of the government and the scientific advisory bodies attached to it.

THE CHANGING STATUS OF RELIGION AND SCIENCE

Up until now the long-term historical view suggests that science is more likely to be dominant in the future than is religion. Secularization has put much of social life under the domination of the rational processes of science — and under the control of bureaucratic and technological structures whose logic and legitimation is derived from science. Yet, the issue has not yet been closed. Much that has occurred in the last few years can be seen as a radical and remarkably strong counterassault on the domination of science and its rational existence, and a plea for the restoration of some sense of the sacred to human life, even though many of those involved had no conception of a religious orientation. (Many in fact were conventionally

[53] See Barry Commoner, *Science and Survival* (New York: The Viking Press, Inc., paperback edition, 1967), pp. 58–59.

[54] See Commoner, *op. cit.,* p. 48.

[55] See Committee on Science in the Promotion of Human Welfare, American Association for the Advancement of Science, "The Integrity of Science," *American Scientist* (June 1965).

antireligious or at least antiestablished religion.) In the widest possible sense the counterculture can be taken as resistance to any further rationalization of life—of which the secularization of religion is one aspect—and as an attempt to restore nonrational values to a central place in human life.

It would be incorrect, however, to think that the resistance to rational science began with today's counterculture. It has deep roots in modern history, as the controversy over the "two cultures" makes evident.

The Two Cultures: Science and Humanism

The scientific culture seems to be one that few nonscientific intellectuals have ever shared or, for that matter, even understood. This is the theme pursued by C.P. Snow in *The Two Cultures and the Scientific Revolution*.[56] By *two cultures* Snow meant the one of science and the other of humanist intellectuals. He saw these two cultures as complete opposites: "the intellectual life of the whole of western society is increasingly being split into two polar groups."[57] Scientists, Snow argues, know too little of the world of literary culture; and literary intellectuals do not have even a glimmer of understanding of the world of science. From his own experience as both scientist and novelist, he documents this mutual ignorance. Snow sides with the scientists; he believes ignorance of science is the more deplorable failing because it is dangerous for the future of the human race.

Snow opts for industrialization and tech-

nology and the science that makes this possible. He sees in the scientific revolution of modern, electronic technology a potential force for eliminating the great gap between rich and poor that now plagues the world.

The Pessimism of the Humanists

Humanists over the past century have been pessimistic to the point of despair. They saw the world becoming increasingly rationalized—more and more calculable, planned, and unspontaneous, and in that sense less free.

Humanists were repelled, not so much by the ugliness of industrialism as by its relentless intent toward uniformity, manipulation, and rationalized bureaucratic control. Science, from this perspective, is the servant of the bureaucrat and the modern politician. The scientist is not only partner to the crime he is its intellectual godfather.[58]

Generations of talented humanists (including religious thinkers) for over a century now have raged against an ever more scientific and rational society. It has bred in them a deepened sense of disenchantment with the world. They are one with Weber in despairing about the future of man in a thoroughly rationalized universe; yet they saw no reason to believe that the course of history could be altered.

Here are two radically opposed ways of viewing the world. The viewpoint of science is abstract, analytical, and piecemeal; and it approaches all phenomena with the single intention of viewing them objectively and with no value preference. Its world view is congruent with much in a

---

[56] *See* C.P. Snow, *The Two Cultures and the Scientific Revolution* (New York: Cambridge University Press, 1961).

[57] *See* Snow, *op. cit.*, p. 4.

[58] Cesar Grana has provided a brilliant sociohistorical analysis of the development of this humanist perspective. *See* his *Bohemian versus Bourgeois: French Society and the French Man of Letters in the Nineteenth Century* (New York: Basic Books, Inc., 1964).

Figure 16.5 Some young people in the counterculture have turned to Eastern religion, such as this group of Hare Krishna. *(Monkmeyer, Bayer.)*

technologically and bureaucratically organized world, which looks to science, not literature, for its standards and norms. The humanistic mind rejects that same world and rebels against it.

This rebellion is the source and fountain of the counterculture as well as for the development of a contemporary attitude among many other youths. It is also the source of a renewed effort to restore the sacred to spheres of human life from which the powerful processes of secularization have removed it. For that reason, religion, in possibly strange and never before experienced forms, is moving back to the center of human experience.

Restoring the Sacred

Much of what is countercultural is religious, a fact missed by those who tend to see religion only as established Christianity. Perhaps the mass-media emphasis

on drugs, sex, and long hair and sloppy dress have missed what is essential. And perhaps it is all just momentary. But one serious and sympathetic sociological observer feels otherwise:

I see it as symptomatic of a deepening spiritual crisis, a disillusionment with science, planning and rationality similar to the disenchantment with Enlightenment that spurred the cultural revolution of romanticism. Here is something that we cannot dismiss as a passing fad.[59]

The most significant aspect of the counterculture has been a turning away from Western rational knowledge to the Eastern mystics—holy men, gurus, and the like. Rather than political action, meditation offers a way to oneness with God.

[59] *See* John Raphael Staude, ''Alienated Youth and the Cult of the Occult,'' in Morris L. Medley and James E. Conyers, eds., *Sociology for the Seventies* (New York: John Wiley & Sons, Inc., 1972), p. 91.

"Mysticism offers a sense of identity with the original and all-inclusive Source and Goal of the universe, the one eternal principle, God."[60]

For adherents of rational scholarship much of the counterculture seems irrational, a failure to face the more unpleasant aspects of reality, a grasping for certitudes in times of rapid change—and worst of all a return to the irrational and antiintellectual attitudes of an earlier day. The close relation of drugs to countercultural experiences, particularly those concerned with consciousness, heightens this sense of dangerous potential. Even strong defenders of the counterculture acknowledge an antirationalist strain that could have dangerous consequences: "The cult of the unconscious as a source of liberating wisdom can easily lead to the *Blut und Boden* ideology of Nazi Germany."[60]

Yet sociologist Staude sees a reason for viewing the counterculture optimistically, and most of all for seeing validity in its coming into existence:

The youth of the counterculture, having broken with the Western rationalistic individualist's skeptical tradition of the last 300 years in favor of communal, personalist, "committed" life style, now are searching for sacral foundations to sustain and celebrate their new identity. This quest for the sacred in an odd amalgam of Eastern and Western terms is itself another sign of how deeply alienated from the immediate Western intellectual and cultural tradition the counterculture actually is.[61]

THE FUTURE OF SCIENCE AND RELIGION

Those who have long hailed a world without religion are likely to prove to be poor prophets. But those who have raged against soulless science are no more likely to be accurate predictors of the future.

It would seem there are two issues for the future of *science:*

1. Science has suffered enormously in prestige from being a too willing partner of worldly power and for letting go so much of its once prized autonomy. Critics both outside and inside science are now engaged in a struggle over the responsible uses of science, so that science is no longer a tool of governments and corporations but puts into practice some larger sense of purpose.
2. More basically, science has suffered for its basic contribution to bureaucratic, technological domination in an over-rationalized world. To recognize that science is a powerful instrument for dealing with nature but not, as Weber well knew, a source of ultimate wisdom is the beginning of understanding both the power and limits of science. Weber's point was that science cannot tell us how to live our lives; at best, it may be one of the means of achieving a desirable world. But science alone is not enough. What is *desirable* in the world is a political and moral matter, not a scientific one.

For *religion* there are also two important developments:

1. The long humanistic resistance to stripping life of sacredness has resurged powerfully in our time, but in new, unforeseen ways. The vitality of religion probably cannot be measured by bank accounts and membership lists of the established churches. A renewed sense of the sacred in life challenges the domination of science and rationality, while raising as yet unanswered questions about life in postindustrial society.
2. Religious groups, even established churches, caught in renewed tension with society, break partnership on a worldwide scale with secular powers and seek social change to provide justice in this world. At least, they no longer passively look on while in-

---

[60] *See* Staude, *op. cit.,* p. 94.
[61] *See* Staude, *op. cit.,* p. 92.

justice holds sway. This puts religion in opposition to governments and ruling classes, and creates a movement to withhold legitimacy from societies as they now are.

The consequences of these new developments are not yet fully apparent. But it is unlikely that science or religion can long remain unchanged.

SUMMARY

A division between the *sacred* and the *profane* distinguishes religious and nonreligious activity.

A *functional* interpretation of religion stresses how sharing in religious belief creates moral cohesion and thus legitimizes society. This makes religion an important instrument of social control.

The *ecclesia* is an inclusive religious organization that accepts the world as it is; while *sects* are small religious groups which are in but not of society, for they reject worldly society.

Denominations are often sects grown into stable churches which have made peace with the world; while *cults* are small, almost formless religious groups which attract the alienated in society.

Religious organization reflects the *class structure* of society, usually in the proportion of members it draws from different social classes. In industrial societies the established churches have had least success in holding on to the working classes. But when working-class people form sects, these often compete with radical politics.

Among the oppressed, religion may produce *nativistic* and *revivalistic* movements in criticism of those members of society who rule them. In the United States religion has been a powerful force in the black community, providing dignity and self-respect. While this has often meant accepting the social order, it has also been an important source of support for civil rights.

Weber described the *Protestant Ethic* as a powerful set of religious ideas that contributed enormously to the development of both capitalism and rational science.

Secularization, the process of removing sectors of society from sacred domination, has been a pervasive process in the modern world. This is a way of rationalizing the world. Science is also a rational process.

There is a scientific *community* sharing an ethos of scientific values, including the *autonomy* of science.

Big science has developed since 1940, and is based on vastly increased funds for scientific research provided by government and a new involvement of scientists in making decisions about scientific development. Scientists also make decisions about the uses of science by government, including the military.

This has put science into *politics,* reduced its autonomy, and opened it to criticism about the role of scientists in advocating *secrecy* (as, for example, where the military is involved) and in directing funds to purposes other than the development of pure science.

As a consequence there is a changing status for both science and religion in modern society. New tensions between these two forces occur as a renewal of the sacred challenges the dominance of science in intellectual life. Both also experience further tension in their present relationship to society.

Suggested Readings

Peter Berger, *The Sacred Canopy: Elements of a Sociological Theory of Religion* (Garden City, N.Y.: Doubleday & Company, Inc., 1967). A foremost sociologist of religion maps the range and concerns of sociology in examining religion.

J.D. Bernal, *The Social Function of Science* (Cambridge, Mass.: The M.I.T. Press, 1967). An American reprinting of an influential English scientist's analysis of the place of science in society—first published in 1939.

Zbygniew Brzezinski, *Between Two Ages: America's Role in the Technotronic Era* (New York: The Viking Press, Inc., 1970). A hard-headed analysis of this nation's place in a world radically transformed by science and technology.

Barry Commoner, *Science and Survival* (New York: The Viking Press, Inc., 1966; paperback edition, 1967). A highly articulate plea for a humanely responsible science, by a scientist actively involved in criticizing the inadequate structure of science.

Nicholas J. Demerath III, *Social Class in American Protestantism* (Chicago, Ill.: Rand-McNally & Company, 1965). A sociological analysis of the relation between status and religiosity among American Protestants.

Émile Durkheim, *The Elementary Forms of Religious Life,* Joseph Ward Swain, trans. (New York: The Free Press, 1948). Durkheim's classic study which established religion as a social phenomenon and developed a functional theory of religion.

H.H. Gerth and C. Wright Mills, *From Max Weber: Essays in Sociology* (New York: Oxford University Press, 1946). Weber's superb essay, "Science as a Vocation," remains as fresh today as it was in 1918. *See also* three fine essays on religion.

Charles Glock and Rodney Stark, *Religion and Society in Tension* (Chicago, Ill.: Rand-McNally & Company, 1965). Religiosity is measured against the influence of stratification and the processes of secularization.

Joseph Haberer, *Politics and the Community of Science* (New York: Van Nostrand Reinhold, 1969). A penetrating examination of the relations of science to politics, including the politics of science under the Nazis, and a good review of the Oppenheimer episode in the 1950s.

Spencer Klaw, *The New Brahmins: Scientific Life in America* (New York: William Morrow & Company, Inc., 1968). A very readable account of how science and scientists have changed from little to big science, with particular emphasis on the lives and careers of scientists.

Thomas Luckmann, *The Invisible Religion* (New York: The Macmillan Company, 1967). The persistence of religion, but without the organized church, is predicted by a sociologist of religion.

Derek M. de Solla Price, *Big Science Little Science* (New York: Columbia University Press, 1963). A distinguished historian of science weighs the significance of the emergence of "big science."

Louis Schneider and Sanford M. Dornbusch, *Popular Religions* (Chicago, Ill.: University of Chicago Press, 1958). A study of the "Americanizing" of religion from the middle of the nineteenth century to now.

Norman W. Storer, *The Social System of Science* (New York: Holt, Rinehart and Winston, Inc., 1966). A good example of how the sociologist examines science as a social process.

Guy E. Swanson, *The Birth of the Gods* (Ann Arbor, Mich.: University of Michigan Press, 1960). A sophisticated effort to relate the development of religion to the development of social structure.

Max Weber, *The Protestant Ethic and the Spirit of Capitalism* (New York: Charles Scribner's Sons, 1958). This is perhaps the greatest classic, certainly the most influential, in the sociology of religion. The magnificent range of Weber's scholarship is evident in his *The Sociology of Religion* (Boston, Mass.: The Beacon Press, 1963).

Bryan Wilson, *Religion in Secular Society* (Baltimore, Md.: Penguin Books, 1969). Britain's foremost sociologist of religion explores the modern process of secularization and what it means for both religion and modern society.

Milton Yinger, *Sociology Looks at Religion* (New York: The Macmillan Company, 1961). A leading sociologist of religion surveys what we know about the relationship of religion to society. *See also* his more comprehensive text, *The Scientific Study of Religion* (New York: The Macmillan Company, 1970).

PART VI

COLLECTIVE
BEHAVIOR

About things on which the public thinks long it
commonly attains to think right.
— *Samuel Johnson*

Chapter 17

Crowds
and Publics

For the most part people interact within the patterns set by social structure,
within the routines that give form and stability to social life—but never
completely. The clash of whites and blacks in a race riot or the violence
between striking workers and police that destroys property and injures
people are both instances of action that is neither routinized nor governed
by the social norms that control more institutionalized action.

Some social interaction exhibits a specific set of norms that define and
limit people's conduct; other situations do not. There are population aggregates with no clear definition of group membership, little division of labor,
no clear role expectancies, no established authority, and an absence of stable
leadership. Compared to bureaucracy or the highly integrated folk society,
these are "loosely" structured.

Social scientists label such phenomena *collective behavior.* It encompasses
three major areas:

Crowds: fighting, violent mobs; great masses of spectators; ceremonial crowds
either happy or solemn as the occasion requires.

Publics: physically dispersed aggregates of people who share an interest in some
event or issue, political or cultural.

Handwritten notes (top left):

unstructured - emotional, spontaneous
behavior   unpredictable

Went unconscious
derive + repressed wishes.

vigilante

1. Informal structure assoc.
2. Impending disaster - lose conf.
of formal structure of gov't, law.
3. Changes in values.
4. Emotional contagion - can be constructive
or distructive.

Figure 17.1 The difference between a crowd in the sociological sense and in everyday parlance can be seen in this group of people hurrying home on the subway—there is no common focus between them; they are probably not even aware of each other. *(Monkmeyer, Rogers.)*

Social movements: collective action of social groups or classes seeking to bring about or resist social change—a matter of social protest, of reform, or revolution.

THE CROWD: TYPES AND FUNCTIONS

In everyday language the presence of large numbers of people at a shopping center or of people pouring out of office buildings at the end of the work day is usually called a crowd. A mob bent on violent attack on others is also a crowd; so is a political demonstration.

These varied situations have in common only the fact of the physical presence of many people. But these people may have no common concern, no particular awareness of one another. Busy shoppers and people hurrying home from work are involved in their own private objectives, making a purchase or catching the next bus. There is only minimal social concern. In the sociological sense there is not a *crowd*.

A crowd emerges when an aggregate of people share a common focus. They are no longer merely individuals; there is a common interest or concern, as well as interaction and communication.

Casual Crowds

People on the street watching the police handle an accident, or watching a building going up, or listening to a pitchman trying to sell his wares are *casual* crowds, whose interest is moderate and whose emotional involvement is low. The individual has little difficulty detaching himself from the crowd. Nor do the norms of conventional behavior lose their force. The *casual* crowd occurs without being deliberately brought together; indeed, its presence in some situations hampers the work going on, as when a crowd gathers to watch a fire.

Conventional Crowds

But the deliberate planning of a crowd situation does occur; and any culture sanctions certain crowd situations and the accompanying crowd behavior. These are *conventional* crowds. They are not completely unstructured; some definite patterning of action occurs. In a spectator sports crowd, or a crowd at a concert or convention, or a crowd in church on Sunday morning there are differences in behavior and mood, yet each has conventional ways of expressing itself.

Expressive Crowds

Conventional crowds sometimes provide an opportunity for release of emotions in ways that are not socially threatening, as, for example, at a football game. These are *expressive* crowds. They give people an opportunity to express themselves freely and to release emotions and tensions. People can scream, yell, cheer, boo, wave their arms, stamp their feet, and shout at the tops of their lungs. When the game is over, they may be both physically and emotionally exhausted.

Huge political rallies may also be expressive crowd situations. By reasserting values and invoking common symbols, the political rally may serve to reinforce these values and strengthen the attachment of the individual to the group, whether that be the party or the state.

Audiences

Conventional crowds called *audiences* are generally more restrained in their be-

havior. A concert or lecture audience may be more passive, and individuals, intent on the speaker or performer, may be less conscious of the audience. There are, nonetheless, appropriate opportunities for emotional expression in the audience situation, particularly at the end of a performance, when applause expresses approval and a standing ovation may express appreciation for a particularly good performance.

Different audiences reflect different cultural expectations. The audience for a symphony concert responds differently than does the youthful audience at a rock concert. Recently, audiences are beginning to make more audible responses to good and bad performances and plays, so that the once more restrained conventional behavior is undergoing some change.

The Acting Crowd

The fears aroused by the thought of a crowd are not from casual or conventional crowds, not even expressive ones, but fear of the crowd in action, violent and destructive, bent on riot. In situations of conflict and tension, whether these are political struggles, labor disputes, or race conflicts the possibility of such crowd action emerges.

There have always been such crowds throughout history, and they have often been a significant political force, even a revolutionary one.[1] An intellectual tradition emphasizing the irrationality and destructiveness of crowds developed in Europe, and particularly in France, throughout the nineteenth century, as the aftermath of a legacy of revolutionary action by street

---

[1] *See* George Rudé, *The Crowd in the French Revolution, 1730–1848* (New York: John Wiley & Sons, 1964).

Riot - extentron action crowd - result

crowds. The rise of mass-based Socialist parties only added to a great fear of the people held by the propertied middle classes.

In this context of conservative reaction, a French scholar, Gustave LeBon, in the 1890s created an image of the crowd that was to have enormous influence on the sociological ideas of crowd behavior throughout the twentieth century.[2] LeBon perceived the crowd not as a mere collection of individuals but as an organized aggregation with a collective mind, in which the person loses his individual mentality. The crowd mind gives free play to the subconscious, and highly emotional qualities and instincts become dominant. The crowd, therefore, is not capable of highly rational or intellectual effort but reflects the common mediocrity of its members. The modern age, according to LeBon, was an age of crowds, instead of an age of a competent elite, and the rule of crowds typically characterized periods of disintegration and decay in civilization. LeBon was giving voice to strong, antidemocratic sentiments.

American social scientists stripped LeBon's theory of its antidemocratic bias, but otherwise developed his work into a conception of crowd behavior built on two assumptions:

1. That collective behavior was radically different from the "normal" actions of the individual, controlled as these usually are by social norms.
2. That the basic explanation for such "abnormal" action of the individual lies in contagion induced by a crowd situation; the usual predispositions of the individual are overcome by unanimous, intense feelings that permit action otherwise blocked by the normative controls of the social structure.

Why the individual loses control of himself in a crowd situation has been explained by such psychological mechanisms as emotional contagion, imitation, and suggestion, as well as the anonymity of the crowd and its restricted attention. Perhaps suggestibility due to contagious excitement and a sense of power in the crowd has been the most frequent explanation. The result, presumably, is an irrational and deviant individual, stripped of his civilized veneer.

Such contagion produces an acting crowd characterized as suggestible, destructive, irrational, emotional, paranoid, spontaneous and uncontrolled, and made up largely of the lower classes. Sociologist Carl Couch calls these terms stereotypes of the acting crowd.[3] He makes the point that irrationality, for example, is a component of many aspects of social life, not just crowd behavior, and that what is called rational and what is irrational is often an official definition that makes rational whatever supports the established system while opposition to current institutions is considered irrational. In similar manner Couch challenges each of the other stereotypes as providing an inadequate sociological analysis of the crowd.

Jerome Skolnick, a sociologist who directed a Task Force of the National Commission on the Causes and Prevention of Violence, has also seriously challenged this conventional contagion theory of crowd behavior, on the basis of the analysis done by his Task Force of the urban racial vio-

[2] See Gustave LeBon, *The Crowd: A Study of the Popular Mind* (London: Benn, 1896; paperback edition, New York: The Viking Press, Inc., 1960).

[3] See Carl Couch, "Collective Behavior: An Examination of Some Stereotypes," *Social Problems*, vol. 15 (Winter 1968), pp. 310–322.

lence of the 1960s.[4] Available evidence, Skolnick notes, "suggests that (a) armed officials often demonstrate a greater propensity to violence against persons than [do] unarmed civilians; and (b) these actions often escalate the intensity of the disorder . . ."[5]

The Emergent Norm Theory

An effort to move beyond an inadequate psychologizing about collective behavior has been developed most deeply by sociologist Ralph Turner, long a student of collective behavior.[6] Turner insists that crowd behavior must be incorporated into the same theoretical framework of structure and process as other collective and group processes. His central thesis is that, even in the most violent and dangerous crowds, there is also social interaction, in which a situation is defined, norms for sanctioning behavior emerge, and lines of action are justified and agreed upon. Turner calls this an *emergent norm* theory.

The emergent norm perspective has particularly challenged the empirical description of crowd situations so often produced in the past, descriptions which seem to overemphasize the unanimity of the crowd and the contagion which captures the emotions of all. Rather, careful observers of crowds note that many people stand around, not involved actively or even emotionally, and some are opposed to the dominant

orientation of the crowd. A crowd is rarely, then, unanimous or undifferentiated.

There is a *developmental* process in crowds in which interaction builds up justification for action, selectively choosing from among "facts" supplied by rumor. Nor are the norms that emerge from such a development strikingly different from the norms which are usually operative; rather, as Turner notes, the crowd supplies "an atypical resolution of a long-standing normative conflict, defining a situation in which 'emergency norms' can be invoked, or providing sanction for the conviction that the usual normative order has ceased to operate."[7] There are also limits to the development of crowd emotion and action; that is, there is a normative control that places limits on the crowd, an observable fact about many historic events that the contagion theory has seriously neglected.

The search for a theory of crowd behavior, then, has moved away from the older perspective that viewed the individual as coming under the sway of the crowd and losing his capacity for rational judgment before the onsweep of an overpowering emotional contagion. Sociologists such as Turner explain crowd behavior by the same sociological concepts that explain social groups. Crowds are best understood as a *developing collectivity*, in which interaction leads to defining what its members feel to be justifiable action, even when this violates established ways or proceeds in the face of official opposition.

Yet even then there must be the proper combination of elements before a crowd becomes an acting crowd. A crowd must be able to direct hostility against a definitely focused object; there has to be

---

[4] *See* Jerome Skolnick, *The Politics of Protest, A Report of the Task Force on Violent Aspects of Protest and Confrontation of the National Commission on the Causes and Prevention of Violence* (New York: Simon and Schuster, Inc., 1969), Ch. IX, pp. 329–346.

[5] *See* Skolnick, *op. cit.,* p. 335.

[6] *See* Ralph Turner, "Collective Behavior," in Robert E.L. Faris, ed., *Handbook of Modern Sociology* (Chicago: Rand-McNally & Company, 1964), pp. 382–425. *See* especially pp. 384–392.

[7] *See* Turner, *op. cit.,* p. 392.

something to act *against.* The interaction must build up an unambiguous imagery of friend and foe, *we* and *they.*

When this is done, the prevailing culture comes into play. It provides symbols—whether of nation, class, or race—which clearly and sharply define the object of hostility, simplify the character of the threat or problem, and create the situation in which it becomes possible to define as legitimate a course of action that would usually be defined as immoderate.

In the confusing situation in which a crowd gathers, *rumor* plays an important part in defining the situation for the crowd in such a way as to encourage direct action. In race riots, for example, rumors have swept through crowds, presenting some actual event in such a way as to arouse either whites or blacks to violent action. Rumor is the act of dealing with ambiguous situations when institutionalized forms of communication do not provide sufficient information; the resulting improvised definitions of what is happening is then a form of news, not necessarily false.[8]

Even when a crowd acts violently, not everyone present in the crowd does so. Sometimes only a small active core commits any action, while the larger part of the crowd watches. But they do give moral support and serve both to encourage and protect the active core. Usually young males will make up the active core, with females, older people, and even children constituting the larger supporting crowd. (Perhaps it is evidence of cultural change

that young women have recently been in the forefront of political demonstrations.)

Many potential situations do not produce an acting crowd, which is evidence that one or more of the necessary elements is not present. Perhaps the crowd cannot focus on a common object of hostility, or the symbols are too ambiguous to provide a clear definition of the situation encouraging action. The gathering of crowds in tense situations always presents the *possibility* of crowd action, of mobs and riots, but it does not guarantee it.

Crowds and Violence

Although mob behavior may seem spontaneous and the least predictable of human actions, it is possible to find some rough relationship between crowd violence and social structure. Violent crowds are most likely to occur around issues and situations that mark the deepest cleavages of values and interests within the society, where there is the least consensus to provide controlling norms, and where conflict between social groups and classes is the most bitter. They are, then, largely political phenomena, though only infrequently are they viewed that way.

In the United States, at the present time, the race riot comes most readily to mind, for race relations is an issue of conflict within the American social structure. Once labor was also an issue of conflict. Indeed, violence has characterized American life since before the American Revolution.[9] Violent action in revolt against economic

[8] Tamotsu Shibutani, *Improvised News: A Sociological Study of Rumor* (Indianapolis, Ind.: The Bobbs-Merrill Company, Inc., 1967). For a discussion of rumor in collective behavior *see* Turner, "Collective Behavior," pp. 399–406.

[9] For an historical review *see* Richard E. Rubenstein, *Rebels in Eden: Mass Political Violence in the United States* (Boston, Mass.: Little, Brown & Company, 1970); for a briefer treatment *see* his "Rebels in Eden," in Roderick Aya and Norman Miller, eds., *The New American Revolution* (New York: The Free Press, 1971), pp. 97–142.

loss and destitution has been characteristic of American farmers for over two
centuries. In the 1930s, bankrupted by
mounting debts and little income, farmers
burned crops, obstructed sheriffs' fore-
closure sales of farm property, and even
bought back foreclosed properties for mere
pennies at "shotgun sales"; they threatened
to shoot any outsider who tried to bid on
a property.

The struggles of blacks, of Chicanos,
immigrants, Indians, farmers, and of workers in the United States is a long, unrelieved record of periodic violence during
most of American history. Action against
the draft in the 1960s pales by comparison
with the extensive destructiveness of the
draft riots in New York City in 1864. An
impoverished immigrant minority, the
Irish, attacked conscription offices, merchants, policemen, and blacks who were
recruited as strike-breakers.

Nor is the use of violence only a weapon
of the disadvantaged. Employers in the
nineteenth and early twentieth centuries
employed private armies, hired strike-
breakers and then employed armed guards
to protect them, and called on police and
militia to use force to subdue strikers and
protesting crowds. In the South the Ku
Klux Klan epitomized the white capacity
for deliberate force and terror to keep
blacks "in their places," while the usually
spontaneous lynch mob was a white
weapon to punish alleged black offenders
against white women and by that means
to terrorize the entire black community.

Labor and Violence

From the Civil War until the 1930s labor
strife periodically broke out in the United
States. In fact, according to two noted students of labor relations: "The United States

has had the bloodiest and most violent
labor history of any industrial nation in
the world."[10]

Labor unions during this period were
much smaller and weaker organizations
than at present, and there was no labor
legislation to legitimize the workers' right
to organize and to be represented in collective bargaining. Furthermore, law enforcement in the form of police and courts
was usually on the side of the employer.
A strike, therefore, pitted the superior
number of the workers against the superior force and legal power of the employer.
Such a combination of numbers against
power led often to violent action, usually
resulting in bloodshed, injuries, and death,
largely of the strikers, and to jail and
imprisonment for the strike leaders. The
presence of even a potentially acting crowd
was usually sufficient excuse for authority
to direct organized violence against strikers.

Violence and Politics

Most of the significant violence in American history, then—and there has been a
lot—is the violence of rebellion and protest. It can only be understood by putting
it into a political context. It is political
because it is an act of violence against a
prevailing situation of power, after efforts
to use more institutionalized and conventional political means have failed, either
because political authority was unresponsive to appeals, or because disadvantaged
people were also disenfranchised and
otherwise lacked legal rights.

It is for this reason, Skolnick argues,

[10] Philip Taft and Philip Ross, "American Labor Violence: Its Causes, Character, and Outcome," in Hugh
Davies Graham and Ted Robert Gurr, eds., *The History of Violence in America, A Report to the Commission on the Causes and Prevention of Violence* (New
York: Bantam Books, Inc., 1969), pp. 281–395.

Figure 17.2 What makes a crowd turn to violence? Protest over the problems of society—for example, decent pay for the black worker—can be precipitated from orderly process to devastating violence, often by a trivial incident that is last in a long series of such manifestations. *(A. Devaney, Inc., N.Y.)*

that analyzing riots in terms of "tensions" and "frustrations" is inadequate:

It is not that this perspective is wrong, but that it tells at once too little and too much. Too little, because the idea of "tension" or "strain" does not encompass the subjective meaning or objective impact of subordinate caste position or political domination. Too much, because it may mean almost anything; it is a catchall phrase that can easily obscure the specificity of political grievances. It is too broad to explain the specific injustices against which civil disorders may be directed; nor does it help to illuminate the historical patterns of domination and subordination to which the riot is one of many possible responses.[11]

Racial Violence

Racial violence, both before and after slavery, has been persistent in American life—though the 1960s manifested a sustained pattern of urban violence probably unmatched in our history.[12]

An outbreak of violence which rent Harlem in the summer of 1964 was soon followed by similar violence in seven other cities, including Brooklyn and Chicago. In the summer of 1965 there was extensive rioting in Watts, the black area of Los Angeles, among five cities where violence erupted. Violence flared in twenty cities in 1966; and then in 1967 there were well over twenty outbreaks of violence, including the major burnings and destruction in Newark and Detroit.

[11] *See* Skolnick, *op. cit.*, pp. 337–338.

[12] *See* Allen D. Grimshaw, ed., *Racial Violence in the United States* (Chicago, Ill.: Aldine-Atherton, Inc., 1969). For a brief review *see* Louis H. Masotti, Jeffrey K. Hadden, Kenneth F. Seminatore, and Jerome R. Corsi, *A Time to Burn?* (Chicago: Rand-McNally & Company, 1969), Ch. 5, "Racial Violence in American History."

Unlike the great race riots of the past (Chicago, 1919; Detroit, 1943), these were not a direct confrontation between white and black crowds. Nor was this an invasion by whites of black areas with attacks on black people. These were riots by blacks directed primarily against white-owned property in the ghetto, accompanied frequently by looting.

The results were devastating. Between 1964 and 1967 about 130 civilians, mostly black, and 12 civil personnel, mostly white, were killed.[13] There were 4,700 people, again mostly black, injured, and over 20,000 persons were arrested during the riots. Property damage was in the hundreds of millions of dollars. Whole areas of cities like Newark and Detroit looked as if they had been destroyed in war.

Besides white-owned property, white police were singled out for attack. Relations between black ghetto inhabitants and white police have always been strained, if not outright hostile. Race prejudice is one simple factor for this. The police have generally acted toward blacks as they have toward poor and socially powerless people — with little restraint in physical attacks, verbal harassment, and ignoring of civil rights.

But the attack against the police is due to more than the failure of police to be considerate of minorities and poor people. For blacks in ghettoes, men in blue are seen as heavy-handed authority. They represent more than enforcement of law and maintenance of order: "they are viewed as members of an occupying army and as an oppressive force acting on behalf of those who rule their environment but who fled it for greener pastures."[14]

---

[13] Joseph Boskin, "The Revolt of the Urban Ghettoes, 1964–1967," *The Annals,* vol. 381 (March 1969), p. 7.

[14] *See* Boskin, *op. cit.,* p. 13.

The Kerner Report

In an effort to understand these race riots the National Advisory Commission on Civil Disorders, appointed by the President, undertook an ambitious and extensive study. Its comprehensive *Report*[15] (called the Kerner Report after the Commission's chairman, Otto Kerner, then Governor of Illinois) analyzed events in twenty-three cities, ten of which had had serious disorders during 1967.

In describing the pattern of disorder the *Report* notes that there was no "typical" riot. Riots did not always spring from a single precipitating incident; and the rioters were not "hoodlums," criminals, or the least educated. They were more knowledgeable than the average ghetto-dweller, even though they were also largely young high-school dropouts. But they were race-conscious, race-prideful young men, hostile to both whites and middle-class blacks.[16] Furthermore, a large segment of the community supported them, though passively, and took satisfaction in the results, viewing riot as a useful and legitimate form of protest.[17]

Although denying that the riots fitted any preconceived popular or even social-scientific pattern, in examining a very large body of data the Commission felt that it had identified a "chain" made up of:

... discrimination, prejudice, disadvantaged conditions, intense and pervasive grievances, a series of tension heightening incidents, all culminating in the eruption of disorder at the hands of youthful, politically-aware activists.[18]

---

[15] *See* The National Advisory Commission on Civil Disorders, *Report* (New York: Bantam Books, Inc., 1968). The official *Report* has also been published by the Government Printing Office.

[16] *See Report,* p. 111.

[17] *See* Skolnick, *The Politics of Protest,* pp. 147–148.

[18] *See Report,* p. 112.

Often the final incident that led to an outbreak of violence was too trivial to create a riot, but it must be understood as the last in a series of exacerbating incidents. In Newark in 1967, for example, these incidents included the arrest of fifteen blacks for picketing a grocery store, an unsuccessful effort by blacks to oppose the use of 150 acres in the black area for a medical-dental center, an unsuccessful effort to get a black-appointed secretary of the Board of Education, and the resentment at the participation of Newark policemen in a racial incident in East Orange. When, on July 12th, a black cab driver was injured in a traffic incident, a crowd gathered before the precinct police station, and later in the evening, as the crowd grew in size, Molotov cocktails were thrown. The police dispersed the crowd, and window-breaking and looting followed. One of America's most destructive riots had begun.[19]

An important point in the *Report* is its effort to deal with riots at two distinct levels of analysis: the long-run factors that are the "basic causes," and the "more immediate factors" that may generate widespread rioting.[20] It identifies the former as basically three: *pervasive discrimination and segregation, black migration and white exodus,* and *black ghettoes.* But these factors are not sufficient to cause riots, except as more "immediate factors" that have "begun to catalyze the mixture" are also present. These the *Report* identifies as the *frustrated hopes* that surfaced when the judicial and legislative victories and the civil-rights movement produced great expectations that were not realized; a *legitimation of violence,* when white terrorism against black demonstrators, and open defiance of law by state and local officials resisting desegregation, encouraged a climate that legitimized the use of violence. The open preaching of the use of violence by black militants has added to the problem, as has a sense of *powerlessness,* of being used and exploited by the white "power structure," which contributed to the idea that there is no way to move the system except through violence. When both basic causes and immediate factors are present, a seemingly trivial incident can ignite a terrible explosion.

Violence and Order

Riots are destructive events, and when they occur there is usually a call for law enforcement accompanied by pious assertions by civic leaders that there are better ways to accomplish worthwhile goals. But if more legitimate forms of social action—the courts and legislation—cannot seem to accomplish significant change, if a group continues in its powerlessness and its felt oppression, a resort to violence may seem morally defensible. At least to many young blacks it did during the urban riots of the 1960s.[21] And so it has throughout history with other peoples.

The moral case against violence is a preference for more rational and humane action. But any moral case must rest on the assurance that democratic society offers alternatives for effecting significant social change. When these alternatives do not prove effective for those who feel oppressed, the moral argument against violence becomes less and less convincing. It is then that situations of collective behavior produce redefinitions of norms to sanction legitimate action that would earlier have been illegitimate.

---

[19] *See Report,* pp. 118–119.
[20] *See Report,* Ch. 4, "The Basic Causes," pp. 203–206.

[21] *See* Boskin, *op. cit.,* pp. 12–13.

Authority and Violence

Violence is always a threat to the established order and so always brings a response from those in authority, sometimes more violent than the violent actions they would quell. When authorities make official explanations of riots, they do not concede any merit to them and insist, instead, that they are senseless and irrational outbursts, even if they may be the product of pent-up frustration. As Skolnick notes, "The essential problem with this perspective is that it neglects the intrinsically political and rational aspects of collective protests and fails to take seriously the grievances that motivate riots."[22]

In addition, the official position is always that violence can accomplish no good purpose: "Violence cannot build a better society," or "violence will not solve problems," and the like. But to claim that "violence doesn't pay" is to make a moralizing judgment, not an historical or sociological one. Rioting by different social groups and classes in the past has, in fact, produced social reforms intended to get at the very source of the grievances that produced the riots. Not to make such concessions in the face of deeply felt grievances is often to invite escalation of the conflict. The only alternative is a ruthless repression, itself notably violent, and possibly the extermination of the group that is in revolt.

To say this is not to celebrate violent riots: This is not to maintain that violence always works or is always necessary. We do not wish to create a new myth—a myth of violent progress—which could be disposed of easily by citing examples of violence without much progress (like the American Indian revolts) and progress with little violence (as among Scandinavian Americans). The point is that political

and economic power is not as easily shared or turned over to powerless outsiders as one had thought.[23]

And just because power is not shared, or a more sensitive responsiveness in authority is not developed, acting crowds seek to achieve by violence what people have been unable to achieve more peaceably.

PUBLICS AND PUBLIC OPINION

Publics and public opinion are creations of the revolutionary changes that created democratic society. Democratic elections and freedom of speech and of the press made possible free discussion of issues on which public decisions had to be made. The growth of newspapers provided both information and partisan opinion, and contributed to the importance of public opinion in democratic societies.[24]

The Public

The public lacks the structure that one associates with well-organized groups; it has no officials, though there may be opinion leaders; there is interaction and communication, though there is no definition of membership. The public, furthermore, has no process of physically coming together—its interaction is not face-to-face.

The concept of the public includes several elements:

1. Some (but not all) members of a society who have some concern or interest in a public matter.
2. An issue that requires resolution or decision within that society.

---

[22] *See* Skolnick, *The Politics of Protest*, p. 340.

[23] *See* Rubenstein, "Rebels in Eden," p. 111.

[24] *See* Hans Speir, "Historical Development of Public Opinion," *American Journal of Sociology*, vol. 55 (January 1950), pp. 376–388.

Figure 17.3 Among the political issues of concern to many people in the United States is racial discrimination. Here, a demonstration of anti-segregationists takes place in front of the White House. *(Monkmeyer, Paul Conklin.)*

3. A process of discussion among these interested individuals, carried on through available means of communication.
4. The emergence of public opinion from this discussion.

From these elements it would seem that the concept of public denotes not so much a group of people as a social process—a process of public discussion leading to the formation of one or more widely-shared opinions as to the advisability or desirability of a public policy or a mode of action by government.

In everyday discussion the concept of public is commonly used to refer to the fans of movie stars and the more devoted followers of public figures. It is also used to refer to the idea of everyone without restriction, as "the public is invited." Another use is to denote the customers and clientele of mass producers of entertainment and material goods: the movie public, the auto-buying public, and so on. In these cases what might be called public opinion is usually *mass customer reaction* to products offered for consumption. Although this mass reaction may certainly influence production policies, it is not public opinion in a sociological sense.

There are other common misconceptions about the nature of public. One is to speak of *the* public as if it included everyone in the society. Potentially it does, but in practice it is more restricted. If the public includes those who are interested in an issue and participate in public discussion of the merits of that issue, this excludes those who are not interested and have not participated.

Furthermore, there is not *the* public— there are *publics*. Different issues are of concern to different segments of the population: school bussing, abortion reform, ecology, taxes, tariffs, and national defense are issues that do not interest the same people or the same number of people. The public concerned with tariffs will be smaller than that concerned with taxes. The public concerned with national defense has been in the past larger than that conserved with conservation, but this may no longer be true.

The Public: A Political Process

If public refers to the discussion of public issues, then the public is a *political* process. According to sociologist Hans Speier, public opinion is:

. . . opinion on matters of concern to the nation freely and publicly expressed by men outside the government who claim a right that their opinions should influence or help determine the actions, personnel, or structure of their government. . . .

Public opinion, so understood, is primarily a communication from the citizens to their government and only secondarily a communication among the citizens. Further, if the government effectively denies the claim that the opinion of the citizens on public matters be relevant, in one form or another, for policy-making or if it prevents the free and public expression of such opinions, public opinion does not exist.[25]

Ideally, then, the public is a process of political citizens—rational, intelligent, informed—discussing fully and seriously the important social issues facing the society, with free access to all relevant facts through the media of communication. Rational people in a free society—this is the image of the public. Only a democratic society could fill the requirements set forth from this perspective.

In totalitarian societies there is a great concern by the controlling elite with the

mass distribution of attitudes and opinions. A free discussion of issues, however, does not take place. There is no public, then, only controlled mass opinion. The controlling elite is always concerned with mass opinion and response as it affects morale and work performance. Also, the elite monopolizes all sources of information in order to inculcate mass opinion in support of the regime.

The State of Public Opinion

The actual state of public opinion in modern democratic society falls short of the ideal process. For over forty years now, beginning with an influential work by journalist-intellectual Walter Lippmann,[26] social scientists, marketing researchers, journalists, and professional pollsters have been measuring public opinion in the United States, and more recently throughout the literate world. We now know a vast amount about public opinion on a vast array of issues.

What comes through from even a modest sampling of expressions of public opinion is this: Often the public seems neither well informed nor deeply concerned with many issues. Nor does public opinion seem to be the outcome of informed and serious public discussion.[27] The image of the public that emerges from analyses by many social scientists is a sorry one, dam-

[25] *See* Speier, *op. cit.*, p. 376.

[26] *See* Walter Lippmann, *Public Opinion* (New York: Harcourt, Brace, Jovanovich, 1922).
[27] For a review of the status of public opinion as measured by polls *see* Herbert H. Hyman and Paul B. Sheatsley, "The Current Status of American Public Opinion," in J.C. Payne, ed., *The Teaching of Contemporary Affairs* (Washington, D.C., National Council for the Social Studies, 21st Yearbook, 1950), pp. 11–34.

aging to the hope for an enlightened public who make a significant contribution to the democratic process.

Dismay at the seemingly low state of public opinion is based on the expectation that (1) all issues are within the intellectual grasp of the public, and (2) all citizens ought to be rational participants in public discussion. But many social scientists have come to the conclusion that what we know about public opinion warrants no such confident position. Even though the late V.O. Key, a distinguished political scientist, wrote a sober defense of the rational capacity of the voting public, challenging seriously the unflattering image now so widespread, this low estimation of public opinion persists.[28]

Yet such a judgment may be unduly pessimistic in assessing the possibilities of intelligent public opinion, while expecting too much from things as they now are. It does not follow, for example, that people are not rational when they take opinion cues from leaders and group representatives whom, they believe, are closer to an issue and understand all its implications better. Nor could we sociologically expect that people would approach public issues with a blank mind, innocent of any predispositions. Before they belong to publics, people belong to social groups and classes, and they think about the world in ways shaped by these group memberships. Through these, they are made conscious of their interests, so their participation in public discussion is shaped by these prior experiences in social groups. We say "rationally" because it is not irrational for people to be aware of their values and interests and to assess issues against these in developing an opinion.

The Problem of Public Opinion

The shaping of public opinion does not occur in a social vacuum. It occurs within the framework of political parties and their contests for public office. One cannot understand public opinion except as one also understands something about parties, their leadership, and the structure of power in American society. And none of these encourage the development and expression of a rational public opinion.

Sociologist Richard Hamilton makes the point that the *concerns* of citizens do not necessarily become public *issues*. "A concern is not necessarily a subject for widespread public discussion nor is it in any way *necessarily* of interest to political parties."[29] Most issues are rooted in widespread social concerns, but sometimes concerns are not translated into issues, and sometimes issues selected by political leaders are of no great concern to masses of citizens.

The connection between the public and the political leader, does not require the translation of every serious concern into an issue, which results in legislative action. The political system is not that responsive. Why not? Why should it be that, according to Hamilton, ". . . there are some rather solid reasons for parties to refuse the mobilization of potential support"?[30]

To understand why the political parties are only partly and incompletely responsive to the opinions of their presumed

[28] V.O. Key, Jr., *The Responsible Electorate: Rationality in Presidential Voting, 1936–60* (Cambridge, Mass.: Harvard University Press, 1966).

[29] Richard Hamilton, *Class and Politics in the United States* (New York: John Wiley & Sons, Inc., 1972), pp. 83–84.

[30] *See* Hamilton, *op. cit.,* p. 84.

constituency, the following need only be noted:

1. Party organization is controlled by professionals, who link two basic groups: the mass of citizens, who supply votes, and the organized interest groups, who supply money—a point we discussed in Chapter 15. Whatever the party does is, at minimum, a compromise between those two interests.

2. The mass of voters, then, are not in direct control of the parties. They can translate their opinions into political action only by choosing the limited and often unclear options offered by the parties:

> The general population, for the most part, only reacts to the leaders' overtures. The options open to them, again for the most part, are very limited; people may choose one or the other of the two parties, or they may choose not to vote at all. With

only rare exceptions, the general population has not been able to intervene in the "political process" in order to make clear the direction of majority sentiment.[31]

3. The diversity of American society—a wide range of social groups and strata, differentiated by class, race, region, religion, education, age, and other factors—is often pointed to as reason for difficulty in achieving a consistent majority, either liberal or conservative or something else. Groups that coalesce on one issue will differ on another.

But Hamilton's careful, detailed analysis of public opinion surveys disputes that conclusion. He argues, first of all, that: "Contrary to common belief, majority sentiment in the United States is solidly liberal with respect to domestic economic welfare issues," by which he means government ac-

[31] See Hamilton, *op. cit.*, p. 138.

TABLE 17.1 Public Opinion on Job Guarantee and Medical Care

I. *"The government in Washington ought to see to it that everybody who wants to work can find a job."*

	1956	1960
Agree strongly	43% ⎤	47% ⎤
Agree but not very strongly	13 ⎦ 56	11 ⎦ 58
Not sure; it depends	7	8
Disagree but not very strongly	11 ⎤	7 ⎤
Disagree strongly	16 ⎦ 27	11 ⎦ 23
Don't know, no answer, no opinion	10	11
Percent liberal of those with opinions	67	72

II. *"The government ought to help people get doctors and hospital care at low cost."*

	1956	1960
Agree strongly	39% ⎤	48% ⎤
Agree but not very strongly	15 ⎦ 54	11 ⎦ 59
Not sure; it depends	8	11
Disagree but not very strongly	8 ⎤	5 ⎤
Disagree strongly	18 ⎦ 26	14 ⎦ 19
Don't know, no answer, no opinion	12	11
Percent liberal of those with opinions	67	76

Source: Richard Hamilton, *Class and Politics in the United States* (New York: John Wiley & Sons, Inc., 1972), pp. 89–90.

Figure 17.4 Although a voter takes political action in an election, his expression of opinion is limited by the options offered by the political parties. *(A. Devaney, Inc., N.Y.)*

tion in guaranteeing jobs and medical care[32] (*see* Table 17.1).

Such issues as foreign affairs, the internal threat of communism, civil liberties, and civil rights are often cited as crosscutting issues that break an otherwise consistent majority. Again, Hamilton's analysis of opinion surveys through the 1950s and 1960s disputes this:

. . . the use of foreign affairs issues to "break" the liberal majority appears to be a procedure having only limited efficacy. The "masses," we have suggested, prove to be the least pugnacious element in the population and hence the least easily mobilized for such ventures. The ready aggressiveness is found with much greater frequency in the upper-middle classes . . . The attitude cleavage that occurs on such issues tends to run along the same line that sepa-

rates economic liberals from the economic conservatives.[33]

In the area of civil rights Hamilton points out that much survey material suggests two things: first, that there has been an increasingly more liberal sentiment on race issues, as measured in opinion survey, since the 1940s; and second, that the majority of the white population in the United States is neither "liberal" nor "illiberal," neither fully integrationist nor fully segregationist. As we noted in Chapter 13, these attitudinal trends do not easily translate themselves into support for programs, as the issue of school bussing demonstrates—but then school bussing is not a legislative program of any political party either.

4. The parties and candidates do not deliberately make "unmistakably clear" what they stand for or will do; instead, they often deliberately obscure the issues. Elections

---

[32] *See* Hamilton, *op. cit.,* p. 87.

[33] *See* Hamilton, *op. cit.,* p. 127.

are interpretable in a number of ways as to what if any "mandates" were given by the voters. Indeed, the intention of the majority can be so obscured, says Hamilton, that it becomes "a relatively simple matter to 'misdefine the majority.'"[34]

When political leaders define issues, the public can make sense of their positions and respond in support or not. Hamilton cites evidence of strong government support of medical care in 1956, when neither of the parties had taken any position.

In the 1960s the Democratic administration backed a program in medical care, and the public responded by clearly distinguishing one party from another on this matter. In 1960 in response to the question as to which party was more likely to do more in medical care 34 percent said the Democrats would, but another 30 percent said there was no difference in the parties. By 1962, 45 percent picked the Democrats and 24 percent said no difference; by 1964, the same percentages were 55 and 14.[35]

What had been a concern only up to 1960 became formulated into a political issue in the 1960s, and the public became quite aware of how the parties stood on the matter. Such data as these, Hamilton notes, support the observation that:

. . . the presumed irrationality and ignorance of "the people" results more from the parties and their failure to make or clarify the issues than from any fundamental lack of ability on the part of the populace.[36]

The discrepancy between what the people want and what the parties deliver is considerable, and most Americans know

that. Neither the parties nor politicians are held in high esteem, as we noted in Chapter 15. More to the point, a sizable number of Americans have constantly recorded their suspicion and distrust of the parties, the political leaders, and of government.[37]

National surveys have only infrequently asked the kinds of questions that would elicit data on how the public feels about its political leadership. But in 1958 and 1964 the Survey Research Center of the University of Michigan, in its continuing national study, did ask some questions to test the degree of trust and confidence people had in the national government.[38] From these we can glean some degree of a persistently disaffected element.

1. In 1958 on the question of whether people running the government are crooked, 26 percent said hardly any were, but 23 percent said quite a lot; in 1964 the respective percentages were 18 and 29. (In this and the following cases there is also an in-between category.)
2. In 1958 on whether the government wastes tax money 10 percent said not much, but 42 percent said a lot; in 1964 the respective percentages were 7 and 47.
3. In 1958 on how much of the time can you trust the government 15 percent said always, but 23 percent said only some of the time; in 1964 the respective percentages were 14 and 22.
4. In 1958 on whether people running the government knew what they were doing or not 56 percent said they did, but 36 percent said

[34] See Hamilton, op. cit., p. 135.
[35] See Hamilton, op. cit., p. 92.
[36] See Hamilton, op. cit., p. 92.

[37] For a recent survey that suggests a crisis of confidence of the American people in their society see Albert H. Cantril and Charles W. Rall, Jr., *Hopes and Fears of the American People* (New York: Universe Books, 1972).
[38] These data are reported in Hamilton, op. cit., pp. 107–109.

they did not; in 1964 the respective percentages were 69 and 27.

5. In 1958 on whether the high-up people in government give everyone a fair break or pay more attention to big shots only 17 percent thought everyone got a fair break and 74 percent thought that big shots got more attention. This question was not asked in 1964; instead, people were asked whether government was run for the benefit of all or for a few big interests. 64 percent said for the benefit of all, and 28 percent said for a few big interests.

These data point up that a disaffected perspective ranges over time and varies considerably, depending on what kind of question is asked. But from one-fifth to one-fourth were disaffected on every issue; and on some issues the figures included most of the adult population.

Such data as these do not suggest that apathy in the public can be traced primarily to a comfortable sense that all's right with the country, but instead to a widespread feeling that government and party act in ways determined by other than the interests or wishes of the majority. Public opinion cannot help but be affected by that feeling.

Public Opinion and Expertise

Even for many educated and concerned people, some public issues are so complex that an informed public is unlikely. Furthermore, leaders who must make decisions—such as legislators, governors, and presidents—cannot be expertly informed on so many matters. As a consequence, they are guided by the advice of experts, as well as by the positions taken by the spokesmen for groups with definite interests in the issue. Interest groups, in turn, employ experts to advance their causes—

disabusing us of any notion that experts are always objective and disinterested. It is often to the advantage of administrators, experts, and elites to let the public assume its own incompetence to judge technical matters.

Few citizens expect that major decisions over national defense, such as the problem of choosing among alternate weapons systems, are matters to be decided by public opinion—and not because so much relevant information is a military secret. Even if the information were not secret, the technical complexity of the matter can exceed the capacity of all but the specially trained. Even where issues are not as technical as military weapons systems, the issues are still complex—involving economic, political, administrative, financial, and tax factors understood only by those trained in these specialties. As a consequence, any concern for the function of public opinion in a democracy must recognize that the average citizen does not expect—and is encouraged not to expect—to have an informed opinion on such matters. He does expect the nation's political leadership to be able to make informed judgments, with the assistance of disinterested experts, and to be held accountable for the decisions made. How to be confident of the disinterestedness of experts, and how to hold political leadership accountable, becomes a serious issue for the public as an electorate.

Interest groups often deliberately obscure and becloud issues, rather than clarify them. While lobbying and pressuring within the legislative and administrative structure, they intervene in the opinion-making process with deliberately constructed appeals. They resort to propaganda.

Propaganda: The Manipulation of Public Opinion

The formation of public opinion is rarely left to chance. Interest groups always seek to shape it to suit their own ends. As a consequence, it is rarely the spontaneous outcome of public discussion; rather, *manipulation by propaganda* is a major factor.

Propaganda is the deliberate dissemination of partisan communication in order to influence the formation of public opinion. It may be, but does not have to be, untruthful. What distinguishes propaganda is its intent: To focus attention on an issue

PUBLICS AND POLLS

For forty years now public-opinion polls have been carefully developed and refined; by now *Gallup* is a household word in the United States. After literally hundreds of polls a vast amount of information has been gathered. Can we now make any assessment of the place of polls in American society? The following are some useful points in attempting any assessment:

1. *Techniques.*   After much experience, and some embarrassing failures (such as *Liberty Magazine's* prediction of Franklin Roosevelt's defeat in 1936, and Gallup and other polls' prediction of Dewey's election over Truman in 1948), careful probability sampling now permits a surprisingly small number of respondents to provide an accurate sample of the population as a whole. A sample of 3,000 is sufficient to predict the outcome of a national election within a very small and measurable range of error.

   Sampling is not everything; the questions asked must be clear and unambiguous in their meaning to respondents, but even here much experience has sharpened and refined the techniques of asking questions.

2. *Predicting elections.*   The polls are most successful in predicting elections; now they rarely miss by more than 2 percentage points. This is because they ask people their *intention* shortly before people actually have an opportunity to act on that intention. Perhaps their greatest technical problem lies in the number who express an opinion but fail to vote.

   But is this technical success of any social value? Are elections any better because pollsters can tell us the weekend before how it will come out? And is the result itself affected by the publishing of polling results?

3. *Testing political support.*   Polling is now a standard tool used by politicians and parties to sound out in advance how voters might respond to a candidacy, and how they are responding during a campaign. It is of practical use, therefore, in deciding on candidates and on shaping campaigns to make the greatest appeal.

   But only some of these polls are public. Those done for candidates and parties are often kept secret. If politicians then know what others do not know, particularly what the public does not know, are such polls contributing to public understanding or to public manipulation?

4. *Public opinion.*   Polls have provided much information on attitudes and

background shapes persons public opinion

in such a way as deliberately to create a choice in public opinion and reduce the probability of alternative choices of opinion being made. Unlike academic scholarship and science propaganda's concern is not the pursuit of truth but to convince people of a point of view. This does not mean that propagandists are intentionally dishonest, only that they are highly partisan about an issue.

In modern society propaganda is a major factor in public life, diffused extensively through the mass media. Systematic, professional work in propaganda comes from those skilled in mass communication and from the communication professions.

opinions of the adult population on a wide range of important issues; on how opinion has changed over time; and on how such opinion varies in the population by age, race, occupation, income, region, religion, sex, and other pertinent variables. Through persistent polling we know a great deal more about the state of public opinion in the United States than ever before.

5. *But is it public opinion?* What is measured by opinion polls, however, is not public opinion—a crystallized and widely shared opinion developed after much public discussion—but the aggregated mass opinions of the population. It is individual opinion counted and added up, including in this mass aggregate many individuals who really have no opinion, are not concerned with an issue, and may even know little if anything about it. Often, polling occurs before any public discussion has occurred, or at least before it has advanced very far.

6. *Is the opinion poll useful?* What value do we derive from its information? Social scientists, and eventually historians, have much to learn from it, particularly in terms of trends measured over time. Carefully assessed within its limits, then, it has a scholarly usefulness.

   But is the opinion poll useful to society, not just to scholars? No ready answer can be given. It depends on what *uses* are made of the poll, and here we know much less than we know about the polling process itself.

7. *Polls and policy-making.* We do know that a favorable opinion poll does not guarantee that an issue will become policy. Gun control, for example, wins in the polls but loses in the legislative chambers. Polls may have some role in policy-making but other factors do also—the successful pressure of various groups, the power differentials in the society.

   However, no one claims that polls should be translated directly into legislation. Decision-making by polls, given their character as expressing aggregate mass opinion rather than public opinion, would not be better democracy than what we now have.

Judiciously used, the opinion poll can be one important communication between citizens and their government. But we need to know more about this and other possible functions of the poll before we can arrive at any adequate assessment of its place in democratic society.

Advertising and public relations provide a source of skilled propagandists. Public-relations firms in the United States have become major businesses manufacturing propaganda for clients. For example, when President Harry Truman advanced his program for national medical insurance, the American Medical Association employed a California public-relations firm, Whittaker and Baxter, specialists in political campaigns, to carry out a national program of opposition.

Political campaigns are now carried on with the aid of professional propagandists, who do more than write speeches. They plan a campaign in detail to create images favorable to their parties or candidates.[39]

Corporations, trade associations, government agencies, and the military now regularly employ the skills of propagandists, who work artfully to "fool all of the people all of the time," though they do not succeed all of the time. They are never called propagandists, though; their activity is labeled press relations, public relations, public information.

The basic task of these professionals is to provide the mass media with information, just as much information as they want made public—no more—selected and organized so as to put the best possible light on the organization and its interests. This is often done by a *press release,* written in the form of a news story. By using a press release an unambitious journalist can let the propagandist write his news story for him—and it happens. Fuller and more accurate information requires the probing of investigative journalists intent on finding out what was withheld or played down, in order to make possible an independent interpretation of the issue at hand.

The Hidden Persuaders

In contemporary America terms like "hidden persuaders" and "Madison Avenue" symbolize public awareness of these efforts to manipulate opinions about products, personalities, politicians, issues, and ideas. Vance Packard's *The Hidden Persuaders* became a national best seller by exposing the techniques by which advertisers and public-relations practitioners sought to influence opinion.[40] Its very title implies a sinister process; its major theme was that people did not know so much of the material in mass communication to which they were exposed was deliberately contrived, without their knowledge, to shape their opinions.

How do mass persuaders persuade? A propaganda message is built by appealing to *values* and *attitudes* in order to influence opinions. The propagandist invokes *symbols* of these underlying values and attitudes to link his particular objective to these values and, as a consequence, mold opinion in the desired direction. Freedom, equality, socialism, private enterprise, individualism, big government, bureaucracy; these are some of the major symbols, both negative and positive, that signify underlying values and attitudes. For example, when Whittaker and Baxter undertook to direct the AMA's campaign against President Truman's program for national medical insurance, they labeled it "socialized medicine" so effectively that the label remained attached to the program until the mid-sixties.

---

[39] For several case studies of the techniques employed by such professionals *see* Stanley Kelly, *Professional Public Relations and Political Power* (Baltimore, Md.: Johns Hopkins University Press, 1956).

[40] Vance Packard, *The Hidden Persuaders* (New York: David McKay Company, Inc., 1957).

Figure 17.5 The American flag is a virtue symbol which seems to sanctify those who invoke its use—and what they stand for. *(Magnum.)*

Labeling is an example of *name-calling*, one of seven major "tricks of the trade" employed by propagandists. These were enumerated in an enlightening little book, *The Fine Art of Propaganda*.[41] If *name-calling* means to place a bad label on something, *glittering generality* means to place a good label on it, using such "virtue words" as *American, democratic, individual,* and the like. Two other tricks, *transfer* and *testimonial,* refer to the process of transferring the prestige or esteem of respected symbols, or of obtaining statements from respected persons, to support or oppose an issue. *Plain folks* is a process of identifying the propagandist's ideas with the people. *Card stacking* refers to the development of an argument that so arranges

facts and falsehoods as to lead people to a particular conclusion; while *band wagon* seeks to build support by leading people to believe that everyone is for the idea, and therefore they had better "get with it."

The Influence of Propagandists

What accounts for the influential role of propagandists in shaping public opinion to suit special interests? The unstable character of public opinion in a changing society is bound to bring efforts at influencing it. Powerful groups of one kind or another develop vast stakes in programs and activities, and are not going to allow public opinion to develop spontaneously if that opinion has some bearing on their interests. Furthermore, the complexity of many public issues allows the propagandist to present simplified answers in acceptable

[41] Alfred McClung Lee and Elizabeth Briant Lee, *The Fine Art of Propaganda* (New York: Harcourt, Brace, Jovanovich, 1939; reprint, Octagon Books, 1972).

435

symbolic terms. Nor does the mass media itself always present rational, objective discussions, free of propaganda.

In America the fears and anxieties of masses of people about world trends; about the prospects for world peace; their insecurities about a changing, uncertain future, individual and collective; their unspoken concerns about shifts and transitions in power—all these concerns give the propagandist an opportunity to influence the shaping of public opinion. Such a situation not only sets the stage for the manipulation of mass opinions it damages belief in an informed and intelligent public opinion as a function of democracy.

Social science has contributed considerably to this damaged image of democracy by its emphasis on the low state of public opinion and the manipulation of it by propagandists. But students of social science must keep clear the distinction between the present state of affairs—*what is* —as objectively described by social sci-

ence, and an image of a future, more ideal state of affairs—*what might be.* The present state of public opinion is not in itself sufficient reason for abandoning a belief in the possibility of a more rational process of forming public opinion, but it is a basis for understanding the present gap between the reality and the ideal, and also for understanding what characteristics of modern society prevent the ideal from being more nearly approximated.

The state of public opinion is not low because people are stupid or irrational— and is probably not as low as social scientists have been saying—but because too many interests are served by confusing, not clarifying public issues. In the face of technical complexity, ordinary citizens are encouraged to assume their own incompetency and so to rely on experts to shape public opinion. But experts are only sometimes disinterested; often they are partisan actors in struggles for advantage and gain.

SUMMARY

Collective behavior includes all those loosely structured collectivities for which there is little division of labor, no established authority, no clear definition of membership; these include *crowds, publics,* and *social movements.*

A crowd is more than an aggregate of people in one place; it emerges when interaction among such individuals gives them a common focus and concern.

It is the *acting crowd* that is the major concern of crowd theory, beginning with LeBon's, which emphasizes the loss of individuality in an emotional *contagion.* But the *emergent norm* theory argues that a crowd is a *developing collectivity,* in which a situation is defined, norms emerge, and lines of action are agreed on.

Crowd *violence* occurs around issues that mark deep cleavages of the values in a society, such as racism and unions in the United States. Such violence is a form of *political protest,* which may or may not produce social reform.

Publics came into being in a democratic society, and are a *political rela-*

tionship between citizens and government. There are publics of varying size, depending on issues. They presumably engage in *rational* processes of discussion and opinion-formation, but the reality is less than the ideal.

The public is not as irrational or uninformed or apathetic as many have said. Political leaders and parties often confuse rather than clarify issues, for publics are often unresponsive to many concerns.

Interest groups intervene in the opinion-forming process to *propagandize*. Skilled experts in mass communication are professionals at this task.

Suggested Readings

Hugh Davies Graham and Ted Robert Gurr, eds., *The History of Violence in America, A Report to the National Commission on the Causes and Prevention of Violence* (New York: Bantam Books, Inc., 1969). A review of violence that painfully reminds us just how much there has been, and how significant it is in American history.

Allen D. Grimshaw, ed., *Racial Violence in the United States* (Chicago, Ill.: Aldine-Atherton, Inc., 1969). A collection of papers that covers the long historical record of violence in race relations in the United States.

Richard Hamilton, *Class and Politics in the United States* (New York: John Wiley & Sons, Inc., 1972). This is a very thorough, detailed study of what survey research tells us about class and political opinion. Hamilton's Chapter 3 in particular bears directly on this subject.

Gustave LeBon, *The Crowd: A Study of the Popular Mind* (New York: The Viking Press, Inc., 1960). This great classic, antidemocratic in its sentiments, had an enormous impact on social-scientific ideas about crowds.

Alfred McClung Lee and Elizabeth Briant Lee, *The Fine Art of Propaganda* (New York: Harcourt, Brace, Jovanovich, 1939; reprint, Octagon Books, 1972). After more than thirty years this remains a little gem that never loses its informative value.

Walter Lippmann, *Public Opinion* (New York: Harcourt, Brace, Jovanovich, 1922). The classic and still readable work that began scholarly concern with public opinion.

The National Advisory Commission on Civil Disorders, *Report* (New York: Bantam Books, 1968). Known as the Kerner Report, this is the most influential of the government-inspired reports that seek to make sense of racial violence in the late sixties.

Vance Packard, *The Hidden Persuaders* (New York: David McKay Company, Inc., 1957). A popular but nonetheless informative work on the techniques and practices of "hidden persuaders."

Richard Rubenstein, *Rebels in Eden: Mass Political Violence in the United States* (Boston, Mass.: Little Brown & Company, 1971). A study that emphasizes the political meaning of violence in American history.

George Rudé, *The Crowd in the French Revolution, 1730–1848* (New York: John Wiley & Sons, Inc., 1964). A French historian's examination of the role of crowds in French political struggles.

Jerome Skolnick, *The Politics of Protest, A Report of the Task Force on Violent Aspects of Protest and Confrontation of the National Commission on the Causes and Prevention of Violence* (New York: Simon and Schuster, Inc., 1969). A major sociological analysis that places violence in a political framework.

The study of social movements reminds us of the irrepressible conviction of sentient men that they can collectively, if not individually, change their culture by their own endeavors.
— *Lewis M. Killian*

Chapter 18

Social Movements

For the most part change occurs in society as an unplanned and unintended process, often not well understood by those whose lives are affected. To look at change this way invokes an image of people reacting blindly to circumstances not of their making, mere puppets swept along by the great flow of human events. History has often been written in just that way.

However, people rarely accept change without making some effort to give it direction, to reshape things according to some human design — an old order to be restored or a new one to be created. *Social movements* are the conscious attempts of masses of people to bring about change in the social structure by collective action.

Social movements have arisen throughout history, from all social classes and groups: peasants and farmers, workers and shopkeepers, oppressed minorities and declining classes. Some of them are limited in their objectives; *reform* movements accept the basic values and institutions of society but seek to change what they define as abuses, defects, or inadequacies. The labor movement is a reform movement when it seeks changes benefiting the worker without altering the basic structure of capitalism.

Revolutionary movements try to bring about a fundamental change in

438

structure, as in replacing capitalism with socialism.

Identifying Social Movements

Like crowds, social movements have been hard to study, for they are large and complex processes. Rarely can they be observed at one time or at one place. They differ from crowds and publics, however, in that they develop some structure—a core of organization, however weak and inconsistently integrated, even fragmented—and they develop a leadership.

Yet the study of social movements "is not the study of stable groups and established institutions, but of groups and institutions in the process of becoming."[1] A definition of social movement that fits our conception is: "A collectivity acting with some continuity to promote or resist a change in the society or group of which it is a part."[2]

That people act collectively, not individually, to promote or resist change is Killian's basis for claiming there are four salient features of a social movement:[3]

1. The existence of *shared values*—a goal or an objective, sustained by an ideology.
2. A sense of *membership* or participation—a "we-ness," a distinction between those who are for and those against.
3. *Norms*—shared understandings as to how the followers should act, definitions of outgroups and how to behave toward them.
4. A *structure*—a division of labor between leaders and followers and between differ-

ent classes of each. This is not a comprehensive structure, however.

From the sociological perspective, therefore, a social movement is an ongoing social process for social change, one in which people are consciously assessing and evaluating their society and initiating efforts to alter its structure in ways that more nearly fit their values.

THE NATURE OF A SOCIAL MOVEMENT

Although it would be correct to say that social movements arise because people want to change the order of things, this is hardly an adequate statement of why social movements come to be. To some extent people always and everywhere would like to change things. In fact, one long and persistently puzzling question about human life is why more people do not rebel against the circumstances of their lives, why they so patiently endure oppressive and burdensome circumstances.

One reason is that many people see their life circumstances as a peculiar and individual fate of their own, unrelated to the life circumstances of others. In societies dominated by an ideology of individualism—of which the United States is a prime example—this isolation is more likely to occur. In other cases dominant ideologies, particularly if they have religious sanction or even take religious form, provide people with beliefs that make them endure rather than revolt. Recall examples we have already cited: the religious justification of caste relations, even the degrading lot of the untouchables (Chapter 10); the use of Christianity to teach slaves to be compliant, and its use to terrorize the poor

[1] *See* Lewis Killian, "Social Movements," in Robert E.L. Faris, ed., *Handbook of Modern Sociology* (Chicago, Ill.: Rand-McNally & Company, 1964), p. 427.

[2] *See* Ralph H. Turner and Lewis M. Killian, *Collective Behavior* (Englewood Cliffs, N.J.: Prentice-Hall, Inc., 1957), p. 308.

[3] *See* Killian, "Social Movements," p. 430.

with fear of fire and brimstone (Chapter 16); and the religious—instead of political —form of dissidence and rebelliousness, which develops sects that reject this world as evil but do not seek to change it, instead, expecting Christ to do so when the heralded millenium comes.

The emergence of a social movement, then, is not an automatic process. For one thing, individuals must communicate their dissatisfactions and share with others a *collective* sense of a common lot in life. They must identify with others who share their same fate. Spontaneous acts of rebellion and protest, silent acts of sabotage and vandalism—these may signify an underlying sense of grievance. So may voting "Communist" (or whatever is most heretical), or a withdrawal and refusal to be involved in society. In these ways a sense of grievance shared by a segment of a society is acted out, but none of these may constitute a social movement. The emergence of a social movement from the appropriate underlying conditions requires the development not only of a sense of collective fate but of a belief in the chance to act collectively toward new goals that will bring a new life. In the absence of any *hope,* there will be no social movement.

Many social scientists believe that a social movement is most likely to occur when, by an objective measurement, the life of an oppressed people has improved. A mood of *rising expectations* then makes people impatient with the actual pace of social change, and a movement develops intent on bringing change more quickly.

Yet this explanation fits some movements and not others. It does not fit movements that emerge among once-dominant classes and groups, who try to resist change that benefits others to their disadvantage. The radical right movement is a fairly re-

cent example;[4] the Southern white movement against blacks came earlier;[5] and the Know-Nothing movement against immigrants in the 1840s and 1850s is still an older one. Nor does it fit native movements among colonized peoples, who reject their rulers' culture but do little to change the relations of power and control. (*See* the discussion of nativistic movements in Chapter 16.)

Many social scientists agree that objective conditions alone will not create a social movement. There must be a social consciousness that finds a basis for hope, as we have seen, however protracted the struggle may be; only then can people define the possibilities for action. For this to happen, says Louis Killian, there must be leadership, an active nucleus sharing a "vision, a belief in the possibility of a different state of affairs, and there must be enduring organization devoted to the attainment of this vision."[6]

This, then, is the crux of a social movement: Not merely that people are in situations which lead to a strong sense of grievance, dissatisfaction, and resentment but that they develop a perspective which makes concerted, collective action possible. Working out such an interpretation of things is the function of ideology.

THE IDEOLOGY OF A SOCIAL MOVEMENT

For any class or group generating a social movement, their ideology expresses a sense of grievance and injustice about society, provides a specific criticism of the

[4] *See* Daniel Bell, ed., *The Radical Right* (New York: Anchor Books, 1963).

[5] *See* David Chalmers, *Hooded Americanism* (New York: Doubleday & Company, Inc., 1965).

[6] *See* Killian, "Social Movements," p. 435.

existing social structure, and projects goals which are to be sought by collective action. (In turn, dominant groups and classes develop defensive ideologies to resist change.) An ideology interprets an historical situation from the perspective of group or class in order to legitimate modes of social movement.

Ideology performs *four* functions for a social movement:

1. It links *action* and *belief*. Ideology gives politically-oriented expression to basic beliefs about justice, rights, human nature, freedom, and property, among others; thus, it interprets these basic values in concrete human situations to justify action. As political scientist David Apter points out: "ideology helps to make more explicit the moral basis of action."[7] In that way ideology provides the deepest of moral sanctions—and possibly passionate support—for political action.

2. Ideology is *unifying*. It concentrates the energies of people onto specific projects and unites them around symbols and slogans that give specific content to their hitherto vague feelings of discontent. Thus, it provides *solidarity* for what might otherwise be a diffuse and weakly organized collectivity.

3. It provides a *collective sense of identity*. Ideology defines *we* against *them*—and *we* may be the people, the working class, *la raza* (the race), the chosen ones, the nation, or whatever is the collective basis of the solidarity. It also helps shape personal identity, particularly for the young (*see* box on "Erik Erikson: Ideology and Identity").

4. It makes a utopian future seem both *believable* and *attainable*. A movement's ideology generates a *utopian* mentality that fastens firmly on belief in a future state of affairs. The utopian myth may seem to reach for impossible goals, but the effort to reach utopia may radically change society, even though it is not utopia which is eventually constructed.[8]

But the same ideology which offers a vision of heaven also offers a vision of hell. It warns of dire consequences if things are not changed. Thus, the white segregationist movement warns of a society made inferior if blacks are allowed full citizenship and if intermarriage produces "mongrelization." Integrationists, in turn, warn of burning cities and oppressive responses that will unintentionally destroy democracy if whites do not grant full citizenship to blacks.

Ideology often simplifies the real world for masses of people. It thus distorts reality by defining "they" and "us," our side and their side, in relatively simple contrasting terms. It may moralize great human events and designate scapegoats. "Vulgar" Marxism, for example, projected a stereotype of the greedy, exploitative Capitalists, though Karl Marx was concerned not with evil men but with a social process. Ideology, therefore, always functions at several intellectual levels, from the most simple and uncomplicated to the most scholarly.

ORGANIZATION AND LEADERSHIP OF A SOCIAL MOVEMENT

A social movement is not the same thing as an organization, yet it needs some degree of organization if it is to mobilize

---

[7] *See* David Apter, "Introduction: Ideology and Discontent," in David Apter, ed., *Ideology and Discontent* (New York: The Free Press, 1964), p. 17.

[8] For a brilliant exposition of the political meaning of utopian myths for the modern world *see* Karl Mannheim, *Ideology and Utopia,* Louis Wirth and Edward A. Shils, trans. (New York: Harcourt, Brace, Jovanovich, 1936).

ERIK ERIKSON: IDEOLOGY AND IDENTITY

While most students of ideology have emphasized its functions of creating solidarity and legitimizing action and program, Erik Erikson has in complementary fashion pointed to the place of ideology in the formation of personal *identity*. Maturation in the person comes when personality is shaped by the search for identity and role. Because youth are the ones who have not yet found themselves, who are searching for an identity, they become particularly responsive to ideologies, for ideology helps to provide identity. That is why youth are so much more easily mobilizable for social movements than are adults, and why youth is particularly responsive to dramatic action.

In his explanation of the appeal and significance of ideologies for youth, Erikson says:

Ideologies offer to the members of this age-group overly simplified and yet determined answers to exactly those vague inner states and those urgent questions which arise in consequence of identity conflict. Ideologies serve to channel youth's forceful earnestness and sincere asceticism as well as its search for excitement and its eager indignation toward that social frontier where the struggle between conservatism and radicalism is most alive. On that frontier, fanatic ideologists do their busy work and psychopathic leaders their dirty work; but there, also, true leaders create significant solidarities.*

*Erik Erikson, *Young Man Luther: A Study in Psychoanalysis and History* (New York: W.W. Norton & Company, Inc., 1958), pp. 38–39.

---

people for collective action. A political party, for example, usually provides the organized core for political movements, but so can civic organizations and labor unions. While organizational membership provides the most stable source of support for the social movement, sympathetic supporters may not all be organization members.

It is the organization which plans rallies, publishes newspapers and pamphlets, holds meetings, and determines the strategy of the campaign. It is organization which provides a leadership with the resources with which to function.

The Social Base

The *social base* of a movement is that particular group or class in whose interest the movement speaks and who provide most, if not all, of the support for the movement. Thus, workers are the social base of the labor and Socialist movements, though the latter also gets considerable middle class and intellectual support.

The social base of a movement is often fairly obvious, as when farmers or peasants constitute an agrarian movement. In other instances the social base is less clear. Fascism, for example, has frequently been characterized as middle class, but this obscures how well it drew from other social classes and how much opposition to fascism came from the middle class. Fascism does not obviously identify itself as middle class in the same way that socialism identifies itself as working class.[9]

[9] *See* Seymour Lipset, "Fascism—Left, Right, and Center," in his *Political Man* (New York: Doubleday & Company, Inc., 1960), pp. 131–176.

Among social movements today, the social base is often unclear and perhaps not what spokesmen for the movement claim. The youth movement of the 1960s was very largely a college student movement, and even as yet women's liberation is still largely based on the support of younger, middle-class, college-educated women.

There is, then, often some conflict between the purported base of a social movement and its actual social base in the population. A movement's adherents may want to speak for a broader base, but something in its ideology or actions, or both, may limit its appeal. The Black Muslims, for example, had its strongest appeal among the mass of ordinary blacks, yet many of these same blacks resist its anti-Christian ideology.[10]

Whatever the social base of a movement logically is, however, it can draw to it many other people looking for a cause. Some of these are the *true believers* that Eric Hoffer talked about, who see dedication to a movement as a way of giving meaning to their lives. (*See* box on "The True Believer.")

Leadership

The leadership of a social movement is not necessarily drawn entirely from its

[10] *See* C. Eric Lincoln, *The Black Muslims in America* (Boston, Mass.: The Beacon Press, 1961).

THE TRUE BELIEVER

Mass movements attract large numbers of alienated and disaffected persons, who find a meaning for their lives in a complete dedication to the movement. In doing so, they may find a solution to their personal problems or at least some therapy for them. Eric Hoffer—a brilliant, self-educated intellectual who worked most of his life as a longshoreman—called such people *true believers.* The *frustrated*, the *rejected*, and the *disaffected* who flock to a social movement give to it some of their unreasoned zeal and enthusiasm, according to Hoffer, regardless of what that movement is all about.*

But care must be taken not to confuse the true believers with others who are strong and devoted adherents of a movement, but are not in any way disoriented or incapable of rational judgments. It would be a poor and very biased analysis to claim that a social movement emerges because people are irrationally disoriented by the problems of their own lives. The bias, obviously, is to make it seem that those attracted to a movement demanding social change are people with psychological problems, while more rational people are not attracted to any such movement. This kind of conservative psychologizing is inadequate sociological analysis. When great mass movements arise, it is because established institutions are not meeting the interests and demands of large numbers of people, and they then turn to a movement as a way of remedying their lot in life.

* Eric Hoffer, *The True Believer* (New York: New American Library, 1951).

social base; many leaders of movements of the oppressed classes are themselves from more advantaged status. But whatever their social origins, leaders of emerging social movements are *charismatic;* they can rally masses of people in opposition to the established order, and they require no institutionalized positions in bureaucracies or traditional social structures to legitimize their leadership.

A social movement needs pragmatic leaders who are skilled organizers, as well as those who can devise strategy and tactics. Emphasis on charismatic leaders and intellectuals, in fact, has neglected the crucial role of the organizer, particularly in the early days of a movement.[11]

There is nothing to prevent one person from filling several leadership roles, but rarely does one person possess the necessary qualities and skills. Although one leader may be charismatically identified with a social movement, there is in fact usually a group of leaders in whom the several functions and skills necessary to carry out the collective action of the movement are combined.

Another function of leadership in a movement is to provide *intellectual* direction and focus. Intellectuals may create ideologies, adapt and alter them to fit changing circumstances, translate great visions like Marxism to the specifics of time and circumstances, and in a number of other ways provide a coherent rationale for the actions of the movement.

Legitimation and Leadership

Just who the leaders of a social movement are is a matter of consensus, not of constitutional validation or even necessarily a matter of organizational office. A charismatic leader, as Weber pointed out, is a leader because of his following alone. This consensus about leadership may frequently be less than complete, however, and competing claims to leadership are often a source of internal conflict in a movement.

In part this may be a struggle for leadership as a coveted prize; the most dedicated of men and women are not always without personal ambition. But often it also represents different interpretations of the goals and intentions of the movement. A struggle over leadership may be the first visible evidence of internal tensions and potential splits within a movement.

Competing Organizations

There can also be competing organizations in a social movement. The civil-rights movement in the South, for example, never focused around one organization. There was Martin Luther King's Southern Christian Leadership Conference;[12] but there was also the National Association for the Advancement of Colored People (NAACP),[13] the Student Non-violent Coordinating Committee (SNCC, called "Snick"),[14] the Congress of Racial Equality (CORE),[15] and other, more local groups as well.

In this case, as in others, several organizations were in existence at the outset of

---

[11] For a brief discussion *see* Jo Freeman, "The Origins of the Women's Liberation Movement," *American Journal of Sociology,* vol. 78 (January 1973), pp. 806–807.

[12] *See* Martin Luther King, Jr., *The Triumph of Conscience* (New York: Harper and Row, 1968).

[13] *See* Langston Hughes, *Fight for Freedom: The Story of the NAACP* (New York: W.W. Norton & Company, Inc., 1962).

[14] *See* Howard Zinn, *SNCC: The New Abolitionists* (Boston, Mass.: The Beacon Press, 1964).

[15] *See* Inge Powell Bell, *CORE and the Strategy of Nonviolence* (New York: Random House, Inc., 1968).

Figure 18.1 A leader in a social movement, who can spark the popular imagination into following him, exercises charisma—at least for a time. *(U.P.I. Photo.)*

the movement. New organizations came into being as the movement developed, usually over differences of ideology and tactics, for when some degree of success makes an organization more moderate, a more radically uncompromising organization may be created by those who refuse to come to terms with society. In other cases, a failure of strategy may lead to new groups that invent new strategic approaches. In the radical movement of the 1960s, the original Students for a Democratic Society (SDS) splintered into factions, such as the Maoist-oriented Progressive-Labor Party and the Weathermen.

Social movements are not neat and tidy affairs; they are never completely systematic, and they are usually a battleground of people who fight each other over the meaning of the movement just as strongly as they fight the common enemy. Claims and counter-claims as to who "legiti-

mately" speaks for the movement and can act in its name and in terms of its values remain unsettled during much of the history of the movement.

Unity and Cohesion

Factors that make for division and disagreement are always present in any social movement, yet the effectiveness of a movement depends greatly on unity and cohesion. Social movements are strong to the extent that the leaders can mobilize the members for concerted action; disagreement and division weaken their efforts. Unity is thus a major value for a movement's leaders and its most committed members. The labor movement's slogan of "solidarity forever" is recognition and promotion of this idea.

A movement, according to sociologist Herbert Blumer, must therefore develop an *esprit de corps,* an identification of its

445

members with one another, a sense of being an in-group.[16] An ideology, as we have seen, can provide this, as can a dynamic and appealing charismatic leader. Informal patterns of interaction, which give members an opportunity to interact with leaders, help to maintain identification with the movement.

Thus, social movements thrive on *enthusiasm*, which is less essential for more ordinary institutions and groups. But enthusiasm is hard to maintain day in and day out, and particularly in the face of adversity—and no social movement escapes some defeats and disappointments. A deeper conviction and commitment of the members of a movement is necessary to maintain *morale*.[17] Again, the charismatic leader probably best maintains morale during struggle and conflict. His own actions must help to sustain unshakable convictions about the unchallenged rightness of the cause, faith in its ultimate success, and a sense of a "sacred mission."

THE CAREER OF A MOVEMENT

A social movement begins at some point in history, at a time of crisis and dissent; but eventually it ceases to exist. It grows; it develops; and then it dies away or becomes a stable organization—a pressure group, most likely—that has made its peace with society. There is no one cycle through which all movements go, no one pattern they all follow.

When a new social movement emerges from a background of dissent and discontent, new leadership expresses a reformulation of values to clarify a new set of goals. The vagueness of mere discontent gives way to the pursuit of specific goals; strategies are formulated and tactics determined. No matter what the movement's origins, or the appeal of its ideology, it must confront the world; as Blumer noted, ". . . a movement has to be constructed and has to carve out a career in what is practically always an opposed, resistant, or at least indifferent world."[18]

A young and relatively untried social movement may engage at first in appeals, in efforts to clarify both to itself and to others what its grievances and objectives are. It may emphasize converting others to the justice of its claims, if not to joining the movement itself. But eventually it usually engages in some concerted action and puts to the test its claims that social change must be made.

The response within society to a developing social movement is crucial for its further development and for the nature of its career. When a movement arouses fear, its activities may bring strong and possibly punitive responses. (This happened to the Black Panthers; a number of its leaders died in shoot-outs with police.)[19] People killed or jailed become martyrs; and the leaders may become more embittered and more alienated from society than they were initially. The movement's ideology emphasizes the evils of society and the need for a more radical or even revolutionary change.

If reaction to the movement is so in-

[16] *See* Herbert H. Blumer, "Collective Behavior," in Alfred M. Lee, ed., *Principles of Sociology* (New York: Barnes & Noble, Inc., 1951), pp. 167–222.
[17] *See* Blumer, *op. cit.,* p. 208.

[18] Herbert Blumer, "Collective Behavior," in Joseph B. Gittler, ed., *Review of Sociology: Analysis of a Decade* (New York: John Wiley & Sons, Inc., 1957), p. 147.
[19] *See* Gene Marine, *The Black Panthers* (New York: New American Library, 1969); *see also* Bobby Seale, *Seize the Time: The Story of the Black Panther Party and Huey P. Newton* (New York: Random House, Inc., 1970). Bobby Seale is a founder of the Black Panthers.

Figure 18.2 Protesters outside the 1970 Black Panther trial in New York City, where thirteen Panthers were charged with conspiracy to bomb public places and with attempted murder and arson. *(U.P.I. Photo.)*

tolerant as to drive it underground, it can become a secret and conspiratorial organization, engaging in efforts at subversion and practicing deceit and subterfuge, including terrorist tactics such as bombing. Among radical youth groups the Weathermen became such an organization.

Between the tolerance of a society that is unworried about a movement and the intolerance that feels threatened by one there is a range of other possibilities. Thus, some social classes may feel severely threatened, while others may be somewhat sympathetic, giving the movement some measure of support and perhaps some allies in crucial circumstances. Public opinion may be split on the merits of a movement along lines of class, region, religion, or race; and support for a movement may shift in response to its tactics or in response to sanctions against it. *White violence* against young, nonviolent black

demonstrators in the South in the early 1960s, for example, won widespread white, middle-class support for civil rights; but *black violence* in Northern cities after 1965 quickly dissipated much of that same support.

The career of a social movement is like the career of a person: What happens in the early and middle stages affects its final outcome. The experiences of the members and leaders in pursuing goals in an uphill struggle can shape a movement in different ways. It was, for example, the bitter and disillusioning experiences of young black activists (like Stokely Carmichael) in civil-rights actions in the South, when they were committed to nonviolence, that led to a rethinking and reassessing of the meaning of the movement. From this re-evaluation came the concept of black power and a radical change in the ideology, goals, and the strategies. What had been an *integrated* civil-rights movement became a *black* movement struggling for black identification and community, though as yet ambiguous as to what specific form that community should take.

When Movements Succeed

A movement may succeed in achieving at least some of its goals, or it may fail. If it succeeds, it is transformed from a protest movement into a legitimate participant in the established order. This is what happened to the labor movement of the 1930s, which finally won legal status as unions became representatives of workers entitled to engage in collective bargaining. *Legitimation and recognition*, then, meant a significant new status for unions. They were no longer illegitimate organizations; they were no longer underdogs; and they were no longer carrying on something resembling a class struggle.

Unions were transformed by this very process. The labor movement became organized labor—less a social movement, more integrated into society, less alienated from it. This transformation brought a change in leadership as well. Old leaders who had excelled at the organization of workers and the leading of strikes now had to excel at negotiations around the bargaining table; those who could not make the change lost out to newer leaders who could. Walter Reuther survived as a leader of the automobile workers because he could organize; he could bargain; and he could remain a charismatic figure while skillfully administering a large organization.

The attainment of recognition and a legitimate status was an immediate and pragmatic goal of unions, one on which all those in the labor movement were agreed. But many also held other, longer-range goals. They saw the labor movement as an organization of workers which would overthrow capitalism and create a new kind of society. Communists, Socialists, Trotskyites, and other radical positions were all actively represented in the labor movement of the 1930s. With the achievement of the pragmatic goals for collective bargaining, those who wanted separate political action by labor—perhaps a labor party—fought with others for whom the immediate goals were sufficient. A decade of internal factional struggle followed, ending when the more radical ideological groups lost out.

Labor's gradual loss of the verve and orientation of a movement was evident in the late fifties and sixties, when the new consciousness about race, peace, and poverty found organized labor either taking no significant part or even standing in opposition to protesting movements. Labor was no longer the representative of the poor; its position on race was compromised by practices of discrimination in some unions; and much of its top leadership (with some notable exceptions) were unsympathetic to the various peace groups and their demonstrations, particularly over the Vietnam conflict.

Labor found itself no longer thought of as an underdog, and no longer the spokesman for underdogs in this new period. In fact, labor was defined by the new social movements as part of the "establishment." The New Left's efforts to create a movement turned to students, poor people, black people, to strongly antiwar segments of the middle class, and to women for its social base. Despite this diversity, however, the New Left remained largely a white, middle-class movement.

When Movements Fail

When a social movement fails to attain power, and when it fails to convert any significant number of people to its cause, frustration and bitterness and sometimes more desperate action may result. More importantly, the inability to achieve any significant goal deprives the movement of the morale-sustaining idea that the future lies with it. It loses adherents, retaining perhaps only a core of the most dedicated. Even the true believers may seek answers in more promising movements. In time, a failing movement withers to a small handful of loyal followers and a leadership increasingly remote from the salient issues of society.

But whether a movement fails or succeeds is not an obvious matter. Socialism, by all normal accounts, failed in the United States. Yet Norman Thomas, the Socialist Party's candidate for president for six elections, has quite correctly pointed out that one of the factors in the "failure" of socialism was that its pragmatic program of social reform was "stolen" by the major parties, though not its more radical measures.

What happened to the Socialist Party has been the fate of most third parties in the United States. The reforms they introduced and promoted on behalf of various disadvantaged groups gradually won acceptance and were politically adopted. Legislation on behalf of working women and children, the eight-hour day, unemployment compensation and social security, union representation—these once "radical" measures have in time won wide acceptance and become social policy.

In this way presumably "unsuccessful" movements may in fact perform a vital function for a democratic society: They champion significant reforms when these are still unacceptable, and they begin the difficult task of converting people into supporters. They are a significant force for social change even though they do not gain power.

THE MAJOR SOCIAL MOVEMENTS AND IDEOLOGIES

In the nineteenth century major social movements were generated by protest against industrialization, as in the case of peasants and farmers, or against the conditions imposed by industrial capitalism, as in the case of workers. The *labor* movement and *socialism* were the outstanding social movements of the past century.[20]

Labor

In protest against harsh conditions of life, the working class struggled to organize labor unions without having any long-range ideology for the reorganization of society. The specific remedies that were advanced were varied and diverse, but they can be defined as an effort to reduce the insecurities and poverty of working-class life by gaining some control for workers over the job and by modifying capitalism's subjection of the worker to the vagaries of the market.[21]

Without being revolutionary, the labor movement in the nineteenth century was a constant challenge to the supremacy in society of the institutions of capitalism and of the property-owning middle class. Some-

[20] For an analysis of these historic social movements see Rudolf Heberle, *Social Movements* (New York: Appleton-Century-Crofts, 1951).
[21] For a classic interpretation of labor in these terms see Selig Perlman, *A Theory of the Labor Movement* (New York: Augustus Kelly, 1949). This is a reprinting of a book originally published in 1925.

times, particularly in Europe, the labor movement accepted socialism and became the social base for that movement.

Socialism

As the dominant social movement of the late nineteenth and early twentieth century, socialism offered a clearly defined alternative to capitalism and a program for a revolutionary reorganization of society. Throughout Europe, and somewhat less in the United States, the socialist movement mobilized millions of people against capitalism.[22] Its broad appeal signified the failure of the ideology of capitalism to find support in all segments of society. Although this was particularly true of the workers, the poor, and the propertyless, socialism also won converts from the middle class, particularly from professionals and intellectuals, who provided much of its leadership. Though it was dominant, capitalism failed to achieve a complete integration of modern society around the symbols of the free market and private property.

If socialism did not succeed completely in its struggle with capitalism, it nonetheless altered the structure of industrial societies. Most of the reforms that changed *laissez-faire* capitalism into *welfare* capitalism originated in the Socialist movement. European socialism, embodied in powerful Socialist parties, became a permanent part of the political structure of democratic societies.

But the more this influence was felt, the less did socialism remain a social move-ment. Powerful bureaucratized Socialist parties, often holding the reins of government, increasingly controlled by the middle class, not the workers, are far different from the revolutionary social movements they were when they first started. Most of them since World War II, in fact, have disavowed their original Marxian goals and dropped the more revolutionary rhetoric. Nor do they any longer seek to socialize all private property.

It is this that has led many social scientists to proclaim that there is an end of the seemingly irreconcilable ideological struggle between socialism and capitalism that dominated so much of the politics of the nineteenth and early twentieth centuries.

The End of Ideology?

The nineteenth century has been called an "age of ideology," suggesting that it was a time in which great contending ideologies, such as socialism and unregulated capitalism, took hold of the minds and imaginations of intellectuals and non-intellectuals alike.[23] They called people to a great struggle to shape human society according to some grand design.

Is this any longer the case? It is not, assert some sociologists; there is now an *end of ideology*. In the twentieth century, according to sociologist Daniel Bell, ". . . ideology, which was once a road to action, has come to be a dead end."[24]

The power of ideology can convert ordinary people into a passionately acting col-

---

[22] For a discussion of socialism in America *see* Donald D. Egbert and Stow Persons, eds., *Socialism and American Life* (Princeton, N.J.: Princeton University Press, 1952); *see also* James Weinstein, *The Decline of Socialism in America 1912–1925* (New York: Random House, Inc., 1967).

[23] *See* Henry D. Aiken, *The Age of Ideology: The 19th Century Philosophers* (New York: New American Library, 1956).

[24] *See* Daniel Bell, *The End of Ideology* (New York: The Free Press, 1960), pp. 369–375. The quotation is from p. 370.

lectivity. They come alive, not in contemplation or in abstract philosophical inquiry but in deeds. Their emotional energies are channeled into politics; from this come social movements. Bell observed that "a social movement can arouse people when it can do three things: simplify ideas, establish a claim to truth, and, in the union of the two, demand a commitment to action."[25]

Why can ideology not do this in the twentieth century? Because too much has happened, Bell and others claim, to give ideology the grip on human commitment and the capacity to arouse passion that it once did. First of all, there had been an unrelieved progression of calamitous events: two world wars breaking out within a quarter of a century; the rise of fascism in Europe; Naziism coming to power in Germany, thought to be one of the more advanced human cultures; the painful realization that the new revolutionary workers' state in Russia had, under Stalin, become totalitarian; and the use of gas chambers in Germany and concentration camps in both Germany and Russia. Few utopian perspectives could survive this onslaught.

Something else, though less fearful, had also happened. The world had changed and was no longer what the ideologies were talking about. Unregulated capitalism had given way to the welfare state; the new legitimate status of unions undercut the passionate case against capitalism. Furthermore, the proponents of capitalism no longer argued that the state should play no role in the economy, and the welfare state was no longer regarded as "the road to serfdom." According to Bell:

In the Western world, therefore, there is

today a rough consensus among intellectuals on political issues: the acceptance of a Welfare State; the desirability of decentralized power; a system of mixed economy and of political pluralism. In that sense, too, the ideological age has ended.[26]

Not all scholars accept the end-of-ideology thesis as accurate, and in the 1960s the emergence of protests and demonstrations and a youthfully passionate New Left seemed to deny that ideology had lost its appeal.[27] A new generation of youth discovered radical thought and action, the writings of Karl Marx and the Marxian Herbert Marcuse, even the idea of anarchism. Among blacks, too, radical perspectives and revolutionary ideas flourished. A pragmatic, passionless politics, given to compromise and pluralistic coalitions, no longer described American political life.

Though Marx was read again, much about the renewed ideology of the left seemed inadequate for humanizing and democratizing the vast bureaucratic structures of modern society. Working out an ideology for the advanced capitalism of the late twentieth century was too difficult to accomplish in such a short time. The end of ideology, then, is a partial truth. Old ideologies have been exhausted, but not because the search for a more humane society is over, and not because the capacity for passionate commitment is gone. After the outburst of political movement in the 1960s, one thing has happened: millions of people no longer accept as legitimate the practices, institutions, and beliefs they once accepted uncritically. It was the novelist, Thomas Wolfe, who said,

[25] See Bell, *op. cit.*, p. 372.

[26] See Bell, *op. cit.*, p. 373.

[27] See Chaim I. Waxman, ed., *The End of Ideology Debate* (New York: Funk & Wagnalls Company, 1968).

"you can't go home again." There are still people today awaiting a movement that is seeking an ideology.

SOCIAL MOVEMENTS TODAY

In recent years the issues of race, peace, and women's status have generated new social movements in the United States.

From Civil Rights to Black Liberation[28]

There was resistance and rebellion among blacks even in slavery, for they have never willingly accepted their inferior status in white America. Protest, even violent rebellion, followed by forceful repression, is part of the long history of blacks in this society.[29]

A civil-rights movement has been going on in American society almost throughout this century. It has been largely a middle-class movement, joining whites and blacks in common action. In that form, with Martin Luther King providing inspired leadership, it enlarged the scope of protest in the South in the early 1960s. Its most active members were recruited from the black colleges, where there was a disciplined commitment to follow King in nonviolent action and passive resistance.

Integrating schools, eliminating *de facto* segregation, and expanding educational and job opportunities for blacks were

basic objectives of the movement. If state and local government in the South was the enemy and needed to be changed, federal government was seen as an ally. This was particularly apparent in the effort to strike down Jim Crow restrictions on the use of public facilities: bus terminals, restaurants, parks, swimming pools, and the like. (Remember: it all began by sitting in at a lunch counter.) No less important was the effort to get blacks registered to vote.

However nonviolent the commitment of the movement was, the response of whites was not. Civil-rights activists, both black and white, were beaten and shot, attacked with dogs and fire hoses, their property dynamited—four small children died brutally in the dynamiting of a church in Birmingham, Alabama—and they were jailed by local police, harassed by local authority, and denied equal justice by local courts.

None of this was unexpected. But strong federal protection and the determined assistance of white liberals had been counted on, and that was not forthcoming. The experience was bitter. Increasingly, it became apparent that neither white liberals nor the federal government could be relied on to bring about the extent of social change in racial practices that the movement was seeking. Such disillusionment produced a hard rethinking. When Stokely Carmichael declared "Black Power" in 1965, the strictly Southern phase of the movement was over, and a new sense of direction had come about.

What had evolved from painful experience was a new set of objectives:

1. Instead of assimilation, the goal was independence—maintaining an existence as a black people with a history and a culture to be celebrated, not to be discarded for white culture. *Cultural autonomy* then became a valued end.

[28] Among a number of useful sources *see* Jerome Skolnick, *The Politics of Protest* (New York: Simon and Schuster, Inc., 1969), Ch. IV; and *also* Lewis M. Killian, *The Impossible Dream?* (New York: Random House, Inc., 1968), Ch. IV.

[29] *See* John H. Bracey, Jr., August Meier, and Elliott Rudwick, *Black Nationalism in America* (Indianapolis, Ind.: The Bobbs-Merrill Company, Inc., 1970); and *also* Rayford W. Logan, *The Betrayal of the Negro* (New York: Collier Books, 1965).

Figure 18.3 During the 1960s the civil-rights movement in the South was aimed at ending Jim Crow restrictions at public facilities. It all began with a lunch-counter sit-in. *(Wide World Photos.)*

2. Instead of nonviolence and passive resistance, *self-defense* by any means necessary. This found widespread appeal among young blacks from the ghetto, whose entrance into the movement, accompanied by the withdrawal of white activists, changed the social composition of the movement radically. The militant style of action of the Black Panthers, for example, helped *politicize* young ghetto blacks.

3. Independence also meant *community control*, particularly of schools, but in principle over all social institutions in which decisions are made affecting the lives of black people.

4. New educational programs were sought for a different set of needs. First, black history, then a more encompassing black studies, followed by an emphasis on widening opportunities to enter colleges and universities.

As new and competing leaders and organizations emerged, there was no single thrust to the developing movement and no single strategy. More moderate developments competed with more militant ones; strategies of confrontation contrasted with strategies of legal petition and conventional political action. Peaceful marches led to peaceful demonstrations, but sometimes also to violence. And there were urban riots.

Two threads run through the seemingly diverse array of activities. One is *cultural*, a growing sense of independence and collective identity, strongest among youth. This was a rejection of assimilation into the culture and institutions of a white society, a beginning effort to redefine the place of blacks in white America. The second was *political*, concerned with finding ways to change the economic and social inequality of blacks. Some of these were:

1. Getting commitment for federal programs— model cities, affirmative action in employment, job training—which continued some programs first sought by the earlier civil-

453

rights movement but often found by blacks to promise much more than was delivered.

2. Building political power based on population concentrations in central cities.

3. Building community in the ghetto, without which a power base for wider action was not possible.

An identification with a world-wide struggle by nonwhite people to throw off the colonial controls of white nations created for blacks a whole new perspective on America, a new sense of their place in this nation. Black America became defined as an internal colony.

There are different ideas about what this means. The most radical position is that of a separate black nation, with a separate territory within the continental limits of the United States. If few blacks now seem to think that feasible, many others look for ways to promote economic advancement, cultural autonomy, and political freedom in some new set of institutional patterns, perhaps not yet imagined. Black liberation, as of now, is a still developing movement.[30]

The Anti-war Movement

A tiny pacifist movement has long been a part of American society, but the Vietnam War brought into being a large if amorphous base of opposition that was never one organization and was never united around a single ideology. From the outset, the movement was overwhelmingly a middle-class one, and was also predominantly white.[31]

[30] See August Meier, ed., *The Transformation of Activism* (Chicago, Ill.: Aldine-Atherton, Inc., 1970).

[31] See Skolnick, Ch. II, "Anti-war Protest," pp. 27–78; see also Irving Louis Horowitz, *The Struggle Is the Message: The Organization and the Ideology of the Anti-war Movement* (Berkeley, Calif.: Glendessary Press, 1970).

Opposition to the war had a variety of bases. Some people were opposed to any war; they were truly pacifists. Others maintained an historic "isolationist" position, opposing American involvement in foreign controversies. But most opposed, not war in general but the Vietnam War in particular, from a political perspective that opposed American intervention in the social and political struggles in southeast Asia.

From the start the anti-war movement had to fight for its legitimacy. It suffered the stigma of not being thought patriotic by many Americans. Support for military symbols and activities—respect for the uniform, for undertaking military service voluntarily, for flag-saluting and pledging allegiance—were all natural sources of support for the war, even among many Americans who thought involvement in Vietnam was a mistake. When opposition to the war produced draft resistance among college youth—including in some cases flight to Canada—"draft dodging" was seen by many as a further sign of disloyalty to the country.

For millions of Americans there was a deep, conflicting response to the war; their natural inclination to support their country in time of military and political crisis abroad, and their growing doubts as to the wisdom of having ever become involved in Vietnam.

The peak of the anti-war movement was reached in 1968, when President Johnson decided not to run again for office and Richard Nixon, a previous supporter of the Vietnam program, promised to end the war. What the anti-war movement succeeded in doing was shifting the bulk of public opinion from approval to opposition. The vigorous debate over the legitimacy of the war undermined confidence

Figure 18.4 Those who opposed the American participation in Vietnam held a variety of ideological beliefs, ranging from pacifism to isolationism. *(Wide World Photos.)*

in the validity of its objectives and in the purported reason for being in Vietnam, as well as making painfully apparent the cost of the war in lives, in national unity, and in international respect.

For young Americans who became involved in the protests against the war, the experience often had further implications. It led them into a critical position on the military, its place in American society, and its ties with corporate power—the military-industrial complex. It made them conscious of the natural affinity between business; patriotic, civic, and veterans organizations; and the military, which coalesced around conservative stands. It brought them into contact with ideas about American imperialism, the Cold War, and a third world struggling to be liberated from the controls of great dominating powers, of which the United States was perhaps the strongest. In short,

it was a radicalizing experience. From that time on, the United States could never be "my country, right or wrong."

The finish of the Vietnam War might very well end the movement as it functioned from 1965 to 1973, but some of the changes it brought about will have permanent consequences. *End to draft.*

Feminism

Movements protesting the lot of women and seeking to change it have been prominent in American society for over a century.[32] The suffrage movement—to make women voting members of society—brought militant protest by women into

[32] *See* William L. O'Neill, *The Woman Movement: Feminism in England and the United States* (Chicago, Ill.: Quadrangle Books, 1971); *see also* his *Everyone Was Brave: The Rise and Fall of Feminism in America* (Chicago, Ill.: Quadrangle Books, 1969).

the political arena, until it succeeded in getting a constitutional amendment granting the vote to women in 1920. The cause of equality for women continued, but in recent years has taken on new spirit and direction, activating a large number of women under the banner of *women's liberation,* or *feminism.*[33]

Like other social movements, women's liberation has no single organizational core, no one set of objectives, no single ideological orientation. "Women's libbers" can and do vary considerably on what changes they seek in the lives and status of women. Nonetheless, there are two important points worth making about the current movement.

One is that the movement is now overwhelmingly white and largely middle class in composition. Though women's liberation addresses itself to the conditions of all women, its active involvement has come largely from white, middle-class, college-educated women. It is they who have forthrightly taken up arms against *sexism.* The movement is more evident at universities and in the professions than elsewhere, and its greatest successes to date have been in advancing equal employment and education for professional women.

A second point is that, as so often occurs in social movements, there is a moderate, reformist wing as well as a radical wing.[34] The distinction is not hard and fast, and many women engage in both kinds of activities. Calling them "reform" and "radical" is now quite common, but political scientist Jo Freeman notes that "these terms tell us very little, since feminists do not fit the traditional Left/Right spectrum . . . Structure and style rather than ideology more accurately differentiate the two branches, and, even here, there has been much borrowing."[35]

Women's Rights

Reformists emphasize the rights of women in legal and economic spheres, stressing equal access to careers and elimination of the barriers of sexism that so often shunt young women off into "women's careers," as well as marriage and family. More women as scientists and doctors, not merely as technicians and nurses; more women as executives and administrators, not merely as secretaries, clerks, receptionists; more women on university faculties, not merely as elementary-school teachers and librarians—this is a major reformist aspiration.

The reformist branch of women's liberation, then, is a civil-rights movement, seeking to enlarge the social opportunities for women, as well as encouraging more women to pursue goals once thought to be strictly male. Any success in achieving such goals will have profound implications for the man-woman relationship. Accepting women as equal competitors for all occupations and offices in the society will slowly undermine the set of assumptions about male superiority that most men and many women still share.

The most prominent organization of the reformist branch is the National Organization for Women (NOW), formed in 1966 with Betty Friedan as its first president. Its members are politically and profession-

[33] Probably the most useful source on its development is Judith Hole and Ellen Levine, *Rebirth of Feminism* (Chicago, Ill.: Quadrangle Books, 1971).

[34] An informative description of both the origins and nature of the two branches is offered by Jo Freeman, "The Origins of the Women's Liberation Movement," *op. cit.,* pp. 792–811.

[35] *See* Freeman, *op. cit.,* p. 795.

ally active women, and its officers are mostly from the professions, government, and the communications industry. Though not large in numbers, with no significant mass base, its members know how to use the media to publicize their concerns, particularly the demand for enforcement by the Equal Employment Opportunity Commission (EEOC) of the "sex" provision to Title VII of the Civil Rights Act of 1964, which forbids any job discrimination on the basis of sex.

Besides NOW there are Women's Equity Action League (WEAL), a lobbyist group; Human Rights for Women, a legal foundation; over twenty women's caucuses in professional organizations; and numerous separate organizations of women in various professions and occupations.

Women's Liberation

In contrast to the reformist branch of the women's movement, the more "radical" branch was organized by younger women, most of whom had had prior experience in the several protest movements of the 1960s. While these movements had attracted women, as Jo Freeman notes, they found themselves "quickly shunted into traditional roles and faced with the self-evident contradiction of working in a 'freedom movement' without being very free."[36] Radical men, it seemed, were no less chauvinists than other men. (Stokely Carmichael in 1964 remarked that "the only position for women in SNCC is prone.")

Young women utilized the contacts and ties of the radical movement, as well as its rhetoric and perspective, both to develop a more radical ideology of feminism and to organize on the community level. Shaped by the radical experience which came to suspect the highly organized group as authoritarian and dominated by leadership elite, these groups have remained loosely organized and not tied closely to one another. As a result, there is no national organization, no top nationally recognized leadership. Their power, therefore, is diffuse, unfocused on any national target.

Less concerned with political change, the emphasis has been on personal change as a basis for determining what political change is necessary. "The primary instrument has been the consciousness-raising rap group which has sought to change women's very identities as well as their attitudes."[37]

Radical "libbers" want to change the personality structure and consciousness of women, to remove passive personality attributes and attitudes of traditional femininity that lead women to assume their inferiority to aggressive, dominant men. This requires stressing *sex roles* of all kinds—the traditional division of labor between men and women—not merely jobs and education. To *de-sex* social roles is not only to change these roles but also to change the men and women who take these roles.

Desexing the social structure does not deny that there are differences between men and women; it seeks to break down many of the cultural myths and assumptions built on the biology of sex. While women, not men, go through pregnancy and bear children, radical "libbers" would not allow this fact to restrict women's rights, or to confine their roles to family roles alone—or to construct the personality of women around mothering as a central activity. The radical extension of women's

---

[36] *See* Freeman, *op. cit.,* p. 799.

[37] *See* Freeman, *op. cit.,* p. 809.

liberation is an assault on the traditional family as the institution that more than any other defines for women their roles, their acceptable activities, their very personalities.

Women's liberation has deep and subtle implications for men, too. First of all, it would reduce the claim men have upon privileged activities and opportunities not hitherto shared with women. Women jockeys and legislators, women astronauts and police, as well as women athletes suggest an invasion of precincts once thought of as belonging exclusively to men. Furthermore, the accompanying sexual revolution alters the hitherto double-standard of sex relations, devalues virginity, and then changes the subtle psychological relation of men and women to each other in that most intimate of relationships, that of love and possibly marriage.

Women's liberation intends a radical transformation of women's roles and status that will eventually alter male roles and status and the male's personality. Men will then be liberated from the demands and compulsions of a culturally defined male-ness—whether they now want this or not.

For that to happen the movement will have to progress beyond its present state. While the resurgent feminist movement has tapped an enormous flow of energy, it has not yet channeled this energy into directions that will create structural changes. Jo Freeman's comment seems to the point:

. . . most of the movement is proliferating underground. It often seems mired in introspection, but it is in fact creating a vast reservoir of conscious feminist sentiment which only awaits an appropriate opportunity for action.[38]

[38] *See* Freeman, *op. cit.,* p. 809.

One Movement or Many?

During the 1960s and the early 1970s people sometimes spoke of "The Movement," by which they meant closely related and mutually supporting separate movements: the black movement, the peace movement, women's liberation, ecology, and student protest. These were all seen as specific dimensions of a general social movement to change society radically. Different people came into the movement through different activities, but the radical reorganization of society and its reshaping into a freer, more equal, more humane society was presumably agreed upon.

It is not at all obvious now that there is such an encompassing single movement. For one thing, the black movement does not share goals and aspirations with others. It is sometimes hostile to others, such as to women's liberation or ecology; or at least it is simply indifferent. As the black movement has developed its objectives through struggle, cooperation in shared activity between blacks and whites has declined.

There is not, secondly, the broad and exciting sense of movement on university campuses and among middle-class youth that once prevailed. Activity has dwindled, as enthusiasm has often been replaced with disenchantment and withdrawal. Young people in particular have returned to privatize activities, or to more conventional ones, or even to a more limited, specific involvement. Women, for example, concentrate their time and energies on women's liberation.

Such limited activity can proceed without an encompassing ideology about how to radically transform this society into a more humane one. Yet there is a strongly

Figure 18.5 Younger women have generally focused on a more radical ideology of feminism, employing such protest tactics as strikes and marches. *(A. Devaney, Inc., N.Y.)*

felt need for such an ideology. Until that is developed there will be various movements, but not "The Movement."

THE SIGNIFICANCE OF SOCIAL MOVEMENTS

Many social scientists have viewed social movements as much shouting and shoving by people who feel keenly the consequences of changes in culture and social structure that have long been developing. Perhaps movements are interesting, the scientists say, even exciting, because of their drama and conflict, but they are of little importance in understanding society and its changes. When people commit themselves to social movements they assume their actions can make a difference. But can they?

The outcome of a great social transformation, such as the Industrial Revolution, may be inevitable and perhaps would have occurred without the shouting and shoving. Some social scientists imply that people can do no more than adjust to inevitable social change. This is the underlying assumption of the famous *culture-lag* theory advanced by sociologist William Ogburn.[39]

For Ogburn, the adequate use of technological and scientific innovation was incompatible with older cultural ways, producing the "lag" of cultural and social processes behind technological change. Social organization had to adapt to technology, rather than the other way around.

But this thesis leaves the issue unresolved. Social change may be necessary and inevitable, but *what* social change? Does moving from an old order mean that the shape of the new order is predeter-

[39] William F. Ogburn, *Social Change* (New York: The Viking Press, Inc., 1922).

mined? Or are there some choices, some options for historical actors? Industrialization and technology make social change unavoidable, but do such changes demand that any one form of social organization supersede the old one? It would seem not. Both Capitalist and Communist structures, and an infinite variation within these, are institutional arrangements compatible with advanced technology.

Only a true believer in free will would assert that people can change society in any manner they choose. Probably all social scientists agree that people are bound within the framework of social institutions by which they are socialized and from which they get a perspective on the world. Karl Marx once said:

Men make their own history, but they do not make it just as they please; they do not make it under circumstances chosen by themselves, but under circumstances directly encountered, given and transmitted from the past. The tradition of all the dead generations weighs like a nightmare on the brain of the living.[40]

Somewhere between a position that sees people as unconscious puppets of vast historic processes, and an opposing position that sees people freely able to choose what history will be, lies a defensible ground. When people want to change their world, they rethink and re-assess and judge; and they act. What they do makes a difference, though what comes about may not be what they intended.

That is why studying social movements is useful. It tells us something important about the conscious efforts of people to

---

[40] Karl Marx, "The Eighteenth Brumaire of Louis Bonaparte," in Karl Marx and Frederick Engels, *Selected Works* (Moscow: Progress Publishers, 1968), p. 97.

determine their destiny *within limits,* and to direct the processes of change in terms of their values and goals.

A Perspective on Society

Studying social movements has another value for students of society. Social movements reveal: 1. latent conflict that has long existed but may have been overlooked; 2. the depth of passion and intensity of group hostility that was not evident until a social movement provided an outlet for its expression; and 3. the manner in which seemingly stable social institutions and dominant values concealed the extent of force and coercion in making a particular society viable. Change and conflict as a perspective on society suggest how much any society is less an integrated social system and more an historical product of group conflict and domination, in which some segments of that society may have never accepted its institutions and values as fully legitimate.

COLLECTIVE BEHAVIOR: A CONCLUDING NOTE

If the evidence of collective behavior is to be taken seriously, society is not always as well integrated as some sociologists seem to believe. Nor is *modern* society as highly integrated or as tightly structured as administrators try to make their bureaucracies or as traditional societies seem to be to our Western eyes. In many spheres modern people have less well-defined roles, more ambiguous normative arrangements, and less stability in social relations than would seem true of society on the surface. It is a sociological error to impute more structure to society than in fact exists. Similarly, modern society lacks the cohesion to be derived from a set of unchallenged legitimizing traditions, where stable and unquestioned beliefs can clearly and authoritatively order social relationships in stable patterns of long endurance.

Collective behavior points up a major historical development: the emergence of masses of people to direct involvement in the great decisions of modern times. Even if they are manipulated, and their anxieties and aspirations exploited, even when elites cheat them and mislead them, their demands nevertheless count and cannot be ignored. The masses are never so completely integrated into any social structure but that they cannot be mobilized by charismatic leaders into challenging the legitimacy of the established social order. The masses may not rule, but no elite can rule without persuading the masses.

SUMMARY

Two ways deal with society
1. Withdraw - protest-
2. Be [Revolutionary] active part to change — reform.

① Reform-change in existing social structure
② Revolutionary—change entire social structure.

A social movement is a collectivity with some continuity to promote or resist change. Its basic features are shared *values,* a sense of *"we-ness,"* shared *norms,* and a *structure.*

While movements arise out of social conditions breeding grievances, they do not occur unless people have reasons to be *hopeful.*

Ideology performs four functions for a movement: it links action and belief; it provides a collective sense of identity; it unifies; and it makes a future seem both believable and attainable.

A movement must have some *organization* and *leadership,* built on a *social base* of the class or group for whom the movement speaks. Most movements are characterized by competing organizations.

Movements have a *career:* they emerge, develop, and either die out or become stable organizations. What happens to an organization is largely a consequence of its experiences in its early and middle stages. A failure, however, may occur because other groups, such as political parties, take over those of its programs that have greatest popular appeal.

The *labor* movement and the *Socialist* movement were the major social movements of the nineteenth and early twentieth centuries, an era marked by great ideological conflict. Now some social scientists say there is an *end of ideology;* the great ideologies no longer arouse passions as they once did. And the world is now greatly changed; unregulated capitalism, for example, has become welfare capitalism. But not all scholars accept this idea. The New Left effort to build a movement did not manage to create an overarching ideology appropriate to the vast bureaucratic structures of modern society.

In the 1960s the issues of *race, peace,* and *women's status* generated new social movements, each of which developed in its own way. However, these remain separate movements; there is not yet a single "Movement."

Suggested Readings

Henry D. Aiken, *The Age of Ideology: The 19th Century Philosophers* (New York: New American Library, 1956). A philosopher probes into the intellectual structure of the great nineteenth-century ideologies.

David Apter, ed., *Ideology and Discontent* (New York: The Free Press, 1964). A collection of essays on the place of ideology in the modern world. See in particular essays by Apter and Clifford Geertz.

John H. Bracey, Jr., August Meier, and Elliott Rudwick, *Black Nationalism in America* (Indianapolis, Ind.: The Bobbs-Merrill Company, Inc., 1970). A collection of readings that makes it clear that black nationalism in varied forms has been a black movement for two centuries.

Betty Friedan, *The Feminine Mystique* (New York: Dell Publishing Company, Inc., 1963). More than any other, this book inspired the feminist movement of today.

Rudolf Heberle, *Social Movements* (New York: Appleton-Century-Crofts, 1951). The author analyzes historic social movements and ideologies, as well as providing a sociological understanding of them.

Eric Hoffer, *The True Believer* (New York: New American Library, 1951). A long-shoreman-intellectual analyzes how social movements attract the frustrated, disaffected, and rejected to their cause.

Judith Hole and Ellen Levine, *Rebirth of Feminism* (Chicago, Ill.: Quadrangle Books, 1971). Probably the best single study of the women's liberation movement.

Irving Louis Horowitz, *The Struggle Is the Message: The Organization and the Ideology of the Anti-war Movement* (Berkeley, Calif.: Glendessary Press, 1970). A review of the organization, ideology, and mobilization of the movement against the Vietnam War.

Lewis M. Killian, *The Impossible Dream?* (New York: Random House, Inc., 1968). A fine study of the origins and dilemmas of the black movement in the United States in the 1960s.

Karl Mannheim, *Ideology and Utopia,* Louis Wirth and Edward A. Shils, trans. (New York: Harcourt, Brace, Jovanovich, 1936). A twentieth-century classic on the political meaning of utopian myths for the modern world.

William L. O'Neill, *Everyone Was Brave: The Rise and Fall of Feminism in America* (Chicago, Ill.: Quadrangle Books, 1969). A fine history of the feminist movement that brought women the vote among other gains.

Jerome Skolnick, *The Politics of Protest* (New York: Simon and Schuster, Inc., 1969). Skolnick examines several of the movements of the 1960s: black militancy, the anti-war movement, and student protest.

Guy E. Swanson, *Social Change* (Glenview, Ill.: Scott, Foresman and Company, 1971). Chapter 4 places social movements in the context of social change.

Ralph H. Turner and Lewis M. Killian, *Collective Behavior* (Englewood Cliffs, N.J.: Prentice-Hall, Inc., 1957). A perceptive text that puts the social movement into the context of collective behavior.

Chaim I. Waxman, ed., *The End of Ideology Debate* (New York: Funk & Wagnalls Company, 1968). The pros and cons of the end of ideology as enunciated by Daniel Bell and others are debated in this well-selected set of essays.

Alfred F. Young, ed., *Dissent: Explorations in the History of American Radicalism*

(DeKalb, Ill.: Northern Illinois University Press, 1968). A useful collection of essays that explores some important historical experiences of dissent and radicalism in America's past.

Howard Zinn, *SNCC: The New Abolitionists* (Boston, Mass.: The Beacon Press, 1964). An enlightening treatment of the early days of the civil-rights movement in the South.

PART VII

THE STUDY
OF SOCIETY

We are indeed travellers bound to the earth's crust . . . Yet we collectively behave as if we were not aware of the problems inherent in the limitations of the Spaceship Earth.
—*René Dubos*

Chapter 19

Society and Environment

To focus on society, as sociologists do—on such phenomena as groups and classes, structure and social change—is to risk losing sight of the fact that human society is embedded in an environment. It is also to risk losing sight of the fact that the human being is first and foremost an animal, sharing living space with other animal species in an environment on which they are mutually dependent. We forget that fact only at our peril.

It may be useful as we approach the end of our introduction to the study of society, to restate some fundamental points we have made throughout this book:

1. In Chapter 1 we argued that society exists because a human population must be organized in some way in order to collectively adapt to a natural environment. The cooperative activity necessary to provide the material basis for life is fundamental to the formation of society. While technology can radically alter the terms of human adaptation to the environment, modern populations are nevertheless not released from the need to adapt.

2. In Chapter 4 we pointed out that culture, like society, emerges from the human effort to survive, and that from this perspective, culture is an adaptation to environment, a body of knowledge based on perceptions and techniques developed by man as *homo faber* (the maker of things). We introduced the concept

of *ecology* as the study of the relation of individual organisms to environment; and the concept of *ecosystem* as the interconnected, interdependent system of relations between organisms and environment.

The growth of culture includes the growth of *technology*, whereby people are able to extract more sustenance from nature, and so to support a larger population. The *evolution* of human society from wandering bands of food-gatherers to vast urban-industrial societies has its source in this development of technology, permitting new levels of integration of ever-larger populations, accompanied by greater internal differentiation (division of labor and class structure) resulting in greater social complexity.

3. In Chapter 6 we examined the relation of technology to levels of social integration. When improvements in technology provide a greater capacity to harness energy—thus making possible increased production—this is followed by *ecological expansion*, a process of absorbing once unrelated populations extending over wide territories into a single society.

In the slow evolution of human societies, domestication of animals and cultivation of crops made possible larger, settled populations and more expanded societies. The Industrial Revolution occurred as a radical transformation in the adaptation of man to environment, which enlarged human society to undreamed of scope and permitted population growth to unprecedented size.

4. In Chapter 14 we asserted that without sustenance and shelter no other human activity is possible, and that this necessary economic activity has an enormously shaping impact on all other aspects of social life.

We also examined empires and colonies, in which, through an international division of labor, the colony provided raw materials and a market for finished goods, while the dominant Western nations used the raw material to manufacture goods for both domestic and foreign markets. Such ecological expansion required a political system of domination and subordination—an imperialist structure—to make the economic structure possible.

Though nineteenth-century colonialism is a phenomenon of the past, a group of modern nations, including the United States preeminently, are twentieth-century imperialists, wielding enormous political control over other nations, maintaining a flow of raw materials from underdeveloped nations (former colonies), and competing with one another for sources of raw materials and markets for finished goods.

These economic processes, always including trade and exchange, have rarely been contained within the boundaries of a single society. Now there is a world economy. Markets are worldwide; rich economies penetrate poor ones; and third-world peasants and American farmers alike find their economic fate far beyond their individual control yet dependent on remote political events and distant markets.

It then becomes necessary to think of the world as a single ecosystem—a complex intricately interrelated process of environment interacting with population on a global scale. However sophisticated technology may be, that population still must derive its sustenance from that planetary environment. Whatever the powers of science and technology, and however removed urban people feel they are from raw nature, the link that ties human beings to nature can never be broken—not, at least, if they are to survive. Mankind cannot escape its dependence on planet earth.

The Ecological Perspective

A human ecology does not let us forget that society is but one component of human life. A society is the *organization* of a *population*, but the size and characteristics of any population depend also on the sustaining *environment*. Organization is a collective potentiality for interacting with environment; cooperative effort will be more productive than will single individuals working alone. *Technology* is a crucial factor in the interaction of people with the environment. It changes the terms and conditions of that interaction; it provides more sustenance, and permits population to grow. But in turn it compels a more complex organization of society, more specialization and differentiation.

There is, then, a complex interactive process among population, organization, technology, and environment. The student of society legitimately concentrates on the study of social organization only if he maintains a perspective in which these other factors are duly noted.

Technology and Ecology

The relation of human populations to nature has always been mediated through technology. As sociologist Otis Dudley Duncan notes:

. . . apart from language, the most distinctive feature of ecosystems that is due to the inclusion of man is the modification, or even the creation, of flows of materials, energy, and information occasioned by technology . . . From this point of view, technology is an *extension* of the species capacities—often a very great extension indeed . . .[1]

Of these extensions, the greatest one has

been the Industrial Revolution. Yet the ground for it was set by a long history of technological development in Europe, from perhaps as early as the eighth century. The use of fossil fuels, beginning with coal, thoroughly altered the relation of man to environment. From 1850 to 1950, according to Duncan, population increased at a ratio of 6.5:1, but work output grew by 65:1.[2]

Population expanded enormously, as new and unprecedented ecological expansion linked Western and non-Western peoples in systems of production and exchange, while standards of living in the Western world grew to undreamed of levels for larger numbers of people.

Such a revolutionary development apparently encourages the naïve and illusory notion that technology has freed man from any dependence on the environment. What can and sometimes does happen is that technology frees people from a complete dependence on the environment of a limited region, but only because technology enables a dominant people to successfully exploit the environment of another people. Thus, imperial control of other people's regions only extends human dependence on the environment to a wider area. Human populations cannot escape dependence on environment any more than animal populations can, even if the artificial urban environment fosters such an illusion among many people.

The power of modern technology is immense, and its often indiscriminate use has altered the environment in ways unimagined only a few decades ago. As Duncan notes: "Taking more from the environment and reacting back upon the environment in more drastic and varied

[1] *See* Otis Dudley Duncan, "Social Organization and the Ecosystem," in Robert E. L. Faris, ed., *Handbook of Modern Sociology* (Chicago, Ill.: Rand-McNally & Company, 1964), p. 42.

[2] *See* Duncan, *op. cit.*, p. 62.

ways, industrial man has carried the process of 'living into' the environment beyond any precedent."[3]

The cumulative consequences of this technological growth have produced a crisis in the relation of society to environment, the full implications of which seem yet to be "unthinkable" to complacent Western people unable to imagine that large-scale and wasteful consumption cannot be carried on indefinitely, if not extended. All the assumptions of growth and development so basic to Western ideology and social science are challenged by the somber messages coming from the ecological scientists. If we interpret those messages correctly, they tell us that some change in social organization—and probably a quite radical one—has to occur.

THE ECOLOGICAL CRISIS

Throughout most of human existence the earth seemed large and limitless, and what human beings could do to it was little enough compared to what nature could sometimes do to them. It required back-breaking toil for most people to wrest a living from nature, and their actions, however temporarily or locally harmful, had no long-run or widespread malconsequences for the environment.

That point in human history is now behind us. The immense power of technology, the spreading poison of man-made chemicals, the insatiable demand of huge populations for food and water, the vast polluting processes of modern industry—

[3] *See* Duncan, *op. cit.,* p. 69. For an effort to assess just how the environment has been altered, *see* the scientific symposium edited by W.L. Thomas, Jr., *Man's Role in Changing the Face of the Earth* (Chicago, Ill.: University of Chicago Press, 1956).

all these threaten the environment more severely than most people realize. There is an ecological crisis on the human population.

Social and cultural life as it has evolved in recent centuries is evidently on a collision course with environmental processes. What is done destructively to the environment as a consequence of sustaining that way of life tells us that something has to give. How radical a change in social life will be necessary, and how soon this will take place, is a matter of disagreement. But the future cannot simply be an extension of the United States of the 1970s—not even in the United States.

The crisis in the relation of society to environment appears in a number of different forms, each one of which is technically complicated and each of which is related to the others. We can summarize this crisis in terms of four issues:

1. *Population.* The rapid growth of population in recent centuries, and its continued growth throughout the world, presses hard on the adequate supplies of food and water, even in a technologically sophisticated world. Experts acknowledge that some limit on the human population is essential, though just what limit achieved how soon by what means remains a source of much disagreement.

There is some popular tendency to define the ecological crisis almost exclusively as the threat posed by the population "explosion." But population growth is intricately related to the organization of society, as well as to the distribution of resources among the societies of the earth. Even if population were to level off now, the accelerating use of energy, for example, would not, for per-capita consumption of natural resources is on the increase. (We will pursue the issue of population in a little more detail later in this chapter).

2. *The depletion of natural resources.* If the environment is conceived of as a complex of natural resources, some of these are finite and irreplaceable — the fossil fuels (coal, gas, and oil) and minerals — supplies of which cannot last but a limited time into the future, particularly given the present rate of consumption — and the continuing technological development increases this rate of consumption.

Land used for food production is increasingly lost to urban development, to soil depletion by erosion and overuse. In the same manner *usable* water diminishes.

Furthermore, raising the standard of living throughout the world threatens to exhaust the environment even faster. To bring everyone in the world up to present American standards would require 75 times as much iron, 100 times as much copper, 200 times as much lead, 75 times as much zinc, and 250 times as much tin as is now extracted annually from the earth.[4]

Plants, too, interact in complex food chains with animals. But land clearance, deforestation, the paving over of arable land, the destruction of many wild plant species, the overuse of grazing land, the building of dams, and liberal application of defoliants destroy organisms, deprive others of a food supply, and simplify the ecosystem. Cutting trees, for example, leads to erosion of soil, which diminishes the water-retaining capacity of an area, reduces the supply of fresh water, and causes silting of dams.

Human activity, it seems, has already produced a great increase in desert and wasteland throughout the world. "In 1882 land classified as either desert or wasteland amounted to 9.4 percent of the total land on earth. In 1952 it had risen to 23.3 per-

cent."[5] Such great deserts as the Sahara in Africa and the Thar in India are largely man-made, due to deforestation and overgrazing, and the potentiality for more such areas in the world is considerable. Both deserts are spreading at the rate of several miles per year.

3. *Depletion of living organisms.* People often act as if they were the only living organisms with a right to exist. The destruction of other animals, from insects to elephants, even other human beings, occurs deliberately and also unintentionally, but no less effectively. Animals are deprived of living environments as human beings take over more space; or they are slaughtered to make room, or to be used. Many species have vanished in the last two hundred years or so, and many more are on the endangered list.

Living organisms interact in complex ecosystems, but when some are wiped out, the ecosystem that connects one organism with another is simpler, and in that danger lies. A disruption in a simple system is threatening in the extreme to its very existence and all the organisms dependent on it, including the human one. (*See* "Food Chains and Ecosystems.")

4. *Pollution and poison.* Not only does human activity use up natural resources but it also pollutes and poisons. Pollution of water and air is probably the best known to our publics, for drinking water and recreational use is at stake, and air fit to breathe is an issue everyone can grasp, even without knowing the technical facts. Still, there is too little understanding by everyman of the pollution potential in modern industrial processes. As Ehrlich and Ehrlich note: "Nowhere is man's ecological naïvete more evident than in his assumptions about the capacity of the atmosphere, soils, rivers, and oceans to absorb pollution."[6]

Industrial waste, spilled oil, and insecti-

[4] *See* Paul R. Ehrlich and Anne H. Ehrlich, *Population, Resources, Environment: Issues in Human Ecology* (San Francisco, Calif.: W.H. Freeman and Company, 1970), pp. 61–62.

[5] *See* Ehrlich and Ehrlich, *op. cit.,* p. 166.
[6] *See* Ehrlich and Ehrlich, *op. cit.,* p. 159.

Figure 19.1 Man has almost wiped out a number of animal species for his own selfish ends, species like this South African leopard. *(Wide World Photos).*

cides also creep into ecosystems and food chains to poison living organisms, deplete available food, and simplify ecosystems dangerously. Poisons seeping into water enter into organisms which feed in the water, and the poison collects in their systems in a higher concentration than is found in the water itself. (Again, *see* "Food Chains and Ecosystems.") An outbreak of cholera in Naples, Italy, in September 1973, for example, was traced to the eating of mussels, which came from the highly polluted Bay of Naples. A desperate government tore up the mussel beds in the bay, destroying the livelihood of many small fishermen.

Air pollution has spread from industrial cities out over oceans even to the North Pole. It kills people and destroys crops and forests. "A 1968 UNESCO conference concluded that man had only about 20 more years before the planet started to become uninhabitable because of air pollution alone."[7]

The destruction of the environment is proceeding rapidly and efforts to halt it and reverse its direction are as yet small and feeble. In part this is because too many people have a naïve notion that the magic of science will ultimately solve all our problems. More significantly, powerful and dominant societies, such as that of the United States, contribute disproportionately to the ecological crisis as a consequence of enjoying a disproportionate share of the world's goods. Its political-economic structure cannot stop destroying the environment without being radically modified. But neither can there be a remedy until there is a change in long-accepted beliefs and values. The roots of the eco-

[7] *See* Ehrlich and Ehrlich, *op. cit.,* p. 118.

FOOD CHAINS AND ECOSYSTEMS

Human beings and other animals survive only by obtaining energy and nutrients for growth, development, and sustenance by eating plants, or by eating animals which have eaten plants, or even by eating animals which have eaten animals which have eaten plants. Whatever the length of the *food chain* may be, it begins with plants.

Through the process of photosynthesis green plants capture energy in the form of radiation from the sun, and use it to bond together small molecules into the large (organic) molecules characteristic of living organisms. When animals eat plants, they break down these organic molecules and use some of the energy in daily activity and some of it to build up the large molecules of animal substance. Animals that eat other animals repeat this process of breaking down the large molecules, thus putting its energy to use.

In this way energy flows through a food chain, which can be several steps long—as when insects eat from plants, small fish eat insects, large fish eat small fish, and birds and humans eat fish. Humans may kill and eat the birds as well.

Sometimes there are several interlinked food chains within an ecosystem. Then organisms feed on several other organisms, and prey organisms are attacked by more than one predator.

These interlinked food chains make up a more complex ecosystem, which is then also more stable; it can the more easily compensate for changes imposed on it.

Complex communities, such as an oak-hickory forest, are stable and persist unless interfered with by human beings. A corn field, in contrast, is a very simple community, consisting of a man-made stand of a single kind of grass. It is unstable and easily subject to ruin unless constantly managed.

When toxic substances enter the food chain through, for example, a river, poison is not dissipated but is concentrated in organisms at each trophic (feeding) level. In predatory birds, for example, the concentration of DDT may be a *million* times as high as that in estuarine waters. Oysters constantly filter the shallow water in which they live, and it is in this water that pollution is concentrated. As a consequence their bodies contain much higher concentrations of radioactive substances or lethal chemicals than does the water from which they got them.*

*For these and other examples *see* Paul R. Ehrlich and Anne H. Ehrlich, *Population, Resources, Environment: Issues in Human Ecology* (San Francisco, Calif.: W.H. Freeman and Company, 1970), pp. 159–161.

logical crisis go deep into Western history, and are not simply the consequence of industrial profit and the thoughtlessness of complacently affluent people.

The Roots of the Crisis

There is a message of some import in recognizing that the people most success-

Figure 19.2 Air pollution has spread out from cities like Pittsburgh, Pennsylvania, over rural lands, the oceans, and as far as the North Pole. *(A. Devaney, Inc., N.Y.)*

ful in ecological expansion—the people of Europe and America, builders of a complex industrial society—are the people of the earth who seem least of any to respect nature or see themselves as part of it.

The Religious Root

According to historian Lynn White, Jr., Christianity must bear much responsibility for this perspective, for it has long taught that man has dominion over the world and all its creatures. White called Western Christianity the most anthropocentric (seeing the universe in human terms) religion the world has seen.

Christianity, in absolute contrast to ancient paganism and Asia's religions (except, perhaps, Zoroastrianism), not only established a dualism of man and nature but also insisted that it is God's will that man exploit nature for his proper ends.[8]

By destroying the pagan religions which paid respect to the spirits residing in natural objects, Christianity bred in people an indifference to feelings in nature:

The whole concept of the sacred grove is alien to Christianity and to the ethos of the West. For nearly 2 millenia Christian missionaries have been chopping down sacred groves, which are idolatrous because they assume spirit in nature.[9]

The Scientific Root

The early roots of modern science lie in religious motivations, for generations of early scientists studied nature for the better understanding of God. It was not until

---

[8] *See* Lynn White, Jr., "The Historic Roots of our Ecologic Crisis," in Fred Carvell and Max Tadlock, eds., *It's Not Too Late* (Beverly Hills, Calif.: Glencoe Press, 1971), p. 22. This article originally appeared in *Science,* vol. 155 (March 10, 1967), pp. 1203–1207.

[9] *See* White, *op. cit.,* p. 24.

the late eighteenth century that scientists outgrew this religious underpinning of their scientific work.

But the basic *man-conquers-nature* perspective remained. Ecology critic Barry Weissberg reminds us of such statements as Descartes' in exclaiming the benefits of his new method for a more rigorous science: "To render ourselves the masters and possessors of nature"; and of Francis Bacon's: "Our main object is to make nature serve the business and conveniences of man."[10]

Science also reflects values that promote destruction rather than the protection of nature. This is particularly the case when science is linked to technology and practical goals. The natural world becomes a thing apart and hostile, and man must conquer it.

Unfortunately, to bastions of applied science such as the Army Corps of Engineers, conquering nature means paving it over with dams, highways, and airports, poisoning all the bothersome insects, killing off the wild animals that could frighten or attack people, filling in the swamps, chopping down the trees, and installing several chlorinated swimming pools where there was once a lake . . . there has to be a radical rethinking of the initial premise that the universe is something "out there" apart from us and hostile to us.[11]

The Technological Root

For many centuries now Western people have been superb technicians. They advanced technology well before they developed science. According to historian White,

between 800 and 1000 A.D. Europe moved well ahead in technological development — not merely in craftsmanship — far outstripping the more sophisticated cultures of Byzantium and Islam. By the end of the fifteenth century the technological superiority of Europe enabled its small nations to conquer, loot, and colonize much of the rest of the world.[12]

Ecology and Capitalism

Western Capitalists have shared this orientation to nature that had its origin in Christianity — man as master of nature. From this perspective, land, water, minerals and fossil fuels, forests and animals — all the components of the environment — are but commodities in a market system — *valuable* if they can be used for producing goods or sold for some human use; *worthless* if that is not the case.

Competitive Capitalists were long unrestrained in their exploitation of natural resources — and of human beings, too — dumping waste material into streams and cutting down forests without regard to the needs of future generations. In the early decades of this century American Capitalists recognized that their own self-interest was not any longer served by such wanton destruction of natural resources, and made conservation their own cause. But by this time competitive capitalism was giving way to corporate capitalism, whose leadership sought rational control of the market rather than unrestrained competition.

Though American corporate capitalism may have adopted conservation as a useful cause, other practices destructive of the environment have multiplied — the pollution of rivers, for example, as we have

[10] *See* Barry Weissberg, *Beyond Repair: The Ecology of Capitalism* (Boston, Mass.: The Beacon Press, 1971), p. 17.

[11] *See* Anthony D'Amato, "The Politics of Ecosuicide," in Leslie L. Roos, ed., *The Politics of Ecosuicide* (New York: Holt, Rinehart and Winston, Inc., 1971), p. 25.

[12] *See* White, *op. cit.,* p. 19.

seen. Even now, land and natural resources are not yet defined as a national resource. The logic of private property still applies; land and oil and minerals, even water, are defined as the property of individuals (including corporations), to be used in the market as they see fit for making profit. Whether the private entrepreneur is the sole individual or the large corporation, the conception of environment as an aggregate of property for profit largely prevails. The very fact that economic growth, a central value of a Capitalist economy, depends on increased consumption of energy, and that such consumption is a major source of corporate profits, suggests a fundamental conflict between capitalism's basic practices and the attaining of an ecological balance.

Capitalism and Social Costs

One reason that capitalism has apparently been so successful in providing us with a mass of consumer goods and thereby increasing the standard of living is that all the costs of production are not added in under present systems of cost accounting or of economic analysis. Many of the social costs of production are shifted to individuals or to the community or even to future generations.

According to economist K. William Kapp, social costs are those "all direct and indirect losses suffered by third persons or the general public as a result of private economic activities."[13] It includes those consequences of production which do damage and cost someone something to repair — air and water pollution, depletion of animal and energy resources, soil erosion and depletion, or deforestation, for exam-

ple. But social costs include the impairment of human beings through injury, disease, and loss of livelihood. The long and as yet not fully successful struggle to assign medical and other costs arising from "black lung" disease among coal miners to the coal industry as a necessary cost of production is a striking example.

Given the ideology of free enterprise, it has always been difficult to measure and assess these costs (which economists call "externalities"); and even more difficult politically to fix the responsibility for such costs on private enterprise. Forcing industry to take steps to reduce pollution leads many businessmen to complain that their individual competitive position will be reduced by additional costs, or to seek to enlist consumer support on the ground that such costs will have to be passed on to the purchasing public.

The production of automobiles that no longer contribute to making physically harmful smog will raise the price of such products to the consumer. Apply that to a large range of products — from residential construction to transportation to food and clothing — and it becomes clear that the high material standard of living produced by capitalism has been possible only by transferring social costs to individuals and publics or to future generations, or sometimes leaving the cost unpaid, as when polluted Lake Michigan beaches are simply closed and withdrawn from public use.

Kapp's thesis that private enterprise escapes paying the social costs of doing business, and that this is a major factor in the ecological crisis, is not intended to place sole responsibility for ecological damage on capitalism alone. When a municipality dumps raw sewage into a river and pollutes someone else's water supply, or when a Socialist government builds up

[13] *See* K. William Kapp, *The Social Costs of Private Enterprise* (New York: Schocken Books, 1971), p. 13.

industrial production with little thought to water pollution, as the Soviet Union has done, "they sacrifice the quality of the environment for revenues by choice: that is, their action is similar to that of a private firm operating in accordance with the principle of investment for profit. Both try to maintain an artificial, purely formal short-run financial solvency by ignoring social costs."[14]

POPULATION

In recent years popular emphasis on the "population explosion" has pointed to high

[14] See Kapp, op. cit., p. xvi.

COUNTING PEOPLE: THE CENSUS

The effort to make an accurate count of the people in a region or a country is very old; in Babylon and China there were population censuses as far back as three thousand years before Christ.

Yet these censuses were never popular with ordinary people—and for good reason. Too often it meant conscription, confiscation, or higher taxes. It was an instrument of political and economic control; and for that reason, rulers tried to keep results secret, even as the people tried to escape being counted.

Modern censuses began in the French and British colonies in what is now Canada in 1665, then took place in Iceland in 1703. A census was introduced in Sweden in 1748, in Denmark in 1769, and in the United States in 1790, followed by Great Britain in 1801. Russia did not undertake a full enumeration of its population until 1897, and Turkey not until 1927.

The United States census was provided for in the Constitution (Article I, Section 2) as the basis for determining apportionment among the states of representatives in Congress. Thus, congressional seats are always reapportioned after every census.

By now, the census does not merely count the number of people in the country. It enumerates them by age, sex, race, national origin; it records their education, occupation, income, and place of residence. It counts their houses, with and without plumbing or electricity. It records their migration from rural place to city, from city to suburb, from one state and region to another. It also undertakes censuses of manufacturing, farming, and business every five years.

Nor does the Bureau of the Census, first established in 1902, content itself with decennial (every ten years) counting. In between, it undertakes samples of changes in population characteristics, so that fairly accurate projections can be made each year.

In tracing the movement of population from rural to urban places, the Bureau of the Census invented such things as the small census tract, and defined for us what we have come to mean by urban, by metropolitan area, the urban fringe, and the central city.*

* See "Measuring the Urban Population" and "Defining the Metropolitan Area" in Chapter 5.

Figure 19.3 It is often the public who pay for pollution, such as that which closed Lake Michigan beaches. *(Wide World Photos.)*

birth rates throughout the world, attributing to them an alarming growth of the world's population. But this only obscures the complex processes of population growth or stability that must be understood if population is to be examined as one component of the ecological complex.

There is a subtle but profound relationship among population, organization, technology, and environment. Significant changes in the structure of society usually produce changes in the composition or characteristics of population, and these interact with the environment—usually altering it in some fashion—which then has a further impact on society and population. Population, then, is but one factor in a dynamic process of ever-changing relationships.

The specialized activity that studies the characteristics and composition of human populations is *demography*. Its most basic

and reliable information is obtained by census. (*See* "Counting People: The Census.") As yet, there is no fully reliable census data for much of the world, so that demographers must still estimate some population factors from various indices and indirect information.

The demographer studies three basic phenomena: *births*, *deaths*, and *migration*. Taken together, these describe the growth and decline of a human population in a given region or geographical area. On a world basis migration cannot add or subtract from the total, but the shift of population from rural to urban, or from one continent to another, is still an important factor in understanding population growth. It is an outcome of a profoundly complex interaction among environmental, social, and cultural factors.

Environmental factors begin with the fertility of the soil, the abundance of game, the character and distribution of plants and other vegetation, the availability of water, and the climate. But these components do not remain virginal. Human practices may, for example, hunt out game or reduce the fertility of the soil, either reduce the water supply or pollute some of it, or destroy useful vegetation. Thus the environment is always modified in interaction with a food-producing population, and that modification has implications — sometimes severe — for the level of population that can be sustained by the environment.

Cultural factors include knowledge and skills of a practical kind for producing food, warding off disease, and promoting nutrition. But customs about mate selection; religious and moral beliefs about conception and birth; values concerning marriage, family, and children; dietary habits; sanitation and health practices — these and other cultural factors influence the population structure of a society.

Social factors must also be taken into account: the degree of urbanization, the efficiency of the social organization to exploit technology and environment, the formation of a labor force, the class structure, migration patterns, the organization of the economy, and the level of technology.

Fertility and Mortality

Demographers measure the growth of a population by the relationship between birth rates and death rates, between fertility and mortality. (For an explanation of demographic terms *see* "The Language of Demography.") Migration can add to or subtract from this measurement.

If we start with the idea that the birth rate can be high or low, and the death rate

can also, we can allow for four logically possible combinations:

1. high birth rates and high death rates
2. low birth rates and low death rates
3. high birth rates and low death rates
4. low birth rates and high death rates.

The first three of these occur frequently enough to be useful for analysis.

The combination of high birth rates and high death rates is the pattern that has been most common throughout human history. It is the pattern even now in many agrarian, nonindustrialized sections of the world, just as it was in the Western world prior to the Industrial Revolution.

In tribal and peasant societies the large extended family is the basic organizing unit of social life, the work group of an agrarian economy. Such societies put a high value on fertility, which is built into their very way of life, for high fertility has been necessary for survival in societies in which life expectancy was short and the infant mortality rate high. In some past societies perhaps most infants failed to live to a reproducing adulthood.

In these societies, then, a high birth rate is balanced by a high death rate. A low standard of living, hard physical toil, exposure to disease, poor diet, a lack of sanitation, even periodic famine in some cases, and a limited technology all promote a high death rate and a short life expectancy. According to demographer Irene B. Taueber, life expectancy typically fluctuates around twenty-five years, and the death rate averages around 40 per 1,000 total population.[15]

This often means that such societies

---

[15] *See* Irene B. Taueber, "Population and Society," in Robert E.L. Faris, ed., *Handbook of Modern Sociology* (Chicago, Ill.: Rand-McNally & Company, 1964), pp. 87–88.

THE LANGUAGE OF DEMOGRAPHY

There are a number of terms that demographers use, each of which is given a statistical expression. Some of the more basic ones are:

The *birth rate* is computed on the basis of every 1,000 persons in a specified population in a given year. Thus, a birth rate of 18 means an average of 18 births for every 1,000 persons in the population.

This is a *crude* birth rate, in contrast to *specific* birth rates, computed on the number of births per 1,000 living persons of designated age, sex, or family status in a specified population in a calendar year.

Like the birth rate the *death rate* is computed on the basis of every 1,000 persons in a specified population in a given year.

The *fertility rate* is the number of births in a particular population for every 1,000 women of childbearing age, generally defined as from fifteen to forty-five.

The *population growth rate* measures the growth of a population as a percent annual increase. A growth rate of 2 percent, for example, means that 20 persons per 1,000 (2 per every 100) are added to the population each year. The rate of *natural increase* (or *decrease*) is obtained by subtracting deaths from births. In addition, gains or losses by migration need to be counted in order to measure population growth.

have a higher proportion of their population below the age of fourteen than any modern society does, and also a much smaller proportion over sixty-five years of age—even a smaller proportion over forty. The birth rate fluctuates with circumstances, but averages forty per 1,000 population. Although population changes both upward and downward in the short run, there is no persistent trend in either direction.

The Western Demographic Transition

Over the last three hundred years or so the Western world has gone through a major change in the relation of births to deaths—a process usually called the "demographic transition"—that has led to an enormous gain in population. Economic, technological, and social development in the seventeenth and eighteenth centuries, followed by increased industrialization in the nineteenth, reduced the death rate dramatically, while the birth rate changed only moderately. It gave Europe a tremendous growth in population, from 103 million in 1650 to 274 million in 1850, while millions more migrated to the Western hemisphere.

However, the great surplus of births over deaths, which increased the European population so much and produced a doubling of population once every 23.5 years between 1790 and 1860 in the United States, was only a transitional phase. In due time birth rates fell. The gap between births and deaths that produced such leaps in population growth occurred in a demographic transition from a high birth rate-high death rate society to a low birth rate-low death rate society.

Mortality

Unlike fertility, death is not a major positive value in any society. That people are mortal is accepted from one or another orientation, but any society will reduce the death toll by whatever means is available to it, except where such means would violate sacred values. Until recently, few societies had any effective means for warding off an early death, and life for the vast majority of people was short. Poorly fed populations were ravaged by diseases that they did not understand and over which they had no control.

The first year of life has always brought the greatest danger of death; death in this first year—infant mortality—is always high in impoverished, agrarian populations. In the United States infant mortality has only dropped significantly since 1900, when the infant death rate was 162.4 per 1,000 live births. By 1930 it was 64.6; by 1958 it was down to 26.9; and by 1968 to 22.1.[16]

This reduction in the death rate has increased life expectancy in the United States and in other societies in which the same kinds of changes have taken place. By 1968 life expectancy in the United States was seventy-one years—fairly typical for a modern society.

When the decline in mortality increases life expectancy, significant changes occur in the population. Since people live longer, a higher proportion of the population is in the older age brackets. In the United States those over sixty-five have increased not only in absolute numbers but as a proportion of the population. They have in

[16] Source: United Nations, Demographic Yearbook, 1963 and Population Reference Bureau, World Population Data Sheet, 1969.

fact increased from 4.1 percent of the population in 1900 to 9.8 percent in 1970.[17]

Because more people live longer, but not necessarily better, either physically or psychologically, there has been an accelerated interest in the field of gerontology (the study of the aging process) in the last two decades. The physical, mental, and social needs of people who are mostly retired from regular employment, voluntarily or not, and who are allowed no

TABLE 19.1   Crude Birth Rates in the United States, 1920–1972

Years	Number of Births per 1,000 Population
1920	27.7
1930	21.3
1940	19.4
1950	24.1
1960–1961	23.9
1961–1962	23.0
1962–1963	22.3
1963–1964	21.6
1964–1965	20.4
1965–1966	19.0
1966–1967	18.2
1967–1968	17.6
1968–1969	17.7
1969–1970	18.0
1970–1971	18.0
1971–1972	16.4

Source: 1920–1950: U.S. Department of Health, Education and Welfare, Vital Statistics of the United States, 1964, vol. 1 (Washington, D.C.: Government Printing Office, 1966), Table 1–2, pp. 1–4; 1960-61–1971-72: U.S. Bureau of the Census, Current Population Reports, Series P-25, no. 493, "Projections of the Population of the United States, by Age and Sex: 1972 to 2020" (Washington, D.C.: U.S. Government Printing Office, 1972), p. 11.

[17] Source: U.S. Bureau of the Census, Current Population Reports, Series P-23, no. 43, "Some Demographic Aspects of Aging in the United States" (Washington, D.C.: U.S. Government Printing Office, 1973), p. 5.

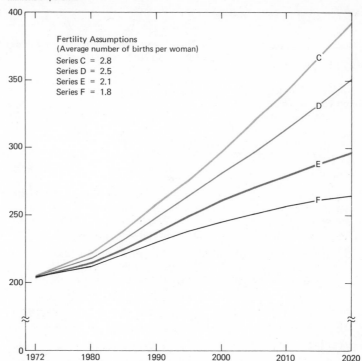

Millions of persons

Fertility Assumptions
(Average number of births per woman)
Series C = 2.8
Series D = 2.5
Series E = 2.1
Series F = 1.8

Figure 19.4 Projections of total population, 1972-2020.

Source: U.S. Bureau of the Census, *Current Population Reports*, Series P-25, #493, "Projection of the Population of the United States, by Age and Sex: 1972 to 2020" (Washington, D.C.: U.S. Government Printing Office, 1972), cover.

useful, respected role in society, has made aging a social issue of growing importance. Despite much bathetic rhetoric about "senior citizens" and "golden years," the lack of any useful function for most people over sixty-five years of age robs increased life expectancy of the kind of cultural and moral value it could have.

Fertility

In most Western countries a long-run decline in the rate of fertility has occurred. In the United States the low was reached in the mid-1930s, but then it increased again, and the birth rate also increased (*see* Table 19.1), contrary to what demographers had expected.

The increased crude birth rate peaked at 26.6 in 1947, but remained around 25 through the 1950s. Since then it has moved down to 16.4 for 1971–1972.

The Future American Population

Since 1970 there has been a sharp decline in fertility, and over the past five years an equally sharp decline in the birth expectations of young wives. This has led the U.S Bureau of the Census to develop new projections for the future of the population, including the possibility of achieving zero population growth (each person reproducing only himself, so that a couple would limit itself to two children).

A new set of assumptions of completed cohort fertility (average number of births per woman upon completion of childbearing) range from a high of 2.8 to 2.5 to 2.1 to 1.8. The difference is 1.0 child per woman; between 1970 and 2000 such a seemingly small difference of one birth per woman for future childbearing cohorts means a difference of about 50 million in the population by the year 2000. There would be 300 million Americans in the

TABLE 19.2   First Year of Zero Growth and Population Attained under Selected Projection Series Assuming No Immigration

	Series T	Series V	Series W
First year of zero growth			
Early timing pattern*	2,062	2,028	2,038
Late timing pattern*	2,058	2,028	2,034
Total population in first year of zero growth (in millions)			
Early timing pattern*	310,187	255,426	294,522
Late timing pattern*	297,933	249,433	276,224

* Mean age of childbearing: early timing pattern, 25.0; late timing pattern, 27.8.
  Series T: Total fertility rate remains at 1970 level until 1980, and then declines to 2,110 (replacement level).
  Series V: Total fertility rate drops to 1,500 by 1980, and then gradually increases to 2,110.
  Series W: Total fertility rate drops immediately to 2,110.

Source: U.S. Bureau of the Census, Current Population Reports, Series P-25, no. 480, "Illustrative Population Projections for the United States: The Demographic Effects of Alternate Paths to Zero Growth," (Washington, D.C.: U.S. Government Printing Office, 1972).

year 2000 if the higher assumption prevailed, 250 million if the lower assumption prevailed (*see* Figure 19.4). A very small change in the birth rate, then, can have large consequences for the rate of population growth, given the already large population and relatively high proportion of females in the childbearing years.

TABLE 19.3   Demographic Aspects of Selected Developed and Underdeveloped Countries

Developed Countries	Birth Rate	Death Rate	Infant Mortality	Life Expectancy	Population under 15 Years (percent)
United States	17.4	9.6	22.1	71	30
Great Britain	17.6	11.2	18.8	71	23
Sweden	15.4	10.1	12.6	74	21
West Germany	17.3	11.2	23.5	71	23
USSR	18.0	8.0	26.0	70	32
Hungary	14.6	10.7	38.4	70	23
Japan	19.0	6.8	15.0	71	25
Underdeveloped Countries	*Birth Rate*	*Death Rate*	*Infant Mortality*	*Life Expectancy*	*Population under 15 Years (percent)*
UAR (Egypt)	43.0	15.0	120.0	50–55	43
Ghana	47.0	20.0	156.0	40–45	45
Tanzania	45.0	23.0	189.0	35–45	42
India	43.0	18.0	139.0	45	41
Philippines	50.0	10–15.0	73.0	47	47
Indonesia	43.0	21.0	125.0	42	42
Mexico	43.0	9.0	63.0	58–64	46
World	34.0	15.0		53	37

Source: Population Reference Bureau, *1968,* and *1969 World Population Data Sheets.*

Zero Growth When?

Under certain assumptions zero population growth in the United States could arrive by the year 2028, which is seventy-six years from projections based on the 1972 data. Under other assumptions it could be as late as 2062. The first assumption is that the total fertility rate moves down to 1500 (equivalent to 1.5 birth per woman) in 1980, and then gradually moves to 2110 (2.11 per woman, which is the level of fertility required for a population to replace itself exactly under projected mortality rates and in the absence of immigration). Table 19.2 provides some examples of projecting the year of zero growth and the size of the American population when that is achieved. Figure 19.5 contrasts the distribution of the American population by age and sex in 1970 with an ultimate stationary population brought about by zero growth.

World Population Growth

Whatever the prospects for limiting population growth in the United States may be, such prospects for the world's population are quite another matter. The present trends in Europe and the United States differ considerably from those in other parts of the world, particularly in the underdeveloped countries.

Measuring the world's population is at best a hazardous process, and even now large areas of the world possess no accurate census. Careful estimates of population and of rate of growth are necessary.

The following table is a demographic assessment from the best available evidence of world population since 1650:[18]

Year	Population (in millions)
1650	545
1750	728
1800	906
1850	1,171
1900	1,608
1950	2,406
1969	3,551

What these figures say is that world population is increasing rapidly, and that it has increased almost sevenfold since 1650. Prior to that, demographers believe, it increased only slowly, with high birth rates offset by high death rates.

The growth rate of world population is given in the *1969 World Population Data Sheet* as 1.9, meaning nineteen people are added to each 1,000 in the world population. At this rate world population will double again in thirty-seven years. As demographer Irene Taueber acknowledges:

> Given at least three billion people increasing at rates of growth four or five times those of recent centuries, simple forward projections for a few more centuries yield numbers that are not possible on a finite earth.[19]

Comparing Developed and Underdeveloped Worlds

Even a simple contrast built on a few statistics makes it plain that the developed world stands in sharp contrast to the underdeveloped world in its demographic structure. Table 19.3 compares a selected set of countries in both the developed and underdeveloped worlds on some

---

[18] *See* United Nations Department of Social Affairs, Population Division, *The Determinants and Conse-* *quences of Population Trends* (New York, 1953), Table 2, p. 11. The figure for 1969 is from the Population Reference Bureau, *1969 World Population Data Sheet.*

[19] *See* Taueber, *op. cit.,* pp. 85–86.

basic demographic phenomena: birth rates and death rates, infant mortality rates, life expectancy, and population under fifteen years of age.

Within the developed countries the range on any one of the rates is exceedingly small. The birth rate ranges from 14.6 (Hungary) to 19 (Japan); while the death rate ranges from 6.8 (Japan) to 11.2 (West Germany and Great Britain). There is a somewhat greater range in infant mortality, from Sweden's 12.6 to Hungary's 38.4. The life expectancy range is narrow, from 70 to 74. The percentage of people under fifteen years of age ranges from 23 percent (Hungary and Great Britain) to the United States' 30 percent (because of a relatively higher birth rate up to the last five years).

The underdeveloped countries, by contrast, offer a strikingly different profile. Birth rates run from 43 to 50, death rates from 15 to 23, and infant mortality from 63 to 189. Life expectancy is much lower, and the percent of their populations under fifteen years of age is in every case over 40 percent—from 41 to 47—suggesting what an enormous potential they have for sustaining a high birth rate in the near future, and consequent population growth—even if fertility should decline.

An inspection of Table 19.3 reveals that the underdeveloped nations have a greater gap between their birth and death rates than do the developed ones. Mexico has a death rate lower than some developed nations. In part, this is because such countries have so large a proportion of their populations in the younger age categories; the age structure in a country affects the death rate.

But since 1940 underdeveloped countries have experienced a greater decline in their death rates than in their birth rates, and have done so without significantly altering their social structures. Rather, deliberate intervention by developed countries has helped to control infectious diseases and to introduce public health measures. The Ehrlichs call this "exported death control." Control of malaria, yellow fever, smallpox, cholera, and other infectious diseases has been responsible for sharp reductions in the death rates of most of the underdeveloped countries.

In the decade 1940–1950 the death rate declined 46 percent in Puerto Rico, 43 percent in Formosa, and 23 percent in Jamaica. In a sample of 18 undeveloped areas the average decline in death rate between 1945 and 1950 was 26 percent.[20]

Implications of Population Growth

Whatever may have been the intention and justification for controlling diseases and reducing the death rate in these underdeveloped countries, humanitarian or otherwise, the consequences for the future are sobering. Ehrlich and Ehrlich assert that by lowering the death rates in these societies, "the world growth rate moved from 0.9 (doubling time 77 years) in the decade 1940–1950 to a rate of 1.8 percent (doubling time 39 years) in the decade 1950–1960."[21] By 1969 the doubling rate of world population was thirty-seven years.

The rapid growth of population in poor countries will not only contribute to world population growth but will also mean that the population in underdeveloped countries will grow faster than in developed countries, and thus become a larger proportion of the world population. Table 19.4 gives projections done in 1963 by the United Nations based on different assump-

[20] See Ehrlich and Ehrlich, op. cit., p. 22.
[21] See Ehrlich and Ehrlich, op. cit., p. 23.

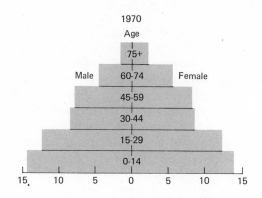

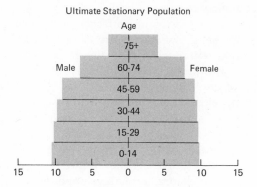

Figure 19.5 Percent distribution of the population by age and sex, 1970, and ultimate stationary population.

Source: U.S. Bureau of the Census, *Current Population Reports*, Series P-25, no. 480, "Illustrative Population Projections for the United States: The Demographic Effects of Alternate Paths to Zero Growth" (Washington, D.C.: U.S. Government Printing Office, 1972), p. 5.

tions, from a low growth that assumes quite effective controls over population growth to a conservative estimate of only moderate controls to one that assumes no change in present fertility levels.

If the present fertility rates in the world do not change between now and the year 2000, the world population will more than double, going from 3.5 billion to 7.5 billion people.

The Limits of the Earth

The earth is a limited ecosystem, capable of sustaining only a limited, though perhaps quite large, population. The sources of food and water are not infinitely ex-

TABLE 19.4 Population Estimates of Growth of World Population, 1960–2000 (population in millions)

	1960	1970	1980	1990	2000
Low variant	2998	3544	4147	4462	5448
Medium variant	2998	3591	4330	5187	6129
High variant	2998	3659	4550	5689	6993
Constant fertility	2998	3640	4519	6564	7522
Estimate of world population, mid-1969: 3551 million					

Note: A more detailed report of these estimates, giving breakdown by regions, can be found in Paul R. Ehrlich and Anne H. Ehrlich, *Population, Resources, Environment: Issues in Human Ecology* (San Francisco, Calif.: W.H. Freeman and Company, 1970), Appendix 2, pp. 336–340.

Source: United Nations Population Studies, no. 41, "World Population Prospects as Assessed in 1963."

pandable. The world's population, however, is increasing so rapidly that it cannot
go on growing indefinitely at its present
rate without insuring disaster.

The problem is not simply one of population and environment. In the underdeveloped societies population is growing
most rapidly, but in the developed societies the much higher standards of living
consume greater quantities of the earth's
finite resources. If the underdeveloped societies change into developed ones, they
will also evolve a different population
structure, one of lower birth rates and
lower death rates. The rising standard of
living that accompanies modernization
may threaten the finite limits of the earth
even more than population growth.

Indeed, from the perspective of the present social organization of human populations and accompanying technology, there
may already be too many people:

Taking into account present population densities and the other factors involved in carrying
capacity, we arrive at the inescapable conclusion that, in the context of man's present patterns of behavior and level of technology, *the
planet Earth, as a whole, is overpopulated.*[22]

The Ehrlichs' sober comment is one with
a growing school of scientists who have
warned that we are soon to exceed—if we
have not already—the earth's carrying
capacity. A British scientist, Hugh Nicol,
offers even more grim prospects for the
human future:

So far from there being grounds for the
prevailing euphoria about indefinite progress
in food-supply or with any other application of
technology, it is shown that population of the
world, as a whole and locally, must within
foreseeable time undergo a decline, in company
with every form of comfort and amenity.[23]

[22] *See* Ehrlich and Ehrlich, *op. cit.*, p. 201.
[23] *See* Hugh Nicol, *The Limits of Man* (London: Con-
stable & Co., Ltd., 1967), p. 1.

Nicol's grim prophecy is based on the
principle that the production of food depends on the availability of fossil fuel,
which is diminishing and for which there
is no substitute. As a consequence, he sees
a future not of growth but of reverting
back (devolution) to a technology based on
wood fuel and to a world population of
1–2 billion people (there are already $3\frac{1}{2}$
billion people in the world and there will
be 5 to 7 billion by the year 2000).

A group of European and American
scientists dubbed the Club of Rome have
recently added fuel to this growing scientific and public debate.[24] They, too, have
offered grim analyses of human prospects
for a foreseeable future.

Challenges to and critiques of these
"models of doom" have come from other
scientists, who see a greater possibility for
solution of the problem.[25] Yet, there is
small comfort in their critiques. The argument is not whether we are doomed or not,
but about how soon and about alternatives
for staving off disaster. There is no disagreement, apparently, that the present
course means doom; there is only disagreement about whether we have enough time
and know enough to do anything to prevent our downfall.

Population Growth in Perspective

From the time of Malthus to now, this
sobering prospect of more people than the
earth can feed, with consequent human
misery, has been a specter of fear and

[24] *See* Jay W. Forrester, *World Dynamics* (Cambridge,
Mass.: Wright-Allen Press, 1971); and Donnella H.
Meadows and Dennis L. Meadows, et al., *The Limits
to Growth* (New York: Universe Books, 1972).
[25] *See*, for example, H.S.D. Cole, et al., eds., *Models
of Doom: A Critique of the Limits to Growth* (New
York: Universe Books, 1973); and John Maddox, *The
Doomsday Syndrome* (New York: McGraw-Hill Book
Company, Inc., 1973).

Figure 19.6 Nations, like India, with the largest populations do not consume most of the world's natural resources. Their standards of living reflect this lack of economic development. *(The Population Council).*

concern (*see* "Malthus: The Problem of Human Survival"). Yet to make sheer population growth the central factor in the present ecological crisis may—conveniently, for the people of the developed nations—shift concern to birth rates in underdeveloped countries and in effect define them as the culprits for the world crisis. That would be a distortion of a complex problem.

To put population in perspective—the basic issue is that sustaining a population requires an adequate supply of food and water. But the largest populations do not necessarily consume the most. Living standards vary considerably, as we have seen, and the Asian nations with the most people still do not consume most of the world's natural resources. The *richest* nations, of which the United States is first, do that.

Moreover, the underdeveloped countries, who now have almost 70 percent of the

world's people, will have between 75 and 80 percent by the year 2000. The domination of underdeveloped countries by developed ones becomes even more politically strained than it is now when population growth increases the poor countries' share of the world's people but not of the world's wealth.

Underdeveloped nations, whose resources are exported for consumption to rich nations, and whose poor and uneducated populations are also young and restless, anxious to share in opportunity and material comfort, may become increasingly responsive to militant anti-imperialist ideologies—calling for nationalism, nationalization, and socialism, with or without democratic processes.

The threat of world population growth, then, is not merely a threat of an impending Malthusian disaster at some future time or of famine and starvation among the least fortunate. It also implies increas-

MALTHUS: THE PROBLEM OF HUMAN SURVIVAL

In 1798, in his "Essay on the Principle of Population," Thomas Malthus (1766–1834) advanced the proposition that population growth tends to exceed the food supply. Specifically, Malthus postulated that population grows at a geometric ratio of 1:2:4:8:16, whereas the food supply grows only at an arithmetic ratio of 1:2:3:4:5. When this happens, human misery in the form of war, famine, plagues, and infanticide increases until population is checked.

These *positive* checks occur if people do nothing to prevent population from exceeding the food supply. *Preventive* checks, which Malthus advocated, are basically a moral restraint: abstention from sexual relations outside of marriage, postponement of marriage for the individual male until he can support a family, even celibacy for some. But Malthus was pessimistic about very many people being capable of practicing such restraints; accordingly, he foresaw misery in the human future.

Demographers have long since abandoned the details of Malthus' theory, but his basic thesis—that population tends to grow in excess of food supply—has come alive again as one of the significant issues of our time. In the shorter run of time, for a century beyond Malthus' life, his dire predictions seemed not to fit the Western situation. Even though population grew, the rapid spread of industrialization and the opening up of the grassy plains of North America to cultivation seemed to negate Malthus' warnings. Even Malthus acknowledged he did not anticipate the great increase in arable land, nor the improvement in agricultural techniques that increased food production several times over.

But the growth of world population in the last half-century or less, and its projected growth if unchecked in the next thirty years, coupled with an insatiable consumption of natural resources—particularly in rich societies—all become aspects of an ecological crisis that makes Malthus' concerns, if not his specific theory, relevant again.

ing political struggle and a revolt against the now quite unequal distribution of the planet's sustenance among the *have* and the *have-not* peoples of the world.

RESHAPING SOCIETY: FINDING AN ECOLOGICAL BALANCE

We started this chapter by making a basic point: That human society is necessarily linked to the environment and that human beings, organized into human societies, are not and can never be independent of that environment. Now, in the twentieth century the relationship of society to environment has become critical. No society has ever survived by remaining persistently out of balance with nature. It is the arrogance of an advanced technological society that it could forget that basic point, or ignore it.

The critical problem of society and environment—the ecological crisis—is a complex matter. The difficulty of providing enough food for the needs of the world, while unchecked population growth continues; the exhaustion of finite resources by the consumption practices of affluent societies; and their destruction of the environment by pollution and poison constitute much of what is basic to the ecological crisis.

But no statement of the problem would be complete without recognizing that the relation of developed to underdeveloped society is also basic to the world's unbalanced ecology. America, the most advanced technological society with the highest standard of living and the greatest capacity to waste and pollute, has often served as a model of what an advanced society could become. Perhaps the most difficult lesson to learn is that the whole world cannot imitate the United States if ecological balance is to be achieved.

America: The Impossible Model

The United States is a society with a voracious appetite for natural resources. Though it has but 6 percent of the world's population, it consumed (in 1966) over a third of the world's tin; over a fourth of its phosphate, potash, and nitrogenous fertilizer; half of its newsprint and synthetic rubber; more than a fourth of its steel; and about a fifth of its cotton.[26]

To do that, and to be the world's most industrially productive society, the United States is highly dependent on foreign sources for most of its basic industrial raw materials, except coal. Since 1961, for example, we have been importing 90 percent of our nickel and 30 percent of our copper.[26] Though the United States now imports only about 4 percent of its oil from the Middle East, it expects to increase this to about 25 percent by 1980, to keep pace with economic growth.[27]

To raise other countries to the standards of the United States would require seventy-five times as much iron as is now mined annually, 100 times as much copper, 200 times as much lead, 75 times as much zinc, and 250 times as much tin. With the exception of iron, this would exceed all known or inferred reserves.[28] Biochemist H.R. Hulett, for example, asserts that "... (about) a billion people is the maximum population supportable by the present agricultural and industrial system of the world at U.S. levels of affluence."[29] The population of the earth is already three and a half times that maximum.

Not only is the United States not a viable model for other nations but efforts to develop to the same level of affluence and consumption threaten to add to an already overpolluted global system, and to use up even faster already depleting natural resources. The sheer competition for oil and for minerals necessary for industrial production threatens to produce a destructive conflict of worldwide and possibly global proportions.

The United States (and other industrial developed societies) can only retain their own levels of production and consumption and maintain their cherished process of growth if they manage to maintain relations of domination and control over other parts of the globe; in short, to maintain a pattern of imperial relations. The present position of the United States depends on this. If the United States is to overconsume, other countries must remain largely underdeveloped and must underconsume.

[26] See Ehrlich and Ehrlich, op. cit., p. 61.

[27] See Newsweek, September 17, 1973.
[28] See Ehrlich and Ehrlich, op. cit., pp. 61–62.
[29] See Ehrlich and Ehrlich, op. cit., p. 202.

Finding Solutions

Many Americans maintain an illusory faith in technological "fixes"; that is, in technological solutions that will miraculously clean the environment, produce abundant food, and find new sources of inexhaustible energy at little cost and requiring no sacrifice. It would be foolhardy to say that is impossible, but few scientists today maintain an optimistic view. Ehrlich and Ehrlich, for example, note that "no conceivable increase in food supply can keep up with the current population growth rates for long."[30]

Many technological solutions require more time for scientific development than the ecological crisis may allow; and others will be so costly as effectively to reduce the standard of living. Other solutions pose further ecological threats. In any case, there is no basis for complacently assuming that scientists and engineers will solve all our problems.

Some technological fixes would have serious economic consequences for already established businesses, and thus bring opposition. Oil companies, for example, have apparently resisted geothermal development, which could provide a new source of clean, nonpolluting energy. At the same time these giant firms have tried to move into other sources of energy production.[31] There is, then, a politics to the

ecological crisis and a set of vested interests able to exercise power in their own behalf.

As the Alaskan pipeline controversy, among others, has made clear, new sources of conventional energy pose additional threats to an already threatened environment. Strip mining for coal in the Western states, for example, offers the possibility of despoiling the environment on a scale hitherto never imagined by most Americans.

The effort to pursue a variety of sources of energy for continued growth, even though it means more pollution to the environment, has enormous power behind it. There is, ideologically, the appeal to growth, consumption, and a high standard of living. There is corporate profit and the immense power of a corporate-controlled political economy.

Against that there is a spreading concern for ecological values by the people, and an unfocused and sporadic environmental movement; but as yet there is little political power. Nonetheless, the effort to act on the many diverse aspects of the problem-ridden ecosystem suggests that struggles over conflicting interests and goals will be central to American political life for decades to come. In American society at the present time there is as yet no significant movement toward a solution of this crisis. A minimum fix perspective now dominates, while more articulate movements are developing.

The Minimum Fix

A dominant approach, reflected in the national administration, is to accept grudgingly that *something* must be done about the environment, but to put most emphasis on increasing the supply of energy. Thus, as little as possible is changed, and the minimum necessary is

---

[30] *See* Ehrlich and Ehrlich, *op. cit.,* p. 112. For a more detailed analysis *see* George Borgstrom, *Too Many, A Story of Earth's Biological Limitations* (New York: The Macmillan Company, 1969).

[31] For a critical review of the place of oil firms in dominating energy policy *see* Weissberg, Ch. V, particularly pp. 115–145. For a fuller treatment *see* Robert Engler, *The Politics of Oil* (Chicago, Ill.: University of Chicago Press, 1967); and Michael Tanzer, *The Political Economy of Oil in Underdeveloped Countries* (Boston, Mass.: The Beacon Press, 1969).

spent to stave off disaster. Laws for clean air and water are based on minimum standards of what is ecologically safe—and many scientists and physicians often urge much higher standards—and business firms rarely do more than minimally comply. Even then, laws are poorly and sporadically enforced. This position accepts national growth as an unquestioned value and seeks to maintain American access to raw materials the world over— and even to extend such sources where possible.

Movement and Conflict: Conservative and Radical

But minimum fix will not provide a long-run solution for the ecological crisis, perhaps not even a short-run one. In the decade of the 1970's and the 1980's a complex and probably conflict-ridden ecological social movement will be the central focus of efforts in the United States to bring society into balance with the environment.

Beyond minimum fix the leadership of established institutions—corporate and governmental—are beginning to think toward solutions that will (1.) maintain the economic and political structure of the society and its dominant place in world affairs; and yet (2.) provide restraints and controls that will ward off disaster. The minimum fix seeks compromise between the values of ecological survival and the maintenance of the institutional structure. This calls for the corporate elite joining with the ecology movement, even as the corporate leadership at the turn of the century embraced the conservation movement to impose rational and efficient controls on the uses of natural resources.[32] Such

a rationality assumes centralization of effective control structures, strengthening federal government at the expense of local government. Life is to be even more regulated. Family planning and control of the birth rate as a national policy will be a key feature not only for the United States but for the rest of the world as well.[33]

The assumption that underlies this conservative effort is that sufficient measures can be taken to preserve the environment, check pollution, and encourage sensible conservation policies without basically altering the economic or political structures of American society. Whether that assumption is a safe risk or not depends on one's reading of the analysis of the ecological crisis.

In contrast to this high risk-taking, conservative effort to restore ecological balance, a radical analysis is organized around the basic idea that survival begins with taking seriously the imperative that ecological balance cannot be avoided for very long or even compromised with or technologically fixed. Antiecological practices, from a radical perspective, are not the actions of irresponsible individuals but are practices consistent with institutions committed to growth, profit, and hierarchy. Only another set of institutions, repudiating these values and invoking other, more humane ones offers a chance at ecological survival that will also keep life from reverting to a barren struggle for existence. As one radical ecologist put it:

Either ecology action is revolutionary action or it is nothing at all. Any attempt to reform a social order that by its very nature pits humanity against all the forces of life is a gross decep-

---

[32] The best study of the minimum fix is by Samuel P. Hays, *Conservation and the Gospel of Efficiency* (Cambridge, Mass.: Harvard University Press, 1959).

[33] For suggestions on what policies might be instituted by a conservative-controlled ecology movement *see* Ehrlich and Ehrlich, Ch. 10, "Family Planning and Population Control."

tion and serves merely as a safety valve for established institutions.[34]

A radical solution begins with belief and institution, and these must be overcome — the legacy of the spirit of domination and hierarchy so long embedded in religious, scientific, and economic thought, and made evident in institutional patterns of property relations, of family, and of state. All of these are to be thoroughly altered.

The reconstruction of society consistent with ecological principles from a radical perspective emphasizes, among other things, a *decentralization* of social life that would eliminate gigantic urban sprawl and replace it with communities scaled to human dimensions and to the carrying capacity of its ecosystem. A diversity of communal patterns would replace bureaucratic organizations and the dominating state.

This radical perspective, however, does not preach reversion to a primitive tech-

nology, as some communes seem to do. Rather, it projects an advanced technology which does not require great urban clusters and huge bureaucratic corporations but permits instead small-scale communal patterns.[35] Such a technology would then be used to meet true human needs, not advertising-induced ones, and its production would be carefully gauged to the necessary recycling of wastes.

Neither of these perspectives — conservative or radical — offers blueprints to the future. But their clashing and incompatible definitions of what can and must be done by generations now living will provide the scientific and ideological content for basic political conflict. From these perspectives probably immense decisions of fateful consequences will be made — perhaps before the end of the century or at least within the next fifty years.

---

[34] *See* Murray Bookchin, "Toward an Ecological Solution," in Editors of Ramparts, *Eco-catastrophe* (San Francisco, Calif.: Canfield Press, 1970), p. 51.

[35] *See* Murray Bookchin, "Toward a Liberatory Technology," in C. George Benello and Dimitrios Roussopolos, eds., *The Case for Participatory Democracy* (New York: The Viking Press, Inc., 1971), pp. 95–139.

SUMMARY

Society is but one component of human life and is never independent of an environment; there is a complex, interactive process among *organization (society), population, technology,* and *environment.*

Technology extends the human capacity to modify environment, but indiscriminate use of technology is the root of an *ecological crisis.* This crisis takes the forms: (1.) of a rapid growth of world population, (2.) of the depletion of natural resources, (3.) of the depletion of living organisms, and 4. of the pollution and poisoning of the environment.

Its *roots* can be traced to:

A *religious* perspective (Western Christianity) that viewed man as apart from and destined to be master of the natural world — *man-conquers-nature.*

A *scientific* perspective that absorbed this attitude toward nature from the religious one.

A superb *technology* which enabled the small nations of Europe to conquer, loot, and colonize much of the rest of the world.

Western *capitalism* also absorbed this perspective, defining natural resources as commodities in a market system — valuable or worthless only in terms of exchange value. Corporate capitalism, however, puts some restraints and rational controls on previously unrestrained competitive capitalism, as in conservation practices. Capitalism has also pushed many *social costs* of production onto individuals, publics, and future generations.

The study of population — *demography* — examines three basic phenomena: *births, deaths,* and *migration.* A change from high birth rates and high death rates to low birth rates and low death rates is the *demographic transition,* which Western nations have gone through and which largely differentiates their populations from those of underdeveloped societies.

A recent sharp decline in fertility in the United States makes *zero population growth* possible anywhere from 2028 to 2062.

The population of the world has grown seven times since 1650, and its present rate of growth of 1.9 will double it again in thirty-seven years, a rate of growth that cannot go on indefinitely.

Developed and *underdeveloped* countries contrast sharply on such major demographic factors as birth rates, death rates, infant mortality, life expectancy, and percent of population below age fifteen. For underdeveloped countries birth and death rates are higher (with some exceptions on death rates), as is infant mortality and the percent of population under age fifteen; life expectancy is lower. Death rates have been lowered in underdeveloped countries by public health measures introduced by developed countries. This has further increased population growth in these societies.

The implications of these facts are: a *rapid world population growth* that threatens the carrying capacity of a finite planet and renews Malthusian fears of disaster in the future; and *increased political strains* between developed and underdeveloped nations, particularly since developed nations will be perhaps only 20 to 25 percent of the world's population. In addition, further development increases the rate of consumption of natural resources; the developed societies, and particularly the United States, now consume far more than do underdeveloped societies, despite their greater populations.

If ecological balance is to be achieved, America is an *impossible model* for the world, for its consumption of resources is at a rate that could not sustain more than a billion people, and there are now 3.5 billion people on the earth.

Within the United States little has been done as yet in reshaping society to find an ecological balance other than *minimum fix,* a minimum adjustment to environmental threats but no basic change in perspectives in social practices or in institutional arrangements. A conflict over *conservative* and *radical* solutions will undoubtedly occur in the 1970s and 1980s. A conservative solution looks to greater imposed restraints to ward off environmental threats while preserving economic growth and America's domination.

A radical perspective seeks the creation of a new institutional structure consonant with ecological balance as the only possible hope of ecological survival and a humane future.

Suggested Readings

Harrison Brown, *The Challenge of Man's Future* (New York: The Viking Press, Inc., 1954). A renowned study of population and resources.

Rachel Carson, *Silent Spring* (Boston, Mass.: Houghton Mifflin Company, 1962). The classic work that did more than any other to awaken people to the dangers of destroying their environment.

Fred Carvell and Max Tadlock, *It's Not Too Late* (Beverly Hills, Calif.: Glencoe Press, 1971). A useful set of readings on ecology, combining serious analysis with hope.

Editors of Ramparts, *Eco-Catastrophe* (San Francisco, Calif.: Canfield Press, 1970). A series of radical essays on ecological issues that originally appeared in *Ramparts* magazine.

Paul R. Ehrlich, *The Population Bomb* (New York: Ballantine Books, Inc. 1968). A foremost spokesman for population control outlines problems and solutions.

Paul R. Ehrlich and Anne R. Ehrlich, *Population, Resources, and Environment: Issues in Human Ecology* (San Francisco, Calif.: W. H. Freeman and Company, 1970). A wide-ranging, informative review of all aspects of the ecological crisis.

Ronald Freedman, ed., *Population: The Vital Revolution* (New York: Doubleday & Company, Inc., 1964). Professional demographers analyze population growth and related problems.

Amos H. Hawley, *Human Ecology: A Theory of Community Structure* (New York: The Ronald Press Company, 1950). A work that has influenced the development of an ecological perspective among sociologists.

K. William Kapp, *The Social Costs of Private Enterprise* (New York: Schocken Books, 1971). An economist's examination of the failure to include social costs in economic analyses of private enterprise.

John Maddox, *The Doomsday Syndrome* (New York: McGraw-Hill Book Company, Inc., 1973). A British scientist sees more hope than do other scientists in solving the problem of population pressure on a limited earth.

Donnella H. Meadows and Dennis L. Meadows, *et al., The Limits to Growth* (New York: Universe Books, 1972). A Club of Rome analysis of the perils of population and ecology on spaceship earth.

Leslie L. Roos, Jr., *The Politics of Ecosuicide* (New York: Holt, Rinehart and Winston, Inc., 1971). A collection of essays that stresses possibilities and problems in instituting change.

William Thomas, Jr., ed., *Man's Role in Changing the Face of the Earth* (Chicago, Ill.: University of Chicago Press, 1956). A scientific symposium on what has been done by humans to the one planet they inhabit.

Barry Weissberg, *Beyond Repair: The Ecology of Capitalism* (Boston, Mass.: The Beacon Press, 1971). A highly readable introduction to the radical perspective on ecology: problem and solution.

. . . by their work all students of man and society
assume and imply moral and political decisions.
   — C. Wright Mills

Chapter 20

Social Issues and the Uses of Sociology

Too often people feel that the troubles that mar their lives are crosses they bear alone. They do not readily see how structural changes and social conflicts lie behind the personal traps from which they cannot manage to escape. They often lack the sociological imagination that would enable them to place their own troubles in a wider context of social issues. When a society like that of the United States emphasizes personal action—"stand on your own feet"; "do for yourself"; "take care of number one" or, as President Richard Nixon once suggested, "ask what you can do for yourself"—the effect is that people see their troubles as only their own private affairs.

Take the matter of the city—decaying, getting poorer and uglier, losing its middle class, finding its streets less safe. The personal solution for this has been, for those with the means, to move to the suburbs. Those without the means—the older, the minorities, the poor—stay behind, the quality of their lives declining along with their neighborhoods. For others—realtors, builders, merchants—the suburban drift has been an opportunity to make money by constructing sprawling housing developments and large shopping centers. The spread of suburbia steadily engulfs farms and green space, while behind it urban blight moves relentlessly outward from the black ghetto and inner-city slums to lap threateningly at the edges of older suburbs. Insofar as dying cities and urban sprawl are the outcomes of leaving urban growth to the irrational processes of profit-making and unregulated markets, the troubles of urban life cannot be altered by private actions.

It is the essence of the sociological imagination—as C. Wright Mills told us—to understand our *private* troubles to be *public* issues.[1] If this is so, it is the task of the sociologist to cope with social issues, to make clear to people how and why their troubles are located in the arrangements of social structure.

Sociologists have always paid serious attention to social *problems*, the term they use more commonly than issues. Yet, there has always been some tension for sociologists between the desire to be socially relevant, with its implications for supporting reform and change in society, and the desire to build a scientific sociology free from bias and the contamination of value judgment.

In an earlier day sociologists made strong moral judgments about social conditions that needed to be attended to, using concepts like social *pathology* and social *disorganization* to characterize such behavior as crime, delinquency, prostitution, and family desertion.

The increasing emphasis on building a scientific sociology not only pressed sociologists to turn away from social issues but made them sensitive to the ill-concealed place of conventional value judgments in their work. But the persistent desire of some sociologists to be scientific while confronting social issues set the stage for re-

ceptivity to the concept of social *problems*, developed first in two essays by sociologists Richard Fuller and Richard Myers.[2]

Social Problems

Those conditions or situations which members of the society regard as a threat to their values were defined by Fuller and Myers as social problems. Social problems are what people say they are. Two things must be present: (1.) an *objective condition* (crime, poverty, racial tensions, and so forth) the presence and magnitude of which can be observed, verified, and measured by impartial social observers; and (2.) a *subjective definition* by some members of the society that the objective condition is a "problem" and must be acted upon. Here is where values come into play, for when values are perceived as threatened by the existence of the objective condition a social problem is defined.

Recognizing an undesirable condition and defining it as a social problem, however, are two different things. There can be disagreement if some people believe the situation, though undesirable, is unavoidable—part of the human condition or the price we pay for "progress." For most of human history poverty was the common lot of the mass of people; given a primitive technology, the existing economies were those of scarcity.

Until the invention of automobile seat belts and shoulder straps, and the speaking out of such critics as Ralph Nader, the steadily rising rate of accidental deaths in-

[1] See C. Wright Mills, *The Sociological Imagination* (New York: Oxford University Press, 1959; paperback edition, Grove Press, 1961).

[2] See Richard C. Fuller and Richard R. Myers, "Some Aspects of a Theory of Social Problems," *American Sociological Review,* vol. 6 (February 1941), pp. 24-32; and "The Natural History of a Social Problem," *American Sociological Review,* vol. 6 (June 1941), pp. 320-329.

Difficulty Fuller & Myrer — Does not specify what people are, but tell what they think they are.

volving automobiles in the United States was considered to be unavoidable. Only then did automobile safety become a social problem. Whether auto manufacturers sacrificed safety for speed and salability finally became a public debate and a matter for Congressional investigation.

But some people may define a condition as not a problem because it is to them desirable and natural, not to be lamented but to be sustained. Racial discrimination is not a problem for those who believe the races to be naturally unequal. They would deny that differential treatment is "discrimination." (For them, integration is a threat to their values, and thus a social problem.) It requires the value of human equality to define a problem of discrimination and to interpret the objective conditions of differential treatment as a threat to such a value.

There are significant cultural differences in the readiness to accept objective conditions as inevitable. Some people in the world are more ready to bow to the inevitable, to be philosophically resigned to the vicissitudes of nature and society than are others. Western people, however, have generally been more activist in their orientation. The outlook that characterized the Protestant Ethic, the emergence of science, and the development of numerous technical inventions is one of activist mastery of the environment. Such an outlook is more likely to demand the alteration of objective conditions, and thus to define them as social problems. In American life this leads to the frequent demand that somebody (usually government) "do something."

Two Types of Social Problems

Sociologists make a distinction between problems seen in terms of the relationship of the individual to society and problems

seen in terms of the way in which the community or society is organized. The adjustment of the individual to society involves *deviance* or *deviant behavior*, the conduct of those who turn away from established modes of action and rules of society. Delinquency is a problem in deviance, as is some (not all) criminal behavior; drug addiction, particularly among young people; homosexuality; and mental illness.

Other problems have to do with relationships between groups, such as whites and blacks, or labor and management; and some with the organization of the community, such as housing, slums, and urban renewal. These are basically problems of *social organization*.

Many people possess an individualistic outlook which leads them to see all problems primarily in social *adjustment* terms. A man who believes that blacks suffer from inadequacies of their own making and not from social discrimination is likely to interpret the race issue as a problem requiring blacks to "pull themselves up" as other groups have done. Similarly, a person who sees poverty as a consequence of individual laziness or moral failure is likely to see this problem as one of inducing poor people to act as middle-class people do. It requires a particular definition, and a very sociological definition at that, to see such problems as those of social organization rather than social adjustment.

DEVIANT BEHAVIOR

The study of deviant behavior by sociologists—and by psychologists—has deep roots in problems of conformity and social control. In an effort to understand deviant behavior the major effort of past social research for at least half a century has concentrated on the *deviant person*. Criminals, juvenile delinquents, prostitutes, and the like have been studied in detail, with an emphasis both on their psychological characteristics and their environment. Criminals, for example, have been viewed as having a weak ego structure, a poorly developed moral sense; meaning, in short, a psychic inability to meet the demands and expectations of society. This, in turn, was seen as the outcome of some type of environment: a broken home, poverty, association with other deviants, and so on.

The focus on the individual sought to find the cause of deviancy in some psychological attribute or characteristic of one person. Much of this focus was an effort to counter an even older conception of deviant behavior as inherent — born criminals, for instance — and thus as genetically caused. The shift to a social perspective instead of a biological one retained a focus on the individual; but now he or she was viewed as becoming deviant because of psychological attributes emerging from a deviant-producing environment.

This approach concentrated on the deviant and asked: Who is he? How did he get to be a deviant? But social research failed to provide any clear answers. The studies only partly supported one another, and many provided contradictory findings.

A British scholar, Barbara Wooten, for example, undertook a careful, systematic critique of the research on juvenile delinquency.[3] She selected twelve factors most commonly reported in both the popular and professional literature as being causes of delinquency and then examined what twenty-one major empirical studies in three countries over a period of four dec-

ades had discovered.[4] Her results produced a bewildering array of findings, frequently noncomparable, and usually subject to overgeneralization. Her voice was one among others declaring that the study of the individual offender as a bundle of traits or deviant-producing factors had about exhausted its value. A new perspective was emerging.

A New Perspective on Deviancy

What was most common to the new effort to define deviancy was an insistence that sociological analysis had to focus on deviant *behavior*, rather than some conception of deviant *personality*. One of the leading students of delinquency, Albert Cohen, insists that "much — probably most — deviant behavior is produced by clinically normal people."[5]

If deviancy is not in the attribute of a person, as Cohen claims, it must be rooted in the structure of society. An earlier, influential essay by sociologist Robert Merton had pointed out one way for deviancy to occur as a consequence of structural conditions: in the gap between goals and means in society.[6] Becoming a "success,"

---

[3] *See* Barbara Wooten, *Social Science and Social Pathology* (New York: The Macmillan Company, 1959).

[4] For a brief summary and analysis of these twenty-one studies and the twelve hypothetical causative factors *see* Louise G. Howton, "Evaluating Juvenile Delinquency Research," in Bernard Rosenberg, Israel Gerver, and F. William Howton, eds., *Mass Society in Crisis,* 2nd ed. (New York: The Macmillan Company, 1971), pp. 290–294.

[5] *See* Albert K. Cohen, "The Study of Social Disorganization and Deviant Behavior," in Robert K. Merton, Leonard Broom, and Leonard S. Cottrell, Jr., eds., *Sociology Today* (New York: Basic Books, Inc., 1959), p. 463.

[6] *See* Robert K. Merton, "Social Structure and Anomie," *American Sociological Review,* vol. 3 (October 1938), pp. 677–682. Reprinted in Robert K. Merton, *Social Theory and Social Structure,* rev. ed. (New York: The Free Press, 1957), pp. 131–160.

Figure 20.1 The ''Black Magic Gang'' in the Bronx, New York, has created symbols of its own, including the clenched fist on the shoulder as a gesture of farewell. *(U.P.I. Photo.)*

for example, is traditionally achieved by hard work and education. Yet a good education is not equally accessible to all social classes, and some people, despite hard work and education, may be held back by discrimination.

People adapt to cultural expectations, according to Merton, and are conformists; or they adapt in other ways and are deviants. Sociologists like Merton defined a deviant as one whom most people *called* a deviant, making a social-scientific concept out of the labeling conventional people apply to unconventional people. In reaction to this redefinition, a newer generation of sociologists undertook to redefine deviant behavior.

The Outsiders

Perhaps the most provocative work has been that of sociologist Howard S. Becker,

who refuses to accept society's definition that people *are* deviant, but recognizes that in fact society does *label* people as deviants.[7] And the majority do so when others violate the rules that the majority have made and insist on. Becker says:

. . . *social groups create deviance by making the rules whose infraction constitutes deviance,* and by applying those rules to particular people and labeling them as outsiders.[8]

Once an individual becomes involved in actions defined as deviant, association with fellow deviants provides support for deviant behavior, as well as rationalizations and justifications for the rule-breaking behavior and protection from the enforcers of the rules and those who clearly disapprove

[7] *See* Howard S. Becker, *The Outsiders: Studies in the Sociology of Deviance,* 2nd ed. (New York: The Free Press, 1973).

[8] *See* Becker, *op. cit.,* p. 9.

499

of such behavior. Deviant society allows the deviant behavior to occur without criticism or even detection, and among those who approve of it. Becker studied drug-taking among jazz musicians, where progressive involvement by the individual over a period of time was strongly encouraged by his association with other jazz musicians, who defined themselves as different from "squares" in every way.

For many, becoming a career deviant may be simply the brutal fact of being caught in a single deviant act and then being labeled a deviant—a delinquent, a criminal, a dope addict, or insane—regardless of any other act on his part. Thus, defined by others as deviant, his only viable role might be to move toward a deviant career and closer association with other deviants.

Deviant Groups

There are also social groups whose marginal or disadvantaged status in society leads them to generate a cultural perspective that is labeled deviant. Groups of delinquent boys are an example. Such a group rejects at least some of the rules and norms of the larger society and develops norms of its own. The key idea in this approach is that individuals *learn* to be deviant through their association with others; they are *socialized* to deviant norms.

This takes for granted that delinquency *areas* and delinquent *gangs* already exist, and then focuses on the fact that those exposed to these groups naturally learn to be delinquent also.

Delinquent Subcultures

In time, sociologists shifted from thinking about the socialization process by which a boy learned delinquency to the conditions from which delinquent gangs emerged. The key concept became *delinquent subculture,* which points to the existence of norms and values that place a positive outlook on delinquent behavior and that confer status on gang members for delinquent acts.[9] Such a subculture also defines the attitudes to and behavior toward those outside the group.

The source of the subculture lies in the experiences of boys low in social status, who suffer when judged by "middle-class measuring rods" (as Cohen called them). Their family and class origins leave them disadvantaged in the middle-class world of education, and they find themselves facing low social status in adult life. They try to create a more rewarding status by developing social groups in which their own skills and abilities are prized, and which then give them a basis for self-esteem and for being esteemed by others. This often means fighting, aggressive behavior, and acts directed against the larger society and its social institutions, particularly the school.

Gangs are not highly structured and disciplined units organized to pursue single activities. Sociologists Richard Cloward and Lloyd Ohlin describe three different types of delinquent subcultures: one organized to engage in violent activity with rival gangs; a second to engage in theft; and a third around such escapist activity as taking drugs.[10]

The extent of such quite distinctive subcultures are in any large urban area is not obvious. Some sociologists have argued that perhaps only in very large cities, like

---

[9] *See* Albert K. Cohen, *Delinquent Boys: The Culture of the Gang* (New York: The Free Press, 1954).

[10] *See* Richard Cloward and Lloyd E. Ohlin, *Delinquency and Opportunity: A Theory of Delinquent Gangs* (New York: The Free Press, 1960).

New York and Chicago, can specific differentiation of youthful gangs be made evident. One investigation found that delinquent groups tended not to be so specialized but to shift their activities from one form of delinquency to another.[11] Sociologist Lewis Yablonsky has argued that the formally organized group with a definite membership is less common, and that a shifting temporary membership and an irregular involvement in activities is more characteristic of what he calls "near-groups."[12]

The lack of opportunity for achieving conventional social goals creates problems of status in society for which delinquent subcultures are one solution. Those who share common problems develop collective solutions in the form of organized group activities oriented around norms and values peculiar to the disadvantaged group, as we have said, and provide rewards of esteem and status from within their own ranks.

The Significance of Deviant Subcultures

Delinquency provides one of the more obvious examples of a deviant subculture. Homosexuals, drug addicts, and adult criminals are others. Drug addicts, for example, need a systematic organization for obtaining and distributing drugs; it cannot be done by one person. Such a sub-

culture also provides a set of beliefs and attitudes that justify deviant behavior, and define both deviant and conventional status and the interaction between them. Deviants, in short, take a stance toward the conventional world, and this is the very essence of a deviant culture.

Deviant subcultures also are forms of protection for the individual deviant. They define a world of friends and foes, and mark out the values that bind those who share this world, those who aid one another against the pressures and threats of the conventional society. Codes of secrecy are often part of it. Homosexuals, for example, find protection from a hostile society in a homosexual community as well as psychic support for sexual interests condemned by most others. They also find opportunity for a homosexual life not otherwise possible.

Situational Delinquency

There has long been much evidence that delinquency declines sharply among youths as they enter adulthood. Not all of them, or even most of them, become adult criminals. This observation has suggested to sociologist David Matza that delinquency is not, for many at least, so deeply rooted.[13] It may be that delinquency occurs where there is less effective control by the family and other primary groups, where socialization has failed to create strong inner restraints against deviant impulses, where there are poor checks and surveillance by the community, and where there are those who have little to lose in a delinquent act. This suggests that delinquency is frequently the taking advantage of opportunities presented in the immedi-

---

[11] See James F. Short, Jr., and Fred L. Strodtbeck, *Group Process and Gang Delinquency* (Chicago: University of Chicago Press, 1965).

[12] See Lewis Yablonsky, "The Delinquent Gang as a Near-group," *Social Problems*, vol. 7 (Fall 1959), pp. 108–117. *See also* his *The Violent Gang* (New York: The Macmillan Company, 1962). For a critical analysis of this conception of delinquency *see* Harold Pfautz, "Near-group Theory and Collective Behavior: A Critical Formulation," *Social Problems*, vol. 9 (Fall 1961), pp. 167–174.

[13] See David Matza, *Delinquency and Drift* (New York: John Wiley & Sons, Inc., 1964).

ate environment, rather than the creation of alternative life styles to achieve status.

Mental Illness

Some forms of deviant behavior, it should be noted, do not easily provide a basis for a deviant group or a deviant subculture. Mental illness is one. Becoming mentally ill isolates the individual from his everyday groups, but does not provide him with deviant groups to which he might turn for support or protection.

Labeling Deviants: A Caveat

Sociological usage has developed the concept of deviancy from that of a deviant person to deviant behavior to deviant groups and cultures. A deviant person or deviant behavior was thought of as a problem in conformity and control. Since deviance was a violation of group norms, applying deviant labels defined the boundaries of acceptable behavior for the group. The sanctions that followed labeling pressured the individual to change his behavior to conform, to hide his deviant behavior from observation, or to leave the group—and he could be made to leave by being ostracized or expelled.

But when deviants come together to form groups and create a subculture, is there still deviancy? There are now groups with contrasting, even contradictory norms. A majority of the population, or larger and more influential groups, may label as deviants smaller and less influential ones. Are homosexuals, for example, deviants, or are they now an alternative life style? What may be legal—and punishable— deviancy, like homosexuality, depends on majority views. But these change over time, are sometimes vague, and are always inconsistently applied.

Deviancy is a normative term. It is easy to forget that sociologists call deviant those who are labeled deviant from the perspective of the dominant, more compelling (but by no means universal) norms of society. Exaggerations of normative consensus lead some sociologists to label as deviancy all rule-breaking behavior, forgetting that rules reflect power as much as consensus, and that it is the more influential people in society who make the rules. It is doubtful, also, if there is any gain, sociologically, in labeling as deviant organized crime or the evasions of moral standards by corporations. The concept of deviancy needs to be used with care if its scientific value is to be maintained.

PROBLEMS OF SOCIAL ORGANIZATION

Although there has been a predominant interest in problems of deviant behavior in recent years, problems of social organization—such as race relations, poverty, slums, and urban renewal—persist as compelling issues. Most such problems prove to be significantly interrelated; and this interrelatedness makes it hard for the sociologist to study a single problem as if it existed without reference to others. Housing as a problem, for example, involves poverty (low-income housing) and race (segregated housing).

It may be useful to sort out three ways in which sociologists pursue the study of social problems. The distinctions are not precise; they simply suggest different ways of focusing on complex issues:

1. Some sociologists follow a basic issue, such as race, across institutional areas like the economy and education, and across levels from interpersonal interaction to community processes to national policy-making.

2. Others focus on a single institution, such as education, which is one locus for a problem like race and a source of problems of its own.

3. Still others analyze the often grievous inadequacies of structures and programs built to handle social problems.

Basic Issues

Some complex issues pervade the entire social structure, having no single institutional locus, for they are not exclusively economic, political, or educational problems; they are all of these. *Racism*, for example, ramifies throughout the social structure, creating problems of job discrimination, educational disadvantage, community tensions, and many others. It complicates other social problems: housing, poverty, the schools, urban renewal, law enforcement, and the like. Few aspects of social life escape its contamination.

Another such problem is *poverty*. It, too, affects education, housing, and employment. It is a problem of the changing labor force, of upgraded job requirements, of unneeded workers with few skills, of school dropouts, of poor housing and poor health, of malnourished children and impoverished elders, of inadequate welfare programs, and basically of the social neglect by all societal institutions of the lower economic fifth of the nation.

The *status of women* is another encompassing issue, one that shows up in the practices and policies of almost all social institutions and groups. All three of these —race, poverty, and women's status—are basic issues (as we saw in Chapter 10) because they are rooted in one of society's most fundamental and difficult matters: the problem of inequality.

Ecology is a different, though similarly pervasive, issue. It concerns the practices of community, government, and industry about waste disposal, pollution of air and water, preservation of wildlife, protection of natural resources, development of land for profit, and provision of recreational facilities. It cuts across the *vested* interests of a wide range of social groups and classes while demanding attention to a more compelling *public* interest.

Institutional Problems

Other social problems have an institutional locus.

Education becomes a social problem— more accurately a set of social problems —when performance in education fails to meet people's expectations and needs. The value placed on equal educational opportunity, for example, may be threatened by obvious differences in educational chances provided for different social classes and racial groups. There is seemingly no end to educational problems: teacher strikes, school dropouts, inner-city schools, segregated schools, schools and delinquency, teaching deprived children, updating curricula, and community control of schools.

Government is a social problem when it responds too slowly to changing needs and demands, or when, in the United States, its democratic character is violated by special-interest control, or when its growing bureaucracies impinge increasingly on those very civil liberties government is supposed to protect.

The *law* is a social problem when its dispensation of justice fails to treat people equally, so that being poor or a member of a minority means less chance for justice than being rich or a member of a majority; or when courts take so long to bring criminal and civil cases to trial that witnesses are unavailable, making impossible the retribution or restitution the law presumes to provide.

Even the *family* does not escape being a social problem. To many who claim that the family is a basic institution, it seems to have been weakened; others see it as unable to socialize children adequately. The fate of children with divorced or working parents, the problems of adoption, the difficulties of marital relations in a changing moral climate, the women's liberation challenge to male domination—all these suggest the family as a set of social problems.

The *economy* is a set of social problems, too: unemployment and underemployment, racial and sex discrimination in hiring and promoting, inflation, the working poor, the changing needs of the labor market, and the inability to provide without subsidy adequate housing for low-income people. There is also the concentration of economic control in huge conglomerates, and the as yet uncharted functions and powers of multinational firms.

When Solutions Are Problems

Agencies of society intended to carry out social policy, remedy ills, and solve problems become each in time a social problem. The mental hospital is one example. The harsh treatment of the mentally ill is a often-told history, and the long struggle for humane treatment in such institutions has reached a fairly wide level of acceptance in modern society. At the core of this struggle has been the effort to win public acceptance of mental illness as just that, an illness, to be treated not punitively but with therapy.

Yet mental hospitals in the past have not been organized primarily for the purpose of *therapy* but for *custody* of mentally disturbed people who are socially disruptive in their normal surroundings. Hospitals, in this case, take the mental patient out of and away from society.

Erving Goffman characterizes mental hospitals as one among the "total" social institutions of modern society that are organized to move whole blocks of people through routines of activity according to schedules, to keep close surveillance on them, and to enforce close association with others, so unlike ordinary life.[14]

Recent sociological work has shown how the internal social organization of hospitals affected patients, particularly their chances for recovery.[15] Many features of the ordinary routines of the mental hospital, it seemed, detracted from recovery, particularly the rather insensitive and impersonal "handling" of patients by nonprofessional attendants, by which dignity and respect were effectively denied. The need for radical alteration of hospitals if they were to be genuinely therapeutic was shown. Alternatives to mental hospitals, such as an out-patient program, the "halfway house" for those patients who were not quite ready to cope with society, and community mental health clinics for early detection and treatment of people with mental problems have now been proposed.

Some other examples of societal agencies that themselves become problems are: *Prisons,* which are intended to reform criminals. But the "reformatories" badly need reform. They are inefficient and fail

---

[14] *See* Erving Goffman, *Asylums: Essays on the Social Situations of Mental Patients and Other Inmates* (New York: Doubleday & Company, Inc., 1961).

[15] *See,* for example, Alfred Stanton and Morris Schwartz, *The Mental Hospital* (New York: Basic Books, Inc., 1954); William A. Caudill, *The Psychiatric Hospital as a Small Society* (Cambridge, Mass.: Harvard University Press, 1958).

Figure 20.2 Poverty—among the unskilled, the poorly educated, and the elderly—is one of the basic issues pervading the social structure of American society. *(A. Devaney, Inc., N.Y., S.W. Hersch.)*

to improve the actions and attitudes of most of those assigned to them. In many cases they are breeders of criminal careers and attitudes; inmates become brutalized as a condition of survival; prisons contribute, in short, to the problem they were once designed to solve.

Welfare, where rolls inflate, yet inefficiency and redtape deprive many of what is legally their due. Welfare agencies can be degrading to many poor, yet these agencies do little if anything to assist the poor in getting out of poverty. The welfare system was designed in the 1930s for temporary but widespread depression-induced unemployment and economic insecurity. The set of problems today is entirely different.

Housing aid was undertaken to help low and moderate income people to get decent shelter, but doing so has produced some horrendous results. Public housing agencies built enormous high-rise apartment buildings inhabited by many welfare poor and fatherless families, often racially segregated (though no longer by official policy). Frequently their corridors became unsafe from muggers, the haunts of criminals and dope peddlers; in a short time they were badly vandalized and fell into disrepair. As environments, they are in some cases socially if not physically worse than the slums they were to replace.

More recently the effort to subsidize single-family homes for the poor in presumably sound, older homes in the inner city turned into a fraudulent game perpetrated by property owners, realtors, and even some housing officials, a scandal that robbed poor people of money and housing opportunity, the government of public funds, and seriously discredited the Department of Housing and Urban Development (HUD).

Each of these institutions reflects in specific ways the carrying out of social policies that encompass older solutions to social problems. Sometimes these programs never were adequate for the task; sometimes circumstances have changed too much. These institutions have taken on a life of their own with a vested interest in their continuity and perpetuation. Once they were an effort to solve problems; now they are part of the problem, complicating the social ills that brought them into being. By emphasizing the failures of official agencies and programs, sociologists can raise questions about the official (and sometimes also popular) definition of the problem, pressing for a new understanding of causes and sources as a basis for new efforts at resolving the problems.

Perhaps one could also put in this category the numerous regulatory agencies of the community, state, and the federal government. A municipal agency intended to regulate construction or protect public health becomes corrupt or bureaucratically slowed down, or both; a federal agency with vast regulatory powers over railroads, or airlines, or public utilities, or public lands becomes an agency of the regulated, when these groups provide most of the experienced experts who serve as professional staff or even as commissioners. Public interest gives way to self-interest.

What should be apparent is not only that there are many social problems but that there is *very little that is not a social problem*. Our social institutions are each a set of social problems; so are all large social groups and organizations; and so are all social agencies claiming to act on social problems. Every aspect of American society is a social problem.

But if everything is a social problem, can the concept of social problems be useful to us any longer? To answer that we must examine critically what is assumed when we label some things as social problems.

The Problem of Social Problems

To speak sensibly of social problems sociologists assume

1. A *reformist* conception of social problems as dealing only with limited aspects of society.
2. A *consensus* model of how problems come to be defined.
3. A *welfare* model of how problems come to be taken care of in society.

The existence of social problems presumably denotes some unsatisfactory and value-threatening dimensions of an otherwise satisfactory society. Society is not a problem, but it contains a limited number of social problems. The concept of social problems, then, implies a *reformist* approach to society. There is no quarrel with basic values and institutional structure, only a concern with some limited features.

Given this assumption, the source of social problems is seen in terms of three not wholly separate ideas:[16]

1. Social problems occur because modern society is so complex, so intricate in its in-

---

[16] Lacking any consistent social problem theory, social problems textbooks make varied constructions of these ideas with different emphases. *See,* for example, Harry Gold and Frank R. Scarpitti, *Combatting Social Problems: Techniques of Intervention* (Holt, Rinehart and Winston, Inc., 1967), pp. 1–10; Robert A. Dentler, *Major American Social Problems* (Chicago, Ill.: Rand-McNally & Company, 1967); pp. 3–17; and Robert K. Merton and Robert A. Nisbet, eds., *Contemporary Social Problems* (New York: Harcourt Brace Jovanovich, 1961), pp. 3–18.

ternal organization that an unavoidably inconsistent and loosely meshed social structure cannot help but generate strains and social tensions.

2. Even if highly productive and highly rewarding in status and goods for so many, modern society still has a dark side to it. There are costs and casualties to any social system; progress has its price.[17]

3. Social change continually alters social structure and therefore disrupts established relations among social groups, redefines social roles, renders outmoded or dysfunctional once respected and productive beliefs and behavior patterns. From this come social problems.

This conception of the sources of social problems suggests a social perspective that is cautiously reforming. Society cannot be perfect—no matter how successful—so utopian expectations are unwarranted. The kind of social problems we have are the price we pay for the kind of society we have; we can expect always to have them, though specific social problems will change as the society changes.

There is a major difficulty in this conception. As we have seen, most problems are intricately interwoven with others, so that a social problem cannot be fruitfully examined in isolation from related problems. Increasingly, we see social problems to be the undesirable aspects of existing social institutions, and these undesirable aspects loom more significantly as time goes on. It may no longer be radical to say that American society does not *have* social problems, American society *is* a social problem.

The Politics of Social Problems

When a social problem is defined as an objective condition that threatens established social values, and when society is defined as organized around a consensus of values, then it leads easily to the assumption that a society readily achieves consensus on what its social problems are. But successfully defining a social condition as a social problem is a complex political process that involves struggle among unequally competing groups, some more powerful, some with little capacity to get recognition. It is, says Herbert Blumer, "a highly selective process," and those most "harmful" conditions are not necessarily the ones to receive attention and be defined as problems.[18]

There are, as Blumer points out, conflicting interests and differences in power in getting public attention for social problems, in developing the institutional and official backing that legitimizes a condition as a problem. Similarly, interests conflict in assessing the problem—vested interests depict it one way, victimized groups another—as they do in accommodating conflicting pressures to provide official solutions. When implemented, the official program is bent to meet the pressures that arise from affected groups and to suit the ideologies of professional staff. Conflict, accommodation, compromise, bargaining, pressuring, and propagandizing —these are the elements by which a condition becomes defined as a problem and is acted upon. In that process differences of social power are decisive. When sociologists study what have been proclaimed to

[17] This is the emphasis given in Harry C. Bredemeier and Jackson Toby, *Social Problems in America: Costs and Casualties in an Acquisitive Society* (New York: John Wiley & Sons, Inc., 1960).

[18] *See* Herbert Blumer, "Social Problems as Collective Behavior," *Social Problems,* vol. 18 (Winter 1971), p. 302.

be social problems, they are often uncritically accepting only those problems defined by the political process just described.

The Welfare Model of Social Problems

Sociologists have usually shared with other professionals a dislike of the political process, and thus have helped define and legitimize a welfare model of social problems.[19] By promoting a liberal stance that chooses *rehabilitation* over *punishment*, the more humane goal nonetheless still presumes social controls over deviants or over victims of problems—such as the poor—who are to be handled within an administrative structure in programs designed by experts "instead of being debated by the very publics who are supposedly menaced."[20] This is the process we have identified before—turning political conflict into manageable issues that can be legally and administratively controlled. (Turning class conflict into collective bargaining between unions and management is perhaps the outstanding historical example of this process).

When this is done, professionals are the crucial actors in an *apolitical* atmosphere, where, however benignly, authority controls and makes decisions about and for others: deviants, the poor, delinquents, the minorities, and all those confined to "total" institutions, such as prisons and hospitals. *Super*ordinates exercise power over subordinates, and the superordinate's

definition of the problem prevails. Because deviants and others have not been politically organized, their conception of the problems is not heard or given consideration.

It is just this apolitical situation, claim Horowitz and Liebowitz, that is changing. Social problems become political and enter the arena of political conflict when the deviants, the poor, or the minorities offer *their* definition of the problem and organize to act on it. Youth have exercised political pressure on drug laws and on the draft; welfare mothers have organized; homosexuals have fought openly to end being labeled deviant; blacks have created new modes of political action and consequently have redefined the problem of race as political, evident in the power differentials of whites and blacks. Moreover, blacks in prison define themselves as political prisoners, not social deviants.

When this redefinition occurs, conflicting perspectives come into the open and problems are politicized. Alternatives beyond rehabilitation and punishment are offered.

The perspective of sociologists on social problems no longer rests firmly on a set of unchallenged assumptions. Social problems are so numerous and extensive that the prevailing social structure itself becomes the problem, as we have seen. Nor can sociologists assume that social problems represent a societal consensus about what conditions threaten values. The welfare model for handling problems assumes an apolitical context of professional authority and administrative control that no longer applies to many problems.

But it is not only the concept of social problems that needs to be redefined. For that is but a part of a more encompassing issue: the uses of sociology in society.

[19] Irving Louis Horowitz and Martin Liebowitz, "Social Deviance and Political Marginality: Toward a Redefinition of the Relation between Sociology and Politics," *Social Problems*, vol. 15 (Winter 1968), pp. 280–296.

[20] *See* Horowitz and Liebowitz, *op. cit.*, p. 281.

Figure 20.3 Homosexuals, and other groups previously defined as deviant, are beginning to take open political action against such labeling by the majority in society. *(Monkmeyer, Carolyn Watson.)*

THE USES OF SOCIOLOGY

The pragmatic temper of American life could be expected to make use of sociological knowledge. What else is it for, if it is not useful? Sociology has proved to be moderately useful to institutional administrators and decision-makers, particularly in solving the complex problems that beset urban communities, large-scale organizations, and deeply troubled institutions, such as education.[21] The *applied* uses of sociology have attracted various kinds of policy-makers.

Sociologists can and do argue—sometimes vociferously—about how their discipline should be related to society. Not all sociologists think sociology should give emphasis to being useful—at least not yet. But probably most do, though with many differences about what useful means.

There are three major positions defining the place and tasks of sociology in society around which sociologists cluster, some closely, some marginally. One of these gives exclusive priority to the development of sociology as a rigorous science, and so tries to avoid being useful now when sociology is too poorly developed scientifically to provide potential users with the capacity for precise prediction

[21] Three recent books devoted primarily to this issue are Alvin W. Gouldner and S.M. Miller, eds., *Applied Sociology: Opportunities and Problems* (New York: The Free Press, 1965); Paul Lazarsfeld, William Sewell, and Harold Wilensky, eds., *The Uses of Sociology* (New York: Basic Books, Inc., 1967); and Arthur B. Shostak, ed., *Sociology in Action: Case Studies in Social Problems and Directed Social Change* (Homewood, Ill.: The Dorsey Press, 1966). There is also a book of readings, Donald M. Valdes and Dwight G. Dean, eds., *Sociology in Use: Selected Readings for the Introductory Course* (New York: The Macmillan Company, 1965).

and control. Such a position is not opposed to sociology being useful, only that it cannot be useful *in the long run* unless sociologists now focus on making it a science.

A second position is that of the sociologist as liberal-meliorist. For such people sociology must be useful in inducing social change and an applied sociology is thus accepted. The viewpoint is that "the implementation of goals" reflects "the prevailing uses of sociology," and the clients for this type of sociology are most likely to be established organizations.[22]

A third position is that offered most eloquently by C. Wright Mills. He argues for a truly independent stance, for the sociologist as social critic, whose conception of social issues includes the structural arrangements that place elites and organizations in positions of dominance and control over the lives of masses of people, control which prevents them from realizing their own potential as free and rational human beings.

The Applied Uses of Sociology

Perhaps the one common denominator of applied sociological research is the careful discovery and identification of relevant facts. This is an important function in its own right, for often there are myths and misconceptions about social situations that can only be dispelled by accurate description. But mere fact-gathering, without analysis and interpretation, never qualifies as sociological work.

Evaluation Research

A careful gathering of facts, done in such a way as to evaluate adequacy of performance, is the goal of evaluation re-

[22] *See* Lazarsfeld, Sewell, and Wilensky, *op. cit.*, p. xiii.

search. The question for this kind of research is how effective is action in attaining goals. Many of the new programs intended to effect changes in poverty or in educational disadvantage have a built-in requirement for research that evaluates the program itself. This means that the subjects of research are both the subjects of the program—the poor or disadvantaged children in schools, for example—and the administrators of the program. Research of this kind moves beyond fact-gathering. The sociologists doing the study must interpret the facts and make judgments, with the objectives of the program serving as the standard for making these judgments. Does a Headstart program in fact give to deprived children entering school a start roughly equal to that of more advantaged children? Evaluation is one of the processes developed to accomplish this end, but the end itself, the goal of the program, is unchallenged.

When the sociologist accepts as a given the goals of a program or the policies of an organization his work fits into an engineering model.[23] He is trying to make somebody else's programs work more effectively; he is telling someone in authority *how to do* what authority wants to do. His role is *instrumental;* he is a "servant of power."[24]

Reanalyzing Social Goals

The sociologist, however, may put goals and social policies themselves to critical analysis. Here the *clinical* model prevails. The clinical sociologist makes an inde-

[23] *See* Alvin W. Gouldner, "Explorations in Applied Social Science," in Gouldner and Miller, eds., *Applied Sociology* (New York: The Free Press), pp. 5–22.

[24] A phrase taken from the title of a book concerned with the uses of social science in industry. *See* Loren Baritz, *The Servants of Power* (Middletown, Conn.: Wesleyan University Press, 1960).

pendent diagnosis of the client's problems, for he assumes that what those in authority think is wrong or needs to be done is not necessarily an adequate formulation of the problem. As a professional, *he* determines what is wrong and what needs doing; he diagnoses and prescribes.

If his diagnosis and prescription rudely challenge his client's assumption about the validity of goals, the clinical sociologist nonetheless does not ignore the *interests* of his client. He is still a servant of power. When his client is an organization, for example, the sociologist's actions must protect that organization's interests against others: publics, consumers, employees, competing or even opposing organizations, and the like. However much he criticizes and inititates reform, a clinician is loyal to his clientele; their interests necessarily circumscribe his. This places limits to the questions he can pose, to how far he can push his analysis.

With integrity intact and in good conscience, a sociologist can function as an applied researcher or advisor in both the engineering and clinical ways. Both models allow for honest performance, and for highly competent and effective service to society. This is so when the sociologist's values are sufficiently consonant with that of the group or organization served. Probably for most sociologists there is a group —a party, a movement, a church, a civic group, or even a government agency— which he can serve wholeheartedly with the satisfied feeling that he has used his sociology to make a contribution to the improvement of social life.

Sponsorship and Autonomy

Applied sociologists nevertheless face difficult problems of sponsorship and autonomy, problems that are largely political and ethical. Autonomy and independence can be impinged upon in various ways by those who feel threatened by the publication of research results or by particular lines of research. The sociologist, Joan Moore, for example, reported how political considerations affected a large-scale study of Spanish-Americans by bringing about "a modification of structure, techniques, and location of research . . ." during a year of preparation for the study.[25]

When research is conducted by research centers and institutes that depend on the good will and even official sponsorship of specialized publics, powerful social organizations, and perhaps influential leaders there is a potential for pressure on research, either planned or undertaken. Jane Record, a sociologist, has described four cases in which established research centers yielded to pressures from their "constituency": (1.) deleted a chapter from a book; (2.) failed to publish a monograph; (3.) left a social scientist of national reputation out of a study after he had demonstrated a highly critical approach to the strict controls over the research to be utilized by the sponsor, a federal agency; and (4.) managed to get a scholar to return a contract to conduct a public administration study after it was discovered he was not acceptable to the mayor of one city to be studied because of what he had written in an earlier book.[26]

Just as often the ideological perspective of the researcher which shapes his work is at issue. Not even clinically reformulating the problem keeps many sociologists from accepting uncritically large segments of

[25] *See* Gideon Sjoberg, ed., *Ethics, Politics, and Social Research* (Cambridge, Mass.: Schenkman Publishing Co., 1967), pp. 225–244.
[26] *See* Jane Cassels Record, "The Research Institute and the Pressure Group," in Sjoberg, *op. cit.,* pp. 25–49.

the problem as given, particularly those which have to do with authority and competence—the unquestioned authority of the client, the unquestioned incompetence of the subordinates. As liberals, sociologists often want to make programs more humane, yet do not undercut the built-in hierarchy, its power structure and distribution of rewards. After all, sociologists do research mostly *for* management *about* the workers, *for* the governing *about* the governed.

It comes more naturally for sociologists to see problems from the perspective of the upper half rather than the lower half of society. This is so because, though liberal sociologists believe genuinely in reform to improve the lot of the "other half," they more nearly share a world view with their clients than with those they study, despite some real differences between sociologists and businessmen. To the extent that sociologists see themselves as professionals, they identify with professional concerns and values, implicitly sharing assumptions about the authority and competence of professional expertise and the incompetence of the professionally "unqualified." Also, sociologists are among the highly educated, and they share what common perspective derives from similar education. As professionals and as part of the highly educated stratum, then, sociologists unconsciously share common viewpoints with those of the same class position, not often realizing how they differ from the perspective of others in society. And it is those others who are most often the subjects of sociological research; people like sociologists, in turn, are the beneficiaries of the research.

Useful to Whom?

Such considerations of the uses of soci-

ology asks useful to whom? In whose interest and for whose problems is applied research conducted? An applied sociology tied too closely to established clienteles and constituencies, and to their intellectual perspectives and their definitions of their problems, can easily be a servant of power, not a force for human liberation.[27]

Concern for the effect of the social acceptance of sociology by various establishments has been sounded loud and clear for some time now by a small number of sociologists. Alfred M. Lee, for one, feels that well-funded research often threatens to involve the sociologist in a manipulation and "integration" of society which reduces human freedom and choice:

> Many a social scientist has turned from the rocky path of creative individualistic investigation and criticism to be embraced in the lush sympathy and support given those who deal "constructively" (i.e., protectively) with the problems of constituted authority, and who do not irritate their clients with critical analysis.[28]

When Lee says *"constituted authority"* and *"clients,"* he specifies where the source of applied sociology's political and ethical problems lies. The discipline has served the interests of clients who were constituted authority—governmental agencies, school boards, police departments, juvenile agencies, human relations agencies and others—who are the "organizational consumers" of social research—the mili-

[27] For a severe critique by a radical sociologist in these terms *see* Martin Nicolaus, "The Professional Organization of Sociology," in J. David Colfax and Jack L. Roach, eds., *Radical Sociology* (New York: Basic Books, Inc., 1971), pp. 45–60.

[28] *See* Alfred M. Lee, "Items for the Agenda of Social Science," in Gouldner and Miller, eds., *op. cit.,* pp. 421–428. The quotation is from p. 422.

tary, the law, corporate management, and the like.

C. Wright Mills called this being *adviser to the king*—rather than being philosopher-king—and saw it as currently the most usual role for sociologists. It is the one in which a *client* is designated as the person or agency for whom research is done and advice is provided. A *clinical* relationship between the sociologist as *professional* and the user of sociology as *client* is now the model preferred by sociologists. It is preferred over the engineering model for the greater freedom and professional autonomy and the greater status as expert that it gives the sociologist. It allows him more nearly to set the terms on which he will serve others.

While there is much social utility in this model, it nonetheless has built-in constraints. Like all professional roles it functions in a political and administrative context in which larger structural features are taken as given, and the problems are therefore always located elsewhere. But when the administrators of prisons and their programs, for example, are as much the problem as are the prisoners, then the professional-client relationship may put limits to the sociological imagination. While the professional sociologist can tell his client that his program is outdated, his goals are confused or misplaced, his procedures are counter-productive, he cannot tell the client that *he* is the problem in terms that undercut the client's power and status without destroying the professional-client relationship.

Though some sociologists claim that the professional sociologist can also be a *social critic*, powerful clients do not usually want social critics; they want practical advice. And for them practical advice does not raise questions about their legitimacy. It

does not redefine the clients' problem to suggest they disband their structure, give away power, share status and privileges with those they have long controlled. Yet just such advice may be advantageous and called for, if one frees the imagination from established assumptions about what is and what is not changeable in social institutions.

In the past, even as now, many sociologists have moved beyond these constraints. A strong case could be made that sociology has been, and indeed continues to be, most useful to society in providing a sociological perspective by which larger publics can interpret the significance of cultural and social events. Sociology provides meaningful clues to what is going on around us, to the outlines of a complex and changing social reality.[29]

To the extent that sociology makes a significant contribution to people's efforts to understand themselves and their social world, their problems and their dilemmas, it attains a significance that is unmatched by its value to people of practical affairs. This is why sociology is always found in popular versions, and why its vocabulary moves so quickly into the mainstream of contemporary discourse. Concepts such as *socialization, alienation, social status, peer group, identity, power structure, power elite, subculture, bureaucracy,* and a host of others have become part of the intellectual tool kit of contemporary generations. They are means for constructing interpretations and explanations of the ongoing social processes of modern society; in short, for constructing reality. Through them sociology has become a useful intellectual perspec-

[29] *See* Marvin Bressler, "Sociology and Collegiate General Education" and Nathan Glazer, "The Ideological Uses of Sociology," both in Lazarsfeld, Sewell, and Wilensky, *op. cit.,* pp. 45–77.

tive for *the changing definition of the situation* in the contemporary world.

The Sociologist as Social Critic

It was C. Wright Mills who advocated that sociologists place less—or at least not exclusive value—on the role of advisor to the king and opt for another: "to remain independent, to do one's own work, to select one's own problems, but to direct this work *at* kings as well as *to* 'publics.' "[30] This definition is not the role of professional working for a client, but that of sociologist as social critic.

Yet such a role cannot function in an intellectual vacuum. A sociologist of this kind needs to communicate with some other people, to have an audience, to direct his work toward users other than clients. Who can these people be? Mills suggests three: *parties*, *movements*, and *publics*. But, he says, they must be in areas within which ideas can be truly debated and they must be capable of influencing decisions. Such a process could lead to a "truly democratic" society.

A democratic society of this kind does not now exist, but there is no reason to despair, according to Mills, for the formal legalistic democracy we have is still vastly preferable to the absence of such, as in the Soviet Union. Furthermore, there are audiences who want to know who they are as actors in historical time, where they are historically located, and what the choices for possible action are. Yet, even here, there must be an avoidance of a *partisan* commitment that would make of the sociologist a hawker of party lines. There is no more value in a "radical" sociologist uncritically spouting party dogma than there is in a "conservative" sociolo-

---

[30] *See* Mills, *op. cit.*, p. 181.

gist preaching official doctrine. Each is an ideologist in the most pejorative and disparaging sense of that word.

Problems: Sociological and Social

We have come some distance in this chapter, beginning with the sociologist's concern for social pathology and social disorganization, moving to the liberal conception of social problems and to the confusion about what a problem is today, and finally ending with the nature and limitations of applied sociology. A newer generation of sociologists, taking Mills very seriously, have sought to enlarge the scope of sociological analyses on social issues. They want to make the institutional structures—economy and polity, in particular—a basic component of the social issues they examine, for the sources of problems lie in normal functioning, not malfunctioning, of these institutions. Going back to Robert S. Lynd, they have asked what knowledge is for, what uses it serves; they have wanted to put knowledge to a larger, more compelling use than that of serving only the powerful and the established.

Most of our private troubles are embedded in some way in public issues; they are symptoms of structural arrangements whose consequences are not always evident to us from casual inspection. The sociologist at his best explores the full range of social issues in order to find the structural consequences that bind people into unreal choices or into no choices at all. He does not accept what those in places of power and authority say are social problems, for frequently these are only *their* problems, defined in terms of their interests. Their interests may be *part* of the problem; but defining problems only to suit their interests does not enhance human values like freedom and opportunity.

The liberal tradition of social problems and applied sociology assumes a distinction between *sociological* problems — those scientific problems by which basic research advances theory — and *social* problems — those value-threatening conditions present in the society which sociologists help resolve by applying sociological knowledge to people's interests. Perhaps this distinction between sociological and social problems is too simple to be real, as illusory as the image of a value-free social science. Robert Lynd thought so, as did C. Wright Mills, who said:

> . . . by addressing ourselves to issues and to troubles, and formulating them as problems of social science, we stand the best chance, I believe the only chance, to make reason democratically relevant to human affairs in a free society, and so to realize the classic values that underlie the promise of our studies.[31]

[31] *See* Mills, *op. cit.*, p. 194.

SUMMARY

For sociologists, a social problem is defined as an *objective* condition defined as posing a *threat* to *values*.

There are two types of social problems: problems of *deviance* and of *social organization*.

Deviants were first defined as deviant *persons;* then deviancy was defined as a matter of a group and culture to which the person had been socialized. More recently, deviants are defined as those *labeled* deviants by the majority or by powerful groups. Thus, deviancy is a normative term, not a scientific one.

Problems of social organization include these *basic* issues: race, poverty, women's status, and ecology; as well as *institutional* issues: education, government, law, family, and the economy, within which there are many specific problems.

In addition, many past solutions — welfare, housing, and mental hospitals, for example — have themselves become problems. Not only are there many problems but there is very little that is not a problem.

Sociologists assume a *reformist* conception of social problems, *consensus* on the definition of problems, and a *welfare model* of how problems are taken care of.

On this basis the source of social problems is seen in terms of (1.) the *complexity* of modern society, (2.) the *costs* and *casualties* of progress, and (3.) social *change*. This is a cautiously reforming approach to social problems.

But Blumer stresses how conflict, bargaining, pressuring, and propagandizing affects what problems get public attention. While sociologists generally assume that problems are *apolitical*, they become political when the poor, the deviants, or minorities offer and press for *their* definition of the problem.

Sociologists hold three positions on the *uses* of sociology: the priority of rigorous science over problem-solving, the liberal-meliorist, and the independent sociologist-critic.

Applied sociology can be the *evaluation* of programs, an *instrumental* function which accepts the program's goal uncritically; or *reanalyzing social goals,* in which the sociologist applies a *clinical* model.

Problems of sponsorship of applied sociology raise important questions about control of research, autonomy, and usefulness.

Sociology has perhaps been most useful not in serving powerful clients but in enlightening publics about their social world, their problems, and their dilemmas.

Suggested Readings

Loren Baritz, *The Servants of Power* (Middletown, Conn.: Wesleyan University Press, 1960). A critique of the use of social science to serve vested interests in industry.

Howard S. Becker, *The Outsiders: Studies in the Sociology of Deviance,* 2nd ed. (New York: The Free Press, 1973). A provocative presentation of the idea of labeling as basic to understanding deviance.

Richard Cloward and Lloyd E. Ohlin, *Delinquency and Opportunity: A Theory of Delinquent Gangs* (New York: The Free Press, 1960). The subcultural variations in big-city gangs is explored here.

Albert K. Cohen, *Delinquent Boys: The Culture of the Gang* (New York: The Free Press, 1954). An influential study defining lower-class delinquency as a subcultural process.

J. David Colfax and Jack L. Roach, eds., *Radical Sociology* (New York: Basic Books, Inc., 1971). A collection of articles on how radical sociologists view sociology's relationship to social issues, with some replies by nonradical sociologists.

Alvin W. Gouldner and S.M. Miller, eds., *Applied Sociology: Opportunities and Problems* (New York: The Free Press, 1965). An interesting collection of essays on what is involved in seeking to apply sociology to social issues.

Paul Lazarsfeld, William Sewell, and Harold Wilensky, eds., *The Uses of Sociology* (New York: Basic Books, Inc., 1967). Establishment sociology's most thorough examination of how sociology has been and can be used in society.

Robert S. Lynd, *Knowledge for What?* (Princeton, N.J.: Princeton University Press, 1939; paperback edition, 1966). The issues Lynd raised about the uses of sociology are still relevant to any contemporary discussion.

David Matza, *Delinquency and Drift* (New York: John Wiley & Sons, Inc., 1964). That delinquency does not in most cases lead to a delinquent career is the theme of this thoughtful study.

C. Wright Mills, *The Sociological Imagination* (New York: Oxford University Press, 1961; paperback edition, Grove Press, 1961). Our private troubles must be seen as public issues, or we cannot understand what happens to us.

James F. Short, Jr., and Fred L. Strodtbeck, *Group Process and Gang Delinquency* (Chicago, Ill.: University of Chicago Press, 1965). A review and analysis of the group basis of delinquency.

Arthur B. Shostak, ed., *Sociology in Action: Case Studies in Social Problems and Directed Social Change* (Homewood, Ill.: The Dorsey Press, 1966). A selected set of examples of using sociology in action on defining problems and producing some social change.

Gideon Sjoberg, ed., *Ethics, Politics, and Social Research* (Cambridge, Mass.: Schenkman Publishing, 1967). A well-selected set of essays detailing the problems and pressures experienced by social researchers from those who stand to profit or lose by the research.

L'Envoi: The Promise of Sociology

Sociology, we said early in this book, began in circumstances of great disruption and social dislocation. Large numbers of people were uprooted, thrust out unwillingly from countryside and peasant life into industrializing cities with dense populations. Aristocracy lost out to a rising bourgeoisie, and power centered in newly forming nations; a new kind of social world came into being. The pressing need to make sense of it brought sociology into being.

Whatever else, sociology has always been a *perspective,* an effort to see ourselves not as isolated persons but as actors moving within historic social structures that are shaped and reshaped by unceasing human interaction. Human beings construct their societies without necessarily understanding what they have done or how they have done it—and without always wanting or liking the outcome. It is sociology's task to probe beneath the surface of our social worlds, to enable us to see more clearly the always imperfect social structures within which we are enclosed with others in a shared existence. Only then can we, freely and rationally, take conscious responsibility for the shape of our society.

We have said it before: Sociology has always lived in tension between two competing, sometimes contradictory, sometimes compatible imperatives. One is to become a science, the other is the ethical and moral imperative to be relevant to the problems and issues of society. This *internal* compulsion to be scientific has been the strongest factor in creating the methodological emphasis that is significant in the discipline today, and also in creating more formalized conceptions of theory. But the imperative to be relevant has never allowed sociology to ignore for long the pressing social issues that beset society. For this reason there is no single orthodoxy for sociology.

In a time when the great ideologies of the past have lost their hold, and when religious orthodoxies no longer command the unquestioned faith of believers, sociology is a humanistic as well as a secular and scientific effort to provide perspective on the collective enterprise that is society. It seeks to offer some knowledge by which people can be more rational and more humane in the decisions they make about the collective organization of their lives, its quality and magnitude, and the direction of conscious change. Such an enterprise, however modest in its skills, is surely a worthy one.

Glossary

Accountability. The means of holding private and public groups to the service of public interest rather than their own or other special interests.

Acculturation. Absorption of ethnics into the dominant culture.

Alienation. Individual feelings of powerlessness, meaninglessness, and isolation from the society as a whole.

Anarchism. An antipolitical doctrine opposed to centralized political authority, strongly valuing individualism, and seeking new and freer forms of human association. "Too socialist for the liberals; too liberal for the socialists."

Androgynous marriage. A marriage in which no sex-role differentiation exists.

Anomie. According to Durkheim, a possible endpoint of change where social relations have disintegrated until moral rules no longer effectively regulate social action.

Applied science. Practical research which uses existing knowledge for the solution of everyday problems.

Assimilation. The absorption of ethnics into the dominant culture (acculturation) and into structural positions to the point where separate ethnic identity is lost.

Attitude. A way of thought or opinion that predisposes a person to act in a particular way.

Audience. A conventional crowd that reflects a shared cultural expectation.

Authority. Legitimate power; the right to make decisions or exercise control over others in social organization.

Automation. A continuous process of production whereby machines control movement from one part to another without human aid and where a feedback system by machines allows for machine control of this process.

Autonomy. Acting separately and with independence; not under the authority of others.

Basic Science. Pure research which advances fundamental and theoretical knowledge.

Bias. Lack of objectivity in social research (*see* Objectivity).

Negative attitudes toward persons because of their group membership (*see* Prejudice). *Collective bias.* The shared perspective or world view of a class or profession that basically shapes their views of what is "real."

Big science. The growth in science attended by increased funds for scientific research and the support of the government and military for scientific activity.

Birth rate. See Crude birth rate.

Bourgeois. The ideal man of capitalism, whose life style is sober, disciplined, respectable, logical, acquisitive, and conformist.

Bureaucracy. The means by which large units of people are administered rationally.

Capitalism. See Corporate capitalism, Laissez—faire capitalism.

Cargo cult. A system of belief and ritual in Melanesia beginning in the late nineteenth century, whereby native independence could be gained and the white man defeated.

Caste. A permanent, very rigid form of social stratification sanctified by religion.

Census. The effort to make an accurate count of the people in a region or country.

Centralization. Political and administrative processes for concentrating control and decision-making in a small, core group.

Channel of communication. The network by which information moves through a group or organization, either by formally provided means or by informal networks, such as grapevines or rumor mills.

Charisma. Literally a gift of grace; now a quality of leadership that attracts a following.

Church. See Ecclesia.

Clan. A social group made up of a number of families with a common ancestor.

Class system. An open system of stratification (in contrast to caste and estate) in which mobility from lower to higher strata is not forbidden by religion or law (*see* Social Class).

Clique. A small circle of people who recognize each other and keep out non-members.

Collective behavior. The relatively structured interaction which occurs when people come together without prior definition of the situation and from which new social forms may emerge.

Colonialism. An international division of labor with the colony providing raw materials and a market for finished goods and the dominant na-tion manufacturing goods for its own and foreign markets.

Colonization. The forced entry of a colonial people into the dominant society with the simultaneous attempt by the colonizing power to control and transform the colonial people.

Comarital adultery. A husband and wife who engage in sexual relations with other persons and with each other's consent.

Commune. A small community, often called a family, which rejects a status hierarchy, believes in the value of small communities over larger ones, and adopts a consciously antibureaucratic structure.

Community. The social organization which meets the problems of providing common residence and sustenance for a population sharing a limited territorial space (village, town, city). Also, the integration and unity around shared sentiments and values and a common life style originally found in small localities, now sought elsewhere.

Community control of schools. The attempt to give the local district real power over the schools in the neighborhood in opposition to the drift toward national control.

Concepts. Terms denoting a general class of objects rendered as precisely as possible.

Conformity. Action by an individual consistent with the norms and expectations of the group.

Conglomerate. A process of corporate diversification achieved by buying a controlling interest in firms in other industries.

Consensus. A social act of communication and agreement shared by a group of people.

Contra-normative. Norm-violating.

Corporate capitalism. An economic system which effectively concentrates large investments, technology, and manpower in a relatively few dominant corporations.

Counterculture. A confrontation and contradiction of the dominant culture, especially concerning the rebellion among American youth in the 1960s.

Crowd. Large numbers of people who share a

common focus or interest and who interact and communicate.

Crude birth rate. Computed on the basis of every 1,000 persons in a specified population in a given year.

Crude death rate. Computed on the basis of every 1,000 persons in a specified population in a given year.

Cult. A small and almost formless religious organization grouped around a charismatic leader.

Cultural relativism. The assertion that all human cultures are equally legitimate.

Culture. The symbolic world of meanings and understandings built up through social interaction into an ordered system.

Data-gathering. A process of observing the world by techniques and tools designed for this purpose: sampling, questionnaires, interviews, fieldwork, and so on.

Death rate. See Crude death rate.

Decentralization. The removal of concentrated power and authority from a core group and extending participation in decision-making to a wider set of actors.

De facto segregation. Segregation in schools not legally required but the unplanned consequence of other restrictive practices such as residential segregation.

Deferred gratification. The ability to save, to postpone pleasure for future rewards.

Definition of the situation. People act in a situation consistent with what they define that situation to be.

Delinquent subculture. The existence of norms and values among delinquent actors that place a positive outlook on delinquent behavior and confer status on those who commit delinquent acts.

Demography. The study of the characteristics and composition of human populations.

Denomination. A stable church that does not withdraw from the world but does not seek to control it either, and does not monopolize a territory.

Deviant behavior. The conduct of those who act contrary to established norms of action and the rules of society.

Differentiation. Specialization of roles, groups, and institutions which creates a more complex social structure (*see* Division of Labor).

Discrimination. Differential (therefore unequal) treatment of persons because of their race or ethnic status.

Division of labor. A process whereby specialization in social roles leads to a more complex social structure.

Dysfunctional. Destructive of established social relations and producing social disorganization.

Ecclesia. A basic type of religious organization that is both in and of the world and seeks to be a power in society.

Ecology. The study of the relations of organisms to the environment.

Economy. The organization within a society to produce and distribute material goods so as to promote the basic sustenance of life.

Ecosystem. The interconnected, interdependent system of relations between organisms and environment.

Education. The process by which the young are inducted into the culture and trained in necessary values and skills.

Elite. Those at the top of an hierarchical social system who control decision-making in the system.

Embourgeoisement. Becoming middle class.

Emergent norm theory. The idea that even in a violent crowd social interaction takes place which defines the situation and establishes norms for sanctioning behavior.

Empirical. Based on observation or experiment, thus factual.

Endogamy. Where marriage partners are chosen from within a group.

Entrepreneur. A Capitalist who owns the machinery and materials that go into the production of goods by virtue of putting up the capital for an enterprise.

Equalitarianism. The denial that inequality is either just or necessary in society.

Estate. A series of social strata in medieval Europe rigidly set off from one another and supported by custom and law.

Ethnic group. People who are visibly different from others by virtue of their cultural patterns and life styles.

Ethnocentrism. Using one's culture as the standard by which all other cultures are judged.

Ethos. Characteristic and distinguishing attitudes and actions that set one group apart from others.

Exogamy. Where marriage partners are chosen outside of the group.

Family. A social arrangement to legitimize mating and the care and socialization of the young.

Family group. A kinship group that regulates and controls the relationship of the sexes in an institutionalized manner and provides for mating in order to reproduce.

Feral children. Those who grew up in virtual isolation from human contact and were thus denied the humanizing influence of the socialization process.

Fertility rate. The number of births in a particular population for every 1,000 women of childbearing age.

Folk society. Small groups of people who are organized on a kinship basis, with little specialization of occupation or economic function but with a shared culture.

Folkways. Customary ways of doing things that are usually accepted as the right way.

Food chain. The interlinked system by which animals and human beings survive by obtaining energy and nutrients from plants.

Formal structure. Rational and impersonal coordination of the actions of many people toward a single objective in a structure with a hierarchy of offices and a centralized authority.

Formalization. A process of making organization increasingly formal in structure.

Functional. Actions and beliefs which sustain the social system of which they are a part.

Ghetto. A section of a city where many members of a minority or disadvantaged people live.

Goal specificity. Clearly and precisely defined aims of a formal organization.

Group. A plurality of persons sharing in a common pattern of social interaction.

Group marriage. Multilateral marriage satisfying the need to find community with others.

Ideational phenomena. Language, myth, philosophy, custom, and the like.

Identity. An image obtained from membership and a role in a group that is particularly valued.

Ideology. The interpretation of an historical situation from the perspective of a group or class in order to legitimate modes of social action.

Imperialism. Political control of colonies by a dominant society.

Indicators. Particular observations from which sociological inferences about invisible phenomena (such as morale) are made for research purposes.

Individuality. The uniquely individual character of each person.

Industrial Revolution. The beginning of the machine age—around the middle of the eighteenth century in England—which changed the social and economic life of the population.

Industrialization. The transformation of society from predominantly agricultural to predominantly industrial forms of production of goods, which then radically alters other institutions of the society.

Informal sanctions. Non-official mechanisms invoked for social control.

Informal structure. The network of spontaneous, unplanned social relations in a bureaucracy that are not formally prescribed.

Inner city. The area beyond the central business district that includes transient residential areas, slums, and racial ghettoes.

Institution. A complex of norms supported by strong group consensus and sanctions for violations; the social acts which these norms govern.

Integration. The meshing of the total pattern of human activity in a group or society into an interdependent process.

Internalization. Taking the role of another so as to learn to feel and think as the other person does; especially true of children.

Invisible phenomena. Aspects of the social world which cannot be "seen," such as attitude, morale, or goal.

Kinship group. A group based on descent or marriage.

Laissez-faire capitalism. An economic system of small, competitive, individual producers in a free market based solely on demand and supply.

Language. A complex system of verbal, written, and gestural symbols created to convey meaning.

Laws. Mores put into a written code with specific punishments for violations enforced by designated authority.

Mass society. Society developed into an undifferentiated cultural sameness.

Matriarchal. Where authority is held by the mother.

Meritocracy. A society based on assignment of position and greater social reward for those presumed to be more qualified.

Metropolitan. A concentration of urban population distributed among a central city and a complex of the smaller satellite cities and villages surrounding the central core.

Minority. Members of society who are blocked from full and equal participation in all phases of social life because of their racial or ethnic status.

Modernization. Radical changes in the institutional structure of traditional societies to become modern societies.

Monogamy. One man married to one woman.

Mores. Those standards which people regard as crucial for the welfare of the group.

Multinational corporation. A process of expansion achieved by investment, purchase, or creation of subsidiaries by a conglomerate across national boundaries.

Multiversity. The functions and responsibilities of a university which give it multiple goals and a highly diversified academic effort, according to Kerr.

Nation-state. A politically integrative unit which extends national loyalties among diverse human populations as a result of the ecological expansion created by industrialism.

Negative sanctions. Formal and informal mechanisms of control used to contain action within established limits. These range from ostracism to a jail sentence or execution.

Norms. Rules of conduct that specify what "should" be done in social situations.

Nuclear family. A husband, wife, and children who carry out the activities of the family.

Objectivity. Social observation and analyses undistorted as far as possible by personal attitudes, emotions, values, and dislikes.

Office. Specific duties and functions in a bureaucracy which exist separate from the person who holds the office.

Oligarchy. The rule of the few over the many.

Open admission. College admission granted simply on the basis of application and high-school graduation, and unaffected by grades or test scores.

Open marriage. Interaction and involvement with others, including sexual relationships, to eliminate the sense of possessiveness of one partner for another.

Other-directed personality. Someone who is particularly sensitive to the demands and expectations of the immediate situation and the cues indicated by the actions of others.

Parapolitical groups. Associations of citizens formed for nonpolitical functions (labor, business, and so on) who also seek to influence government and change social policy in their own interests.

Participant-observation. Taking part in the social life of a group or community to observe what happens from an insider's viewpoint.

Party. A political structure organized to acquire power and achieve domination.

Patriarchal. Where authority is held by the father.

Peer group. A group of equals, who provide significant experiences in learning how to interact with others, how to be accepted by others, and how to achieve status.

People. A population that shares a common language and heritage.

Politics. The process whereby humans utilize power and authority to make decisions.

Polity. The distribution of power and authority in a society for making decisions and exercising control.

Polyandry. A woman married to several husbands.

Polygamy. A plurality of mates.

Polygyny. A man married to several wives.

Population growth rate. A measure of the growth of a population as a percent of the annual increase.

Power. The distribution of influence, pressure, and authority for the making, executing, and legitimizing of decisions.

Prejudice. Attitudes and feelings toward people because of race or ethnic status.

Prestige. The ability to impress others, conferred by status.

Primary group. A social relationship that permits socialization to occur within a small, intimate group.

Primary relationship. Direct, face-to-face interaction; a relationship valued as an end in itself.

Production. Land, capital, labor, and organization combined in a cooperative effort to produce goods.

Progress. Change that signifies a welcome improvement in material conditions or a lessening in coercive social relations.

Propaganda. The deliberate dissemination of partisan communication in order to influence the formation of public opinion.

Protestant ethic. A religious orientation to the world which encouraged self-discipline, hard work, initiative, material acquisition, and competitive individualism.

Public. Some members of a society who are interested in a public matter that may require decision or resolution by the society. A process of discussion by which such decisions can be made, and the emergence of public opinion from such discussion.

Pure science. *See* Basic science.

Racism. Beliefs about the inherent superiority of one race over another, and practices based on such beliefs. *Institutional racism*. Control of social institutions by one social group (whites) to the disadvantage of another (blacks).

Reform movement. A social movement that accepts the basic values and institutions of society but seeks to change what are defined as abuses, defects, or inadequacies.

Religion. Explanations that transcend mundane, factual knowledge, expressed in symbolic form and acts, which relate a people to the ultimate conditions of their existences.

Resocialization. Socialization later in life that makes a sharp break with an individual's past.

Revolutionary movement. A social movement that tries to bring about a fundamental change in the structure of society.

Role. The patterned way in which people in various social positions interact with others based on mutual expectations.

Role differentiation. Specialization in occupational and other social roles.

Role set. A differentiated set of role expectations that orient an occupant of a role toward other actors who are in different relations and situations.

Role strain. When an actor in a role cannot seem to meet expectations for one role fully without violating another role.

Sample. A small proportion of the total population drawn so that the variation in the characteristics of the population will be present in the sample in the same proportion as they appear in the universe of the study.

Scarcity. Where the demand for goods exceeds the supply.

Science. A rational and empirical process for creating validated theory; the institutional roles and structures for carrying on scientific work.

Sect. A basic type of religious organization that is small and exclusive and whose members voluntarily join it.

Secularization. The decline of religious influence on other social institutions.

Segmentalization. The emergence of differentiated subgroups from a single structure.

Segregation, racial. Separate facilities—such

as schools—for people based solely on race.

Sexual revolution. A change in attitude, and perhaps behavior, regarding greater permissiveness for sex outside of marriage.

Sign. A physical thing or event that stands for another thing or event.

Social base of a movement. A particular group or class in whose interest the movement speaks, and who provide much of the support of the movement.

Social change. Any alteration in roles, relations, or in the structure of a group or society.

Social class. Economic strata distinguished by unequal rewards from participation in the production processes of the society.

Social conflict. A struggle over values or over scarce resources in which two contesting groups seek to improve their definition of the situation.

Social control. The use of negative and positive sanctions (punishment and reward) to get people to act in conformity with group norms and expectations.

Social evolution. The growth and development of human society by greater spans of integration and control of population, accompanied by greater internal differentiation and complexity.

Social mobility. When property and position are open to all individuals and are not transmitted through a system of inheritance.

Social movement. A collective action to promote or resist change which includes shared values, a sense of membership, shared understandings, and a structural system between leaders and followers.

Social problem. A condition or situation which members of the society regard as a threat to their values, according to Fuller and Nyers.

Social process. Modes or forms of interaction—such as cooperation, competition, accommodation, assimilation, and conflict.

Social relation. Interaction between people in a somewhat stable and persistent pattern.

Social solidarity. The cohesion of social groups into a unified structure, according to Durkheim.

Social structure. The integration of social roles into a relatively coherent pattern of social interaction.

Socialization. The basic process by which the human being becomes a person and a functioning member of society.

Society. All the systems of action sustained by a given societal population; that is, the self-perpetuating inhabitants of a territorial area.

State. A political organization that claims binding authority and a legitimate monopoly of force within a territory, according to Weber.

Status. A position in society; often used to classify someone as high in rank.

Status group. A number of individuals who occupy a similar position in the prestige ranking of their community and who regularly interact with one another and recognize each other as equals.

Stereotype. Culturally based images of a category of people, attributing to them uniformly a common set of characteristics.

Stratification. The division of society into a series of levels, ranking one above the other by virtue of the unequal distribution of social assets such as power and privilege.

Subculture. Distinctive versions of the dominant culture carried by particular segments and groups of the society.

Suburban community. Residential facilities beyond the city limits, usually for the more prosperous segment of the population.

Suffrage. The right to vote, particularly associated with making women voting members of society.

Symbol. Human-made signs—objects including words—for which human beings have a set of shared meanings and values.

Symbolic interaction. Interaction that proceeds through the communication of meanings by language and other symbol-using processes.

Technology. The application of knowledge and skill through tools, machines, and instruments for practical purposes.

True believer. Someone who sees dedication to a social movement as a way of giving meaning to his life.

Urban ecology. The distribution of people, functions, and services in a community, and the location of the community in its physical environment which influences its shape and form.

Urbanism. The values and life styles associated with urban life.

Urbanization. A shift of the population from predominantly rural to predominantly urban locations.

Values. End states that people would like to achieve; conceptions of what is good and desirable in society.

Zero growth. The level of fertility required for a population to replace itself exactly under projected mortality rates and in the absence of immigration.

Name Index

Aiken, Michael, 361–362
Alinsky, Saul, 366
Alpert, Harry, 22
Apter, David, 441
Aristotle, 199

Bacon, Francis, 472
Bales, Robert, 142
Balzac, Honoré de, 11
Barnard, Chester, 155
Becker, Howard S., 499–500
Bell, Daniel, 125, 127, 223, 450–451
Bell, Wendell, 183
Bellah, Robert, 396
Bendix, Reinhard, 219
Benedict, Ruth, 232
Bensman, Joseph, 174, 187
Berger, Bennet, 184
Berger, Peter, 14, 396
Berkley, George, 164
Bernard, Jessie, 286
Berrigan, Daniel, 395
Berrigan, Phillip, 395

Blake, Judith, 66
Blau, Peter, 161, 162
Blauner, Robert, 244–245, 337, 389
Blood, Jr., Robert O., 278–279, 280
Blumer, Herbert, 445, 446, 507
Bookchin, Murray, 368
Booth, Charles, 11, 22
Boskoff, Alvin, 177
Bowles, Samuel, 305–306
Broder, David, 355
Bronfenbrenner, Urie, 88
Burgess, Ernest, 144, 176, 178
Burnham, James, 214

Calvin, John, 326, 392
Caplovitz, David, 251
Carmichael, Stokely, 235, 236, 244, 447, 452, 457
Cassirer, Ernst, 44
Centers, Richard, 217
Chagnon, Napoleon A., 120
Chavez, Caesar, 237, 367
Chinoy, Eli, 221
Clark, Burton, 291, 297

Subject Index